"Like the supposedly conformist and complacent 1950s, too long eclipsed by the drama and turbulence of the 1960s, so has Dwight Eisenhower too long been dismissed as a distracted codger compared with the youthful president who succeeded him, John F. Kennedy. Now William I. Hitchcock's trenchant and compelling book convincingly redresses the balance. . . . Persuasively portrays Eisenhower as an engaged and thoughtful leader who deeply shaped the nation's destiny for decades to come."
—David M. Kennedy, Donald J. McLachlan Professor of History Emeritus, Stanford University, and Pulitzer Prize– winning author of *Freedom from Fear*

"William Hitchcock has given us an absorbing account of an era that looms large not only in the long history of the West but in our time. . . . Ike's achievements on the battlefield and in the public square of peacetime are towering, and we live still in their long shadow."
—Jon Meacham, author of *Destiny and Power: The American Odyssey of George Herbert Walker Bush* and *American Lion: Andrew Jackson in the White House*

"Lays to rest the widespread notion that Eisenhower was a laissez-faire, golf-crazed president swept along by the times. . . . Authoritative."
—*The Economist*

"The definitive single-volume account of this understudied but highly consequential presidency."
—Alvin S. Felzenberg, *The Claremont Review of Books*

ALSO BY WILLIAM I. HITCHCOCK

The Bitter Road to Freedom: A New History of the Liberation of Europe

*The Struggle for Europe: The Turbulent History of a
Divided Continent, 1945–Present*

*France Restored: Cold War Diplomacy and the Quest for Leadership
in Europe*

The Human Rights Revolution: An International History
(coedited with Petra Goedde and Akira Iriye)

From War to Peace: Altered Strategic Landscapes in the 20th Century
(coedited with Paul Kennedy)

THE AGE OF EISENHOWER

AMERICA AND THE WORLD
IN THE 1950S

WILLIAM I. HITCHCOCK

Simon & Schuster Paperbacks

NEW YORK   LONDON   TORONTO   SYDNEY   NEW DELHI

Simon & Schuster Paperbacks
An Imprint of Simon & Schuster, Inc.
1230 Avenue of the Americas
New York, NY 10020

First Simon & Schuster trade paperback edition March 2019

SIMON & SCHUSTER and colophon are registered trademarks of Simon & Schuster, Inc.

For information about special discounts for bulk purchases, please contact Simon & Schuster Special Sales at 1-866-506-1949 or business@simonandschuster.com.

The Simon & Schuster Speakers Bureau can bring authors to your live event. For more information or to book an event, contact the Simon & Schuster Speakers Bureau at 1-866-248-3049 or visit our website at www.simonspeakers.com.

Interior design by Paul Dippolito

Manufactured in the United States of America

10   9   8   7   6   5   4   3   2   1

The Library of Congress has cataloged the hardcover edition as follows:
Names: Hitchcock, William I., author.
Title: The age of Eisenhower : America and the world in the 1950s / William I. Hitchcock.
Description: First Simon & Schuster hardcover edition. | New York : Simon & Schuster, 2018. | Series: Simon & Schuster nonfiction original hardcover | Includes bibliographical references and index.
Identifiers: LCCN 2017026867 | ISBN 9781439175668 | ISBN 1439175667
Subjects: LCSH: Eisenhower, Dwight D. (Dwight David), 1890–1969—Influence. | United States—Politics and government—1953–1961. | United States—Foreign relations—1953–1961.
Classification: LCC E835 .H56 2018 | DDC 973.921092—dc23
  LC record available at https://lccn.loc.gov/2017026867

ISBN 978-1-4391-7566-8
ISBN 978-1-4516-9842-8 (pbk)
ISBN 978-1-4516-9843-5 (ebook)

For my father,
David I. Hitchcock, Jr.,
who was there

CONTENTS

PART III: RACE, ROCKETS, AND REVOLUTION

PROLOGUE

"When I think about Dwight Eisenhower," wrote Capt. Edward Beach Jr., Eisenhower's naval aide, "I like to recall an incident that took place aboard the presidential yacht *Williamsburg* shortly after he was inaugurated for his first term in 1953."

The *Williamsburg*, a steel-hulled vessel of 1,800 tons, had served as President Harry S. Truman's pleasure craft; he used it for cruises with friends and political cronies. In May 1953 President Eisenhower ordered it decommissioned. He thought the ship frivolous and wasteful and felt it should be used for recreation by GIs who had been injured in the Korean War. One evening the president met the ship at the dock in the Washington Navy Yard as it returned from a cruise on the Potomac.

"As Eisenhower boarded the *Williamsburg*, he stepped in among the soldiers, brushing aside his Secret Service guards with words to the effect, 'Just let me be for a while. I know these men.'" Captain Beach remembered the scene:

> The soldiers crowded in around him. They were young men whose bodies had been ravaged by war in some way; some lacked an arm or a leg, some hobbled on crutches, others had heartbreaking facial disfigurements. . . . They gathered as close to the President as they could get, and I heard him talking to them.
>
> This was an Eisenhower that the public never saw. He talked to the soldiers of love of country, and of sacrifice. He said their country would never let them down, but no matter how much it did for them it was nothing compared to what they had done for it. And then he said that even with all they had already given, they must yet be prepared to give more, for they were symbols of devotion and sacrifice and they could never escape that role and its responsibilities.

Beach never forgot the electricity of Eisenhower's presence and the impact it had on these wounded warriors. "His voice had a deep friendly warmth, with a somewhat different timbre than I had ever heard before. It reached out and grabbed the men around him, so that they kept crowding in closer and closer as he talked, as if an unseen magnet were pulling at them."[1]

Historians who study Eisenhower know how those men felt in his presence. Ike draws you in. He radiated authenticity, idealism, sincerity, and charisma, and these personal qualities were the keys to his political success. Between 1945 and 1961 no person dominated American public life more than Eisenhower. He was the most well-liked and admired man in America in these years. And he was also the most *consequential*. This book argues that the era from the end of the Second World War up to the presidency of John F. Kennedy deserves to be known as the Age of Eisenhower.

Such a claim would once have prompted chuckles and even sneers from historians, journalists, and politicians. From the start of his active pursuit of the presidency in 1951, right through eight years in office, and for a decade after he retired to his farm in Gettysburg, Pennsylvania, critics styled Eisenhower as a lightweight, an amateur, an orthodox pro-business do-nothing president, a lazy leader who, despite all his grinning, was often callous and distant, more interested in golf than governing. The Washington press corps depicted him as unimaginative, slow-witted, out of touch, and frankly uninterested in the daily affairs of the country. Even as the nation enjoyed a period of unprecedented prosperity at home and a stable if fragile peace abroad, and even as the American people grew ever more fond of Ike, his political rivals were scathing about his shortcomings as a leader. It is the central paradox of the Eisenhower presidency: that a man so successful at the ballot box and so overwhelmingly popular among the voters could have been given such poor marks by the political class.

His critics never grasped the profound appeal of the man and never appreciated the depth of his political talent. His two-time opponent for the presidency, Governor Adlai Stevenson of Illinois, mocked Eisenhower as dim and tongue-tied and declared him little more than a tool of wealthy right-wingers. President Truman, campaigning on Stevenson's behalf in 1952, went further: he told whistle-stop audiences across the country that Eisenhower had only "a military mind" and that voters should "send Ike back to the Army where he belongs." The radical muckraker I. F. Stone, writing what many liberals felt, predicted that Ike, a "rather simple man who enjoys his bridge and his golf and doesn't like to be too much bothered," would be a "president *in absentia*." Even after his resounding triumph at the polls in 1952, Eisenhower still earned nothing but scorn from his critics. "Poor Ike," Truman said on his way out of office. "It won't be a bit like the Army. He'll sit here, and he'll say, 'Do this! Do that!' And nothing will happen."[2]

His presidency changed few minds among the commentators. A 1958 book by journalist Marquis Childs described Ike as a "captive hero," a man unable to make decisions, passive, complacent—little more than a ventriloquist's dummy who mouthed words prepared by others. That same year the *New York Post*'s Washington columnist William V. Shannon drew up a balance sheet and concluded that Eisenhower had largely sustained the policies of his Democratic predecessors in both the domestic and the international realm and had made almost no major initiatives of his own. "The Eisenhower era," he wrote, "is the time of the great postponement."[3]

Norman Mailer, the novelist, was nastier. In a celebrated 1960 essay in *Esquire* that hailed the nomination of the youthful and energetic John F. Kennedy for president, Mailer derided Eisenhower's era of "security, regularity, order." The 1950s for Mailer was a time when "many a mind atrophied from disuse and private shame." Mailer struck a note that has continued to reverberate ever since in some circles: "Eisenhower's eight years have been the triumph of the corporation. Tasteless, sexless, odorless sanctity."[4]

With Eisenhower's departure from office in January 1961, critics gleefully got out their spades and began to bury the ex-president. On the eve of Kennedy's inauguration, *New York Times* journalist James Reston wrote an essay on the Eisenhower years that read like an epitaph. Eisenhower "was not in tune with the world-wide spirit of the age, which was convulsive and revolutionary." He was merely "a good man in a wicked time; a consolidator in a world crying for innovation; a conservative in a radical age; a tired man in a period of turbulence and energetic action." Scholars agreed. In July 1962 Harvard historian Arthur Schlesinger Sr. published the results of a poll that asked 75 historians to rank the presidents. Eisenhower placed 22nd out of 31 chief executives, nestled between Chester A. Arthur and, incredibly, Andrew Johnson. President Kennedy himself had a good chuckle about this; after all the adulation and public frenzy, Eisenhower would now see "how he stood before the cold eye of history—way below Truman; even below Hoover."[5]

Indeed Camelot almost killed Ike. Not only did Kennedy run a brilliant campaign for president in 1960, contrasting his youth and dynamism with the septuagenarian Eisenhower, but his tragically shortened life only enhanced the sense of his sparkling singularity. Arthur Schlesinger Jr., who had served as special assistant to JFK, rushed out an elegiac account of the Kennedy presidency. In his 1965 testament, *A Thousand Days*, Schlesinger used the complacent Eisenhower as a foil to better reflect sunlight upon the glittering years of Camelot. In every respect the comparison between the two men and the ideas that inspired them was unflattering to Eisenhower.[6]

By the time of his death, on March 28, 1969, at the age of 78, Eisenhower had been largely forgotten by the press. Obituaries summed him up as a worthy man whose greatest role had been played on the European stage in the Second World War and whose presidency was a postscript to a life of noble military achievement. The *New York Times* asserted that as president he "had governed effectively through sheer force of his popularity among average Americans"—a distinctly backhanded appraisal. *Time* magazine commented that many Americans would remember Ike "not as the 34th president whose stewardship may long be disputed, but as 'the soldier of peace' who led the greatest alliance of armies the world has ever seen." By the close of his years in office, *Time* concluded, he was "more figurehead than president" and "out of touch with his people." As a politician Eisenhower seemed destined to be written off as a benign mediocrity.[7]

Tides, once having ebbed, always come back in. The revival of interest in Eisenhower began in the late 1960s, prodded perhaps by the deep national crisis that his successors, John Kennedy, Lyndon Johnson, and Richard Nixon, had confronted and exacerbated. In an era of student protest, war in Vietnam, racial upheaval, and economic malaise, the 1950s began to look curiously alluring. One of his most acerbic critics, the shrewd *New York Post* columnist Murray Kempton, penned a 1967 essay that almost single-handedly gave rise to a new school of thought about Eisenhower. He was neither benign nor mediocre, Kempton concluded, but malevolent and brilliant. His skills ran not to governing but to manipulation, dissimulation, and guile. He sought always to profit from the success of others and to avoid the taint of any failures, especially his own. Eisenhower was "cold," "immoral," determined to conceal "his marvelous intelligence from admirer and critic alike." Kempton summed up Eisenhower's political motto: "Always pretend to be stupid; then when you have to show yourself to be smart, the display has the additional effect of surprise."[8]

The theme of a devious and effortlessly political Eisenhower appeared in Garry Wills's masterful 1970 study of the early Nixon, in which "the Great One" was the perfect contrast to the restless, insecure, and nakedly ambitious Nixon. The relationship hinged upon Nixon's desire to supplant Eisenhower and his awareness that he never could. Eisenhower's supreme self-confidence, his immense popularity, his ability to compel others to serve him while never appearing to ask for such loyalty—all these were mysteries of character Nixon could never hope to understand, let alone emulate. Eisenhower, Wills believed, "had the true professional's instinct for making things look easy. He appeared to be performing less work than he actually did. And he wanted it that way. An air of ease inspires confidence." It was in *Nixon Agonistes* that a leading intellectual of the era first called Eisenhower a "political genius"—a far cry from the smirks and chortles of the Camelot clan.[9]

The picture really began to change, though, in the late 1970s, when the voluminous archives held at the Dwight D. Eisenhower Presidential Library in Abilene, Kansas, became available to scholars. In a 1982 book titled *The Hidden-Hand Presidency*, political scientist Fred Greenstein added depth and detail to the sketch offered by Kempton and Wills. Drawing on new evidence, Greenstein argued that Eisenhower's apparent aloofness and absenteeism had been part of a deliberate governing strategy. Greenstein believed that Ike hid his abilities and his own engagement with the issues in order to exercise power more effectively. He used intermediaries to do his political dirty work, baffled reporters with garbled syntax, refused to publicly acknowledge political rivals by name, delegated responsibility to cabinet secretaries, and fed the public reasoned, calm, simple bromides about the American way of life. "Eisenhower went to great lengths," Greenstein concluded, "to conceal the political side of his leadership."[10]

A "hidden" Eisenhower, then. Perhaps. But later work, drawing on much more material than Greenstein could access, suggested otherwise. During the 1980s and 1990s the boom in Eisenhower studies gained momentum, sustained not principally by biographers but by historians of U.S. foreign relations. Scholars who wanted to know about the origins and course of the cold war; the Korean War; the rise of covert operations and the CIA; grand strategy and nuclear weapons; American policies toward China, Latin America, Europe, and the Middle East; the rise of the Third World—all trekked to Abilene to inspect the Eisenhower archives in hopes of finding hitherto unseen treasures. The subsequent cascade of studies on Eisenhower's cold war policies shattered forever the myth that Ike was disengaged from the running of government. And it became increasingly difficult to sustain the idea that he "hid" his power and authority.[11]

The Eisenhower era suddenly looked, well, *interesting.* The new research revealed a complex president who at times showed exceptional restraint in the use of America's power but who also had a taste for daring and even recklessness, especially when ordering the use of covert operations against left-wing governments. The documents portrayed a deeply engaged leader struggling to forge policies in a vast array of fields, from civil rights to economic policy, infrastructure, science and education, religion, communist "subversion" on the home front, and national security policy abroad. Eisenhower now appeared principled but adaptive, ideological at times but usually pragmatic, a problem-solver who dominated his cabinet, the military, and the bureaucracy and put his imprimatur on the age.[12]

Above all, the evidence showed how hard Ike worked over eight years. The allegation that he had been a golf-playing no-show was deeply unfair. "No man on Earth knows what this job is all about," he said one afternoon in 1954. "It's pound, pound, pound. Not only is your intellectual capacity taxed to the utmost, but your physical stamina." It wasn't so easy after all.[13]

This book stands on the shoulders of the many previous Eisenhower scholars who have worked diligently for years to unearth the secrets of the period and to flesh out our understanding of the man and his era. It also benefits from many newly declassified documents that have become available only recently, thanks to the efforts of the dedicated staff at the Eisenhower Library. Taking into account all this material, this book offers a comprehensive account of the president and his times and concludes with a decisive verdict: Dwight Eisenhower must be counted among the most consequential presidents of modern American history.[14]

Eisenhower shaped the United States in at least three lasting ways. First, he dramatically expanded the power and scope of the 20th-century warfare state and put into place a long-term strategy designed to wage, and win, the cold war. This book deals with national security and foreign relations a good deal because Eisenhower spent much of his time forging a global role for the United States. Unlike the isolationist faction in his own party, he believed that to defend freedom and liberty at home, Americans would have to defend these principles overseas as well.

These views did not lead Eisenhower to seek war. On the contrary, he ended active hostilities in Korea, avoided U.S. military intervention in Indochina in 1954, deterred China's military adventures in the Taiwan Straits in 1955 and 1958, compelled Britain and France to reverse their ill-conceived invasion of Egypt in 1956, and even established stable personal relations with the Soviet leader Nikita Khrushchev. Eisenhower worked hard, and successfully, to keep the peace. His global strategy required the steady accumulation of immense national power and a willingness to deploy that power when necessary. Building on the legacy of Truman, who laid the foundations of the cold war state, Eisenhower deployed American economic muscle, diplomatic leverage, generous deliveries of arms, and a global nuclear shield to deter and intimidate America's enemies. He mobilized science, universities, and industry to boost American military power, even going so far as to take the first steps in the militarization of space. He presided over a significant expansion of America's secret intelligence agencies and ordered them to conduct covert operations and coups d'état around the world. He frequently evoked the image of an "America in peril" and in so doing generated an enduring national consensus to support his robust cold war policies.

Eisenhower built the United States into a military colossus of a scale and lethality never before seen and devoted an enormous amount of the national wealth to this effort. Biographers have often hailed his tight-fisted budget policies, but when it came to national defense, he was not stingy. In the Eisenhower years the United States spent about 10 percent of its GDP each year on the military establishment—a higher percentage than any peacetime administration before or since. This book offers abundant evidence that the man who warned later generations about the military-industrial complex did a great deal to build it.

Second, Eisenhower recast domestic politics by strengthening a national consensus about the place of government in the lives of American citizens. Before Eisenhower, the political pendulum had swung from the archconservative nostrums of Warren Harding, Calvin Coolidge, and Herbert Hoover to the bold, all-encompassing activism of Franklin Roosevelt and the New Deal. Eisenhower, perhaps the least partisan president of modern times, sought to stop the pendulum in dead center. To be sure, when he ran for president in 1952, he thundered against the "statism" of the New Deal and its expansive federal programs. But once in office he adopted centrist and pragmatic policies that fairly reflected the preferences of most of his fellow citizens. Early on he made his peace with the New Deal, expanding social security, raising the minimum wage, and founding the Department of Health,

Education, and Welfare. He even suggested ideas for a national health insurance system. Eisenhower found a way to make government work without making it too big; his interstate highway system is a good example. Though building its thousands of miles of roads cost billions of dollars, most of the money came from user fees in the form of a gas tax, used to replenish the Highway Trust Fund. The burden on the U.S. Treasury was relatively minor.

In confronting the greatest social and moral challenge of his times, the civil rights movement, Eisenhower—like many white Americans of the era—responded with caution and wariness. Crucially, though, he did not obstruct progress on civil rights. Instead he channeled it along a path that aligned with his own ideas about managing social change. Knowing that he was out of his depth on such matters, he accepted guidance from the most consequential cabinet officer of the decade, Attorney General Herbert Brownell. Together these two men worked quietly through the courts to weaken Jim Crow segregation. They appointed five moderately progressive jurists to the U.S. Supreme Court and ushered the Civil Rights Act of 1957 through a skeptical Congress. The Act was a landmark only because it was so rare: the first civil rights law since Reconstruction. Eisenhower took an enormous risk, and one that was deeply uncharacteristic, when he ordered federal troops to surround Central High School in Little Rock, Arkansas, to ensure that court-ordered desegregation proceed despite the hostility of local authorities. It is true that Eisenhower never publicly or personally embraced the fundamental demand of African Americans for equal justice, but he did use his power to aid rather than halt the work of a courageous generation of civil rights crusaders who were just emerging onto the American scene.

Third, Eisenhower established a distinctive model of presidential leadership that Americans—now more than ever—ought to study. We might call it the *disciplined* presidency. Raised in a strict and frugal family and trained for a career of soldiering, Ike believed that discipline was the key to success. Not only did he apply discipline to his own person, maintaining his weight at a trim 175 pounds and quitting a four-pack-a-day cigarette habit overnight, but discipline infused his governing style. Coming into Truman's disorganized and improvisational White House, Eisenhower imposed order on it, establishing clear rules of procedure. Each Monday he met with leaders from Congress; Wednesday he held his weekly press conference with the print, radio, and (after January 1955) television reporters; Thursdays he chaired the National Security Council; Fridays he met with his cabinet.

Truman did not convene his NSC often, and Kennedy simply dismissed it. Eisenhower, by contrast, endowed the NSC with enormous importance. He used the weekly meetings of this body to craft, review, and approve policies. In his eight years in office, the NSC met 366 times, and Eisenhower was present at 329 of those meetings—a 90 percent attendance rate. It is easy to lampoon this bureaucratic drudgery, but for Eisenhower good government required such constant focus. "Plans are worthless, but planning is everything," he often remarked. "If you haven't been planning, you can't start to work, intelligently at least." In the hour of crisis Ike wanted a disciplined, well-trained staff and system already in place, ready to work.[15]

Discipline carried over into Eisenhower's approach to the economy and defense. A champion of the free market, Ike told Americans that prosperity would come only to those who worked hard and made sacrifices; the government would do no more than clear a path so that individual Americans could demonstrate their God-given talents. It is no accident that Eisenhower's closest friends were self-made millionaires who, like him, had started out in life with little. He also told Americans they needed discipline to wage and win the cold war. From his first inaugural to his Farewell Address, he insisted that to prevail in the struggle against global communism, Americans needed to demonstrate vigilance and steadfast purpose. They needed to pay taxes, serve in the military, and rally to the defense of their country. They needed to spend wisely on defense so as not to jeopardize the health of the economy or trigger inflation. Most significant, he believed, the American system could endure only if citizens willingly imposed *self-discipline* and prepared themselves to bear the common burden of defending free government. Americans like to think of themselves as the inheritors of Athenian democracy, but Eisenhower, a soldier-statesman who believed his nation faced a dire threat from a hostile ideology, also drew inspiration from the martial virtues of Sparta.[16]

Ike's insistence on vigilance, discipline, restraint, and individual self-reliance sometimes worked against him politically. He was never comfortable in the role of a purely partisan leader. He did have strong views on many issues, and he presented himself at election time as a conservative, small-government, budget-balancing Republican. But he considered the president a national leader, above the partisan fracas. This tendency to leave the job of party politics to others got him in trouble. In the elections of 1954, 1956, and 1958 Republicans lost 68 seats in the House and 17 seats in the Senate, and Eisenhower had no good answer for this implosion. When

Democrats attacked him from late 1957 on for his alleged lapses on a series of issues, from national defense to economic growth and social programs, Eisenhower failed to mount an effective partisan rebuttal to these charges. In 1960 Senator John Kennedy got a jump-start in the presidential campaign, running against the allegedly cold and complacent Republican Party, and nimbly raced to victory.

Yet one of the reasons Americans admired Eisenhower was his indifference to narrow party advantage. Though voters put Democrats in charge of Congress, they loved Eisenhower: he garnered an astonishing average approval rating of 65 percent during his eight years in office, higher than Ronald Reagan (53 percent) or Bill Clinton (55 percent). More striking, Eisenhower found support in both parties. Over eight years, 50 percent of *Democrats* approved of his performance. In our more polarized times, such cross-party affinity is rare. On average only 23 percent of Democrats approved of George W. Bush during his eight years in office, while a mere 14 percent of Republicans offered their approval of Barack Obama during his two terms. Eisenhower had that rarest of gifts in politics: he brought Americans together.[17]

And so we come back to that scene on the deck of the *Williamsburg* depicted so movingly by Captain Beach, a scene filled with pathos and deep humanity, and in a way the perfect metaphor for the Age of Eisenhower. There sat the most powerful man in the world, relaxed in a circle of wounded soldiers, men who had given so much for their country, men who would never be whole again. It was a moment of quiet intimacy, a gathering of brothers. "I know these men," Ike had said.

These kindred spirits felt bound to one another not by their desire for power or their yearning for material rewards or their partisan affiliation. Instead, these men formed a family because of their belief in the ennobling act of personal sacrifice and public service. In their midst, Ike drew their attention not to the benefits they could now expect from their government but to the additional role they must play as exemplars of the American spirit. Nothing could more perfectly capture the hopes and the enduring appeal of the Age of Eisenhower.

PART I

DUTY

CHAPTER 1

ASCENT

*"The homely old saw had proved to be true: in the
United States, any boy can grow up to be president."*

I

"NO PRESIDENT HAD EVER HAD SO LITTLE EXPERIENCE OF POL-
itics and so little firsthand experience of American life" as Dwight D. Eisenhower, asserted the veteran political journalist Marquis Childs in his 1958
book, *The Captive Hero.* And many critics echoed this claim: after a long
career in the protective, isolated world of the American military, including
lengthy postings overseas in Panama, the Philippines, and Europe, Eisenhower, upon taking office as president, knew little about the basic rhythms
of ordinary American life and was unschooled in the ways of politics.[1]

True, Eisenhower had spent his adult life in the hierarchical, rule-
bound world of the army, and he'd never been elected to anything in his life.
But Childs was doubly wrong. Eisenhower was intimately familiar with the
nature of rural American life, having been raised by God-fearing, dutiful,
and frugal parents in the Kansas farmlands, and he left Kansas at the age
of 20 to enter upon a career in the most political of institutions, the U.S.
Army, in which he rose, over many years of patient labor, to a position of
preeminence.

His humble origins and his extensive leadership experience were the
twin sources of Eisenhower's popular appeal and his political success. He
had deep roots in Middle America, of which he remained proud and by
which he set his moral compass. At the same time he learned how to operate
in, and finally dominate, a massive bureaucracy filled with ambitious egos
hungry for glory. As Garry Wills memorably wrote, Eisenhower made his
ascent to power by climbing "a slippery ladder of bayonets."[2]

Not only did he achieve greatness in the American armed services; during the Second World War he asserted control over the British Army as well, forging its fractious, skeptical generals into a cohesive fighting force alongside the Americans. Together—and under his command—they defeated the Germans. His leadership of the combined Allied armies in Western Europe required vision, patience, compromise, goodwill, and inexhaustible persistence: precisely the skills that prepared him for the White House. As chief of staff of the U.S. Army just after the war, he faced huge problems of winding down the national military establishment while retooling for a global cold war. For four years he was president of Columbia University, where he navigated the complexities of academia. And in his final post before winning the presidency, as supreme commander of NATO, he directed 12 nations toward the common goal of mutual defense and rearmament.

Far from being inexperienced upon taking office in 1952, Eisenhower could reasonably look upon the presidency as a job for which he was extraordinarily well prepared—far more so certainly than his predecessor, Harry S. Truman, had been upon taking office after Franklin D. Roosevelt's sudden death, and certainly more than his 43-year-old successor, John F. Kennedy, the junior senator from Massachusetts. Expressing supreme confidence in himself, Eisenhower jotted down this remarkable observation at the end of his first day in the Oval Office: "Plenty of worries and difficult problems. But such has been my portion for a long time—the result is that this just seems (today) like a continuation of all I've been doing since July 1941—even before that."[3]

It is hard to imagine a man with a stronger sense of himself and his origins and a man as tested by war, the burdens of command, and the politics of world leadership as was Dwight D. Eisenhower on the day he took office as the 34th president of the United States.

II

There was nothing inevitable in this ascent. Eisenhower's forebears had emigrated from the Susquehanna Valley of Pennsylvania to Abilene, Kansas, in 1878. They formed part of a colony of prosperous Mennonites who were searching for a new start in the wide-open plains of the West. The family patriarch, Jacob Eisenhower, a minister of the River Brethren Church, saw opportunity in Kansas and desired greater distance from the influence of modernity that was starting to encroach upon the Plain People of south-central Pennsylvania. In Abilene, Jacob bought hundreds of acres of rich farmland, built a large homestead with ample room for gatherings of his church flock, and settled into a life of farming and worship.

Jacob's son David Eisenhower, not drawn to the rigors of a life on the land, hoped to establish himself in business. He spent a year at Lane University in Lecompton, Kansas, improving himself, learning Greek, and studying mechanics. At Lane he also met a pretty young woman whose family hailed from Virginia, Ida Elizabeth Stover. The two were married in the Lane University chapel in September 1885. David went into the dry-goods business in the nearby town of Hope. For two years the store succeeded, and David and Ida began to raise a family. But David lost interest in the store and moved his family to Texas in search of a new start. He found work in the small town of Denison. Just south of the Red River and the Oklahoma state line, Denison had been established only 20 years earlier and was little more than a huddle of buildings surrounding the intersection of rail lines on the Missouri-Kansas-Texas Railroad. Far from home and penniless, David and Ida had a third son, born on October 14, 1890. They named him David Dwight, and he was brought into the world in a rented home facing the railroad tracks in an isolated, rural Texas town, as far from the halls of power as an American could be at the turn of the century.[4]

David, Ida, and their three boys could endure the heat and the limited prospects of Denison for only two years. In early 1891 they moved back to Abilene, where David was embraced by the extended Eisenhower clan and employed as a mechanic by the large Belle Springs Creamery, a dairy-processing plant owned and operated by members of the Brethren Church community. Cautious about spending money, David raised his family in modest and at times difficult circumstances. Combining hard work with a devout faith, he and Ida built a stable and happy life, though they always lived close to the margins and never knew financial security.[5]

Abilene was a small frontier town with a population in 1892 of about 5,000. It had been settled by cattlemen in the 1850s to serve as the end point of the Chisholm Trail, along which millions of cattle were driven from ranches in Texas to stockyards and railheads in the heart of the country. Despite an early reputation as a town of loose morals and dangerous gunslingers (Wild Bill Hickok served as the sheriff in 1871), Abilene by the turn of the century had settled down to become a quiet mid-American small town, with a main street of handsome Victorian homes and a downtown of a few dozen brick buildings running north from the train depot and stockyards.

No longer a rough outpost, Abilene then had 14 churches, four schools, paved main streets, a theater, two daily and four weekly newspapers, and was home to the Dickinson County Courthouse. The community valued modesty, piety, plain speaking, and family. Townspeople shared the view that hard work was a duty as well as proof of a person's worth.

The Eisenhowers lived in a small, white clapboard two-story home at 201 Southeast 4th Street, with tall narrow windows and a slender ribbon of porch running along the front. The home sat on a three-acre parcel just a block south of the main rail line that marked a frontier of sorts: Eisenhower's family lived on the wrong side of the tracks and would have had limited social interaction with the more affluent families. David's job at the creamery demanded long hours, six days a week. Stern, religious, and diffident, David was "the breadwinner, Supreme Court and Lord High Executioner" of the family, his son later recalled. Ida provided quite a contrast. Vivacious, intellectually curious, and clever, her one year of college at Lane—almost unheard of among women in Kansas in the late 19th century—revealed her passion for learning. This she passed on to her six boys, to whom she dedicated her life.

But the Eisenhower household was no bevy of free-thinkers: as parents, David and Ida were disciplinarians, and family life revolved around work and Bible study. "Everybody I knew went to church," Eisenhower remembered. "Social life was centered around the churches," and in the Eisenhower family that meant close association with the Mennonite River Brethren community and its intense devotions. Every evening the family gathered in the small living room to listen as David read out loud from the family Bible. Later in life Ida and David both became Jehovah's Witnesses, a sect devoted to Bible study, evangelism, and pacifism. Eisenhower knew his Scripture, yet it is noteworthy that after leaving home for the army, he did not attend church until 1953, when he joined the National Presbyterian Church in Washington and was baptized there at the age of 62.[6]

Eisenhower was the third son and known affectionately as "Little Ike." His larger, older brother Edgar was "Big Ike." Arthur, Edgar, Dwight, Roy, Earl, and Milton (another brother, Paul, died in infancy) shared two bedrooms; Eisenhower shared a bed with Roy. They all became successful in their chosen fields, the youngest, Milton, becoming one of the country's leading academic administrators. A president of Kansas State University, Penn State, and Johns Hopkins, Milton served as Eisenhower's closest and most intimate personal adviser for the duration of his presidency. The boys shared in the manual labor of the household, whether working in the vegetable gardens, doing chores, or attending to the animals the family kept in a barn. Eisenhower spent summer weekends selling home-grown vegetables from a cart he pulled up and down the residential streets, earning the family a few additional cents.

In these early years Eisenhower turned in an average performance in school. Intensely competitive and a gifted athlete—strong, agile, and quick—he ran with a group of South Side boys, defending the honor of his neighborhood against the wealthier and socially more prominent lads from north of the tracks. He bloodied a few noses in frequent scraps and developed prowess in boxing. He grew to a height of 5'10", tall for the time, and sported a shock of blond hair. Throughout his life he loved to be outdoors. His relationship with nature had nothing of the masculine, self-improvement hyperbole of Theodore Roosevelt or Robert Baden-Powell, two leading figures of the day then urging teenage boys to pursue the strenuous life as a way to build character. Eisenhower was simply a country boy who, when not working or in school, spent the happiest moments of his youth fishing, hunting, camping, or playing in the breezy vastness of the plains or along the banks of the shallow Smoky Hill River.

Like any boy who has grown up in the country, he always felt cooped up inside, and as president he yearned to get into the open air, whether on the golf course or on occasional fishing and hunting trips with friends. Eisenhower never tried to hide his humble country origins behind the accumulated honors of his stunningly successful career. "The life we had together," he wrote, "had been complete, stimulating, and informative, with opportunity available to us for the asking. We had been poor, but one of the glories of America, at the time, was that we didn't know it. It was a good, secure small-town life, and that we wanted for luxuries didn't occur to any of us."[7]

After he finished high school, Eisenhower went to work in the creamery alongside his father, a job he held for nearly two years. But this was not a fulfilling life for a smart, quietly ambitious young man. He wanted to go to college, inspired by his brother Edgar, who matriculated at the University of Michigan in 1909. Edgar's tuition was paid for in part by Eisenhower's wages at the creamery. The boys agreed that after a year they would switch places, with the older boy working to put the younger through a year at Ann Arbor. But Eisenhower was too impatient to wait for this long-term plan to unfold. In his 20th year, urged on by his friend Edward Everett "Swede" Hazlett Jr., who was planning to attend the Naval Academy, Eisenhower sought and gained admission to the U.S. Military Academy at West Point; he enrolled in June 1911, age 20 years and eight months. Here was his ticket out and up, into a world he could never have glimpsed from Abilene.[8]

III

He could not have known it at the time, but Eisenhower entered West Point at a propitious moment. In the coming three decades his class of 1915 provided many of the general officers for a rapidly expanding U.S. Army that would wage two world wars and grow into the most powerful military the world had ever seen. Of the 164 men who graduated in his class, 59 would rise to the rank of brigadier general or higher. Eisenhower and his friend and classmate Omar Bradley both attained the exalted rank of general of the army, a five-star general. In time their class was aptly named "the class the stars fell on."

This rise to stardom, however, took a long time. For all his later glory, Eisenhower did not distinguish himself at West Point. He struggled with the Academy's obsessive attitude toward discipline and rules, though he persevered. His years of manual labor in Abilene prepared him for the rigors of cadet training. Life at West Point, Eisenhower thought, "was hardest on those who were not used to exercise or who had been overindulged." But he confessed to "a lack of motivation in almost everything other than athletics." His one true passion, football, occupied most of his time. "It would be difficult to overemphasize the importance that I attached to participation in sports," he later wrote, and yet this was a pleasure denied to him after suffering a knee injury in 1912, his second year at the Academy.

Though his playing days were over, he became a cheerleader for the football team, then the coach of the junior varsity squad. He showed great talent as a motivator and student of the game. He was inclined later in life to see football as a great school for leadership: "Perhaps more than any other sport, [football] tends to instill in men the feeling that victory comes through hard—almost slavish—work, team play, self-confidence." His knee injury nearly cost him a commission in the army, but he had gained a reputation as a natural leader, despite his average academic performance. He graduated 61st in his class in June 1915 and in September received a commission as a second lieutenant in the U.S. Army, along with three months' back pay and orders to report to Fort Sam Houston in San Antonio, Texas.[9]

The fates now conspired to deny Eisenhower the one thing that every officer silently yearns for to spur his advancement up the ranks: war. When he left West Point, his timing seemed perfect for a combat command. In 1915, the year Eisenhower received his commission, a German submarine sank the British passenger liner *Lusitania*, killing 128 Americans and putting America and Germany on course toward war. After further provocations from Germany, President Woodrow Wilson asked Congress for a declaration of war in April 1917—the start of America's 30-year confrontation with German militarism.

For Eisenhower, the outbreak of war promised action, combat, and promotion. But when war came, he did not go to France; he went to Fort Oglethorpe in Georgia, to train officer candidates. He yearned for orders that would get him into the war, and they seemed in the offing when he was posted to Camp Meade in Maryland, there to train an engineering battalion. But Eisenhower's organizational abilities had been noted, and instead of being shipped to Europe he went to Camp Colt in Gettysburg in the spring of 1918, where he was tasked with building a new Tank Corps. Rather than face the trials of the battlefield, he confronted the arduous duty of transforming a derelict outpost in the Pennsylvania countryside into a major training ground for men destined to be shipped to France.

"Now I really began to learn about responsibility," he recalled. He had to find tents for his men; equip these rudimentary quarters with stoves, fuel, bedding, and food; and develop a training regimen for a Tank Corps that as yet did not even have tanks. In midsummer the camp received its first shipment of the new wonder weapons: three French-built Renaults, about seven tons in weight, without guns. To train the men, Eisenhower laconically wrote, "we improvised." He became known as a rigid disciplinarian, but one who was fair and consistent. When he caught an officer cheating at cards, he had no doubts about what to do: the man was given a choice of immediate resignation or court-martial. More serious challenges came in September 1918, when Spanish influenza swept through the camp, leaving 175 men dead in just a week. Eisenhower now had to organize isolation tents, a hospital, a rotation of doctors, and a morgue.

On his 28th birthday Eisenhower was promoted to temporary lieutenant colonel, but his real present came the following month, in orders to ship out to France. Too late: the German Army was close to collapse, and on November 11 the war came to an end. It was a bitter disappointment to him. "I had missed the boat in the war we had been told would end all wars. . . . I was mad, disappointed, and resented the fact that the war had passed me by."[10]

What was to become of an army major, the rank to which he now reverted, without combat experience, in a peacetime army? His prospects were limited, but it is a testament to Eisenhower's talents that he rose even in these circumstances to a position of influence. Two factors worked for him: his own hard work and the support of some powerful patrons. His posting to Camp Meade led to an introduction made by a dashing, aristocratic officer named George S. Patton, whom Eisenhower had befriended, to one of the most influential and respected men in the interwar army, Brig. Gen. Fox Conner. As operations officer for the American Expeditionary Force during the war, Conner had won a reputation as one of the army's finest minds and most respected senior officers. Eisenhower and Conner developed a strong relationship based on mutual admiration, and Conner adopted Eisenhower as a protégé. When Conner was sent to the Panama Canal Zone to command the 20th Infantry Brigade at Camp Gaillard and oversee the U.S. military presence in this new vital waterway, he got Eisenhower assigned to him as his executive officer.

From January 1922 to September 1924, under Conner's command, Eisenhower burnished his reputation as a hard-driving, exacting officer who brooked no slouching from the men. When he was not working or shooing bats and insects out of his vine-covered quarters at Camp Gaillard, Eisenhower read texts assigned to him by the deep-thinking Conner. Under the general's guidance Eisenhower sweated out the tropical evenings in his tin-roof barracks devouring the classics of strategy, including Carl von Clausewitz's complex treatise *On War*, the memoirs of Napoleon, and campaign histories of the American Civil War. He even dove into Plato and Nietzsche, borrowing books from Conner's splendid personal library. After their daily duties were complete, the two spent many hours exchanging ideas and provocations about history, philosophy, and leadership. These sessions were invaluable to Eisenhower, and he later acknowledged Conner's enormous impact on his intellectual development. He was therefore supremely well-prepared for the yearlong course in strategic studies he took at the Command and General Staff School at Fort Leavenworth in 1925–26. At the end of the year Eisenhower graduated first in his class.[11]

In July 1926 Eisenhower marked an important milestone: the 10th anniversary of his marriage to a slender blue-eyed beauty named Mamie Geneva Doud. He had fallen for her when he was just a year out of West Point and she just 18. They met in San Antonio, where Mamie's well-to-do family spent part of the year; her father had made a prosperous living in the meat-processing industry and also owned a large home in Denver. Mamie and Eisenhower were married in the Doud home in July 1916.

It proved a wonderful match. Though they had few resources—Eisenhower's pay was paltry, and despite small subventions from Mamie's father, they lived in cramped officers' quarters for years—they were both outgoing and warm, a pair that collected friends and hosted parties with eager, unfeigned pleasure. "She was not technically beautiful," one portrait-ist wrote. "Her nose was a millimeter too long, her mouth too generous, and her shining brown hair swirled down her high forehead in a curious untamed style of her own. On the other hand, her long-lashed eyes were the dark blue of a piece of sky reflected in a well, and her skin actually seemed translucent." Though fragile-looking, she possessed "the warm earthiness of the people of the western plains and mountains. She was restful to be with, yet her enthusiasm for life was expressed in constant movement, so that she rippled in the breeze of her own excitement." In Mamie, Eisenhower had found a vital partner, a woman of energy, charm, and sociability who devoted herself to his career.[12]

Their happiness was touched by tragedy in the late winter of 1920, when their three-year-old son, Doud Dwight, whom they had nicknamed Icky, contracted scarlet fever. The young couple had been amassing armfuls of Christmas presents and putting them under a spindly Christmas tree in their cramped Camp Meade quarters. But the gifts were to remain unwrapped, for by Christmas Day Icky's condition had worsened, his fever soared, and he drifted in and out of consciousness. In the early hours of January 2, 1921, he died. Eisenhower's own words, written almost a half century later, cap-ture his despair: "I do not know how others have felt when facing the same situation, but I have never known such a blow. Within a week he was gone. I didn't know what to do. . . . This was the greatest disappointment and di-saster in my life, the one I have never been able to forget completely. Today when I think of it, even now as I write of it, the keenness of our loss comes back to me as fresh and as terrible as it was in that long dark day soon after Christmas, 1920."[13]

"For a long time," Mamie would reveal many years later, "it was as if a shining light had gone out in Ike's life." She too was shattered, as a plaintive letter to her parents, written three weeks after Icky's death, reveals: "I find the hardest time is when I go to bed and I can't tuck him in—and the many times I think I hear him in the night." Not until August 1922, with the birth of their son John, did the Eisenhower family begin to feel whole again. But every year on Icky's birthday, Eisenhower sent Mamie a bouquet of roses.[14]

The Conner connection that had taken Eisenhower to Panama continued to open doors. Conner secured for Eisenhower a position working for Gen. John "Black Jack" Pershing, the commander of American forces in the First World War, who by 1927 was directing the American Battle Monuments Commission. This organization erected cemeteries and monuments across Western Europe to memorialize and honor America's fallen servicemen, and Pershing asked Eisenhower to prepare its official guidebook. This job gave him the opportunity to work with the army's most senior officer and to earn a glowing commendation letter from Pershing that referred to Eisenhower's "superior ability" and "unusual intelligence." He also made the acquaintance of a man whose name he had often heard praised by General Conner: Col. George C. Marshall, whose star was on the rise.

After further academic training at the Army War College in Washington, D.C.—from whose yearlong course he graduated first in his class in 1928—Eisenhower went to Paris to continue his work for Pershing's Battle Monuments Commission. It was a heavenly 14 months for Eisenhower, Mamie, and young John. They lived in an apartment on the rue d'Auteuil, in the western part of the city, near the Bois de Boulogne. Eisenhower and Mamie entertained often, drawing on the large American community in Paris for social company. They half-heartedly studied a little French and spent a good deal of time on the road visiting military cemeteries and monuments on behalf of the commission. One memorable holiday junket with Maj. William Gruber and his wife, Helen, in late summer of 1929 took them through Belgium, Germany, and Switzerland. Traveling in a rented Buick, drinking plenty of wine along the way, staying in country hotels, and picnicking on the roadside, they especially enjoyed the Rhine Valley. Eisenhower found the countryside of Bonn, Coblenz, Heidelberg, and Konstanz "gorgeous," with its vistas of pine woods, hills, and castles. The couple was entranced, he noted in his journal of the trip, by "the people as well as beautiful landscapes." Everywhere they went, they were met with courtesy and kindness. "We like Germany!" he gushed.[15]

Eisenhower could not know it then, but he would return to these same lovely landscapes 15 years later as the commander of a gigantic armed force set upon destruction and conquest.

IV

If Fox Conner, in his dank quarters in Panama, had given Eisenhower a graduate seminar in strategy, the 1930s would immerse this talented but un-fulfilled officer—now nearing 40 years old, he'd been a major for ten years—in another kind of learning: the bureaucratic and institutional politics of Washington, D.C. In the fall of 1929, Eisenhower was assigned as an aide to Brig. Gen. George Van Horn Moseley, then serving as executive assistant to Frederick Payne, assistant secretary of war. After a delightful but marginal assignment in France, Eisenhower was able to observe and participate in the making of national defense policy. "Except for the fact that I do not like to live in a city," he confided to his diary, "I am particularly pleased with this detail. The General is alert and energetic and certainly enjoys a fine reputation for accomplishment in the Army. I am also looking forward to the opportunity of learning something about the economic and industrial conditions that will prevail in this country in the event of a major war."[16]

For two years Ike studied the problems of industrial mobilization in wartime, the start of a lifelong concern with the problem of America's mili-tary preparedness. In the late 1920s the U.S. Army was in dreadful shape, with barely 120,000 men. (By comparison, Eisenhower would have three million men under his command in Europe at the close of World War II.) Congress had slashed the army's budget, and as a consequence the links between industry and the military procurement process had withered. All this would have to be restarted from scratch in the event of war. Ike labored valiantly in studying America's industrial capabilities and the need for close government-industry cooperation in wartime. After months of inspection tours of factories, workshops, and rubber plantations, Eisenhower declared in a journal article published under the name of the assistant secretary that the most important lesson of the First World War was this: "When great na-tions resort to armed conflict today, the readiness of each to meet promptly the needs of its armed forces in munitions, and of its civilian population in the necessities of life, may well prove to be a decisive factor in the contest." As early as 1930 he grasped the need for modern states to build a standing "military-industrial complex."[17]

Eisenhower had a way of being noticed by senior officers, and by 1931 the new chief of staff of the U.S. Army, Gen. Douglas MacArthur, had come to see in Major Eisenhower a valuable talent. MacArthur was America's leading soldier. He'd had a legendary career at West Point, graduating first in his class in 1903. Fighting on the Western Front in World War I, he rose to the rank of brigadier general, won the Distinguished Service Cross twice, and earned the Silver Star for valor in action seven times. He had served as superintendent of West Point, did a tour of duty in the Philippines, and in 1930, though the youngest major general in the army, became chief of staff. MacArthur was an impressive figure, but he was also egotistic, vainglorious, and somewhat operatic, besotted with his own self-made legend and sensitive to the least slight. Eisenhower found him "forceful" and "blessed with a fast and facile mind." But he disdained MacArthur's obsession with politics. Most officers tried hard to respect the line drawn by tradition between politics and the military, while MacArthur "chose to ignore it." As a result Eisenhower's duties under the chief of staff began "to verge on the political, even to the edge of partisan politics." Over time, close association with MacArthur provided Eisenhower with a role model of the kind of military leader he did not want to be.[18]

In 1931 MacArthur gave Eisenhower the job of writing the army's annual report, then rewarded him with a commendation for his work and roped him into his entourage. Ike was now ensconced in the higher reaches of the military, but he paid a price for his proximity to the ostentatious chief of staff. In the summer of 1932 MacArthur brazenly led the army into the streets of southeast Washington to evict 20,000 destitute war veterans who were demanding payment of back wages for their war service. Eisenhower counseled him against using army troops as policemen. "By this time," he recalled, "our relationship was fairly close, close enough that I felt free to object. I told him that the matter could easily become a riot and I thought it highly inappropriate for the Chief of Staff of the Army to become involved." MacArthur ignored this wise advice and ordered Eisenhower to don his uniform, mount up, and ride along with him to conduct the operation.

MacArthur's assault on the "Bonus Army" led to disaster. Ignoring orders from the secretary of war not to provoke a larger confrontation by crossing the bridge over the Anacostia River, MacArthur led his cavalry forces directly into the encampments. Federal troops were thus turned on the former military men in the streets of the nation's capital, and the huts of the protestors were set ablaze. The event haunted Eisenhower for years, and though he obediently wrote MacArthur's official report of the incident, he privately railed against the chief's lack of restraint. "The whole scene was pitiful," he felt.[19]

Eisenhower's value to the chief of staff was so great that he was given increasingly large tasks to perform, as MacArthur lobbied Congress heavily for increased army budgets. It was hard going, and four years of intense work in the War Department took a terrible toll on Eisenhower's health: severe back problems and attacks of abdominal pain—the start of a long affliction that would finally be diagnosed as ileitis—left him exhausted. But with Eisenhower helping him, MacArthur got results, and the fate of the armed services slightly improved under his leadership. After an unprecedented five years as chief of staff, MacArthur received orders in 1935 to go to the Philippines to create a new army for the soon-to-be-independent nation. He had no doubt which officer he wanted to serve as his military adviser.

Eisenhower endured a difficult four-year tour in the Philippines under MacArthur. The task he had been set, to plan for the construction of a Philippine army and the defense of the islands, was almost impossible, since the Philippine government had no money to pay for such a force, nor did it have any sort of military tradition or infrastructure from which to begin. Eisenhower had to devise a 10-year plan for training an officer corps, building up a reserve, equipping this armed force with everything from uniforms and rifles to aircraft, designing a network of training facilities, and putting together a curriculum for officers: all without the needed funds. MacArthur left the work to Eisenhower while he basked in the adulation that came to a man of high rank. (He managed to appoint himself field marshal of the nonexistent Philippine army.) MacArthur loved a stage, and Eisenhower, on a 15-man staff, was obliged to serve as audience while the general fulminated about President Roosevelt or bored his subalterns with soliloquies about his West Point days. MacArthur may have been America's most distinguished soldier in these years, but his patronage did Eisenhower little good as long as he was stuck in the Pacific, without a combat command, drafting plans for a phony army that would never see the light of day. "The sooner I get out of here, the better I'll like it!" he privately wrote.[20]

World events would soon reshape Eisenhower's career path. In early September 1939, sitting in a friend's living room in Manila, Eisenhower heard a crackling, barely audible radio broadcast from London, carrying an astonishing message from Prime Minister Neville Chamberlain. In a voice that was "stricken" with defeat and sorrow, Chamberlain declared that all his peacemaking overtures to Hitler had failed. His country was at war with Germany. Though a tragedy for the world loomed, Eisenhower must secretly have rejoiced. "I hoped a field command awaited me," he admitted. The task ahead was one "for which all my life I had been preparing."[21]

V

When war broke out in Europe in September 1939, Eisenhower was a 49-year-old lieutenant colonel stuck in a distant outpost in the Pacific. Less than three years later, in June 1942, General Eisenhower took command of the entire European Theater of Operations in the war with Germany. Some contemporaries expressed wonder and sheer bafflement at this meteoric rise to fame and power by the once-obscure staff officer who had never commanded troops in the field. Yet inside the armed forces and in Washington, D.C., Eisenhower had developed a reputation for planning brilliance, hard work, supreme organizational skills, and personal qualities of tact, loyalty, devotion to duty, and optimism. Eisenhower himself said it best: he had been preparing all his life for this moment, and he would make the most of it.

First he had to get out of the Philippines as fast as possible. He begged MacArthur to let him transfer to a combat command, and MacArthur, perhaps now seeing in Eisenhower a rival, seemed glad to be rid of him. Pulling strings with friends in the States, Ike secured an appointment to the 15th Infantry Regiment at Fort Lewis in Washington State. He kept moving up, first to chief of staff of the 3rd Division at Fort Lewis, and in March 1941 to chief of staff to the IX Corps. With that post came a promotion to colonel. But he had no time to rest on his laurels. In June he became the Third Army's chief of staff, with orders to relocate to San Antonio.

With war in Asia and Europe brewing, the U.S. Army at last roused itself from its long interwar slumber and began to knock off the rust of two decades. Congress, which in September 1940 had passed legislation creating the country's first peacetime draft, reluctantly extended the law in August 1941. Millions of young men were now registering for what would soon become a huge expansion of the armed forces. As Third Army chief of staff, Eisenhower had to prepare these raw recruits for real fighting. In the late summer of 1941 he staged a military exercise in the swampy Louisiana backwoods, a war game that involved half a million men and 19 divisions in a mock clash between two armies, spread out over 3,400 square miles. Eisenhower's staff work helped lead to a smashing victory by his Third Army forces, and it also got him his first star. He was promoted to brigadier general on October 3, 1941. Powerful figures in Washington took note.

Certainly the new army chief of staff, Gen. George C. Marshall, noticed. Marshall, the man identified by Fox Conner a decade earlier as the army's finest officer, had begun to assemble the brightest minds he could find to staff the War Plans Division in Washington. Just days after the December 7, 1941, attack on Pearl Harbor, Marshall ordered Eisenhower to report for duty in the nation's capital. After a brief stint as the deputy of war plans under his friend Brig. Gen. Leonard "Gee" Gerow, Eisenhower took the helm as chief of the War Plans Division in February 1942. The appointment was reported by the *New York Times*, the first time Eisenhower had his picture in that paper.[22]

Once again Eisenhower had been snatched up by a powerful patron— first Conner, then Pershing, MacArthur, and now Marshall—who needed his competence, his hard work, and above all his confidence in making large decisions. Marshall placed enormous trust in Eisenhower, and Ike always honored him for it. "I must have assistants who will solve their own problems," Marshall told him, "and tell me later what they have done." The historian of Eisenhower's presidency can draw a direct line between these words and Eisenhower's own management style as chief executive, when he too would look for powerful and confident lieutenants and allow them the freedom to run their own departments.[23]

Marshall and Eisenhower made a dynamic team, among the best general officers the U.S. Army ever produced. The two men collaborated in developing America's grand strategy for the war. The United States faced the awful dilemma of choosing between fighting Japan or Germany, for it could not engage both fully right away. With MacArthur pinned down by the Japanese invasion of the Philippines and desperately short of everything, the temptation to try to rescue the American and European position in the Pacific was powerful. But Marshall's new chief of war plans saw the larger picture. "We've got to go to Europe to fight, and we've got to quit wasting resources all over the world, and still worse, wasting time," Eisenhower confided to his diary. "If we're to keep Russia in, save the Middle East, India and Burma, we've got to begin slugging with air at West Europe, to be followed by a land attack as soon as possible."[24]

President Franklin Roosevelt and Prime Minister Winston Churchill, meeting in Washington for three weeks from December 22, 1941, to January 14, 1942, reached the same conclusion, but translating this broad idea into operations would prove immensely complex. To speed things up, Eisenhower had his War Plans Office flesh out the "Germany-first" plan. The first stage would be a massive buildup of U.S. forces in Britain, code-named Bolero, followed by a cross-channel invasion of France. General Marshall tried to sell the plan to the British, who were apprehensive about rushing onto the continent too quickly with too few resources. As Anglo-American strategic conferences fought over the precise timetable and direction of the cross-channel attack, Eisenhower sketched out the creation of a European Theater of Operations, supervised by a London-based Allied headquarters. In June, after showing Marshall the plans he had devised, the chief of staff assigned Ike "the biggest American job of the war": he was to become commander of the entire Allied war effort against Hitler.[25]

On June 24, 1942, Major General Eisenhower arrived in London and assumed command of the Allied war in Europe. He started his tour of duty in typical Eisenhower fashion, as the *New York Times* wryly noted: he "talked informally off the record with British and American correspondents, giving an excellent demonstration of the art of being jovially outspoken without saying much of anything."[26]

VI

Eisenhower's three years in command of the Allied armies in Europe featured an almost unimaginable series of crises, decisions, conflicts of personality, disappointments, and setbacks. Yet with perseverance and exhausting effort, and the heroic sacrifice of millions of soldiers from dozens of nations, Eisenhower led the Allied forces to victory over Germany. These were years that could have broken any man; they certainly took a terrible toll on Eisenhower's health. Yet he came through the ordeal as a revered, universally acclaimed military leader, a man recognized for his decisiveness, tact, unfailing goodwill, penetrating intelligence, and absolute commitment to victory. In preparing him for a future career as a political leader and commander in chief of the United States, the war years steeled him as no other experience could have done.

As the military leader of a multinational alliance, Eisenhower faced a preeminently political task: to fuse together the British and American military establishments, with their wholly contrasting traditions, organizations, and operational doctrines, into an effective fighting force. Such an amalgamation proved enormously difficult for, as historian Max Hastings has recently shown, American opinion toward the British in mid-1942 was low indeed. The Americans thought the British were shy of fighting after their licking at Dunkirk in May 1940, and British reluctance to open up a second front in France sustained this opinion. One English visitor in America declared that "anti-British feeling was beyond belief," especially among senior army officers.[27]

Eisenhower had to reverse this tide, quickly. Upon his arrival in London he set the tone in terms that would come to mark the Eisenhower style. In his first day on the job, he demanded "that an atmosphere of the utmost earnestness coupled with determined enthusiasm and optimism character-ize every member of this staff . . . that pessimism and defeatism not be toler-ated, and that any person who could not rise above the recognized obstacles and bitter prospects that lie in store for us has no recourse but to ask for instant release from this theatre."[28]

The British high command placed the first obstacles in Eisenhower's path. Churchill had very definite ideas about how the war should be run. He wanted to attack the "soft underbelly" of the enemy in the Mediterranean, North Africa, and Italy. Eisenhower and Marshall strongly opposed this plan, which they considered a diversion of men and resources into a the-ater with little real strategic significance. Victory must come by slaying the German dragon in its lair, namely, Germany. But Churchill and his military commanders, especially the Chief of the Imperial General Staff Gen. (later Field Marshal) Alan Brooke, would not relent. In any case, it had become clear that Eisenhower's favored alternative, an immediate cross-Channel at-tack in France, would not be ready in 1942. Roosevelt ordered his generals to stand down. The Americans had to get into the fight somewhere, and in 1942 it would be in North Africa. Eisenhower now had to lead Operation Torch, the invasion of Morocco, Algeria, and Tunisia, a plan against which he had vociferously fought.[29]

All this was unknown to the wider world, of course. Publicly Eisen-hower cultivated the image of a sturdy American fighting man, all business and little fun. The press played up these traits: a profile of the general on the eve of the North African campaign described him as "tall and lean with hard muscles around his jaws and lips that can straighten into an Archi-medean line, blue eyes that glint like marbles—he is as tough as hell." The reporter wrote that the general was known informally as "Ike," the nick-name he'd had since childhood. "He is the best liked and least social of any American officer in London. The town is full of stories about him, but hardly anyone outside military circles knows him." Early in his London tour he ceased attending clubs and social events, seeing such frivolity as time-consuming and wasteful. "He has established the seven-day week for his officers and eliminated any idea of the eight-hour working day." The press relished Eisenhower's public persona as a driven, tough, relentless military mastermind.[30]

It was hard to live up to the hype. The North African campaign, once under way in November 1942, did not go well. Within days of the landings in Morocco and Algeria, Eisenhower had to make a political judgment that nearly upended his career. By welcoming into the ranks of the Allies the collaborationist French leader Adm. François Darlan, who was in North Africa at the time of the invasion, Eisenhower seemed to be coddling the enemy and rewarding the treacherous behavior of Frenchmen who had made common cause with Hitler. Eisenhower's view was simple: Darlan's popularity in North Africa meant that the French Army, which deeply resented the Anglo-American invasion of their empire, would come over to the Allies without further bloodshed, allowing Eisenhower to turn on the real enemy, the Germans, all the more swiftly. But at home and in Britain, Eisenhower's "Darlan deal" triggered a good deal of negative press.[31]

More important, Eisenhower's operational plan in North Africa was unduly cautious and slow, giving the Germans ample time to counter the invasion and reinforce Tunisia. Terrible weather, a thin supply line, inexperienced troops, and a chaotic command structure slowed progress. It would take seven months of heavy fighting to gain control there, and the Germans made the green American soldiers pay dearly. The British generals sharpened their knives: According to General Brooke, Eisenhower was "at a loss as to what to do, and allowed himself to be absorbed in the political situation at the expense of the tactical." In late December, Brooke huffed in his diary, "Eisenhower as a general is hopeless! He submerges himself in politics and neglects his military duties."[32]

Still, Eisenhower retained the confidence of the men who mattered. On January 23, 1943, General Marshall visited him in his headquarters in Algiers and reaffirmed his belief in Eisenhower's talents. Shocked by Eisenhower's harried, anxious appearance, Marshall instructed Eisenhower's naval aide, Capt. Harry Butcher, to "look after him. He is too valuable an officer to overwork himself."[33]

Surviving the political and military missteps of North Africa, Eisenhower was now saddled with another operation he opposed: the invasion of Italy. This too reflected British strategic interests, asserted at the Casablanca conference in January 1943, and was another waste of precious resources. But once committed to it, Eisenhower toiled to make it work. The invasion of Sicily and the southern tip of the Italian peninsula during July–

September 1943 featured many of the same mistakes made in North Africa. The Americans lacked daring, relied instead on a slow buildup of materiel before taking decisive action, and again the Germans escaped a decisive engagement. Eisenhower was not above self-criticism. In August 1943, with Sicily just about fully in Allied hands, he was still assessing previous operations and identifying mistakes. "The trouble with Ike," Butcher noted, "is that he has no harness for his brain cells. They keep poring over problems both real and imaginary as ants swarm over an anthill."[34]

By the end of 1943 Eisenhower's forces had been fighting in the European theater for over a year but had yet to land a mortal blow on the German Army. Even so, Eisenhower emerged as a popular public figure, in large part because of his excellent relations with the press and his candid, upbeat personality. He was the embodiment of Allied unity and optimism. His zeal in waging a war for freedom never waned, and the public could see the sincerity of his commitment. "In no other war in history," he wrote to his friend Swede Hazlett in a letter typical of his unfeigned devotion to the cause, "has the issue been so distinctly drawn between the forces of arbitrary oppression on the one side, and on the other those conceptions of individual liberty, freedom and dignity under which we have been raised in our great Democracy." He confessed he had become "a crusader in this war."[35]

The press became devoted to Eisenhower, in large part because he confided in journalists and trusted them to act as his partners rather than his enemies. Butcher called Eisenhower "the keenest in dealing with the press I've ever seen, and I have met a lot of them, many of whom are phonies." Even the skeptical British commanders respected him and liked him more than any other American general (most of whom they openly loathed). With Marshall too valuable as chief of staff to be sent to the field command he yearned for, Roosevelt made the obvious choice to place the invasion of France in Eisenhower's hands. "Well, Ike, you're going to command Overlord," Roosevelt casually told him in the backseat of an armored Cadillac in Cairo in December 1943. It was the biggest command job of the war. Eisenhower earned it through his competent management of the troops, his disciplined strategic focus, and his scrupulously fair treatment of his resentful and frequently embittered British allies. Overlord was the turning point in Eisenhower's career. The fame and accolades he earned leading the invasion of France in 1944 and then the final assault on Germany in 1944–45 transformed him into the face of American victory and set spinning the wheels of fortune that would carry him to the White House precisely nine years after being told of his new command.[36]

In planning the invasion of France, Eisenhower's skill and experience shone. Not only did he attack the operation with his usual logistical and planning talent, but he had to fight strong headwinds from none other than Churchill, who never liked the prospect of an invasion of France and thought it likely to end in disaster. By now Eisenhower was an old hand at dealing with strong personalities: his days were full of exchanges with men such as Patton and the always difficult British combat commander Gen. Bernard Montgomery, to say nothing of Churchill and Roosevelt. In planning for Overlord Ike revealed a growing confidence in himself and his powers as supreme commander. He fought ferociously with the British and American air services, demanding that they limit assaults on Germany and instead dedicate air power to destroying rail lines into Normandy. He fought with Churchill and Brooke, who still wanted to keep pressing in Italy when he wanted troops diverted from the Mediterranean for Overlord. He fought with everyone to get more landing craft to carry as large a force as possible onto the Normandy beaches, even though this required him to delay the operation for an additional month.

Tellingly, he won these battles and imposed his will on the operation. He was consumed with the challenges of directing 6,000 ships that would carry 150,000 soldiers across miles of roiling sea to be thrown against mines, tank obstacles, barbed wire, and concrete bunkers filled with thousands of well-prepared German defenders. In conference with his commanders and in public, he exuded confidence, but privately he agonized. "No one who does not have to bear the specific and direct responsibility of making the final decision as to what to do," he wrote three days before D-Day, "can understand the intensity of these burdens."[37]

He could occasionally lay down these heavy cares at the small home he occupied, called Telegraph Cottage, hidden in the then-remote suburbs southwest of London, near Richmond Park. Here he found time to unwind, play cards with his band of devoted aides, listen to records, stroll in the garden, and rest. In those days at Telegraph Cottage, among his ersatz family, he developed an amorous reliance on his pretty Irish driver and helpmate Kay Summersby. At a time of immense stress and anxiety, Eisenhower welcomed the attentions and ministrations of this lively young woman who gave him something else to think about than war. It is unknown if their friendship ever became sexual; the story is veiled by the fog of war. To say that they were for a time devoted to and dependent on one another is enough. The supreme commander did not live like a viceroy, nor behave like one. He was no MacArthur. He knew at any moment a turn in the fortunes of war would bring him ignominy and defeat, and he seemed never to forget the "grisly, dirty, tough business" that lay ahead.[38]

Eisenhower's burdens hardly abated once the Normandy landings began in June 1944. Overlord started auspiciously, and within three weeks over a million Allied soldiers were ashore in France. But 60 divisions of well-trained and determined Germans did not break and run. It took all summer until a combination of overwhelming air, artillery, and ground assaults shattered the German defenses; by September 1944 France was cleared of Germans, Paris had been liberated, and the Allies had pushed on into Belgium. But an inexcusable delay in seizing the vital river approaches to the port of Antwerp meant that until November 1944, Allied armies could not be resupplied except by vehicles from the Normandy beachheads. Without fuel, weapons, and replacement soldiers, progress ground to a halt, and the Allied armies bogged down in a long winter war on Germany's doorstep. The war that Eisenhower hoped might end by Christmas had another six months left.

Hitler's fateful gamble in December 1944—the counteroffensive through the thinly defended Ardennes Forest in eastern Belgium that would go down as the Battle of the Bulge—confronted Eisenhower with his last great test of the war. Hitler sent a quarter of a million troops into a weak American sector, hoping to divide the Allied armies, race to the sea, and retake Antwerp. For perhaps six days the situation was dangerous, though not catastrophic. Eisenhower's cool handling of the crisis revealed yet again that by the end of 1944 he had learned how to manage such moments without succumbing to panic. He "acted instantly and with the greatest vigor," according to his admiring chief of staff, Gen. Walter Bedell "Beetle" Smith. If Eisenhower was surprised by the attack, it was because its chances of success were so slim. Hitler's westward penetration created a menacing bulge in the Allied line, but it also opened up both German flanks to counterattack, as Eisenhower anticipated. "It is easier and less costly to us to kill Germans when they are attacking than when they are holed up in concrete fortifications in the Siegfried Line," he assured Butcher. "The more we can kill in their present offensive, the fewer we will have to dig out pillbox by pillbox."[39]

With fighter-bombers pummeling the Germans from the air and a stalwart American defense on the ground, especially at surrounded Bastogne, the bulge was contained, then destroyed. This was desperate fighting in freezing temperatures, with a terrible harvest of lives. But it was the end-game: failure in the Ardennes cost Hitler dearly. Since D-Day the Germans had lost 400,000 casualties, while 860,000 soldiers had surrendered. If victory in Normandy had ensured the liberation of France, victory in the Ardennes ensured the defeat of the Third Reich. By January 1945 Eisenhower could say that he had broken Hitler's army in the West.

The operations in March and April 1945 would deliver the coup de grâce: after crossing the Rhine, Allied armies encircled the remaining German divisions in the Ruhr and snapped up 325,000 POWs. Eisenhower was brimming with confidence by now, exulting over the news from the front. Butcher said Ike acted like "a football coach whose team had just won a big victory and he couldn't help talking about the accomplishments of his players." Eisenhower wrote Swede Hazlett that he "knew on March 24"—when Allied forces crossed the Rhine—"that the enemy was absolutely whipped. . . . He had not the slightest chance from then on." By the end of April the German Army had simply disintegrated and over a million soldiers surrendered. On April 30 Hitler shot himself. A week later Gen. Alfred Jodl, chief of the German Army's General Staff, appeared at Eisenhower's headquarters in Reims, France. At 2:41 a.m. on May 7 he signed the surrender, effective the next day. The war with Germany was over.[40]

In a typically unadorned telegram, Eisenhower reported to the Combined Chiefs of Staff the result of his campaign in Europe: "The mission of this Allied force was fulfilled at 0241 local time, May 7, 1945." He and his staff retired at five o'clock in the morning. When Butcher looked in on Eisenhower a few hours later, he was in bed, awake, thumbing through the pages of a western pulp fiction novel titled *Cartridge Carnival*.[41]

CHAPTER 2

STAR POWER

"I haven't the effrontery to say I wouldn't be president."

I

THROUGHOUT THREE TERRIBLE YEARS OF TOIL, EISENHOWER had given himself over wholly to his role as leader of the Allied armies. From North Africa to Italy, France, and then Germany itself, he had worked inhumanly long hours and suffered from anxiety, back and stomach problems, hypertension, and rasping respiratory troubles, much aggravated by his smoking four packs of cigarettes a day. He had often daydreamed about retirement in letters to Mamie and his son John. Just before Christmas 1944 he wrote to Mamie, whom he had seen only once in two years, "I sometimes chuckle when I think of how much 'talking' you and I will have to do when this is all over. We'll have to take a three month vacation on some lonely beach—and oh lordy, lordy, *let it be sunny.*"[1]

But if he imagined he could slip back into the quiet anonymity of his prewar days, he was wrong. His achievements were too great for that. Even the normally restrained chief of staff of the U.S. Army, General Marshall, exulted in his success, writing a glowing personal tribute to him on V-E Day: "You have completed your mission with the greatest victory in the history of warfare. You have commanded with outstanding success the most powerful military force that has ever been assembled. . . . You have made history, great history for the good of mankind."[2]

Within days of the German surrender, Eisenhower's headquarters filled up with congratulatory letters from heads of state, generals, friends, and citizens. Prominent among these was an invitation from the British prime minister to receive recognition from the people of London and to be named to the Order of Merit by King George VI. On June 12, 1945, Eisenhower traveled to London to receive the key of the city and to give an address at the bomb-shattered gothic Guildhall, the ancient seat of London's lord mayor. Eisenhower worked on his Guildhall speech for three weeks, hoping to strike the right notes at this august occasion. He wanted to stress that the war had been won by soldiers, not generals. He wanted to acknowledge that Britons had suffered more acutely and fought longer than Americans during six years of war. And above all he wanted to emphasize that Britain and America together formed the bulwark of freedom that had vanquished tyranny. His instinct at this moment of great personal triumph was to share the glory with others.

The Guildhall had nearly been destroyed by the German incendiary raid of December 29, 1940, an attack that set much of the City on fire and nearly razed St. Paul's Cathedral. The building had been hastily repaired, its roof still showing temporary patches covering gaping holes. Eisenhower was carried through the city streets in a phaeton drawn by two horses, with his wartime deputy commander, Air Chief Marshal Sir Arthur Tedder, at his side. The British government leaders, including Churchill, were there to welcome him.

As Eisenhower mounted the rostrum in the Great Hall, the audience of dignitaries offered him a thunderous ovation. In his speech, during which he struggled to master his emotions, he demonstrated the Eisenhower touch: gracious humility, plainspoken earnestness, and a willingness to give credit to others. "The high sense of distinction I feel upon receiving this great honor from the city of London is inescapably mingled with feelings of profound sadness," he began, striking the somber note of a battle-weary commander. "Humility must always be the portion of any man who receives acclaim earned in the blood of his followers and the sacrifices of his friends." The honors a warrior may win in battle "cannot hide in his memories the crosses marking the resting places of the dead. They cannot soothe the anguish of the widow or the orphan whose husband or father will not return." It is impossible to imagine Patton or MacArthur sounding so mournful in this moment of high honor or deflecting the proffered acclaim onto the hallowed memory of fallen soldiers.

Eisenhower repaid the compliment London gave him by recalling the city's tragic passage through the war. He praised the residents for their courage as they endured Hitler's air attacks at a time when Americans were still oblivious to the great sacrifices the British were making. He recalled the shock of the green American soldiers who arrived in Britain and saw first-

hand what war had done to this proud and defiant people. And he emphasized the common commitment of America and Britain to freedom. In a
flourish that linked his humble hometown to the majestic British capital,
he declared, "To preserve his freedom of worship, his equality before the
law, his liberty to speak and act as he sees fit, subject only to the provision
that we trespass not upon similar rights of others—the Londoner will fight.
So will the citizen of Abilene!" The speech even melted the icy heart of one
of Eisenhower's most ferocious critics, Field Marshal Lord Alanbrooke, as
he was now, who confided in his diary: "Ike made a wonderful speech, and
impressed all hearers in the Guildhall including the Cabinet. . . . I had never
realized that Ike was as big a man until I heard his performance today!"[3]

The warm and heartfelt adoration of London paled in comparison to the
reception he received upon his return to the United States. On June 19 more
than four million New Yorkers welcomed Eisenhower during a long open-
car journey through the streets of the city. All the way down Fifth Avenue,
then all the way up Broadway an avalanche of ticker tape and confetti rained
down on the beaming general. It was at the time the largest parade crowd
in the city's history. Mayor Fiorello La Guardia proclaimed June 19 "Eisenhower Day" and declared a holiday for city employees, urging New Yorkers
to hang flags and give the general a full-throated welcome. In his address at
City Hall, Eisenhower paid tribute to the soldiers still on the battlefields of
Asia, as well as the productive forces on the home front that had made victory in Europe possible. He insisted, "There is no greater pacifist than the
regular officer. Any man who is forced to turn his attention to the horrors
of the battlefield, to the grotesque shapes that are left there for the burying
squad—he doesn't want war. He never wants it." And he called for a great
effort to return the world to peace: "As I see it, peace is an absolute necessity to this world." Americans "should be strong but we should be tolerant.
We should be ready to defend our rights but we should be considerate and
recognize the rights of the other man." He had begun his transition from
soldier to statesman.[4]

At this moment of triumph Eisenhower was 55 years old and the world's
best-known and most-respected soldier. He embodied America's victory
over fascism and Nazism. He possessed extraordinary political gifts and
had been able to find compromise and consensus among headstrong Allied
leaders where rivalry and bickering predominated. Raised in the solitude of
the Kansas plains, he now knew every corner of the globe and had worked
intimately with great men of state. He remained comfortable in his own

skin, a characteristic that made him a natural communicator with the press, with his fellow military commanders, and especially with the soldiers he sent into battle, whose company he loved. For a man of such skills and abilities, the future was his for the asking.

President Truman understood this. A practiced politician, he had a nose for winners. In mid-July, Truman traveled to Europe to meet with Churchill and Premier Josef Stalin of the Soviet Union at the great postwar conference at Potsdam, Germany. By this time Eisenhower had returned to Europe in his role as commander of the military occupation of the defeated nation, and he welcomed Truman to Germany. The two had met only a few times before, though the president obviously had a high opinion of America's foremost soldier. Truman had mused in his diary the previous month about the varying quality of U.S. generals: "Don't see how a country can produce such men as Robert E. Lee, John J. Pershing, Eisenhower and Bradley and at the same time produce Custers, Pattons and MacArthurs."[5]

In Berlin, Truman found a moment to talk politics with Eisenhower. "One day," Eisenhower later recalled, "when the president was riding with General Bradley and me he fell to discussing the future of some of our war leaders." Eisenhower told Truman he hoped to retire soon. "I shall never forget the president's answer. . . . Now, in the car, he suddenly turned toward me and said: 'General, there is nothing that you may want that I won't try to help you get. That definitely and specifically includes the presidency in 1948.'"

It was a striking thing for Truman to say. It may have been meant as a gesture of flattery. Perhaps Truman was still feeling somewhat out of his depth in the new job; he'd been president for only three months. Perhaps he wanted to ingratiate himself with a man who was far better known worldwide and far more popular in America than he was. But it might also be that Truman perceived in Eisenhower what the general did not yet perceive in himself: star power. His countrymen now revered him, world leaders everywhere knew and trusted him, and the end of hostilities with Germany, far from bringing an end to his career, would open up new vistas for the "soldier of democracy."

Eisenhower was "suddenly struck in his emotional vitals" by this "astounding proposition," and once the shock had passed he tried to laugh it off. This was the position he adopted whenever the question of a political career came up: he wanted to retire, he said; failing that, he thought he might run a small college, write his memoirs, and do some public speaking.

"Nothing could be so distasteful to me as to engage in political activity of any kind," he wrote one eager supporter in August 1945. His own desire, as he told Marshall that same month, was to find "a remotely situated cottage" in which to hide and "to let someone else have both the headaches and the headlines."[6]

II

No such luck. The job he now faced as governor of occupied Germany presented him with extraordinary troubles, for the defeated Reich lay prostrate, its cities ruined and clogged with rubble and refugees. "The country is devastated," Eisenhower wrote Mamie. "Whole cities are obliterated. And the German population, to say nothing of millions of former slave laborers, is largely homeless." The country faced acute shortages of food and coal for heating and cooking, and millions of war-weary refugees swarmed across the charred landscape. "It is a bleak picture," he wrote. "In my wildest nightmares I never visualized some of the things now thrown at me."[7]

As he tried to navigate these complexities, he was extremely fortunate in having one of the ablest military administrators in the army as his deputy, Lt. Gen. Lucius D. Clay, who bore on his shoulders much of the daily work of running the occupation zone. Clay, the son of a U.S. senator from Georgia and a West Point graduate, had known Eisenhower since they served together in the Philippines. An engineer, Clay had overseen the construction of hundreds of airfields in North America during the war and in 1944 served alongside Eisenhower again in Normandy, winning a Bronze Star for his heroic efforts in getting the Cherbourg harbor up and running after the Germans had mined it. Eisenhower and Clay set up shop in the huge office complex of the chemical giant I. G. Farben (the firm that had manufactured the poison gas used to asphyxiate Jews in Hitler's extermination camps). Ike hated the job. He came in for sharp criticism from the press for the long delays in getting the troops home, for failing to arrest all the top Nazis, for lapses in delivering food, clothing, coal, and other supplies. Fighting the Germans seemed easier than trying to govern them. He was, as his son John noted, "a lonely man, let down after the excitement of the war."[8]

Eisenhower did his best to develop a good working relationship with Marshal Georgy Zhukov, the commander of the Soviet zone of occupation in Germany. If they could cooperate inside the Allied Control Council, which was set up in Berlin and acted as the four-power joint headquarters for the running of the occupation, then all the subsequent problems would resolve themselves much more easily. "Berlin, we were convinced, was an experimental laboratory for the development of international accord," Eisenhower wrote. Success in Berlin could be translated into a "world partnership" with the USSR. He liked Zhukov, a true soldier and not a Communist Party hack, and he felt he understood the Soviet outlook: they had sacrificed more than any other nation to defeat Hitler's armies and wanted to be sure the job of breaking Germany was done once and for all. All that was needed was "a friendly acceptance of each other as individuals striving peacefully to attain a common understanding." It was a characteristically optimistic, even naïve view of world affairs.[9]

To cultivate the friendship, he agreed to visit Moscow in August. It was an eye-opening trip. "When we flew into Russia in 1945," he recalled, "I did not see a house standing between the western borders of the country and the area around Moscow—a distance of over 500 miles." Arriving on August 12 from Berlin in the company of Zhukov, as well as his son John, Eisenhower was welcomed by an honor guard at the airport and the American ambassador, Averell Harriman. According to John, the people of Moscow looked very shabby, and "the houses were dingy, crowded and miserable looking."

But the following day, in the presence of the sinister warlord Stalin, Eisenhower observed the astonishing spectacle of the Physical Culture Parade in Red Square. Thousands upon thousands of athletes, dancers, musicians, acrobats, and members of youth organizations, all resplendent in gleaming native costumes, marched or danced jubilantly past the reviewing stand where the Soviet leadership stood. Early in the proceedings, Eisenhower received an invitation from Stalin to join the Generalissimo on Lenin's Tomb, an extraordinary honor for a foreigner. Stalin beamed as the endless parade unfolded over the course of five hours. "This develops war spirit," he remarked. "Your country ought to do more of this." And then, as an afterthought, he added coldly, "We will never allow Germany to do this."[10]

The visit lasted three days, during which Eisenhower toured the Moscow subway, a collective farm, a fighter aircraft factory, and the Kremlin itself. On August 13 Stalin hosted a banquet at the Kremlin; John recalled, "All the Soviet officers wore white tunics; and this, combined with the glistening tablecloth and gigantic crystal chandeliers, gave an aura of brilliance that I have never seen elsewhere." At the American Embassy the next night, in an atmosphere of growing cordiality, American and Soviet generals drank rivers of vodka and champagne, locking arms and breaking into a hearty chorus of "Song of the Volga Boatmen." The evening was topped off when Ambassador Harriman arrived with joyful news: the Japanese had surrendered. The war was truly over. It is not without reason that Eisenhower could look back at this moment and conclude, "The late summer and early autumn of 1945 represents the peak of postwar cordiality and cooperation that we were ever able to achieve with the Soviet officials."[11]

Soon after his return to Berlin, Eisenhower received a letter from General Marshall. The chief of staff wrote that he planned to retire and that he had urged Truman to appoint Eisenhower as his successor. Eisenhower had suspected this was coming, and dreaded it. To be sure, this was the top job in the American military, and he told Marshall that he was "willing to attempt anything that my superiors may direct." But he knew it was going to be a terribly hard assignment, overseeing the dismantling of the huge military apparatus that the United States had assembled at such great cost. Nor did he wish to go back to Washington. "It all leaves me very cold," he wrote Mamie. "If the President wants me to take the job at any given time it is, of course, my duty to do so. But you are certainly in no doubt as to what the effect on me will be. That city really bears down on me!"[12]

Still, staying in Germany was no better. He had been in Europe for over three years, missed his wife terribly, and was ready to go home. In November 1945, while on a visit to the States to testify before Congress and speak at the American Legion conference, he fell ill with pneumonia and had to be hospitalized for two weeks at the Greenbrier Hotel (which had been converted during the war to an army rest facility) in White Sulphur Springs, West Virginia. When he emerged at the end of the month, rested and healed, he went directly to work in Washington as chief of staff of the U.S. Army. "No personal enthusiasm marked my promotion to Chief of Staff," Ike later admitted.

Almost immediately, Eisenhower faced trouble. In January 1946 a serious crisis broke out over the demobilization of U.S. soldiers. They wanted to get home fast, but getting eight million soldiers back to the States would take some time. Congress, under siege by voters and "Bring Daddy Home" clubs that had sprouted up across the country, was pressing the army to move faster. By the end of 1945 four million soldiers had already been discharged; the aim was to get another two million home by June 30.

But on January 4, 1946, the army disclosed a new policy: in order to maintain occupation troops overseas sufficient to keep order, demobilization would have to be slowed. Within days thousands of GIs in Manila, Seoul, Guam, Hawaii, Le Havre, and Paris staged loud protests, marching with picket signs reading "Bring the GIs Home" and "No Boats, No Votes." The commander of the U.S. Eighth Army in Yokohama declared a "general breakdown in morale and discipline." In Frankfurt a loud group of soldiers marched to the doors of the American military headquarters and were met by a barricade of military police, bayonets fixed. The *New York Times* called it "the worst administrative and morale crisis that the Army has faced."[13]

Eisenhower moved decisively to grapple with the problem. He delivered detailed and comprehensive testimony to a joint session of Congress on January 15, then issued a radio broadcast explaining his plans. He promised that all three million soldiers eligible for discharge would be out of uniform by the first of July. But he reminded Congress and the country that the army still had a job to do in occupied lands and needed manpower to do it. As long as the policy of the government was to help stabilize the postwar world, the United States would need to keep some soldiers overseas. Those who had seen combat would have priority for returning home, while those newly entering the army through the Selective Service System would now have to do their part. Eisenhower seemed to have doused the flames of the crisis, but in a private letter to MacArthur, he seethed: "No amount of persuasive argument, based on logic, reason, and National duty, has had material effect in combating hysteria generated by pressure groups." This was to become a common refrain as he labored through his new assignment at the Pentagon.[14]

While Americans were ready to be done with the war, Eisenhower preached a sermon of preparedness. He did not want to dismantle the armed forces so completely as to leave America unprepared, as it had been on the eve of World War II. He called for the continuation of the draft into peacetime and strongly supported Truman's proposal, made in October 1945, for some kind of mandatory military service for all 18-year-old males. "If we are to retain any semblance of military power," he wrote to an old wartime colleague, the American financier Bernard Baruch, "we can only do so by establishing a ready reserve of trained manpower to support our regular military establishments."[15]

But Congress refused to consider it: the war was over and the public's appetite for sacrifice had waned. Ike found it no easier to impose order over the services. His effort to unify the command of the three branches, in hopes of limiting interservice rivalry, streamlining command decisions, and reducing cost, was opposed strongly by the navy, and all of his appeals to common effort and selflessness did little to overcome their ingrained mutual suspicions. Eisenhower discovered that the unrivaled power and influence he exercised during the war had shrunk; he was now just another bureaucrat, going to Congress hat in hand. And Congress was in no mood to spend on military appropriations. Too often, he wrote, "my recommendations were ignored." It was a cruel fate: the massive fighting force Eisenhower had led in wartime withered away on his watch.[16]

Though Eisenhower usually refrained from criticism of political leaders, his exasperation occasionally spilled out into public. In a speech he delivered in April 1946 to the American Newspaper Publishers Association, he decried an American tendency "to ignore, in time of peace, the basic military problems of the country." Following a two-week tour of military installations across the United States, he concluded that because of the pell-mell demobilization, it would take a year of hard work just to get the U.S. military back to its 1940 state of readiness—a low threshold indeed. "In the shadow of the most costly conflict of all time," he boldly declared, the country was ignoring the chief lesson of war: that peace can be assured only through military strength. The speech received a warm reception, but all his sincerity and frankness could not sway Congress, which barely passed an extension of the Selective Service Act—and then only by allowing a nine-month "holiday" and exempting 18-year-olds from service. As for universal military training, that idea died.[17]

No wonder Eisenhower grew annoyed with life in Washington. Replying to a letter from his old Abilene friend Swede Hazlett about a rumor that he might become a candidate for the presidency, Eisenhower squashed the idea: "When trying to express my sentiments myself I merely get so vehement that I grow speechless, if not hysterical. I cannot conceive of any set of circumstances that could ever drag out of me permission to consider me for any political post from Dog Catcher to 'Grand High Supreme King of the Universe.'" He often expressed his wish to retire altogether. And yet to his son, who was still in Germany, he fretted about the absence of strong leadership in the country: "The most noticeable thing here at home is the great confusion, doubt and haziness that seem to prevail in all circles, high and low, both in governmental and private life. I talked to many civilians during my recent trip and find that all of them are puzzled as to what to do about management and labor, about taxes, about investments, about foreign policy and about the strength and character of our Army and Navy. No one

seems to have a complete program on which he is ready to stand or fall."
Just possibly Eisenhower could provide such a program. The idea began to
germinate.[18]

III

The year 1946 was a tough one for Harry Truman, still struggling to find
his footing in the White House. The end of the war led to dramatic layoffs
across the country as demand for war-related industrial products declined.
A wave of strikes by workers anxious about loss of pay reached a peak in
1946, when almost five million workers downed tools and took up pickets. It
turned out to be the worst year of labor strife in the nation's history. Truman,
a New Dealer, had plenty of sympathy for the workers and their unions, but
when coal miners and railroad workers went on strike, halting the nation's
economy, he exploded and threatened to draft striking rail workers into the
military. The conflict created an uproar across the country, jeopardizing the
coalition that underpinned the Democratic Party.[19]

In November 1946, in the midterm congressional elections, the Democrats took a beating, their worst since the 1920s. They lost 55 seats in the
House of Representatives and 12 in the Senate and, for the first time since
1930, surrendered majority control of both chambers. (Two legislators of
later significance for Eisenhower came to Washington in the 1946 freshman
class. Richard M. Nixon of California was elected to the House of Representatives, and Joseph McCarthy of Wisconsin won a Senate seat.) The newspapers began to write Truman's political obituary, while Republicans sensed
that "the presidency [was] a ripening plum" well within reach.[20]

With Truman embattled, speculation swirled around Eisenhower. In
late September 1946 Arthur Krock of the *New York Times* predicted that
in 1948 both parties would be looking to soldiers as possible presidential
candidates. In a time of domestic turmoil, seasoned military leaders like
Marshall, MacArthur, and Eisenhower might draw a great deal of national
support. Eisenhower seemed especially attractive, thought Krock. "His is
the one military name that crops up in both Republican and Democratic
groups when they surround and peer into the crystal ball."[21]

Eisenhower repeatedly poured cold water on this kind of talk. "There is
no possibility of my ever being connected with any political office," he told
reporters in late September. Eisenhower found that people did not believe
his denials. On the eve of a much-needed vacation in December, he con-

fided to his diary, "[Reporters] don't want to believe a man that insists he will have nothing to do with politics and politicians."[22]

But just what did he want to do, once his army career came to an end? "From time to time," he wrote to his father-in-law in January 1947, "prominent people in the commercial and financial world approach me with offers" of future employment, and the offers came with large salaries. Eisenhower was tempted by these, though he was afraid of being used as a corporate figurehead. He mulled over the prospect of retiring with Mamie to Denver or San Antonio, but he was still only 56 years old. He confessed that he was "definitely puzzled as to the future."[23]

By the spring of 1947 he had reached his breaking point. He told his friend Walter Bedell Smith, now ambassador in Moscow, that the army chief of staff job was "even more irritating and wearing than I had anticipated. We are still in the latter stages of destroying the greatest machine that the United States ever put together." He was confounded on every hand by "prejudice, lack of understanding, and outright self-seeking. . . . So many things seem to be placed above the welfare of the country." This was a swipe at Congress but also at Truman, who had not taken Eisenhower into his confidence nor made him a key player in mapping out his global military strategy. Eisenhower was on the outside looking in, and he was tired of it.[24]

In late May 1947 Thomas J. Watson, the founder of IBM and a member of the Board of Trustees of Columbia University, offered Eisenhower the position of president of the university. In fact it was the second time he had made the offer: the first was in April 1946, and Eisenhower had declined. But now Eisenhower was searching for a way out of Washington, although he doubted his own ability to succeed "in an enterprise so different from all my own experience." He discussed the offer with Truman, who encouraged him to take the job. Eisenhower worried that Mamie would be burdened with a busy social schedule at Columbia, and living in bustling New York City was a fearful prospect to the man from Abilene. Once he was reassured that his social obligations would be light and that he could easily secure a getaway house in the nearby countryside for relaxation, he was willing to take the plunge. "The finger of duty seems to point in the direction of Columbia," he told the chairman of the Board of Trustees on June 23, 1947.[25]

Moving to Columbia did nothing to curtail speculation about his entering politics. Without the army to shield him from overtures by political factions that wanted him to enter the presidential sweepstakes, he found himself the target of renewed speculation. Supporters across the country immediately set up a "Draft Eisenhower for President" headquarters in Washington to get him on the Republican ticket in 1948. Eisenhower, who still had many months to go to complete his tour as chief of staff, decried the draft campaign. "Frankly, I deplore the organization," he said publicly in early September 1947 in an effort to stop the momentum. "It is a mistaken idea." On a visit to New York City to meet with officials at Columbia, he said he thought soldiers should stay out of politics. In any case, he wasn't interested. Yet still the draft talk continued. By mid-October there were draft organizations in 13 states, and "I Like Ike" buttons began to pop up on the streets of major cities.[26]

Eisenhower bore some responsibility for the draft movement because he wouldn't issue a definitive refusal to run. "I haven't the effrontery to say I wouldn't be president," he had said in July 1947, in words that poured fuel on the fires of speculation. In private letters to two men he deeply trusted, Beetle Smith and his brother Milton, he tried to explain his reasoning. "I do not believe that you or I or anyone else has the right to state, categorically, that he will not perform any duty that his country might demand of him," he wrote Smith. If a political "miracle" happened and he was genuinely drafted by a national outpouring of acclaim, a refusal would be tantamount to betrayal: "It would be almost the same thing as a soldier refusing to go forward with his unit."[27]

The pressure on him continued to mount. In January 1948 the Draft Eisenhower group announced that it had filed a complete slate of delegates to run in the New Hampshire primary in March. If elected, the delegates would go to the Republican National Convention pledged to Ike. Just as the movement seemed to be reaching critical mass, Eisenhower definitively squashed it. On January 22, in a carefully phrased public letter to Leonard V. Finder, the publisher of the *Manchester Union-Leader*, who had endorsed Eisenhower for president and egged on the New Hampshire draft movement, Eisenhower stated his desire to be left out of the political sweepstakes. He repeated his view that "lifelong professional soldiers, in the absence of some obvious and over-riding reason, [should] abstain from seeking high political office." If he had been slow to withdraw from contention it was only because he did not wish to seem presumptuous. His decision to stay out of politics was, he stated, "definite and positive." He was off to New York, to Columbia University, to enjoy the freedom of a civilian for the first time in nearly four decades.[28]

IV

With his arrival in New York City in May 1948 as America's most famous college president, Eisenhower now had a platform from which to speak openly and a position of rank and status at the center of American public life. It was an exciting time. Free from the strictures of the army, he could imagine a new role for himself as a wise man, a leader in the field of ideas, and a source of guidance for the nation as it faced growing troubles on the world stage. From mid-1948 on, Eisenhower began to shape his public persona as a man to whom the country could turn for vigorous, competent, disinterested leadership. He might not have been running openly for president, but he did everything to prepare himself for a call he felt certain would come. While denying any interest in the presidency, he made himself appear to be the only—the inevitable, the indispensable—man for the job.

At Columbia he and Mamie moved into the newly refurbished presidential mansion at 60 Morningside Drive, a six-story home built in 1912 by McKim, Mead and White. Eisenhower had no idea what lay in store for him as a university president; the only man he knew at Columbia was Lou Little, the football coach, who had once led a Georgetown squad against an Ike-coached Army team in 1924. He didn't even know what to wear: Thomas Watson had to send Ike a private tailor to provide him with a wardrobe of suits of a style and quality consistent with his new civilian status.

Eisenhower attacked the job with his usual energy and impatience, but he found academia a strange new world. He thought he would diagnose Columbia's problems and fix them simply by drawing up a plan and ordering others to carry it out. It surely could not be as difficult as invading Normandy. And yet he found he was temperamentally unsuited to this sort of work. He wanted to move fast; the university moved slowly. He wanted decision-making power in his hands; the trustees often derailed his plans. He expected it would be easy to call on great men for significant donations; these proved hard to secure. The faculty expected Ike to open the president's home for social occasions; instead he and Mamie entertained only army friends and old acquaintances, shunning the academic community. Before long it was clear that Eisenhower did not fit in.

Global affairs also distracted him from his academic duties. In June 1948, just a few weeks after Eisenhower had unpacked his bags in New York City, the Soviet Union triggered a major crisis in Berlin, cutting off road and rail access into the western portions of the occupied city. It was the first major eruption of the cold war, and it brought the United States and the Soviet Union to the brink of war. The Allied powers launched a major airlift to keep the city supplied with food and fuel, and the Great Powers faced off in an icy staring match across an increasingly hostile border. Until now Eisenhower had generally preached a sermon of toleration toward the Soviets. But with the crisis in Berlin, he sharpened his criticisms. "I am beginning to think," he wrote Secretary of Defense James V. Forrestal in September, "that they may push the rest of the world beyond endurance."[29]

Two weeks after his formal inauguration as president of Columbia in October 1948, he swept down to the Pentagon to meet with the chiefs of the armed services to discuss military preparedness. Sounding eager to be back in the thick of things, he reassured Forrestal that no obligation at Columbia would stand in the way of his serving in Washington: "I can scarcely think of any chore that I would refuse to do" for the cause. In December, Forrestal took him up on this offer and asked him to serve as a senior military adviser and work with the Joint Chiefs of Staff to bring some unity into defense planning. Eisenhower did not wish to be sidelined in the ivory tower.[30]

Indeed he was almost incessantly active in the public sphere, offering his views on a wide range of topics—almost as if he were running for national office. In October 1948 alone, he gave 20 speeches in 30 days; this was the pace he set for much of the next two years. He clearly believed the country faced a crisis of national leadership. And though he always prided himself on articulating a "middle way" between left and right, Eisenhower in the late 1940s drew heavily on the vocabulary of the emerging conservative movement in America.[31]

In particular he was formulating a broad political argument that would in due course become the centerpiece of his political ideology. In Eisenhower's view, the great issue of the day was freedom. As he put it in his Columbia inaugural address on October 12, 1948, "Human freedom is today threatened by regimented statism. . . . In today's struggle, no free man, no free institution, can be neutral." Americans must fight for freedom at home and abroad or risk losing it to forces of subversion, tyranny, and a paternalist state. On the world stage he called for vigilance against Soviet aggression and tyranny, but much of his criticism was directed at the home front. There, freedom was threatened by the unchecked growth of the federal government, which arrogated to itself too much power over the citizen and the free market. After 20 years of the New Deal and its extension under Truman, Americans had grown content to let the government take care of them, to provide for them, and to make their decisions for them. The result was a creeping socialism that he likened to a stealth dictatorship.[32]

Truman's narrow reelection in November 1948 over New York's governor Thomas E. Dewey distressed Eisenhower intensely. The New Deal, he feared, would live on for another four years, leading to bloated government while suffocating individual initiative. Eisenhower wrote in his diary at the start of 1949, "In the name of 'social security' we are placing more and more responsibility upon the central government—and this means that an ever growing bureaucracy is taking an ever greater power over our daily lives." As he put it in a letter to a faculty colleague at Columbia, "Each increase in centralized bureaucratic control of our national life increases the danger of bankruptcy in spirit and enterprise as well as finance, and facilitates a potential dictator's seizure of power." In a speech to alumnae of the Seven Sisters colleges he proclaimed, "We are drifting toward something we hate with all our hearts . . . centralized government." If Americans did not strive to combat this "constant trend," they could expect "a kind of dictatorship" to emerge.[33]

In private Eisenhower began to sound downright cynical about his fellow citizens. In a letter to an old friend, the publisher of the *Fort Worth Star-Telegram*, Amon G. Carter, he confessed that "for many years" he had been growing anxious about the aspirations of common Americans: "Many of us seem to want only a powerful and beneficent central government which will insure us nice jobs during our active years and a comfortable old age when we're too old to work." While admitting that government had a role to play in modern society by cushioning the harsh blows of the free market, he rejected the claims of those who "insist that only through collectivism, with centralized control of all our affairs, can justice, equity and efficiency be maintained." Liberals just did not understand the real world, he claimed. They were "essentially humanitarian and altruistic in purpose," but by making the working man dependent on the state for his well-being, they were advancing the country "one more step toward total socialism, just beyond which lies total dictatorship." Such people think "the government owes us a living because we were born." Dependence upon state handouts, he asserted, "must be repudiated everywhere."[34]

These kinds of sentiments, spoken openly in speeches or in private correspondence, fed the Ike-for-president speculation. Eisenhower received a flood of entreaties and appeals to enter the political arena. One, from Clare Boothe Luce, struck a deep chord. A former Republican congresswoman and the wife of publisher Henry R. Luce, she was someone Ike admired. In his diary he recounted the discussion: "She believes I may turn out to be the one who could provide the leadership she believes to be mandatory" for the survival of the country. A failure of leadership now means "increasing use of federal subsidies; growth of paternalism; weakening of community responsibility and individual rights," and nothing less than "dictatorship." Even Governor Dewey, twice the standard-bearer for the Republican Party—and twice defeated—now lobbied Eisenhower to make himself available to the country. "He remains of the opinion that I must soon enter politics or, as he says, be totally incapable of helping the country when it will need help most. He is most fearful (as are thousands of others, including myself, in varying degree) that we, as a nation, will fail to see the dangers into which we are drifting." For a man who claimed no interest in politics, Eisenhower had begun to sound quite political.[35]

V

In February 1950 the Custom Tailors Guild released its annual poll of the best-dressed men in America. The top 10 included Clark Gable, the dashing screen superstar; dancing impresario Arthur Murray; and Secretary of State Dean Acheson, whose bespoke suits, made by Farnsworth Reed, had won him best-dressed honors in 1949. But Acheson was a distant second in 1950 to none other than Eisenhower. The Guild declared that Columbia's president "shows perfect judgment in wearing clothes which reflect the dignity of his office and his role of elder statesman."[36]

For those who may recall Eisenhower as a somewhat sedate, rumpled, and even sickly president, it may come as a surprise to find that in the early 1950s he was considered the very paragon of American masculinity. His personality and his vigor were essential to his political appeal. According to Emmet Hughes, his speechwriter, "Upon first encounter, the man instantly conveyed one quality—strength." He had "blue eyes of a force and intensity singularly deep, almost disturbing, above all, commanding." He carried himself with "healthy self-confidence" and an "easy air of personal authority." He weighed about 175 pounds and maintained this trim weight for most of his adult life. He was broad shouldered, had a narrow waist, walked leaning slightly forward, and was agile and quick. "Irrespective of their actual age," one senior adviser would note, "some people move 'old'; some move 'young.' Ike moves 'young.' It is noticeable in the spring of his walk as he enters a room. It is noticeable in the flashlike speed in which he moves from sitting to striding in his office in the middle of an interview."

As he aged, he gained gravitas. He had a gift for commanding a room. People wanted to be near him. Arthur Krock, the *New York Times* columnist and veteran Washington reporter, identified his key features: "physical vigor, a ruddy and pleasing countenance, a personal warmth of manner, high intelligence, professional competence, and a most infectious grin." His self-confidence and cheerful face enchanted those around him. When Eisenhower was serving as army chief of staff, Secretary of Defense Forrestal quipped, "Ike, with that puss you can't miss being president." Yet there was steel behind that smile. Robert Cutler, who would serve Eisenhower as national security adviser, recalled his first meeting with him in 1948: "His uniformed figure appeared trim and poised, compact and full of power. . . . His speech was incisive, crisp, the speech of one accustomed to command. Never lacking in courtesy, but pressing to dig in and get to the heart of things."[37]

By 1950 many seasoned political observers agreed: Ike was, politically speaking, "a natural." Philip W. Porter of the Cleveland *Plain Dealer* laid it out for his readers in a gushing, breathless column in April 1950: "There's something about the common sense of his remarks, the clarity of his English, the homely charm of his smile, and the natural humility of the unaffected, un-swellheaded man who has had greatness thrust upon him, that would bowl over the workers and the young people, the very groups that the opposition to Truman must reach. I defy anyone to watch Eisenhower in action, to see him personally, and not be convinced of this." His column ended with a flourish: "He's got it. He can really sweep the country."[38]

Simply put, Ike was a winner, and it is no surprise that many men of power, success, and influence in 1950s America sought him out and desired to be in his company. He was shrewd enough to take advantage of many of them. From 1948 on, Eisenhower developed a posse of wealthy, politically active Republican friends who had made their fortunes in manufacturing, oil, finance, and publishing and who served him as an informal kitchen cabinet. These men, hugely successful in their own right, virtually worshipped Eisenhower and set out to coax him into the political world. They made their considerable resources available to him, helped him develop a network of contacts across the country, and, perhaps most important, provided him with access to the private, elite world of Republican grandees. He was a constant guest at the most exclusive country clubs in America, where he played golf on the finest courses. At private estates he could pursue his passion for hunting and fishing and bridge in the company of like-minded men. He was made an honorary member of the Bohemian Grove in 1950, the secretive northern California resort for conservative and wealthy Republicans who gathered in luxurious camping sites under the benevolent sponsorship of former president Herbert Hoover.

The central figure in this network was William E. Robinson, a discreet, dignified, and politically calculating advertising and newspaper executive. Ike and Robinson had met during the war, when Robinson was running the *Herald Tribune* from behind Allied lines in recently liberated Paris. He was awed by the general and described him as "natural, alive, alert, spirited," and possessing an "intense amount of unloosed energy, both intellectual and physical." In 1947 Robinson persuaded Ike to write his memoirs and introduced him to Douglas Black of Doubleday. *Crusade in Europe*, which appeared in 1948, had netted Eisenhower about half a million dollars—the first real money he'd ever had—and Robinson had been its midwife.

Robinson, an excellent golfer and frequent winner of country club charity matches, also introduced Eisenhower to the pleasures and privileges of one of the nation's most exclusive playgrounds, Augusta National Golf Club, the setting that would become Ike's favorite presidential retreat. Robinson was a self-made man who worked his way from a paper route in Providence, Rhode Island, to New York University and into the advertising and publishing business. He was a gifted leader and joined the boardrooms of a number of newspapers before becoming executive vice president of the *New York Herald Tribune*. In 1954 he would move over to Coca-Cola as head of its marketing department and eventually would become chairman of the board. He was a devoted Catholic, a member of elite clubs in New York and Florida, and a civic leader, serving on the board of trustees of New York University. In his later years Robinson kept two things on his mantelpiece: a gold bottle of Coca-Cola and a bronze head of Eisenhower.[39]

If Robinson was avuncular, tolerant, known to be a soft touch to old friends with money troubles, Clifford Roberts was just the opposite: a cold, driven perfectionist who made his living as an investment banker in New York but made his reputation as the cofounder and dictatorial chairman of the Masters golf tournament at Augusta National. Originally from Iowa, he moved to New York in the 1920s and quietly built a powerful client list whose interests he deftly managed to protect from the Wall Street Crash of 1929. (His firm, Reynolds and Co., merged with Dean Witter in 1978.)

Roberts's lifelong passion was Augusta: he created the club in 1933 as a springtime retreat for well-heeled friends, and of its 80 original members, 60 were New Yorkers. At a time when the country was still in the grips of the Depression, Roberts oversaw the purchase of the land and the construction of the course and clubhouse, and then hired a special train with Pullman sleeping cars to whisk the wealthy members down to Georgia for a sneak preview in January 1933.

Roberts had the brains, connections, and money to build Augusta. His partner was the perennial amateur golf champion Bobby Jones, a native Georgian and one of the most well-known sportsmen of the era. The two made a powerful team and created a cult around Augusta that endures today. It was an exclusive, invitation-only club and strictly segregated: Augusta National did not invite a black man to play there until 1974 and did not include black members until 1991. (Not until 2012 did Augusta invite two women to join; one of them was an African American, former Secretary of State Condoleezza Rice.)[40]

W. Alton Jones, known as Pete, was another self-made man in Ike's inner circle. He was born in 1891 in southwest Missouri on a hardscrabble 40-acre farm, one of seven siblings. His first job was as a janitor and meter reader for the Webb City and Carterville Gas Company. By 1952 he was making $150,000 a year as president of Cities Service Company (today CITGO), a network of oil, gas, and utilities services that Jones built into a billion-dollar corporation. He had one year of college education, at Vanderbilt; the rest of the business he learned on the job. His talents as an engineer and administrator were put on display during the war, when he was tasked by the government to build an oil pipeline from Texas to the East Coast, and to do it in time for the D-Day landings so American trucks in France would not run out of gasoline. He was awarded the Presidential Certificate of Merit in 1948. He served as chairman of the board of the Richfield Oil Corporation, a director of the Chrysler Corporation, Tiffany's, and the Morgan Guaranty Trust Company. Jones owned a 2,300-acre estate in Rhode Island, where he pursued fishing avidly and frequently hosted Eisenhower. Upon his death in 1962 in an airplane crash, Eisenhower called him "one of my dearest, closest and best friends."[41]

The richest man in Eisenhower's circle was Robert W. Woodruff, the longtime chief executive of the Coca-Cola Company. Even among these titans of industry and finance, Woodruff was a kingpin. He made Coke into the sugary black gold that transformed Atlanta and the South. Woodruff grew up in Georgia, the son of a successful businessman and banker. But he did not have his fortune handed to him: he quit college after a year and set out to earn his own living, working his way up through the auto business to become vice president of White Motor Company in Cleveland, Ohio. In 1923, when the Coca-Cola Company in Atlanta offered him the job of leading the struggling soft-drink concern, he jumped at the chance. He was only 33 years old, and he would run the company for the next six decades, turning it into the most recognized brand in the history of American capitalism. His greatest coup came during the war, when he announced that every GI fighting overseas would be guaranteed a bottle of Coke for five cents wherever he was serving. This was a great morale booster for the troops and a savvy business move. At a time when sugar was rationed, the government now exempted Coke from the restrictions to allow more production and paid for transportation of the fizzy drink around the world. Woodruff used the opening to build over 60 bottling plants to slake the soldiers' thirst. By the end of the war, GIs had guzzled five billion bottles of Coke and the brand was a global powerhouse.[42]

Woodruff, known to his company as "the Boss" and everyone else as Mr. Bob, was a true tycoon, though a publicity-shy one. He served on the boards of dozens of the country's largest banking, steel, railroad, and insurance companies, but he always shunned the press. He was an avid outdoorsman, devoted to quail hunting, and he used his money to acquire 30,000 acres of land in southwestern Georgia to use as a sportman's paradise. He called it Ichauway, and there he entertained in country grandeur. The grounds were studded with giant oaks and strewn with Spanish moss. The stables included dozens of mules that were hitched to elegant little wagons and used to transport his guests into the scrub in search of quail. He kept great numbers of pointers for the hunt, and when they died he buried them in a dog cemetery; each tombstone displayed an enamel picture of the beloved hound. In the evening, back at the lodge, a fleet of black servants in starched white coats quietly offered visitors Havanas from burnished humidors. Woodruff was rarely seen without a cigar clenched in his teeth.

He was not an intellectual, to say the least: according to his longtime personal secretary Joseph W. Jones, he never read a book, never made a public speech, never listened to music, rarely attended the theater, and had no passions other than hunting and golf. Naturally he was an original member of Augusta National and a close friend of Bobby Jones. Even after he donated millions of dollars to Atlanta arts organizations, he was never seen enjoying the music, theater, or exhibitions his wealth had made possible. His gift of $100 million to Emory University in 1979 was at that time the largest single donation in the history of American philanthropy; overall he gave away some $350 million of his fortune to civic, arts, and educational institutions. This, from a man who dropped out of college because, he said, he was bored.[43]

Eisenhower's friends, then, were not simply wealthy: they were among the richest and most powerful businessmen in postwar America. And they were all birds of a feather. Like Eisenhower, they started out in life with little and had grown up as outsiders, working in small towns in the Midwest or South. They had little formal education and considered themselves men of action rather than ideas. Like Eisenhower, they were workaholics, intensely competitive, and demanding. Deeply hostile to the New Deal and its expansive federal programs, they shared a profound belief in what Eisenhower liked to call the "American system," that is, capitalism tempered by personal responsibility and good corporate governance. They felt that government interference in the free market they had mastered was a kind of betrayal of the American ideal. Although they behaved like elitists, retreating behind a high wall of wealth and privilege, they held themselves up as proof that pedigree was no requirement for success in America. They had earned their status by working hard for it, and this developed in them a zealous belief in free enterprise and a guiltless devotion to luxuries that their fabulous wealth allowed.

Ike enjoyed their company and had no qualms about accepting their largesse. It is easy to see why. He shared their outlook on life, shared their views on politics, and mirrored their personal intensity, drive, and ambition. He also liked their wealth, which he saw as evidence of talent and industry. Eisenhower himself did not own a home of his own until the fall of 1950, when he bought a dilapidated farmhouse in Gettysburg. His wealthy friends could provide him with comforts on a much grander scale. They threw a protective cordon around him, gave him their absolute loyalty, and furnished him with ideas as well as political and social connections of a kind the general did not yet have. Their help would prove invaluable in opening doors for him and, at critical moments, whisking him out of the limelight for periods of rest and recuperation.

And the friendships worked both ways. Eisenhower had something none of these men possessed: star power. He was a global phenomenon, one of the few men whose face was instantly recognizable around the world and whose name stood for victory and integrity. His friends knew a good product when they saw it and were determined to see Eisenhower become president. Over the course of many weekends of golf, bridge, and hunting, they had ample opportunity to relate their fears of "statism" and a bureaucratic seizure of power. America was in trouble, they believed, and Eisenhower was the only man who could save it.

CHAPTER 3

CALL TO DUTY

"It is not easy to just say NO."

I

"WE ARE JUST NOT CAPABLE, IN THIS COUNTRY, OF CONCEIV-ing of a man who does not want to be president," Eisenhower wrote at the start of 1950. It was a long diary entry, and it read like the draft of a speech—one he was obviously rehearsing for the many visitors who came to see him at 60 Morningside Heights to talk politics. "I do not want a political career," he insisted. "I do not want to be publicly associated with any political party." He would do anything for the public good, as a "military officer instantly re-sponsive to civil government." Yet he wished to ride above the partisan fray. He wanted to use his Columbia presidency as a platform to laud the virtues of "the American system," a political order he considered "far superior to any government elsewhere established by men."[1]

Yet the country would not leave Eisenhower alone. The Gallup poll in the spring of 1950 showed him ahead of Truman by 30 points in a head-to-head matchup of presidential contenders. Richard Rovere, the skilled reporter with an acute ear for political whispers, wrote in *Harper's*, "The second Eisenhower boom is underway." In June, Governor Dewey, the twice-defeated GOP presidential aspirant, hinted that he would not run again and that his favored replacement was Ike.[2]

The Korean War, which broke out on June 25, 1950, with a surprise in-vasion of South Korea by communist North Korea, upended world affairs as well as domestic politics in the United States. Truman responded quickly, committing U.S. troops under a United Nations flag to defend South Korea, but the war was a disaster for the allied forces that fought there. South Ko-rean forces were woefully unprepared; they were almost wiped out by the invading North Korean Army, which reached the southern end of the Korean peninsula by mid-September. General MacArthur, based in Tokyo and named commander in chief of UN forces, launched a daring and successful amphibious landing at Inchon on September 15. Sending 75,000 troops onto Korea's western shoreline in a bold outflanking maneuver, MacArthur caught the North Koreans by surprise. The UN forces appeared to have a rout on their hands, as they snapped up hundreds of thousands of North Korean POWs and rushed northward, taking Pyongyang in mid-October. But this swift advance of American-led UN forces triggered Chinese intervention, and by early November American soldiers were fighting Chinese troops and getting beaten. By Christmas 1950 U.S. forces had been badly mauled by the Chinese and were forced to abandon almost all of North Korea. A few days after New Year's Day 1951, the Chinese and North Koreans retook Seoul, the South Korean capital. A bloody and tragic stalemate now took hold.

The outbreak of war punctured the already sagging balloon of Truman's presidency. Not only did the war go badly, but America's unpreparedness to confront the global communist threat could be laid at Truman's door. The record showed that Eisenhower had been speaking out publicly in the months before the war about the erosion of American military power and in particular about Truman's defense budget, which he thought too low. The fiasco in Korea now proved Eisenhower right, and Truman had to scramble to expand the military to meet the new war effort. The image of an improvisational war president contrasted poorly with the reputation of the steady Ike, whose prophesies had been borne out.[3]

There was no time for recrimination. Truman needed help, and he desperately reached out to the men who had led the nation in World War II. On September 12, 1950, he fired his feckless defense secretary Louis Johnson and in his place appointed George C. Marshall. The lion of the armed services, Marshall had left government service in 1949 to take up the presidency of the American Red Cross. His health was somewhat fragile and he dreaded going back to the Pentagon. But Truman had gone in person to Marshall's home in Leesburg, Virginia, and begged him to take the job. As Marshall put it in a letter to his goddaughter, "When the president motors down and sits under our oaks and tells me of his difficulties, he has me at a disadvantage."[4]

Truman and his leading advisers feared that the war in Korea might be just the start of a broader communist offensive around the world, perhaps in the Middle East or Western Europe. While trying to halt the North Korean onslaught, therefore, Truman also sought a major expansion of U.S. military forces in Europe in order to deter any possible Soviet threat there. In the summer of 1950 Truman asked Congress for dramatic increases in military spending, army personnel, and aircraft forces, as well as atomic weapons capabilities. Most of the money would be spent enhancing U.S. and allied forces in Europe, where the stakes were highest. The United States could survive the loss of Korea, but if the USSR attacked Western Europe and overran Germany, America's world position would be imperiled.[5]

Only one American soldier had the prestige and reputation to go to Europe to lead this rapid rearmament. On October 27, 1950, Truman asked Ike to take the job of commander in chief of all allied forces in Europe. The North Atlantic Treaty Organization (NATO) had been formed in April 1949 but still had no integrated military structure and no commander to lead it. Truman needed Ike to go to Europe, galvanize the allied nations, spur their military rearmament, and forge them into a fighting force powerful enough to hold back any Soviet assault. Eisenhower of course could not say no. If Truman believed that sending Ike to Europe would eliminate his most formidable obstacle to reelection in 1952, neither he nor Ike ever mentioned it. If anything, Eisenhower seemed happy to leave Columbia and take the NATO command. "I rather look on this effort," he wrote to Swede Hazlett, "as about the last remaining chance for the survival of western civilization."[6]

Back in Washington, Eisenhower found the U.S. military establishment in a state of woeful disarray. He considered Truman far too complacent and prone to accept the armed services' expressions of confidence at face value. In his diary he wrote that Truman was "a fine man who, in the middle of a stormy lake, knows nothing of swimming. Yet a lot of drowning people are forced to look to him as a life guard." As the news from Korea worsened in late November, Eisenhower confided to one of his close friends, Lt. Gen. Alfred Gruenther, that he was "puzzled" by "a lack of urgency in our preparations." American actions had been far too slow and cautious, especially on the home front, where mobilization of the economy and armed forces for war had lagged. "Something is terribly wrong," he wrote in his diary in early December.[7]

Such criticism had little merit. In 1950 the United States spent $14 billion on defense, but after the outbreak of war, defense spending skyrocketed. Truman's 1951 budget called for $23 billion for the military, and almost double that for 1952, when defense spending hit $46 billion—a threefold increase in just three years. More dramatic, on December 16 Truman declared a state of national emergency, freezing prices, forcing striking railroad men back to work, and appointing Charles Edward Wilson, the head of General Electric, as the director of defense mobilization, with sweeping powers over war production.[8]

Eisenhower welcomed these bold actions. He took a leave of absence from Columbia and in January 1951, with Truman's approval, set off for a three-week trip to European capitals to make a preliminary assessment of the political and military picture there. The nation's attention was fixed on Eisenhower. He was no longer a university president; he was a returning hero, called back to lead a military alliance in a time of crisis. He was in his uniform again, still trim and straining at the bit, recalling to his countrymen past days of martial glory. If Truman was weighed down by six years of a combative, bitter presidency—a man many had come to respect but few to like or revere—Eisenhower's dignity and confidence reassured the country that one of America's great military men was back at the helm.

Eisenhower had to draw on these reserves of prestige to win congressional approval for building up NATO forces. It is important to recall that in 1951 public opinion largely opposed sending significant numbers of American troops to Europe so soon after the Second World War. The United States had already spent some $12 billion through the Marshall Plan to restart the economic engine of the Old World, and many in Congress wondered why the Europeans could not do more to defend themselves. Meanwhile, at home, the U.S. economy was struggling; inflation had soared due to the Korean War, and powerful voices called for a policy of global restraint. In late December 1950 Herbert Hoover, the godfather of the Republican Old Guard, publicly asserted that the Korean War was lost, that more military aid to Europe would be wasteful and provocative, and that America should instead rely on naval and air supremacy to defend itself.

Many Republicans, joined by some conservative Democrats, voiced similar doubts about Truman's proposals to rebuild Western Europe's military capabilities. Senator Kenneth S. Wherry, Republican of Nebraska, argued the constitutional point: the president simply could not send U.S. soldiers overseas without congressional approval, and Congress had not yet been asked to approve the military action in Korea, let alone troops for Europe. In early January 1951 Senator Robert Taft, a perennial Republican presidential candidate and recognized leader of the isolationist faction, spoke against Truman's policy for over two hours before a packed gallery in the Senate.

The "principal purpose of the foreign policy of the United States," he argued, "is to maintain the liberty of our people. It is not to reform the entire world or spread sweetness and light and economic prosperity" to all those who might want it. Furthermore, sending troops to Europe would surely be seen as provocative by the Soviets and "make war more likely." A big military buildup in Europe was unnecessary and dangerous.[9]

In this atmosphere of gloom and partisan criticism of his foreign policy, Truman deployed his secret weapon: Eisenhower. The general returned from Europe on February 1, 1951, to address a joint session of Congress. Speaking from the heart on a subject that deeply moved him, Eisenhower captivated his audience. He began, as he often did in public addresses, by emphasizing his respect for the legislators and the difficult decision they faced in preparing the country to defend itself. He stressed the connection between a strong Europe and America's own security. Should Europe, with its talented people and great industrial resources, fall under the sway of the enemy, America would be "gravely imperiled." The defense of Europe was not America's responsibility alone, he said to applause. But the United States must take the lead: "What nation is more capable, more ready of providing this leadership?" He appealed to his listeners' sense of moral purpose: "The cost of peace is going to be a sacrifice, a very great sacrifice, individually and nationally. But total war is a tragedy: it is probably the suicide of our civilization." He spoke with conviction and quiet urgency.[10]

His speech was a huge hit. "Eisenhower's Magic Wins Over Capitol Hill Suspicion," headlined the *New York Times*. James Reston's accompanying article called it a "personal triumph" for Eisenhower. He was confident, direct, and heartfelt. The performance cemented his reputation as America's most respected leader on national security issues: "When General Eisenhower addresses a large audience or a committee, even the most cynical Congressman cannot dismiss him with a wisecrack. It is this capacity to command respect and confidence; this combination of knowledge, experience and achievement; this quality of objectivity, of being non-attached to any of the local political warriors; this quality of directness, of toughness, of being the same inside and out that Washington has been seeking."[11]

At just this moment, with his prestige running as high as ever, Eisenhower decided to take the fight directly, though privately, to Taft himself. He invited the senator to meet him at the Pentagon, discreetly, with no press coverage. The general laid his cards on the table. "Would you," he asked Taft, "agree that collective security is necessary for us in Western Europe and will you support this idea as a bipartisan policy?" If he answered yes, Eisenhower would make a public statement withdrawing his name from the presidential contest in 1952, leaving the field clear for Taft. But Taft would not offer such assurances. He opposed NATO and opposed spending money on bailing out other nations. Eisenhower failed to budge him. After Taft departed, Eisenhower tore up a piece of paper on which he had earlier written out a pledge to withdraw from political activity. He wagered, "It might be more effective to keep some aura of mystery around my future plans."[12]

Eisenhower's public performance on behalf of Truman's troops-for-Europe plan had been so effective that opposition largely melted away. Taft could do little to stop the momentum that Eisenhower had created. A face-saving resolution was passed in the Senate in March calling for the president to get congressional approval before sending American soldiers overseas, but it was toothless. Soon after, in early April, the Senate passed a resolution, 69–21, approving Eisenhower's appointment to command NATO forces and asserting the vital security importance of building up U.S. forces in Europe. The great debate was over, and once again Eisenhower had been crucial to victory.

At a time when Truman's presidency was in trouble, Eisenhower offered a stark contrast. He combined a determined confidence with an unashamed embrace of the rhetoric of freedom. He showed in his speech to Congress, as the *Washington Post* observed, that "faith and ideas are the things that move nations and civilizations." His intervention in the NATO debate revealed his immense stature in the country and the world. The presidential buzz around him was humming: he was, in the words of one reporter, "the most attractive and the most intriguing figure in American public life today." Millions of Americans agreed.[13]

II

When Eisenhower returned to Paris to take up his new post as NATO commander, he faced what he called "one of the most irksome jobs ever designed by man." Europe still languished in the postwar doldrums. Money was tight; the scars of the war had barely healed. Many Europeans were wary about NATO, seeing it as provocative to the Soviets. Neutralist sentiment ran strong. In this atmosphere, Eisenhower had to develop a common military identity for 12 distinct nations and get them to commit to rearming a continent that had just passed through history's most destructive war.

Even more awkward, he wanted the Germans to play a role in the new alliance. The idea of rearming Germany so soon after the war struck more than a few Europeans as bitterly ironic. In fact the Germans too were against the idea: a poll in the newspaper *Frankfurter Allgemeine Zeitung* found 67 percent strongly against participation in Western defense. Eisenhower's diplomatic talents and skills of persuasion would be severely tested.[14]

There was another aspect of the NATO job that troubled Eisenhower: he had become, by default, the Truman administration's most effective ambassador, yet he personally disagreed with Truman on a wide range of policy issues. As president of Columbia, he had been free to speak his mind. Now, back in uniform, his military duty required him to be silent on all political matters. Privately, though, he insisted that he was not Truman's man. In a letter to Edward Bermingham, a financier at Lehman Brothers, a Columbia trustee, and a savvy Republican insider, Eisenhower wrote, "You are quite well aware of the extreme degree in which I differ with some of our governmental foreign and domestic policies of the past years." But there was work to be done. The simple truth was that America faced a "deadly danger": international communism. It was "ruthless in purpose and insidious as to method," and its goal was "world revolution and subsequent domination of all the earth." The only way to stop Soviet expansion was to build a formidable military alliance and to rally all Americans to that purpose. Such concerns—not political loyalty to Truman—had drawn Eisenhower back into uniform.[15]

Eisenhower may have differed with Truman on politics, but he had a scrupulous respect for the chain of command. While working at Supreme Headquarters, Allied Powers in Europe (SHAPE), he refused to utter a word in public that could be construed as critical of the president. By contrast, his former mentor Douglas MacArthur knew no such restraint. MacArthur had been in command of American and allied forces in Korea since June 1950, and his handling of the war had ranged from tragically inept to breathtakingly bold. He had presided over costly defeats and the daring amphibious landing at Inchon in September 1950. But MacArthur's apparent desire to free the entire Korean peninsula from communist control—pushing much further than merely defending South Korea—had triggered Chinese intervention in the war in October and led to a series of bloody reversals for his troops.

MacArthur chose to shift any blame for the failure to win in Korea onto Truman, and he did so openly, while serving in the field. In March 1951 he called for expanding the war by taking the fight directly to communist China, using air power and perhaps atomic weapons. He also called for the use of Chinese Nationalist forces from Formosa (Taiwan) to fight against Mao's communists. Anything less, MacArthur implied, was tantamount to appeasement. In a letter that was read on the floor of the House of Representatives by its recipient, Congressman Joseph W. Martin Jr. of Massachusetts, MacArthur stated, "Asia is where the Communist conspirators have elected to make their play for global conquest. . . . If we lose the war to communism in Asia the fall of Europe is inevitable." In a shocking act of disrespect, MacArthur rebuked Truman for his unwillingness to take the fight directly to the Chinese.[16]

Truman could take no more of this. On April 11 the president relieved MacArthur of his command, setting off one of the biggest controversies of the decade. For MacArthur was not just an army officer. To his admirers, he was an icon, the most storied military man of his generation, the liberator of the Philippines, the proconsul of the American occupation of Japan, and the daring strategist who had rescued a precarious American position in Korea. His dismissal triggered an eruption of hostility toward Truman across the country. "It is doubtful if there has ever been in this country so violent and spontaneous a discharge of political passion as that provoked by" Truman's action, according to two sharp contemporary observers. "The American citizen . . . took MacArthur's recall as if it were an outrage to his own person." Telegrams calling for the president's impeachment poured into Congress. Senator Joe McCarthy, the right-wing Red hunter who had been attacking the administration for over a year for allegedly coddling communists, called the president a "son of a bitch" and declared the firing "the greatest victory the Communists have ever won."[17]

Some Republicans now believed that MacArthur should challenge Truman for the presidency. Sympathetic congressmen engineered an invitation to the general to speak to a joint session of Congress. There, on April 19 MacArthur, newly arrived stateside from his Asian posting, delivered an astonishing valedictory. When China intervened in the Korean War, MacArthur said, he had demanded a bold new military strategy to deal with this threat, but was denied. Thus Korea had become "an indecisive campaign with its terrible and constant attrition." Truman's allegedly passive, defensive attitude was to MacArthur an outrage. His peroration rang through the halls of Congress and echoed across the country: "Once war is forced upon us, there is no other alternative than to apply every available means to bring it to a swift end. War's very object is victory, not prolonged indecision. In war, there is no substitute for victory."

The following day MacArthur traveled to New York City and was met with a reception even more rollicking and tempestuous than that which Eisenhower had enjoyed in 1945: millions of New Yorkers acclaimed Mac-Arthur a returning hero as his open car drove slowly through 15 miles of city streets under a hail of confetti. Steamboats and tugs in the harbor belched thunderous bass notes of welcome; fireboats sprayed jets of water in the air; columns of marching bands blared triumphant music. At the steps of St. Patrick's Cathedral, where the general dismounted from his car, Francis Cardinal Spellman and six bishops welcomed the general and clasped his hands, as if anointing him with holy powers.[18]

III

The Truman-MacArthur imbroglio roiled the waters of domestic politics. Truman's approval rating sank below 30 percent and stayed there for all of 1951. His weakened position opened the path to a Republican presidential victory in 1952, but so far the only serious contender was Robert Taft. He had angled for the nomination three times before, losing out to Wendell Willkie in 1940 and Thomas Dewey in 1944 and 1948. Perhaps, many in the GOP argued, it was Taft's turn. He had much support in the conservative and isolationist midwestern and western states. The Democrats had been in control of the Executive since 1933, and the country seemed ready for a change. Surely 1952 would be a Republican year.

The thought of a Taft presidency alarmed Eisenhower's closest friends, none more so that Lucius Clay. Since returning from running the American occupation forces in Germany in 1949, General Clay had been working as CEO of the Continental Can Company and serving on various corporate boards. He was one of Eisenhower's closest and most savvy wartime colleagues: supremely intelligent, politically sensitive—his father had been a senator—and enormously respected for his wisdom and organizational skill. He was also one of the great architects of America's position in Europe: he had helped implement the Marshall Plan, helped cement the Western alliance and NATO, and was a stout believer in the Western security program Eisenhower was now building. Clay believed that if Taft became president, all this work would be wiped away. "We cannot let the isolationists gain control of government if we are to endure as a free people over the years," he wrote Eisenhower in mid-April 1951. Within weeks Clay had formed a small group of moderate Republicans to start organizing a political campaign committee to win the GOP nomination for Eisenhower. "This involves no commitment on your part," Clay reassured the general. But there was urgency in his message: "It is time to move now."[19]

Eisenhower, on active duty in Europe as the NATO commander, could not condone such partisan activity. But while he told Clay that his own personal attitude toward a political career was "flatly negative," he left the door open a crack: "Now, as to what others may or should do, I have always insisted upon the right of every free-born American to do what he pleases." He went on, somewhat unpersuasively, "I am not trying to duck any difficult question, or to be evasive or coy. . . . My present duty is to help develop the defensive power of twelve countries. If I ever have to do any other, I shall have to be *very clear* that I know it to be a *duty*."[20]

Did Eisenhower want to be president? He said repeatedly to his closest friends that he did not want a political career. But he was not immune to the arguments that reached him in Paris. He believed the country's global interests would be profoundly harmed by a Taft presidency, and he believed Truman's leadership on domestic policy had been disastrous. He wanted the country to move in a sharply different direction. He understood his own popular appeal and was sensitive to the clamoring of hundreds of friends and acquaintances that he was the right leader for these difficult times. But he had serious reservations. His reputation could be tarnished by a bruising political fight. Politics was a dirty business, and he had little respect for its leading practitioners. He had already given 40 years of service to his country and was ready for an easier life. There was also the possibility that if he ran for office, he might lose.

In mid-1951 the pressure on him mounted. In late June, Bill Robinson spent 10 days with Eisenhower in Paris. During golf, luxurious dinners at Le Coq Hardi, a few trips to the horse races, and a short jaunt to London, the two friends regularly talked politics. Robinson updated Eisenhower on Dewey's efforts behind the scenes to stop Taft. Robinson told him directly that he had "not the slightest doubt" that Ike would be nominated by the Republicans "and would be elected." He suggested that Eisenhower "make his plans for the future on that assumption."[21]

Just two days after Robinson left Paris, Massachusetts senator Henry Cabot Lodge Jr. called on the general at his SHAPE headquarters. Lodge was a close associate of Dewey and was known as a promising young talent in liberal Republican circles. He knew Eisenhower very slightly from the war years, when Lodge had been a junior officer. But now Lodge felt it a duty to press him to run for president. Eisenhower was surprisingly eager to talk politics. He and Lodge spoke from 9:00 a.m. until lunch, after which Lodge stayed for further conversation. He left the meeting feeling that Eisenhower would be open to a draft from the Republican Party, though Ike's refusal to campaign would make winning the nomination difficult.[22]

Clay drove this point home and made a proposal to Eisenhower that only a close and respected friend could have suggested: "I would hope that sometime in the early part of next year you would request your release [from the NATO command]. . . . No matter how badly you may be needed in Europe, you are needed even more here, and perhaps if you do not return, nothing accomplished there would have any real permanency." Soon after, Ed Bermingham beseeched Eisenhower to declare his party affiliation so he could be registered in party primaries across the country. Such a statement would "unloose the energies and activities of your friends all over America who want to get the delegate machinery moving in your behalf." Eisenhower tried to resist these entreaties, but in his diary he revealed that the pressure was getting to him. He wrote plaintively, "It is not easy to just say NO."[23]

In mid-October Eisenhower gave his friends the first real sign that he could be persuaded to enter the political battle. The occasion was a visit from a West Point graduate and fellow Army football player, Gen. Edwin N. Clark, to Ike's headquarters in Paris. Clark had served on Eisenhower's staff in the war, then practiced law and run an international consulting business. He brought to Eisenhower a message from James Duff, a senator from Pennsylvania and a former governor. Duff had been working hard in Congress to peel away moderate and liberal Republicans from Taft and bring them to Eisenhower's side. To do this effectively, he needed the general's personal assurance that Eisenhower was a Republican and that he would run if drafted. So far Eisenhower had refused to give any such assurances. But Clark had more success. After a marathon session, Clark and Eisenhower worked out a statement that was to be given, in strictest secrecy, to Senator Duff. The letter, in Eisenhower's handwriting, was dated October 14, 1951—his 61st birthday. It stated, "I have been and am an adherent to the Republican Party and to liberal Republican principles." He reiterated his inability to campaign for the nomination while on active duty. However, he promised that if nominated, "I would resign my commission and assume aggressive leadership of the party." Clark promptly returned to the United

States, showed the letter to Duff, and locked it away for safekeeping. There could be little doubt now: Eisenhower was preparing to run for president.[24]

Truman, his canny instincts bristling, sensed the political threat Ike posed. The president remained uncertain whether he would run for reelection in 1952; his decision depended largely on Eisenhower. In November he summoned Ike to Washington, supposedly for a meeting on NATO matters. The reunion was overshadowed by a new poll from Gallup reporting that if Eisenhower ran against Truman in 1952, he would capture 64 percent of the vote against a mere 28 percent for Truman. On November 5 the two men had a private lunch at Blair House and spent more than an hour closeted together. No record was kept of the meeting, and Eisenhower later denied there had been any political talk; they discussed NATO and national security issues, he said. In fact Truman did ask Eisenhower about his political intentions. And he went further: the president would bow out of the race if Eisenhower accepted the *Democratic* nomination. Eisenhower, probably appalled that Truman would bring up the subject, replied that he had serious differences with the Democrats on domestic politics, especially on labor and social issues, and he could not accept such a scenario. He tried to change the subject, and Truman let it drop.[25]

Ike affected a lack of interest in politics for Truman's benefit, but immediately after his lunch with the president, he flew to New York, and while parked on the tarmac of LaGuardia Airport in his official airplane, the *Columbine*, he held an impromptu strategy session with his close friends. Bill Robinson, Cliff Roberts, and his brother Milton, among others, talked to him for three hours about politics and the plan now in place for winning the nomination. Eisenhower continued to say that he would not actively campaign, but by now he was clearly giving enough support to the draft effort to banish the idea that he was merely a disinterested bystander.[26]

With Eisenhower's word that he would accept a draft from the Republican Party, the momentum began to pick up. In a press conference on November 17, Lodge announced the formation of an Eisenhower-for-President organization. Wearing an "I Like Ike" button on his lapel, the tall Bostonian declared, "We've got a candidate and we've got the one who is sure to win. . . . I know he is a Republican, period. I can assert that flatly. There is no doubt about that."[27]

Working out of the Commodore Hotel in New York, the organization picked up speed. Dewey, much loathed by the Old Guard Republicans, kept a low profile so as not to tarnish the operation, but behind the scenes he provided talent and access to wealthy backers. The money began rolling in, much of it from John H. "Jock" Whitney, the multimillionaire heir to the Payne Whitney fortune, and Sid Richardson, the Fort Worth oilman. The group reached out to Sigurd Larmon of the Young and Rubicam advertising agency, which would play a major role in the election, churning out billboards, radio and television commercials, and reams of newspaper ads pushing Eisenhower's candidacy. From New York tentacles reached out across the country to coordinate Citizens for Eisenhower groups. Eisenhower was kept abreast of all these developments by various correspondents, and while he continued to profess no interest in politics, he did tell Robinson that he could imagine enjoying the freedom to be outspoken once again. "If I ever get into this business, I am going to start swinging from the hips and I am going to keep swinging until completely counted out."[28]

The New Hampshire primary, set for March 11, 1952, would be a crucial test of Eisenhower's appeal among rank-and-file Republicans. The issue of placing Eisenhower's name on the ballot in New Hampshire had triggered a detailed round of secretive correspondence and plotting among the many cooks in the Eisenhower-for-President kitchen. Over the Christmas holidays of 1951, Robinson had spent five days in Paris with Eisenhower. Upon his return he reported back to the team in New York: Eisenhower agreed to be placed on the ballot in New Hampshire. This was breaking news, the first public confirmation by Eisenhower of his party affiliation. *Life* magazine, owned by the admiring Henry Luce, rushed out a powerful endorsement of Eisenhower's candidacy, giving four reasons why Ike should be president: "he understands war," "his administrative ability," "his political principles," and his "gift for leadership." Eisenhower understood that the first requirement of leadership was "moral strength, the conviction that we are right." He himself surely possessed this virtue. "What a boost he could give to the national morale!"[29]

The storm was gaining force, and on January 7, 1952, Eisenhower released a message of his own. Buried inside a few paragraphs of the usual statements about his devotion to NATO and his inability to campaign in person, he confirmed his party affiliation and acknowledged that a nomination to be the Republican candidate for president would constitute "a duty that would transcend my present responsibility." Somewhat reluctantly, he had set in motion a great national effort that would carry him to the White House.[30]

IV

Winning the nomination for president is hard enough for an active and will-ing candidate. Eisenhower was neither. He seemed to think that he could be drafted as the GOP nominee without having to lift a finger. But the odds were sharply against a draft. The only 20th-century presidential candidate to be offered his party's nomination without openly seeking it was Charles Evans Hughes, who, then serving on the Supreme Court, was drafted as the 1916 Republican nominee to face President Woodrow Wilson. And Hughes had been a consensus candidate, facing little opposition. Eisenhower's forces, by contrast, had to contend with the determined and resourceful Taft machine. His legions of backers in New York knew that to be nominated, Ike would have to get off his high horse and descend into the muck of politics.

To persuade Ike of the groundswell in his favor, a group of well-heeled enthusiasts concocted a rather brazen effort to charm the reluctant can-didate. On February 8, with an eye on the New Hampshire primary just four weeks away, they staged a rally in New York's Madison Square Garden to demonstrate the wide base of Eisenhower's popular appeal. Billed as a "Serenade to Ike," the affair was organized by John "Tex" McCrary and his stunning wife, the model and actress Jinx Falkenburg, who together had pi-oneered a number of radio and television talk shows. McCrary was a Texan but had schooled at Exeter and Yale, where he joined the DKE fraternity, was tapped for Skull and Bones, and played football. He was a journalist, editor, and public relations consultant with wealthy friends like fellow Yalie Jock Whitney, who bankrolled the event. McCrary made sure the "Sere-nade" was broadcast by NBC to radio and television markets in a dozen major cities, though with the time difference, Eisenhower in France was sleeping soundly while the raucous event unfolded.[31]

McCrary used his connections to rope in some of the country's most famous talent to tout the Ike-for-President movement. Clark Gable, Henry Fonda, Ethel Merman, television hostess Faye Emerson, Noel Coward, and a dozen other high-profile entertainers popped up on the stage. Fred War-ing, the universally popular bandleader, acted as emcee for the night and led the audience in songs from the popular Broadway shows *South Pacific* and *The King and I.* Merman belted out "There's No Business Like Show Business" to delirious applause. Irving Berlin crooned a humorous confec-tion called—what else—"I Like Ike" and was joined on stage by a comical Truman look-alike, who received the loud jeers of the crowd. To top it off, the composer Richard Rodgers accompanied singer and Broadway actress Mary Martin in a rendition of "I'm in Love with a Wonderful Guy"—the theme of the night.[32]

By all accounts, this foolishness was a great success, not so much for its impact on the electorate as for its impact on Eisenhower. Two days after the rally, on February 11, Jacqueline Cochran, a former World War II flying ace, pioneer of the Women Air Force Service Pilots, and a close collaborator of McCrary's in mounting the "Serenade," packed up reels of film of the whole event, boarded a TWA flight to Paris, and arrived breathlessly at SHAPE headquarters with what Eisenhower called "burning enthusiasm and the spirit of the crusader."[33]

Eisenhower knew Cochran from the war years and was also close to her husband, the wealthy investor and utilities owner Floyd Odlum. Watching the film of the "Serenade" with Mamie at his side in the theater they had installed in their Paris residence, Eisenhower was overcome by the outpouring of enthusiasm he saw among the New York well-wishers. He broke down, openly sobbing in front of his guest. Cochran did not hesitate: she pressed him to declare himself a candidate, resign from the NATO command, and return to the United States to campaign. After a long and emotional conversation, Eisenhower concurred: he told her he would run. The next day he composed a brief note in his diary: "Viewing [the film] finally developed into a real emotional experience for Mamie and me. I've not been so upset in years. Clearly to be seen is the mass longing of America for some kind of reasonable solution for her nagging, persistent and almost terrifying problems. It's a real experience to realize that one could become a symbol for many thousands of the hope they have!"[34]

On February 16, just four days after Cochran's dramatic visit, Eisenhower arranged to meet Clay in London, where Eisenhower was attending the funeral services of King George VI. Meeting secretly in the home of Brig. James Gault, Eisenhower's British military aide, Clay pushed Eisenhower to settle the issue once and for all: Would he come home to run for the nomination? It took some hours of heated discussion before Eisenhower agreed. "He dreaded a campaign," Clay recalled later. "He'd never been in one, and it represented a rather awesome undertaking. And I think he didn't like being pressed for a decision. As a matter of fact, he got quite provoked with me when I kept on insisting that we had to have a decision."[35]

Eisenhower finally told Clay he would ask Truman to be relieved of his post. He would then resign his commission and return to the United States around June 1, after a crucial round of NATO meetings was wrapped up. At long last, after a year or more of prevarication and delay, he was ready to get into the fight. "I only ask," he wrote to Clay a few days later, "that you people regard my own position with some sympathy."[36]

V

Eisenhower's decision to seek the GOP nomination could not yet be made public. He wanted to finish his NATO assignment without the distraction that his resignation would create, and he needed Truman's permission to relinquish his command. So even though he knew he was going to run, he continued to feign indifference toward the political dogfight now shaping up in the Republican primary in New Hampshire. As it happened, that contest of March 11, 1952, would have a major impact on the course of the election. Both parties had candidates on the primary ballot in New Hampshire. Truman's name would appear for the Democrats, though he had made no formal announcement of his intention to run for reelection. His challenger was the Tennessee senator Estes Kefauver, a political maverick who had made himself a national figure by chairing the televised Senate special committee on organized crime. Truman's low popularity made him vulnerable, but no one gave Kefauver much of a chance against the sitting president. The fact that Kefauver was a southerner and campaigned while wearing a coonskin cap only emphasized his eccentricity and novelty in New England.

In the Republican primary voters would elect 14 delegates to send to the national convention in Chicago in July. The ballot also featured a "beauty contest," a simple expression of preference for president. The stakes were high: not only were delegates to be accumulated, but the winning candidate would gain valuable momentum going into the subsequent primary contests.

With Eisenhower mutely observing from France, Taft had the field almost to himself, and he swung into the primary with confidence and a strong message. The weather during his three-day tour through the state was cold and wet, with snow drifts melting into the thick slush of early spring. But his stump speech was red-hot, and he gave it 30 times in as many towns. Taft ran as the true conservative in the race and a man of principle who would offer a sharp contrast to the Democrats. He promised voters that he would launch "an all-out attack on the unlimited spending and taxing, the bureaucratic regulation of the Fair Deal; on the disastrous foreign policy which has led to Russian power and unnecessary war, and on the immorality of this Administration." In a swipe at Dewey and the liberal Republicans, Taft declared, "We cannot win by a modification of our principles. . . . We must shun a 'me-too' campaign," such as Dewey had run in 1948 that only sought to continue the FDR legacy of the New Deal. It was time to stop the growth of government, time to end the terrible war in Korea, and time to throw out an administration that "had been dominated by a strange Communist sympathy." Taft reserved a number of pointed barbs for Eisenhower. "You would not choose someone," he told a rain-soaked crowd in Laconia on March 6, "who never ran for office in his life and doesn't know how to conduct a campaign." Besides, Ike had expressed no political views at all and had worked closely with Democratic administrations.[37]

With Eisenhower still in Paris, the Ike-for-President team relied on the powerful influence of New Hampshire's governor Sherman Adams. A pro-Eisenhower Republican, he had selected a very strong and well-known slate of candidates whose names were on the ballot as Eisenhower delegates. Many were proven vote-getters; they included Adams himself, the former governor Robert O. Blood, Representative Norris Cotton, and the head of Phillips Exeter Academy William Saltonstall.[38]

On the night of March 10 a heavy blanket of wet snow fell, but this did not depress the turnout on the following day: twice as many voters came out to the polls as in the primary of 1948. And the results were stunning: not only did Eisenhower sweep the delegates, winning all 14, but he topped the popularity poll decisively, garnering 46,661 votes to Taft's 35,838. Perhaps more significant for the 1952 national election, Kefauver edged out Truman, winning even labor-heavy districts in Manchester. The president had not campaigned in New Hampshire, but even so it was a blow to lose to a dark-horse senator from the back woods of Tennessee.

Eisenhower had been helped by his enormous popularity, by the argument that only he could beat the Democrats, by the strength of his slate of delegates, and by Taft's stiffness and wooden manner on the stump. Taft later implied that Governor Adams had arm-twisted state employees to vote for Eisenhower, and the right-wing *Manchester Union Leader* darkly hinted that unnamed Wall Street bankers had flooded the state with slush funds for Eisenhower. But saner observers understood the significance of the vote: Walter Lippmann, the dean of national political columnists, asked rhetorically, "Is there any serious doubt that Eisenhower is the Republican who has by all odds the best chance to capitalize upon the discontent within the

Democratic party?" Lippmann went on, putting words to what Eisenhower himself had already concluded. He was "no longer just a popular General" but "an active candidate" and so should no longer be in uniform. He must "ask the president to relieve him of his military command."[39]

In Paris, Eisenhower took careful notice of what was going on. In mid-March he sent a discreet letter to New York lawyer Herbert Brownell, inviting him to his headquarters. Brownell, a longtime Republican power broker and the manager of Dewey's 1948 campaign against Truman, had been working with Clay and others to get Eisenhower into the race. He quickly accepted Ike's invitation and made his way to Paris, incognito, for a meeting with the general on March 24. The two men had "a confidential and extremely candid exchange of views." Over the course of a full day, they discussed politics, ideas, and strategy. Brownell leveled with Eisenhower. He would not get the nomination through a draft; if he wanted it, he would have to campaign for it. Taft might have lost the beauty contest in New Hampshire, but he already had 40 percent of the delegates needed to win the nomination, and Ike could not delay declaring his candidacy any longer.[40]

Truman too had a decision to make. The double blows of New Hampshire—the Eisenhower and Kefauver victories—had concentrated his mind: if he were to run for reelection, he would not only face a wildly popular war hero and political superstar, but he would have to lead a badly divided Democratic Party into the campaign. Kefauver's win in Yankee New Hampshire had shown the northern liberals and labor supporters were ready for a change of leadership, and down in Dixie just a few weeks earlier, Senator Richard Russell of Georgia, an opponent of Truman's civil rights policies, had announced his own candidacy. The segregationists in the Democratic Party were once again threatening to secede, as they had done under the Dixiecrat Strom Thurmond in 1948. It was a depressing political landscape, even for a talent as wily and indefatigable as Truman. At the annual Jefferson-Jackson Day dinner on March 29, 1952, Truman made his announcement. He rose to the podium at 10:30 at night, before a crowd of 6,000 elegantly attired party faithful who had just dined on beef tenderloin, baked potatoes, and ice cream molded into the shape of a donkey. After a long-winded and barbed attack on the Republican Party and a full-throated defense of his own record, he declared his decision to retire from the fray: "I shall not be a candidate for re-election."[41]

Truman had concluded that Eisenhower would run and that he would win. The president could not have been surprised to find, just two days later, a letter from Eisenhower on his desk, dated April 2, 1952: "I am requesting the Secretary of Defense to initiate action to bring about my relief from my current post as Supreme Commander, Allied Powers Europe, on or about June 1st of this year." It "makes me rather sad," Truman replied in a handwritten note, perhaps thinking not only about his own departure from office but about the decision of one of his idols to step into the dirty work of politics. "I hope you will be happy in your new role."[42]

CHAPTER 4

CRUSADE

*"You have summoned me on behalf of millions of
your fellow Americans to lead a great crusade."*

I

IT HAS LONG BEEN ASSERTED THAT EISENHOWER SWEPT INTO
the White House as the 34th president on a wave of personal popularity
rather than for any set of ideas or policies. Certainly Eisenhower was popular, universally known and admired for his war service. Yet in the election of
1952 he did not rely on his reputation as an apolitical soldier to stay above
the fray of the campaign. Quite the opposite. Rather than playing it safe, rising above faction and controversy, coasting on his name recognition, Eisenhower jumped into the mess of electoral politics with gusto. In running for
president, he was vehement, polemical, and partisan. He lambasted the Truman administration, heaped abuse on the New Deal, and curried favor with
the right wing of his party.

Why did he do so? Eisenhower deeply believed in the conservative,
small-government, balanced-budget positions he celebrated on the hustings; he maintained an instinctive aversion toward New Deal policies and
bureaucracies. But he was a much shrewder politician than he let on. In
1952 he effectively pulled off a brilliant political conjuring trick. He pretended to be a nonpartisan political amateur, just an "old soldier" incapable
of duplicity, while in fact he followed a ruthless and successful strategy: attack your opponent relentlessly, stress ideological themes in order to stir up
enthusiasm in the base, and promise to "fix the mess in Washington." He
posed as an outsider, speaking for the average American. For a man who
had been a government employee since 1915, who had worked in Washington for many years, whose friends were among the wealthiest power brokers

in the nation, and who had aligned himself closely with Truman's foreign policies, this was as neat a political bait and switch as American politics has seen in the 20th century. And Ike did it all with a smile.

His campaign for president started in Abilene on June 4, 1952, a date the hometown selectmen hastily named "Eisenhower Day." Fifty thousand people flocked to this quiet Kansas hamlet to see the great war leader open his bid for the White House. Every hotel and rooming house for 40 miles was booked by reporters and television crews. Hawkers of popcorn, candy apples, foot-long hot dogs, and trinkets lined Abilene's main street. Two (Republican) elephants were shipped into town on a long trailer from Kelly's Circus in Holyoke, Colorado. Eisenhower, who had returned from Paris to Washington on the first of June, flew into Kansas City that morning and took a special train to Abilene. It was set to be a terrific day.

An hour before the general was scheduled to make his nationally televised speech to a crowd of well-wishers in Abilene's "stadium" (a generous term for an open field of weeds and dirt ringed by a few bleachers), the skies erupted. Rain poured down, churning the ground into ankle-deep black mud. Onlookers fled for their cars or nearby shelters, leaving Ike almost alone on a simple wooden platform, a few flags snapping in the wet wind behind him. "Like his invasion of Europe eight years ago," one reporter quipped, "General Eisenhower's political invasion of the Middle West turned out this afternoon to be an amphibious operation."[1]

It was a miserable start, and it looked even worse on television, as Eisenhower donned a pair of foggy spectacles, bowed his head, and read out a long prepared speech devoid of much punch or pizzazz. A few wisps of hair blew from his bald pate, and his wet slicker made him look like an elderly crossing guard on a windswept street corner. Back in New York, Governor Dewey and his team of professionals were appalled as they watched the speech. Herbert Brownell, who was going to play a central role in getting Ike elected, recalled that "everything went wrong." It was "absolutely dismal," he said of the kickoff event, "about as disappointing an opening campaign speech as I've ever experienced."[2]

Through the rain and wind, though, Eisenhower's speech carried an accusation: 20 years of Democratic rule, from Roosevelt's New Deal to Truman's Fair Deal, had left America feeble, anxious, and vulnerable. The nation faced terrible problems, he asserted, from persistent labor unrest to unchecked inflation, a spike in taxes, a bloated national debt, the spreading tentacles of a grasping bureaucracy, and pernicious corruption inside the federal government. All these problems he laid at Truman's doorstep. It was time, Eisenhower argued, to scale back the government and return to "thrift, frugality and economy." James Reston of the *New York Times* likened the speech to an old revivalist Chautauqua meeting, in which "the virtues of frugality, austerity, honesty, economy, simplicity, integrity" were solemnly invoked.[3]

The next day Eisenhower held his first press conference as a candidate in Abilene's Plaza Theater and revealed his skill at handling the news media. The Eisenhower team wanted to dispel accusations from the Taft camp that Ike was out of touch with America's problems after his long service overseas. To the astonishment of his interrogators, Eisenhower was masterful. He reaffirmed his lifelong support for the Republican Party and its principles, saying he had "never voted the Democratic ticket." He spoke frankly about the Korean War, insisting that there was no "clear cut answer" to the conflict because of the size and scale of the Chinese military forces now in the region. Asked about civil rights legislation, he gave what would become a sort of mantra for him: "I do not believe we can cure all of the evils in men's hearts by law." This was both his personal belief and a pitch to southern white voters that he would be no crusader in this field.

In reply to a question about compulsory national health insurance, a policy Truman wanted but failed to secure, Eisenhower invoked his opposition to socialism: "Beyond pure socialism lies, I believe, dictatorship." He deftly reaffirmed his anticommunist credentials while distancing himself from Joe McCarthy. "No one could be more determined than I am that any kind of communistic, subversive influence be uprooted," he said, but it could be done "without besmirching the reputation of any innocent man." Combined with his opening speech, this press conference aimed to deflect Taft's accusation that Eisenhower was just another "me-too" Republican, willing to accept the legacy of the New Deal. Ike tried to reassure the Old Guard Republicans and put the Democrats on notice that he intended to bring the fight to them.[4]

Watching Eisenhower in action, Stewart Alsop, writing in the *New York Herald Tribune*, called him the "most effective personality to emerge on the political scene since the death of Franklin Roosevelt." He had a kind of "political magic," Alsop wrote, evident from the "electric undercurrent of excitement" that filled the room. His words mattered less than his sincerity and his lack of guile. Alsop concluded, "He will be a remarkably hard man to beat."[5]

II

And yet there was nothing inevitable in his winning the Republican nomination at the national convention in Chicago in July. While Eisenhower had been stationed at NATO headquarters in Paris, Senator Taft had been working hard to secure the commitment of state delegates across the country. Taft had won many state primaries and had used his enviable political connections with governors, senators, and congressmen to nail down an impressive slate of committed delegates. The states would send 1,206 delegates to the convention; a nominee would need 604 to win. By the time Eisenhower gave his speech in Abilene, Taft could say with some confidence that he had already lined up 500 delegates. Eisenhower showed strength in northeastern and mid-Atlantic states and the Pacific coast and had won almost 400 delegates. But Taft was ahead. "The campaign has gone just about as we programmed it," Taft said. He expected to have the nomination within reach by the time the convention opened.[6]

With both sides fighting so fiercely for every slight advantage, it was perhaps inevitable that a bit of old-fashioned political chicanery would erupt into a national scandal just a few weeks before the convention. In Texas, with 38 delegates at stake, the Republican Party was deeply divided over which candidate to support. In local precinct elections the voters went for Eisenhower, but the party bosses were pro-Taft, and they appointed a Taft slate of delegates anyway, claiming that many Democrats had voted for Ike in the primary—they were legally allowed to do so—and had thus skewed the results. The Eisenhower forces promptly labeled the affair "the Texas Steal."

So serious was the issue that Eisenhower himself traveled to Dallas in late June to give a searing speech denouncing the tactics of a "small clique" of Texas Republicans who were trying to steal delegates. He pointed out that no party could "clean up the government of the United States unless that party—from top to bottom—is clean itself." In the meantime the pro-Eisenhower forces in Texas named a rival delegation to go to the national convention, where they would continue the fight to be recognized. This nasty conflict loomed as the convention opened.[7]

There was further drama over which side would win the votes of state delegations controlled by "favorite sons," that is, state leaders who had won their own state primaries and whose name would be placed in nomination in the distant hope that a rally to them might occur at the convention. Governor Earl Warren of California held 70 delegates—a powerful voting bloc in a tight race—and former Minnesota governor Harold Stassen held 28. The Michigan, Pennsylvania, Georgia, and Louisiana delegates were uncommitted or in dispute, and in the close race it was unclear which way these vital votes would turn. Taft's men dominated the Republican National Committee, but the dynamics of a convention were impossible to predict. The pressure was on: everything would come down to the politicking on the floor of the convention, which opened on a blazing hot July 7 in the International Amphitheatre in Chicago's south side, just across the street from the vast reeking works of the Union Stockyards.

With Eisenhower ensconced in his suite of rooms in the Blackstone Hotel and watching the convention on television, the four days of mayhem and chaos began. The first stage of the battle was led by the clever veteran Brownell. He had been Dewey's campaign manager in 1948 and had intimate knowledge of how the convention process worked. It was his idea to attack Taft's weakness: his reliance upon delegations whose votes were contested. Brownell wrote a "Fair Play" amendment to the convention rules that proposed that contested delegates not be allowed to vote on the seating of other contested delegates. It was a technicality, but an important one, for it meant that only secure and legitimate delegates would be allowed to vote on which slate of delegates—Taft's or Eisenhower's—would be seated from the contested states.

Brownell and his allies, especially Governors Sherman Adams of New Hampshire and Arthur Langlie of Washington, appealed to the convention on moral grounds: the GOP nominee would fight the Democrats on the issue of corruption, so he had to guarantee integrity in his own campaign. This accusation put the Taft forces back on their heels; in a series of narrow votes the convention agreed to accept the "Fair Play" language and awarded to Eisenhower the delegates from Louisiana, Georgia, and Texas. The tumultuous first day was, as Brownell put it, "a disastrous day for Taft." He was stuck 100 votes short of the nomination, and the momentum was moving swiftly toward Eisenhower.[8]

Behind the scenes, Brownell, Dewey, Adams, Henry Cabot Lodge, and the Eisenhower team now put intense pressure on the delegates to get on the Eisenhower bandwagon. They made a simple and powerful argument: Taft could not win a national election, and Eisenhower could. With Ike on the ticket, the Republicans would be back in the White House after 20 years. It worked: early in the afternoon of Friday, July 11, the balloting began, and as state after state voted, it became clear that Eisenhower was leading—slightly. By the time the last delegate had spoken—the Virgin Islands named its single delegate for Eisenhower—the vote stood at 595 for Eisenhower, 500 for Taft, 81 for Earl Warren, 20 for Harold Stassen, and 10 for Douglas MacArthur. Ike was nine votes short. The leader of the Minnesota delegation, Senator Edward J. Thye, leaped to his feet and asked to be recognized, whereupon he switched his state's votes, formerly pledged to Stassen, to Eisenhower. Other delegations rose to do the same, making a second ballot unnecessary. By the time all the votes were counted, Eisenhower had 845 votes to 280 for Taft. Governor Warren, still hoping a deadlocked convention might turn to him as a fallback choice, held on to his delegates until the bitter end.[9]

And for the Taft delegates in Chicago, the end was indeed bitter. The sharp-tongued *New Yorker* correspondent Richard Rovere took the measure of the Taft supporters: "Nominating Dwight Eisenhower was an act of hard sacrifice and self-denial for most delegates here. It was clear from the time the first throngs began to gather in the lobby of the Hilton that a lot of them, including those who wore "I Like Ike" buttons the size of saucers, really did not like the General at all. . . . They grumbled publicly over a fate that forced them to reward a man they regarded as a parvenu, an amateur, a boob, and a heretic of sorts." Said one forlorn delegate about Taft, "My God, I love him. . . . It kills me to have to do this to him." In fact the right wing of the party would never forgive Eisenhower or be reconciled to his leadership.[10]

Eisenhower could offer an olive branch to these disaffected Tafties in his choice of a vice-presidential running mate. He and his advisers would not consider the darlings of the Old Guard like Taft himself or MacArthur, but Dewey suggested just the right man for the job: the junior senator from California, Richard M. Nixon. At first glance Nixon was not an obvious choice. He was only 39—the youngest Republican in the Senate. He'd been in politics for all of six years, and before that had been a struggling lawyer fresh out of the navy. In late May a poll of national political reporters discounted Nixon as a nominee for the second spot on the GOP ticket. They expected Warren or Senators Everett Dirksen of Illinois, William Knowland of California, or Henry Cabot Lodge of Massachusetts. Of the 50 leading writers interviewed by *Newsweek* magazine, only one thought Nixon would be chosen.[11]

Yet Nixon did have some attractive features for the Eisenhower team. His youth would counteract Eisenhower's 62 years; his home state of California would balance out Eisenhower's New York residency (and the impression of

Dewey's influence); and he was both a conservative and an internationalist who had the respect of the Old Guard and the Taft camp while not being beholden to them. He had also developed a reputation—appalling to some, thrilling to others—as an avid Red hunter, the man who unmasked Alger Hiss, the dapper State Department official who had passed secret documents to a communist spy. "Nixon seemed an almost ideal candidate for vice-president," Brownell suggested. "He was young, geographically right, had experience both in the House and Senate with a good voting record, and was an excellent speaker." According to Sherman Adams, "Eisenhower wanted above all a vice-presidential nominee with a demonstrable record of anti-Communism." The Eisenhower campaign strategists needed an aggressive campaigner on the ticket. In Nixon, they got their man.[12]

Dewey had had Nixon in his sights for some time. In May 1952 he invited Nixon to speak to an audience of leading New York Republicans at a dinner at the Waldorf Astoria. Dewey introduced the young senator as the tough courageous fighter who had exposed Hiss. Nixon knew the speech was an audition for national office and treated it as such. "I devoted a full week to preparing it," he later admitted, though he spoke without notes, having memorized his remarks. He laid out a strategy for winning the presidency, stressing the "survival of the nation," which was under siege by international communism. After the speech, Dewey invited Nixon to his suite at the Roosevelt Hotel and told him he was on the short list for vice president.[13]

At least two weeks before the Republican Convention, Dewey, Clay, Lodge, and Brownell settled on Nixon as their choice. Just after Eisenhower's nomination was secured, Brownell and Dewey convened a meeting of two dozen leading Republicans at Chicago's Hilton Hotel to consider vice-presidential nominees. For an hour or so, a desultory discussion considered and ruled out Taft, Dirksen, Knowland, and Governor Daniel Thornton of Colorado. Dewey then spoke up. "What about Nixon?" he asked, as if the name had suddenly popped into his head. He spoke eloquently about the strengths Nixon would bring to the ticket, and within a few minutes it was settled. Brownell left the room to place a call to Eisenhower, who approved the choice.[14]

Brownell then called Nixon, who was napping in his underwear in a stifling un-air-conditioned hotel room near the convention hall, and told him to come meet Eisenhower at the Blackstone Hotel. Nixon and his trusty aide Murray Chotiner jumped into a limo with a police escort, dashed uptown to the hotel, and were ushered into Eisenhower's suite. Nixon, always sensitive to slights of any kind, was acutely aware of the enormous gap of prestige and power that separated the two men. Just a few years earlier he had been a junior naval officer doing desk work in New York City when Ike was driven through the streets to a hero's welcome; peering out a window on the 20th floor, Nixon could just make him out through the snowstorm of confetti. Now he stood before the famous general, who formally asked him to join his "crusade."

Nixon accepted eagerly. "July 11, 1952 was the most exciting day of my life," he wrote 10 years later. But there was no warmth here. "Despite his great capacity for friendliness, Eisenhower also had a quality of reserve which, at least subconsciously, tended to make a visitor feel like a junior officer coming in to see the commanding General." And no matter how hard he tried over the next decade, Nixon would never close the distance between them.[15]

With the ticket now set, Eisenhower delivered his acceptance speech to the convention. He declared that he would "lead a great crusade for freedom in America and freedom in the world." "Today is the first day of our battle," he told his Republican followers. "The road that leads to November 4th is a fighting road. In that fight I will keep nothing in reserve." And by his side would be the brawler Dick Nixon. In a memorable backhanded compliment, Eisenhower praised Nixon to the assembled delegates as "a man who has shown statesmanlike qualities in many ways, but has a special talent and an ability to ferret out any kind of subversive influence wherever it may be found."[16]

III

Was there any Democrat in 1952 who could beat Eisenhower? With Truman out of the picture, the Democratic Party seemed rudderless. Estes Kefauver desperately wanted the nomination, but he was a nakedly ambitious, self-centered maverick and widely disliked in his own party. Vice President Alben Barkley, much loved by Democrats after many decades of public service in Congress, was, at age 75, too old. Averell Harriman, with a distinguished career as an ambassador and public servant, had close ties to the liberal wing of the party, but he was painfully awkward as a public speaker and probably too rich to be appealing to Democratic voters. And there really was no one else. Except, perhaps, for the one-term, reform-minded moderate governor of Illinois, Adlai Stevenson.

Stevenson, a rumpled, affable man with a bald pate and a fringe of dark hair around his ears, looked like everyone's favorite English professor, or perhaps the town pediatrician. He had a gift for combining lighthearted wit with soaring idealism. At the Democratic National Convention, also held in Chicago, the delegates heard a kind of talk they thirsted for like weary travelers crossing a desert of parched rhetoric. "Intemperate criticism is not a policy for the nation," Stevenson said, chiding the Republicans. "Denunciation is not a program for our salvation. . . . What counts is not just what we are against but what we are for." Listening to the convention over the radio 1,000 miles away in New Hampshire, a young aspiring reporter named Mary McGrory heard Stevenson's words crackling through the night. "Stevenson's speeches seemed beautiful to me," she confessed. "Politically speaking, it was the Christmas morning of our lives."

Although Stevenson had deep reservations about running for president, his party clamored for his leadership and, on July 26, nominated him as its standard-bearer. To reassure southern Democrats, the convention added Senator John Sparkman of Alabama to the ticket, a New Dealer but a man who had consistently opposed civil rights for African Americans. Liberals, ignoring Sparkman, cheered Stevenson's high-minded invocations of good government and his paeans to FDR. Where Eisenhower spoke the simple vernacular of the parade ground, Stevenson's speeches were carefully written gems, suited for a university lecture hall. Eisenhower relied on clichés and leaden one-liners; Stevenson quoted St. Francis of Assisi, Thomas Jefferson, Lincoln, even Christ himself. Was he too sophisticated for American politics? His liberal supporters didn't seem to mind. "He lighted up the sky like a flaming arrow," his young aide George Ball remembered.[17]

Republicans, by contrast, did not rely on oratory. They had a blunt election slogan: "Time for a change." After 20 years of Democratic rule, this resonated. "Indignation," observed Rovere, was "the emotional keynote of Eisenhower's campaign." Allegations swirled around Truman's administration that a New Deal agency, the Reconstruction Finance Corporation, had been approving loans in return for political favors. Republicans cried foul, condemning corruption in high places. They bemoaned bloated federal budgets and expansive bureaucracy, reviled Truman's alleged failure to combat communist subversion at home, and denounced the stumbling diplomacy that had lost China and invited North Korean aggression in June 1950. Senator Karl Mundt of South Dakota tried to summarize the case against the Democrats in a scientific formula: "K_1C_2"—Korea, Communism, and Corruption.[18]

Eisenhower chose to make the Brown Palace Hotel in Denver his head-quarters, the better to stress his western roots and to escape to the mountains for an occasional weekend. From there he would make forays across the country by train on the elaborately decorated *Eisenhower Special*, 24 Pullman cars crammed with 150 aides, journalists, bodyguards, a teletype machine, and Ike's personal physician, Brig. Gen. Howard Snyder. The Denver staff and the campaign train were tightly managed by Sherman Adams, the taciturn New Hampshire governor with cropped white hair, a natty bow tie, and razor-sharp elbows, who brooked no guff from anyone and kept a close hand on the reins. Robert Cutler, a Boston bank president who had served under Secretary of War Henry Stimson and Army Chief of Staff George Marshall during the war, rising to the rank of general, vetted policy papers and speeches and later became Eisenhower's first national security adviser. James Hagerty, a seasoned reporter for the *New York Times*, signed on as press secretary. Back in New York, a large staff of advisers, speechwriters, researchers, and typists, as well as political hacks mostly from the Dewey machine, took over the ninth floor of the Commodore Hotel under the loose direction of Herbert Brownell. They produced countless speeches and briefing papers, cabled across the country to the Eisenhower campaign train.[19]

Eisenhower covered 20,000 miles by rail and flew 30,000 miles across the country, visiting 45 states and 232 towns and cities. In every town where he appeared, an advance team arrived many hours before in a giant truck labeled "The Eisenhower Bandwagon." From this emerged an army surplus jeep with a shrieking sound system that blared out "I Like Ike" songs and broadcast the message that Eisenhower would soon be passing through town. The campaign used new technology, saturating the airwaves with pioneering television commercials. Eisenhower (who grumbled about it) made a series of short ads in which citizens asked him questions about high prices, taxes, military preparedness, and more. Viewers would then see Eisenhower respond directly with a few lines of campaign boilerplate, always ending with "It's time for a change!"

Stevenson, facing this well-funded, media-savvy Eisenhower juggernaut, needed to attack early. He went after one of Ike's most tender spots, asking whether he condoned the shameful behavior of the Republican senator Joseph McCarthy, who for over a year had been attacking the distinguished public servant and war hero George Marshall. McCarthy, along with William Jenner of Indiana and a few other zealots in the Senate, alleged that Marshall, as Truman's envoy to China after the war, bore responsibility for the loss of China to the communists. Marshall's actions were so inept, they claimed, and so beneficial to the communists that the only explanation was treason. The wartime chief of staff, alleged McCarthy, was part of a conspiracy "spun from Moscow."[20]

Only after great prodding by the press did Eisenhower make a statement, rather impromptu, about his former boss. He told a press conference in late August, "General Marshall is one of the patriots and anyone who has lived with him, worked with him as I have, knows that he is a man of real selflessness." There was "nothing of disloyalty in General Marshall's soul." However, when pressed by reporters if this implied a rebuke to McCarthy, Eisenhower said he would not discuss "personalities" and would support all Republican candidates for election to ensure Republican control of Congress, even if he did not agree with all their methods. That meant supporting McCarthy and Jenner for reelection. And worse, in September Eisenhower spoke at Butler University in Indianapolis, where he delivered a sharply partisan speech and allowed Jenner—who had called Marshall "a front man for traitors" and "a living lie"—to stand next to him, clasping his arm while waving to the crowd.[21]

For a man who claimed to dislike politics as a profession, Eisenhower certainly leaned into campaigning. His speeches were combative, vague on policy proposals, and full of biting criticism of the Democrats. In Joliet, Illinois, on September 15 he reminded his audience, "We are waging a crusade, a crusade to get out of the governmental offices not only these people who are tempted by money but the people who have been venal enough and weak enough to embrace Communism and still have found their way into our government. Let's get rid of them!" Journalist Marquis Childs observed that Ike enjoyed making these "blunt and even brutal denunciations of the Truman Administration that draw cheers from orthodox Republicans."[22]

Thin on substance, Ike's speeches thrilled his crowds anyway. Cutler said that on the campaign trail he saw "an extraordinary personal intercommunication" between Ike and the voters. "People who saw, in the flesh, the candidate's tall, straight figure and ruddy, smiling face, and who heard from his own lips his straightforward, un-oratorical talk, caught again something they remembered from their youth. He didn't quip; he didn't sound erudite; he was like a member of the family." The effect was noticed by the press. "Eisenhower's stock is rising," observed Roscoe Drummond of the *Christian Science Monitor*. "Ike is no fancy orator . . . and he occasionally will trip over his syntax." But his audiences were huge, sympathetic, and star-struck. "He is good on the hustings not because of what he says or the way he says it but because he projects a dedicated personality. More than one listener has remarked to me after a rally: 'That man sure is sincere.'"[23]

IV

And then, just as the campaign was gaining momentum, Eisenhower's running mate threw a wrench into the gears. On September 18 the *New York Post* revealed that Senator Nixon had established a fund into which wealthy California backers had occasionally deposited contributions. The money was used to cover the cost of campaigning and disseminating political material. The sum involved was not large—about $18,000—and the fund was not illegal. It soon emerged that Adlai Stevenson also had such a fund. But one of the legs of the Republican K_1C_2 tripod was the cry of "Corruption," and Nixon's fund looked dubious. Eisenhower did not like surprises, and this was a nasty one.[24]

Whatever its legal status, the fund was a political disaster. It conjured up the cartoon-like image of a band of unnamed wealthy backers handing sacks of cash to a young congressman in return for political favors. After all, such an image squared with the very picture Nixon himself had been painting of corruption in Washington. The fund crisis swiftly brought to the surface the subterranean divisions within the Republican Party. The Taft men, who were still in control of the party machinery, insisted that the story was nothing but "a left-wing smear," in Karl Mundt's words. Herbert Hoover was roused from his slumbers to offer stalwart praise for Nixon's integrity. GOP chairman Arthur Summerfield gave Nixon his full support. But the men in Ike's inner circle, the pros in New York, reacted with grave concern. Brownell, Clay, Dewey—they wondered if they'd bought a pig in a poke. The official organ of liberal Republicanism, the *Herald Tribune*, whose publisher, Bill Robinson, was Eisenhower's boon companion, immediately put out an editorial calling for Nixon to step down. Privately Robinson told Eisenhower that Nixon's place on the ticket "seriously blunts the sharp edge of the corruption issue and burdens you with a heavy and unfair handicap."[25]

Yet Eisenhower worried that dumping Nixon might do more damage to his candidacy. He directed Paul Hoffman, an old friend who was now head of the Ford Foundation, to undertake a careful investigation of Nixon's records with the help of the accounting firm Price Waterhouse. He asked

Nixon to release all documents relating to the fund; the senator would have to be "clean as a hound's tooth" in order to continue the fight against corruption—a remark that, when reported to Nixon, struck him like a punch to the solar plexus. Ike told the press, "I believe Dick Nixon to be an honest man," and then clammed up, awaiting developments. To hedge his bets, he alerted California's other senator, William Knowland, to join the campaign train in case he was needed to replace Nixon.[26]

If Eisenhower assumed Nixon would immediately offer to step off the ticket, he was wrong. Nixon showed what would become his trademark resilience and refused to be bullied. He believed there was nothing illegal or unethical about the fund. He wanted to tell his story, and he had support within the Taft-dominated Republican National Committee, which swiftly raised the money to buy half an hour of television time so Nixon could explain himself. The campaign headquarters approved the television appearance, but Governor Dewey, calling Nixon from New York just minutes before his televised speech, told him that the campaign staff expected him to offer his resignation at the conclusion of the broadcast.

Nixon refused. Instead he gave a performance on September 23 that rescued his political career from almost certain destruction. Known as the "Checkers" speech for its unctuous reference to the Nixon family dog, it was a landmark in modern American political history. Its most notable feature was that it was broadcast live on television and that 60 million voters watched it. Nixon spoke from the El Capitan Theater in Hollywood. The stage had been decorated to look like a middle-class sitting room, with bookshelves and drapes and a plush armchair in the corner on which his young wife, Pat, reposed in mute admiration. The senator, looking thin and pale, sat at a desk and faced the camera, speaking slowly with quiet emphasis.

His integrity had been questioned, Nixon began, and he wanted to reply. He had "a theory that the best and only answer to a smear . . . is to tell the truth." He explained the need for the fund as a simple expedient to spare the American taxpayer the cost of supporting his political activities. He pointed to the audit that had been done and said it showed that he had not taken a dime for himself. His conscience was clear. He continued with a pathetic accounting of his modest finances, enumerating his income, debts, mortgage payments, even the value of his 1950 Oldsmobile. Nixon summed up with a sigh. "Well, that's about it. That's what we have and that's what we owe. It isn't very much but Pat and I have the satisfaction that every dime we've got is honestly ours." Except, of course, for the dog, Checkers, which had been a gift to the Nixon daughters from an enthusiastic Texan. "Regardless of what they say about it, we're gonna keep it."

Then Nixon went on the attack. He noted acidly that Governor Stevenson, who had inherited a fortune from his father and never had to worry about money, also had a political fund and had revealed nothing about it. Senator Sparkman, the Democratic vice-presidential candidate, had bilked the taxpayers by putting his wife on the federal payroll. The establishment newspapers had attacked Nixon when he went after Alger Hiss and were attacking him now. Above all, President Truman allowed corruption to thrive in his administration while thousands of fine young American men died in Korea. It was natural that such people would want Nixon out of the way, that they would use "smears to silence me, to make me let up. Well, they just don't know who they're dealing with." Nixon would not give up. "I'm not a quitter," he insisted. Defying the directive from New York to leave the ticket, he asked his viewers to send a telegram to the Republican headquarters in Washington to tell them what *they* wanted.[27]

Watching the broadcast from a campaign stop in Cleveland, Eisenhower was furious. But although Nixon had disobeyed him by not offering to resign, Ike had to grant his running mate some respect for fighting. At the end of the speech Eisenhower strode out onto the stage of the Cleveland Public Hall, where 15,000 people had been waiting to hear his previously scheduled address. The audience had just heard Nixon's broadcast through the loudspeaker, and the atmosphere in the hall was electric. Eisenhower knew he had little choice but to offer praise for Nixon. "I have been a warrior and I like courage. Tonight I saw an example of courage," he began. "I have seen many brave men in tough situations. I have never seen any come through in better fashion than Senator Nixon did tonight." The audience responded with tumultuous applause. Still, Eisenhower prolonged Nixon's agony another day by ordering Nixon, through a public telegram, "to fly to see me at once" in Wheeling, West Virginia, where Ike would be campaigning the next day and would render his verdict in person.[28]

Although to contemporary viewers the Checkers speech appears saccharine and insincere, colored by Nixon's wounded pride and class resentment, at the time it was hailed as an honest and, above all, gutsy demonstration. The *New York Times* ran a digest of editorial opinion from the nation's newspapers on September 25, in which the speech was seen as "a smash hit," and Nixon was described as "honest" and "sympathetic." The *Los Angeles Times*, which had backed Nixon from the start, declared him "an adversary of evil and a champion of right." The *Dallas Morning News* even styled him "the sort of he-man who has made this country what it is."[29]

Hundreds of thousands of telegrams flooded into the Republican National Headquarters calling for Nixon to stay on the ticket. His painstaking assessment of his debts and his modest income, combined with his antagonism toward liberal elites, resonated with millions of viewers. Nixon revealed an uncanny ability to identify with the financial insecurities and ideological anxieties of the American Everyman—who wanted to see him rewarded. There was no way to dump a fighter like Nixon. For once, Eisenhower had been outmaneuvered. "You're my boy," Ike told him when they met the next evening in Wheeling, but Eisenhower's big grin hid the menace of that remark.[30]

Nixon had saved his skin and his career. But at what cost? Ever after, Ike would treat him with suspicion and a certain disdain. Nixon's failure to fall on his sword, his public pleading, his naked ambition, his almost painful self-exposure on television—all this repelled the proud Eisenhower. He could admire the way Nixon had fought for survival. But he could never trust him.[31]

V

Just when the fund crisis seemed to be dissipating, the Eisenhower campaign stumbled again. In early October the *Eisenhower Special* rolled into the battleground state of Wisconsin, whose 12 electoral votes went to the Democrats in 1948 by a narrow margin. The state had a tradition of progressive politics but in 1946 had sent Joseph McCarthy to Washington. Despite his controversial reputation in the country at large, McCarthy was popular in Wisconsin and seemed sure to win reelection. Eisenhower needed McCarthy's support. Even the moderate Republican governor of Wisconsin, Walter J. Kohler, who loathed McCarthy, found it necessary to swallow his principles and endorse the senator for reelection. Kohler concluded that a break with McCarthy would injure the party and possibly tip the scales toward the Democrats in November.[32]

The press was well aware of the friction between Eisenhower and the Red-baiting senator. McCarthy had made known his suspicions about Eisenhower's faith in the anticommunist crusade, while Eisenhower was bitter about McCarthy's continuing attacks on George Marshall. Ike's New York–based team of speechwriters, representing the liberal faction within the campaign, urged him to use the visit to Wisconsin to speak out on Marshall's behalf, indirectly rebuking McCarthy. They penned a speech that, while full of harsh anticommunist rhetoric, carried several lines of support for Marshall.[33]

But those words would never be spoken. The night before Ike arrived in Wisconsin, McCarthy met him in Peoria, Illinois. McCarthy knew about the speech and asked Eisenhower to omit the statement of support for Marshall. Ike refused, outraged by the presumption of the junior senator. But the next day, when the train crossed into Wisconsin, McCarthy jumped on board and appeared on the back platform alongside the candidate. At the day's first stop, in Green Bay, Eisenhower endorsed all the Republican candidates running for office in Wisconsin, and specifically referred to McCarthy. "I want to make one thing very clear," he said. "The purposes he and I have of ridding this Government of the incompetent, the dishonest and above all the subversive and the disloyal are one and the same. Our differences have nothing to do with the end result that we are seeking. The differences apply to method." At the next stop, in McCarthy's hometown of Appleton, the senator stood next to Ike on the back of the train and introduced the general as a man "who will make an outstanding president."

Inside the train, however, a fierce debate had broken out. Governor Kohler was urging the Eisenhower team to change the speech their man planned to make that evening in Milwaukee. The paragraph of support for Marshall would be seen as provocative, a slap in the face to McCarthy, and it would damage Eisenhower's chances of winning the state. Sherman Adams agreed, but the New York team was appalled: Why buckle under to McCarthy? Surely Eisenhower would win more votes nationwide by showing his independence from the toxic senator.[34]

To his everlasting regret, Eisenhower did in fact buckle, allowing his praise of Marshall to be excised from his speech. Why? The answer that is often given is that he was a novice in politics and didn't understand the significance of the issue. But nothing could be further from the truth. Eisenhower understood exactly what he was doing. To win in November he felt he needed to shore up his support from the Old Guard and the right wing of his party; the moderates would be for him anyway. He would grit his teeth and appease McCarthy.[35]

That night in Milwaukee, Eisenhower delivered a blistering attack on the Democrats and the Truman administration that sounded very much like a speech that could have been given by MacArthur or Nixon. Unbeknownst to Eisenhower, however, his staff had released to the press the original text of the speech, including the praise for Marshall. Journalists who had been expecting a bold statement of support on behalf of Marshall listened in vain. Eisenhower's condemnation of the communist penetration of government, delivered in McCarthy's home state and shorn of any tempering words of praise for Marshall, left him open to a wave of criticism that he had caved in to the worst demagogue in his party. And so he had.[36]

Truman was roused to fury by the events in Milwaukee. He adored Marshall, and he was outraged at Eisenhower's decision to place party unity above personal loyalty. Truman decided to go on the attack. In speeches in Oakland and San Francisco just a day after Eisenhower's Milwaukee fiasco, Truman linked Eisenhower with "a wave of filth" that he claimed Republicans were spreading. The president spoke with unabated anger about his old associate: "The surrender has been complete—to the Old Guard—to the lobbies—to the mossbacks of every description. But it is more than a surrender. It is the tragedy of an able and amiable human being, torn out of the life he was trained to follow and shoved around as a tool for others."[37]

The following day, in a speech in Colorado, Truman blamed Ike for appeasing those "moral pygmies," Senators Jenner and McCarthy. Such "moral blindness brands the Republican candidate as unfit to be president of the United States." Hearing these attacks, Eisenhower swore that if he won the presidency, he "would never ride down Pennsylvania Avenue" with Truman. "How low can you get!"[38]

Truman's attacks compelled Eisenhower's speechwriting team to attempt to change the focus of the campaign away from McCarthyism and the Marshall affair and toward an area of strength for the general: foreign relations and, in particular, Korea. In Detroit on October 24, Eisenhower offered his personal pledge to grapple with the ongoing crisis in Korea and to do everything possible either to win or to end the war there. If elected, he vowed "I shall go to Korea." Here at last was a concrete promise to fix a problem most Americans cared deeply about, far more than communists in government. The comment infuriated Truman, who was in the midst of negotiating an armistice in Korea. But politically it was a powerful move, conjuring the image of America's most successful soldier finally bringing an end to a bitter war. When reporters on the campaign train saw the text of the Detroit speech, they simply concluded, "That does it—Ike is in."[39]

On November 4, Eisenhower won a smashing electoral and popular victory, amassing 55 percent of the vote to Stevenson's 44 percent. The electoral total was crushing: 442–89. Stevenson won only nine states, all in the South, and he lost his home state of Illinois by 10 percentage points. Eisenhower even chipped away at the Democrats' southern stronghold, picking up Virginia, Tennessee, Oklahoma, Texas, and Florida, all of which Truman had won in 1948. At age 62, Eisenhower was the oldest man to be elected president since James Buchanan in 1856.

The 1952 election was not Eisenhower's finest hour. He made regrettable mistakes on the campaign trail, allowing Nixon to outmaneuver him during the fund scandal, refusing to break with right-wing zealots like McCarthy and Jenner, and failing to rally to the defense of George Marshall, his mentor and a true national hero. His criticisms of Truman were acidic and hypocritical, given his own role in forging America's security policy under Truman's leadership. The campaign needlessly poisoned his relations with the outgoing president.

But then election campaigns do not often bring out the best in politicians. And despite the gaffes and the overblown attacks, Eisenhower genuinely moved millions of Americans. Voters in 1952 were tired of Truman, tired of war, labor strife, inflation, big government, and the communist peril. Eisenhower legitimated these grievances because he shared them. His view of government was skeptical, distant, and wary. He urged voters to turn away from the material promises of the New Deal and return to a time of entrepreneurial spirit, to revive American traditions of independence and self-reliance. For Ike, the virtuous American was the businessman, the farmer, the innovator, the laborer: men who understood the value of money, men tempered by a decade of war and who drew sustenance from their faith in God and from the stern lessons of the marketplace. In addition to the message, Americans rallied to the messenger. Eisenhower drew people to him because he was indisputably a *winner*, a man touched by success, comfortable in command, unafraid of great responsibility. With some reason Americans had come to believe that Eisenhower, invested with the great power of the American presidency, could change the country and quite possibly the world.

PART II

AN AGE OF PERIL

CHAPTER 5

SCORPIONS IN A BOTTLE

"Freedom is pitted against slavery; lightness against the dark."

I

ON NOVEMBER 5, 1952, THE DAY AFTER HIS TRIUMPH AT THE polls, Eisenhower slipped away from the hubbub of New York City in the company of Mamie, her mother, his press secretary Jim Hagerty, his pals Bill Robinson and Cliff Roberts, and flew south to the pleasant confines of Augusta National Golf Club. Here the president-elect spent 10 days playing golf (including a round with golf legend Byron Nelson), writing notes to his loyal campaign staff, and conferring with his inner circle of advisers, especially Lucius Clay and Herb Brownell, to pick the members of his cabinet. Clay would take no official role in the administration but exercised enormous informal influence; Brownell was offered the post of attorney general. Sherman Adams, the wiry and taciturn New Hampshire governor who had managed the campaign, was given a special portfolio—assistant to the president—a position later called chief of staff. Robert Cutler, a wartime assistant to General Marshall who had shown administrative genius during the campaign, took the post of special adviser on national security affairs. Cutler would lead an extensive beefing-up of the procedures of the National Security Council and turn it into the most important decision-making body of the administration.[1]

The name of one cabinet nominee was already etched in stone: John Foster Dulles would be named secretary of state. He had been a diplomat and lawyer for half a century and was a Republican grandee, an internationalist, and a leading anticommunist hawk with ties to both the Dewey and the Taft factions of the GOP. His imprimatur could be found on the 1952 Republican platform, with its strident demand for the "roll-back" of communism from

Eastern Europe and Asia. Although a leading figure of the Establishment, during the campaign Dulles had been sharply critical of Truman's handling of foreign affairs and the Soviet threat. Arguing that containment was passive and likely to invite aggression, he called for a more robust strategy to defeat the communist bloc. His personality seemed suited for the times: he was "tough, self-centered, suspicious, insensitive"; he could also be a bore, "ponderous and Jesuitical," according to one biographer. Eisenhower respected his knowledge and experience but found his lengthy interventions in the cabinet tiresome. More important, Eisenhower kept Dulles's hawkish instincts in check. Eisenhower made sure that Dulles was surrounded by reliable, steady men whose loyalty was to the president: he named Gen. Walter Bedell Smith undersecretary of state and Robert Murphy, a wartime colleague in North Africa and France, deputy undersecretary for political affairs. Dulles was a zealous and aggressive cold warrior in public; in private he took his lead from Eisenhower.[2]

On Clay's advice, Eisenhower appointed Charles Erwin Wilson, the millionaire head of the General Motors Company (nicknamed "Engine Charlie"), to run the Pentagon. A successful engineer and industrial manager, his central qualification for secretary of defense was that he had led GM during the Second World War and had worked with the government to rapidly expand production of trucks, tanks, armored cars, and aircraft engines for the war effort. One close observer called Wilson "bluff and hearty, a passionate and uncompromising simplifier of issues, fresh from General Motors with abundant confidence that his corporate experience in Detroit's automobile industry would guide his path through all snares of politics." Yet he was politically an outsider, and Eisenhower paid a price for picking a man with few political connections and no common touch. Ike later confessed that Wilson never found a way to "sell himself and his programs to the Congress" and proved no match for the service chiefs in the Pentagon, who ran circles around him.[3]

Clay urged the president-elect to appoint George M. Humphrey as secretary of the treasury. Humphrey, president of M. A. Hanna, a large iron ore–processing company in Cleveland with subsidiary interests in steelmaking and other industries, was jovial, earnest, midwestern, and unaffected. According to one observer, he was "a businessman's businessman: a pleasant, vigorous figure, working hard and playing hard, with a mind of impressive clarity, a passion for facts, and an assumption that New Dealism was spending the country into bankruptcy." Eisenhower came to like Humphrey personally a great deal. He frequently vacationed at Milestone, Humphrey's plantation in Thomasville, Georgia, where the two men enjoyed the excellent quail shooting. In the cabinet Humphrey volubly intervened in debates, calling for less spending in every quarter. His stolid judgment and parsimonious inclinations played a major role in the administration.[4]

The Eisenhower cabinet, not surprisingly, felt and looked much like a corporate boardroom, though it retained accents of a military headquarters. For example, Robert Cutler, the national security adviser, maintained a "formidable protocol" when the National Security Council convened. According to one participant, "Bobby would come striding into the room and in a stentorian voice announce 'Gentlemen, *the president!*' Everyone stood up, and Ike would enter quietly and take his place without further fanfare. Cutler occasionally tended to embellish this ritual, and it was rumored that the president finally suggested that he moderate the pomp and ceremony."[5]

The cabinet epitomized what the left-wing sociologist C. Wright Mills called in 1956 "the power elite" when he observed that power in modern America tended to flow toward a small, dynamic coterie of men with shared experiences, ideals, values, and ambitions. Through military service, corporate leadership, and government work, and sometimes all three, these men had developed a network of influence and connections. They agreed, as Wilson would tell Congress in his confirmation hearings, that "what was good for General Motors was good for America, and vice versa." No one in the cabinet found such an idea objectionable. Nor would they have doubted for one moment the thesis that America was in peril, fighting for its life against communism, or that disloyalty must be rooted out of public life, or that government itself was something to be looked on with suspicion, an impediment to the healthy functioning of the free market and the pursuit of individual happiness. These men had not been brought into the cabinet for their diversity or heterodox ideas. Quite simply they embodied the Age of Eisenhower.

II

Two weeks after the election, Eisenhower wrapped up his vacation at Augusta and headed north. His first stop on November 18 was to call on Truman at the White House. There had not been an orderly change of presidential administrations since 1933, and both Eisenhower and Truman wanted to show the world that even as the office changed hands, there would be basic continuity in government. But it was a bitter moment for Truman. When Eisenhower arrived at Washington National Airport, he was met by an army band and cheering crowds, and his motorcade wound through the city past half a million well-wishers. Standing in the backseat of a brown open-top Cadillac, Eisenhower raised his arms in the air in a V shape and beamed at the flag-bedecked lampposts and banners hung across the streets declaring "Welcome Ike." At 10 minutes before 2:00 p.m. he arrived at the White House. Truman did not step outside to greet him.[6]

The two men had burned their bridges during the campaign. In the Oval Office, Truman tried to make some idle chatter to warm things up, but, as he recalled in his memoirs, "Eisenhower was unsmiling." Their conversation remained formal, touching on the many pressing international issues of the moment, such as Korea, Indochina, Iran, and the hydrogen bomb. Secretary of State Dean Acheson, Secretary of Defense Robert A. Lovett, and Secretary of the Treasury John W. Snyder made presentations to the president-elect and discussed setting up liaisons between the incoming administration and key executive offices. Yet Truman and Eisenhower remained palpably uneasy with each other. Truman later chalked this up to Eisenhower's inexperience, writing that Eisenhower "had not grasped the immense job ahead of him. . . . He may have been awe-struck by the long array of problems and decisions the President has to face." Nonsense. The architect of Overlord was no stranger to daunting jobs. Simply put, Eisenhower could not forgive Truman for his outrageous attacks during the campaign, accusing Eisenhower of "betraying his principles" and of "moral blindness," among other calumnies. A novice in politics, Ike had not yet developed a thick skin to shield him from the barbs of partisan politics. He was still sore, and it showed.[7]

Later that day Eisenhower flew to New York City and the familiar embrace of the Columbia president's mansion at 60 Morningside Heights. For 10 days he held meetings with a stream of Republican Party leaders, senators and congressmen, advisers and friends. But in the early hours of November 29, under cover of darkness, he was ferried by car to Long Island and Mitchell Field, from which he departed for his promised trip to Korea. The offer to "go to Korea" had been one of the defining moments of the 1952 campaign; now, in secrecy, General Eisenhower was going to fulfill his pledge.[8]

It is not clear what Eisenhower thought he would learn by going to Korea that he did not already know: the war was a bloody morass, a stalemated conflict that neither side wished to prolong and neither side dared to lose. The trip was logistically complex: a 10,000-mile flight via San Francisco, Hawaii, Midway Island, and Iwo Jima, to Seoul, in the company of his old friend and now chairman of the Joint Chiefs of Staff Gen. Omar Bradley, as well as Wilson, Brownell, and Hagerty. A second plane with a small team of handpicked newsmen, sworn to secrecy, followed. The arrangements were handled personally by Defense Secretary Lovett, and ships and aircraft around the world were put on high alert. The president-elect stopped on Iwo Jima for the night and slept in a brand-new Quonset hut just a few yards from the foaming strand where so many marines, storming this barren citadel, had been scythed down by Japanese machine guns in February 1945. The next morning Eisenhower rode in a jeep to the summit of Mt. Suribachi, passing remnants of Japanese entrenchments and dugouts; from the top he looked with reverence upon the black volcanic beaches below.

The reality of war was a constant companion on this trip. Upon arrival in Seoul on the evening of December 2, Eisenhower's party drove from the airfield into the war-scarred city center. Seoul had changed hands numerous times in the seesaw battles of the previous two years, and it was a charred ruin. Hagerty was shocked by the hundreds of thousands of refugees crouched over cooking fires in the darkness and bitter cold. "Block after block of what had once been buildings were leveled flat. . . . The Korean Capitol building was all shot up, bombed and vacant." Propaganda banners with slogans such as "Destroy Communism" snapped in the wind in the burned streets. Through this misery Eisenhower's motorcade drove on toward a large university complex, now the heavily fortified headquarters of the U.S. Eighth Army, whose commander, Gen. James Van Fleet, welcomed the president-elect. In the next three days Ike toured American military installations, met with commanders in the field, visited wounded soldiers, and ate army rations. He felt the sting of the bitter winter wind that made Korea such a misery for the soldiers and toured the battle front in a light L-19 Cessna aircraft that allowed him to see the mountainous terrain below. He quickly confirmed his own hunch that this war could not be won without a dramatic increase in firepower, men, and risk.[9]

While in Seoul, Eisenhower met twice with South Korean president Syngman Rhee. The 77-year-old lobbied Ike hard for an immediate and aggressive attack on the North. "An all-out drive to the Yalu River"—the Chinese border—"is the only alternative to break the stalemate," Rhee believed. Naturally he had no desire for a permanent division of his country; now was the moment to unleash a crippling blow on the North and unify the peninsula—under Rhee's leadership, of course. Eisenhower met these calls for a wider war with stony silence. He knew such an attack might trigger a global war with China and the Soviet Union, but he was convinced the present bloody stalemate must end: "We could not stand forever on a static front and continue to accept casualties." Eisenhower made it his first priority to bring the war to an end, either through an armistice or through an all-out drive for victory.[10]

For the long journey home, Eisenhower chose to take the 17,000-ton cruiser USS *Helena*, which he boarded in Guam. The six-day sea journey to Pearl Harbor, Hawaii, afforded him some time to relax, play bridge, and meet with senior advisers. Dulles joined the party at Wake Island, along with George Humphrey, Budget Director–designate Joseph Dodge, Adm. Arthur Radford, commander of the U.S. Pacific Fleet (and soon to replace Bradley as chairman of the Joint Chiefs of Staff), and speechwriters Emmet Hughes and C. D. Jackson. This floating presidential administration naturally aroused a great deal of comment and speculation in the press once the news blackout was lifted on December 6. Hughes recalled that press secretary Hagerty played up the "portentous strategic decisions" being made during this "epic mid-Pacific conference." There were broad discussions about Korea and the strategic options available to the new president; the general outlines of Eisenhower's first budget proposal were also discussed. But the cruise was principally a time for the chief players on the new team to get to know one another and discuss in broad outlines the goals for the coming year.[11]

Upon his return to New York on December 14, Eisenhower found a controversy brewing. Truman had labeled Ike's trip to Korea "a piece of demagoguery" in a press conference on December 12. Truman also lambasted General MacArthur, the embittered former allied commander in Korea, who had told the press that he alone had a "secret plan" to end the war. Truman demanded that MacArthur reveal the plan; MacArthur announced he would share it instead with Eisenhower. The slight was deliberate and Truman seethed with anger and contempt. Eisenhower tried to walk a fine line: he accepted MacArthur's offer to meet and discuss Korea, though he privately dismissed MacArthur's plan, which was little more than an atomic ultimatum to the Reds: end the war in Korea or experience all-out atomic attack. Instead Eisenhower issued a statement that was measured and restrained: there was "no simple formula for bringing a swift, victorious end" to the Korean War; he wanted a "satisfactory solution" and an "honorable peace," and in the meantime Americans would continue "our world-wide struggle against Communist aggression." Privately, though, he was furious at Truman for disparaging his Korean trip as a political stunt.[12]

On January 20, 1953, a cloudy and mild day, Eisenhower went to the East Portico of the U.S. Capitol to take the oath of office. Truman, his sour and mute companion in their limousine ride down Pennsylvania Avenue, now stood across from him, his face unmoved and distant. Chief Justice Fred Vinson faced Eisenhower, holding in his left hand two Bibles: one, used by George Washington in 1789, opened to II Chronicles 7:14 ("If My people who are called by My name will humble themselves, and pray and seek My face, and turn from their wicked ways, then I will hear from heaven, and will forgive their sin and heal their land"), and Ike's own personal Bible, opened to Psalm 33:12 ("Blessed is the nation whose God is the Lord; and the people whom he hath chosen for his own inheritance"). Behind Eisenhower stood Vice President Nixon, who had been sworn in just moments earlier. Eisenhower raised his right hand, solemnly took the oath of office, and then turned to the gathered crowd.

He had agonized over his inaugural address, working closely with Hughes for weeks to craft it. He started with a hastily written prayer—a telling overture to a presidency that would attempt to place piety and devotion at the center of American public life—then launched into a remarkably unmerciful 20-minute speech, keynoted by overtones of conflict, war, ideological division, and sacrifice. "Forces of good and evil are massed and armed and opposed as rarely before in history," he began, and continued in this somber tone. Americans, he said, faced a deadly and insidious enemy who "know no god but force, no devotion but its use. They tutor men in treason. They feed upon the hunger of others. Whatever defies them, they torture, especially the truth." The battle between communism and democracy was truly a clash of civilizations: "Freedom is pitted against slavery; lightness against the dark."

Americans would not shrink from the struggle against communism, he insisted. They would fight, with full conviction of the moral rightness of the American way of life, and without compromise or appeasement. "We shall never try to placate an aggressor by the false and wicked bargain of trading honor for security. Americans, indeed all free men, remember that in the final choice a soldier's pack is not so heavy a burden as a prisoner's chains." Eisenhower preferred war with honor to peace with dishonor. "We must be ready to dare all for our country. For history does not long entrust the care of freedom to the weak or the timid." The great task of the second half of the 20th century was to wage freedom's battle and persuade the world to join in that struggle against tyranny. "This is the hope that beckons us onward in this century of trial," he concluded. "This is the work that awaits us all, to be done with bravery, with charity, and with prayer to Almighty God." Dark and ominous, Eisenhower's speech conjured a vision of struggle, conflict, and sacrifice. The Great Crusade was off to a cheerless start.[13]

III

President Eisenhower had reason to be anxious. His first year in office, and indeed his entire presidency, unfolded under the shadow of an intensifying arms race. Just three days before his election, on November 1, 1952, the Atomic Energy Commission oversaw the test of the first hydrogen bomb— to that date, the largest explosion detonated by man. The device had been built on the coral island of Elugelab in the South Pacific and weighed 80 tons. The 10.4-megaton explosion—500 times more powerful than the bomb that devastated Hiroshima—sent a mushroom cloud of steam and radioactive coral 100,000 feet into the sky. When the Soviets tested their first hydrogen bomb, in August 1953, detonating a 400-kiloton bomb in the remote steppe of Kazakhstan, the world's peoples faced the no longer fantastical prospect that the superpowers could, between them, end human life on Earth.[14]

To drive home the strategic significance of these "super" weapons, the outgoing secretaries of state and defense, Dean Acheson and Robert A. Lovett, prepared an alarming report for the new administration. Their message must have made Ike's blood run cold: despite its increasingly powerful arsenal of atomic bombs, the United States could do almost nothing to halt a Soviet first strike. "As of mid-1952," Acheson and Lovett wrote, "probably 65–85% of the atomic bombs launched by the USSR could be delivered on target in the United States." Only a crash program of investment in building a continental defense shield of interceptor aircraft and radar stations could help improve the nation's ability to survive such an onslaught.[15]

A panel of distinguished experts reinforced this chilling message. Chaired by J. Robert Oppenheimer, the father of the atomic bomb, the group arrived at some depressing conclusions. The time was very near, they predicted, when the Soviet atomic arsenal would be large enough to destroy the United States many times over. Of course the Soviets knew that any attack on the United States would lead to their own certain destruction from a devastating retaliatory strike. Even so, the United States was vulnerable as never before to a surprise attack from its principal enemy. Oppenheimer's team concluded that the United States had to improve its air defenses to locate and intercept any Soviet bomber aircraft that might seek to deliver an atomic payload on American soil. The government also had to do a better job of informing the public about just what was at stake in the arms race. When Oppenheimer summarized the findings of the panel's report for publication in the journal *Foreign Affairs*, he penned an enduring metaphor for the nuclear age: "We may anticipate a state of affairs in which two Great Powers will each be in a position to put an end to the civilization and life of the other, though not without risking its own. We may be likened to two scorpions in a bottle, each capable of killing the other, but only at the risk of his own life."[16]

What was to be done? How should the United States wage the cold war in an era of thermonuclear weapons? Should the president, in light of the ever-increasing power of nuclear weapons, pursue a policy of conciliation with the Soviets and propose a halt to the arms race? Or should the new administration intensify America's efforts to expand its nuclear arsenal, intimidating the Soviets with an array of fearsome nuclear weapons and perhaps even pushing the Soviets into retreat? The dilemma shaped Eisenhower's first year in office.

Secretary of State Dulles had no hesitation about which course to take. He counseled Eisenhower to adopt "a policy of boldness" in world affairs. The leading hawk in the cabinet, Dulles rejected Truman's strategy of containment as nothing more than a "treadmill policy" that offered no chance to win the cold war. What was needed was a "dynamic" and "active" approach, combining nuclear deterrence—he spoke of hitting the enemy with "shattering effectiveness," if necessary—with a determined effort to "liberate" the enslaved peoples behind the Iron Curtain. Eisenhower himself echoed these sentiments in his State of the Union address on February 2, 1953. The president declared, "The free world cannot indefinitely remain in a posture of paralyzed tension, leaving forever to the aggressor the choice of time and place and means to cause greatest hurt to us at least cost to himself." It was time for a "new, positive foreign policy." Following Dulles's lead, Eisenhower denounced Franklin Roosevelt's wartime deal with Stalin at Yalta, which, according to the Old Guard, legitimated the Soviets' "enslavement" of Eastern Europe. The president also signaled that he would no longer restrain the Nationalist Chinese in Taiwan, and their leader, Chiang Kai-shek, from waging war against mainland communist China. The "unleashing" of the Nationalists upon the communists had long been an ardent fantasy of the GOP hard-liners.[17]

But on March 5, 1953, Josef Stalin died, and the landscape of the cold war briefly shone in a new light. Eisenhower, sensing an opportunity, asked his advisers: Did Stalin's death open up the chance for a thaw in the U.S.-Soviet conflict? Secretary Dulles and the CIA answered no: the Soviets, they argued, would remain just as hostile and aggressive under Stalin's successors as they had been since the birth of the Soviet Union more than three decades earlier. If anything, Moscow might be even more inclined to take risks now, as a show of strength during the transition to new leadership in the Kremlin.[18]

Eisenhower bridled at this unimaginative attitude. Perhaps naïvely, he hoped Stalin's death might create an opportunity for a new departure in world affairs. And the new Soviet leaders were making surprising gestures. Just 10 days after Stalin's death, Georgy Malenkov, who had stepped out from behind the Kremlin's cloak of secrecy as the leading figure of the new regime, expressed the hope of a settlement of East-West differences in terms unimaginable in Stalin's day. "At the present time," Malenkov averred on March 15, "there is no disputed or unresolved question that cannot be settled peacefully by mutual agreement of the interested countries. This applies to our relations with all states, including the United States of America."[19]

Such overtures merited consideration, Eisenhower thought. The world wanted peace. Perhaps this was the moment to seize it? "We do need something dramatic to rally the peoples of the world around some idea, some hope, of a better future," he told the National Security Council. As he put it to speechwriter Emmet Hughes, "We are in an armaments race. Where will it lead us? At worst, to atomic warfare. At best, to robbing every people and nation on earth of the fruits of their own toil." He asked his advisers to sketch a bold proposal that contained "no double talk, no sophisticated political formulas, no slick propaganda devices. Let us spell it out, whatever we really offer." He told his cabinet, "If we must live in a permanent state of mobilization, our whole democratic way of life would be destroyed in the process."[20]

Despite Dulles's reservations, C. D. Jackson, the senior adviser for cold war strategy and psychological warfare, hammered out a plan of action for the president. Eisenhower, he argued, should announce an immediate offer to the Soviets to unify Germany, end the war in Korea, and place firm limits on armaments production. Jackson felt this plan would seize the moral high ground, put the Soviets on the defensive, bolster allied unity, and quite possibly lead to an uprising inside the communist world or even a negotiated settlement to end the cold war. The death of Stalin offered "the greatest chance we have had in decades . . . to move history in the right direction without war." If the president wanted a dynamic foreign policy, Jackson was ready with one. Eisenhower liked the idea of making some kind of opening gambit toward the Soviets, and over the next four weeks, he and Hughes prepared a quite extraordinary text that Ike delivered on April 16 at the annual meeting of the American Society of Newspaper Editors at the Statler Hotel in Washington.[21]

The speech came to be known as "The Chance for Peace." In it the president stressed the terrible waste of the superpower arms race and painted a picture of a world that could be turned toward more productive pursuits:

The cost of one modern heavy bomber is this: a modern brick school in more than 30 cities. It is two electric power plants, each serving a town of 60,000 population. It is two fine, fully equipped hospitals. It is some 50 miles of concrete highway. We pay for a single fighter plane with a half million bushels of wheat. We pay for a single destroyer with new homes that could have housed more than 8,000 people. This, I repeat, is the best way of life to be found on the road the world has been taking. This is not a way of life at all, in any true sense. Under the cloud of threatening war, it is humanity hanging from a cross of iron.

If the superpowers could agree on arms reductions and limitations, "this Government is ready to ask its people to join with all nations in devoting a substantial percentage of the savings achieved by disarmament to a fund for world aid and reconstruction. The purposes of this great work would be to help other peoples to develop the undeveloped areas of the world, to stimulate profitable and fair world trade, to assist all peoples to know the blessings of productive freedom." All that was needed, apparently, was goodwill and sincerity. "We are ready, in short, to dedicate our strength to serving the needs, rather than the fears, of the world."[22]

Among the finest words Eisenhower would utter in his time in the White House, his speech was acclaimed as a heartfelt appeal for peace and arms reductions. The text was circulated in printed brochures around the world; the Voice of America rebroadcast it in 45 languages. The world press commented on it. His chief of staff Sherman Adams called it "the most effective speech of Eisenhower's public career." Yet it did not alter the course of the cold war or even temper the arms race. It proved an empty gesture.[23]

Why so little impact? "The Chance for Peace" failed to ease the cold war because Stalin's death did nothing to alter the fundamental ideological and geopolitical rivalry between the United States and the Soviet Union. Each superpower still saw the other as a looming threat to its security, its belief system, and its vision of the future. The ideological trenches were dug too deep, and the risks of appearing weak or engaging in appeasement were too great, for either side to commit to a genuine thawing of relations. The Soviet Union was now in the hands of a nervous team of men who had risen in the Soviet system by slavishly attending to Stalin's every caprice. For a brief moment, Malenkov, Nikita Khrushchev, Lavrenti Beria, and Nikolai Bulganin had hoped that a thaw with the West would buy them time to transition to a post-Stalin period of rule. But they dared not loosen the reins over the communist bloc for fear of letting it slip away. In June 1953 East German workers rose up in open defiance of the communist government in East Berlin, and the Soviets were obliged to send in tanks and soldiers to restore control. The post-Stalin thaw evaporated after just three months.[24]

Meanwhile Eisenhower, despite his inspiring rhetoric about the terrible waste of the global arms race, seemed unwilling to move from words to deeds. He approved a surprisingly belligerent speech that his secretary of state delivered a mere 48 hours after "The Chance for Peace" hit the airwaves. Aiming to reassure both the right wing of the GOP and allies abroad that the United States was not seeking peace from a position of weakness, Dulles publicly itemized the many ways in which the new administration had aggressively beefed up the U.S. military presence around the world. Dulles boasted that the United States was arming Western Europe, intensifying its operations in Korea, "speeding delivery of military assistance" to the Nationalist Chinese, pouring arms into French Indochina, and strengthening ties to governments in the Middle East and Latin America. The United States would not accept any settlement of the cold war that perpetuates "the captivity of hundreds of millions of persons" behind the Iron Curtain. If the Soviets wanted to ask for peace, the administration would listen to their proposals, but "we do not play the role of suppliants." Two days after "The Chance for Peace" speech, Dulles put the world on notice: America was still waging the cold war and would seek nothing less than victory.[25]

Eisenhower's actions following Stalin's death set something of a pattern for his presidency. He was emotionally and personally attached to the idea of peace. He spoke eloquently about the horrors of war and his desire to turn the productive capacities of humanity away from swords and toward plowshares. But Eisenhower was not an impulsive man. As a general he had developed a reputation as a master planner, a man who husbanded power, amassed resources, and always fought from a position of overwhelming strength. As president he followed the same strategic principles, choosing to wage a long, patient struggle with the USSR in which American power would eventually win out, rather than make any sudden or risky move that could leave the nation vulnerable. There would be many sincere words of peace during his presidency, but Ike was always preparing for war.

IV

To win the cold war, Eisenhower believed, the United States must remain economically dynamic, robust, and expansive. Spending huge sums on armaments and national defense might be unavoidable, but it had to be done carefully. Since 1940 the United States had swung between extremes, from a total lack of preparedness to breakneck and improvised rearmament programs. In a long confrontation with the Soviets, the watchword must be balance: the nation must build a permanent strategic defense capability while also avoiding inflation, spending prudently, and encouraging private innovation and economic growth. Rather than turn the country into a garrison state built upon a command economy, Eisenhower proposed to wage the cold war along free-market principles moderated by wise fiscal management.

His first budget reflected these convictions. Truman's last budget had proposed total spending of $78.6 billion against revenue of $68.7 billion, thus leaving a deficit of $9.9 billion—a shocking gap, as far as Eisenhower was concerned. Ike called for belt-tightening, though since 70 percent of Truman's 1953 budget went toward defense spending and the costs of the Korean War, the cuts would have to come from the military. Treasury Secretary Humphrey strongly supported this approach. He told the National Security Council, "The money and resources required by the great security programs which had been developed since Korea to the present time simply could not be borne by the United States unless we adopted essentially totalitarian methods." By that he meant that continued massive overspending on behalf of the military would make the United States no different from its nemesis, the Soviet Union. Humphrey told the president that "we were at a fork in the road and a decision would have to made." The country needed "to make basic changes in national security policies and programs."[26]

Designed by Joseph Dodge, a Detroit banker of vast international experience, Eisenhower's 1954 budget made real cuts to Truman's spending plans. Truman had wanted to spend $78.6 billion; Ike trimmed that figure to $72.1 billion, a reduction of 8 percent. Instead of a budget deficit of $9.9 billion, Eisenhower expected a budget deficit for 1954 of $3.8 billion—still large but far less than Truman had proposed. Where Truman's defense budget for 1954 was $45.4 billion, Eisenhower's was $41.6 billion. An additional $1.4 billion was cut out of the Mutual Security Program, that is, military and economic aid to nations in Western Europe, Asia, the Middle East, and Latin America.

These cuts had been hard to achieve. Secretary of Defense Wilson had to wage a long battle with the service chiefs, as the budget savings were attained mainly by cutting noncombat personnel by 250,000. This decision had a knock-on effect because a smaller military workforce meant slower training, production, and procurement of weapons systems, especially aircraft. Advocates of air power in Congress, including prominent Democrats like Representative George H. Mahon of Texas and Senator Stuart Symington of Missouri (Truman's former secretary of the air force) laid into the administration for slowing the expansion of airpower, leaving America, they said, with merely the "world's second best Air Force." (This would be a constant refrain from hawkish Democrats right up to the 1960 presidential election, when John F. Kennedy criticized the Eisenhower administration for its weakness on national security.) But Eisenhower persevered.[27]

Not only did Democrats and the armed services object to the new budget. So too did the right wing of the GOP. To balance the budget, Eisenhower appealed to Congress to extend Truman's Korean War taxation measures—chiefly the excess profits tax on big business—and he asked for a delay in the reduction of personal income taxes that Congress had approved. This left conservative Republicans deeply distressed. On April 30 Senator Taft, now majority leader of the newly Republican Senate, went to the White House to complain. After looking over the numbers, he exploded. Eisenhower wrote in his diary that Taft "broke out in violent objection" to the modest cuts to Truman's budget and derided the reductions as "puny." Having failed to deliver tax cuts, the GOP would take a beating at the polls in 1954, Taft predicted, and he announced that he would fight against the proposed budget.

Eisenhower was stunned, then deeply offended and angered at what he considered a "demagogic" tirade. But Taft's outburst was a harbinger: despite months of work to trim the budget, Eisenhower would get no easy pass from the GOP Old Guard. The archconservative Republicans mistrusted Eisenhower and were ready to pounce on any sign that he would simply carry on Truman's policies.[28]

Taft was right about one thing: Eisenhower had no intention of drastically reducing defense spending. The numbers show that Eisenhower instituted a new era of steady, generous defense appropriations. In 1940 the United States had spent a mere $1.6 billion on national defense. In 1945, after four years of global war, the figure had soared to a staggering $83 billion. These huge expenditures were drastically cut back after the war; by 1950 defense spending had shrunk to a mere $13.7 billion, leaving the military hollowed out. Ike, as army chief of staff, had tried to sound the alarm, to no avail. With the outbreak of war in Korea in 1950, Truman turned on the spigots once again, and defense spending shot up to $53 billion by 1953. Eisenhower abjured these drastic swings in spending; they suggested an unwillingness to think ahead and stay prepared for future conflict. In his time in office defense outlays remained remarkably steady and substantial, averaging $46.5 billion a year. This was a huge sum, representing roughly 50 percent of annual federal budget outlays during his administration. Put another way, the United States consistently spent 10 percent or more of its GDP each year on defense during the Eisenhower years, a higher percentage than any peacetime administration in U.S. history, before or since.[29]

Eisenhower allocated fewer dollars to defense than Truman did at the height of the Korean War. But Ike presided over nearly eight years of peace, and his annual defense budgets were still more than three times what Truman's administration had spent in 1950, before Korea. They were living in an age of peril, the president had said. "Security based on heavy armaments is a way of life that has been forced upon us and on our allies," he explained to the American public on April 30. "We don't like it; in fact we hate it. But so long as such an unmistakable, self-confirmed threat to our freedom exists, we will carry these burdens with dedication and determination."[30]

There was a Spartan tone to Ike's approach to national defense—fitting for a lifelong soldier. He viewed democratic government as a collective enterprise in which great benefits came to a free people only through common effort and shared sacrifice. As long as the nation faced grave threats, taxes would stay high and citizens must remain on alert. "We expect to live as a free state," he told the country in a public radio address, "which means we must develop a [defense] program that can . . . carry the security burden for a long, long time if that is necessary, and we will do it without complaining because we prize our freedoms that highly." This was a maxim to live by in an age of peril.[31]

V

Having imposed a degree of restraint and order on the federal budget, Eisenhower now turned to the bleeding wound of the Korean War. To Eisenhower as well as many Americans, the war seemed a tragic waste. It was costly, it placed a terrible drag on the domestic economy, it sapped public morale, and it did not enhance America's global position. Eisenhower had no specific plan to end the war, but he knew it must end, somehow.

He had inherited a difficult tangle in Korea. By the start of 1953, the battle lines had stabilized along a front that was fairly close to the 38th parallel, the prewar border between North and South Korea. Since June 1951 the combatants had been in fitful discussions about signing an armistice, though these talks had been interrupted regularly by fierce outbursts of fighting, with the result that the war was an open sore, hurting both sides but achieving little strategic purpose. After painstaking negotiations over many months, the Truman administration had managed to settle with the Chinese and North Koreans almost all the outstanding issues—except for the question of repatriating thousands of Chinese and North Korean prisoners of war in American hands who expressed an earnest desire not to be sent home. The communist nations consistently refused to accept the American position that captured soldiers should be allowed to choose their subsequent fate, and demanded that they all be returned. The United States, by contrast, viewed forcible prisoner repatriation as morally wrong: it would not agree to surrender, against their will, North Korean and Chinese prisoners who were begging to be spared the return trip. A top-secret staff study declared that a forcible return of prisoners would "constitute appeasement of the most serious sort" and "the grossest betrayal of trust."

The domestic politics of any such deal were also toxic: President Roosevelt at the close of the Second World War had in fact agreed to the forcible repatriation of Soviet POWs, whose destiny thereafter was to languish in the Gulag. This was part of the hated legacy of the Yalta agreements. A Republican administration could never agree to follow such a precedent.

Thus the negotiations stalled, while both sides lashed out at one another on the battlefield with periodic attacks designed chiefly to enhance their bargaining position at the peace table. It was grotesque: American soldiers were dying on behalf of a war that no one was trying to win. Eisenhower considered this situation "intolerable," and he wanted to bring the whole unfortunate mess to an "honorable end."[32]

But how? For many years biographers have asserted that Eisenhower's plan for achieving an armistice in Korea was breathtakingly simple: he threatened to expand the war into China and to use nuclear weapons in the process. Ike's so-called "bluff" scared the Chinese and brought them to accept a reasonable deal at the peace table. This example of Eisenhower's bold leadership was promoted initially by none other than John Foster Dulles, when in 1956 he told a *Life* magazine reporter, James Shepley, that Eisenhower had settled on his plan to use the nuclear threat to achieve a peace deal as early as the conversations aboard the *Helena* in December 1952. When the Chinese and North Koreans refused to accept reasonable terms for an armistice, Shepley reported, Dulles passed along Eisenhower's ultimatum to the Chinese through the intermediary of India's leader Jawaharlal Nehru, whose country was acting as a go-between. The results were immediate: "Within two weeks of his trip to New Delhi, Dulles received word from Korea that the Reds appeared to have begun to negotiate seriously." The communists accepted what was a "propaganda defeat" for a simple reason: "because they had had an unmistakable warning that further delays would no longer be met with U.S. indecisiveness." Many admiring historians and biographers, eager to highlight Eisenhower's decisive leadership style, have adhered to this explanation.[33]

However, the facts do not bear out the "atomic bluff" theory. When Eisenhower came into office, he, like Truman, had no secret plan or magic bullet with which to end the war. Threats of nuclear attack offered no quick fix; Truman had already tried that, to no avail. Eisenhower, assessing the long-running efforts of the Truman team to arrange an armistice, had come to the conclusion that negotiations would not work either; the communists could not be trusted to keep a deal. Therefore Eisenhower's first inclination was not to seek a negotiated end to the war but to *widen* the war in search of a major victory on the battlefield. There was no bluff about his seriousness on that score.

To that end, in early February he broached the idea with his advisers of using "tactical atomic weapons" on the Chinese in North Korea. Although the chairman of the Joint Chiefs of Staff, his former classmate Omar Bradley, discouraged this, Eisenhower laid down a marker: "We could not go on the way we were indefinitely." On March 21 he reiterated the possibility of building up United Nations conventional forces "in order to deliver a massive blow and reach the waist of Korea," that is, push even farther north, to about the 39th parallel, and then impose a settlement upon a defeated enemy. He knew such a military objective would likely require an attack directly on the territory of China. Ten days later Eisenhower seemed to be settling on a plan that would significantly expand the war in Korea. The minutes of his statement at the NSC meeting record his chilling reasoning:

> If, he said, we decide to go up to the strength which will be necessary to achieve a sound tactical victory in Korea—for example, to get to the waist—the Russians will very quickly realize what we are doing. They would respond by increasing the Communist strength in Korea, and, as a result, we would be forced into a situation very close to general mobilization in order to get such a victory in Korea. . . . The President then raised the question of the use of atomic weapons in the Korean war. Admittedly, he said, there were not many good tactical targets, but he felt it would be worth the cost if, through use of atomic weapons, we could 1) achieve a substantial victory over Communist forces and 2) get to a line at the waist of Korea.

Eisenhower knew that America's allies would be very reluctant to follow such a course, but "somehow or other the tabu which surrounds the use of atomic weapons would have to be destroyed." There was no bluff in these words; Eisenhower was deadly serious. If compelled to wage a prolonged war in Korea, he would do so with one end in sight: victory.[34]

But Ike got lucky. He never had to make the terrible decision to launch nuclear weapons in Korea. It is a paradox that while American officials were contemplating a significant increase in the intensity of the war, the Chinese and Soviets were moving in the opposite direction. The Chinese foreign minister Zhou Enlai, in Moscow for Stalin's funeral in mid-March, held discussions with the new Soviet leaders about the Korean War. The Soviets, still seeking to ease global tensions, decided that it was "urgently necessary" to end the war and instructed the Chinese to give in on the POW issue. As it happens, the North Koreans too were ready to end the war. The intensive American bombing had devastated virtually the whole of the North, so much so that Pyongyang had been obliterated. Kim Il-sung, the North Korean dictator, seemed positively relieved at the Soviet decision. On March 31 the Soviet Council of Ministers made it official, stating that China, North Korea, and the USSR were all agreed on seeking an end to the war.[35]

Yet these hopeful signs were as yet unseen in Washington and so did not immediately influence American planning. On April 2 the NSC Planning Board submitted to the president its staff report, titled "Possible Courses of Action in Korea." The document's authors assumed that the stalemate at the negotiating table would not be broken and that the war would continue. In such a case there seemed two broad policy choices: to continue the war while avoiding any attacks directly on China and thus ensuring the war did not widen or drag in the USSR, or to intensify the war by combining a large-scale offensive in Korea with air and naval attacks against targets in China, including the use of atomic weapons. Instead of offering a path to peace, the NSC envisioned more war on the horizon.[36]

Fortunately Eisenhower did not have to choose between these two poisoned cups. Following their discussions with the Soviets, the Chinese began to make surprising new concessions at the armistice talks in Panmunjom. On April 11 Gen. Mark Clark, the commander of UN forces in Korea, informed Washington, "The sense here is that the Communists probably want an armistice," which they demonstrated by agreeing to an exchange of sick and wounded prisoners in mid-April. Between April 19 and May 3, 700 United Nations POWs came back across the battle lines in exchange for 7,000 communist POWs.

The communists seemed ready to compromise, a fact not lost on South Korean president Syngman Rhee. He was staunchly opposed to the division of Korea and alarmed at this sudden change of heart by the Chinese. He wrote an anguished letter to Eisenhower denouncing any kind of armistice that would leave Korea divided. Eisenhower coolly replied that "it would not be defensible to refuse to stop the fighting on an honorable basis." And in early May hopes were raised again by a major communist concession at the negotiating table: they agreed to the creation of a commission of neutral nations to take custody of the soldiers who refused repatriation and to screen them independently. A long debate ensued about which countries would provide this service—Poland, Czechoslovakia, Switzerland, Sweden, and India were eventually enlisted—but by the beginning of May 1953 an armistice was in reach. And no nuclear threats had been made to the Chinese or Soviets.[37]

Even as these encouraging steps were being made, American military planners, and the president himself, were preparing for the possibility that a peace deal might fall through. Over the previous three years the communist side had often used prolonged armistice negotiations as a screen for reinforcing their military positions. Eisenhower was determined not to be caught unprepared. During May and June, as peace talks were inching their way to a conclusion, he held numerous discussions with the Joint Chiefs of Staff about developing a contingency plan for widening the war and hitting the enemy savagely if the talks failed. In these conversations Eisenhower rather breezily discussed the use of atomic weapons against the enemy in the event that the war should continue. "He had reached the point," he told General Bradley, "of being convinced that we have got to consider the atomic bomb as simply another weapon in our arsenal."

The Joint Chiefs, aware of the president's predilections, incorporated the use of atomic weapons into their contingency planning. They concluded that the only way to impose a solution on the battlefield was to increase bombing of North Korea so as to "destroy effective Communist military power in Korea." This would also require extensive bombing of targets in China. Yet it is important to note that these plans were to be used only in case the armistice talks collapsed and the war continued to 1954.[38]

To make America's position clear, Secretary Dulles, in India in late May, dropped hints to Nehru—hints he hoped would be passed along to the Chinese—that the Americans were quite prepared to continue the war and to significantly widen it if the talks failed. However, Dulles said nothing to Nehru about using nuclear weapons, only that "if the armistice negotiations collapsed, the United States would probably make a stronger rather than a lesser military exertion, and that this might well extend the area of conflict." But the United States had been saying much the same thing publicly for many months, and this vague comment can hardly be considered a nuclear ultimatum. In any case, Nehru never reported this conversation to the Chinese. And by now threats were unnecessary: the communists had decided two months earlier to seek a deal to end the fighting and had already made substantial concessions to secure an armistice. Nuclear saber-rattling had been irrelevant to the whole affair.[39]

If there were any American ultimatums delivered in this delicate stage of the armistice talks, they were directed not at the communist enemy but at America's purported ally, Syngman Rhee. The South Korean leader did not want the war to end and the Americans to leave without having won a decisive victory and the unification—under his rule—of the Korean peninsula. He opposed the armistice tooth and nail. In an attempt to sabotage the carefully structured agreements on prisoner-of-war exchanges that the combatant states had worked out over many months, Rhee ordered his military to release 25,000 North Korean prisoners, all of whom had declared their opposition to being repatriated.

Eisenhower was stunned by this deceitful act. In the privacy of a National Security Council meeting, he fumed that if Rhee continued in this way, "it was 'goodbye' to Korea": American forces would simply withdraw, leaving South Korea to its fate. Eisenhower sent Rhee a scorching letter to this effect. But Secretary Dulles had a hunch—a correct one, as it turned out—that "the Communists really want an armistice so badly that they will be willing to overlook the release" of the prisoners. The real problem was Rhee: Would he accept an armistice and not start the war again on his own authority? On July 2 Eisenhower directed his military staff to make a show of planning for the exit of U.S. forces from Korea. Just days later Rhee agreed to accept the armistice in exchange for a mutual security pact with the United States and substantial financial aid to assist in reconstruction.[40]

Having reeled in his reluctant and high-strung ally with a combination of threats and incentives, Eisenhower now had a settlement in reach. On July 27, 1953, the armistice was signed and a much-hated war came to an end. "Three years of heroism, frustration and bloodshed were over," he reflected. Forty-five thousand Americans had been killed or went missing in Korea; over 200,000 North Koreans and as many as 400,000 Chinese died in the war. And yet Korea remained divided, its new frontier scarcely different from where it had been three years earlier.

What had Eisenhower learned from the Korean experience? Above all, he concluded, no more Koreas. Yet he also came to believe—erroneously— that America's warlike disposition and atomic threats had been essential in bringing the Chinese to the armistice table. These twin conclusions—avoid quagmires and carry a big nuclear stick—would shape Eisenhower's strategic thinking for the duration of his administration.

VI

These strategic principles now found their way into official policy. During the summer and early fall of 1953, Eisenhower directed his national security team to prepare a top-secret document that articulated America's grand strategy for the global cold war. Before drafting this new statement of policy Robert Cutler put together an elaborate staff study exercise, called Operation Solarium, named after the White House parlor in which Ike and Dulles had first hatched the project. Cutler assembled three teams of leading policy and military officials under elaborate security precautions at the National War College, on the grounds of Fort McNair in southwest Washington, D.C. For six grueling weeks each team evaluated one of three policy hypotheses: that America should continue with a more robust version of Truman's policy of containment; that America should "draw a line" on the world map to demarcate its sphere of influence and go to all-out general war if the Soviets crossed that line; or that America should not wait any longer but go on the offensive now and attempt to roll back the Soviet bloc.[41]

The voluminous planning documents reveal how seriously each team took its mission. But the exercise remained at best an intellectual one, for the president had already settled in his mind the broad contours of America's cold war strategy. This was made perfectly clear on July 16, when the three teams presented their conclusions to Eisenhower in an all-day meeting in the White House Conference Room. After listening to the reports, Eisenhower thanked the teams for their hard work but reflected that "the only thing worse than losing a global war was winning one." The American people had no desire to wage a war of annihilation against the USSR and then find itself responsible for yet another long-term project of rehabilitation of a defeated enemy. The best policy for the nation must be one of strategic patience, resilience, and vigilance. Great Power war in the nuclear age was simply unthinkable. As one shrewd participant noted, Ike flatly contradicted the rhetorical fulminations of Dulles: "Roll-back sank, it was finished off as of that day."[42]

Eisenhower now directed his national security team to draft the strategic concept paper that would define the basic principles of American policy for a long cold war with the Soviet Union. What emerged in October 1953 was the document "Basic National Security Policy," referred to by its numerical designation, NSC 162/2. In a briskly written 27 pages, the NSC staff described a strategy for "meeting the Soviet threat" while avoiding any "serious weakening of the U.S. economy or undermining our fundamental values and institutions." It was one of the most important statements of American security policy ever written, for within it lay the plans for the creation of the military-industrial complex.[43]

NSC 162/2 lucidly defined the main global threat faced by the country:

"Soviet hostility" toward the United States combined with a rapidly growing Soviet military and a communist Chinese regime that had established itself in Asia. The communist bloc was large, populous, and ideologically menacing. Even if the likelihood of a Soviet attack on the United States remained small, NSC 162/2 asserted that the Soviets could sustain a long ideological struggle, hoping to spread their doctrine in the Third World among newly independent nations and stirring up instability and revolution around the world.

To defend against such a devious global enemy, the United States would above all have to develop and expand its arsenal of nuclear weapons, for here was the key deterrent to keep the Soviets in check. As long as the United States maintained "a strong military posture, with emphasis on the capability of inflicting massive retaliatory damage by offensive striking power," the Soviets would not risk general war. Eisenhower accepted that nuclear weapons were now a part of the landscape of world affairs, and he would use them if necessary. "In the event of hostilities," NSC 162/2 stated, "the United States will consider nuclear weapons to be as available for use as other munitions."

But nuclear weapons were only one part of the grand strategy. Eisenhower's planners called for full mobilization of American society to ward off the communist threat. NSC 162/2 demanded not merely more and bigger nuclear weapons, along with the aircraft to deliver those bombs; it also called for a robust intelligence network to analyze Soviet behavior, coupled with elaborate security measures to combat domestic spying. It outlined a nationwide manpower program, emphasizing scientific and technical training to serve military needs. It insisted upon military readiness through stockpiling and securing of vital raw materials and key industrial plants. The concept paper envisioned huge continental defense systems, with early-warning radar and a large air force that could meet Soviet intruders. It called for the overhaul of military service requirements for American citizens, with longer tours of duty for draftees, inclusion of women into the armed services, and the enlistment of civilians for maintenance work. And the strategy insisted on a better public effort to explain to the American people why such a militaristic mobilization of their society was needed.

Eisenhower's policy, then, cannot be called restrained or passive. To be sure, it envisioned patience rather than provocation and war. But to wage a prolonged geopolitical and ideological struggle with the communist bloc required a transformation in American capabilities and mentalities. In these first months of his presidency, Eisenhower laid down a blueprint for the warfare state—an official plan to mobilize the nation and put it on a permanent war footing. The military-industrial complex had begun to take shape.

VII

As commander in chief, Eisenhower could impose his new strategy on his subordinates. But selling it to America's allies proved more difficult. In early December 1953 he traveled to Bermuda for a conference with his wartime comrade Winston Churchill, once again serving as the British prime minister. (The two men were joined by their French counterpart, Prime Minister Joseph Laniel, who developed a high fever as soon as he arrived and was thus sidelined for the duration of the conference.) Churchill had just turned 79. The previous June he had suffered a stroke that left him weakened and diminished. His hearing too was failing, and his family and inner circle of advisers thought it was time for him to cede power to his longtime protégé and foreign minister, Anthony Eden. Churchill refused. With a supreme effort he worked to recover his mobility after the stroke, and by December he had gained enough strength to travel to Bermuda for a week of discussions with the American president. The leaders used the Mid Ocean Club as their gathering place, a large white-stucco Colonial-style hotel that looked out across gently rolling golf links to pink beaches and a shimmering blue sea.

Churchill had gone to Bermuda with one goal in mind: to arrange a four-power summit of America, Britain, France, and the USSR to discuss all the major issues in the cold war, especially the possible unification of Germany. The death of Stalin seemed to him to open the prospect of ending the cold war, if only the world leaders could grasp the moment. Churchill yearned to play the role of honest broker, bringing together the hawkish Americans and the suspicious Soviets and sealing a grand bargain that might significantly improve world relations. Such a deal might place the capstone on his storied career, whose days were clearly numbered.[44]

Yet in Bermuda, Churchill found an Eisenhower who was in no mood for compromise. The smiling Ike of the war years, the genial consensus-builder, was gone. In his place was a man of firm opinions and deep anti-Soviet sentiment. In reply to Churchill's appeal at the conference's opening session for a real effort to strike a deal with the new leaders of the Soviet Union, Eisenhower delivered a vulgar tirade in front of all the diplomats and officials of the three national delegations. Churchill's private secretary, John

Colville, recorded the scene: "[Eisenhower] said that as regards the prime minister's belief that there was a New Look in Soviet policy, Russia was a woman of the streets and whether her dress was new, or just the old one patched, it was certainly the same whore underneath. America intended to drive her off her present 'beat' into the back streets." Colville noted "pained looks all round."[45]

In a gesture of conciliation designed to accommodate European anxieties, Eisenhower said he would offer a constructive proposal to the Soviets. For some months he had been mulling over the idea of asking the UN to create an international agency to share research on the peaceful uses of atomic energy. If the Soviet Union and the United States created a "pool" of atomic material, dedicated to civilian energy use, the two nations could find common ground in deploying their nuclear knowledge for the betterment of the world. Eisenhower's own advisers were cool on the idea, but they understood its propaganda value. If the Soviets rejected the overture, they would bear the responsibility for turning away a constructive proposal.[46]

At Bermuda, Eisenhower discussed this scheme with the British. "The world was in a rather hysterical condition about the atomic bomb," he said, and he wanted to use an invitation he had received to speak at the UN General Assembly to point to the "constructive capabilities of atomic energy." America "wished to appear before the world as we really were—struggling for peace, not showing belligerence or truculence." Surely, he mused, a proposal to gather the world's scientists into a great collaborative effort to use atomic energy for peaceful purposes "would bring a large number of people to our side."[47]

However, Eisenhower was quick to point out to his British allies, this scheme for sharing atomic energy was not to be confused with a disarmament proposal. No indeed: the United States planned to rely heavily on nuclear weapons to deter communist misbehavior. In an exchange that left his British partners deeply glum, the president declared that "atomic weapons were now coming to be regarded as a proper part of conventional armament." If, for example, the North Koreans and Chinese broke the armistice so recently achieved in Korea, they would be struck with atomic weapons. This had been expounded in NSC 162/2 and was now American policy.

Eisenhower's cool assertion triggered a mournful outpouring from Churchill: any use of atomic weapons by America would lead to Soviet retaliation in Europe and to the "destruction of all we hold dear, ourselves, our families and our treasures; and even if some of us temporarily survive in some deep cellar under mounds of flaming and contaminated rubble, there will be nothing to do but take a pill to end it all." Colville noted in his diary that Eisenhower's announcement of his intention to use nuclear weapons in the case of war, even a peripheral war like Korea, was news "which far outstrips in importance anything else at the conference."[48]

Eisenhower expressed some annoynace at the British in his diary that night: "We have come to the conclusion that the atom bomb has to be treated just as another weapon in the arsenal"; the British, by contrast, still see atomic weapons as marking "a completely new era in war" and "cling to the hope (to us fatuous) that if we avoid the first use of the atom bomb in any war, that the Soviets might likewise abstain." Secretary Dulles, in his own account of these exchanges, noted that American "thinking on the subject was several years ahead" of Britain's and that the British leaders worried that "there was a danger of our taking action which would be morally repellant to the rest of the world." It was a striking moment: America's closest ally viewed the evolution of America's nuclear strategy with growing alarm.[49]

With the anxieties of the British fresh in his mind, Eisenhower went forward with his proposal for U.S.-Soviet collaboration in the field of nuclear energy research. He and his White House staff flew from Bermuda directly to New York, where at the United Nations on December 8 Eisenhower delivered his surprising offer. The speech carried both a warning and a promise. In the first passages of his address, Eisenhower walked through a catalogue of horrifying statistics about the consequences of nuclear war. But he soon pivoted toward hope instead of fear. In a stirring passage he said that the atom bomb should be taken "out of the hands of soldiers" and given to those "who will know how to strip its military casing and adapt it to the arts of peace." He wanted "to hasten the day when fear of the atom will begin to disappear from the minds of people." It was time to declare that the Great Powers were "interested in human aspirations first, rather than in building up the armaments of war." In creating the International Atomic Energy Agency, and turning over to it some quantity of uranium and fissionable material to be used to supply electricity to the developing world, the Great Powers would show their desire to use science to improve the world rather than to destroy it.[50]

While the press responded with hearty praise for Eisenhower's "dramatic," "eloquent," and "moving" address, the Soviets quite predictably called his bluff, responding that instead of discussing nuclear sharing, the Great Powers should agree to ban all atomic weapons. Since the United States had no interest in halting atomic weapons production, the Soviet counteroffer was swatted away, and the arms race continued unabated. Indeed it might be asked: Was Eisenhower really committed to moderating the cold war or to altering his recently designed cold war strategy? The evidence suggests he was not.[51]

"Atoms for Peace" was sold to the public as an earnest declaration of Eisenhower's desire to turn atomic weapons into plowshares—a desire to end the arms race and instead invest in science and technology for the betterment of mankind. But it was not a disarmament proposal at all; Eisenhower had decided that the United States would commit itself to a major expansion of its nuclear weapons. The Soviet Union, he believed, remained bent on world domination. Only deterrence and a credible threat to use nuclear weapons would halt Soviet expansionism. Eisenhower's UN speech certainly held out the hope that atomic energy might aid the developing world in the long run, but he nowhere suggested that he was ready to stop the rapid expansion of America's nuclear arsenal.[52]

Nothing could make this clearer than the delivery, shortly after the UN speech, of a strikingly bellicose declaration by Dulles to an audience gathered at the Council on Foreign Relations in New York in January 1954. Speaking from a text edited by the president himself, Dulles looked back over the first year of the Eisenhower administration. He spoke of how Truman's national security policies had been improvisational, expensive, reactive to Soviet threats, and unsystematic. The United States, Dulles announced, had inaugurated a new strategy to deter the USSR from any aggressive action. From now on America would "depend primarily upon a great capacity to retaliate instantly by means and at places of our choosing." Eisenhower and Dulles, just one month after the "Atoms for Peace" speech, declared that America was ready and willing to use nuclear weapons to protect its interests anywhere in the world against Soviet provocation.[53]

Eisenhower's cold war strategy soon earned the nickname the "New Look"—a riff on the term used to describe the newest women's fashions then being featured in society magazines. Driven by a desire to cut the costs of defense, the New Look relied heavily upon a powerful nuclear deterrent instead of a large ground army. To be successful, the New Look had to create the impression that America was willing to unleash nuclear war to protect itself and its allies. And Dulles seemed to relish the opportunity to declare this willingness. "The free world," he wrote in *Foreign Affairs* in April 1954, "must make imaginative use" of its powerful weapons, whether air power, naval power, or atomic weapons. "A potential aggressor should know in advance that he can and will be made to suffer for his aggression more than he can possibly gain by it." Whether on a wintry Korean hillside, in a tropical Vietnamese jungle, on an arid Middle Eastern desert, or even in a charming German village, American interests all around the world would be backed by nuclear weapons. The goodwill generated by the "Atoms for Peace" speech evaporated like a warm breath on a cold evening.[54]

As if timed to reinforce this message, on March 1, 1954, less than a year after Eisenhower's soaring "Chance for Peace" message and three months after the "Atoms for Peace" proposal at the UN, the United States set off the largest nuclear explosion in history up to that time. Code-named "Castle Bravo" and detonated on the Bikini Atoll in the Marshall Islands, the H-bomb test was measured at 15 megatons, 1,000 times the power of the Hiroshima bomb. The first year of Eisenhower's presidency had ended just the way it began: under the shadow of an ever-widening mushroom cloud.

CHAPTER 6

CONFRONTING McCARTHY

"I don't believe we can live in fear of each other forever."

I

"I'D LIKE TO MAKE SOME CHANGES RIGHT AWAY," SAID MAMIE Eisenhower, blowing smoke from a freshly lit cigarette as she sat upright in bed. She had just passed her first night in the White House, and she didn't like it. She had been quartered alone in a small dressing room used by Bess Truman and given a narrow single bed. The room had one small dark closet. It would not do. She summoned the White House domestic staff and announced that the Eisenhowers would move into the large sitting room next door and use it as a bedroom. She ordered a king-size bed with a headboard upholstered in pink. Unlike the Trumans and Roosevelts, the Eisenhowers would share a bed. That way, "I can reach over and pat Ike on his old bald head any time I want to!"[1]

After seven years of the unvarnished, unpretentious Bess Truman, the White House now had an imperious, demanding, outgoing, dynamic, and crackling first lady. Mamie Eisenhower, with her curly bangs, her pink ribbons and ruffles, her devotion to high fashion and her lively personality, became central to the Eisenhower style that defined Washington in the 1950s. Ever since John F. Kennedy took office in 1961, all first ladies have been measured against the incomparably glamorous and graceful Jacqueline Kennedy. Yet it was Mamie Eisenhower who inaugurated a new image for the presidential spouse. She was highly visible, trend-setting, and fashion-conscious. Her personality was lively, witty, genial, brisk, at times common and jokey, with a certain folksy affectation. According to the long-serving chief usher of the White House, who worked with her every day, she was "feminine to the point of frivolity," an "affectionate and sentimental" person who "adored the pomp and circumstance and grandeur that went along with the nation's top job." Yet she ran the house with intense devotion to detail and a hawk-like watchfulness for overspending, waste, or inefficiency. Every morning she combed the newspapers, looking for bargains. She approved every menu served at the White House, met daily with the White House chef, and insisted that food never be wasted. She had grown up in a well-off Denver family, but her life had been shaped by the same scrimping and saving that every officer's wife endured in the interwar army. For all her love of luxury, she took pride in sticking to a tight budget.[2]

Mamie's style matched Ike's. Together they were exemplars of a new American sense of self that marked the decades of the 1950s: outgoing and convivial, they combined an air of success and achievement with a good degree of contented ordinariness. In later years, especially during the Kennedy era, the Eisenhower style would come to be seen as middle-brow, plain, even vulgar and undignified for the White House. Yet America in the 1950s compared Mamie with the homespun, self-effacing Bess Truman and the earnest, admirable and slightly tragic Eleanor Roosevelt. In truth there had been no genuine glamour in the White House since Woodrow Wilson had married the lovely and aristocratic Edith Galt in 1915. Ike and Mamie brought an altogether new and refreshing change.

The American public seemed to relate to the confident, pragmatic, and accessible Eisenhower style. An admiring account in *U.S. News and World Report* welcomed the new attitude. "Harry Truman surrounded himself with cronies," the magazine lamented. "Eisenhower picks men for what they can do. Franklin D. Roosevelt dealt in political theories. Eisenhower distrusts theories. Herbert Hoover held himself aloof from people. Eisenhower is warmly human. Calvin Coolidge was a silent New Englander. Eisenhower talks easily and frankly." Eisenhower's traits seemed to align with a new ideal of American masculinity that was visible across the decade of the 1950s. The practical, extroverted, can-do man of business was in; the reflective intellectual, the man of irony, the calculating politician were out. Richard Nixon had called Adlai Stevenson an "egghead" on the campaign trail, and the epithet stuck: in the Eisenhower White House, businessmen were preferred over professors. As for Mamie, *U.S. News* declared her to be "an adaptable, easy hostess, used to moving about and meeting people. She makes a home for her husband, handles social affairs with aplomb, likes people and gets along with them." No greater compliment could be paid, apparently, than acknowledgment of these domestic virtues.[3]

President Eisenhower was a hardworking man who regularly put in 9- and 10-hour days in the Oval Office. Yet politics was his job, not his life, and he insisted on frequent informal gatherings of friends and family. He kept up his card-playing, his regular rounds of golf at Burning Tree Country Club, his dabbling in paints; he even worked on his putting and chip shots on the White House lawn. When his son John returned from Korea he brought his family to visit often; the footfall of the Eisenhower grandchildren—David, Anne, Susan, and Mary Jean—could often be heard clattering through the family quarters of the presidential mansion. Eisenhower was always happy to get out of Washington; while the family farm in Gettysburg was undergoing renovations until 1955, Ike took delight in the presidential retreat in Maryland's Catoctin Mountains. Franklin Roosevelt had called the place Shangri-La. This Ike vetoed ("too fancy for a Kansas farm boy") and found a name that echoed his days in military encampments: Camp David, named after his grandson. Inevitably the president had a three-hole golf course installed. There was trout fishing in the mountain brooks nearby, a handsome stone barbeque pit to grill steaks for a few friends, and even skeet shooting—just the ticket for an avid outdoorsman. The evenings featured screenings of favorite western films. It was a middle-class paradise on a presidential scale.

Washington society had some trouble adapting to the rather humdrum tastes of the first family. Long lunches and late nights were frowned upon; cabinet officers were expected to turn down most invitations to elegant soirees. Ike did not much like to attend parties, and elite Washington hostesses declared themselves baffled by a president who preferred to stay at home in the evenings to watch television. Ike preferred light entertainment, such as the CBS television variety show put on by Arthur Godfrey and western movies in the family quarters. The new domesticity did not please everyone. Collier's magazine sniffed that Mamie and Ike, "living in what is probably the world's most publicized hunk of architecture," were "playing it strictly suburban. . . . The fact is that the atmosphere of the White House these days is more reminiscent of Dubuque than of Versailles." And that suited Eisenhower just fine.[4]

If the White House was not turned into a stage for sparkling entertainments, Eisenhower did rely heavily upon formal evening dinners with members of the "power elite." He kept up a heavy schedule of men-only dinner parties to entertain political supporters, hear from business leaders, and receive reports on public opinion from men he had reason to trust.

Each dinner followed a script: about 15 guests would arrive at 7:30 and chat casually before being seated at 8:00. A menu of national specialties, from Alaska salmon to Texas pheasant, duck, or steak, would be served. Eventually Eisenhower would steer the discussion to a particular topic that was on his mind and ask for his dinner companions' opinions. The afterdinner conversation would end promptly at 11:00. In his first two years in office, he gave 38 stag dinners and welcomed over 550 men to these functions at the White House. Overwhelmingly the guests were drawn from the corporate and business world, as befitted a pro-business president. Others included administration officials and congressional leaders. Perhaps a tenth came from the press, and smaller numbers from universities, labor organizations, and philanthropic foundations.[5]

In one crucial respect Eisenhower chose to use the White House as a public stage. On February 1, 1953, just 10 days after his inauguration, he was baptized and welcomed into the National Presbyterian Church by the Rev. Edward Elson. He remains the only president to have been baptized while in office. Although the ceremony itself was private, Eisenhower made every effort to place faith at the center of national life during his years in office, and the numbers suggest that Americans followed his lead. The 1950s was a time of extraordinary religious revival: church membership rose from 49 percent in 1940 to 69 percent in 1960. His own heart-felt prayer had prefaced his inaugural speech; his cabinet meetings began with a moment of silent prayer; he initiated the National Prayer Breakfast and welcomed Rev. Billy Graham into the White House as a spiritual adviser. He heartily approved when, in 1954, Congress inserted "under God" into the Pledge of Allegiance and later made "In God We Trust" the official motto of the United States, even placing these words on the paper currency.

Eisenhower's own civic religion was ecumenical and inclusive. He had no interest in doctrinal differences or religious debates. His upbringing in a devout though nonconformist household of Bible readers left him with both an abiding spiritual belief and a mistrust of organized churches. But he knew that as president he must publicly proclaim his faith in God so as to encourage all Americans to do the same. For Eisenhower religious faith was the single most important distinction between the free world and the communist world. The Soviet bloc was a monstrous tyranny that sneered at spirituality. Americans, by contrast, held to the belief that every individual was God's creation. Human rights were therefore divine and not to be trampled underfoot by an all-powerful government. Eisenhower never tired

of repeating his fundamental belief that democracy, which empowered individuals to govern themselves, offered the only form of government that
could fulfill God's purpose on Earth. If the cold war was to be won, spiritual
power would be every bit as important, Eisenhower believed, as material
and military might.[6]

II

Eisenhower's tastes and social outlook, his loyalties, friendships, religious
beliefs, sense of right and wrong—these matter if we are to understand his
handling of the greatest domestic political issue, and perhaps the thorniest
moral issue, of his first two years in office: McCarthyism.

It has long been a subject of debate among historians: How well did
Eisenhower handle the "Red Scare" and its sinister impresario, Senator
Joe McCarthy? Contemporary observers in the press, intellectuals across
the political spectrum, and quite a few of Eisenhower's friends and close
advisers agonized over what they saw as his timid approach to the whole
business. Despite his popularity and his enormous political capital, they
believed, he refused to engage directly with McCarthy or to confront the
paranoia the senator so effectively cultivated. By avoiding McCarthyism,
some writers asserted, Eisenhower allowed it to continue unchecked. By
contrast, later scholars working from the documentary record perceived a
design in Eisenhower's approach to the senator, and indeed have gone so far
as to conclude that Eisenhower had a "strategy" for dealing with the relentless inquisitor. That strategy was what military theorists call the "indirect
approach": Eisenhower avoided a direct attack on McCarthy but cut off his
supply lines by blocking his access to the information and people he needed
to sustain his investigations. The political scientist Fred Greenstein, for example, argues that Eisenhower's handling of McCarthy provides evidence of
a "hidden hand" style of government. In this interpretation, Ike rode above
the fray of politics while secretly pulling levers and using White House influence to stymie McCarthy and his allies.[7]

Like most debates among historians, the pendulum has swung from one
extreme to the other. It would be unfair to say that Eisenhower failed to
confront McCarthy; he did challenge McCarthy, repeatedly, and with the
broader purpose of trying to defuse the explosive Red hunter. Yet it also
overstates the case to claim that Eisenhower had a strategy. Rather Eisenhower in 1953 *improvised* in dealing with McCarthy, at first trying to ignore

him, then trying to outdo him in the Red-hunting business, then trying to seduce him with promises of new legislation to destroy communism in America. None of these tactics worked. Not until the spring of 1954, when an emboldened McCarthy turned his investigatory resources on the U.S. Army and on members of the administration, did Eisenhower choose to fight back.

To understand his reluctance to tangle with McCarthy, consider that by the time Eisenhower came into office, anticommunism had flourished in America for over three decades. Since the Bolshevik Revolution of 1917, the U.S. government had viewed communism as a sinister, secretive, revolutionary ideology hostile to freedom, to religion, and to private property—in short, entirely un-American. In the 1930s politicians hostile to the New Deal tried to stymie Roosevelt's plans for social reform by invoking the specter of communism. Anxieties about subversive activities inside the country led to the passage of the Smith Act in 1940, which compelled resident aliens to register with the government and made it illegal to advocate the overthrow of the U.S. government.

In the immediate postwar years, as the reaction against the New Deal mounted, left-wing labor activities were an easy target of the anticommunist forces, and the 1947 Taft-Hartley Act required all union officials to swear that they were not members of the Communist Party. In March 1947 Truman issued Executive Order 9835, which established the federal Loyalty Review Board with a remit to purge the federal government of any "disloyal" employees. At the same time the House Committee on Un-American Activities held hearings about the alleged communist penetration in Hollywood, the labor movement, government, universities, and elsewhere. It was here that the young Nixon made his name in unmasking the communist spy Alger Hiss. In 1949 the Justice Department indicted 11 leaders of the Communist Party of the United States for violation of the Smith Act; after a year-long trial they were found guilty.

International events, in particular the discovery in September 1949 that the Soviet Union had tested an atomic bomb and the fall of China to communist forces the following month, heightened American anxieties. In January 1950 the country was shocked to learn that a British scientist named Klaus Fuchs, who had worked at Los Alamos during the war, had been a Soviet spy. Fuchs confessed and identified his courier, Harry Gold, who in turn led investigators to discover more atomic spies in the Manhattan Project, notably Julius and Ethel Rosenberg, who were indicted in August 1950.

The outbreak of war in Korea completed the picture of a communist enemy that seemed to be on the march both on the battlefield and deep inside the American home front. And all this predated the arrival on the political scene of Senator Joe McCarthy.[8]

Republican critics of the Truman administration—and there were many—had been employing the communists-in-government issue with great success since Nixon's tangle with Hiss. In February 1950 McCarthy, still a relatively unknown legislator from Wisconsin, announced that he had come into possession of shocking new evidence that 205 members of the Communist Party were still working for the State Department, even though their names had been turned over to top government officials. The charge would have been comical in another time and place: McCarthy had no list of names, and he had no new evidence. But the Democrats who controlled Congress could not be complacent, and they launched hearings into Mc-Carthy's charges, which were soon shown to be fanciful. In response Mc-Carthy simply made up more. Aided by key GOP senators, including Robert Taft, who took unrestrained pleasure in seeing McCarthy take on the Truman administration, as well as a press corps that never tired of covering accusations of subversion, McCarthy was able to keep his circus going for three years.[9]

And he did not act alone. Congress, sensitive to the climate of fear surrounding the communist-in-government issue, passed the Internal Security Act in September 1950. Also called the McCarran Act after its chief sponsor, archconservative Nevada Democrat Pat McCarran, it gave the federal government sweeping powers to investigate allegations of subversion. It compelled communist-front organizations to register with the government, created a Subversive Activities Control Board to track down suspicious persons, and enacted an emergency detention statute that allowed the government to detain suspected spies or saboteurs. President Truman vetoed the bill, declaring, "We would betray our finest traditions if we attempted, as this bill would attempt, to curb the simple expression of opinion." The proposed law "would make a mockery of the Bill of Rights and of our claims to stand for freedom in the world." But Truman stood alone: Congress swiftly and easily overrode his veto, with many Democrats voting in favor.[10]

The electoral appeal of the communist issue became apparent in November 1950, when the GOP picked up five seats in the Senate and cut the Democratic lead to two; in the House the Republicans picked up 28 seats. These results inoculated McCarthy from any charge that his anticommunist antics were harming the GOP: quite the contrary, he was manifestly helping his party and landing body blows on the Truman administration. He carried on his attacks on Truman, Secretary of State Dean Acheson, George Marshall, and others associated with what McCarthy labeled a foreign policy of appeasement of the Soviet Union, cowardice toward Red China, and treason of their own nation. Privately many Republicans worried that McCarthy was debasing the Senate and would soon harm the party, but publicly few leaders wished to gainsay the Wisconsin senator. Eisenhower had tried to avoid commenting on McCarthy while running for office in 1952. He did not like to deal in "personalities," he had said. Besides, McCarthy was a fellow Republican, and a popular one at that. The tactic seemed to work. Not only was McCarthy reelected in November 1952, but the Senate passed into Republican control by a razor-thin majority of two seats.

Eisenhower and Nixon had won the election in part on a pledge to sweep the communists and the crooks from government. Far from seeking to halt McCarthyism, Eisenhower stated his intention to adopt a policy of vigilance and ruthlessness toward domestic subversion. Upon entering the White House he found waiting for him an opportunity to administer a firm hand in such matters.

III

Julius Rosenberg, an electrical engineer and ardent communist since the 1930s, had been identified during the investigation of Klaus Fuchs as a key figure in an atomic spy ring. During the war Rosenberg's brother-in-law, David Greenglass, a U.S. Army engineer, was assigned to work at the most secret American scientific project: the atomic bomb research effort at Los Alamos. Rosenberg, delighted by this turn of events, enticed Greenglass to pass along any information he could find that might be useful to the Soviet Union in its own search for the atomic bomb. Greenglass complied and passed some secrets to Rosenberg and to a courier named Harry Gold. (The value of this information remains disputed.) Questioned by the FBI in June 1950 about these activities, Greenglass swiftly confessed and also named his brother-in-law as part of the spy ring. But Rosenberg, when picked up by the authorities, did not confess. The FBI, hoping to ratchet up the pressure, arrested his wife, Ethel, on flimsy charges of helping him.

Ethel turned out to be a feisty woman and strong communist who refused to turn against her husband under questioning. Accused of typing up some of the notes for Julius that had been secreted out of Los Alamos, she steadfastly disavowed any role in espionage. There now opened one of the most celebrated trials in American history, in which Greenglass became the star witness against his own sister and his brother-in-law, supporting the government's case that the husband-and-wife team had helped the USSR get the atom bomb. Following their trial in March 1951, a jury found the pair guilty, and the judge in the case, Irving Kaufman, promptly issued death sentences for both.

The harsh sentences set off an international outcry. The court in its zeal had gone too far, many believed; at least Ethel, the mother of two children who was only peripherally involved, should be spared. During the two years of appeals that followed, many activists in the United States and especially abroad clamored for leniency in the case, calling on President Truman to commute the sentence. The State Department prepared a summary of the European press showing that while the far left was predictably vehement in its denunciations of the verdict, even the noncommunist press was calling for mercy for the condemned pair. In France, Belgium, Italy, and West Germany, centrist writers and political figures cast doubt upon the guilt of the Rosenbergs and argued that, in any case, the American government should not succumb to the hateful passions of the anticommunist frenzy.[11]

President Eisenhower remained unmoved. He was inclined to follow the previous administration's position: the case had been tried, it had been reviewed, and justice had been done. To overturn the sentences would be to interfere in the workings of American justice, something he found abhorrent. Besides, the case, he told the cabinet, was "clear cut." On February 11, 1953, Eisenhower issued a statement that had actually been drawn up by the Truman White House: there would be no act of executive clemency in the case. The crime of passing atomic secrets to the USSR was heinous, involving "the deliberate betrayal of the entire nation" that could "result in the death of many, many thousands of innocent citizens."[12]

Thousands of letters and telegrams poured into the White House, asking the president to stay the execution. Seven thousand protestors thronged the gates of the White House and held a silent vigil on the National Mall. The eldest Rosenberg child, Michael, sent Eisenhower a poignant handwritten note in childish cursive, asking, "Please let my mommy and daddy go and not let anything happen to them." Sophie Rosenberg, Julius's mother, begged Eisenhower to show mercy to "an old woman whose days are spent in weeping."[13]

Yet Eisenhower never wavered. The reasons are not hard to divine. He believed above all that the accused were surely guilty of espionage (and Julius's guilt was later confirmed by declassified materials). The case had been tied up in the courts for two years, and every appeal had been heard. The Rosenbergs had had their day in court. But there was also a powerful institutional momentum that carried Eisenhower along. His administration was composed of hawks who were determined to show no mercy toward subversion, lest they be tarnished with the "pink" brush that had been used on the Truman administration. Attorney General Herbert Brownell later confirmed Ike's view that clemency for the Rosenbergs "would have been interpreted as a tremendous victory of Communist propaganda." Eisenhower's adviser C. D. Jackson put it in the most vulgar way possible: the Rosenbergs "deserve to fry a hundred times for what they have done to this country."[14]

In two letters, one to a former Columbia colleague and the other to his son, Eisenhower developed his position on the case. He believed that if the Rosenbergs were spared, "Communist leaders" would surely conclude that Americans were "weak and fearful and that consequently subversive and other kind[s] of activity can be conducted against them with no real fear of dire punishment." In a striking passage in the letter to John, he wrote that the Rosenbergs had to be executed as an example to other would-be traitors. Eisenhower recalled his days as supreme commander during the liberation of Europe: "One month in Normandy, we had so many cases of assault, murder and rape that the citizens of the region were driven to desperation." He had decided to make an example of two American soldiers, convicted of rape and murder in occupied France. "Under my direction, this was made a semi-public execution, with representatives of all units, citizens, police forces, and churches present." Thereafter assaults declined dramatically, he claimed.

Eisenhower also swept away the argument that Ethel should be spared because she was a woman and a mother. To do that would simply invite the Soviets to deploy "only women in their spying process." What is more, Eisenhower had concluded that Ethel "has obviously been the leader in everything they did in the spy ring" (a remarkable and inaccurate claim). Julius was a "weak" man, but Ethel was a "strong and recalcitrant character," and so deserved no mercy. In the end Eisenhower advanced the argument that the Rosenbergs "exposed to greater danger of death literally millions of our citizens." For this they would have to die.[15]

On the evening of June 19, 1953, after a last-minute refusal of the Supreme Court to hold up the trial any longer, and after Eisenhower declined again to intervene, Julius and Ethel Rosenberg were put to death in the electric chair at Sing Sing Prison.[16]

IV

If Eisenhower had hoped to win plaudits from the Red hunters in his own party for his unsentimental handling of the Rosenberg case, he was soon disappointed. From the very first days of the Eisenhower administration, Senator McCarthy had set out to test the new president on the genuineness of his desire to root out subversion from government. McCarthy had a new stage on which to perform: with the Republicans in the majority in the 83rd Congress, he took over as chairman of the Committee on Government Operations as well as the Permanent Subcommittee on Investigations, which he used to call countless witnesses and launch numerous fishing expeditions in his search for communist subversion. When Eisenhower nominated his most trusted wartime colleague, Walter "Beetle" Smith, as undersecretary of state, McCarthy told the press he would hold up the appointment because Smith had once expressed support for John Paton Davies, a former "China hand" who, McCarthy alleged, had been sympathetic to the Chinese communists. McCarthy wrote a letter to Eisenhower on February 3, 1953, stating that he was "strongly opposed" to the appointment of Harvard president James B. Conant as high commissioner to Germany because Conant had been insufficiently aggressive in rooting out communists from Harvard, professors who "have been up early every morning doing the work of the Communist Party." Conant could not be relied upon, McCarthy said, "to safeguard the American Embassy at Bonn from Communist penetration."[17]

McCarthy was toying with the new president and chose not to make a direct attack in the Senate on Smith or Conant. But he did not show any restraint when Eisenhower nominated Charles "Chip" Bohlen as ambassador to the USSR. To McCarthy, Bohlen was the epitome of the professional pin-striped Ivy League diplomat. A Harvard degree, a long career in the State Department, an interest in all things Soviet, previous service in Prague, Paris, and Moscow, and his work in setting up the United Nations in 1944–45—all this hinted at the kind of worldly cosmopolitanism that drove McCarthy mad. Worse, Bohlen had worked closely with Marshall, Acheson, and Truman, and, most damning of all, he had been present at

Yalta, the much-derided 1945 meeting when Roosevelt was alleged to have surrendered Eastern Europe and Manchuria to Stalin. Bohlen, fluent in Russian and a longtime Foreign Service officer, served as a translator and adviser to Roosevelt, and it was inevitable that, given the toxicity of the Yalta connection—it was the same conference, after all, where Hiss advised the president—Bohlen was going to come under close scrutiny.

Yet in his March 1953 confirmation hearing before the Senate Foreign Relations Committee, Bohlen refused to be intimidated. The Yalta accords, he patiently explained, did not sell out China or turn over Eastern Europe to Stalin. At Yalta, FDR was trying to win Soviet entry into the war against Japan as well as cooperation in the newly formed United Nations. The USSR was granted a lease to Port Arthur and ownership of southern Sakhalin Island. As for Poland, the Yalta accord demanded the inclusion of democratic elements into the postwar Polish government. The Yalta agreement, Bohlen pointed out, was designed to forestall Soviet control of Poland, not surrender it. Bohlen's firm defense of Yalta inflamed the Red hunters. Senator Styles Bridges of New Hampshire, one of the GOP's senior leaders, called on the president to withdraw Bohlen's name. Democratic senator Pat McCarran announced his opposition too, saying that Bohlen's presence at Yalta "was enough" for him to vote against the man. Senator Homer Ferguson of Michigan pressed the White House to withdraw the nomination. Majority Leader Robert Taft managed to stave off open rebellion by announcing his support for Bohlen and calling him "well qualified," and Eisenhower too signaled that he was going to stand firm behind his nominee. Bohlen was, he said in a press conference, a personal friend, a good family man, and the "best-qualified man for the post."[18]

But McCarran and McCarthy were not finished with Bohlen, for they knew that in conducting a security review of the nominee, the FBI had dragged out various hints that Bohlen's brother-in-law, Charles Thayer, a Foreign Service officer who was then stationed in Munich, was a homosexual. Bohlen had known Thayer for many years and had once shared an apartment with him when both were junior officers stationed in Moscow. Thayer had introduced his sister, Avis, to Bohlen, and the two married in 1935. But rumors had circulated about Thayer, and now they wound up in Bohlen's FBI file. Had Bohlen known of his brother-in-law's sexuality? Was Bohlen covering up for him? Was this evidence of a homosexual ring in the State Department? Was Bohlen himself a "queer"?

Bohlen's FBI file and its contents now sat at the center of a struggle between Congress and the Executive. The senators wanted to inspect the file. Herbert Brownell, the attorney general, and even FBI director J. Edgar Hoover, were against it: it would set a precedent for congressional inter-ference in Executive branch business, and in any case the FBI files were highly confidential. But McCarthy kept the pressure on. He demanded that Eisenhower "examine the entire file on Bohlen"; if he did so, he would cer-tainly "withdraw the appointment." Secretary Dulles declared that he had seen the FBI file and that there was nothing in it that tarnished Bohlen's name. He asked the Senate to take him at his word, but McCarthy and Mc-Carran accused Dulles of a cover-up. McCarthy was using Bohlen to attack Dulles and Eisenhower for being "soft" on internal security. According to the Washington columnists Joseph and Stewart Alsop, the Bohlen case was "war, and make no mistake about it."[19]

That Bohlen had contact with, even shared an apartment with an alleged homosexual was potentially devastating in the climate of the early 1950s. Hostility toward gay men was extreme in American public life at this time, and in the context of the Red Scare, sexual "deviance" of federal employees was considered a security risk since it was assumed that gay people could easily be blackmailed. In 1950 the Senate held hearings on the matter and is-sued a report titled "Employment of Homosexuals and Other Sex Perverts in Government," which concluded that homosexual conduct was "so contrary to the normal accepted standards of social behavior that persons who engage in such activity are looked upon as outcasts by society generally." Further-more homosexuals "lack the emotional stability of normal persons" and have weak "moral fiber," and so could not be trusted with government secrets.[20]

This intolerance toward homosexuality meant that the merest whiff of such behavior on the part of a high-ranking government official could be ruinous. In Chip Bohlen's case, therefore, it was essential that the FBI file be shared with the Senate so that it could be seen just how flimsy the ru-mors relating to Thayer really were. Yet the constitutional prerogative of the Executive branch had to be protected. On the eve of the Senate debate on Bohlen's nomination, Taft suggested a compromise: two senators, one from each party, would be tasked with viewing the report and informing their colleagues of its contents. Taft himself and Democratic senator John Sparkman then duly inspected the documents and found, as Taft put it, "nothing in all the testimony which would create the most remote 'guilt-by-association' accusation that can be thought of." McCarthy, on the floor of the Senate, howled about a cover-up, declaring that the American people had voted Eisenhower into office to "clean house: This means get rid of Acheson's lieutenants—including all the Bohlens."[21]

Bohlen was confirmed by the Senate in a vote of 74–13. (Thayer, meanwhile, resigned from the State Department under duress.) Eleven Republican senators, in opposing Bohlen, voted against their newly elected and immensely popular president; they also voted against Taft, against Dulles, and against the privilege of the Executive to choose its own envoys. Eisenhower won, but it had cost him a great deal of bad blood with the right wing of his own party and showed that McCarthyism was in no sense diminished simply because the Republicans had taken control of the White House.

Eisenhower was personally frustrated by the Bohlen affair. He wrote to his brother Edgar at the start of April 1953 that the Bohlen file was full of "completely baseless, wholly unsubstantiated rumors that he had been associated some fifteen or twenty years ago with some unsavory characters." McCarthy, he wrote in his diary, had stirred the pot "in order to secure some mention of his name in the public press." But Eisenhower refused to confront the senator and his hijinks directly: "Nothing will be so effective in combatting his particular kind of trouble-making as to ignore him. This he cannot stand."[22]

V

Ignoring McCarthy was not the only plan for dealing with the publicity-hungry senator. The Eisenhower administration also tried another tactic: to seize the initiative in the anticommunist crusade. On April 27, 1953, just after the Bohlen confirmation, the Eisenhower White House issued Executive Order 10450, announcing new procedures for combing out any security risks from the federal government. The order took aim not only at those with politically disloyal ideas but also those with a dubious "moral" record. Federal employees could not demonstrate "any criminal, infamous, dishonest, immoral, or notoriously disgraceful conduct, habitual use of intoxicants to excess, drug addiction, or sexual perversion." The Red Scare had subjected the political attitudes of government employees to careful scrutiny; now their moral, personal, and sexual conduct would be supervised by the federal government for any sign of "deviance." The Executive Order was a sober reminder that Eisenhower, for all his antagonism toward McCarthy, was determined not to be outflanked on the issue of loyalty and subversion by the right wing of his own party.[23]

On June 3, 1953, Eisenhower went on national television along with four cabinet members, one of whom was Attorney General Brownell. Eisenhower wanted Brownell to give the nation a report on how well the new team was doing in "keeping the internal house secure against the boring of subversives and that sort of thing." Brownell's statement was full of praise for the "fine investigative work of the FBI arm of the Department of Justice under J. Edgar Hoover," as well as the administration's new loyalty program. He stressed that the Eisenhower team's approach to federal employee security, unlike Truman's, was to go after people who, because of their "personal habits," were security risks. The politically active person who had "traitorous thoughts" of course had to go. But so too did anyone "who might be subject to blackmail" due to shameful behavior. The principle of denying access to government service for allegations of immoral behavior was now a settled rule for the new team.[24]

Eisenhower was never personally comfortable with the business of security investigations. Although he understood the political need to demonstrate vigilance against security risks in federal employ, he took pains to say publicly that he wanted to conduct investigations in a way that protected the rights of the accused. The personal attacks, innuendo, and slander that McCarthy relied upon were obnoxious to Eisenhower. When he learned that Roy Cohn, the general counsel for McCarthy's committee on investigations, had been trolling American libraries in Europe, digging out and allegedly destroying literature from the shelves written by left-wingers and communist enthusiasts, he used a public address at Dartmouth College to denounce such paranoid behavior. Taking the podium at the graduation exercises, he spoke off the cuff:

Look at your country. Here is a country of which we are proud. . . . But this country is a long way from perfection—a long way. We have the disgrace of racial discrimination, or we have prejudice against people because of their religion. We have crime on the docks. We have not had the courage to uproot these things, although we know they are wrong. Now, [your] courage is not going to be satisfied—your sense of satisfaction is not going to be satisfied, if you haven't the courage to look at these things and do your best to help correct them. . . . It is not enough merely to say I love America, and to salute the flag and take off your hat as it goes by, and to help sing the Star Spangled Banner.

He concluded his rambling remarks in a clear rebuke to the close-mindedness of the McCarthyites: "Don't join the book burners. Don't think you are going to conceal faults by concealing evidence that they ever existed. Don't be afraid to go in your library and read every book, as long as that document does not offend our own ideas of decency. That should be the only censorship. How will we defeat communism unless we know what it is, and what it teaches, and why does it have such an appeal for men, why are so many people swearing allegiance to it?"[25]

Yet such public expressions were all too rare. Just three days later Eisenhower replied to a letter from Philip Reed, the chairman of the board of General Electric and an adviser in the 1952 campaign, explaining why he would avoid direct confrontation with McCarthy. Reed had sent the president an anguished letter reporting on public opinion among Europeans, who saw McCarthy as "a potential Hitler . . . a typical totalitarian, a demagogue, a ruthless purger of those with whom he disagrees." The ousting of diplomats like Thayer, the combing of libraries, and the allegations of treachery, all this was "to them a familiar and frightening scene." Reed felt the "stature of [Eisenhower's] administration" was "impaired" overseas, and he hoped to see "strong statements" that countered McCarthy's allegations. Eisenhower calmly replied, "To attempt to answer in terms of personal criticism is to place yourself in the hands of the attacker." If the president were to "point his finger at any particular individual, meaning to name anyone specifically, he automatically gives to that individual an increased publicity value. This is exactly what many people are seeking and I decline to be a party to it." To his Abilene friend Swede Hazlett, Eisenhower explained that he would not "crack down" on McCarthy because to do so would only increase the attention paid to his scandalous activities.[26]

Instead of standing up to McCarthy, Eisenhower preferred to point to his own success in "cleaning up the mess in Washington." On October 23 the head of the Civil Service Commission, Philip Young, delivered the news to the press that the administration had dismissed "1,456 subversives" from federal service. The number was never precisely explained, and the dismissed employees were not identified. What seemed to matter most was that all but five of the 1,456 were holdovers from the Truman years.[27]

There soon came further revelations, clearly designed to seize the communist issue from McCarthy while embarrassing the previous administration. On November 6 Attorney General Brownell—with Eisenhower's prior approval—announced that he had information showing that President Truman had been informed in late 1945 that a high-ranking treasury official, Harry Dexter White, was a Soviet spy, and yet the following month Truman nonetheless nominated White to serve as the top U.S. representative to the International Monetary Fund. (White served in that post until 1947, when he got wind that the Justice Department was on his trail. He died of a heart attack in August 1948.) Brownell, speaking before the Executives Club in Chicago, declared, "It is a source of humiliation to every American that during the period of the Truman Administration, the Communists were so strikingly successful in infiltrating the Government of the United States." Brownell laid it on thick: "The records in my department show that White's spying activities for the Soviet Government were reported in detail by the FBI to the White House." But Truman had not acted.[28]

Brownell's accusation that Truman had knowingly advanced the career of a high-ranking Soviet agent triggered what the *New York Times* called "the most rancorous political brawl of the year." Of course the charges were deeply embarrassing to Truman. But Brownell's attack on the former president was depicted in the press as a crude political ploy designed to make the new administration appear zealous in the hunt for communist subversives. Sherman Adams later admitted that the Brownell report was designed precisely to "take away some of the glamour of the McCarthy stage play" and put Ike in the limelight as the leading actor in the anticommunist drama. But the attack on Truman made Brownell look like a political hack who was using privileged access to FBI files to dredge up evidence of Democratic malfeasance. Marquis Childs, the *Washington Post* journalist, wrote, "Many who were behind Mr. Eisenhower in the campaign last year believed he would end the divisiveness and distrust; that he would help give America a new unity and a new confidence." Instead the Eisenhower team widened the partisan divide.[29]

The White House press corps battered Eisenhower with questions about the White affair at his November 11 news conference. Standing behind a desk in the ornate Indian Treaty Room of the old State Department building, he experienced "some of the roughest minutes of the Eisenhower Administration," according to *New York Times* journalist James Reston. Eisenhower was compelled to admit under questioning that he had approved Brownell's anti-Truman charge in advance. He also was forced to cut the ground from under Brownell by stating that it was "inconceivable" that Truman had knowingly appointed a spy to high office. When one reporter asked if Eisenhower was "virtually putting a label of traitor on a former president," Eisenhower visibly tensed up and said, "I reject the premise. I would not answer such a question." He tried to kill the clock with a rambling statement about the need to fight subversion in government while attending to just and democratic principles. But the damage was done: it was clear that Brownell's assault had opened Eisenhower up to the charge that his Justice Department was raking through the files in search of politically damaging material against the Truman administration. "The partisan feeling here to-night," wrote Reston from Washington, "is bitter."[30]

The most incendiary criticism of Brownell's announcement came, pre-dictably, from Truman himself, who gave a nationally televised address on November 16 from Kansas City to rebut the suggestion that he had bungled the White case. Truman insisted that the information he had seen was not damaging enough to fire White in 1945, that an ongoing investigation at that time was still under way; and that even in 1947 a federal grand jury had tried and failed to indict White because the evidence was too flimsy. But the real issue, Truman said, going on the attack, was that President Eisen-hower "has fully embraced for political advantage McCarthyism. . . . It is the corruption of truth, the abandonment of due process of law. It is the use of the big lie and the unfounded accusation against any citizen in the name of Americanism or security. It is the rise to power of the demagogue who lives on untruth." Truman offered this withering barb: "In Communist countries, it is the practice when a new government comes to power to ac-cuse outgoing officials of treason, to frame public trials for them, and to degrade and prosecute them." Brownell was engaged in just such "political skullduggery."[31]

Eisenhower had walked into a political minefield and found himself with no easy way out. Either he could press forward and engage Truman's blistering speech; or he could backtrack and so abandon his attorney gen-eral. In his November 18 news conference he did neither. He simply refused to answer questions on the matter. But the press reported to him that Leon-ard Hall, the chairman of the Republican National Committee, had recently stated that the communists-in-government issue was going to be the major theme of the 1954 midterm elections and that "we have not seen the end of it." Eisenhower directly contradicted the party chairman: "I hope that this whole thing will be a matter of history and of memory by the time the next election comes around. I don't believe we can live in fear of each other forever, and I really hope and believe that this administration is proceeding decently and justly to get this thing straightened out." Pressed further, he said he hoped "the suspicion on the part of the American people" that the government was infiltrated by subversive elements "will have disappeared through the accomplishments of the executive branch."[32]

This was a clear message to the right wing of his party in Congress. The Eisenhower administration was cleaning up the government, and as soon as possible it would declare victory in the Red-hunting effort and move on to less divisive issues. To one listener such a statement came as a direct challenge. McCarthy had no intention of ceding the role of top prosecutor to Brownell or Eisenhower. Relishing the prospect of tangling with Truman again, McCarthy pressured the television networks to let him respond to Truman's address. On November 24, from a studio in New York, McCarthy gave a classic and outrageous performance. He scorned the "phoney, deluded, fuzzy-minded liberals in whose book it is a mortal sin ever to expose or criticize a Communist." And he depicted Truman's pointed attack as payback "because I took some part in the exposure of the Communist infiltration of his administration." But attacking Truman was not the main purpose of the address. The second half of his televised remarks was aimed squarely at Ike.

"A few days ago," he said, "I read that President Eisenhower expressed the hope that by election-time in 1954, the subject of communism would be a dead and forgotten issue. The raw, harsh, unpleasant fact is that communism is an issue and will be an issue in 1954." Eisenhower's "batting average" in rooting out communists was quite low, McCarthy went on. John Paton Davies, whom McCarthy had hounded for alleged softness on communism, was still on the State Department payroll. More worrisome, America's allies in Europe, many of them recipients of Marshall Plan money, continued to trade with communist China, the same nation that was still holding American prisoners of war. "How free are we when American aviators . . . are being brainwashed, starved, or murdered behind an Iron or Bamboo Curtain?" Eisenhower's policy toward Red China and Dulles's inability to get European allies to conform to America's wishes were signs of "whining, whimpering appeasement."[33]

Even for McCarthy this was a loopy, unhinged performance. Jim Hagerty privately called McCarthy's address "sheer Fascism." Yet it was perceived by Washington observers as a "blunt warning" to the president, in the words of Stewart Alsop. McCarthy made clear what he was after: not the purging of dubious employees but the "Administration's public acceptance that he, McCarthy, is the leading symbol of Republicanism. He will be satisfied, in a word, only by the abject surrender of President Eisenhower." Alsop grasped that the Eisenhower team had underestimated McCarthy, "as the Administration strategists who believe they could undercut him by 'fighting fire with fire' must surely have noticed." An open breach between McCarthy and Eisenhower was now "inevitable."[34]

Eisenhower's advisers recognized that McCarthy had flung down the gauntlet, and some of them begged the president to pick it up. C. D. Jackson, who was at that moment toiling hard over the "Atoms for Peace" speech, argued that McCarthy had declared war on the president and needed to be hit hard. McCarthy had set himself up as the leader of the Republican Party and had called out Eisenhower for harboring communists. Ignoring McCarthy—playing what Jackson called the "three little monkeys act"—was not working, and the president had to show some leadership. In a heated phone conversation with Dulles on December 1, Jackson raged that Ike's tepid replies to McCarthy were failing. "The Olympian dialectics are superb," Jackson sputtered, "but when your house is on fire you don't put it out by oratory." The timid behavior of the White House was reminiscent of the "disastrous appeasement" of McCarthy that had started in September 1952 on the campaign trail in Wisconsin. Yet even now it was very difficult for Jackson to budge the president, especially as Vice President Nixon, Chief of Staff Adams, and Gen. Wilton "Jerry" Persons, the congressional liaison, were against any open breach with McCarthy.

On December 2, however, Dulles struck back at McCarthy, with Eisenhower's approval, sharply denouncing McCarthy's criticism of the administration's foreign policy. Jackson wanted the president to back up Dulles in his scheduled news conference that afternoon, and presented a draft statement that struck at McCarthy. Eisenhower slammed the text on his desk, saying, "I will not get in the gutter with that guy"—a point that had become his guiding principle on this issue. But Jackson kept up what he called his "needling" and "goosing" and managed to get Eisenhower to agree to a mild rebuttal to McCarthy's latest criticisms. In a prepared statement that he read to the press, Eisenhower backed Dulles and reinforced his earlier message: his administration was successfully purging the federal government of disloyal Americans and doing it through "fair, thorough and decent investigations." By 1954 the issue of disloyalty would "no longer be considered a serious menace." Far more important was to enact a "progressive, dynamic program enhancing the welfare of the people of our country." So fraught was the atmosphere in Washington that even this mild statement was taken by the press as a direct counterstroke to McCarthy. An editorial in the *Washington Post* was titled simply "Ike Takes Command."[35]

VI

That surely overstated the case. In fact the president faced serious disadvantages in taking command over the anti-McCarthy forces. Perhaps most important, his own party was deeply divided over the matter. The Old Guard Republicans in the Senate shared many of McCarthy's prejudices and fears and were sympathetic to his brand of reactionary, isolationist, conspiracy-laden, communist-obsessed, vulgar populism. Eisenhower might have had a stronger hand to play if Majority Leader Taft had not died of cancer in July 1953, just six months after the new administration took office. Taft, though ideologically at odds with Eisenhower, had played a crucial role in salvaging the Bohlen nomination and could have helped at least keep McCarthy in check. Unfortunately Taft's successor was William Knowland, a 44-year-old from California—the youngest ever to hold the post of majority leader—and an ambitious, politically naïve, and inflexible politician who consistently disappointed Eisenhower as a congressional ally. Knowland had long been a rival of Nixon's, and he held a grudge against the administration. Harry McPherson, a longtime staffer for Senator Lyndon Johnson, acidly noted that Knowland's "mind had a single trajectory—flat—and a point-blank range." He was conservative, unimaginative, bullish, and proved deeply hostile to any interference by the Executive branch in McCarthy's Senate activities.

Behind Knowland stood a team of Old Guard senators who distrusted Eisenhower and the moderate leaders of the GOP. Styles Bridges, the most senior Republican in the Senate, was a true reactionary and deeply suspicious of the Eisenhower program. He became notorious for hounding a Democratic senator, Lester Hunt of Wyoming, to his death. When Hunt's son was arrested for soliciting homosexual sex in a Washington, D.C., park, Bridges compelled Hunt to resign by threatening to publicize the case; distraught, Hunt killed himself. William Langer of North Dakota, Homer Ferguson of Michigan, Bourke Hickenlooper of Iowa, Homer Capehart of Indiana, John Butler of Maryland, William Jenner of Indiana, and Herman Welker of Idaho—these bilious conspiracy theorists served as a gleeful cheering section for the junior senator from Wisconsin. Even Everett Dirksen, who served seven terms in the House before moving to the upper chamber, lent support to McCarthy. Dirksen's almost comical theatricality, his goggle-eyed, bespectacled face topped by an unruly mop of gray curls, his deep baritone and love for posturing and oratory, made him much-loved by Senate colleagues. He was known mainly for changing his views on almost every issue of consequence, and he often proved helpful to Eisenhower. Yet on one issue he remained consistent: he never wavered in his support for Joe McCarthy.[36]

Another leading Republican antagonist of Eisenhower in this period was John Bricker of Ohio, a silver-thatched, handsome former governor who had been Thomas Dewey's vice-presidential running mate in 1944. His obsession was the passage of an eponymous constitutional amendment to restrict the power of the president to sign foreign treaties. In these years, when FDR's personal diplomacy with Stalin had come under attack and when the newly formed United Nations seemed to be probing into domestic matters such as racial inequality, many American legislators felt that it was important to make more precise the relative powers of Congress and the president to forge international agreements that might impinge upon domestic law, especially the rights of states. In Congress there was a surprising degree of support for the Bricker amendment, since it was seen as a way to clip the wings of a secretive or willful Executive branch like Roosevelt's. But Eisenhower furiously resisted it, knowing it would weaken presidential powers and tip the balance of power decisively toward Congress. A long fight with the Old Guard over the Bricker amendment finally led to a narrow defeat for the proposal in February 1954, but not without creating more bad blood between Ike and his right wing.[37]

No wonder, then, that when Eisenhower in December 1953 sought to frame a strategy to handle McCarthy he did not plan on a frontal attack. He had too few foot soldiers from his own party to follow him into battle. Instead he turned to the man closest at hand who would be seen as a trusted emissary to the Senate's Old Guard: the former senator and now vice president Richard Nixon. Nixon and William Rogers, the deputy attorney general, invited McCarthy to visit Nixon on vacation in Key Biscayne, Florida. The two men "double-teamed" McCarthy, urging him to continue to go after communists when necessary but to "move into some new areas lest he become a 'one-shot' Senator." Perhaps he could pursue tax fraud and the like. But McCarthy could not be won over. "Frankly," recalled Nixon, "we tried to mediate with McCarthy until we were blue in the face."[38]

Eisenhower and Attorney General Brownell continued their efforts to seize control of the internal security issue. A few weeks after the Harry Dexter White case broke, Brownell began to discuss with Congress new legislation to update the 1950 Internal Security Act. He wanted to strengthen the federal government's hand by securing legislation to allow for evidence from wiretapping by the FBI to be used in court. He also wanted legislation that would give immunity from prosecution to witnesses who helped expose communist subversion, and new tools to ban unions that were led by Communist Party activists. Brownell reported these proposals to the National Security Council on December 28, clearly as part of a strategy to seize the communist issue from McCarthy and place it into Brownell's hands.[39]

But McCarthy would not go away, nor would he be appeased, bullied, or intimidated. In the spring of 1954 the long-simmering contest between Eisenhower and McCarthy finally boiled over. The crisis came over McCarthy's growing interest in the security procedures of the U.S. Army, of all things. Since the fall of 1953 McCarthy had been holding hearings into allegations of communist sympathies at the Army Signal Corps laboratories at Fort Monmouth, New Jersey—the same institution where the doomed Julius Rosenberg had worked during the war. McCarthy suspected that the spy ring that had harbored Rosenberg might still be operational there. The secretary of the army, Robert Stevens, tried to reassure the senator that the espionage problem had already been investigated and the facility at Fort Monmouth had been cleared. McCarthy doubted it and pledged to pursue the matter. In the process of gathering information about the army's security and loyalty review procedures, he stumbled across the curious case of a dentist named Irving Peress. (Like Julius Rosenberg, Peress was Jewish and had attended New York's City College.) Peress was drafted into the army in 1952 and given the rank of captain, but when he was reviewed for security clearance, he refused to fill out various forms about his political views, which were indeed far left. The army, moving in a plodding bureaucratic fashion, eventually found Peress to be a security risk and recommended that he be discharged. But the army took almost a year before acting on his case, and by that time Peress had actually been promoted to the rank of major.

How could the army have promoted a known communist? The explanation of bureaucratic bungling would not satisfy McCarthy; he imagined a conspiracy at work to protect Peress and possibly others. Perhaps Camp Kilmer, where Peress was stationed, was a hotbed of communists. On February 18, 1954, McCarthy called before his subcommittee Gen. Ralph Zwicker, Camp Kilmer's commanding officer. McCarthy baited and taunted the general, a distinguished career army officer who had earned decorations for valor on Omaha Beach on D-Day. McCarthy accused him of protecting communists under his command; furious because of Zwicker's unhelpful answers, McCarthy declared him unfit to wear the uniform of a U.S. Army officer.

The incident caused an uproar and led Secretary of the Army Stevens to inform McCarthy that no further military officers would appear before his subcommittee unless the senator gave assurances that they would be treated with respect. But Stevens, a wealthy businessman and textile merchant with no political experience, was not cut out for this kind of brinkmanship. McCarthy, in league with Senators Dirksen and Mundt, invited Stevens to lunch in Dirksen's office on February 24 and after two hours of wrangling, threats, and cajoling, forced him to backtrack from his firm position. He would in fact agree to turn over to Congress the names of any army officials involved in the Peress case. The press promptly reported this outcome as an abject surrender to McCarthy by Stevens. A shaken Stevens telephoned Nixon and Hagerty and offered to resign. McCarthy was triumphant and defiant.

Eisenhower's improvisational responses to McCarthy—avoid him, then appease him, then steal from him the role of chief anticommunist prosecutor—had failed. Fifteen months into the Eisenhower administration, McCarthy was as strong as ever. Ike was furious at McCarthy's handling of Stevens and his reckless assaults on the army. "I'm not going to take this one lying down," he fumed in the Oval Office to Hagerty. On March 1, speaking to Republican congressional leaders, he asked why more was not being done to rein in McCarthy and firmly stated, "We cannot defeat Communism by destroying the things in which we believe." Privately he lashed out at the Old Guard, seething, "We just can't work with fellows like McCarthy, Bricker, Jenner, and that bunch."[40]

Hoping to diminish the impact of the Peress issue, Eisenhower drafted a statement that he read to the press corps on March 3, in which he acknowledged that the army had made an error in failing to expel the communist-leaning dentist. However, the president added, members of the administration who were working in good faith would not "submit to any kind of personal humiliation when testifying before congressional committees." He went on to give a lengthy and firm statement of support for army officers, including General Zwicker, whose "courage and devotion have been proved in peace as well as in war." The badgering of witnesses and the impugning of their character must stop, and Ike put the Republican leadership on notice that it was their job to make it stop. "In opposing Communism," he stated, "we are defeating ourselves if either by design or through carelessness we use methods that do not conform to the American sense of fair play."[41]

But McCarthy seemed only to relish the opportunity to engage the president in a personal confrontation. Two hours after the president's press conference, McCarthy held a televised news conference of his own, in Room 155 of the Senate Office Building, and defied Eisenhower. McCarthy declared that he was being criticized for revealing that the U.S. Army had protected and promoted a "Communist Army officer." As to badgering General Zwicker, McCarthy was unrepentant: "If a stupid, arrogant or witless man in a position of power appears before our committee and is found aiding the Communist party, he will be exposed. The fact that he might be a general places him in no special class so far as I am concerned." This was just the kind of tit-for-tat exchange that Eisenhower had feared and sought to avoid, and just the kind of attention that McCarthy eagerly courted.[42]

McCarthy's audacity was taking a serious political toll on Eisenhower. The senator seemed to be breaking the GOP apart, pushing the Old Guard into an open confrontation with the president. Eisenhower beseeched Knowland to control his members in the Senate. "If we pursue the course we have taken so far, the Republican Party will be wrecked," he predicted. But Knowland, whose sympathies were with the Old Guard, was little help. The Democrats, meanwhile, were ready to pounce and exploit these fissures in the GOP. Adlai Stevenson, the nominal leader of the party, took unfeigned pleasure in attacking the president for his "timidity" on McCarthy. Speaking to southern Democrats in Miami Beach on March 6, Stevenson said that the GOP was "hopelessly, dismally, fatally torn and rent within itself. . . . A political party divided against itself, half McCarthy and half Eisenhower, cannot produce national unity or govern with confidence and purpose." The dean of the Washington columnists, Walter Lippmann, added a scathing assessment of the state of play: "There is no doubt whatever that McCarthy is a deliberate aggressor, that he is fighting Eisenhower's leadership and control of the party. . . . The fight is unavoidable because McCarthy refuses to be appeased. Until he is stopped and his power is checked, he will go on until he is the master of the party." Lippmann declared that Eisenhower's "prolonged appeasement has failed."[43]

Perhaps it was Stevenson's barbs that finally prodded Eisenhower into action, for on March 10, in his weekly press conference, Eisenhower's comments about the troubles in the Senate were "punctuated by anger and near-bluntness," according to Anthony Leviero of the *New York Times*. He declared Stevenson's charge of a divided GOP to be "nonsense" and affirmed that Vice President Nixon would rebut Stevenson's claims in a televised speech. Contradicting his own assertions of party unity, however, Eisenhower went on to denounce the "internecine warfare" in the Senate, and in a direct jab at McCarthy he said it was time to put aside "personal aggrandizement" and get on with crafting constructive legislation. "The President," wrote Hagerty in his diary, was "in a fighting mood, and has had it as far as Joe is concerned."[44]

Angry as he was at McCarthy, Eisenhower remained determined to avoid lowering himself to the senator's level. Besides, he had Nixon for that sort of thing. He directed Nixon to go on national television ostensibly to reply to Stevenson's criticisms but in fact to deliver a direct rebuke to McCarthy. On March 13, in a brilliant performance, once again carefully prepared and rehearsed yet delivered in his now-trademark conversational and apparently off-the-cuff manner, the vice president affirmed the success of the Eisenhower administration in rooting out communists from government in a manner that was "fair and proper." Directing his remarks at McCarthy's frenzied and undisciplined Red hunting, Nixon said, "When you go out to shoot rats, you have to shoot straight, because when you shoot wildly it not only means that the rat may get away more easily, you make it easier on the rat. But you might hit someone else who's trying to shoot rats, too. And so we've got to be fair." Nixon stated that certain "men who have in the past done effective work exposing Communists in this country have, by reckless talk and questionable methods, made themselves the issue." When it came to hunting down the bad guys, Nixon seemed to suggest, Ike was Gary Cooper—restrained, cool, and precise—and McCarthy was the angry drunk in the street, his pistols blazing away wildly and shooting up the storefronts. Once again Nixon had proven his worth to the Eisenhower team.[45]

VII

Nixon's speech marked the start of a concerted administration effort to take the offensive against McCarthy. But the real bombshell that burst on McCarthy did not come from the president or Nixon. It was delivered in the form of a dossier of material, carefully prepared by the U.S. Army, which did incalculable damage to the Red-hunting senator. The dossier had been in the works since January 21, when the army's chief counsel, John G. Adams, alerted the White House to a pattern of pressure and bullying of the army by McCarthy and by his committee's chief counsel, Roy Cohn. The two men had been using threats and intimidation to demand that Cohn's assistant, David Schine, who had been drafted into the army the previous November, be granted preferential treatment in the form of light duties, desk work, and plum assignments. Schine was handsome, Harvard-educated, and very wealthy; though he had no legal training, Cohn had brought him onto the McCarthy committee as a staff member and had taken him on the highly public tour of U.S. libraries overseas, when Cohn had discovered dangerous books lurking on the shelves.

When John Adams reported this to Attorney General Brownell and White House Chief of Staff Sherman Adams at the January 21 meeting, the two senior advisers knew they had found dynamite. Sherman Adams directed the army lawyer to prepare a detailed account of what he knew about McCarthy and Cohn's campaign on behalf of Private Schine. John Adams completed his report on February 2, and its contents were astonishing: in great detail Adams revealed how many times McCarthy and Cohn had badgered, harassed, and threatened him in demanding that Schine be given kid-glove treatment. Adams wrote of the "the sustained violence" of Cohn's phone calls and described his "obscenities and vituperative remarks" as shocking and unprintable. "The most consistent remark [Cohn] made," Adams wrote, "was that the Army was requiring Schine to eat [obscenity] because he worked for the McCarthy committee." Cohn threatened to destroy the army through ceaseless investigations unless Schine got special treatment. "We'll wreck the Army," Cohn screamed over the phone at Adams. "We've got enough stuff on the Army to have the investigation run indefinitely." More shocking, McCarthy was present at a number of meetings with Adams and Cohn, and he piled on, asking the army to get Schine a cushy desk job in New York City.[46]

On March 11 the White House sent a streamlined and cleaned-up version of Adams's report to a number of key congressmen. At the same time the White House leaked it to the press. Sherman Adams later admitted his role in the operation: "Not entirely by accident, the Army's report on its troubles with Schine fell into the hands of a few newspaper correspondents. . . . Their stories built up a backfire against McCarthy, as intended." The resulting furor was dramatic and marked the beginning of the end of Joe McCarthy. The accusations were so damaging to the integrity of the Senate's investigatory powers that the Senate itself was now put on trial. If the allegations were true, then McCarthy and Cohn stood guilty of abuse of power. Within days McCarthy was asked to step aside from his position as chairman of the Subcommittee on Investigations. Senator Karl Mundt took the chair in his place and—quite unwillingly—began hearings into the army's allegations against McCarthy. In a dramatic reversal, the senator from Wisconsin was now placed under the spotlight by the very committee he had turned into a national inquisition.[47]

The army-McCarthy hearings began on April 22 and were televised to a national audience that could not avert its eyes from the slow-moving train wreck of McCarthy's self-destruction. This was not a courtroom proceeding but a congressional hearing into charges made by the army against McCarthy and Cohn. But of course McCarthy and Cohn, who acted as their own defense counsel, were free to call and cross-examine witnesses and to plant the seeds of doubt among the "jury"—namely, the millions of television viewers. Therefore McCarthy had every reason to play to the gallery, making countercharges against the army's staff, suggesting dark conspiracies, deploying phony documents to embarrass the army. If McCarthy was going to go down, he was planning to take the army with him. And so it went, on and on, for two months, over 72 sessions featuring 35 witnesses and creating a transcript of nearly 3,000 closely printed pages.

Among the spectators was President Eisenhower, who felt no need to intervene now that the Senate had seized control of the McCarthy affair. To tangle with McCarthy directly, he wrote to Bill Robinson, would "make the presidency look ridiculous." He preferred to let the Senate look ridiculous, and indeed Ike told Swede Hazlett in the midst of the hearings, "It saddens me that I must feel ashamed for the United States Senate." In his press conferences Eisenhower tried to stay above the fray and affected disinterest in the hearings. On May 12 for instance, he told reporters he "was going to take a little vacation" in discussing McCarthy and ignored questions asking him to comment on the hearings.[48]

But Eisenhower could not completely insulate himself from the proceedings. In his testimony of May 11, army counsel John Adams had inadvertently revealed that the army's now-famous report revealing a pattern of bullying from Cohn and McCarthy on behalf of Schine was in fact the brainchild of Sherman Adams and that he had discussed the matter on January 21 with Adams, Henry Cabot Lodge, Herbert Brownell, and William Rogers. Clearly the damaging report on McCarthy had originated not in the army but in the White House itself. The trail was leading back to Eisenhower, and McCarthy caught the scent like the bloodhound he was. It seemed likely that McCarthy would now move to subpoena Eisenhower's principal advisers and cabinet members.

Eisenhower had anticipated this and had been accumulating expert advice on the constitutional question of whether the Executive branch was obliged to submit to congressional investigation. He had asked for a detailed report on the matter from Assistant Attorney General Rogers as far back as March 2. Now, after a weekend golf game at Burning Tree with Hagerty, Ike said he was ready to make his move. On May 17, in a bold preemptive strike on McCarthy, Eisenhower issued a remarkable statement asserting the privileged nature of White House conversations. He explained that "it is essential to efficient and effective administration that employees of the Executive Branch be in a position to be completely candid in advising with each other on official matters" without those conversations being subject to congressional scrutiny. Therefore he blocked all employees of the Department of Defense, including John Adams, from discussing in the hearings any "conversations or communications" that constituted confidential advice to the president or to his advisers. The January 21 meeting was off limits, as were any other conversations in the White House on the McCarthy affair.[49]

Two days later Eisenhower brilliantly explained to the press that his order asserting executive privilege was designed not to cut off information but to keep the hearings from becoming a fishing expedition. "Far from trying to get any investigation off track," he said with no hint of guile, "I was merely trying to keep it on the rails." It was important, he stressed, that "the public know the facts."[50]

With Eisenhower's order blocking testimony by Executive branch personnel, the army-McCarthy hearings became a fruitless sideshow. The army's charges had embarrassed McCarthy, but McCarthy's vigorous and crafty defense showed the army was a bungling bureaucracy, prone to personnel errors and bad judgment. Yet the hearings served one crucial purpose: by putting on national television the brutish, hostile, sneering, and demagogic style of Joe McCarthy, they fatally damaged the senator's reputation. He liked to portray himself as a heroic underdog, daring to challenge the hidden conspiracies and underhanded dealings of a faceless and immoral government. But after two months of pointless outbursts, threats, and farcical allegations, McCarthy looked fatigued, wounded, even broken. It was only a matter of time before the senators themselves, so unwilling to oppose McCarthy when he was popular but so finely attuned to the shift in public opinion, turned on him.

It is sometimes said that Eisenhower played the pivotal role in destroying McCarthy. That is too generous an assessment. The Adams report on Cohn's abuses of power, combined with the president's statement on executive privilege, certainly stymied McCarthy. But these were tactical, parliamentary maneuvers, designed less to hurt McCarthy than to shield Eisenhower. The closest the president came to attacking McCarthyism directly was a speech at Columbia University's bicentennial celebrations on May 31, 1954. Ike wanted to use the occasion to strike out in favor of freedom of thought, and his team of speechwriters prepared a soaring address, whose peroration was aimed clearly at McCarthy. "If we allow ourselves," he told the audience, "to be persuaded that every individual, or party, that takes issue with our own convictions is necessarily wicked or treasonous—then indeed we are approaching the end of freedom's road. . . . Our dedication to truth and freedom, at home and abroad, does not require—and cannot tolerate—fear, threat, hysteria, and intimidation." The speech was interrupted by applause 25 times.[51]

Of course Ike would not mention McCarthy by name. He set a tone, however, and others now moved to take their place by his side. On June 1, the day after Eisenhower's Columbia speech, one of the sharpest attacks on McCarthy ever made was read out on the floor of the Senate by a venerable and largely unknown conservative Republican from Vermont named Ralph Flanders. He seized the moral high ground and beckoned others to follow. A 73-year-old mechanical engineer and bank president, impeccable in his Yankee reserve and disgust for McCarthy's foul antics, Senator Flanders chose to denounce McCarthy in public in words that Eisenhower would never dare utter. Speaking to a dead-silent Senate chamber, just steps away from a furious and seething William Knowland, Flanders pulled no punches, declaring that McCarthy's "anti-communism so completely parallels that of Adolf Hitler as to strike fear into the hearts of any defenseless minority."[52]

It was the start of a patient and successful effort by Flanders to urge his Republican colleagues to be rid of McCarthy and his poisonous behavior. On June 11 Flanders introduced a resolution to strip McCarthy of his chairmanships; on July 20, gaining some momentum, Flanders called for the outright censure of McCarthy. Months of bitter infighting among Republicans postponed the vote, but finally, on December 2, a resolution of condemnation passed, 67–22, all the Democrats voting in favor, and all the nays coming from the unrepentant and anti-Eisenhower phalanx of the Old Guard, McCarthyite to the bitter end.[53]

VIII

How then to assess Eisenhower's role in the denouement of McCarthyism? Certainly the president played his hand well, supervising the accumulation of evidence in the Adams dossier and wielding executive privilege like a drawbridge, swiftly pulled up to stop the attacking hordes. But he was always on the defensive. From mid-1953 on, Eisenhower spoke out against the excesses of McCarthyism without mentioning McCarthy himself. His speeches were often elliptical, hortatory statements and were largely ineffective, too bland to rally others to his cause and too opaque to hurt McCarthy. Indeed it cannot be said that Eisenhower showed much moral courage in confronting what he knew to be a reprehensible demagogue who was holding Congress hostage to his personal crusade against subversives. Ike had approached McCarthy as an experienced prizefighter might have assessed a hard-punching brawler: he played rope-a-dope until McCarthy, exhausted and out of ideas, lowered his guard. Then Eisenhower struck with a series of powerful jabs. But he did not land the fatal blow. Rather McCarthy was undone chiefly by his own reckless behavior, his lies, his aggression, and his limitless appetite for cruelty. Eisenhower protected himself and the presidency from the worst of McCarthyism, but it was the Senate itself that finally brought McCarthy to heel, stripping him of his committee posts, condemning him for his disreputable behavior, and, worst of all, ignoring him. Within a few years his self-loathing and heavy drinking killed him off for good.

The demise of McCarthy did not put an end to Red hunting, however. On the contrary, the Eisenhower administration had long stipulated that it could clean up the government using legal methods. As the army-McCarthy hearings came to their miserable and anticlimactic end in late June, Eisenhower pressed ahead with his own anticommunist agenda, happy to embrace the political benefits of being tough on alleged subversion. At the very moment that Ike was extolling the virtues of freedom of thought in his Columbia address, one of America's greatest free thinkers, J. Robert Oppenheimer, was being slowly cut to ribbons in an excruciating secret hearing before the Atomic Energy Commission.

To read the transcripts of the Oppenheimer hearings held by the Personnel Security Board of the AEC is to see McCarthyism at work without McCarthy. Oppenheimer, the crucial figure in leading the wartime research project that developed the atomic bomb, had been directing the Institute for Advanced Study at Princeton since 1947. He also served as the chairman of the AEC's General Advisory Committee, and in this role he expressed support for the international control of nuclear energy and raised doubts about the moral desirability of building a hydrogen bomb. He grew uneasy about the arms race and hoped that science could be turned away from its wartime function as an adjunct of the national security state. But by 1953 powerful institutional and bureaucratic interests wanted to see nuclear weapons produced at breakneck speed; Oppenheimer's counsel of caution was now considered suspect, perhaps "disloyal." In December 1953 the FBI turned over to the AEC old evidence, much of it accurate, about Oppenheimer's sympathy and support for left-wing causes dating back to the 1930s. In another time, perhaps, decade-old allegations of left-wing attitudes might not have amounted to much. After all, few could doubt that Oppenheimer had proved his patriotism during the war by guiding the production of the atomic bomb. Yet the administration knew that if they were seen as shielding Oppenheimer, they would be vulnerable to accusations of a cover-up of subversion. The issue was "real hot," "the biggest news we've had down here yet," wrote an anxious Jim Hagerty in his diary.[54]

The new director of the AEC, Adm. Lewis Strauss, an old antagonist of Oppenheimer's, was determined to suspend Oppenheimer's security clearance pending an investigation. From April 12 to May 6, 1954, at the height of the army-McCarthy hearings, the AEC conducted a detailed analysis of Oppenheimer's personal history, reviewing material and calling witnesses, including Oppenheimer himself, to discuss the evidence. The hearings, unlike the McCarthy circus, were closed. A three-person board, chaired by a former secretary of the army and now president of the University of North Carolina, Gordon Gray, poured over tidbits of information about Oppenheimer's donations to Spanish loyalist causes in the 1930s, his close friendships with left-wing activists, his cultivation of collectivist ideals, and more. They also delved into his attitudes toward the development of the hydrogen bomb, which he had opposed just at the moment the government deemed this weapon crucial for national security. In a 2–1 decision the board recommended to the AEC that Oppenheimer's security clearance not be reinstated because, although he was "a loyal citizen," he also had "fundamental defects in his character" and so could not be trusted. The national security state was now eating its own.

Eisenhower considered this a sterling example of the proper way to purge the government of subversives. He told Hagerty that his "handling of the Oppenheimer case would be such a contrast to McCarthy's tactics that the American people would immediately see the difference." But would they? Oppenheimer was now labeled a Red, or at least a fellow-traveling Pink. His reputation was ruined, his career in physics largely over, and his great contributions to science and to victory in World War II now tarnished by allegations of communist sympathies. If the Gray board's methods had been more scrupulous than McCarthy's, the results were the same: the personal destruction of a decent patriot whose only crime was a persistent sympathy toward political ideals considered dubious in an age of peril.[55]

From midsummer 1954 on, the administration carefully ignored McCarthy but embraced his Red-hunting agenda. In early June Eisenhower crowed about his record in this area, citing the conviction of 41 communist leaders, the indictment of 20 more, the targeting of 255 political organizations for their communist sympathies, and the deportation of 352 "alien subversives." He told the press, "The constant surveillance of Communists in this country is a 24-hour, 7-days-a-week, 52-weeks-a-year job." By late August the president and Congress had hammered out the Communist Control Act of 1954, which outlawed the Communist Party in America. The CPUSA was not in fact a "party," Congress asserted, but a criminal conspiracy. Furthermore labor unions that contained any communists would be stripped of their legal standing. The Senate passed the bill 79–0, and the House could find but two nay votes against this assault on the political freedoms of American citizens to organize. Eisenhower embraced the bill and hailed its usefulness "in our fight to destroy communism in this country."[56]

CHAPTER 7

DARK ARTS FOR A COLD WAR

"The things we did were 'covert.'"

I

ON FEBRUARY 26, 1953, ALLEN DULLES TOOK OFFICE AS THE DIrector of the Central Intelligence Agency; he held the job for the duration of the Eisenhower administration, departing under a cloud in 1961 after the failed invasion of Cuba's Bay of Pigs. Dulles left behind a significant legacy. The CIA was initially designed to analyze intelligence gathered by a variety of government and military entities. With Eisenhower's active support, Dulles transformed the agency into the operational headquarters of a secret struggle against the Soviet Union and many other nations considered threatening to American interests. Eisenhower's CIA went way beyond intelligence analysis; it engaged in global propaganda, foreign sabotage, subversion, economic warfare, coups d'état, and political assassination. Not until the mid-1970s, when congressional investigations revealed the scale and scope of these activities, was any real restraint placed upon the agency. In the Age of Eisenhower the CIA became fully integrated into the everyday practice of American statecraft, and it remains so to this day.

In the demonology of the cold war, the first few years of the Eisenhower administration hold an especially prominent place. It was then that two major CIA covert operations—in Iran and Guatemala—were launched, in addition to numerous smaller acts of subversion against communist-leaning countries. But these two covert actions, reprehensible and damaging as they were, tend to obscure our perception of the larger canvas. The CIA was more than just a cabal of putschists. In fact the CIA became an incubator for a much wider and arguably more consequential set of ideas and innovations about how America could use its power—its intellectual, scientific, military, economic, and moral power—to defeat communism everywhere in the world. The coups in Iran and Guatemala were symptoms of a larger pathology, namely, the delegation by the American president and Congress of enormous power and resources to a largely unaccountable and opaque agency to conduct a range of subversive and violent operations against the nation's enemies. Here, in the story of the growth of the CIA, is the most striking evidence that Eisenhower, who warned later generations about the dangers of the military-industrial complex, did so much to build it.[1]

The man at the center of the story did not look much like a spymaster. Unlike his older brother, Foster, Allen Dulles was an outgoing, gregarious, and gruffly charming man, a tweed-wearing, pipe-smoking, mustachioed figure, full of hearty Ivy League backslapping and warm guffaws. Where Foster was rigid, ponderous, and boring, Allen was impulsive, intellectually curious, disheveled, and disorganized. Allen was a broad though not necessarily deep thinker. He was the fox to his brother's hedgehog: Foster's singular brooding obsession was the communist threat emanating from Moscow, while Allen saw the world as a kaleidoscope of challenges and possibilities. Unlike the lugubrious Foster, Allen charmed everyone he met—a crucial asset in a man whose career depended on people telling him their secrets. Indeed he was a successful seducer not just of secret agents but of women, with whom he had innumerable affairs.

Outwardly different, Foster and Allen were nonetheless intimate confidantes. They had grown up together and spent summers basking in the sun and fishing on the shores of Lake Ontario at the family summer home. There the boys whiled away evenings transfixed by the stories of their grandfather, former secretary of state John W. Foster, who had served under President Benjamin Harrison. (Their uncle, Robert Lansing, would occupy that office during World War I under Woodrow Wilson.) Allen and Foster schooled at Princeton, practiced law together at the distinguished New York firm Sullivan and Cromwell, and during their Washington years played tennis, swam, and had drinks together regularly at the McLean, Virginia, home of their brilliant sister, Eleanor—another Dulles standout, who earned a Harvard Ph.D. in economics and worked in the State Department as a German expert.

Allen came into intelligence work by chance. He entered the diplomatic service in 1916, just a few years out of Princeton, and served in posts in Austria and Switzerland. He worked alongside his brother at the Paris Peace

Conference of 1919, and then went to Berlin and Constantinople. Although he practiced law beginning in 1926, he never lost his interest in government work, and in the 1930s he did periodic tours of duty at the League of Nations in Geneva. In 1942 he was approached by another well-connected New York–Ivy League–Wall Street Republican, Col. William Donovan, about serving in a new intelligence organization. The Office of Strategic Services (OSS) had been created by FDR to gather intelligence on the nation's enemies, and Donovan wanted a discreet figure he could trust to help run it.

Dulles accepted immediately. Donovan sent him to Bern, Switzerland, in the fall of 1942 to establish a listening post, using an assignment to the American legation as a cover. Over the course of more than two years, Dulles developed a rich list of contacts—European bankers, lawyers, intellectuals, industrialists, bureaucrats, and émigrés—who provided him with useful intelligence about Nazi Germany. He found sources of information through contacts with the French resistance, with anti-Nazi Germans, even inside the German Foreign Office. His success at penetrating the Third Reich became legendary. By early 1944 he had even learned and reported to Washington the details of the "Valkyrie" circle of plotters who were aiming to assassinate Hitler.[2]

The OSS, which had begun as a shoestring operation run by amateurs and oddballs, was by war's end a global enterprise, active in Europe, the Mediterranean, and China. It had 3,500 civilian employees and over 8,000 military personnel. But all this was dismantled after the war as the nation demobilized. Not until July 1947, under the pressures of the intensifying cold war, did President Truman devote attention to building up the intelligence services. The National Security Act created the National Security Council, chaired by the president, which in turned would supervise the new Central Intelligence Agency, whose director reported to the president. Quite quickly the CIA's mandate expanded to include not just the collection of intelligence but active covert offensive operations against the nation's foreign enemies. In June 1948 the NSC created a new division within the CIA. Despite its innocuous name, the Office of Policy Coordination had a breathtaking remit. According to its charter, NSC 10/2, it would be responsible for "propaganda, economic warfare, preventive direct action, including sabotage, anti-sabotage, demolition and evacuation measures, subversion against hostile states, including assistance to underground resistance movements, guerillas and refugee liberation groups, and support of indigenous anti-communist elements in threatened countries of the free world." The only requirement was deniability: these covert operations were to be designed so that "any U.S. government responsibility for them is not evident to unauthorized persons and that if uncovered the U.S. government can plausibly disclaim any responsibility for them." Instead of gathering and analyzing intelligence, the CIA was now going to become an active combatant in the struggle against communism and its allies.[3]

The man tasked to run the Office of Policy Coordination was Frank Wisner, an energetic, imaginative, intensely driven, and finally tragic figure of the early clandestine service. Born in Mississippi in 1909 and educated at the University of Virginia, he was a first-rate student and athlete. Giving up his promising legal career, he joined the navy at age 32 and eventually found his way to the OSS in 1943. With daring assignments in Cairo, Istanbul, Bucharest, and occupied Germany, Wisner burnished his credentials as one of the most eager underground operatives of the era. As head of the OPC, Wisner presided over the rapid growth of the CIA's covert projects. His office soon had 2,800 full-time employees in 47 overseas stations and burned through a budget of $80 million a year. Wisner concentrated mainly on targets inside the European communist bloc. He believed that the thousands of Soviet and East European émigrés who had fled west after the war could be used as the spearhead of a secret anticommunist underground. Many of them were brought in to help staff Radio Free Europe, though whenever they were sent back behind the Iron Curtain they were almost immediately arrested. Wisner found it was extremely hard to penetrate the Soviet bloc, despite millions of dollars and many ingenious projects. By 1951 the CIA would look to softer targets where covert operations could notch up a few easier wins.[4]

As the CIA grew, it was aided enormously by a compliant Congress. Rather than act as a watchdog, Congress ceded control of covert activities to the president. In June 1949 Truman signed into law the Central Intelligence Agency Act, which gave a free pass to the CIA to receive and spend government money off the books: "In the interests of the security of the foreign intelligence activities of the United States," and so that "the Director of Central Intelligence shall be responsible for protecting intelligence sources and methods from unauthorized disclosure, the Agency shall be exempted from . . . any other laws which require the publication or disclosure of the organization, functions, names, official titles, salaries, or numbers of personnel employed by the Agency." A legal blanket was thus thrown over the agency's operations and functions. In addition, money appropriated to the

CIA would not need to be accounted for. "The sums made available to the Agency," the law stated, "may be expended without regard to the provisions of law and regulations relating to the expenditure of government funds; and for objects of a confidential, extraordinary, or emergency nature, such expenditures to be accounted for solely on the certificate of the Director and every such certificate shall be deemed a sufficient voucher for the amount therein certified." The new spy agency thus possessed unparalleled freedom in waging the cold war.[5]

The CIA did not distinguish itself in its early years, however. It failed to anticipate the rapid development of a Soviet atomic bomb, first tested in August 1949, and notably failed to predict the outbreak of the Korean War in June 1950. Truman called on Eisenhower's wartime chief of staff and former ambassador to the Soviet Union, Gen. Walter Bedell Smith, to take the reins of the intelligence agency. Smith, a sour, demanding workaholic and masterful administrator who was nearly incapacitated by painful ulcers, took over in October 1950 and called on Allen Dulles, the experienced wartime spymaster, for help. In January 1951 Dulles took the title of deputy director for plans, with a remit to oversee both intelligence collection and the conduct of covert operations; in late August, Smith appointed him deputy director of the agency, and Wisner took over as the head of plans. The Dulles-Wisner team, now in charge of all covert operations, would have a dramatic impact on American foreign relations in the coming years.[6]

Dulles had long been a believer in the promise of covert activities to frustrate the expansion of communism. He would now get a chance to prove his ideas. Truman approved a policy document in October 1951 called NSC 10/5 that demanded "the intensification of covert operations" in order to "place the maximum strain on the Soviet structure of power." Truman's security team wanted more of everything: the cultivation of secret resistance cells in the Soviet bloc, a vigorous psychological warfare campaign, sabotage, espionage, and even direct guerrilla activities inside the communist states. In April 1952 Smith reported to the NSC on their progress. Between 1949 and 1952 the CIA had tripled its number of clandestine operations. "These cold war projects," he wrote, "are worldwide in scope" and included "psychological warfare as well as paramilitary operations; denial programs with respect to strategic materials; stockpiling on a limited scale in strategic areas to assist the military in the event of war; the organization and planning of sabotage teams to support resistance operations"; and other "stay-behind movements" to be used in the event of war. The CIA that Dulles took over in February 1953 had gone from monitoring and studying the enemy to waging all-out subversive war.[7]

II

President Eisenhower looked at the CIA and its capabilities through the prism of the Second World War. As supreme commander in Europe, he had relied on secret intelligence, especially the priceless information achieved through the decryption of German signals traffic, known as Ultra. Eisenhower had also valued special operations behind enemy lines, such as the use of secret resistance networks to gather information and conduct sabotage, the creation of underground cells, and the dissemination of propaganda. Transposing this experience onto the cold war, he believed that the Soviet regime, like the Nazi Third Reich, aimed to control the geography and resources of Eurasia, to expand across the world, and to destroy America itself. Missiles and armies might deter a Soviet invasion of Western Europe, but the challenge of the 1950s was to halt the communist infection on the periphery, in the Third World especially. America had to find new means to weaken the ties binding the Soviet imperium. The stakes were extremely high, and if Eisenhower had any qualms about the ethics of using secret and often brutal means to destroy America's enemies, he never expressed them.

When Eisenhower looked at the world map in early 1953, he saw a landscape dotted with brush fires. What he called "the free world" faced threats from nationalism, anticolonial liberation movements, socialist and communist agitation, and direct military aggression. The arc of danger circled the globe: from the Caribbean and Latin America to the eastern Mediterranean and Persian Gulf, across Pakistan and India, through Southeast Asia, Taiwan, and Korea, it seemed as if America and its allies were on the defensive. Eisenhower wanted to project American power and contain Soviet influence while avoiding any direct provocation that might trigger war. Covert operations provided one way of squaring this circle. The first chance to go on the offensive came just six weeks into his presidency, not in Asia or in Europe but in the Middle East, in the oil-rich monarchy of Iran.

On March 1, 1953, Eisenhower received a memo from the CIA about the worsening of the Western position in Iran. In words surely designed to catch the president's attention, the CIA reported that "a Communist takeover [in Iran] is becoming more and more of a possibility." This was a dire prognosis indeed. Three days later the National Security Council took up the issue in only its seventh meeting of the new administration. CIA director Dulles summarized the Iranian situation in apocalyptic terms. If Iran should fall to the communists, he told the president, not only would the Soviet Union gain access to Iran's oil, but "there was little doubt that in short order the other areas of the Middle East, with some 60% of the world's oil reserves, would fall into Communist control." His brother, the secretary of state, solemnly agreed. "The Soviets had played their game in Iran very cleverly," he said. Treasury Secretary George Humphrey declared that he was "shocked" at this news and asked Foster Dulles if he really believed that "Russia would ultimately secure Iran." Dulles sadly replied "in the affirmative." Added National Security Adviser Robert Cutler, "With the loss of Iran, we would lose the neighboring countries of the Middle East."[8]

Was the situation so dangerous? Were the Soviets banging at the gates of Tehran? In fact, as Allen and Foster Dulles knew very well, events in Iran were rather more complex and fluid than they represented to the president. But in the forum of an NSC meeting, when many items are competing for the president's attention, a cabinet officer who speaks of complexity and nuance will soon find his voice drowned out by those who insist on simplicity. And the Dulles brothers knew how to make their voices heard.

Iran had been a source of anxiety for the United States for over a decade. In 1941, as the Second World War raged, the Soviet Union and Britain occupied Iran under an agreement that ensured vital Iranian oil would keep flowing northward into the Soviet war machine then fighting Hitler. The two Great Powers pledged to withdraw their military forces within six months of the end of the war. Until that time they used Iran as a valuable supply depot and transit station to supply the USSR in its hour of need. In 1943 FDR, Churchill, and Stalin met at Tehran to discuss war strategy, famously ignoring the 24-year-old shah of Iran, Mohammad Reza Pahlavi, dismissing him as though he were an errand boy. After the war the Soviets were slow to depart; it took more than a year of tense negotiations and Anglo-American pressure to pry them out of northern Iran. Even after they withdrew in 1946, the West understood that the Soviet Union could if it wished sweep down into Iran and seize a valuable geopolitical prize.

Although the Soviets had departed, Britain still exercised enormous influence in Iran through the Anglo-Iranian Oil Company, which since the start of the century had pumped, refined, transported, and sold Iranian oil on the world market. Its principal stockholder was the British government, and for many Iranians the AIOC represented the foreign exploitation of

Iranian resources. The forum for the expression of these grievances was the Iranian Parliament, which under the constitution was subject to the shah but which, given the passivity of the monarch, had come to assume a leading role in public life. Voices within the Parliament from across the political spectrum expressed a desire to take back control of Iran's most valuable asset, its oil resources.

The call to nationalize the oil industry held great political appeal to Iranians. In April 1951 a new National Front government came to power in Tehran, led by a Western-educated, 70-year-old anti-British nationalist named Mohammad Mossadeq, who promised the expulsion of foreign influence from the nation. Mossadeq rallied many Iranians to his cause by arguing that Iran could not modernize, nor democratize, as long as it was ruled by a powerful monarchy and policed by a royalist army, and as long as its principal source of wealth—oil—was controlled by foreigners. Just a few weeks after taking office, Mossadeq won approval from Parliament for the nationalization of the oil industry. His actions pleased Iranians but deeply worried American officials. According to the CIA, "the policy of the National Front at this time plays directly into Soviet hands." The stage was set for an ugly confrontation.[9]

The British briefly contemplated answering this challenge with an armed seizure of the vast British-built refinery works on the island of Abadan, just where the Shatt al-Arab river meets the Persian Gulf. But the risks were too great that the Soviets might intervene in response, and British forces were too small for such a daring operation. Instead the British tried economic pressure as well as diplomacy. The Royal Navy began to seize vessels carrying Iranian oil on the grounds that the cargo was stolen, while other large oil companies also ceased trade with Iran. The result was a virtual blockade of Iran's oil exports. The British also demanded payment from Iran that would compensate them for the investment they had made in the oil industry and refineries. The Iranians refused. In July 1951 President Truman sent Averell Harriman to Tehran to try to broker a deal, but the Iranians did not yield. The British then asked the United Nations to take up their claim, arguing that Iran had violated an international treaty. But the UN decided it had no jurisdiction. Britain's legal claims were exhausted by 1952. Casting Mossadeq as a dangerous, misguided Oriental zealot who could not see reason and whose policies were likely to do his country grave harm, the British government concluded that the only action left open to them was to replace him with a more pliant leader. But in October 1952, sensing that the British were likely to resort to such dirty tricks, Mossadeq severed relations with the British government and expelled all British officials from the country. The end of British predominance in Iran created an opening that the United States was quite willing to fill.[10]

Mossadeq was a populist, a nationalist, and an anti-imperialist, but he was certainly not a communist. The CIA's Iran analysts were smart enough to understand the difference. Yet the problem they faced was that Mossadeq's power and popularity depended upon sweeping anti-British and anti-Western sentiments that, they feared, would surely open the way to more radical political ideas. His period in office had inflamed opinion in Iran against the West, had weakened the role of the shah—already a vacillating and fragile figure—and had triggered a serious crisis in the economy, since Iran's oil income had disappeared. Mossadeq had created an atmosphere of upheaval and intrigue, and rumors in 1952 abounded that either the army or the Shi'a religious leader Abul-Qasim Kashani might attempt a coup to overthrown him. Mossadeq's radicalism had also legitimated the political platform of the Tudeh Party (the Party of the Masses, or communists), which since the early 1940s had emerged as a major political actor in Iran, drawing support from labor groups, youth organizations, and intellectuals. If Mossadeq's government were to fall, the CIA worried, the Tudeh might profit. The Americans came to see Mossadeq as a ticking time-bomb. While CIA analysts believed that an outright communist takeover in Iran was unlikely, Mossadeq had created a dangerously unstable climate that would open the way to communist, and hence Soviet, influence. No wonder, then, that the CIA concluded at the end of 1952, "The USSR appears to believe that the Iranian situation is developing favorably."[11]

In response to this evolving crisis, the British proposed the idea of a Western-organized plot to oust Mossadeq. The idea came from C. M. "Monty" Woodhouse, a senior officer in MI6, Britain's foreign intelligence service. Like so many figures in the covert operations business, Woodhouse was a veteran of World War II: he had fought alongside the anti-Nazi Greek resistance, undertaking many hair-raising and successful acts of sabotage. In 1951–52 he led the MI6 office in Iran, and over the years he had developed close ties to Americans Allen Dulles, Walter Bedell Smith, Frank Wisner, and the U.S. ambassador in Iran, Loy Henderson. He was a trusted figure; a proposal from him would be entertained seriously. Woodhouse, now preaching to the choir, argued to his American friends that Mossadeq was an unwitting Trojan horse for Soviet influence; the longer he stayed in office, the more likely would be the penetration by the Tudeh Party of the Iranian bureaucracy. In mid-November 1952 Woodhouse presented these arguments to Smith, still head of the CIA, and to Kermit Roosevelt, head of the CIA's Near East Division. The Americans were not ready to commit to a violent overthrow of Mossadeq. The outgoing Truman administration still held out some hope that the Iranian prime minister could be pressed one last time to work out an agreement to the oil problem with the British in exchange for greater development aid. But the seed had been planted, and by the time Ike's new national security team was in place, the coup plan had taken root. The Dulles brothers had discussed it informally among colleagues, and in February 1953 Smith, who was on his way out as director, gave approval to CIA planners to draw up a proposal for discussion at the highest levels of government to oust Mossadeq from power.[12]

It is not surprising to find the new Eisenhower team embracing the idea of a coup. This is not because they were reckless—Ike was always cautious about the use of force—but because of a convergence of factors that served to make Iran a critical test case for the new president. The campaign of 1952 had stressed the need for boldness in handling foreign affairs. Republicans had chided Truman for his failures in Korea, his "loss" of China, and his alleged satisfaction with standing on the defensive in the face of the Soviet onslaught. Furthermore the CIA reports that reached the president summarized a complex picture in bold strokes: Mossadeq was not himself a communist, but his regime was letting the communists in through the back door. If he stayed in power, the West would be forever barred from Iran, and the "loss of Iran" would be added to the rolls of ignominy alongside the loss of Czechoslovakia in 1948, the loss of China in 1949, and the invasion of South Korea in 1950. The CIA's most recent National Intelligence Estimate of the Near and Middle East, prepared in January 1953, stated, "The West has a specific and basic concern with the extensive oil resources and strategic location of the area." Given that strategic picture, "the loss of Iran to Communism would be a blow to U.S. and Western prestige and would increase the vulnerability of the remainder of the Middle East and of the Indian subcontinent." For the new president, Iran would be the place where he would draw the line.[13]

Documents from the CIA files (some released quite recently) have allowed scholars to re-create the planning and execution of the coup in great detail. The documents show that, in the words of the 1974 secret CIA history of the operation, the coup was "conceived and approved at the highest levels of government." On April 4, 1953, Allen Dulles approved a budget of $1 million to be used by the CIA station in Tehran for the coup. In mid-May British and American intelligence agents gathered in Nicosia, Cyprus, to hammer out a plan. After two weeks a proposal was sent to London and Washington for approval. The plan, code-named TP-AJAX, was quite simple. The British and American secret services had extensive contacts in the Iranian Army, industrial circles, the press, and police, as well as among politicians who were hostile to Mossadeq. Using these well-placed and well-bribed assets, the CIA would help to stir up intense anti-Mossadeq fervor in the press and on the streets. The shah would then dismiss Mossadeq from office in order to reestablish order. His replacement would be a senior army officer, Gen. Fazlollah Zahedi, a former member of Mossadeq's cabinet, whose supporters in the army would stand at the ready to rally to him and the shah. The shah's role was crucial, for he had the legal authority to act against Mossadeq, even if he proved to be an inconstant and fearful player in this drama. On July 1 Prime Minister Winston Churchill and Foreign Minister Anthony Eden approved the plan; on July 11 President Eisenhower and Secretary John Foster Dulles did the same.[14]

The propaganda campaign against Mossadeq greatly intensified. "Every agent of the press with which we or the United Kingdom had working relations went all out against Mossadeq," stated the CIA's internal after-action report. "There can be no doubt whatsoever that this campaign had reached a very large audience." The CIA Art Department prepared posters and handbills, copied them by the tens of thousands, and flew them into Tehran. These materials purported to show that Mossadeq was a tool of the communists and had secretly secured the support of the Tudeh Party to sustain him in power. The propaganda also asserted that he was planning to lash out against religious leaders and the army.[15]

The coup started out well enough on August 15, when the CIA's man in Tehran, Kermit Roosevelt, secured the shah's signature on two decrees, one dismissing Mossadeq, the other appointing General Zahedi to succeed him. But Mossadeq got wind of the plan just in time, and army and police units that were still loyal to his government arrested a number of conspirators. By the morning of August 16 the coup seemed to have failed, and Zahedi went into hiding. Worse, the shah fled the country, flying to Baghdad and then on to Rome. Mossadeq's allies hailed the failure of the coup and decried the alleged American role in it.[16]

Yet the CIA team in Tehran did not give up. They worked quickly to disseminate the shah's decrees, which legitimated Zahedi as the new prime minister. Roosevelt bankrolled gangs of youths to stage riots and vandalize public buildings while posing as Tudeh supporters, thus stirring fears of a communist takeover. The shah appealed on the radio to respect Zahedi as the legally appointed premier. By August 19 the army, key politicians and clerics, and the Tehran crowds began to move away from Mossadeq. In this atmosphere of crisis and uncertainty, spontaneous pro-shah demonstrations—quite unrelated to CIA activity—began to gather across the capital. Gaining courage, Zahedi came out of hiding and made a radio broadcast claiming he was the rightful prime minister, while soldiers loyal to the shah routed pro-Mossadeq forces in a number of skirmishes that left over 100 people dead. By the evening of August 19 Mossadeq had fled; his home was ransacked and set on fire, and Zahedi's military men imposed a curfew in Tehran and started rounding up Mossadeq's supporters. The aged prime minister himself surrendered in the early morning hours on August 20, and the shah flew back to Tehran two days later to a tense but quiet city.[17]

Eisenhower was kept abreast of developments in Tehran while he was in Denver on vacation, as cable traffic from Washington to Lowry Air Force Base makes clear. In Washington the NSC looked on with relief at the positive turn of events. Meeting on August 27, Vice President Nixon and the NSC team heard the deputy director of the CIA, Gen. Charles Cabell, report on Zahedi's success in shoring up his power. According to Cabell, Zahedi was about to form a new government and eventually hold elections, which "the army will doubtless manipulate" to ensure a desirable result. Most important, "the Tudeh Party will be ruthlessly curbed." Secretary Dulles asserted that "the United States now had a second chance in Iran." In the following months thousands of Mossadeq supporters, National Front members, and Tudeh Party members were arrested. Mossadeq himself was tried and convicted and would spend the rest of his life under house arrest. The bureaucracy and military were thoroughly purged of unreliable elements. Zahedi successfully put into place the foundations of an authoritarian regime that would endure until 1979.[18]

The U.S. government quickly turned on the spigot of economic and military aid to Zahedi and his new government: $45 million in economic aid available right away, plus a $100 million military aid program. The NSC reasoned that although Iran's army was many years away from being an effective force, "military aid to Iran has great political importance apart from its military impact. Over the long term, the most effective instrument for maintaining Iran's orientation toward the West is the monarch, which in turn has the Army as its only real source of power." Military aid would "cement Army loyalty to the Shah and thus consolidate the present regime." This remarkably candid analysis dispelled any notion that the new government in Iran was based on popular support: the army, and American military aid, would prop up the shah for the next quarter century. Nixon, who visited Iran in late 1953 and met with Zahedi, reported back to the NSC in fairly blunt terms: "This government in Iran is ours. . . . Now that Mossadeq is out of the way things should be a lot better. What he did to that country is enough to hang him."[19]

The whole affair looked wonderfully successful from Washington. Naturally Eisenhower dissembled when he spoke in public about Iran. He tended to describe the events there by saying that "Iran threw off a threat of Communist domination and came strongly to our side." But in his diary he was more candid. "The things we did were 'covert,'" he wrote. "If knowledge of them became public, we would not only be embarrassed in that region, but our chances to do anything of like nature in the future would almost totally disappear." He praised Kermit Roosevelt's courage in carrying out the plot, which "seemed more like a dime novel than an historical fact." By sustaining the shah and Zahedi in power, Ike felt, the United States might "give a serious defeat to Russian intentions and plans in that area." That was how he saw the coup: as a strike against Soviet communism in a dangerous part of the world.

Eisenhower had not the slightest concern that the United States had interfered in the parliamentary functions of a sovereign state. The cold war was a long game of position, and every test mattered. By the end of 1954 his assessment of the coup had only improved. "A year ago last January," he wrote in a letter to his brother Edgar, "we were in imminent danger of losing Iran, and sixty percent of the known oil reserves of the world. You may have forgotten this. Lots of people have. But there has been no greater threat that has in recent years overhung the free world. That threat has been largely, if not totally, removed."[20]

III

To Eisenhower and his advisers, the Iran operation fit neatly into a particular view of the world. The Soviet Union sought to penetrate and destabilize vulnerable states and would use any means to achieve its purpose. In response the United States must use its own cunning, as well as inducements of aid and arms, to create strong points around the world to resist such communist subversion. In Iran, the Americans told themselves, Mossadeq was a tool of foreign interests. The shah represented tradition, continuity, and above all constitutional authority. In this telling America had sought to protect Iran from a radical and misguided opportunist. Indeed Kermit Roosevelt, the chief CIA operative in Tehran, titled his memoir *Countercoup* precisely to suggest that it was Mossadeq who was the usurper: the United States merely assisted the shah and the Iranian Army in restoring power to the nation's rightful rulers.

In light of the success of the covert plan in Iran, it was natural that such fictions would be transposed onto other cases around the world. Just as the Iran case was reaching its climax, American planners accelerated their plans to "save" another nation from the perils of communism. Just one week after the ouster of Mossadeq, the leading covert operations planners within the CIA agreed that among their next projects "Guatemala will have number one priority." This was no mere accident of timing. The success in Iran had opened up a new vista for the CIA, which after all was still a fairly small and unproven agency. It was now possible to imagine a panoply of covert actions that could turn the tide of communist subversion around the world. Central America was the next front in this long twilight war, and Guatemala an especially vulnerable sector in what Ike thought of as the battlements of freedom.

And yet the Guatemalan case differed significantly from Iran. Roosevelt, the star of his own Persian drama, could weave a somewhat plausible story about the legitimacy of the shah, the links between the Tudeh Party and Moscow, and the crucial role of the United States in restoring the shah's authority. In Guatemala there was no corollary. This was a small, poor agricultural nation whose principal source of wealth, its land, was owned by a tiny elite of plantation owners and foreign companies. From the start of the 20th century Guatemalan landowners and an authoritarian government had enriched themselves by growing coffee beans and bananas for export and by enticing investment from wealthy American bankers, industrialists, and corporations. The exploitative practices of one such commercial giant, the United Fruit Company, became a rallying cry for left-wing organizers and agricultural workers. In 1944, in the face of widespread unrest from teachers, students, and workers, the country's dictator yielded power. Nationwide elections brought a moderately conservative government to power, which opened up a period of political reform in the country. Guatemalans were writing their own democratic story.

While the army and landed elites continued to wield strong influence in the country, after 1944 political parties flourished, unions were formed in many industries, and Guatemalans had high expectations of future reforms to the social and economic structure of the nation. A federation of workers' unions was formed, and communist activists from other Central American nations found refuge in Guatemala. In 1948 leftist politicians formed the Guatemalan Workers' Party, just at a time of extreme U.S. anxiety about the spread of communist political activity. Corporate interests looked with worry at the formation of labor unions and the spurring of worker activism. The United Fruit Company, owner of huge banana plantations in Guatemala and a company that relied on cheap, nonunionized agricultural labor, pulled strings in Washington to make sure the U.S. government was fully aware of the threats to their interests. By August 1950 CIA officials had locked in on Guatemala as a likely source of anti-American activity in the Western Hemisphere, though even they could not find evidence of direct Soviet interference there.[21]

In late 1950 a charismatic army colonel named Jacobo Arbenz Guzman, a man of progressive, even socialist views who had backed the 1944 Revolution, won the presidential election and took office on March 15, 1951. Though not a communist, he wished to see the glaring inequalities in his nation rectified through a major land reform project, and he counted in his government a number of prominent communist labor leaders. He was influenced by them and shared some of their views about the basic inequalities of the capitalist system. In June 1952 Arbenz signed Decree 900, which sought to expropriate mostly fallow and underused land from large estates, divide it into small parcels, and sell it to farmers. The former owners were to be compensated for their losses. Even the *New York Times* editorial page saw these reforms as "long overdue." The paper argued that "in promoting social justice there should be a relatively fair distribution of the land"; it was wrong to tarnish the plan with the epithet "communistic."[22]

These views were not shared by major private companies like United Fruit, which now waged an aggressive legal and economic campaign to try to force Arbenz to withdraw his proposals. Arbenz's reforms were not directed from Moscow or part of some plot to create a Marxist utopia among the humid plantations of Central America. Arbenz wanted to bring modernity and development to his poor country by stimulating small farming and rolling back the predatory economic practices of large companies and their allies. But the local origins of his policies were lost on the U.S. government. In the highly charged atmosphere of the early cold war, this kind of aggressive land reform aligned with the state-sponsored social reform projects being imposed by socialist and communist governments around the world.

By the spring of 1952 the CIA had come to see Arbenz and his government as "a potential threat to U.S. security," and the agency found a number of allies who shared its desire to be rid of the president. Col. Carlos Castillo Armas, a longtime rival of Arbenz who had launched an ill-fated and disorganized military coup in 1950 and later fled into exile in Honduras, regularly offered his services to anyone who would back him in launching an invasion of Guatemala. The strongman of Nicaragua, President Anastasio Somoza, approached American officials in July 1952 and proposed a plan to use Castillo Armas to oust Arbenz; the Americans just had to supply the weapons. President Truman authorized CIA director Smith to proceed with the plan, and a shipment of rifles, pistols, machine guns, and grenades was assembled in New Orleans for shipment to Castillo Armas. But word of the American support for a military coup leaked, and Truman called off the operation in October 1952. The fate of the Arbenz regime was going to be pushed off onto the new administration.[23]

Over the course of 1953 Guatemala moved rapidly up the ladder of concern. From being an irritant at the start of the year, this small "banana republic" took on menacing characteristics in the eyes of American officials. In January 1953 the State Department worried about the growing influence of the communists in Guatemalan politics and labor unions but believed that Arbenz had "the power to check or break the Communist organization at will." The communists were small in number and still dependent upon the toleration of the regime. The American ambassador there, Rudolf Schoenfeld, considered the goal of the Guatemalan communists to be "the neutralizing of Guatemala" rather than turning the country into a Soviet beachhead in the Western Hemisphere. In March 1953 Eisenhower and his NSC staff approved a general statement of aims for U.S. policy toward Latin America that emphasized the need to encourage economic development in an effort to meet the basic desire of people for an improved standard of living. While the NSC called for the "reduction and elimination of the menace of internal Communist or other anti-U.S. subversion" in the hemisphere, it seemed inclined to believe that economic aid and cooperation were the tools best suited to that goal.[24]

During the summer of 1953 the picture changed. Allen Dulles, newly installed as CIA director, his director of operations Frank Wisner, Undersecretary of State Smith, and Secretary of State John Foster Dulles all grew apprehensive about the state of affairs in Guatemala and clamored for immediate action against the regime. They had intelligence showing that Arbenz was consolidating his position by rounding up various members of Castillo Armas's network inside the country; he also tightened his alliance with the communist activists in the labor unions. Communist influence in the country and the government was "as great as ever," according to one American reporter, and the noncommunist opposition had withered. Arbenz was growing stronger while Castillo Armas was languishing in Honduras, awaiting orders to strike. The government was also proceeding rapidly with its seizure and redistribution of United Fruit land holdings. In February the government announced a plan to seize 250,000 acres of the fruit giant's land along the Pacific and in August took aim at another 174,000 acres on the Atlantic coast. The State Department framed the problem this way: "The immediate Communist objective is the elimination of American economic interests, represented in Guatemala by the United Fruit Company, the International Railways of Central America, and the Guatemalan Electric Company. The loss of these enterprises would be damaging to American interests and prestige throughout Central America." While it seemed that "the Communists are not seeking open and direct control of the Guatemalan Government," their tactics served a nefarious purpose: "to convert [Guatemala] into an indirectly controlled instrument of Communism."[25]

It was time to act. On August 12, 1953—the very same week that the CIA launched the Iran coup—the NSC gave Allen Dulles authority to implement a plan to oust President Arbenz. The scheme was optimistically labeled PB-SUCCESS and became the CIA's "number one priority." Wisner, who took command of the coup planning, instructed the new (and hard-line) American ambassador to Guatemala, John E. Peurifoy, that the CIA was "authorized to take strong action against the government of President Arbenz in the hope of facilitating a change to a more democratically oriented regime." On September 11 Wisner sent a detailed plan of action to Allen Dulles for his approval. Describing Guatemala as "the leading base of operations for Moscow-influenced Communism in Central America," Wisner stated that the CIA would now "reduce and possibly eliminate Communist power" there.[26]

PB-SUCCESS, as described by Wisner, would place Guatemala in an ever tightening vise: sending arms to anticommunist neighbors Honduras,

Nicaragua, and El Salvador; using official channels to condemn any anti-American statements made by the regime and encouraging neighboring pro-U.S. states to isolate Guatemala; deploying "covert economic warfare methods targeted against oil supplies, shipping and vital exports and imports," including attacking coffee exports; and unleashing a massive "psychological warfare operation" inside the country to destabilize the government. After this "softening up," Castillo Armas and his band of U.S.-trained and armed exiles would invade the country and oust Arbenz in a "swift, climactic military action." Just three weeks after the Iran coup, with that victory still casting a warm glow on covert operations, Allen Dulles read Wisner's plan and approved it.[27]

As it turned out, though, Guatemala was a tougher nut to crack than Iran. The CIA possessed none of the advantages that the coup plotters in Tehran enjoyed. The Guatemalan Army was loyal to Arbenz; the president was popular and democratically elected; the exiles were discredited and perceived as right-wing opportunists; neither the CIA nor the exiles had penetrated the Guatemalan press, political parties, church, or bureaucracy and could count on no rallying of these institutions to the cause of Arbenz's overthrow. The most powerful anti-Arbenz force in the country was a rapacious foreign corporation long linked to Yankee colonialism. Most damaging, in September Arbenz himself discovered the details of the plot from a defector from Castillo Armas's group and rounded up a number of conspirators. How could the plan proceed under such unfavorable circumstances?

The answer is that the Eisenhower administration, having elevated Guatemala to such a high level of threat to the national security, had no alternative but to proceed, though with a badly compromised operation. "In view of the growing Communist strength and declining non-Communist cohesion," the CIA concluded, the project "to install and sustain, covertly, a pro-U.S. government in Guatemala" must proceed "without delay." There was also domestic pressure to act: in mid-October the chairman of the Senate Foreign Relations Committee, Republican Alexander Wiley, declared, "Communism has established a strong beachhead in Guatemala," thus putting the Eisenhower administration on notice that inaction in Central America would not be acceptable. When Allen Dulles met with his top CIA planners in mid-November, he told them the coup "is a top priority operation for the whole agency and is the most important thing we are doing. I am under pressure by others to get on with this." On December 9, 1953, he allocated $3 million to PB-SUCCESS and the overthrow of Arbenz.[28]

The CIA set up a large headquarters at the Opa Locka air base in Dade County, Florida, and Allen Dulles appointed a tough, hard-charging army colonel, Albert Haney, to run it. Haney had experience in Korea running underground guerrilla activities; now he led over 100 case officers in plotting the ouster of a democratically elected head of state. In February 1954 Haney's team met with Castillo Armas and drafted a basic plan for channeling funds and weapons to his revolutionary movement. They had hopes that conservatives inside the Guatemalan Army, as well as elite landowners, would provide support and sympathy for a coup. Land reform had been controversial and indeed had antagonized the presidents of neighboring Honduras, El Salvador, and Nicaragua, who worried about the radical plans Arbenz had championed spilling over into their countries. Haney's team worked hard to spread intensive propaganda about the "communist" land reform, even launching a radio program from Miami that broadcast anticommunist messages interspersed with music. Agents put intense pressure on army officers, subjecting them to anonymous phone calls and promoting rumors of what would happen to them if they continued to support the communists. Vivid posters describing the role of Moscow in distorting Guatemala appeared in the streets. The CIA had perfected the tools needed to generate an atmosphere of crisis.

But Arbenz himself may have caused the most grievous wound to his government. In April 1954 he secretly placed a $5 million order with the Czechoslovakian government for the purchase of thousands of tons of arms with which to supply his small armed forces. In mid-May those arms arrived at Puerto Barrios, a port on Guatemala's Caribbean coast, carried by a Swedish freighter, the *Alfhem*. Wisner knew about the shipment of communist bloc arms, and although the CIA tried to intercept the ship, its arrival in Guatemala simply confirmed for the public the nefarious links between Arbenz and international communism. Neighboring Honduras now set aside any reservations it had and offered to support the American plot against Arbenz. U.S. Navy vessels moved into the Gulf of Honduras to impose a blockade, and shipments of tanks and planes now flowed into Honduras, to be deployed by Castillo Armas's band of rebels.

On June 15 Castillo Armas began an invasion of the country from his bases in Honduras, but his "army" amounted to little more than 500 men on foot—hardly a threat to the capital city. Over the course of the following week, however, Castillo Armas relied upon U.S.-supplied aircraft to drop leaflets, strafe government buildings, and occasionally launch a bomb or two on locations near Guatemala City, creating the impression of an imminent invasion. The army, which had begun to reconsider its loyalty to Arbenz, finally turned on the president and pressured him to resign. On June 27, unable to command the loyalty of his troops, he stepped down, eventually making his way to safety in Mexico. Within days a junta of army officers, in conjunction with American intelligence agents, worked out a deal to bring Castillo Armas into power. It was another home run for the CIA, as Dulles and Wisner saw it. "A great victory has been won," Wisner cabled to PB-SUCCESS headquarters in Florida.[29]

But was it such a great victory? Arbenz was no Soviet puppet but a leftist, reform-minded politician who had the bad fortune to face off against powerful foreign interests at the height of the cold war. His country posed no threat to the United States, or other Central American nations. His ouster brought down international condemnation on the coup, which was widely assumed to have been supported from Washington, and fomented anti-Americanism throughout Latin America. And Castillo Armas quickly turned into a pliant, if needy foot soldier for the United States, dependent on handouts of economic and military aid. Thereafter Guatemala endured three decades of repression, civil war, death squads, and terror. Not a legacy the Eisenhower team would wish to celebrate.

But those sorts of assessments would not become apparent until much later. In 1954 the CIA took enormous pride in its record: twice in 12 months it had engineered the overthrow of foreign governments that were seen as hostile to American interests and subject to communist pressure. Eisenhower, who had been informed of the events in Guatemala on a daily basis by the Dulles brothers, seemed fully to believe that Arbenz was little more than a Kremlin-trained operative who had to be squashed. In the days after the coup, he discussed in the NSC "the best means of publicizing the fact that the Arbenz regime had been directed from Moscow, as a means of counteracting the Communist propaganda line that the United States had intervened in the internal affairs of Guatemala." Here was a curious inversion of reality: in Ike's mind, the USSR had become the interfering party, while the allegation of a U.S.-sponsored coup was mere "propaganda."[30]

IV

In the spring of 1954, in the afterglow of the Iran operation and on the eve of the Guatemala coup, the National Security Council issued a policy document that reinforced America's newfound reliance on covert operations as a tool of statecraft in the cold war. Building upon the Truman-era commitment to using covert operations to combat the "vicious covert activities of the USSR," NSC 5412 went even further. It called for a battery of covert operations designed to "exploit troublesome problems for International Communism, impair relations between the USSR and Communist China . . . discredit the prestige and ideology of International Communism . . . counter any threat of a party of individuals directly or indirectly responsive to Communist control to achieve dominant power in a free world country . . . reduce International Communist control over any areas of the free world," and develop secret resistance networks to wage guerrilla operations in the event of war. NSC 5412 reveals the astonishing breadth and ambition of American covert operations. From coups to economic warfare, and sabotage, propaganda, and underground resistance, U.S. secret plans took aim at every aspect of communist power across the globe.[31]

And yet, despite the success of the covert operations in Iran and Guatemala, and despite the determination stated in NSC 5412 to continue to wage a hidden war against communism, Eisenhower was unhappy in mid-1954 with the state of his intelligence agency. Certainly he saw the value of covert operations and he approved NSC 5412 and its call for greater, bolder plans. But Eisenhower had bigger concerns. The "dime novel" capers of Kermit Roosevelt and Al Haney had inadvertently drawn attention away from a much bigger problem that the CIA was not adequately addressing: the need to provide the president with timely intelligence about the intentions of the Soviet Union. What kept Eisenhower awake at night was the Soviet threat, not the Guatemalan threat. The NSC had declared in a top-secret policy paper in February 1954 that with the advent of a Soviet H-bomb the previous August, the danger of the Soviet arsenal had dramatically increased. This new weapon has "placed a premium on . . . improvement of our intelligence regarding Soviet capabilities and intentions." It was the CIA's job to give the president this information, and so far it had failed.[32]

In early July 1954 Eisenhower turned to Lt. Gen. James Doolittle, a former World War II bomber pilot who had gained fame as the first American to launch a strike against mainland Japan in 1942, to ask if he would lead a task force to review the CIA. The project, as Eisenhower explained it to Doolittle, was to review not only the CIA's covert operations but "the entire National Intelligence Program," including the "collection, interpretation and dissemination of intelligence dealing with the plans, capabilities and intentions of potential enemies." Doolittle accepted the job and spent an intensive two-month period studying the CIA, interviewing its top officials, and combing through its records. What he found was unsettling: the CIA employed too many mediocre personnel; it suffered from leaks; the agency's relations with the armed services were terrible, and not much better with the State Department; the covert operations office had become too large and messy and needed a "complete reorganization."[33]

In private Doolittle was even more critical. On October 19, 1954, he met with Eisenhower in the White House and made clear that he thought the CIA's main problem was Allen Dulles himself. Though a man of deep knowledge, passion, and integrity, Doolittle said, Dulles was disorganized, a bad manager, "sloppy," "highly emotional," and surrounded by incompetent people. Also, there was "a complete lack of security consciousness through-out the organization. Too much information is leaked at cocktail parties." Eisenhower defended his CIA director, saying the agency was a "peculiar" organization and "it probably takes a strange kind of genius to run it." Yet the president could not have taken comfort from such a dismal assessment of his intelligence chief.[34]

Eisenhower seemed to anticipate the conclusions of the Doolittle Re-port, because he had already tasked another high-level committee of sci-entists to consider new means of finding out more about the Soviet nuclear threat. On March 27 Eisenhower met with his Science Advisory Commit-tee and told its members of his anxiety about the inadequacy of America's weapons technology, especially the inability to detect and deter a surprise attack by the Soviets on the American homeland. What means could be de-vised to guard against a surprise attack and ensure America's overall safety in the nuclear age?

The man to answer that question was James R. Killian, president of MIT, a skilled administrator who had significant experience dating back to the Second World War in linking his research institution to national defense needs. In the summer of 1954, on Ike's orders, Killian assembled a team of leading scientists and innovators to begin "a searching review of weapons and intelligence technology." Killian formed three task forces: one to explore means of improving America's offensive striking power; one to examine new means of defense and early warning against attack; and one to consider new sources of intelligence on the Soviet threat. The Killian group was officially called the Technological Capabilities Panel, and for five months it examined the problem of using new technology to strengthen America's nuclear and strategic forces. "There was a growing realization," Killian wrote later, "that thermonuclear weapons in the hands of the Soviets posed a threat of terrible dimensions that required urgent efforts to construct new defenses." His final report, sent to the president in February 1955, bore an arresting title: "Meeting the Threat of a Surprise Attack." It offered a breathtaking list of military and technological initiatives that needed urgent attention. The Killian Report, along with NSC 162/2 and NSC 5412, sketched a vision of a powerful and enduring warfare state.[35]

The lengthy report began by discussing the likely evolution of the balance of power between the United States and the Soviet Union in the next decade. In Period I, the current moment, the scientists perceived one great U.S. strength—a significant advantage in air power and deliverable nuclear bombs—and one great U.S. weakness: poor early-warning technology and poor intelligence. America in 1955 was thus vulnerable to surprise attack. By 1960, however—Period II—Killian thought the situation would have changed. The U.S. nuclear arsenal, he predicted, would have grown enormously to include many "multi-megaton weapons," as well as the deployment of intercontinental ballistic missiles. Furthermore the early-warning systems and interceptor fighters would be much improved. "Our military superiority may never be so great again," Killian said of the year 1960. He urged the president to consider that in the late 1950s, the United States would have such strength that it might be able to impose a settlement on the cold war rivalry.

But Killian argued that after the 1960s the picture would change again. In Phase III the Soviets would gradually catch up, building ICBMs of their own, improving their own defenses, and building more powerful nuclear devices. By Period IV there would be a massive arsenal of weapons on both sides that was large enough to survive a surprise first strike and still deliver a massive counterattack. This phase might come by the middle of the 1960s. Rather than bring mutual deterrence and stability to U.S.-Soviet relations, that phase "would be a period of instability that might easily be upset by either side." A small conflict on the periphery, they feared, could easily escalate to a nuclear war. (The Cuban Missile Crisis of 1962 would show that these fears were not wholly misplaced.)

What were the implications of this timetable? For Killian the policy to be followed was clear: the United States needed a program of rapid expansion of all aspects of its weapons technology to stay ahead of the USSR as long as possible. The goal was to prolong Period II and forestall the arrival of Period IV. "We must press forward to develop more sophisticated offenses and defenses," Killian concluded. "We must constantly seek new technological breakthroughs that will bring about significant advances in our military power."[36]

Killian and his scientists delivered the report in a full-dress presentation to the president and the NSC at the White House on March 17, 1955. Their recommendations were vast in scope. In the area of offensive weapons, the report called for an immediate crash program in building an intercontinental ballistic missile that could deliver a nuclear warhead a distance of 5,500 miles. This would prove to be an enormous engineering challenge, and such ICBMs would not be ready for use until 1959. But Killian's recommendations turned what had been a stalled research program into a national effort of the "highest priority." The report also sought the production of an intermediate-range missile that could be placed on ships and submarines. Killian's team pushed for more air fields and bases at which nuclear-armed bombers could be dispersed around the country, and the scientists wanted to see innovations in aircraft fuels and the construction of a larger and more powerful class of nuclear bombs. The report also called for an extended network of early-warning radar stations across the globe and research on antiballistic missiles to shoot down incoming rockets.[37]

These programs were going to have a major impact on U.S. defense planning in the coming years, but perhaps nothing was of such immediate consequence as the recommendations of Killian's intelligence task force. Led by Edwin Land, the inventor of the Polaroid camera and a man Killian described as "an authentic genius," this team insisted that the best defense against surprise attack was more "hard facts upon which our intelligence estimates are based to provide better strategic warning" of Soviet intentions. The best way, perhaps the only way to obtain these hard facts was by sending aircraft over the Soviet Union to take high-altitude photographs of its military installations. Land and the Killian team knew that sending American planes into Soviet airspace was enormously dangerous. Indeed the U.S. Air Force had been doing just that since at least 1946. Using modified bombers such as the RB-29, the air force sent planes mostly along the periphery of the USSR in hopes of spotting and photographing important bases and industrial facilities. But since the major weapons projects were hidden deep inside the Soviet hinterland, these flights did not yield terribly valuable results. In 1951 and 1952 numerous missions were sent across Soviet territory, but Soviet radar and fighter aircraft often spotted and intercepted these flights; a considerable number of them were shot down. Eisenhower continued the practice and personally approved of occasional overflights despite the loss of aircraft and their crews. He had to balance the risk of discovery of these overflights with the urgent need to know about Soviet military hardware.[38]

And the need for intelligence only grew more pressing. In late 1953 Eisenhower learned that the Soviets had begun production of a new class of long-range bomber, the Myasishchev-4, a plane with much greater range and payload capacity than anything the USSR had built before. In May 1954, at the Moscow Air Show, the Soviets flew a number of these behemoths, labeled "Bison" bombers by the United States, over the capital, while American attachés on the roof of the U.S. Embassy snapped photographs. As one former participant in the reconnaissance program recalled, the new plane "generated an intelligence crisis," for now it was assumed that the heartland of the United States was vulnerable to an attack from the Soviet bomber fleet. The prospect of an atomic "first strike" upon the major cities of America could no longer be discounted.[39]

The Killian team was fired up by the challenge of finding a way to learn more about the scope of the Soviet threat. Land was aware that engineers at Lockheed Aircraft Corporation had been drawing up plans for an aircraft that could fly into Soviet airspace at such an altitude as to be beyond the reach of interceptor aircraft, and maybe even radar. The plane they sketched—and would become the famous U-2—was essentially "a jet-powered glider," stripped down to its absolute minimum and carrying high-powered cameras. American engineers believed that Soviet radar could not detect an aircraft flying above 65,000 feet, and also assumed Soviet fighters could not intercept an aircraft at that altitude. Such an airplane, defying Soviet air defenses, could provide instant detailed data about the Soviets' capabilities and perhaps catch them in the act of a sudden buildup of their atomic forces. The U.S. air force, however, wary about diverting more funds into reconnaissance planes and away from the expansion of the bomber fleet, wasn't interested. Curiously the director of Central Intelligence was also wary. Dulles desired the fruits of the new technology but did not wish to divert his resources into an untested project that would take attention away from human intelligence and old-fashioned spycraft.

For Killian and Land, however, the growing Soviet capabilities strengthened their arguments about the need for a secret surveillance airplane. After assessing the Lockheed design, they took the case directly to the president. According to Killian's later memoir, Eisenhower "asked many hard questions" and then approved the concept of the new U-2 spy plane. It was Eisenhower himself who saw the need to keep the plane out of the hands of the military bureaucracy and to allow the CIA to run with it. Energized by this expression of presidential support, Killian and Land now went back to Dulles to press him to accept ownership of the project. They urged him to see the problem as one of bureaucratic control, in which the CIA must control intelligence gathering. "You must always assert your first right to pioneer in scientific techniques for collecting intelligence," Land wrote to Dulles in early November. The secret plane could provide "large amounts of information at a minimum of risk." Within 17 months Lockheed could deliver four operational planes that could sweep across the Soviet skies and record detailed pictures of air bases, missile sites, roads, power grids, railways, and the like: a gold mine of hitherto unavailable intelligence. The spy plane could film a "strip 200 miles wide by 2,500 miles long per flight." Equally important, the whole project would cost only $22 million—a bargain for such valuable results.

Allen Dulles, perhaps feeling the sting of the Doolittle Report, which had charged his agency with failure to grasp the promise of new technologies, set aside his hesitations and embraced the project. In a memorandum of November 24, 1954, he summarized Land's arguments about the high value of the project and the low risk: "There is a definite and urgent National requirement for photographic and electronic reconnaissance overflights of the Soviet Bloc." Dulles took this document to the president on the same day, with a request for $35 million to produce 30 such aircraft. Eisenhower approved on the spot, but also insisted that he personally approve of each and every overflight of Soviet territory. Later that day he reflected on the top-secret technological breakthroughs of his scientists and nervously remarked, "I know so many things that I am almost afraid to speak to my wife."

Though aware of its extreme danger—penetrating Soviet airspace could trigger war—Eisenhower desperately wanted the information the U-2 spy plane could provide. He insisted the plane be funded off the books and that no active military personnel be used as pilots; the CIA would run the show. Within a month the highly secret design project, code-named Aquatone, was under way. By August 1955 the U-2 aircraft was ready for its first test flight. A new chapter in the secret war against the USSR was about to open.[40]

The period from mid-1953 to mid-1955, then, was a crucial one in the evolution of the military-industrial complex and the warfare state. NSC

5412, the March 1954 charter for covert operations, provided an ambitious global plan to counter communism at every turn, by any means. The Doolittle Report of October 1954 called for the CIA to become better organized and better managed precisely so it could also take on a bigger role in the cold war. The Killian Report of February 1955, infused with anxiety about the inability of the United States to predict or deter a surprise attack on the nation, called for a dramatic expansion of new weapons systems, new aircraft, new forms of radar and early detection, bigger and more secure air bases, more powerful bombs, and more aircraft to deliver them.

Eisenhower kept up the pressure on his scientists and engineers and technicians. Especially in the race for a new class of long-range rockets, the ICBMs, he was adamant. In late 1955 he expressed to his senior advisers his frustration at the delay in getting these missiles built. According to official NSC minutes, "he was determined not to tolerate any fooling with this thing. We had simply got to achieve such missiles as promptly as possible, if only because of the enormous psychological and political significance of ballistic missiles." The arms race was not just about a state of readiness, Eisenhower understood, but also about a state of mind: the United States must never seem to be playing catch-up to its allegedly inferior and less developed enemy.[41]

This reliance upon covert operations and high technology to address America's strategic dilemmas reveals an essential characteristic of the Age of Eisenhower. During the 1950s Eisenhower and the political establishment elevated the scientific "expert" to a position of extraordinary power and prominence. Eisenhower himself disdained partisan politics and preferred to place his trust, and the security of the nation, in a cadre of patriotic scientists, technicians, engineers, and veteran military officers to provide innovative solutions to America's strategic problems. The decisions they made—about which weapons systems to build, about how to spend national resources, about which enemies to pursue and what risks should be taken to counter communist expansion—all took place behind closed doors, largely hidden from the scrutiny of Congress or the public. Naturally Eisenhower felt that it was essential to keep American national security policy hidden from the enemy, but he also found it desirable to hide such matters from Congress and even members of his own administration; the U-2, for example, was never discussed in the National Security Council, remaining one of Eisenhower's most closely guarded secrets.

Eisenhower found nothing wrong with this. He was used to making important decisions, and he placed the burden of command on his own shoulders. He personally approved the risky U-2 overflights of Soviet territory and he personally engaged in the coup plotting of the 1953–54 period. But in the meantime he set a pattern that would bedevil America for decades: the closing off of national security decision-making from even the most cursory review by elected officials or the public. It is a paradox, hardly the only one of these years, that a man who so ardently championed America's dynamic, free-market society, and who asserted that America could defy communism while sustaining its democratic values, did so much to obscure the inner workings of the nation's security from public debate. In this sense the Age of Eisenhower would live on long after Ike had passed from the scene.

CHAPTER 8

ASIAN DOMINOES

*"I cannot conceive of a greater tragedy for
America than to get heavily involved now in an
all-out war in any part of those regions."*

I

ON NOVEMBER 2, 1953, VICE PRESIDENT NIXON FOUND HIM-
self riding shotgun in a green military troop transport, enduring bone-
rattling bumps as the truck ground its way along a rutted path in the dank
jungle of southern Vietnam. Alongside the vice president's vehicle, French
and Vietnamese soldiers carried their weapons on their hips and periodi-
cally unleashed bursts of gunfire into the jungle undergrowth at unseen
enemy targets. Suddenly a few mortars landed close by and live rounds siz-
zled overhead. But this was only an exercise. Enthusiastic Vietnamese Army
troops had loosed a few shells to impress the visitor, and some landed a bit
too close for comfort. Nixon, who had never fired a shot in anger during his
wartime navy service, smiled bravely and declared himself impressed with
these fighters for freedom.[1]

Nixon was midway through a 10-week-long goodwill tour of over a
dozen Asian nations, sent by Eisenhower to express American solidarity
with friendly governments there. Of the many stops on his grand tour, however, none had quite the significance of Indochina. France's colonial war
there was entering its eighth year. The French expeditionary force was exhausted and demoralized. The communist independence movement—the
League for the Independence of Viet Nam, or Viet Minh—had paid a high
price in its struggle but by 1953 controlled large swaths of northern Vietnam. It could rely on the support of most of the Vietnamese population, as
well as a steady supply of weapons and materiel from communist China.

The French meanwhile had begun to float the idea of "an honorable peace" that would give them a way to cut their losses and exit Indochina.

Upon arriving in Saigon with his wife on October 30, the vice president delivered a stern and fateful message to the Vietnamese and to his French hosts. "What is at stake in this war is fundamentally the freedom and independence of southeast Asia," he declared. Yes, the Vietnamese wanted independence, and they would have it—just as soon as the communists were defeated. Until then America would support France in its war effort, and the Vietnamese people must rise up against "the common enemy": the communists. If America, France, and the Vietnamese people should fail, the consequences would be grave indeed: Southeast Asia as a whole would be gone forever. "The eyes of the world are fixed on this area, and free people everywhere are vitally interested in what will happen here."[2]

The eyes of the world are fixed on this area. Nixon's words remind us that for American leaders of the 1950s, Asia was the most dangerous theater of the global cold war. Unlike in Europe, where by 1953 the East-West rivalry had settled into a frosty standoff, in Asia the cold war still burned red hot, and the glowing ember at the heart of it all was China. As Nixon later put it, "The major new and unfathomable factor in Asia and the Pacific was Communist China. It was a giant looming beyond every Asian horizon—475 million people ruled by ruthless, disciplined ideologues." And China's influence "was already spreading throughout the area."[3]

Just as Nixon was sweating his way through friendly Asian capitals, Eisenhower and his advisers gathered on November 5 at the usual Thursday meeting of the National Security Council to give final approval to a top-secret paper titled "U.S. Policy toward Communist China." Designated NSC 166/1, it drew an alarming picture. "The emergence of a strong, disciplined, and revolutionary communist regime on mainland China has radically altered the power structure in the Far East," the paper asserted. No one could doubt the fact of China's power. "In the course of half a decade the Chinese Communists have succeeded in defeating and replacing the National Government of China on the mainland, in consolidating, extending, and intensifying the control of the central administration, and in largely rehabilitating the Chinese economy, while at the same time undertaking a Communist political and social revolution of vast proportions."

The Chinese communists would not stop there. They wanted, the NSC asserted, to "recapture the historically Chinese territories which the U.S. and the West now hold or protect," namely Taiwan and Hong Kong. They also wanted the "eventual expulsion of Western or Western-allied forces from adjacent mainland areas," such as Indochina, Korea, and Malaya. And beyond that they desired the "substitution of Chinese Communist influence for that of the West in the other areas of the Far East," especially Japan, Indonesia, and the Philippines.

What should the United States do to halt China's march? The NSC ruled out war. That would lead to "full U.S. mobilization, heavy casualties, the deployment of a major proportion of U.S. armed forces to the China theater, possible use of a significant proportion of the U.S. atomic stockpile and employment of a major proportion of its atomic carriers, almost certainly a split of the U.S.-led coalition, [and the] probability of military intervention by the USSR and a very high risk of global war." Eisenhower had just ended one war in Asia; he certainly did not seek another.[4]

Instead the president preferred to combat communism in Asia using the same method that had worked effectively in Europe: containment. That meant generous economic and military aid to sympathetic governments in the region, along with close political, diplomatic, and personal ties—of the kind Nixon's trip sought to foster. This strategic concept aimed to avoid war, but it also required the United States to turn every outpost of Western influence into a symbol of American resolve. South Korea, Taiwan, French Indochina, British Malaya, the Philippines, and Japan—all had to be defended from communist subversion. Ike's advisers now conceived of East Asia as a single zone of struggle against China and communism from which America could not retreat.[5]

Eisenhower's strategy of containment in Asia faced its first major test in Indochina in 1953–54, and the matter has been a subject of contentious debate among historians ever since. Searching for the long-term origins of America's tragic war in Vietnam, scholars return again and again to that tumultuous moment in the early 1950s when the French Empire was collapsing and communism seemed poised for a stunning victory over the forces of Western colonialism. Eisenhower confronted a terrible dilemma: he could send U.S. military forces to prop up the rotten and unpopular French Empire, or he could stand aside as the communists seized northern Vietnam and took aim at the rest of Indochina.

Most scholars have praised Eisenhower's wisdom and restraint as he worked through this awful problem. Despite considerable pressure from members of his cabinet, his leading military advisers, and the French government, Eisenhower did not commit American military forces to Indochina in 1954. Though willing to rattle his nuclear weapons at the Chinese to deter them from advancing into Vietnam, he "shrewdly vetoed American military intervention," according to historian Robert Divine. Much later scholarship has sustained this argument.[6]

Yet the debate rages on. In his prize-winning study of the long-term origins of the Vietnam War, historian Fredrik Logevall paints a less flattering portrait of the president. Stressing Eisenhower's adherence to the domino theory, Logevall argues that Eisenhower was "fully prepared to intervene with force" in order to halt the fall of Vietnam to the communists. What stopped him from doing so? Not his own innate caution, which Logevall dismisses. Instead he was blocked by external forces, especially the reluctance of the U.S. Congress to give him a carte blanche for military intervention, as well as the opposition of America's crucial ally, Britain, to a wider war in Indochina. In this interpretation it was the restraint of Congress and especially the British government—not Eisenhower—that kept America out of war in Vietnam in 1954.[7]

The argument is difficult to resolve. Was Eisenhower a hawk or a dove? Does he deserve the praise he often receives for avoiding war in Vietnam, or was he truly spoiling for a fight, only to be hamstrung by Congress and his allies? As is typical with Eisenhower, the answer lies somewhere in between. There can be no doubt that he wanted to avoid an intervention by U.S. troops in Indochina; "no more Koreas" was his guiding dictum. Yet in pursuit of his overall strategic goal of containing China and halting the spread of communism, Eisenhower used every other tool at his disposal. He sent arms to fund the French war, spoke menacingly of falling dominoes, and pointedly issued nuclear threats to the Chinese to deter them from seizing Indochina as France withdrew. While his tactics worked in the short run to keep America out of another Asian war, Eisenhower nonetheless committed resources and prestige to Indochina in the cause of containment—and for that cause, just a decade later, Americans would fight and die. Eisenhower avoided war in 1954, but he also sowed many of the seeds that would yield a harvest of sorrow in later years.[8]

II

A French colonial creation made up of three kingdoms—Cambodia, Laos, and Vietnam—Indochina had been France's Asian jewel since the 1880s. Not only did the colony produce rice, rubber, tea and coffee, coal, and zinc, but it demonstrated France's Great Power status. During the Second World War the Japanese conquered Indochina, but in 1945 the French government set out to reclaim its colonial possession. It was not easy. France's plans were foiled by a powerful Vietnamese anticolonial movement that had been much fortified during the war and was led by the well-educated and worldly communist Ho Chi Minh. In 1945 France began a military campaign to suppress the rebellion, inaugurating 30 years of bitter conflict in Vietnam.

The French pursued a two-pronged strategy to defeat the communist insurgency. Using French Foreign Legion and local Vietnamese soldiers supplemented by French regulars, they erected a protective cordon around population centers like Hanoi and Saigon and built static outposts in the countryside from which to launch raids into the hinterland. In addition the French tried to create a plausible Vietnamese nationalist alternative to the charismatic Ho. They transformed Bao Dai, the pliant former emperor of Annam and the scion of the Nguyen dynasty, into a head of state, and they set up a national parliament to provide the illusion of local political autonomy.

The strategy never worked. The communist Viet Minh used its control of the rural areas, especially in the northern province of Tonkin, to build popular support, resupply, strike at vulnerable French targets, and sap French morale. The Viet Minh also relied upon significant Chinese military aid. The French expeditionary force of about 75,000 soldiers, supplemented by 50,000 colonial troops from North and West Africa and 300,000 Vietnamese, rarely took the initiative in the fighting and never inspired confidence among a population that was largely hostile to French rule. Without military success, the political strategy withered, since noncommunist politicians perceived that Bao Dai did not have the leverage to deliver Vietnamese independence from France. The French could win neither on the battlefield nor in the hearts of the Vietnamese.

Initially American leaders looked warily at France's recolonization of Indochina, but with the triumph of Mao's communist revolution in 1949 and the outbreak of war in Korea just eight months later, the Truman administration came to see French Indochina as a front in the global war against communism. By 1952 the United States was paying for at least half the cost of France's war there. Eisenhower and John Foster Dulles believed, as Dulles explained in a speech in early 1953, that the Soviets wanted to control "Indochina, Siam, Burma, Malaya . . . what is called the rice bowl of Asia." Such control would allow them to threaten Japan and India. During the long discussions on board the USS *Helena* after Ike's Korean trip, cabinet officials agreed that Indochina must not fall to the communists.[9]

But how to avoid such a calamity? Upon taking office, Eisenhower and Dulles received dismal reports from the State Department and military officials, who depicted the French war in Indochina as likely to end in a desultory defeat for France. The Joint Chiefs of Staff asserted that the communist Viet Minh held all the initiative in military matters, striking the French at will, and the French forces were too defensive-minded to achieve victory. In language that foreshadowed the grim American experience in Vietnam in the 1960s, one internal intelligence assessment put the issue bluntly: "Although the French have been successful in inflicting severe losses on the Viet Minh, and have considerably disrupted the Viet Minh economy, overall French operations cannot be considered successful because of their failure to arrive at a political solution that obtains the support or patriotism of the Vietnamese people." The picture was dark and getting worse.[10]

Such defeatist opinions did not satisfy the new team in Washington. The incoming chairman of the Joint Chiefs, Adm. Arthur Radford, thought he knew a great deal about Asia. Trained as a navy pilot, he had led a carrier division in World War II, had sailed across every watery mile of the Pacific, and eventually commanded the entire Pacific fleet. An ardent advocate, not surprisingly, of air and naval power, he was also an admirer of General MacArthur and a charter member of the "Asia First" club that stressed the need to go on the offensive against communism in Asia. Radford considered the French poor soldiers, far too passive and defensive in their operations. "Two good American divisions with the normal American aggressive spirit could clean up the situation" in 10 months, he told the top State Department planners. The United States must use its leverage to force the French to adopt bolder tactics. "It was essential," Radford felt, "that we take a more hardboiled attitude with the French in order to get them to adopt a more aggressive policy."[11]

This kind of can-do talk appealed to Eisenhower, who thought Indochina was of critical importance to the position of the free world in Asia. In March 1953, in a private discussion, Ike and his secretary of state agreed that Indochina was "*the top priority in foreign policy*, being in some ways more important than Korea because the consequences of a loss there could not be localized, but would spread throughout Asia and Europe." But merely stating Indochina's importance did not constitute a strategy for saving it. In late May a worried U.S. Embassy in Saigon reported to the State Department, "Despite continuing effort of seven years and material increase in Vietnam[ese] native armed forces, successful termination of war against Communist arms is still as far from sight as ever."[12]

In the meantime public opinion in France was turning ever more sharply against the war, as the moderate center-left newspapers *Le Monde* and *L'Express* called for a negotiated settlement and withdrawal. The maverick politician Pierre Mendès-France, a brilliant lawyer who led the Radical Socialist faction in Parliament (a center-left party despite its name), openly championed an immediate negotiated end to the war; on May 29, 1953, he came within a whisker of winning enough votes in the National Assembly to form a government and take the reins of power. Clearly time was running out on the French war effort.[13]

It may seem paradoxical that at the very moment of his most successful foreign policy achievement—the July 1953 armistice in Korea—Eisenhower expanded America's commitment to the French war in Indochina. Yet in fact these two lines of policy were closely linked. Though hailed by most of the American public, Eisenhower's decision to accept an armistice in Korea prompted much gnashing of teeth among the hawkish, Asia First faction of the Republican Party. To them the deal to cease fighting in a divided Korea looked too much like Yalta, where FDR acquiesced in the Soviet conquest of Eastern Europe. During the 1952 campaign the Republican right wing had been told by Foster Dulles that they could expect rollback and victory, not compromise and containment. Although they could hardly bay for more war after three years of bloody stalemate in Korea, the GOP hard-liners did not like Ike's decision to stop the war short of victory. As the *Los Angeles Times* put it, "The Old Guard is miserable about what's happened at Panmunjom," where the Korean armistice was signed. In order to shore up his right flank, Ike would have to show firmness in his policies toward Indochina lest he ignite a full-scale rebellion in his party over his Asia policy.[14]

Having settled for stalemate in Korea, Eisenhower now looked to Indochina for an outright victory to balance the ledger. In return for more aid to France, America demanded battlefield results against the Viet Minh. To meet this pressure, the French leadership unveiled a new commander of the Indochina war effort in May 1953. Gen. Henri Navarre, a soldier with a distinguished battle record earned in both world wars in the Near East and North Africa, went to Vietnam determined to succeed where his predecessors had failed. He had never been to Indochina, but he believed he could turn the tide of war. Navarre proposed a more aggressive strategy: build up the Vietnamese Army, send more mobile groups of elite French troops into the North to do the heavy fighting, and secure more air- and sea-lift capacity from the United States. All this, Navarre claimed, would bring a kind of victory in two years. Navarre's confidence and aplomb won the approval of the Americans, though his actual plan raised eyebrows among the Joint Chiefs of Staff, who remained skeptical about French fighting capabilities. Nonetheless Navarre's plan was the only game in town, and the Americans embraced it.[15]

But there was a catch: it was going to cost more, much more. And America would have to pay. Congress approved a $400 million package of military aid in July 1953, but this was not enough to meet the needs of the Navarre plan. At the end of July, Prime Minister Joseph Laniel secretly approached the American ambassador in Paris, Douglas Dillon, and made a brazen demand. The French needed *another* $400 million to fund the Navarre Plan. If Laniel did not get these extra funds, he could not commit to the more aggressive strategy, and his government would fall, thus leading the way to a peace-at-any-price government led by Mendès-France. "If funds are not available to carry on in Indochina," Laniel told Dillon, "the only alternative is eventual withdrawal."[16]

Some might call it blackmail, but it was simply a statement of the truth: France could keep the war going only if the United States picked up the tab. And the American leadership accepted the arrangement. In a hastily written report to the National Security Council, the director of the State Department's Policy Planning Staff, Robert Bowie, put the issue bluntly: the United States could "grasp a promising opportunity to further a satisfactory conclusion of the war in Indochina" by spending an additional $400 million, or it could "accept the loss of Indochina and possibly other areas of Southeast Asia." Seen in those terms, the choice looked easy. On August 6 the NSC gave provisional approval for $385 million in increased aid. A few weeks later Eisenhower formally signed off on the additional funds.[17]

Foster Dulles seemed to think it was a good deal. He told his colleagues on the NSC that Laniel and Navarre together promised a "dynamic approach to the military problem in Indochina." If these additional funds would help push France into action, Dulles said, it would be "the cheapest money we ever spent." But the Eisenhower administration was then wrangling with a painful budget-cutting exercise, and Ike had especially targeted the Defense Department for trimming. By providing a total of $785 million to France's war just in fiscal year 1954 alone (equivalent to $6.3 billion today), Ike made plain that the Indochina war stood at the very top of his list of national security priorities.[18]

Eisenhower publicly justified this largesse by invoking the specter of communist victory across Asia. In a speech on August 4 to the 45th annual Governors' Conference in Seattle, he told his audience why he was so concerned with Indochina. "If Indochina goes, several things happen right away," he claimed. India would be "outflanked" and "Burma would be in no position for defense." "How would the free world hold the rich empire of Indonesia? . . . So you see, somewhere along the line, this must be blocked and it must be blocked now, and that's what we are trying to do. So when the United States votes $400 million to help that war, we are not voting a giveaway program. We are voting for the cheapest way we can prevent the occurrence of something that would be of a most terrible significance to the United States of America." Like Dulles, Eisenhower argued that money spent on the French war was money well spent.[19]

In addition to increasing aid to the French, Eisenhower and Dulles decided to put the Chinese on notice that America's determination to hold the line in Asia was undiminished. Dulles took to the airwaves on September 2 to deliver a threat (carefully vetted by Ike) that if China took advantage of the Korean armistice to shift soldiers and resources to the war in Vietnam, the United States would immediately intensify its own military commitments there. If America was drawn into war in Indochina through Chinese provocation, Dulles asserted, the resulting conflict "might not be confined to Indochina." Hinting at a possible nuclear war against China had become the signature Dulles style, no less hair-raising for all its familiarity.[20]

The weak link in all this was of course France, for if the French should falter in their commitment to the war, then America might well have to send in its own troops to rescue Southeast Asia—a prospect Eisenhower strongly opposed. So Eisenhower placed his bets, and his nation's prestige, on the outcome of a war fought in tropical jungles by a beleaguered French colonial expeditionary force against a well-armed and ideologically motivated national liberation army. It was a colossal gamble. And for once Eisenhower's usual luck at games of chance failed him.

III

In late November 1953, as part of General Navarre's new aggressive strategy, the French sent an airborne force to seize a small outpost in Tonkin on the

Laotian border, a hitherto insignificant crossroads called Dien Bien Phu. Navarre planned to build a powerful base from which to defend Laos and also stage offensive strikes against the Viet Minh. American analysts were unimpressed by this strategy, seeing it as too passive. In truth, the CIA believed the French were not trying to win the war in Indochina at all; they simply wanted to "improve their position sufficiently to negotiate a settlement which would eliminate the drain of the Indochina war on France."[21]

Nixon, freshly returned from his extensive Asia journey, confirmed this gloomy picture in a detailed report to the president and the National Security Council on the day before Christmas 1953. His diagnosis confirmed what observers in Indochina had been saying for years: France had not given the Vietnamese people anything to fight for. The French had failed to build a serious Vietnamese army to share the burden of fighting and refused to offer Vietnam full independence. As a result nationalist leaders declined to work with French authorities. Bao Dai was widely seen as a puppet who lacked legitimacy. Vietnam had no powerful figure, like Korea's Syngman Rhee, who could rally the nation to fight the communist foe. Even Nixon, who always tried to align himself with what Eisenhower wanted to hear, could not pretty up the picture. "The Communists have a sense of history," he said, "and time is on their side."[22]

At the start of 1954 Eisenhower held a number of crucial high-level meetings with his advisers to determine how the United States would react if France should suddenly lose its will to sustain the fight in Indochina. Should America fight for Indochina if France would not? The question could no longer be ignored. In the National Security Council meeting of January 8, when his advisers discussed the possible need for the United States to intervene in order to prop up the French war effort, Eisenhower spoke decisively. The minutes record his adamant opposition to sending American soldiers to Indochina: "He simply could not imagine the United States putting ground forces anywhere in Southeast Asia. . . . There was just no sense in even talking about United States forces replacing the French in Indochina. If we did so, the Vietnamese could be expected to transfer their hatred of the French to us. I cannot tell you, said the President with vehemence, how bitterly opposed I am to such a course of action. This war in Indochina would absorb our troops by divisions!" Indeed the U.S. Army had already run the numbers and concluded it would take seven army divisions and one marine division to defeat the Viet Minh. Along with support and logistics personnel, that meant sending 275,000 men to Indochina. Just months after halting a most unpopular war in Korea, Eisenhower clearly had no appetite for such a dramatic move.[23]

Having taken direct combat intervention off the table, however, Ike still had a number of measures open to him. When Admiral Radford suggested that American planes be used to help break the alarmingly large Viet Minh buildup around Dien Bien Phu, Eisenhower warmed to the idea and mused that non-American pilots might be allowed to fly "U.S. planes without insignia." This action "could be done without involving us directly in the war, which he admitted would be a very dangerous thing." Secretary of the Treasury George Humphrey, who loudly opposed such a step-by-step increase of direct military help, put the issue bluntly to Ike: "Suppose the French were to give up and turn the whole country over to the Communists, would the United States then interfere?" Eisenhower confirmed his position, saying, "No, we would not intervene." Offering aircraft and pilots to the French, however, was like sticking your finger in a leaky dike. "And with leaky dikes, it's sometimes better to put a finger in than to let the whole structure be washed away."

The NSC therefore ordered that 40 B-26 bombers and 200 U.S. technicians be dispatched to Indochina. Just this small gesture—sending Americans into a combat zone—proved controversial, but Eisenhower told congressional leaders that this "small project" of a few hundred technical personnel would achieve "a very large purpose—that is, to prevent all of Southeast Asia from falling to the Communists." In his public press conference on February 10 he stressed that he wanted to keep France in the war so Americans could stay out. "No one could be more bitterly opposed to ever getting the U.S. involved in a hot war in that region than I am," Eisenhower declared in front of a room full of reporters. *"Every move I authorize is calculated . . . to make certain that that does not happen."* This became the leitmotif of Ike's Asian diplomacy: to maneuver in such a way that the war could be sustained without direct U.S. involvement. For emphasis he insisted, "I cannot conceive of a greater tragedy for America than to get heavily involved now in an all-out war in any part of those regions."[24]

With public statements about the "tragedy" of war in Indochina clattering across the wire services, the French could be excused for trying to bring their part in the conflict to a close. In February the French government, desperate to appease a restive and war-weary public, successfully managed to secure the agreement of the Great Powers to include discussion of the Indochina war at a summit in Geneva in late April. The purpose of the meeting, initially proposed by the Soviets, was to discuss an easing of tensions in Korea, where the armistice remained fragile and unsteady. But Foreign Minister Georges Bidault, under express orders from Paris, asked the five powers— the USSR, the United States, Britain, France, and communist China—to take up the possibility of a compromise settlement in Indochina. U.S. policy had opposed any such talks for months, especially in the presence of the communist Chinese, whom the U.S. government did not recognize as legitimate representatives of the Chinese people. (The United States recognized Nationalist China, or Taiwan, as the only legitimate Chinese government.) Yet Bidault insisted that if the issue was not placed on the Geneva agenda, the Laniel government would be voted out of office and an antiwar government would be installed. The United States had to accept placing Indochina on the agenda at Geneva as the price of keeping the war going.[25]

By circling a date on the calendar for a Great Power summit to discuss the future of Indochina, France motivated the Viet Minh to improve their bargaining position by winning a big battle in the weeks before the conference. And a large target had conveniently presented itself: the heavily fortified and now surrounded French garrison at Dien Bien Phu. By February, Navarre had transferred 15,000 elite French soldiers there. Engineers refitted and expanded a small airfield to allow DC-3 aircraft to bring in light tanks, howitzers, and plenty of ammunition. Navarre's initial purpose was to use this strongpoint as a base and to sally forth from this heavy redoubt to block Viet Minh forays into Laos. The French military leadership expressed confidence in its ability to fend off the Viet Minh attacks. Indeed they seemed almost to welcome a showdown as an opportunity to draw Viet Minh forces into a large engagement in which heavy French firepower would take a murderous toll on the enemy.[26]

Welcome or not, the attack came. On March 13, 1954, thousands of Viet Minh soldiers threw themselves at the heavily defended outpost under cover of a ferocious artillery barrage. The battle of Dien Bien Phu had begun.[27]

IV

The next eight weeks marked an anxious, stress-filled period for Eisenhower, among the most complicated and controversial days of his presidency. France teetered on the brink of collapse in Indochina, and Eisenhower had to decide: Would the United States, which had fought to save South Korea from communism, now bail out the French in Vietnam?

As the first news reports about Dien Bien Phu reached Washington, American officials did not panic. To be sure, the U.S. ambassador in Saigon, Donald Heath, reported that the opening phase of the battle "gives cause for some concern. Viet Minh artillery is zeroed in on French positions. . . . Both airstrips in consequence are unusable." Right from the start of the battle, the French had to rely on airdrops for their daily supplies of food and ammunition. Even so, CIA director Allen Dulles reported to the NSC on March 18 that the chances for a French victory stood at "50–50"—not great odds, but not desperate either. Viet Minh forces were taking huge casualties. Eisenhower took some comfort from the fact that the French were "fighting from prepared and heavily fortified positions." Allen Dulles even went so far as to suggest that the French in Saigon might be playing up the gravity of the crisis so as to "exaggerate the extent of their final victory." And Navarre confided to Ambassador Heath that even if the Viet Minh should take the besieged garrison, "his capacity to remain in the Indochina war would not be greatly impaired."[28]

Another French emissary delivered the same message of sangfroid. On March 20 Gen. Paul Ély, chief of staff of the French armed forces, arrived in Washington for a week of discussions with the Eisenhower administration. Ély had served as French representative to the NATO Council and knew his American counterparts well. Radford welcomed him and took him to dine with leading members of the government, including Nixon, Allen Dulles, and the army's chief of staff Gen. Matthew Ridgway. Ély, a tall, wiry veteran of both world wars, lauded the stalwart determination of the Laniel government to carry on the war in Indochina and stated that "newspaper reports," especially the left-wing French press, "exaggerate in some degree the defeatist sentiment" in France. He acknowledged the enormous political significance of Dien Bien Phu; a communist victory there would amplify calls in France for a negotiated end to the fighting. But he felt reasonably confident that France could hang on, provided that the United States would send more combat aircraft for use in the battle. Ély did not sound especially worried.[29]

Indeed Ély's demeanor struck Radford as far too calm. In Radford's view, the situation at Dien Bien Phu and in Indochina generally looked catastrophic, and Radford clearly wanted Ély to make bigger demands on Washington while offering to share direction of the war effort. Radford believed that American airpower could save Dien Bien Phu and perhaps crush the Viet Minh altogether. On March 26, in a remarkable act that approached the boundaries of insubordination, Radford tried to get the French general to make a direct appeal to Eisenhower for American military intervention at Dien Bien Phu. Ély was wary, but Radford egged him on, telling him privately that if France would only ask for it, the United States would deliver massive air support to the embattled French outpost. Surprised, Ély reported Radford's zeal to Paris, where this remarkable offer was duly noted and filed away for future use.[30]

While Radford was proffering airstrikes to the French, however, Eisenhower on March 24 repeated his opposition to a wider U.S. role. "We should not get involved in fighting in Indochina unless there were the political preconditions necessary for a successful outcome," he told Foster Dulles. Those preconditions, such as immediate independence for the Indochinese states, full international approval for any military action, and a Vietnamese request for American intervention, were highly unlikely to be in place soon, as Ike knew. Dulles noted for the record that Eisenhower "did not wholly exclude the possibility of a single strike [against the Viet Minh at Dien Bien Phu], if it were almost certain this would produce decisive results." But Eisenhower knew better than anyone that a single airstrike would not dislodge three full divisions of Viet Minh soldiers from their positions around Dien Bien Phu, and in fact the French were already bombing the Viet Minh positions with napalm and 1,000-pound bombs. Ike knew there was no easy way to break the Viet Minh troops, and he did not want Americans tangled up in a jungle war they could not win.[31]

On March 25, when the president met with his National Security Council, Allen Dulles reported that Dien Bien Phu was "relatively quiet" and that the French position had "improved somewhat." The French seemed to be holding their own. Foster Dulles asked the group to take up the question of just how far the United States was willing to go to help the French in the event of their withdrawal from Indochina. Eisenhower asserted that any U.S. role would require the approval of the United Nations as well as an invitation from the government of Vietnam itself. It would also require the approval of Congress. "It was simply academic to imagine otherwise," he said. Since the likelihood of securing UN, Vietnamese, and congressional approval for American military action in Indochina was nil, Eisenhower was indirectly vetoing intervention.[32]

Instead he began to outline what he considered a more constructive path: the creation of a group "of governments and nations who might be approached to assist" in securing Indochina—nations such as Australia, New Zealand, the Philippines, Britain, France, and other "free" Southeast

Asian countries. Might there be a place for some kind of Asian collective security organization that could backstop the French in Indochina? As the former commander of NATO, Eisenhower could easily see that model applied in Asia.

In fact Eisenhower had been thinking about this idea for some time. In mid-January 1954 he had tasked a small group of his most trusted advisers, chaired by Undersecretary of State Bedell Smith, to think broadly about a Southeast Asia "area plan," as he called it, "including the possible alternative lines of action to be taken in case of a reverse in Indochina." In mid-February, while testifying to a closed executive session of the Senate Foreign Relations Committee, Smith revealed that planning along those lines had moved ahead. Rejecting the domino theory, Smith said, "Even at the worst, part of Indochina might be lost without losing the rest of Southeast Asia. . . . One can think of the possibility of an area defense pact which might include Thailand as the bastion, Burma and possibly Cambodia and part of Indochina—and maybe some part of it could be lost without disastrous effect." A man as savvy as Smith, Ike's intimate confidante, would never have said such things unless they squared with the president's thinking. When Senator William Langer asked Smith whether the United States would "go ahead alone . . . if France quits on us," Smith replied curtly, "I do not think so, sir. No."[33]

No unilateral U.S. intervention, then. But a regional confederation of allied states, operating perhaps with the blessing of the United Nations and in concert with free governments to halt communist aggression—this tantalizing vision took hold in the Eisenhower administration. On March 29 Foster Dulles gave a speech at the Overseas Press Club in New York that explained this new policy. The speech had been, as usual, carefully edited by Eisenhower. It called for "united action" against the military interference of China in the affairs of the Vietnamese people and against the ideological imperialism directed from Beijing and Moscow. Dulles spelled out an indictment of the Chinese for aiding the Viet Minh insurrection and declared that communist China had placed all of Southeast Asia in jeopardy. Indochina was in the crosshairs now, but if it fell, the rest of Southeast Asia would soon be targeted. China's subversive tactics constituted "a grave threat to the whole free community" and had to be stopped.[34]

Though full of ominous hints and hawkish bluster, Dulles did not specify what he meant by "united action," and historians to this day disagree on how to interpret his speech. Perhaps his obfuscation was deliberate, designed to keep the Chinese guessing. Or perhaps his policy remained in flux, and his speech aimed to hide the confusion inside the administration. In his weekly news conference two days later, Eisenhower distanced himself somewhat from Dulles's bellicose remarks. Asked by Martin Agronsky of ABC if he was considering direct military intervention, Ike hedged: "I can conceive of no greater disadvantage to America than to be employing its own ground forces, and any other kind of forces, in great numbers around the world, meeting each little situation as it arises." That statement did not rule out the use of force, but it sounded less hawkish than Dulles's remarks. "What we are trying to do," the president went on, "is to make our friends strong enough to take care of local situations by themselves, with the financial, the moral, the political and, certainly, only where our own vital interests demanded any military help."[35]

Eisenhower, it seems, viewed the "united action" concept not as an allied invasion force but as a symbolic assertion of common purpose by the Western and democratic nations to halt communist expansion. "United action" was a shield rather than a sword. Dulles's speech aimed to make the Chinese think twice about extending their reach into Indochina and to show the French that the world would not abandon them in their hour of need. Though bellicose, the speech was in fact a mask of angry words crafted to hide Eisenhower's deep reluctance to enter another Asian war.

V

Eisenhower, a lifelong student of strategy, knew that deterrence could succeed in keeping the peace only if it was backed by a willingness to use force. He wanted to keep America out of war, but perhaps the best way to do that was to prepare for it. That meant sounding out Congress. On April 1, 1954, shortly after a meeting of his National Security Council, Eisenhower tasked the secretary of state to consult congressional leaders: How much appetite did they have for conflict in Southeast Asia? Would they support the use of American forces there? If Ike could tell the world that Congress had approved a resolution giving him the authority to use air and naval power to help the French, China could only conclude that America was truly girding itself for confrontation.[36]

Dulles drafted a congressional resolution and reviewed it with Eisenhower in a meeting on April 2, which Radford and Defense Secretary Charles Wilson also attended. The resolution asked Congress to give the president authority to employ naval and air power "to assist the forces which are resisting aggression in Southeast Asia." Was this a request for a blank check to begin a war in Vietnam? That is not how Ike and Dulles saw it. Dulles expressly told Eisenhower that the resolution was "designed to be a deterrent" and to make the call for united action among the allies seem more credible. Backing Radford into a corner, Dulles insisted that he did not see the resolution as the preliminary step to a military "strike." Wilson agreed and characterized the resolution as an effort "'to fill our hand' so that we would be in a stronger position to negotiate" with the states that would join the new Asian security group. The proposed resolution would give Eisenhower the appearance of a man preparing his nation for war precisely so he could more effectively avoid it.[37]

On Saturday, April 3, at 9:30 a.m., Dulles and Radford held a meeting at the State Department with a number of congressional leaders from both parties. Senate Majority Leader William Knowland, Senator Eugene Millikin, and Speaker of the House Joseph Martin represented the Republicans. Democratic senators Lyndon Johnson (Minority Leader), Richard Russell, and Minority Whip Earle C. Clements were joined by Democratic representatives John McCormack, the minority whip, and J. Percy Priest, the chief deputy whip.

Dulles did not present them with the text of the draft resolution he had given Eisenhower. Instead, according to the summary of the meeting Dulles wrote afterward, he and Radford summarized the administration's well-known view that Indochina possessed extraordinary geopolitical significance and its loss to communism would threaten vital American interests in Southeast Asia. Dulles expressed his belief that in light of the high-stakes battle now being waged there, "the president should have Congressional backing so that he could use air and sea power in the area if he felt it necessary in the interest of national security."

It was a clumsy overture. The congressional leaders sniffed out Dulles's encroachment on their constitutional prerogative to declare war. Other than Knowland, an eager Asia Firster, the legislators demurred. They worried that Eisenhower, if granted such powers, might take actions that could trigger war. "We want no more Koreas," they said, and in this they surely spoke for the great majority of Americans. Dulles and Radford insisted that "the administration did not now contemplate the commitment of land forces," but the distinction between land and air forces did not assuage congressional concerns. The congressmen made the argument that "once the flag was committed," whether attached to a plane or a naval vessel, "the use of land forces would inevitably follow."

Yet for all their caution, the congressmen did not flatly reject Dulles's request. Instead they asked for a demonstration that America's allies, especially Britain, supported the concept of united action and were ready to help create a coalition of nations to come to the aid of French Indochina. If such a public statement of support from allies could be secured, then "a Congressional resolution could be passed."[38]

Later writers invested this meeting with enormous, and probably exaggerated, significance. It became immortalized as "the day we didn't go to war" after one of the men present, Congressman McCormack, leaked the content of the discussion to *Washington Post* reporter Chalmers Roberts. In McCormack's telling, Dulles's request for a congressional resolution as part of a policy of deterrence was overshadowed by Radford's hair-raising briefing in which he laid out a plan for immediate airstrikes on Dien Bien Phu by carrier-based jets in the South China Sea. McCormack turned the encounter into an epic standoff: Radford seemed bent on starting a war, and the Democrats in the room rose to quash the idea.[39]

But Dulles did not think the congressmen had stymied the administration at all. Right after the meeting ended, Dulles called President Eisenhower, who was spending the weekend at Camp David. Dulles was ambiguous at first, saying the meeting went "pretty well—although it raised some serious problems." He did not specify what those problems were. He told Ike that he thought "Congress would be quite prepared to go along on some vigorous action if we were not doing it alone." Eisenhower thought such a position was reasonable; indeed his entire policy depended upon mobilizing allied nations to come to Indochina's defense. That meant Eisenhower and Dulles needed Britain to sign on to united action, and fast.[40]

VI

To win the support of the British government, Eisenhower dipped into his deep reservoir of personal friendship with Winston Churchill. Just before midnight on April 4, 1954, the president sent a powerful, and quite unprecedented, telegram to his old comrade in arms. Drafted by Eisenhower, Dulles, and Counselor of the State Department Douglas MacArthur II, the message sought to appeal to the prime minister's well-known romantic streak by depicting April 1954 as a moment of world-historical importance akin to the early days of the war against Hitler. France was faltering before the onslaught of Chinese-backed aggression. The fall of Indochina would have a "disastrous" effect on the "global strategic position" of the United States and Britain. How could such an outcome be avoided? Eisenhower proposed to Churchill the allied coalition concept that he and Dulles had discussed, namely:

> a new ad hoc grouping or coalition composed of nations which have a vital concern in the checking of Communist expansion in the area. . . . The important thing is that the coalition must be strong and it must be willing to join the fight if necessary. I do not envisage the need of any appreciable ground forces on your or our part. If the members of the alliance are sufficiently resolute it should be able to make clear to the Chinese Communists that the continuation of their material support to the Viet Minh will inevitably lead to the growing power of the forces arrayed against them.

This was the crucial element of the concept: action now by the free powers would compel the Chinese to back off, withdraw their support for the Viet Minh, and cease their inexorable drive into Southeast Asia.

Deterrence required credibility; that is what Ike wanted Churchill to give him. By creating a powerful coalition, Eisenhower asserted, "we will enormously increase our chances of bringing the Chinese to believe that their interests lie in the direction of a discreet disengagement." Ike's bid for Churchill's support was no battle cry; on the contrary, it was a means to deter the Chinese, buck up the French, and keep the dogs of war on a tight leash.

Eisenhower's telegram ended with an egregious and somewhat embarrassing invocation of the dark days of 1938–39, when Britain, against Churchill's advice, preferred to appease rather than confront Hitler: "We failed to stop Hirohito, Mussolini, and Hitler by not acting in unity and in time. May it not be thought that our nations have learned something from that lesson?" To lecture Churchill, whose country fought Hitler for two years before the United States entered war, on the appropriate lessons of history was a shocking act of bad taste. But this reference to appeasement reinforced the basic logic of Eisenhower's policy: in 1938, at Munich, the allies appeased Hitler and war followed; now, in 1954, the allies must stand together and act firmly in the face of aggression so that war could be avoided.[41]

Eisenhower's strategy of deterrence encountered some unexpected trouble late in the evening of April 4. At about 9:45 p.m. the State Department received a cable from Ambassador Douglas Dillon in Paris, reporting that he had been summoned by Prime Minister Laniel and Foreign Minister Bidault. "They said," Dillon wrote, "that immediate armed intervention of U.S. carrier aircraft at Dien Bien Phu is now necessary to save the situation." The Viet Minh were bringing in massive reinforcements and the garrison was in grave jeopardy. The French government was seeking to cash in the chip that Radford had slipped into General Ély's pocket on March 26: a promise to bring American aircraft into battle should France request such aid. Bidault told Dillon that "for good or evil the fate of Southeast Asia now rested on Dien Bien Phu."[42]

Early on April 5 Secretary Dulles called the president and told him about Dillon's cable. Ike was furious. Radford "should never have told a foreign country he would do his best [to get the president's approval for intervention] because they then start putting pressure on us." Dulles tried to protect Radford from Ike's wrath, blaming Ély for the misunderstanding. "Radford did not give any committal talk," Dulles said, untruthfully. Eisenhower rejected the idea of intervention out of hand. It would be "completely unconstitutional and indefensible. . . . We cannot engage in active war." Any military act required congressional approval, the support of allies, and much greater preparation so it could be part of an overall strategy. Piecemeal airstrikes would jeopardize American prestige, anger Congress, and quite possibly draw a Chinese military intervention in response. In short, bombing Dien Bien Phu was about the worst thing Ike could imagine. Within the hour Dulles cabled a reply to Ambassador Dillon, rejecting the French request.[43]

With all these elements of a complex story swirling around—Dulles's united action speech on March 29, the meeting with congressional leaders on April 3, the Churchill telegram and the appeal from the French on April 4—Ike moved up the usual weekly meeting of the National Security Council from Thursday to Tuesday, April 6. The discussion again took up the question of military intervention by U.S. and allied forces in Indochina. Allen Dulles weighed in, noting that if the United States were to intervene strongly enough to bring about the defeat of the Viet Minh, there was a "very great danger" of the Chinese pouring across the border into Indochina, just as they had done in Korea in November 1950. CIA intelligence counted five divisions of Chinese soldiers 200 miles from Dien Bien Phu, just across the Vietnamese border, and an additional 200,000 men within

300 miles of the border. An American intervention would provide justification for these troops to sweep down into Vietnam.

These chilling facts may explain the lack of enthusiasm at the April 6 meeting for military intervention. Eisenhower set the tone: speaking with "great emphasis," according to the note-taker, he said "there was no possibility whatever of U.S. unilateral intervention in Indochina, and we had best face that fact." Following Eisenhower's lead, Foster Dulles now asserted that the NSC did not need to consider a military option at the present time, however desperate the situation at Dien Bien Phu. Instead America must concentrate on "an effort to build up strength in the Southeast Asia area to such a point that military intervention might prove unnecessary." If he could win the support of other allied nations to form a united bloc, "the Communists might well give up their intent to seize the area."

Over the course of a long discussion, Radford, Nixon, and even Foster Dulles tried to keep open the option of using military force as a last resort if united action failed, but Ike seemed to have made up his mind against it. He instead "expressed warm approval for the idea of a political organization which would have for its purpose the defense of Southeast Asia even if Indochina should be lost. In any case, the creation of such a political organization for defense would be better than emergency military action." Eisenhower would not go to war to save French Indochina, but he would gladly lead a collective security organization in Asia that would bolster the "free" nations, draw a line in the sand, and dare the Chinese to cross it.[44]

VII

The president had made his decision: he would not send Americans to fight in Vietnam. He told his advisers confidentially that he rejected the simplistic idea that "because we might lose Indochina we would necessarily have to lose all the rest of Southeast Asia." Privately he argued that the domino theory should not force America's hand. It was possible, he believed, to create a strong Western position in Asia even without Indochina.[45]

But *in public* Eisenhower delivered a very different message. Just a day after telling the NSC that "there was no possibility whatever of U.S. unilateral intervention in Indochina," he strode into the Indian Treaty Room in the Old Executive Office Building for his usual weekly press conference. When journalist Robert Richards of the Copley Press asked the president to comment on the strategic importance of Indochina, Eisenhower became expansive, and in some of his most famous words, asserted the viability of the domino theory. "First of all, you have the specific value of a locality in its production of materials that the world needs," he began. "Then you have the possibility that many human beings pass under a dictatorship that is inimical to the free world. Finally, you have broader considerations that might follow what you would call the 'falling domino' principle. You have a row of dominoes set up, you knock over the first one, and what will happen to the last one is the certainty that it will go over very quickly." He went on to prophesy a total disaster in Asia if Indochina fell. "The possible consequences of the loss are just incalculable to the free world," he concluded darkly.[46]

No wonder his contemporaries were baffled by Eisenhower's strategy toward Asia: while pursuing a policy of restraint and diplomacy, he publicly warned against the catastrophic consequences of communist success and hinted at the most severe American response to any direct challenge.

The consequences of such double-talk were serious. When Foster Dulles arrived in London on April 11 to confer with his British counterparts to try to win their support for the allied coalition to support the French, he found the British both dubious about American objectives and deeply anxious about Eisenhower's warlike words. Churchill and Foreign Minister Eden, longtime friends and partners of the Eisenhower team, fretted about Eisenhower's nuclear saber-rattling. Just a month earlier the United States had tested the world's largest explosive device, a 15-megaton H-Bomb, on a remote South Pacific island. The radioactive fallout reached Japan and Australia and also fell on a boat of Japanese fishermen, killing one and rendering the others gravely ill. The blast set off serious criticism of U.S. policy around the world and in the House of Commons.

The British leaders also vividly recalled Eisenhower's offhand remark in Bermuda the previous December, that "atomic weapons were now coming to be regarded as a proper part of conventional armament." They had heard Foster Dulles on March 29 indict Chinese actions like a prosecutor in a courtroom. They noted Ike's domino principle and his doom-filled prophecy should Indochina fall. They knew of Radford's planning for air strikes against Viet Minh targets. Putting this evidence together, they had come to see American policy as reckless, driven by an obsessive anticommunism that might soon plunge the world into atomic war.[47]

Dulles therefore received a cool reception upon his arrival in London. On the evening of April 11, after dinner at the American Embassy, he made his pitch to his British colleagues. He proposed the creation of a tempo-rary coalition of 10 nations, led by the United States and Britain, that would guarantee Indochinese security, deter further Chinese aggression in Asia, and create a united block at the upcoming Geneva conference so there would be no precipitous French withdrawal even if Dien Bien Phu should fall. Dulles wanted to demonstrate the resolve of free nations to halt the ex-pansion of communism in Asia. The coalition would possess implied mili-tary power, but Eisenhower and Dulles hoped the forming of the coalition by itself would be a sufficient deterrent against future Chinese adventures.[48]

Eden smiled politely and said he would think about it. In fact he had already decided to reject Dulles's proposal. Eden thought the scheme was provocative and dangerous. He preferred what he considered the "least damaging solution—the partition of Vietnam into a communist North and a free South, an idea that was wholly poisonous to the Americas. Such a deal, Eden calculated, could be achieved at Geneva provided it was not undone by any "injudicious military decisions" imposed by the Americans. Threats and nuclear brinkmanship toward China were counterproductive; they could not be "sufficiently potent to make China swallow so humiliating a rebuff as the abandonment of the Vietminh without any face-saving concession in return." And if threats failed, then what? Nuclear war? Eden would have no truck with that. So, to Dulles's immense frustration, Eden rejected the "united action" plan for fear that it would lead to war, not avert it.[49]

Dulles and Eden met again just two weeks later, this time in Paris during a NATO conference. On the evening of April 23, as they gathered for an offi-cial dinner in the ornate and gilded splendor of the French Foreign Ministry on the Quai d'Orsay, Dulles learned that the French government had just received another anguished appeal from General Navarre asking for Ameri-can air intervention against the Viet Minh at Dien Bien Phu. Failing that, the surrounded French position could not last more than three days. Dulles and Radford, admitting that it was now too late to save those embattled French soldiers, nonetheless beseeched Eden to set aside his doubts and announce his support for the creation of a united Western coalition that would defend the rest of Indochina from Chinese aggression after Dien Bien Phu fell.[50]

Eden immediately flew back to England and went to see the prime min-ister at his weekend retreat, Chequers, where he and Churchill discussed and again rejected the American proposal. Churchill hit the nail on the head: a small-scale military intervention would be both ineffective and likely to trigger a wider war with China and the USSR—in short, the worst possible outcome. The partition of Vietnam now appeared a safer and more plausible solution. That could be done at Geneva without paying the heavy price of war. Once again the British stymied Dulles's plans.[51]

These developments left Eisenhower deeply unhappy. He fumed about the foolishness of the French, who kept asking for U.S. military intervention but refused to respond to repeated requests to grant immediate independence to the Indochinese states. He thought the decline of France as a serious power was tragic and that the French government had virtually "abdicated." And he seethed about the cautious British and their "morbid obsession that any positive move on the part of the free world may bring upon us World War III," as he put it to Swede Hazlett. But he did not waver from his basic policy: unilateral intervention by the United States was out of the question. If the coalition idea did not inspire the allies, the United States would not act alone.[52]

On that point Eisenhower was unbending, as he made clear on April 29, when the NSC met again to review the situation. The team heard a depressing report from Radford, who carefully spelled out the dismal predicament of the besieged French soldiers at Dien Bien Phu. When Radford had finished, Harold Stassen, the director of the foreign aid program, spoke up. Stassen had a reputation as a politically ambitious maverick; it must have been embarrassing to all in the room when he burst out with an impassioned plea that the United States intervene unilaterally to save Vietnam from collapse. French and British weakness should not "render the United States inactive and impotent," he declared.

This was a slap in Eisenhower's face, drawing him into a pointed colloquy with Stassen. If the United States moved in to rescue the French, Ike stated, "we would in the eyes of many Asiatic peoples merely replace French colonialism with American colonialism." Furthermore unilateral American intervention "would mean a general war with China and perhaps with the USSR." The only way to sustain America's moral position in the world was through collective action in the name of freedom. To intervene alone in Indochina "amounted to an attempt to police the entire world." Showing his sensitivity to the politics of the matter, he asserted, "We would soon lose all our significant support in the free world. We should be everywhere accused of imperialistic ambitions." Stassen, who obviously did not know when to quit, kept pleading. "To do no more than we have done," he cried, "would be tantamount to giving Britain a veto on U.S. action in Southeast Asia." Eisenhower was unmoved.[53]

Such criticisms of Eisenhower's actions—or inactions—were not confined to the cabinet. Hawks in the press, none more voluble than Joseph and Stewart Alsop, wondered why the Eisenhower team, once so bold in its anticommunism, had lost its nerve. Dien Bien Phu, they suggested, was like Yorktown: its loss will surely be such a "psychological blow" that "Indochina must eventually fall into Communist hands." The normally friendly editorial page of the *Washington Post* questioned why France had been abandoned and why Eisenhower had allowed the "erosion of our vital interests in Asia." Calls for action rang out on the Senate floor, where on May 4 Republican Majority Leader Knowland urged Eisenhower to act. Knowland proposed American military intervention to save Indochina even if the British refused to join the effort. There should be no British veto of American policy, he argued, nor could he tolerate what he labeled an "Asian Munich," a sellout of pro-Western nations in Asia in exchange for a fragile and short-term peace.[54]

And these comments came from *friends* of the administration! When the Democratic Party held its annual Jefferson-Jackson Dinner at Washington's Mayflower Hotel on May 6, party leaders took off the gloves and hit Eisenhower mercilessly. President Truman lambasted Ike for "insulting" America's allies, and Lyndon Johnson, who until that moment had never publicly criticized the president's foreign policy, launched into a bitter attack. Having alienated both Britain and France, he said, America stood "naked and alone in a hostile world." The failure of Dulles to close the deal on his united action program marked "a stunning reversal" of policy. "What is American policy on Indochina?" Johnson asked the assembled Democrats as they dined on roasted capon in the cavernous ballroom. It was nothing more than "a dismal series of reversals and confusions." Worse, "we have been caught bluffing by our enemies." Johnson's attack, which kicked off the 1954 congressional midterm campaign, ended with a cruel barb: "This picture of our country needlessly weakened in the world today is so painful that we should turn our eyes from abroad and look homeward."[55]

The next day, as if on cue, the terrible news arrived: Dien Bien Phu had fallen. Having suffered over 3,500 killed, the French garrison was reduced to about 9,000 wounded, emaciated, and ill Frenchmen who now entered captivity. Many of them would die there. The French Empire in Asia faced total collapse. The dreaded Indochinese domino that Ike had prophesied looked ready to fall. Yet the president had refused to act.

VIII

Although Eisenhower would eventually win the praise of posterity for staying out of the Indochinese war in 1954, at the time most observers believed that he and the United States had suffered a terrible defeat. Critics said that Eisenhower had abandoned France, an old ally, as it was engaged in a death struggle with communist insurgents. The president looked on as Dien Bien Phu and northern Vietnam fell to communist battalions. After much bluster about the domino theory, Eisenhower was compelled to reveal that he did not believe all of Indochina was worth fighting for. Most embarrassing, Ike and Foster Dulles could not even persuade Britain, the most stalwart of friends, to join a coalition to help defend Asia from communism. The *Washington Post* called America's failure on united action "one of the most humiliating diplomatic defeats in its history."[56]

Secretary Dulles wearily rebutted the charges of failure. In a nationally televised address on May 7 he explained that the president had resisted military intervention because the United States did not wish to be seen as propping up colonialism in Asia and did not want to act without allied support. Yet he went on, curiously, to reemphasize the domino principle: if Indochina fell to the communists, the rest of Asia would rapidly follow. The tensions in the policy were obvious: the sky was falling, Dulles said, but America would not act to hold it in place.[57]

Dulles publicly tried to rationalize his administration's policy, but on May 12, while testifying in executive session before the Senate Foreign Relations Committee, he seemed genuinely flummoxed and unsure of himself. America had done everything it could short of war. It tried to press the French to decolonize more rapidly, helped train Vietnamese troops, gave France huge sums of money and military hardware, and sought to build an Asian NATO to rally morale. None of it had worked. His plan for united action was now "in the doldrums," he confessed. American policy "has at the present moment fallen into a state which I would not like to call exactly collapse but a state of suspended animation."

Asked to explain why the French had been so badly beaten at Dien Bien Phu despite having chosen that ground to defend, Dulles blamed poor French intelligence, a greater quantity of Chinese military materiel than was expected, and—inevitably—the "devious" behavior of the Oriental. "Almost always it seems our Western people underestimate the capacity of the Asian troops to move surreptitiously through the jungles at night, through trails that are impassable to white people." The senators nodded in assent.[58]

The Eisenhower administration had no plan for what to do next. The world's attention turned to Geneva, where delegations from the Great Powers had been meeting to discuss Korea and, after May 8, Indochina. (The United States, not a combatant in Indochina, did not officially participate in those discussions.) French foreign minister Bidault, in obvious anguish, was compelled to call for a cease-fire following the fall of Dien Bien Phu. The Viet Minh representatives, working under the close supervision of the Chinese, might well have scoffed at such a proposal: they were winning the war, after all. But unbeknownst to the Western powers, China and, behind the scenes, the USSR, wanted the Indochina conflict to come to an end—perhaps a temporary end, but an end nonetheless. They saw how much the Viet Minh had gained and wanted to forestall an American military intervention. Widening the war, seizing the rest of Vietnam, and planting the red flag across all of Indochina—that would surely tip American opinion toward war. So the communist side floated the idea of a temporary partition of Vietnam in order to separate the warring parties and implement a political process for a postcolonial Vietnam.[59]

The French hesitated: Bidault, an archimperialist who hated to give up Indochina, tried to quash talk of partition. He even engaged in secret and fruitless talks with the Americans about some kind of military operation in southern Vietnam that would resurrect the defunct "united action" scheme. Dulles was sympathetic, for he too opposed partition: it would look precisely like the "Asian Munich" that the GOP had decried. But the military option had been foreclosed by France's collapse in the North, and in any case Eisenhower would not budge from the principle that any intervention had to be coordinated with America's allies.

The Americans instead fell back on the barren idea of launching an all-out nuclear war on China if the Chinese now "overtly" intervened in Vietnam as the French were pulling out. In discussing this position with his senior advisers, Eisenhower revealed that his patience was running out. If the communists tried to snatch all of Indochina now, he said, the U.S. response would be massive: "There should be no half-way measures or frittering around. The Navy and the Air Force should go in with full power, using new weapons, and strike at air bases and ports in mainland China." As Dulles put it to Smith, war with China, "waged primarily with sea and air power and modern weapons"—by which he meant nuclear weapons—was "infinitely to be preferred to the task of intervention in Indochina." Rather than wage an unending jungle conflict, the United States could simply launch a nuclear strike on China.[60]

This war talk illustrated the administration's frustration rather than a plausible policy. In any case, events on the ground in Vietnam made Chinese intervention quite unnecessary. After Dien Bien Phu, soldiers in the French-backed Vietnamese Army deserted at an alarming rate. The confident and powerful Viet Minh redeployed its forces to threaten Hanoi and could if it chose snap up the rest of northern Vietnam without much trouble. Whether at the point of a gun or at the peace table, the Viet Minh was going to take northern Vietnam.

Events in Paris too drove the action. On June 18 the French National Assembly voted Pierre Mendès-France into office as prime minister. Publicly committed to ending the war and signing a peace agreement within one month, Mendès-France dismissed Bidault and set about making a deal that would temporarily cut Vietnam in half, impose a cease-fire, secure some Western influence in the southern portion of the country, and allow for nationwide elections in 1956. Once he had settled a crucial sticking point—the neutralization of Cambodia and Laos and the removal of all Viet Minh troops from those two states—Mendès-France moved rapidly to accept the partition of Vietnam.

The Eisenhower administration, its policy in tatters, had little choice but to make the best of these distressing events. On June 23 Eisenhower and Foster Dulles met with congressional leaders in a private conference. Senator Knowland inevitably frothed that the French were going to agree to a "Far Eastern Munich" and accused the administration of appeasement. Dulles had anticipated this and met Knowland with a coolly reasoned and optimistic reply. The shift in the French position toward partition was "not as black as it might appear on the surface," he said. If the French left Indochina altogether, a South Vietnam could emerge under U.S. tutelage: "There is today the possibility of salvaging something free of the taint of French colonialism." With the French out of the way, the United States could "establish a military line, and we must hold that line." It would cost much more money, perhaps $800 million a year, and commit the United States to defend the free states of Southeast Asia, but this was the path forward. "We must hold the western side of the Pacific or it will become a Communist lake," he concluded. Eisenhower agreed and summed up the new American position: "In simple terms, we are establishing international outposts where people can develop their strengths to defend themselves. We cannot publicly call our allies outposts, but we are trying to get that result." The American era in South Vietnam had begun.[61]

Ike and Dulles had realized that the peace deal in Geneva rescued a confused and contradictory American policy in the region. Rather than working alongside a rotten French colonial administration to suppress a powerful communist-nationalist insurgency in the North, the Eisenhower administration could write off the French experience as a terrible failure. In its place the Americans would use their know-how to construct a new South Vietnam on the ashes of the French Empire. In this emerging state, America could showcase its way of life and its democratic ideals and declare its unalterable opposition to further communist encroachment.

Although the United States was not a signatory to the Geneva Accords of July 21, 1954, which ended the war and divided Vietnam, the Eisenhower administration embraced them nonetheless. Secretary Dulles released a statement on July 23, saying that while the Geneva agreement contained "many features which we do not like," the important thing was "not to mourn the past but to seize the future." With France and its heavy colonial baggage gone, America could begin its own kind of nation-building in South Vietnam. One day this fledgling protectorate might come to look like West Germany or South Korea—other divided nations in which Western resolve had stabilized a dangerous frontier. South Vietnam would become a new test of America's purpose in the cold war.[62]

In August 1954 Eisenhower signed off on a new statement of American policy in Asia. NSC 5429 asserted that, in order to compensate for the loss of prestige the West had suffered due to the communist victory in northern Vietnam, the United States would rededicate itself to shoring up military and economic ties to Japan, Taiwan, and the Philippines, as well as Australia and New Zealand. Laos, Cambodia, and South Vietnam too would come under the American umbrella. A new regional security treaty, the Southeast Asia Treaty Organization, would pull Asian states into a military alliance backed by American power. Rather than being an outdated colonial structure designed to prop up European influence, SEATO would serve as a joint enterprise of Asian states that desired American partnership to keep communism at bay. In discussing this new, muscular policy in the NSC on August 12, Dulles relished its simplicity: "In the Southeast Asia treaty it was proposed to draw the line to include Laos, Cambodia, and South Vietnam on our side. The theory of the treaty was that if the Communists breached the line we would attack Communist China."

Eisenhower agreed. America had suffered a black eye in northern Vietnam, even if the defeat had been France's. Ike welcomed the opportunity to clarify American policy. From now on, with the colonial question out of the way, things would be different. The president wrapped up the NSC meeting with the simplest of statements: "Sometime we must face up to it: We can't go on losing areas of the free world forever."[63]

IX

Within weeks he would have his first chance to demonstrate America's newfound resolve, not in Vietnam but in Taiwan (then called Formosa). Taiwan was the island redoubt of Chiang Kai-shek, the Chinese Nationalist leader. Following his defeat by the communists in 1949, Chiang and his Nationalist Army had fled to Taiwan, where he became one of America's most important allies, much admired by hawks in Washington for his stout anticommunism, his Methodism, and his Wellesley-educated wife, Soong Mei-ling. To communist China, however, Taiwan represented a strategic threat as well as a highly embarrassing piece of unfinished business. Mao Zedong desperately desired the destruction of Chiang's outpost, and in July 1954 he asked the Chinese military to draw up plans for an invasion to "liberate" Taiwan from foreign control. As a preliminary move, China had to seize a group of tiny islands right off its coastline that Chiang's Nationalists had held since 1949 and that could hamper China's military operations. These island groups, collectively called Quemoy and Matsu, became the site of one of the most dangerous confrontations of the cold war.[64]

On September 3, 1954, Mao gave the order to unleash a major artillery barrage on the island of Quemoy and its 50,000 Nationalist troops. Analysts in Washington tried to divine Chinese intentions: Was this the start of an invasion of Quemoy and perhaps of Taiwan itself? Or was China simply testing America's resolve to back up the Nationalists? Either way, the Chinese attack presented the administration with a serious problem. Eisenhower could signal indifference to the shelling, effectively abandoning the small offshore islands to the Red Chinese. But that would undermine Chiang, damage America's prestige in Asia, and cause a firestorm of protest by the Asia First Republicans at home. Or Eisenhower could declare America's unalterable support for the tiny islands and reply to Chinese attacks with a war on China. As Secretary Dulles put it in an NSC discussion, it was a "horrible dilemma."[65]

The NSC debated this awful predicament in mid-September, and its members fell out much as they had over Indochina. Radford urged a swift response to the attacks and wanted to provide air and naval support for Quemoy, knowing full well this would mean war with China. Secretary of Defense Wilson said he "was opposed to getting into war over these 'dog-goned little islands,'" and Treasury Secretary Humphrey agreed. Much as they had done in Indochina, Eisenhower and Dulles tried to find a way to delay, prevaricate, and keep the Chinese guessing. On September 12 Dulles suggested to Ike that sympathetic allies might raise the issue of Chinese "aggression" in the UN Security Council, thus perhaps embarrassing the communist bloc and buying time.[66]

While this ruse played out, the administration debated its next move. Although Eisenhower recognized that the islands were "not really important except psychologically," they could not be given up under duress to the communist Chinese, especially in light of the recent American passivity in Indochina. Yet the islands also could not be defended tooth and nail. These were insignificant islets, little more than seaweed-choked clusters of rock that were not vital to America's security, and for that matter not vital to Taiwan's defense either. In short, they were nothing but symbols. Was America going to attack China with atomic bombs over a few small islands? The stakes were indeed that high. For as Eisenhower chillingly stated to the NSC, "If we are to attack Communist China, [the president] was firmly opposed to any holding back like we did in Korea." This time the war would go nuclear.

Eisenhower certainly did not want the conflict to escalate. His mailbag was filled with letters asking, as he put it, "What do we care what happens to those yellow people out there?" It would be a "big job," he said, to explain why Americans should die for these tiny islands. But the black eye America had received in Vietnam was still bruised and tender. Eisenhower simply could not tolerate any more Chinese provocations.[67]

To find a middle course Eisenhower and Dulles chose to offer the Nationalist government a defensive security treaty that would commit the United States to the defense of Taiwan and the neighboring Pescadores island group. Such an act would demonstrate resolve to domestic critics and reassure Chiang and other Asian allies that America meant to stand up for its friends. But the treaty would leave out any specific mention of Quemoy, Matsu, and other offshore islands. The purpose of this bit of guile was to gain credit for supporting Taiwan while avoiding the burden of an explicit commitment to defend the disputed islands. Eisenhower was a master at delay and evasion, and this action personified his style: Don't make a firm decision until you absolutely must. At the start of December the United States and Taiwan initialed a security pact giving American guarantees to Taiwan but making no mention of Quemoy and Matsu.[68]

But the crisis did not end there. This defense treaty, even with its hedging about Quemoy and Matsu, outraged Mao. He saw it as proof that the United States aimed to create a U.S. military colony in Taiwan. On January 6, 1955, Mao's forces opened up a new artillery barrage, this time on the Tachen island group, located 300 miles north of Taiwan, and seemed poised for further military operations along the offshore islands. As his advisers huddled together in anxious meetings in Washington on January 19 and 20, Eisenhower had to look the problem in the face: Had the time for a show-down with China arrived?

Secretary Dulles advised Eisenhower to pressure the Nationalist forces on Tachen island to abandon their position, which was militarily not significant in the defense of Taiwan, and at the same time to make a public statement that clarified the ambiguous language of the mutual defense treaty to make clear that the United States would defend Quemoy and Matsu against any communist attack. "We could not play a fuzzy game any longer," Dulles concluded. "That game was played out." The Chinese were probing, testing. It was time to take a stand and then "deliver on our commitments." Not only that, Dulles said; now was the time for the president to ask Congress for authority to commit the armed forces to the defense of Taiwan and to secure a congressional resolution to that effect. In short, Ike should publicly prepare for war.[69]

In a memorable meeting of the National Security Council on January 20, Robert Cutler argued that Dulles's proposal was likely to increase the risk of war. Eisenhower firmly disagreed. By making American policy crystal clear and laying down an absolute line, the United States "would actually decrease the risk of war with Communist China." In a reversal of his usual policy of deception and ambiguity, Eisenhower now admitted that America's deliberate obfuscation in Asia—what he called its "dangerous drift"—had backfired. Wilson and Humphrey dissented, just as they had done in the debate over bombing Dien Bien Phu. "It was foolish to fight a terrible war with Communist China simply in order to hold all these little islands," Wilson insisted. Defend Taiwan, yes, but forget about these little islands that were within hailing distance of the mainland.

But unlike in the Indochina crisis, Eisenhower lost patience with a strategy of delay and deception. The offshore islands were not by themselves crucial to the defense of Taiwan, but "abandoning these islands" would crush the morale of the Nationalist troops, who might one day be called on to repel a Chinese invasion. Worse, coming so soon after the Western defeat in Vietnam, it would shatter the reputation of the United States in those East Asian nations that America had pledged to defend. And the domestic politics of any abandonment of territory to the communists would be very troublesome. In a revealing comment at the end of a long and contentious meeting, Ike said "there was hardly a word which the people of this country feared more than the term 'Munich.'"[70]

Thus, on January 24, Eisenhower sent a message to Congress asking for authority to use armed forces to defend Taiwan—indeed to do more than that: to repel attacks on "closely related localities" that might be a preliminary to an attack on Taiwan. That could only mean Quemoy and Matsu. "Our purpose is peace," Eisenhower declared, but then insisted that he be given authority to wage war if the line he now drew was crossed. Four days later the "Formosa Resolution" passed the two houses of Congress with near unanimity. Unlike during the Dien Bien Phu crisis, Eisenhower had laid down a bold red line and signaled to his adversary that he, and his nation, would not retreat.[71]

The passage of the resolution opened a new phase in America's public posturing toward China. Over the course of the next six weeks, administration officials went to considerable lengths to signal to the Chinese their new resolve. On March 8, in a nationally televised speech, Secretary Dulles stressed that America would use "new and powerful weapons of precision" to defend its interests in Asia—a clear reference to atomic bombs. In his press conference on March 16, Eisenhower backed up Dulles, saying, "In any combat where these things [nuclear weapons] can be used on strictly military targets and for strictly military purposes, I see no reason why they shouldn't be used just exactly as you would use a bullet or anything else." In case the press missed the point, he repeated, "Yes, of course they would be used." The next day, in a public speech in Chicago, Vice President Nixon reiterated the government's position that "tactical nuclear weapons are now conventional and will be used against targets of any aggressive force."[72]

Was Eisenhower really considering a nuclear war against China? The evidence seems clear that he was. In contrast to his reluctance to send troops to fight in Vietnam, he seemed prepared to hit China with a devastating nuclear air strike, not just because such a blow could be delivered quickly and without infantry divisions on the ground but also because the Taiwan crisis provided a clear-cut case of Chinese aggression against a U.S. ally. The Dien Bien Phu battle had been a muddle with no easy choices. The Quemoy crisis looked much simpler. A Chinese attack would be met by war.

The nuclear saber-rattling had the desired effect. On April 23 the Chinese foreign minister, Zhou Enlai, announced that China wanted no war with the United States and stressed China's desire for friendship with the American people. The shelling of the islands fell off dramatically and the crisis was dispelled. Eisenhower's threats seemed to have worked. But at what cost? America's use of nuclear brinkmanship made Eisenhower look tough and determined, but it deeply alarmed the European allies, who now feared more than ever that the United States might trigger a global nuclear war. Ike's menacing warnings may also have pushed China into a search for its own nuclear weapon as a counterweight to America's. Just 10 years later, in 1964, China would test its first nuclear bomb.[73]

In evaluating Eisenhower's handling of the twin Indochina and Taiwan crises of 1953–55, it is difficult to support the argument that he demonstrated commendable restraint. Certainly he decided against a unilateral American intervention in Vietnam in the tumultuous spring of 1954, but the problem of confronting communism in Asia was larger than that. His ambition to contain Chinese influence and suppress communist rebellions in Asia led him to make a series of dramatically hawkish public statements that pledged American prestige in Asia, and from which neither he nor his successors could easily walk away. By resorting to nuclear brinkmanship and constantly speaking about falling dominoes, Eisenhower narrowed his options for dealing with future crises. At some point America would have to make the terrible choice between living up to its promises or skulking away.

Yet one can rightly ask: What was the alternative to Eisenhower's policy? War, certainly, was one. Another would have been a politically disastrous decision to turn away from Indochina altogether and leave it to its fate. In retrospect that might look appealing, but presidents do not govern in retrospect. They must make decisions in real time, and Eisenhower tried his best to pursue his broader goal of containment while avoiding war. He himself acknowledged the amount of improvisation that went into his policymaking. Far from claiming that he followed a grand strategy in Asia, he admitted that America "threaded its way, with watchfulness and determination through narrow and dangerous waters between appeasement and global war." To a great degree he managed to accomplish that balancing act. His successors, alas, did not.[74]

CHAPTER 9

TAKING ON JIM CROW

"There must be no second class citizens in this country."

I

HIS MOTHER WANTED AN OPEN-CASKET FUNERAL. SHE WANTED the world to see what they had done to him.

In the early morning of August 28, 1955, in a small Mississippi Delta cotton-mill town along the Tallahatchie River called Money, Emmett Till, a 14-year-old African American boy, was abducted from his great-uncle's home, driven to a nearby barn, brutally beaten, and then shot to death. His naked body, wrapped in barbed wire and tied to a heavy cotton-gin fan, was dumped into the brown slow-moving river, where it lay on the muddy bottom until, three days later, two boys out fishing discovered the mutilated and swollen corpse.

Till was from Chicago, where he lived on the South Side with his mother, Mamie Till Bradley, who had been born in Mississippi but moved to Illinois as a baby with her parents in the early 1920s. Young Emmett had expressed an interest in visiting his extended relatives in the South, where he planned to stay with his mother's uncle, Mose Wright, a sharecropper. Three days after arriving in Money, Till and his cousins went to buy candy at Bryant's Grocery. Something about Till, an extroverted city kid from up north, gave offense to the 21-year-old white woman, Carolyn Bryant, who was working behind the counter. Perhaps he had been impolite, or had looked at her wrong. Mrs. Bryant later claimed that Till made suggestive remarks and had whistled at her. (Many years later she recanted.)[1]

The details did not matter much to Roy Bryant, who returned home on August 27 after working a long shift as a truck driver hauling shrimp from New Orleans to Texas. The idea that a black boy, from the North no less, had leered at his wife in his own grocery store was too much for Bryant to bear. Given the sexual innuendo of the tale Carolyn related to her husband, Roy felt fully empowered to administer the kind of punishment that whites had been doling out to black people in the South for many generations.

It did not take long for Bryant and his half-brother, J. W. Milam, to discover that the boy they believed had insulted Carolyn was staying at Mose Wright's house. They drove there in Milam's pickup truck at 2:00 a.m. on August 28, seized Till, and threw him into the truck. Over the course of the next few hours, Bryant and Milam took the boy to a number of locations, beating him savagely at every stop, until finally they shot him in the head and threw his weighted body into the river.

After Till's disfigured body was recovered, it was shipped back to Chicago. At the Illinois Central train station, Mamie Till Bradley dropped to her knees in anguished prayer upon seeing the wrapped bundle containing her son's remains. "Oh God, my boy, my only boy," she wailed, filling the hall with her wrenching cries. She decided that his death would not go unnoticed. The body was placed in an open casket at the Roberts Temple of the Church of God in Christ at 4021 South State Street. For the next five days, as word spread and the murder became a national story, tens of thousands of people filed past the bier, gazing at the horrific sight. "Mississippi Lynches Boy," screamed the front page of the *Pittsburgh Courier*. "Emmett Till Funeral Saddens City, Nation," was the headline of the *Chicago Defender* above heartbreaking scenes of the funeral. *Jet* magazine published close-up photos of the boy's bashed and swollen, contorted face.[2]

The National Association for the Advancement of Colored People (NAACP) demanded that the Justice Department launch an investigation and put an end to "a state of jungle fury" in Mississippi. Mayor Richard Daley of Chicago sent a public telegram to President Eisenhower asking for swift justice for Till, as did Governor William Stratton of Illinois. In Mississippi, however, the reaction to Till's murder was muted. Governor Hugh White named a special prosecutor, and the two suspected murderers were indicted and put on trial in Tallahatchie County just a few weeks later.

But the white authorities quickly closed ranks. The prosecution was lackluster. The two men admitted to seizing Till but claimed to have released him later. The defense asserted that the body retrieved from the river could not be identified and that Till might still be alive. Witnesses were intimidated. The sheriff of Tallahatchie County, Clarence Strider, announced his opinion that the "whole thing looks like a deal made up by the NAACP."

The trial lasted five days and attracted national press coverage, though black journalists reporting on the trial were segregated from whites in the courtroom. The jury was all white and all male, and on September 23 after an hour of deliberation it returned a verdict: Milam and Bryant were acquitted.[3]

Why did the Emmett Till case become a nationwide controversy? After all, his was not the only murder of a black person in Mississippi in the summer of 1955. In May, Rev. George W. Lee, a local member of the Regional Council of Negro Leadership and an NAACP organizer, was shot to death in Belzoni while leading a voter registration drive. On August 13, a 63-year-old farmer and World War I veteran named Lamar Smith, who was also active in a voter registration campaign, was shot and killed on the steps of the Brookhaven Courthouse. There had been little national attention paid to these murders. By contrast, Till's youth and the particularly vicious details of the murder transformed his case into a national tragedy. And his Chicago roots meant that the northern press and politicians took an immediate interest and helped the NAACP in its efforts to shine a powerful light on Mississippi. When Till's killers walked out of the courtroom free men, the national news media was there to record the scene. And when in early 1956 Bryant and Milam defiantly and publicly admitted killing the boy, the murder case became a symbol of the shame of white supremacy and a rallying cry of the struggle for black freedom that in the 1950s was gaining power across the nation.[4]

For all its self-congratulation as a time of peace and prosperity, the Age of Eisenhower was also a time of racial turmoil and confrontation. Eisenhower found the civil rights crisis a deeply unsettling and troublesome issue, one he was ill-prepared to handle. Yet presidents always confront crises they do not foresee and often do not understand. It is then that history is best able to take the measure of the man. How would Eisenhower respond?

II

Eisenhower had little personal experience with or knowledge of black people. True, his valet, the man who dressed him every day for 27 years, Sgt. John Moaney, was black, but Eisenhower's entire career was spent in the segregated U.S. military. His army patrons—Fox Conner, Douglas MacArthur, and George Marshall—had southern ties, as did most of the general officers he led in the great crusade in Europe, from George Patton (who attended Virginia Military Institute before West Point) to Leonard T. Gerow (a Virginian), J. Lawton Collins (born in New Orleans), Lucian Truscott (a Texan), and Courtney Hodges (from Georgia). Bedell Smith grew up in Indianapolis, where public schools were segregated until 1948, and Omar Bradley hailed from Randolph County, Missouri, where slavery had been practiced until the end of the Civil War.

Soon after he left the army, while testifying before the Senate Armed Services Committee on universal military service, Eisenhower was invited to give his views on racial segregation in the military. His response was quite lengthy. The army, he opined, "is just one of the mirrors that holds up to our faces the United States of America. . . . There is race prejudice in this country, and when you put in the same organization and make live together under the most intimate circumstances men of different races, we some-times have trouble." He spoke about the segregation that was in place when he first joined the army four decades earlier, calling it "extreme" and unnec-essary. But he suggested that "amalgamation" would cause problems. "You always have some men that do not like to mingle freely between the races, and therefore if you have a dance for your soldiers, you have a problem. But I believe those things can be handled."

More difficult, he went on, was the issue of promotion. Black men with-out the opportunities for education that whites might have had would al-ways be at a disadvantage in a desegregated army, Ike said. A better practice was to keep black units intact, thus allowing them to develop a cadre of black officers. Eventually, Eisenhower hoped, "the human race may finally grow up," and such concerns would disappear. But for now, "if we attempt by passing a lot of laws to force someone to like someone else, we are just going to get into trouble." These comments reveal a man who believed that racial segregation in both the army and the nation had an organic quality. It was unpleasant and probably wrong, but because of its history, it could not be eradicated quickly, nor should federal policy be seen as the principal agent of change. Let sleeping dogs lie.[5]

That Eisenhower held such views is not surprising. He had lived in small-town Kansas or on army bases all his life, and he knew nothing of the crisis of black life in modern America. He had seen Jim Crow in operation and given it little thought. He had grown up in a world that was domi-nated by whites and in which black people had no power or prominence. He knew very little about the aspirations of black Americans. He had no black friends, no black teachers, no black role models, and no black colleagues.

His favorite place to unwind was Augusta National Golf Club, a bastion of white male privilege in the heart of the Old South. He simply had no inkling that the struggle for African American civil rights was going to become perhaps *the* defining social problem of his era and of the next half-century.

Eisenhower was hardly alone among white Americans in failing to perceive the depth of black anger and the urgent need for action, although already in the mid-1940s some leaders had begun to press for change. Truman had taken important steps, setting up the President's Committee on Civil Rights in 1946. It produced a landmark report, *To Secure These Rights*, in October 1947, which outlined specific policy proposals to advance civil rights. In July 1948 Truman ordered the desegregation of the federal workforce and the armed services, a major accomplishment. He called for a federal antilynching law and a ban on the poll tax. He also wanted to create a permanent Fair Employment Practices Commission to ensure nondiscrimination in hiring in industries that were working on government contracts. But Truman was stymied by his own Democratic Party, which was deeply cleft on the issue of race. Segregationist southern Democrats held a stranglehold on the Senate; no civil rights legislation had a chance in that chamber. Many of Truman's civil rights policies were stillborn.[6]

During the 1952 presidential campaign, Eisenhower shied away from making strong statements in support of civil rights. In his first press conference as a candidate, held in Abilene on June 5, 1952, he declared his "unalterable support of fairness and equality among all types of American citizens," but quickly hedged: "I do not believe we can cure all the evils in men's hearts by law," an echo of his 1948 congressional testimony. "I do repeat again and again my fear," he told the press in New York on June 7, "that in law itself we do not find the answer always." In Detroit a week later he again extolled equality as "the basic conception of our whole government." But he insisted that he would "never use a coercive law when we might aggravate instead of help to advance the program of pure equality of opportunity in this country."

By September 1952 Eisenhower had broadened his message somewhat, stating that he would eagerly abolish segregation in the nation's capital and continue to expunge it from the armed services. In enforcing Jim Crow segregation in Washington, D.C., he said, "we have the poorest possible example given to those of other lands of what this country is and what it means." But he would not impose new laws on the South. "An ounce of leadership," he said in a speech in Wheeling, West Virginia, "is worth a pound of law." In a major address on civil rights in Newark, New Jersey, on October 17, Eisenhower said his goal was to act "in a spirit of good will" toward states where segregation still persisted. He wished to "enlist cooperation, not invite resistance." Framing his statement as a criticism of Truman's failures to get results, he insisted that what was needed "to deal with the problem of race relations, to provide equal opportunities and to end racism, is leadership." Leading by example and exhortation rather than using federal law: that was Eisenhower's preferred method. On civil rights, it seemed, he planned to speak loudly and carry a small stick.[7]

III

To his credit, Eisenhower followed through on his modest campaign promises on civil rights. In his first State of the Union address just two weeks after his inauguration, he drew the nation's attention to the question of racial injustice: "We know that discrimination against minorities persists [in America]. Such discrimination—confined to no one section of the Nation—is but the outward testimony to the persistence of distrust and of fear in the hearts of men. This fact makes all the more vital the fighting of these wrongs by each individual, in every station of life, in his every deed." He then announced a concrete action: "I propose to use whatever authority exists in the office of the President to end segregation in the District of Columbia, including the Federal Government, and any segregation in the Armed Forces."[8]

Washington was a southern town in the 1950s, and segregation had been in place there for many decades. President Wilson had overseen the formal segregation of the federal workforce upon taking office in 1913, and in a city in which one-third of all jobs were in federal service, this denial of opportunity had a huge economic impact on black city residents. Cafés and restaurants, buses, movie houses, public housing, and schools were mostly segregated. No black person could stay overnight in a downtown hotel. Black citizens who rode trains from the North to the South had to switch to segregated cars in Washington. When Eisenhower came into office, a court case was already pending that challenged Jim Crow in the capital city. The plaintiffs argued that there were already laws on the books in Washington, dating from the Reconstruction era, which banned racial discrimination in restaurants. The laws had been passed by the local government in 1872 and 1873 and had long been ignored but never legally repealed. The case,

District of Columbia v. John R. Thompson Co., made its way to the Supreme Court, where arguments were heard on April 30, 1953.

Eisenhower and his attorney general, Herbert Brownell, showing considerable creativity, seized the opportunity to join the case and filed an amicus curiae brief in support of the plaintiffs. Brownell, who held progressive views on race and civil rights, wanted the Justice Department to deliver on the president's pledge to end segregation in the capital. His brief certainly pleased Thurgood Marshall, the chief legal counsel for the NAACP, who publicly praised the attorney general for his support. On June 8, 1953, the Court unanimously found that the earlier statutes banning "whites only" cafés were valid. At a stroke the Court opened up the capital's dining places to African American patrons, with the overt support of the administration. Movie theaters followed suit. It was only a start: the capital's public schools were still segregated, but that issue was also being taken up in the courts. For the city's African American residents, this was a major victory, and the administration would seek to take political credit for the Court's decision.[9]

Equally impressive was the speed with which Eisenhower embraced the tricky issue of segregation in the military. Of course Truman had started the process to desegregate the armed forces, but much remained to be done. Across the country in the early 1950s army and navy bases were still segregated, including military housing, schools, cafeterias, drinking fountains, and workplaces. In mid-March 1953 Eisenhower was asked at a press conference by an African American journalist, Alice A. Dunnigan, if he was aware that the army continued to operate white-only schools, which seemed incompatible with his declared policy of eliminating segregation in areas of federal responsibility. The question caught Ike off guard. "I haven't heard it; I will look it up," he replied. But he went on to say, "Wherever federal funds are expended for anything, I do not see how any American can justify— legally, or logically, or morally—a discrimination in the expenditure of those funds among our citizens." There was little ambiguity in this message.[10]

The next day Secretary of the Army Robert Stevens produced a memo for the president's press secretary, James Hagerty, that confirmed Dunnigan's assertion: there were indeed segregated schools being operated on military installations in Virginia, Oklahoma, and Texas. These schools, however, were funded by the states and supervised by local school boards. The only way to integrate these schools, Stevens believed, was to have base commanders negotiate with local authorities, and if they proved unwilling to comply, the Department of the Army would have to build and run new, integrated schools. If this happened, wrote Stevens, the administration would surely be attacked in Congress and the press "for needlessly spending public funds." Eisenhower brushed aside this objection and directed the army and navy to conduct a survey of their installations and report on the progress toward desegregation of their facilities.[11]

In early June, however, Congressman Adam Clayton Powell Jr., the charismatic Baptist clergyman from Harlem who had served in Congress since 1945 and gained a national reputation as an outspoken civil rights advocate, made an embarrassing allegation: Eisenhower's own staff was blocking the president's policies. "Your official family," Powell charged in an open letter to the president, "has completely undermined your stated position on segregation." Officials in the Veterans Administration, the navy, and the Department of Health, Education and Welfare were countermanding desegregation orders. "The hour has arrived for you to decisively assert your integrity," demanded Powell.[12]

The accusation stung, and it prodded Maxwell Rabb into action. Rabb, a Harvard-trained lawyer, was officially the secretary to the cabinet, but he was also a seasoned congressional hand and a former aide to Senator Henry Cabot Lodge Jr. By default he had been given the unofficial portfolio of "minorities officer" in the Eisenhower White House. Rabb reached out to Powell and cut a deal: Eisenhower would issue a temperate public reply that promised swift action on Powell's charges. In return, Powell would declare himself satisfied. The deal stuck: Rabb's draft had Eisenhower declare "I will carry out every pledge I have made with regard to segregation." He said his staff was working hard to achieve his program: "We have not taken and we shall not take a single backward step. There must be no second class citizens in this country." Powell, with characteristic overstatement, hailed Ike's pledge as "a Magna Carta for minorities and a second Emancipation Proclamaton." For the black community, so starved for official recognition of their struggle, Ike's commitment marked a breakthrough.[13]

Rabb now pushed White House Chief of Staff Sherman Adams to make sure the president did indeed hold up his end of the bargain. In particular Rabb and Adams put great pressure on Secretary of the Navy Robert Anderson to abolish the last vestiges of segregation on naval bases. Under orders from the White House, two navy officials made visits to the large navy bases at Norfolk, Virginia, and Charleston, South Carolina, to investigate the status of the desegregation effort. Reports came in from dozens of other naval facilities across the South. The picture was entirely predictable:

washrooms, cafeterias, drinking fountains, and some work spaces were still segregated—fully five years after Truman's July 1948 Executive Order that commanded desegregation of the armed forces. Under direct pressure from the president, Anderson moved fast. In August 1953 he ordered the removal of "Colored" and "White" signs over water fountains and toilet facilities. Mess halls were next. By November 1 Eisenhower could proudly and truthfully state that at the 60 naval facilities in the South, segregation had been eliminated.[14]

And he was not finished. On August 13, when he was putting pressure on the armed services to root out the last vestiges of segregation, Eisenhower announced the creation of the Committee on Government Contracts, a body designed to oversee nondiscrimination policies in the allocation of federal contracts. It marked a definite reversal for the president, who in the campaign had rejected Truman's proposal to create a permanent Fair Employment Practices Commission (FEPC). Yet now, under pressure from black leaders, Ike relented. He named Nixon as its co-chairman to indicate the seriousness of the committee. In correspondence with Nixon, he stated that the Government Contracts Committee was "proof of our own faith" in the principle of equality. "On no level of our national existence can inequality be justified."[15]

Of course this was only an advisory body, designed, Ike wrote, to "find out whether existing laws are being enforced." It had no coercive authority. But Executive Order 10479 was hailed by black leaders as a sign of progress. Given the significance of federal contracts in the American economy, Eisenhower was ensuring that a major segment of jobs would now be subject to federal nondiscrimination policy. Walter White, the executive secretary of the NAACP and a frequent critic of Eisenhower, praised the president's action, which "merits the gratitude of thousands who are now denied a chance to work or use their highest skills in the mills and factories that hold government contracts."[16]

Eisenhower's southern friends took notice, as the president learned in July at a lunch with his "great friend," Governor James Byrnes of South Carolina. A former Democratic senator, Supreme Court justice, and secretary of state under Truman, Byrnes had backed Eisenhower in 1952. At their lunch, according to Eisenhower's diary, Byrnes expressed his anxiety that the Supreme Court might soon issue a ruling banning segregation in public schools. If that happened, Byrnes warned, there would not only be "riots, resultant ill feeling and the like," but the southern states would "immediately

cease support for public schools." Byrnes seemed to suggest that while opinion in the South was evolving with respect to the desegregation of public
places, buses, and the workplace, schooling was a different matter: "They are
frightened of putting the children together." Eisenhower wrote that Byrnes
was "afraid that I would be carried away by the hope of capturing the Negro
vote in this country."

But Ike reassured the South Carolinian of his belief that "improvement
in race relations is one of those things that will be healthy and sound only if
it starts locally." Prejudice, Ike insisted, will not "succumb to compulsion,"
and any imposition of federal law on states "would set back the cause of
progress in race relations for a long, long time." This was a classic expression
of Eisenhower's inner convictions: racial discrimination was wrong, but its
remedy must emerge from within the communities and states themselves.
Federal legislation could only make trouble. The president made every effort to signal to white southerners that he did not plan to confront Jim Crow
in the South.[17]

Eisenhower's first eight months in office had brought about meaningful
progress, including the desegregation of restaurants in the nation's capital,
the vigorous attack on the remaining segregated practices in military installations, and the creation of a "little FEPC" in the form of the Government
Contracts Committee. Yet these were relatively easy triumphs, at little cost,
fought on ground chosen by the administration. A far greater test came
when African Americans challenged the segregation of public schools and
compelled Eisenhower to take a public stand: Would he support them in
their bid to open public schools to all, or side with his friends in the South?

IV

The segregation by race of public schools in the United States had won legal
sanction through the Supreme Court's ruling in *Plessy v. Ferguson* in 1896.
In that case the Court ruled that the state of Louisiana could legally separate whites from blacks on public railway cars, provided that the cars themselves were of equal quality. The Court concluded that while the Fourteenth
Amendment to the Constitution enforced the equality of all people before
the law, it did not "abolish distinctions based upon color," nor did it insist
on "commingling the two races." In *Plessy*, the Court implied, people could
be equal before the law but unequal among each other. In society distinctions of race, color, religion, and social status clearly still mattered, and on

such social customs the Constitution was silent. Simply separating citizens according to their color did not imply the inferiority of one race. If separate public facilities provided to black and white citizens were equal, the state was free to decide which citizens could use which facilities. The *Plessy* decision was of monumental significance, for it provided legal validity to racial segregation in "separate but equal" public schools.[18]

For over half a century the doctrine of "separate but equal" served as a legal barrier to black schoolchildren who wished to attend white-only local schools. Seventeen southern and border states required public schools to be segregated by race; other states chose to allow segregation on a school-by-school basis. Not until June 1950 did a few cracks appear in the legal edifice that supported such segregation. In two decisions the Supreme Court ruled that the universities of Texas and Oklahoma had to admit two black men to their graduate schools because they had failed to provide these men with equal facilities to pursue their studies. The Court meant not just equal facilities but equal treatment inside the classroom. The plaintiff in the Oklahoma case, George McLaurin, was studying for a doctoral degree in education. He was forced to sit in a sort of alcove in the classroom, separated from the white students; he was assigned to a separate table in the library and took his meals at a separate table in the cafeteria. The Court objected to this treatment, ruling that "the Fourteenth Amendment precludes differences in treatment by the state based upon race." McLaurin, "having been admitted to a state-supported graduate school, must receive the same treatment at the hands of the state as students of other races." This was a major blow against *Plessy*, for it suggested that the "separate but equal" principle was not in fact protected by the Constitution.[19]

Sensing an opportunity, Thurgood Marshall of the NAACP's Legal Defense Fund decided in October 1950 on a legal challenge to the entire "separate but equal" doctrine in all public schooling. Marshall's team provided legal advice and lawyers to assist plaintiffs in five separate cases, in South Carolina, Virginia, the District of Columbia, Delaware, and Kansas. These cases would be grouped together by the Supreme Court when it decided to hear the case of *Oliver Brown v. Board of Education of Topeka* in December 1952. At the very moment Eisenhower was taking the helm of the nation, the Supreme Court was preparing to pass judgment on one of the thorniest, most explosive social issues in the nation's history.[20]

The anxiety of the Court in facing school desegregation became evident in June 1953. Although it had been mulling over the *Brown* case for six months, the Court announced that it would postpone its decision pending another round of arguments. The legal issues, and the social consequences, were too great for the Court to move rapidly. News reports hinted at divisions among the justices. It is also possible that Chief Justice Fred Vinson was looking for guidance from the newly installed Eisenhower administration. In announcing the postponement, Vinson invited Attorney General Brownell to file a brief as a "friend of the Court," stating the opinion of the administration on the matter of segregation in public schools. The Court, it seemed, wanted to flush out the president rather than bear the burden entirely on its own shoulders.[21]

Eisenhower, who would have preferred to steer clear of the issue, was caught in a dilemma. While vacationing in Denver in mid-August he called Brownell to express his preference that the administration decline the request of the Court to file a brief. He even went so far as to dictate a "Memorandum for the Record" after the phone call, noting his own worry that the Court was unfairly asking him to put his thumb on the scale. Crucially and with great cunning, Brownell talked Eisenhower through the issue and persuaded him that, as attorney general, he could not possibly remain silent: it would be tantamount to shirking his duty. The Court had asked for advice; he must answer. Eisenhower relented and, from this point on, tried to deflect all public discussion of the *Brown* case onto his attorney general.[22]

Brownell took advantage of the leeway Eisenhower gave him. Working behind closed doors for three months with a team of Justice Department lawyers, Brownell did extensive research into the origins of the Fourteenth Amendment. In his brief he asserted that the purpose of Congress in framing the amendment in 1868 was clearly "to strike down distinctions based on race or color" and to establish "equality of all persons under the law." The nub of the issue was this: Did this intent apply to public schools? Brownell admitted the record was inconclusive, but he claimed that Congress did not "enumerate in detail all the specific applications" of the law. Rather, the Fourteenth Amendment's "great and pervading purpose" was "to establish complete equality for Negroes in the enjoyment of fundamental human rights." If the segregation of public schools by state mandate resulted in any form of inequality, Brownell suggested, then it was necessarily unconstitutional and the Court must ban it.[23]

As Brownell was working on his brief for the Court, Washington was hit by the sudden death on September 8, 1953, of Chief Justice Vinson, of a heart attack at the age of 63. The significance of Vinson's passing was enormous. Although an affable and decent Democrat from Kentucky, much liked personally by Eisenhower, Vinson had not been a success as chief justice. It was now up to Eisenhower to appoint a replacement, someone who might determine the outcome of the school desegregation case and who could shape the Court and the nation for decades to come. Ike's choice, settled on quite rapidly, was Earl Warren.

Warren was a dignified national political figure. Tall, broad-shouldered, of Scandinavian descent, he was a three-time winner of the California governorship and a former state attorney general. He had been the GOP vice-presidential candidate in 1948 and had a reputation as a moderate and a man of integrity. Warren had challenged Ike for the GOP presidential nomination in 1952, but this former political rivalry did not hurt his standing with Eisenhower, who, after the general election, told Warren that he hoped to appoint him to the first vacancy on the Supreme Court.[24]

Part of Eisenhower's enthusiasm for Warren sprang from his belief that Truman's Supreme Court appointments had been undistinguished, going chiefly to political friends and cronies. Vinson had been a close friend of Truman's in Congress. Tom C. Clark, appointed in 1949, had been Truman's attorney general; he was a political "fixer" with no judicial experience. Sherman Minton was a New Deal liberal who was also a Truman pal from his Senate days. Even Harold Burton, the one Republican Truman appointed, had come from the Senate. Moreover the Court had been badly divided by ideological and personal feuds between Hugo Black and William O. Douglas on the one hand, and Robert Jackson and Felix Frankfurter on the other. The Court rarely voted unanimously, and Vinson was unable to impose any semblance of unity upon the fractious justices. This state of affairs deeply worried Eisenhower; he wanted men on the Court who were known for integrity, an absence of partisanship, and statesmanship.[25]

Yet, as is so often the case with Eisenhower, there was another angle to the story. The death of the chief justice came just as Brownell was writing his brief for the Court, and just weeks after Eisenhower had his sharp exchange with Byrnes about the role of the federal government in civil rights. Although civil rights concerns did not determine Eisenhower's appointment of Warren, the president knew that these matters would come before the Court soon and he wanted at the helm a proven leader and a statesman— someone, as he put it to his brother Milton, who had been through "the hard knocks of a general experience" in politics. According to a later interview with Brownell, Eisenhower "studied Warren's record long before he was appointed. . . . He admired the way that Warren had governed in California on a non-partisan basis." And Eisenhower "knew about his civil rights record," which was reasonably progressive. Warren was Ike's man, and on September 30, 1953, the president announced his nomination. Congress was in recess at that moment, but Ike, aware that the desegregation cases were already under way, did not wait for Congress to come back into session. He made a recess appointment, and Warren took the oath of office a week later, without congressional approval.[26]

By the fall of 1953, then, Eisenhower had made some key decisions. He had used executive authority to push desegregation in the armed forces; he had aided those seeking to ban segregation in the nation's capital; he allowed his attorney general to present an antisegregation argument before the Supreme Court; and he had appointed a noted California moderate as chief justice. All this on the eve of the arguments in *Brown v. Board of Education*. Perhaps Eisenhower began to feel things were moving too fast. On November 16 he called Brownell to reveal his own unease with the case. He worried that if *Plessy* was overturned, southern states might close public schools altogether rather than integrate them. Brownell, once again reassuring his chief that he was on the right path, told Ike that if the Court chose to strike down segregation in public schools, "it would be a period of years," maybe 10 to 12 years, before integration would take place. Southern leaders like Byrnes could rest easy and "wouldn't have to 'declare war,' so to speak."[27]

But the southern leaders were growing anxious. On November 20 Byrnes and Governor Robert Kennon of Louisiana wrote direct appeals to the president to respect the right of states to run public schools. Kennon, a Democrat who had endorsed Ike in 1952, claimed that "a federal edict" on public schools, "contrary to the established order and customs," would worsen race relations in the South. He went at one of Eisenhower's soft spots, begging him to respect "states' rights, local self-government and community responsibility." Byrnes echoed the same points: "States should have the right to control matters that are purely local." Eisenhower must have felt great pressure: he did believe in states' rights and local responsibility, yet his attorney general, a man he admired and to whom he had given control of the brief, told him the Constitution did not allow states to impose racial segregation.[28]

Defying the opinions of his southern friends, Eisenhower backed Brownell. The attorney general's brief, filed on November 27, was a bombshell. "GOP Backs NAACP," announced the *Pittsburgh Courier* in a banner headline. "Brownell Says Court Should Kill Jim Crow." The president and attorney general "took a calculated and idealistic risk," the newspaper observed, "in riding the trend of modern times." Brownell had boldly confronted *Plessy* head-on by arguing that the issue at hand was not merely "equality as between schools; the Constitution requires that there be equality as between persons." Many southerners howled at this idea. Governor Herman Talmadge of Georgia opined that Brownell was speaking for "radical elements" who "are vying with each other to see who can plunge the dagger deepest into the back of the South." But the die was cast: the Eisenhower administration had decided that racial segregation in public schools contravened the Fourteenth Amendment.[29]

Personally, however, Eisenhower never seemed comfortable taking ownership of the issue. Quite the contrary, in fact. After conferring with Brownell by telephone on December 2, when the two men discussed how to respond to Governor Byrnes, the president sent a letter to Byrnes in which he distanced himself from the *Brown* case. Because the question of the legality of segregation in public schools was a matter for "lawyers and historians," he had been "compelled to turn over to the Attorney General and his associates full responsibility in the matter." Brownell, in writing his brief and advising the Court, had acted "according to his own convictions." This was a remarkable statement: the president asserted that he had delegated one of the most explosive issues facing the nation to his top legal officer. His convictions—not Eisenhower's—would shape the administration's position.[30]

On May 17, 1954, in a unanimous decision written by the new chief justice, the Supreme Court ruled that the segregation of schoolchildren by race "deprived the children of the minority group of equal educational opportunities." To separate students solely on the grounds of race "generates a feeling of inferiority as to their status in the community that may affect their hearts and minds in a way unlikely ever to be undone." The Court's peroration was a damning indictment of the entire structure of Jim Crow segregation: "We conclude that in the field of public education the doctrine of 'separate but equal' has no place. Separate educational facilities are inherently unequal." There was one note of uncertainty in the Court's decision. Taking into account the administrative complexities involved in integrating schools, the Court announced its intention to hear further arguments on how to implement the decision. These arguments would not come for some months; indeed it was not until May 1955 that the Court would address this question fully. Yet this element of caution could not obscure the basic fact: after more than half a century, the nation's highest court had faced American apartheid squarely and condemned it.[31]

It would be wrong to give Eisenhower the credit for the *Brown* decision. That must go above all to the courageous plaintiffs in the separate cases and to the leaders of the NAACP, especially Thurgood Marshall, who over many years had built a legal strategy designed to confront and overturn Jim Crow segregation in the United States. *Brown* was their victory. Yet Eisenhower—perhaps despite his inner convictions—played a crucial role in the story nonetheless, especially by appointing Brownell to run the Justice Department and by placing Earl Warren on the Supreme Court. Things might have worked out quite differently if Eisenhower had named John Foster Dulles, or a southerner he was considering, Judge John J. Parker of North Carolina, as chief justice. At various stages along the way, Eisenhower could have used his power to halt progress. He didn't. Perhaps the best that can be said is this: Eisenhower did not lead the nation toward civil rights reform, but he could sense which way history was moving and did not wish to be left behind.[32]

V

"May 17, 1954, was one of life's sweetest days," wrote Roy Wilkins, the NAACP leader, three decades after the *Brown* decision. "For 58 miserable years" black Americans had suffered under the humiliation of legal segregation. In the Jim Crow South, he wrote, "we had been squeezed into the hollows, alleys, and back streets across the tracks; there we sat in the back of the bus; there for every white man, no matter how low, who passed by, we had to step off the sidewalk, remove our hat, and say 'Sir.'" But now, after *Brown*, "the law was on our side." Wilkins recalled going home and having a glass of Scotch with his wife, Minnie, and drinking a toast to Earl Warren.[33]

It looked like a new day to the African American press too. The *Pittsburgh Courier* printed an editorial titled "Let's Give Thanks," asserting that the *Brown* decision was "the most important affirmation of the ideals of our country since the Emancipation Proclamation." The paper called for a day of prayer and thanksgiving, and acclaimed the role of the president: "Negroes should thank the President of the United States, Dwight D. Eisenhower, for placing this administration in the forefront of the struggle."[34]

Two days after the decision, Eisenhower held a press conference. The remarks he made about *Brown* at this gathering of reporters have sometimes been used by historians to suggest that he was dissatisfied with the decision. But the evidence is open to interpretation. The context is crucially important, for by coincidence, May 17 was a historic day not only because of the *Brown* ruling. That same day Eisenhower had issued his famous letter insisting on executive privilege with respect to the army-McCarthy hearings, ordering Defense Department personnel to refuse any summons or inquiry from McCarthy's committee. It was a major news story, every bit as big as the *Brown* ruling, and in fact it preoccupied Eisenhower and his staff. On May 18, when Ike met with press secretary Hagerty to plot answers for the upcoming press conference, they were chiefly concerned with the issue of executive privilege and how to handle it with the press. Only after working on that issue did they turn to *Brown*. Hagerty's diary records the tenor of the discussion: Eisenhower "would simply say the Supreme Court is the law of the land, that he had sworn to uphold the Constitution and he would do so in this case." Ike also told Hagerty of his worry that "some of the Southern states will take steps to virtually cancel out their public education system," a move that would "not only handicap Negro children but would work to the detriment of the so-called 'poor whites' in the South."[35]

The president had sound reason for concern. Even before the *Brown* decision, a number of southern governors had declared their intention to block integration by closing public schools altogether. Ike rightly feared the consequences. Does this mean he would have preferred that the Court sustain *Plessy*? Certainly not, and the evidence for this is clear: he had approved Brownell's powerful brief for the Court in favor of banning segregation.

When the press conference took place at 10:30 a.m. on May 19, the reporters who gathered in the Indian Treaty Room were in a high state of excitement about the president's recent pronouncement on executive privilege. The first five questions were on this topic, and Eisenhower stood his ground, affirming the importance of the division of powers between the Executive and Congress. He spoke at length on the subject and insisted that whatever discussions had been held in the Executive branch concerning Senator McCarthy's hearings were off limits to congressional investigators. Reporters from the Associated Press, the *New York Post*, the International News Service, the *New York Times*, and the *Washington Star* concentrated their fire on this issue, consuming well over half of the press conference. Only then did a reporter from South Carolina, Harry Dent, ask the president if he had "any advice to give the South as to how to react to the recent

Supreme Court decision." Eisenhower replied, "Not in the slightest," and praised South Carolina governor Jimmy Byrnes for adopting a moderate position in his own public remarks on the decision. Byrnes, Ike said, had advised South Carolinians to "be calm and be reasonable." (In fact Byrnes had not been so temperate; Ike was attributing to him more generosity of spirit than he really showed.) For his part, Eisenhower said, "the Supreme Court has spoken and I am sworn to uphold the constitutional processes in this country; I will obey."

Was this statement an attempt to undermine *Brown*? It was a curt, perhaps strained reply given the significance of the Court's decision, but it was consistent with the words he and Hagerty had planned to use with the press. It was also consistent with his view that the president must not make Supreme Court decisions into partisan political issues. When Dent asked Eisenhower if his Republican administration would pay a political price among southerners for the decision, Ike bristled: "The Supreme Court, as I understand it, is not under any administration." The decision was out of his hands, and voters could draw their own conclusions.[36]

These comments have irked historians for many years. Stephen Ambrose, a prominent (and usually obsequious) biographer, wrote in 1990 that Eisenhower's "refusal to lead [on civil rights] was almost criminal." Eisenhower's failure to laud the *Brown* decision "did incalculable harm to the civil-rights crusade and to America's image." No doubt, looking back many decades after the fact, Eisenhower's reserve in this press conference, and in his later handling of desegregation, strikes the modern observer as lacking sufficient zeal and certitude. At the time, however, he appeared to be taking important strides in support of civil rights. After 80 years of inaction, the federal government and Supreme Court seemed to have found new urgency in facing up to segregation. Eisenhower's actions—appointing Warren, allowing Brownell to argue in favor of overturning *Plessy*, stating his constitutional responsibility to uphold the Court's decision, insisting that Washington initiate desegregation of schools immediately after *Brown* as a model to other cities—were seen in 1954 as evidence of the president's willingness to support civil rights progress.[37]

Nor is there much evidence that Ike resented Warren's handling of *Brown*. In fact he told Hagerty a month after the decision of his satisfaction with Warren: "I wanted a man to serve as Chief Justice who felt the way we do and who would be on the Court for a long time. . . . I am glad I made the decision." Later that fall, in a letter to Swede Hazlett, he described Warren as "a man whose philosophy of government was somewhat along the lines of my own." Ike disowned neither Warren nor *Brown*.[38]

Southerners certainly did not see Eisenhower as moving slowly on civil rights. Quite the contrary. Governor Byrnes said he was "shocked" by the *Brown* decision and asked "how long . . . local government [could] survive" in the face of such powerful assaults on states' rights. He did urge the public to show "restraint" and to "preserve order," but his administration had already secured approval from voters to close public schools rather than integrate them. Governor Talmadge considered the ruling tyrannical and unjust and promised that Georgians would "fight for the right under the United States and Georgia Constitutions to manage their own affairs." He vowed "continued and permanent segregation" in Georgia. Senator Richard Russell, the powerful Georgia Democrat, denounced *Brown* as a "flagrant abuse of judicial power" and spoke of the "tendency of the Court to disregard the Constitution." The Court had become nothing more than a "pliant tool" and "the political arm of the Executive branch." Senators Harry Byrd of Virginia and James Eastland of Mississippi made similar remarks. Southern leaders now saw they could expect no help from the White House.[39]

In truth Eisenhower was caught between two powerful forces, and he did not know how to resolve the tension between them. On the one hand, he believed that equality between citizens and the rule of law were the bedrock ideals of "Americanism" as he understood that term. Therefore defiance of the Supreme Court was unthinkable. Yet he also believed that the federal government must respect local customs, habits, laws, and desires. His speechwriter Emmet Hughes wrote that Eisenhower was determined not to use federal power to push southern states toward dramatic social change: "His political faith rested on the slow, gradual power of persuasion." According to Hughes, Eisenhower insisted, "We can't demand *perfection* in these moral questions. All we can do is keep working toward a goal and keep it high. And the fellow who tries to tell me that you can do these things by *force* is just plain *nuts*."[40]

His go-slow instincts were driven also by certain cultural assumptions that he shared with his southern white friends. For example, the president was not above invoking the specter of race-mixing between black men and white women—an apparition many white people then considered truly horrific—to explain why the South must be allowed time to evolve in its opinions. In a vulgar exchange with Warren at a stag dinner, the president is alleged to have said that white southerners were "not bad people. All they are concerned about is to see that their sweet little girls are not required to sit in school alongside some big overgrown Negroes." This sort of language was regrettably common among men of Eisenhower's inner circle. Byrnes had evoked similar images when speaking to a reporter about the *Brown* decision, painting the following scene: "White girl in shorts plays tennis in the yard of a segregated school; Negro boy enters playground; the basic wall between the species begins to crumble and social chaos has begun."[41]

Even Ike's old chum Swede Hazlett stirred the pot of race and sex in a personal letter to the president. Writing in early 1955 about southern reaction to the ruling, he opined that children had no apprehension about integrated schools and would readily adapt to the new landscape. The problem lay with the "racist parents" who had "visions of walking into their parlour some night and finding a black buck courting their own blonde honey-chile. If honey-chile wants a negro date let her have it. But the chances are 1000 to 1 that she won't—with several centuries of tradition and social usage behind it. When I was a freshman at A[bilene] H[igh] S[chool] Gertie Tyler was a classmate of mine, and a sleek good-looking negress. But I can't recall ever having even thought of social or any other kind of intercourse with her. Ridiculous!" Hazlett thus captured Ike's own racial sensibilities in a nutshell.[42]

The Supreme Court convened its new term in October 1954 and called for briefs to discuss the practical aspects of desegregating public schools. But on October 9 Associate Justice Robert Jackson died, and the chief justice suspended discussion of the matter until a replacement was named. Eisenhower nominated John Marshall Harlan II, the grandson of the Supreme Court justice who, in 1896, had been the sole vote against the *Plessy* decision. A conservative New York lawyer and judge, and a close friend and law partner of Herbert Brownell, Harlan had impeccable legal credentials. Yet to men of the South, he was associated with the work of his famous grandfather, who had declared the Constitution to be "color blind." Southern senators seized on the opportunity of a vacancy on the bench to slow down the work of the Court. The Judiciary Committee elected to delay consideration of the Harlan nomination. The president resubmitted the nomination in January 1955 to the new Congress, but once again hearings were delayed. Not until April 1955, after Harlan's confirmation—in the face of vigorous opposition from southern Democrats—did the Court take up the debate about how to implement desegregation in public schools.[43]

When the debate before the Court resumed on precisely how to advise lower courts in their handling of integrating public schools, the NAACP was ready. Under Thurgood Marshall's direction, NAACP lawyers submitted arguments calling for prompt and immediate desegregation, allowing at most a one-year grace period, until the fall of 1956, by which time desegregation would have to be fully implemented. Marshall said there could be no "moratorium on the Fourteenth Amendment."[44]

The lawyers for the four states that were defendants in the case argued against rapid implementation and asked for time—perhaps an indefinite amount of time—to desegregate the schools. The attorney general of Virginia, J. Lindsay Almond, claimed that a Court order for immediate desegregation "would be pre-emptive of the rights of a sovereign people" and would not be obeyed. The NAACP was asking the Court "to press this crown of thorns upon our brows and press the hemlock cup to our lips." Not to be outdone in fearmongering, I. Beverly Lake, assistant attorney general of North Carolina, claimed that a Court order for immediate desegregation would provoke "racial tension and animosities unparalleled since those terrible days that gave rise to the original Ku Klux Klan."[45]

Which side would Ike take? As in the previous round of arguments, the Eisenhower administration leaned toward the position of the NAACP, but this time it offered an olive branch to the states. The Justice Department brief, submitted on November 24, 1954, at the request of the Court, argued that school boards should be given 90 days to submit plans to end segregation. Federal district courts would then supervise the implementation of those plans, and there would be no hard deadline by which these plans would have to be fulfilled. Arguing that the Court had now decided that the rights of black citizens were being violated, the Justice Department asserted, "Relief short of immediate admission to non-segregated schools necessarily implies the continuing deprivation of those rights." The right of children to attend public schools without encountering racial barriers was "a fundamental human right supported by morality as well as law." That said, Brownell's brief, which was carefully edited by Eisenhower himself, took particular note of the historical context: racial segregation had been practiced for many decades and had long been upheld by the Supreme Court. Therefore, as it was rolled back, local anxieties must be met with "understanding and good will."[46]

When Solicitor General Simon Sobeloff made this case in oral argument before the Court on April 13, 1955, he made it plain that while the government wanted prompt desegregation, it would be content with a "middle course." The government asked that district courts be allowed to supervise desegregation, thus returning to states a role in the process. Yet states must not be allowed "to delay for the mere sake of delay." Local attitudes against desegregation should be taken into account, and local communities should not be ridden over "rough-shod." Even so, "a Constitutional right ought not to depend upon a public opinion poll." States could implement their own plans but must demonstrate a "bona fide advance toward desegregation." Soboloff recognized that states would need some time to act, but "time should not be allowed for paralyzing action." There was more hope than certainty in his argument.[47]

On May 31, 1955, just over a year since the first *Brown* ruling, the Court issued its decision on the remedy in the case, often referred to as *Brown II.* It reaffirmed its 1954 judgment and called for a "prompt and reasonable start toward full compliance" with the previous ruling. The justices took note of administrative and logistical tangles that would emerge as schools integrated but ruled that "the burden rests on the defendants" to show why any delay was needed. The wording of the ruling made it clear that simply disagreeing with the Court was not a valid reason for delay. Therefore desegregation must proceed under court supervision "with all deliberate speed." Following closely the arguments of the Eisenhower team, the Court did not demand immediate desegregation, nor did it set a date by which integration must be completed. This ambiguity would create many problems in the future. But taken as a whole, there could be no doubt that racial segregation in public schools was unconstitutional and must end. "The more I think about it," said Thurgood Marshall two days later, "I think it's a damned good decision!"[48]

VI

Historians who wish to portray Eisenhower as a failure on civil rights cannot look to the first three years of his administration for much supporting evidence. In fact Eisenhower presided over a significant acceleration of civil rights reform. In the summer of 1955, in the wake of the *Brown* decisions, he received accolades from African American leaders for the progress he had encouraged. The NAACP expressed a "debt of gratitude" to the president at its 46th annual convention in Atlantic City, detailing the considerable success of the previous few years: "During 1954, America turned the corner from partial toward full freedom for all citizens." At the end of July 1955 the Republican Party released a report hailing Eisenhower's achievements on civil rights policy, and in early August Eisenhower himself took a victory lap, boasting that his record on civil rights had been "one of action, not words."[49]

Yet in the months after the second *Brown* ruling, as the South erupted in anger and division, Eisenhower's enthusiasm notably cooled. The reaction he had long feared burst out around the country. In Prince Edward County, Virginia, one of the original five school districts in the *Brown* case, the school board refused to pass a budget and planned to close its schools rather than integrate them. In Georgia the attorney general and governor announced that the Court's decision would not be recognized in their state and banned any state funds from being spent on interracial schools. Former Georgia governor Talmadge likened the actions of the Court to fascist tyranny. The Mississippi state education advisory committee declared it would "never compromise on segregation." The Alabama State Senate passed legislation to ensure the continuation of segregation and called for the impeachment of the U.S. Supreme Court. State legislators in Louisiana foamed in anger. "We do not intend by any stretch of the imagination to mix whites and Negroes in our schools, regardless of the Supreme Court decision," said one lawmaker, and funds were to be cut off from any schools than did so.[50]

In the weeks after the second *Brown* ruling, southern whites ran a campaign of intimidation and reprisal against African Americans that was designed to raise the price they would have to pay if they persisted in challenging Jim Crow. Across the South white community leaders formed citizens' councils to spearhead a campaign of economic retaliation against black citizens. New state laws further restricted the right to vote and allowed the purging of voter rolls. State governments sought to close down the activities of the NAACP, and by the middle of 1956 Louisiana, Alabama, and Texas were successful in doing so. State governments sought to seize the membership lists of the NAACP, the easier to target blacks for retribution. Black citizens known to be favorable to NAACP activities lost their jobs or had their bank accounts closed. Mass rallies in southern cities were held at which leading public figures spoke about preserving states' rights, while Confederate flags flapped in the breeze and local marching bands thumped out "Dixie." In December 1955 Mississippi Senator Eastland, a militant segregationist, formed the Federation for Constitutional Government to coordinate the southern white reaction. Eastland's aim: to preserve the "untainted racial heritage" of "generations of Southerners yet unborn." State officeholders across the South flocked to Eastland's side.[51]

The United States was on the threshold of decades of unsettling conflict over civil rights. Perhaps no one in the White House was more sensitive to the emerging crisis than E. Frederic Morrow, the only African American to work on the White House executive staff. The grandson of a Presbyterian minister who was born a slave, Morrow grew up in Hackensack, New Jersey, a town he described as rigidly segregated by custom and habit, if not by law. He attended Bowdoin College, then worked for the National Urban League and then the NAACP in the 1930s, where he came to know Lester Granger, Roy Wilkins, and Thurgood Marshall. He traveled throughout the South, opening up NAACP chapters and raising funds for the organization. When war came in 1941, he volunteered for military service and endured what he termed four years of "ignominy and personal shame" at the hands of the U.S. Army. He was assigned to menial jobs on bases across the South, humiliated by racist officers, and at every step confronted "injustice, segregation, discrimination and dishonest public servants." After the war he entered Rutgers Law School on the GI Bill and earned a law degree.[52]

Morrow was recruited into the Republican Party by Val Washington, a black journalist and advertising executive who had worked for the *Chicago Defender* before becoming an assistant to Herbert Brownell in New York in the late 1940s. By 1952 Washington was the Republican Party's director of minority affairs, and he urged Morrow to join the Eisenhower campaign. After his years in the South, Morrow had no affection for the Democratic Party; he accepted Washington's invitation to work for the GOP and in the fall of 1952 was assigned to the Eisenhower campaign train. Soaking up the hectic, thrilling atmosphere of the presidential race, he befriended Sherman Adams and came to know Eisenhower himself. On the campaign trail he was often mistaken for a butler or asked to stay in black-only hotels away from the rest of the campaign staff. But he enjoyed the work and admired Eisenhower for his decency and integrity. In 1953 he took a position in the Commerce Department, and in mid-1955 Adams appointed him to the Executive White House staff. From there Morrow would be a close observer of Eisenhower's response to the civil rights crisis that was just breaking upon the country.

In the wake of Emmett Till's murder as well as the brazen shootings of Lamar Smith and Rev. George Lee, African American leaders demanded action. In a letter to the president, Roy Wilkins declared that "a reign of terror against Negro citizens of Mississippi" had broken out and urged Eisenhower not to "stand mute and inactive when brutality and violence are used against United States citizens." He wanted a "public denunciation" of such barbarism. The NAACP placed full-page ads in major newspapers: "HELP END RACIAL TYRANNY IN MISSISSIPPI," blazed block-letter text in the *New York Times* above a detailed accounting of murder, intimidation, and voting rights violations.[53]

Inside the White House Fred Morrow also painted a dire picture of the racial climate in the South. Writing to Max Rabb, the cabinet secretary, who also supervised civil rights affairs, Morrow asserted that the country was "on the verge of a dangerous racial conflagration," that mass meetings were being held by angry and bitter African Americans, and that sermons in black churches spoke of little else. Morrow believed that "Negroes in Mississippi have formed an underground" to protect themselves from armed white mobs. "There is a clamor for some kind of statement from the White House," he told Rabb.[54]

Yet it appeared that the White House did not wish to involve itself too directly in the affairs of the South. One reason for this excess of caution lies in the fears stoked by FBI director J. Edgar Hoover that black activists were tools of the Communist Party. In a series of reports to the White House, Hoover connected the national outcry for justice in the Till case to Communist Party activity. Hoover's weekly memos to the president's office and the attorney general painted a picture of a mobilized communist apparatus attempting to use the Till slaying to arouse black opinion, trigger mob violence, embarrass the president, and inflame the South. According to Hoover, "the over-all objective" of communist-planned mass meetings, demonstrations, press articles, and letter-writing campaigns was "to put the heat on Federal authorities and condemn them for not protecting constitutional guarantees in the State of Mississippi."

Hoover sought to link NAACP demands for justice with Communist Party subversion. "Militant resources of both organizations," he wrote, "have been mobilized to attain recognition and favorable action. . . . The potential for violence not only is present but is daily increasing in intensity." One FBI source reported that "some sort of revolt by Negroes in the South" was being planned and that "arms and ammunition were being taken into the South from the North." For a White House already growing wary of black social activism in the South, Hoover's reports provided yet another reason to steer clear of any close affiliation with the civil rights movement.[55]

But events in the South made it hard for the administration to stay quiet. On December 1, 1955, Rosa Parks, a bespectacled 42-year-old African American woman, refused to give up her seat on a crowded Montgomery, Alabama, public bus to a white person. Parks was hardly an accidental activist. She was "deeply rooted in the black protest tradition," according to one historian, and had been ejected years earlier from a public bus for refusing to comply with the Jim Crow rules. She had long-standing ties to E. D. Nixon, the president of the local NAACP chapter. Her arrest that day on charges of violating the city's segregation codes triggered an immediate response among local black citizens, especially the Women's Political Council, which spread the word that until the city changed its rules, African American riders would boycott the buses. To direct the boycott, Nixon founded the Montgomery Improvement Association and on December 5 secured a charismatic 27-year-old Baptist preacher to serve as its president. His name was Martin Luther King Jr., and his nonviolent boycott would soon transform the politics of the South and the country.[56]

Inside the White House, Morrow pleaded with Adams to act in response to the news from Mississippi and Alabama. "The failure of any prominent member of the administration to speak out against and deplore the present condition of terrorism and economic sanction against Negroes," he wrote, "is causing deep concern among Negro leaders in the country today." Morrow reported a widespread feeling that the administration "has completely abandoned the Negro in the South and left him to the mercy of state governments." He urged a public denunciation of the lawlessness in the South as well as a meeting between Eisenhower and a high-level delegation of black political and religious leaders. Yet with Hoover's reports circulating in the White House, linking African American activism with communism, Morrow got nowhere with his suggestions. The White House remained publicly silent.[57]

Only after considerable persuasion from Rabb did the president agree to place a brief mention about civil rights in his State of the Union speech on January 5, 1956. It was a tepid statement, buried deep in a long speech. "It is disturbing that in some localities," Eisenhower said, sounding as if the matter had just been brought to his attention, "allegations persist that Negro citizens are being deprived of their right to vote and are likewise being subjected to unwarranted economic pressures. I recommend that the substance of these charges be thoroughly examined by a Bipartisan Commission created by the Congress. It is hoped that such a commission will be established promptly so that it may arrive at findings which can receive early consideration." Thus Eisenhower kicked the question back to the Congress—the very body that had failed to pass any civil rights legislation for nearly a century.[58]

But events would not wait for a congressional commission. The authorities in Montgomery escalated the tension in that city by denouncing the ongoing bus boycott as the work of "Negro radicals" who the mayor claimed were determined to "stir up racial strife." The city's police commissioner, Clyde Sellers, appeared at a White Citizens' Council meeting to announce that he would join the pro-segregation group; a few days later the mayor did so as well. On January 26 Rev. King was arrested on a trumped-up traffic charge and locked up overnight. Four days later an unknown assailant set off a bomb on the front porch of King's home while his wife and infant daughter were inside. No one was injured, but the firebombing of the young pastor's home confirmed the worst fears of federal authorities: the South was erupting into violent racial strife.[59]

That picture was confirmed by events at the University of Alabama, where a black woman named Autherine Lucy had sought admission to the graduate program in library science. When the university refused her admission, the NAACP helped Lucy take the case all the way to the U.S. Supreme Court, which, in October 1955, unanimously upheld her right to attend the public university. She attended her first class on Friday, February 3, 1956, but when she returned on Monday she was met by a screaming mob of 3,000 people who threw eggs at her and blocked her from entering the school buildings. The police used tear gas to disperse the protestors, and a few weeks later the NAACP filed a complaint against the university for conspiring with the crowd to keep Lucy from going to classes. In response the university expelled her for making "defamatory statements."[60]

Finally Eisenhower saw the writing on the wall: southern schools and universities were going to resort to violence before they accepted desegregation. In a meeting with his senior advisers on February 29, he wondered aloud if "the Federal Government could step in if there was mob action" in Alabama. Adams, Hagerty, and other staff debated just what power the federal government had to enforce the Supreme Court ruling. With great reluctance, and a sense of foreboding, the Eisenhower team now realized that perhaps only military intervention would compel local authorities to desegregate southern schools. Yet publicly Eisenhower dared not hint at such a drastic idea. In his press conference of February 8, he hoped "we could avoid any interference" in Alabama and said he felt sure the governor could "straighten it out."[61]

Meanwhile the harassment of boycott leaders in Montgomery intensified. On February 21, 115 boycott organizers—among whom were King and
23 other clergymen—were indicted by a grand jury for conducting an illegal
boycott. The grand jury held these black leaders responsible for spreading
"distrust, dislike and hatred in a community which for more than a generation has enjoyed exemplary race relations." To this King replied from the
rostrum of the First Baptist Church, where black leaders had gathered in
protest of the arrest warrants, "This is not a war between the white and
the Negro but a conflict between justice and injustice." On February 25 the
Council of Bishops of the African Methodist Episcopal Church appealed
publicly to Eisenhower to use federal authority to intervene in the dispute.
By its 12th week the boycott had become national news. As the *Washington
Post* reported "The eyes of Alabama, the South and now the nation are on
Montgomery."[62]

VII

The administration was struggling to prepare a response to the events in the
South. In fact since December 1955 Attorney General Brownell had been
drafting proposals to present to Congress that would empower the Justice
Department to investigate and prosecute civil rights violations. Brownell
had been frustrated by his inability to do anything in the Till case, and the
blatant violations of voting rights in the South now left him determined to
strengthen the federal government's hand. But there was also a political cal-
culation here. On February 29, 1956, the president announced that he would
run for reelection. At a stroke the White House began thinking about everything through the lens of politics. In a memo to Adams, Rabb went so far as
to call for "a new look at our civil rights policy from a partisan viewpoint." He
felt it was time to break "this iron curtain of silence on our civil rights case"
and seek out northern black voters. With a more active civil rights program
he suggested, "we still can gain, without too much effort, a five to ten percent
increase" in the black vote, "which would be decisive in fringe districts."[63]

Brownell agreed that there might be some electoral benefits from pushing moderate civil rights legislation. But he worried more about determining just what power the federal government really possessed to protect basic
civil rights in the states. Brownell believed he simply did not have enough
authority to mount a successful legal challenge to recalcitrant southerners,
and he wanted to strengthen his hand. He therefore drew up four proposals

that he submitted to the cabinet and the president for consideration. First, he drafted a bill to create a civil rights commission that had subpoena power to investigate ongoing abuses. Second, he wanted a new Civil Rights Division in the Justice Department, with additional authority and resources. Third, and more boldly, he wanted to be able to pursue civil injunctions against defiant local and state authorities who were violating the basic civil rights and voting rights of black citizens. Brownell pitched this idea as a gentle way of exercising federal power: instead of prosecuting local officials for a crime, he could bring civil proceedings against them if they were seen to be interfering with voting rights. And fourth, Brownell wanted broader Justice Department powers to investigate any conspiracy that aimed at the deprivation of civil and voting rights. Taken as a package, these proposals, if they became law, would substantially increase the Justice Department's power to compel desegregation in the South.[64]

Brownell faced some serious headwinds in getting his ideas made into law. In a March 9, 1956, cabinet meeting in which Brownell was scheduled to present his proposals for discussion, Hoover beat him to the punch. The FBI director had been invited to give an update on the racial tensions in the South since *Brown*, and he did not miss his chance. His report to the cabinet was chilling. Once again using the old canard that the NAACP was being infiltrated by the Communist Party, Hoover depicted black activist organizations as provocative and dangerous. Their spokesmen, he said, had declared that "white blood will flow," and he singled out the bus boycott in Montgomery as an example of the NAACP's revolutionary activities. Hoover praised white southerners who had reacted to provocations by forming citizens' councils made up of "bankers, lawyers, doctors, state legislators, and industrialists," that is, "some of the leading citizens of the South." These men were protecting "historic traditions and customs" and would not abandon them "without a struggle." The situation was a powder keg, Hoover darkly declared, and some "over-zealous but ill-advised leaders of the NAACP and the Communist Party" were likely to set off an explosion.[65]

With this remarkable presentation having cast a pall over the Cabinet Room, Brownell introduced his plans for new civil rights legislation. He ran into criticism from Agriculture Secretary Ezra Benson, HEW Secretary Marion Folsom (a Georgian), and others who questioned the need to move quickly on the package of civil rights proposals. Eisenhower backed Brownell but also launched into an impassioned plea for tolerance and respect for the "deep emotions" surrounding this subject. He urged Brownell to moderate the tone of the proposed legislation. "Don't take the attitude that you are another [Charles] Sumner," Ike said, referring to the Radical Republican senator from Massachusetts who had violently denounced slavery during the 1850s and led the fight to grant civil rights to African Americans after the Civil War. The president insisted, "These people in the South were not breaking the law for the past 60 years. . . . Now we cannot erase the emotions of three generations just overnight. . . . People have a right to disagree with the Supreme Court decision, since the Supreme Court has disagreed with its own decision of 60 years standing. But of course the new decision should now be carried out." Eisenhower asked Brownell to resubmit revised and toned-down proposals to the cabinet.[66]

Just two days later, and perfectly timed to complicate Brownell's efforts, a leading Virginia congressman, Howard Smith, and Georgia senator Walter F. George, read on the floor of their respective chambers a "Declaration of Constitutional Principles," which rapidly earned the sobriquet "The Southern Manifesto." It denounced the Supreme Court's decision in *Brown* as an abuse of power, described the Court as having destroyed in a stroke "the amicable relations between the white and Negro races that have been created through 90 years of patient effort by the good people of both races," denounced "outside agitators" who wanted to bring "revolutionary changes," and pledged to halt the implementation of school desegregation. The document was signed by 82 representatives and 19 senators—about one-fifth of the Congress, all Democrats except for two Virginia Republicans. Every one of the signatories, including the 1952 Democratic vice-presidential candidate John Sparkman of Alabama, hailed from the Confederacy. The South now spoke with one voice: it would not recognize federal law. A constitutional crisis loomed.[67]

No wonder, then, that Eisenhower's advisers were becoming exasperated. However, their anger was not directed at southern white leaders but at black activists. Fred Morrow, despondent, wrote a long and revealing entry in his diary about the atmosphere in the administration. Even Max Rabb, normally a close ally, gave Morrow a "tongue-lashing" about black behavior. After all Eisenhower had done, Rabb asserted, "Negroes had not demonstrated any kind of gratitude," and most of the responsible officials in the White House had become completely disgusted with the whole matter. He said there was a feeling that "Negroes were being too aggressive in their demands; that an ugliness and surliness in manner was beginning to show through." What black leaders wanted, Rabb told Morrow, "far exceeded what reasonable white people would grant." And Rabb was Ike's chief adviser on minority affairs.[68]

When the cabinet convened on March 23 to reconsider Brownell's civil rights proposals, the attorney general ran into still more opposition. John Foster Dulles, just back from a trip to Asia, thought the laws Brownell proposed "deviated too far from accepted mores" and should be shelved. Defense Secretary Wilson and HEW Secretary Folsom also pounced on the proposal, saying things were too dangerous already "without adding more fuel" to the fire. The leading members of the cabinet had thus arranged themselves against Brownell's civil rights proposals. The president himself now began to worry "about piling up laws that could not be enforced." On March 20 he spoke with Rev. Billy Graham, who told him that desegregation "would come eventually" but that "the South has a fixed tradition" and could not be forced to move quickly. A consensus was forming: new federal laws to strengthen civil rights protections would only intensify the fury of southern whites. The discussion was brought to a close when Eisenhower asked Brownell to see him after the cabinet meeting had adjourned.[69]

In that closed session Eisenhower broke the news to Brownell: he could not support the controversial third provision of the bill that strengthened the attorney general's hand in fighting civil rights violations. It was just too provocative in an election season. No verbatim record of that meeting exists, but Eisenhower must have sensed Brownell's deep disappointment because he offered some compensation. Brownell could submit parts 1 and 2 to Congress as formal legislative proposals, while merely suggesting that the ideas present in parts 3 and 4 be considered. Brownell would have to present that case to Congress. If there was going to be a fight, he would take the heat. Eisenhower had decided to stay out of it.[70]

Brownell accepted the challenge and began navigating the tricky waters of Congress with great cleverness. Knowing Eisenhower's objections, he softened the proposals that he sent to the House Judiciary Committee. But he also tipped off his New York friend Congressman Kenneth Keating, who ensured that the proposal to strengthen the Justice Department's ability to prosecute civil rights violations was beefed up in the bill's language. It was a clever piece of chicanery, and it allowed Brownell to report to Eisenhower that he had followed the president's instructions, while also posing as a stalwart advocate for bolder civil rights powers for the Justice Department. Crucially, this bit of theater also gave Eisenhower himself some distance from the legislation.

It was Brownell's bill as far as the administration was concerned, and he fought for it with verve. In hearings in Congress in April as well as in public addresses in New York and Washington, Brownell urged Congress to act to protect the right of every American to vote, and in particular to protect black citizens from what he called "haters and opportunists." *New York Times* reporter Anthony Lewis described his words as "the strongest spoken thus far on the racial issue by any member of the Administration." It was an impressive performance, and by early summer a new four-part civil rights bill was working its way through the House of Representatives. On July 23 it passed the House by 276–126 votes, drawing bipartisan support from Republicans and northern liberal Democrats. The first civil rights legislation since Reconstruction now moved on to the Senate.[71]

And there it died, as everyone knew it would. Southern Democrats dominated the Senate committees through which the bill had to pass. Instead of considering the bill, the Senate went on summer recess and would not take it up again until 1957. Eisenhower did not seem to mind. He did not endorse the legislation in public, though privately he assured Republican congressmen he still favored it. Indeed, despite his successes in pushing moderate civil rights reforms in his first term, Eisenhower tried his best to stay clear of the subject during the fall election season for fear of alienating whites in the South who might be tempted to vote Republican. For Eisenhower, it was time to let the civil rights issue cool off a bit.

But it was not for the president to adjust the temperature of the racial conflict that was gaining intensity across the South. Provocations and violence kept the crisis on a high boil. In late August 1956, exactly a year after Emmett Till's horrific murder, a voice Eisenhower would come to hear frequently rose up from the front lines of the racial struggle and called for the president to turn his attention to Montgomery, a city marred by racial violence, the bombing of the homes of religious leaders, mass arrests, and intimidation of black citizens: "Hundreds of Negroes are being arrested daily on trumped up charges and fined. The revival of the Ku Klux Klan is a constant threat and the robed members are allowed to demonstrate in the city without police interference whatsoever. Thousands of Negroes in the city of Montgomery and the state of Alabama are deprived of their right to vote." Surely now was the time for the president to use "the power of your office to see that the proper investigation is made in Montgomery and Alabama to the end that justice and law will prevail." The voice was that of Martin Luther King Jr., still leading the nine-month-old bus boycott in Montgomery, still clinging to the hope that Washington would respond to the outcry of black citizens across the South who clamored for justice.[72]

Eisenhower remained impassive. He would not be drawn into King's movement. Although Ike managed the civil rights problems of 1953–56 with dexterity, compiling a record of progress as good as that of any of his 20th-century predecessors, he refused to lead the country to embrace a new era of civil rights. As resistance to *Brown* increased, and as the battle lines formed for a prolonged period of conflict, Eisenhower retreated from the battle-field, seeking the comfort of the distant hills, while Brownell continued to fight in the trenches below. If this was an example of Ike's "hidden hand," it was a disappointing performance for those who yearned for some sign from America's most powerful and popular leader that their struggle was also his.

CHAPTER 10

GOD, GOVERNMENT, AND THE MIDDLE WAY

*"The Republican Party must be known as a
progressive organization or it is sunk."*

I

JUST AFTER CHRISTMAS 1955 EISENHOWER RECEIVED SOME welcome news from George Gallup, the pollster and director of the American Institute of Public Opinion. Americans, Gallup reported, considered Eisenhower the most admired man in the world, at the head of a distinguished pack that included Winston Churchill, Douglas MacArthur, Harry Truman, Albert Schweitzer, Pope Pius XII, and the Rev. Billy Graham. Yet the president was probably not surprised by the honor. He had also topped the list in 1954. And in 1953, 1952, and 1951. Indeed Ike would be America's most admired man for ten straight years between 1951 and 1960.[1]

Americans also approved, overwhelmingly, of his performance in office. During his eight years as president he enjoyed an *average* approval rating of 65 percent. He was especially popular in his first term, winning approval from 70 percent of the American public in those four years. The lowest score Eisenhower tallied was in the midst of a recession in the spring of 1958, when his approval rating dropped briefly to 48 percent—still higher than the average rating for Truman's entire presidency. In short, Americans loved Ike.[2]

Why? Peace and prosperity helped, though even when crises in Korea, China, Taiwan, Eastern Europe, and the Middle East erupted, Ike remained popular. Nor did significant slowdowns of the economy in 1953–54 and 1957–58 substantially mar his reputation. It would be easy to chalk up Eisenhower's popularity simply to his personality, his charm, his affability, and above all the lingering effect of his wartime laurels. Yet there is more to the story than that, for the key to Eisenhower's success lay in his ability to balance, in his own person and in his policies, the contradictions in American society. People liked him because he seemed to embody so many virtues that they admired—even when these virtues were in tension with one another. As an acute observer of the era, William Lee Miller, noted in a 1958 essay, Ike was ordinary and extraordinary at the same time. He "combined the perennial grandeur of success in battle with the familiar friendliness of the man next door." He found a way to reconcile the cross-cutting tendencies of the American character: the "practical, competitive, individualistic, externally-minded, environment-mastering and success-seeking on the one side, and the spiritual, idealistic, friendly, team-working, moralizing, and reform-seeking on the other. Mr. Eisenhower exactly summarized both."[3]

Actions that might have seemed hypocritical and even schizophrenic in a lesser man appeared, when performed by Eisenhower, to be evidence of a tempered and moderate philosophy that transcended mere politics. He could trumpet the virtues of capitalism and individual success even as he called for Americans to go to church more often and abjure materialism. He insisted on conservative government, demanded tight budgets, and inveighed against the dangers of "statism," yet he also hailed the beneficial role of government in providing public schools, roads and bridges, airports and public housing, hospitals and old-age pensions to American citizens. The last president born in the 19th century welcomed innovation, modernity, new technologies, the space age, and global travel and communication. Liberal intellectuals like Adlai Stevenson and Arthur Schlesinger Jr., as well as right-wing pundits such as William F. Buckley, found Ike's political shape-shifting infuriating. But the voters admired his uncanny ability to float above the partisan scrum.

No wonder, then, that Americans loved Ike. He was big enough to embody their collective hopes and dreams. He was a Texan, a Kansan, a Coloradan, and a New Yorker; a soldier and a peacemaker; a poor country boy and a wealthy elitist; a devoted reader of Scripture who seldom went to church until he was 62; a beer-and–hot dog man who fêted his powerful White House guests with pheasant under glass. With his example in mind, Americans could aspire to riches, power, and personal success without losing their moral compass. They could earnestly talk up the importance of bootstraps and personal responsibility while demanding that their government care for them. They could embrace change and modernity while also venerating their elders and attending church in record-breaking numbers. Here lie the elements of the Eisenhower phenomenon: by personifying and reconciling these contradictions, he made Americans believe that they, like him, could have it all.

II

On Sunday, February 7, 1954, the president and Mrs. Eisenhower went to worship at the National Presbyterian Church in Washington. Immediately after the service the president appeared on a CBS television and radio broadcast to kick off the American Legion's "Back to God" campaign. Started in 1951 as a way to honor the famous "four chaplains"—ministers of four different denominations who died at sea during the war when they gave their life jackets to others on board their sinking ship—the Back to God campaign had become a signature annual event in which leading churchmen and rabbis, gathered in ecumenical fellowship, called upon their listeners to rededicate themselves to a life of godliness and spirituality.

Eisenhower's remarks on the broadcast aimed to link the American experience to religious zeal. "Out of faith in God, and through faith in themselves as His children, our forefathers designed and built the Republic," the president said. He gave a brief civics lesson that recalled the struggles of the Pilgrims, the testing of George Washington at Valley Forge, and the determined battle of Abraham Lincoln to save the Union: all of them shared a steadfast belief in God. The one unifying feature of the American experience, Eisenhower insisted, was faith: "By the millions, we speak prayers, we sing hymns, and no matter what their words may be, their spirit is the same—In God is our Trust." In 1954, as America again faced a time of crisis and struggle, "there is a need for positive acts of renewed recognition that faith is our surest strength."

This brief speech captured perfectly Eisenhower's instrumental view of religion: the doctrinal content of religious devotion need not divide Americans so long as they shared a basic commitment to faith and belief. The differences between sects paled in contrast to the yawning gap between believers and nonbelievers. And of course the seedbed of such nonbelief was "atheistic Communism." To believe in God was itself an act of resistance and defiance of communism; however one worshipped God did not matter, so long as one was willing to acknowledge the power of a higher being.[4]

The president was joined in this televised appeal by two of the leading public religious figures of the day: the Rev. Fulton J. Sheen, a bishop of the Roman Catholic Archdiocese of New York, and Dr. Norman Vincent Peale, pastor of the Marble Collegiate Church in New York City. Bishop Sheen was well known as the longtime host of the radio show *The Catholic Hour* and, since 1951, the impresario of the television program *Life Is Worth Living*. Among the first clergymen to use the new medium of television to reach his flock, Sheen, with his gaunt face and deep-set eyes, could be seen weekly at 8:00 p.m. across the nation. Robed in a full-length cassock, bearing a pectoral cross on a chain around his neck, topped by a small skullcap, Sheen delivered commentary on topics ranging from marriage and alcoholism to freedom, the devil, love, and purgatory. He stood before a chalkboard, occasionally turning away from the camera to jot down a few keywords like a skilled 10th-grade English teacher. He usually started by recounting a humdrum tale of ordinary life, perhaps sent to him in a letter from a viewer. He would mine this for its didactic value and throw in a few light witticisms along the way. Quiet, composed, articulate, Sheen's TV personality entranced millions of Americans, drawing audiences as large as those that tuned in to Milton Berle and Bob Hope.

Peale, a pudgy, bespectacled Methodist with a flair for homespun stories and down-to-earth verities, had become a national phenomenon as the author of wildly popular Christian self-help books. The idea for such guidebooks was not Peale's alone: in 1939, *Alcoholics Anonymous* appeared on America's bookshelves, offering a 12-step method for treating not just alcoholism but other "social" diseases. The crucial step in these programs was the recognition of a "higher power" that could provide spiritual sustenance as one progressed through the prescribed treatment.

Peale saw a church-building opportunity in the yearning of Americans to overcome their personal problems and achieve success. He offered a simple therapy for any affliction: belief in God. In a stream of publications as well as radio and television appearances, he provided audiences simple steps to improve their lives and grasp the financial, personal, social, and professional success they desired. Books like *Inspired Messages for Daily Living* compiled passages from the Bible that could serve as "health-producing, life-changing, power-creating Thought Conditioners" for people experiencing anxiety, insomnia, fatigue, lack of confidence, frustration, and more. These troubles were easily treatable by reciting Scripture. If you wanted to know, for example, "how to break the worry habit" or "how to make your work easy" or "how to get people to like you," Peale offered easy techniques, all of which amounted to reciting a few passages of the Bible, selected by Peale himself. Such spiritual exercises, Peale claimed, amounted to a "magic formula" for personal happiness and success. He found an enormous audience for his Christian home remedies. His book *The Power of Positive Thinking* appeared in 1952 and stayed on the best-seller list for 186 weeks. He became a much-admired public figure and would go on to develop a close personal friendship with Richard Nixon.[5]

If Peale and Sheen were friendly Christian showmen, Ike's own pastor, Rev. Edward Elson, offered sterner counsel. In 1954 Elson published a small book, *America's Spiritual Recovery*, dedicated to the president. (The introduction was written by another parishioner, FBI director J. Edgar Hoover.) Elson declared that America found itself "in a period of real moral sag and deterioration." He drew a desperate portrait of the nation's ills: soaring crime, the "kow-towing admiration for the tycoons of business and the captains of industry," the veneration of money and profit, and the lapse of religious worship. Children, he said, no longer respected their parents. Jazz, modern art, and vulgar films like *Death of a Salesman* and *A Streetcar Named Desire* that glorified "a deteriorating personality" offered more evidence of a collapse of morals. Schools no longer taught Christian precepts. The militant atheism of communism threatened the world.

Yet Elson also found reason for optimism: amid these grave moral threats, "the greatest religious awakening in the history of our nation" was under way. American worshippers were filling the churches and making plans to build many more. "Six out of every ten Americans formally belonged to a church—the highest ratio in the country's history," he wrote. Every week 85 million Americans bowed their heads in prayer in a house of worship. Students on college campuses had shown renewed enthusiasm for religious instruction. The recent best-selling books in the nation included the Bible, books by Rev. Peale and Bishop Sheen, and other inspirational texts and tales. Elson did not mention that this was also the period in which Hollywood produced blockbuster movies on religious themes, such as *Quo Vadis* (1951), *The Ten Commandments* (1956), and *Ben Hur* (1959).

Elson believed that Eisenhower's election to the presidency had triggered this religious revival. Ike had become "the focal point of a moral resurgence and spiritual awakening of national proportions." His inaugural prayer, given on the steps of the Capitol, had signaled the return of faith into public life, as did his decision to start his cabinet meetings with prayer. "It is not an exaggeration to say that the business which receives the attention of the president is surrounded with an atmosphere of prayer." Ike's moral and spiritual leadership could save America from what Elson saw as a grave threat: not only the nation's internal moral collapse but the gathering forces of atheism and communism. Marxism presented such a great danger because it offered a "new world religion" and aimed to unseat Christianity. The philosophies of "the sickle and the cross," Elson said, "are irreconcilable," and only one of them could survive. If Christianity was to triumph, communism must be vanquished.[6]

This kind of public piety, moralism, and prophetic speech saturated the Age of Eisenhower, and it squared perfectly with the language of the new administration. It is not surprising, then, that Ike found himself drawn to and befriended by the most significant evangelist of the postwar years, Billy Graham, with whom he shared many basic ideas about the relationship of spiritual faith to the creation of a well-ordered society. Graham, a tall, rangy Baptist, grew up on a dairy farm near Charlotte, North Carolina, went to college in Wheaton, Illinois, and started his preaching in a Chicago-based organization called Youth for Christ in the mid-1940s. His talent, sincerity, zeal, and sheer charisma sped him on his way to stardom. In 1949 his enormous Los Angeles revival meeting—which he called a "crusade"—attracted nationwide press coverage. In 1951 Texas oil man Sid Richardson urged Graham to add his voice to the chorus then calling for General Eisenhower to run for president. Graham gladly complied, asking Eisenhower to "offer himself to the American people."[7]

Richardson arranged for Graham to meet the general at SHAPE headquarters in Paris in March 1952, just after Ike won the New Hampshire primary. Eisenhower welcomed Graham into his modern, newly constructed office and spoke with the pastor of his spiritual life, especially his upbringing among the devout River Brethren in Kansas; Graham reported on the "crusade" he had recently concluded in Washington, D.C. They sat together for two hours and formed a bond. In August, after Eisenhower won the GOP nomination, he invited Graham to Denver to the Brown Palace Hotel, where he asked Graham to help him find appropriate themes and scriptural passages to work into his campaign speeches.

Graham's influence hung on some of Eisenhower's campaign statements. When Ike was asked to describe his religious beliefs for the *Episcopal Church News* in September 1952, he responded, "You can't explain free government in any other terms than religious. The founding fathers had to refer to the Creator in order to make their revolutionary experiment make sense. . . .

It is ours to prove that only a people strong in Godliness is strong enough to overcome tyranny and make themselves and others free." He concluded, "What is our battle against communism if it is not a fight between anti-God and belief in the Almighty?" America's problems might be easier to solve, Eisenhower opined, if every American "would dwell more upon the simple virtues: integrity, courage, self-confidence, and an unshakeable belief in his Bible."[8]

After the election Graham sent the new president a fairly steady stream of correspondence, updating him on the activities of his ministry. In June 1953 Graham reported that his monthlong revival in Dallas drew 25,000 people a night and was "the largest evangelistic crusade in the history of the United States." He found the American people "hungry for God," and he told Eisenhower that in Dallas a crowd of 75,000 at the Cotton Bowl rose up as one, bowed their heads, and prayed that "God would give you wisdom, courage and strength." To see so many people praying for their president, Graham wrote, "was one of the most beautiful and moving sights I have ever seen." A few months later Graham sent word that the president's "constant references to spiritual needs and faithful attendance at church have done much to help in the spiritual awakening that is taking place throughout the nation."[9]

In November 1953, Graham called on Eisenhower in the White House to update the president on his long-planned crusade in Britain and present to him a startling gift: a book signed by several hundred Chinese and North Korean prisoners who, while being held in South Korean camps, were converted to Christianity. These were POWs who had asked not to be repatriated after the Korean armistice; alongside their names they stamped their fingerprints, using their own blood as ink. Upon leaving the White House that day, Graham told the press that Eisenhower's religious devotion had "inspired the nation."[10]

Graham's ministry suited an era of robust individualism, for the evangelist spoke about the need to bring people to Christ as the answer to the world's problems. "We must be born again," he said. "If we change men, we can change the world. We've got to do something about all the hating, cheating, lying and stealing in the world today." He summed up his approach to the temporal world by saying repeatedly, "Human nature, not the hydrogen bomb, is the world's chief problem." Fix human nature by conversion, and the anxieties of the atomic age would disappear. This emphasis on the freedom of the individual to choose a way of life—to make what Graham called a "decision for Christ"—squared with Eisenhower's belief that religious values, because they bring people to do the right thing, are crucial to a well-ordered society. "Religious principles," Eisenhower told an audience of interfaith leaders in February 1955, "must not be kept in a realm apart from everyday life. . . . Without God, there could be no American form of government, nor an American way of life. Recognition of the supreme being is the first, the most basic expression of Americanism." Human rights, Eisenhower asserted, are granted by God, not the state. And as such they are inviolable. The government must protect and defend these rights; it must never abridge them. Between man and his Creator, no government should intervene.[11]

On March 6, 1955, Graham achieved a milestone: he delivered a sermon directly to an American president. As the guest of Rev. Elson at the National Presbyterian Church, Graham spoke on "Faith in Our Times." Again he stressed the message that the cold war and the H-bomb, juvenile delinquency, racial strife, moral weakness—all these worries could be cured instantly by conversion to Christ. They all sprang from a single source: sinful human nature. Fix that, and the world would be free of trouble. Not every theologian shared Graham's simple answer to the problems of the age. Reinhold Niebuhr, the leading Christian intellectual of the era and a professor at Union Theological Seminary, published a searing essay in the *New Republic* in June 1955 that addressed the surge in popular piety. Niebuhr had no time for the likes of Norman Vincent Peale and Bishop Sheen, whom he described as mere entertainers. Graham he treated with more respect and more venom. Niebuhr attacked Graham's "perfectionist illusions" and his "simple religious moralism," which claimed that "conversion to Christianity could solve the problem of the hydrogen bomb." Niebuhr accused Graham—and Eisenhower—of equating faith with "good plumbing" as the core values of the "American Way of Life." What angered Niebuhr was the smug, complacent, self-regarding contentment of powerful men, both in government and in the churches, who decided that simple "religious faith" would resolve the social and political crises of the age.[12]

Eisenhower dismissed this kind of criticism. He shared Graham's belief that government could at best only ameliorate social problems, not fix them, and that God and gumption formed the true essence of the American experience. In his State of the Union address in January 1954, he said government alone could not make people industrious or enterprising. It was up to them to work hard for their future prosperity. Similarly, he said,

Americans know how to balance God against greed. "Though blessed with more material goods than any people in history," Americans "have always reserved their first allegiance to the kingdom of the spirit, which is the true source of that freedom we value above all material things." He told the annual meeting of the U.S. Chamber of Commerce in May 1955 that America became great by mixing religious faith with the spirit of free enterprise. Yes, government occasionally had a role to play in softening the blows of modern life, but what made America great was its combination of deep religious faith and individualism. With God, prosperity, and individual freedom at work on America's side, "we cannot lose; we simply cannot lose."[13]

III

Thus Eisenhower believed it possible to balance prayer and prosperity, doxology and dollars, godliness and good times. Viewed from a later age, such pairings might appear cynical and hypocritical. But Eisenhower believed in balance, in finding the right calibration between moral purpose and creature comforts. He did not see prosperity as immoral; rather he saw it as a reward for hard work and sacrifice. A blessed nation had earned a bountiful harvest.

Eisenhower could sustain this belief because, to a surprising degree, many Americans shared in the prosperity of the 1950s. Unlike the boom times of the Gilded Age or the dot-com bubble of the 1990s, the prosperity of the 1950s ran both deep and broad. The bane of American society in the 21st century—drastic economic inequality—did not afflict the nation to the same degree during the roaring '50s. Incomes grew at roughly the same pace for all groups, and those at the very top of the economic pyramid paid far more taxes than the wealthy do today. Instead of enriching only a few fat cats, 1950s-era prosperity helped create and nourish what is now a vanishing species: the American middle class. Here lies the source of much later nostalgia for the Age of Eisenhower. The 1950s was the decade in which many citizens appeared to have realized that elusive goal, the American Dream.

Numbers can help tell this story. At the start of the Age of Eisenhower, in 1950, Americans were already making two to three times the hourly wage they had earned in 1935, so they began the decade in an atmosphere of optimism. In 1948–53 unemployment was negligible, averaging just 4 percent. In manufacturing, hourly wages rose from 58 cents an hour in 1935 to

$1.59 in 1950. The average American family income was $4,237 in 1950, a dramatic improvement from the depression-wracked 1930s, but of course prices had shot up as well: in 1950 a pound of butter cost twice what it had 15 years earlier, and the price of meat had tripled. Average family expenditures in 1950 ran to $3,800, so while Americans in 1950 had more money in their pockets, they spent most of it on the high cost of living.

But if economic trends looked promising in 1950, few could have predicted just how prosperous the coming decade would be. The gross national product nearly doubled in the decade, from $285 billion to $500 billion. Average family income in 1960 stood at $6,691, a 58 percent increase from the then-record levels of 1950. Wages rose sharply across the decade in key industries. In manufacturing, mining, construction, transportation, and finance, hourly wages increased well over a dollar an hour—in some cases up 60 percent in just a decade. These numbers were especially important because in the 1950s America was still a nation of factories: in 39 percent of American households, the head of the family was employed in manufacturing of some kind. Overall, manufacturing provided about a third of all employment in the U.S. economy in the 1950s—a postwar high. (Today it is less than 9 percent and falling.)

Despite rising wages and near-full employment, prices rose only moderately across the decade—far less than during the 1940s. Stable prices created a sense of predictability, allowing Americans to think ahead about how to spend their extra cash. Homeownership spiked: more Americans owned their own homes in 1960 than in 1950 (53 percent compared to 48 percent). The newest appliance in those homes was the television, which was present in 87 percent of American households by 1960. As the suburbs expanded, Americans bought more cars. In 1950, 59 percent of families owned a car, but by 1960, 73 percent did. And most of those cars were made in America by one of three companies: General Motors, Ford, or Chrysler. And of course Americans had more babies than ever, creating a significant postwar "baby boom."

These numbers make it plain: Americans in the 1950s enjoyed a higher standard of living than any previous generation in the nation's history. They earned more money, owned their own homes, drove their own cars, and bought nonessential consumer goods. And contrary to popular belief, not only men benefited: female participation in the workforce rose during the 1950s, from 34 to 38 percent. Compared to the world they had been born into—a world of economic depression and war, rationing of scarce goods, social and class conflict, and anxiety about the future—American adults by the mid-1950s saw their lives as unusually prosperous, stable, and secure. Simply put, for more families than ever, life in America was good, and getting better.[14]

IV

Does Eisenhower deserve the credit for this prosperity? Not entirely. America benefited in the 1950s from many positive trends that owed nothing to Ike: a growing population, and a better educated one; pent-up demand among consumers after 15 years of hardship; cheap oil and energy; innovations in technology and science; and the creation of a vast market of consumer goods, stimulated by the rapid expansion of the advertising industry. The global picture was also favorable: Germany and Japan, which would challenge American economic dominance after the 1970s, still faced formidable domestic reconstruction problems. And the world economy still ran on dollars, supporting America's ability to export its wares around the world. The country enjoyed a healthy trade surplus throughout the decade. In such circumstances perhaps any president would look good.

Yet Eisenhower's policies did matter. In seeking a balanced budget, developing tax policy, expanding social welfare benefits, and guiding government investment in infrastructure, Eisenhower made significant choices that reflected his philosophy of government. This he described succinctly: "a liberal attitude toward the welfare of people and a conservative approach to the use of their money."[15]

This language was keenly political and designed to generate a national consensus. Eisenhower knew that Republicans carried the heavy weight of recent failure: the previous Republican administration had been Herbert Hoover's, and on his watch the nation tumbled into a severe Depression. Eisenhower called the Hoover experience the "skeleton in the Republican closet." Hoover had failed to act vigorously to address the desperate economic conditions the nation faced. Austerity had only worsened the Depression, and the lessons of the 1930s indicated that government had to be active and creative. Eisenhower wanted to find the right policies that would allow a proper role for government intervention in the economy while encouraging individual initiative. As he explained in 1954, "Government must play a vital role in maintaining economic growth and stability. But I believe that our development, since the early days of the Republic, has been based on the fact that we left a great share of our national income to be used by a provident people with a will to venture."[16]

His principal obsession, from which all other policies flowed, was the balanced budget. Pursuit of this goal demanded thrift, sacrifice, and discipline—characteristics he equated with virtuous government. A budget deficit represented weakness, both moral and political. And deficits, he believed, produced inflation, which he thought of as simple theft: the stealing of the value of hard-earned savings. Eisenhower inherited a $10 billion deficit from Truman and set his two toughest budget-slashers, Joseph Dodge and George Humphrey, to work on cutting government spending. They cut $4.5 billion out of Truman's last budget, and then, during the first two years of Ike's administration, they slashed still more; they managed to get overall spending down from $74 billion in 1953 to $67 billion in 1954 and $64 billion in 1955. In January 1955 Eisenhower proposed to Congress a balanced budget for fiscal year 1956 (July 1955 to June 1956)—an astonishing turnaround in the nation's fiscal fortunes. Much of this cutting was made possible by the end of the Korean War—which Eisenhower had helped bring about—and by the consequent cuts in government personnel, both military and civilian. This rapid fall-off of government spending, however, tipped the economy into recession in 1954, as economic growth briefly paused and unemployment rose to 5 percent. No matter. Eisenhower believed a balanced budget would eventually provide conditions for a rapid recovery of growth.

Always keen to balance the budget, Ike felt little urgency in cutting personal income taxes. Tax rates in the United States, which had been low before 1940, shot up during World War II. Despite some reduction in 1946 and 1948, tax rates went back up during the Korean War and stayed high throughout the 1950s. In the Eisenhower years marginal tax rates for the *lowest* brackets floated at between 20 and 26 percent; unlike today, working people on the bottom rungs of the economic ladder paid income taxes, in addition to social security payroll taxes. But rates were progressive: the moderately well-off paid much more. A head of household who earned $20,000 in 1953—the equivalent of $175,000 today—faced a marginal tax rate of 52 percent. As for the very wealthy, they were soaked. The top marginal rate was 91 percent in 1953, though very few Americans made enough money (over $200,000) to qualify for that heavy burden. Conservatives decried these high rates and expected that when a Republican president took office, he would slash them. This is what Ike had promised in the 1952 campaign.

But despite intense pressure from his treasury secretary, George Humphrey, as well as the Old Guard in his own party, Eisenhower insisted that taxes not be cut until government expenditures had been tamed. The president abjured what later became known as supply-side economics—the theory that tax cuts would work as a stimulant to business and would pay for themselves by generating economic dynamism. No, he insisted that taxes be trimmed only as a reward for cutting spending. He managed to get Congress to agree to extend a Korean War measure, the excess profits tax, for the duration of 1953. This extension was in effect a tax increase and signaled Eisenhower's position that deficits were a greater worry than taxes. In his 1954 budget proposal, he asked Congress to sustain the corporate tax rate, then set at the remarkably high rate of 52 percent and to keep in place excise taxes on liquor, tobacco, automobiles, and gasoline. These measures, he said, would help balance the budget and stimulate confidence and economic growth.

When, in the spring of 1954, Democrats in Congress called for significant tax cuts, Eisenhower took his case to the public. In a television address he sympathized with his audience. "I know how burdensome your taxes have been," he said, but Americans also wanted certain important improvements, like an expansion of social security, unemployment insurance, more public housing, better health care, and more schools. "These things cost money," and that money would come from taxes. His administration proposed reforms to the tax code that would allow certain classes of lower-income people to get a break, but he opposed across-the-board tax cuts as likely to lead to deficits and inflation. "The good American," he suggested, "doesn't ask for favored position or treatment. Naturally he wants all fellow citizens to pay their fair share of the taxes, just as he has to do, and he wants every cent collected to be spent wisely and economically. But every real American is proud to carry his share of that national burden." In a classic statement of Eisenhower's values, he rejected the idea that some people should get special tax breaks. "I simply do not believe for one second that anyone privileged to live in this country wants someone else to pay his own fair and just share of the cost of his Government."[17]

Yet the president did agree to a variety of new tax policies in the Internal Revenue Act, a major piece of legislation he signed in August 1954 that shaped tax policy for the next 30 years. Rather than focus simply on cutting marginal tax rates, the administration, treasury, and congressional staffs worked during 1953 to craft a new tax code that opened up a variety of favorable tax breaks. The new rules allowed for a greater range of deductions and exemptions dealing with dependent children, medical expenses, child care expenses, and the exclusion of various forms of government assistance from taxation. More favorable rules for the taxing of dividend income were also included, and rules that favored small business. Rather than offer across-the-board tax cuts, Eisenhower kept income tax rates high while giving away a certain amount of revenue through tax loopholes.

Ike resented that some critics called his tax proposal "a rich man's law." He saw it as a thoughtful combination of targeted tax reduction and economic stimulation. He simply did not want to slash revenues and add to the debt. "Every dollar spent by the government," he wrote to a friend, "must be paid in taxes—now or by our children." Although his party supported the bill in Congress and managed to get it past Democratic objections, the lingering effect of the bill hurt Eisenhower's reputation among his own right wing as a man who was prepared to roll back the New Deal. It also left him open to the charge—effectively made by John Kennedy in 1960—that his administration had done nothing to cut taxes.[18]

The impression that Eisenhower had repudiated his campaign tax pledges made conservatives anxious; so too did his warm embrace of the signature New Deal program, the Old Age and Survivors Insurance Program, better known as social security. Since 1935 this scheme had allowed workers and their employers to pay into a retirement fund, to be paid out in installments after a certain number of years of work. As a candidate Eisenhower had denounced what he called the creeping socialism of the New Deal and declared that if Americans wanted "security" they could go to jail and have their meals and housing provided for free. But once in office he adopted a far more generous, and indeed progressive outlook on the provision of social security benefits for working Americans.

Eager to sever any link to the heartless policies of the previous Republican administration, Eisenhower unambiguously embraced the principle of social security in his 1953 State of the Union address. "The individual citizen must have safeguards against personal disaster inflicted by forces beyond his control," he insisted. Three weeks later he used a homely metaphor to reassure Americans: "It is a proper function of government to help build a sturdy floor over the pit of personal disaster, and to this objective we are all committed." Eisenhower would be no Herbert Hoover.[19]

Among his first acts as president, in March 1953, was the consolidation of such programs under a newly created Department of Health, Education and Welfare. Billed as an efficiency move, it also elevated the executive in charge of administering social security to cabinet rank. Oveta Culp Hobby, a Texan who had run the Women's Army Corps during the war, was tapped for the position. She then chaired a commission to recommend ways to extend social security to millions of workers who were not yet included. From its inception in 1935, the program had not been available to many self-employed professionals, including architects, dentists, accountants, lawyers, farm owners, farm workers, domestic workers, waiters and wait-resses, fishermen, and religious ministers. Many government workers and public school teachers were not included either. This gap in coverage hurt the industrious small business owner; it also hurt the women and minorities who toiled in service industries and domestic work without a social safety net. Eisenhower proposed to widen the scope of the program in a move that would add 10 million working people to the social security rolls.

How did Ike square this extension of a welfare program with his con-servative ideas about thrift and self-reliance? In typical fashion, he found a middle way. He rejected the argument that social security was some sort of government handout. In fact it was available only to people who had worked and who had made contributions to the system. By asking workers and employers to set aside money for retirement, the government encour-aged foresight and wise financial stewardship. Eisenhower believed that "retirement systems, by which individuals contribute to their own secu-rity according to their own respective abilities, have become an essential part of our economic and social life. These systems are but a reflection of the American heritage of sturdy self-reliance which has made our country strong and kept it free; the self-reliance without which we would have had no Pilgrim Fathers, no hardship-defying pioneers, and no eagerness today to push to ever widening horizons in every aspect of our national life." In this way of thinking, receiving a benefit check in old age was a right citizens had earned through their industry and labor.[20]

In January 1954 he sent to Congress proposals for a wide array of wel-fare programs and enhancements, making the case in language that would have made his Republican predecessors Hoover and Coolidge choke on their breakfast oatmeal: "We must make greater and more successful efforts than we have made in the past to strengthen social security and improve the health of our citizens. In so doing, we build for the future, and we prove to the watching world that a free Nation can and will find the means, despite the tensions of these times, to progress toward a better society."[21]

Congress embraced Eisenhower's proposals for expanding social security and overwhelmingly approved his request. On September 1 Eisenhower signed the Social Security Amendments of 1954, expanding coverage and benefits to an additional 10 million people. Social security, once an embattled program and a symbol to conservatives of bloated federal spending, had become a permanent part of the American system. In a letter to his brother Edgar, a right-winger who had recently complained about the growth of federal programs, Ike explained this political reality: "It is true that I believe this country is following a dangerous trend when it permits too great a degree of centralization of governmental functions. I oppose this—in some instances the fight is a rather desperate one." But, he added, "the Federal government cannot avoid or escape responsibilities which the mass of the people firmly believe should be undertaken by it." Americans wanted the government to act as a safety net. "Should any political party attempt to abolish social security, unemployment insurance, and eliminate labor laws and farm programs, you would not hear of that party again in our political history." A few "Texas oil millionaires" and the occasional hard-liner might still oppose social security. But, he said, in memorably blunt terms, "their number is negligible and they are stupid."[22]

V

In truth, Eisenhower was not a small-government conservative, although he successfully sold himself as one to the public. He believed government should create the conditions in which Americans could pursue their own ambitions. This implied not a small or diminished government but an effective one. Good government should deliver meaningful enhancements to citizens within the limits of fiscal restraint. Ike believed in making government work "for the little fellow," as he put it, and in particular that meant providing social security, health care and insurance, housing, and highways.[23]

This principle of effective yet restrained government led Eisenhower to champion a program for national health insurance, a policy area of infamous complexity and entrenched interests. As early as his State of the Union message in January 1954, he expressed his convictions on the subject: "I am flatly opposed to the socialization of medicine," he began predictably. But he did believe that with the rising costs of medical care and health insurance, many Americans had no protection against sudden injury or illness. He floated the idea of a "limited government reinsurance program" to backstop private insurance companies and encourage them to offer "broader protection to more families." In March 1954 the administration sent a proposal to Congress that would set up a $25 million fund, which the government would use to guarantee policies given to low-income or high-risk groups. HEW Secretary Oveta Hobby said the scheme would allow insurance companies to offer more insurance to a wider population, while avoiding a national or socialized program.[24]

But in a stunning defeat for the president, the reinsurance bill was killed in the House of Representatives in July. A coalition of 162 Democrats who wanted a national health insurance program and 75 conservative Republicans who wanted no federal role at all in the health insurance business sank the legislation, aided and abetted by the American Medical Association. Eisenhower's frustration boiled over in a mid-July news conference. His goal was to "bring good and fine medical care within reach of the average household budget." The House members who had defeated his bill "just don't understand what are the facts of American life. . . . Our people are not getting the kind of medical care to which they are entitled." The right-wing *Chicago Tribune* hailed the defeat, calling the scheme a political ploy to show the country that the Republicans now embraced the welfare state. But the *Washington Post* argued that the plan was "the most hopeful middle-of-the-way measure" yet devised to make health insurance affordable to 68 million uninsured people. The president reintroduced the proposal in 1955 and in 1956 but could never overcome its varied sources of opposition.[25]

Eisenhower had more success in steering public housing and urban development legislation through Congress. In the early 1950s both political parties could agree that America's cities were facing a serious crisis of decay. As many white middle-class families moved to the suburbs, taking advantage of federal mortgage subsidies through the GI Bill, city centers began to lose residents, businesses, and taxes. In their place less affluent families, immigrants, and African Americans took up residence in city neighborhoods and apartment blocks that were already in decline. In the eyes of many whites who yearned for their slice of the American dream, urban city centers began to look broken and dangerous, whereas modern suburban developments like the Levittowns in New York and Pennsylvania glittered with the appeal of modernity (and remained white, thanks to racially restrictive covenants). The Truman administration developed a huge public housing program that aimed to build 800,000 new units of housing over six years to address the shortage of modern homes, while helping cities to retain residents. But Congress appropriated only a fraction of the money needed to carry out this building program, and most of the promised houses were never built.

Eisenhower believed the federal government should encourage "good housing in good neighborhoods" as a way to produce "good health and good citizenship," as he phrased it in his 1954 proposal to Congress for a new housing law. But simply building homes would make people more "dependent" upon government, so Eisenhower took a different tack. He appointed Albert Cole, a conservative Kansan who was a well-established foe of public housing, as his administrator of the Housing and Home Finance Agency. He also convened the Advisory Committee on Government Housing Policies, staffed entirely by leaders from the business, banking, and construction worlds. Their conclusions pushed Eisenhower to de-emphasize a direct federal role for public housing. Instead he proposed to offer cities loans for slum clearance and land reclamation projects. For medium- and low-income families, the Federal Housing Administration would provide low-interest loans.

These forms of assistance were designed to rehabilitate urban areas and attract residents and new businesses, thus creating a self-sustaining cycle that would in theory repair urban blight while also enhancing economic growth. The *Washington Post* enthused about the plan, calling it a "blitzkrieg against slum living" and "the most ambitious anti-slum battle in the Nation's history." At the same time, though, the government significantly slowed its public housing projects to less than a quarter of what Truman had called for. Signed on August 2, 1954, the Housing Act of 1954 marked a sharp transition from a New Deal era that identified public housing as a responsibility of the federal government to an era of public-private partnership in which the government pursued pro-business policies favoring loans, easier mortgage terms, and urban redevelopment.[26]

Consequential as these achievements were, nothing demonstrates Ike's belief in the constructive possibilities of good government as much as his pursuit of a nationwide interstate highway system, perhaps his most enduring domestic initiative and one that continues to shape the American landscape, environment, and economy. Biographers have long noted that Eisenhower first encountered the woeful American road network when he joined the army's 1919 transcontinental road convoy. This lumbering three-mile-long caravan of surplus war vehicles left Washington, D.C., in early July on a publicity jaunt and arrived in San Francisco two months later.

The conditions of the roads over which the convoy struggled showed Eisenhower that the nation could not flourish without significant internal infrastructure improvements. At a time when other nations, especially Germany, were investing in modern highways to boost economic growth, America remained stuck in second gear.

Many American leaders had arrived at the same conclusion, but in the interwar years road construction was considered a municipal and state matter. Traditionally states planned their own road networks, raised the necessary money through bonds, taxes, and license fees, and then built roads with the purpose of serving local communities. The result was a skein of byways clogged with cars, motels, cafés, gas stations, and stoplights, impeding swift movement across the country. In a report drawn up during the war, federal road planners proposed a major change: the construction of a single integrated interstate highway system, with common design standards and limited access, bypassing congested small-town America and allowing cars and trucks to move faster and farther. These plans led to the 1944 Federal-Aid Highway Act, a blueprint for a 40,000-mile system of interstate highways. Congress, however, did not appropriate enough funds for the scheme, and so it was stillborn. Financing highway projects would be the great stumbling block Eisenhower had to address: Who would pay for such a massive public works project that would soon become "the biggest peacetime construction project of any description ever undertaken by the United States or any other country"?[27]

Eisenhower was preoccupied with the issue from the outset of his presidency, but in the fragile economic climate of 1953–54 he was wary of proposing such a massive project. Instead, with unemployment inching upward, he pushed highway building as a crash jobs program. The administration steered a stop-gap highway bill through Congress in May 1954 that dedicated $2 billion to road maintenance and construction. But this fell short of a full-scale highway system, and Eisenhower kept up the pressure. In July 1954 he declared the nation's highways "obsolete." Traffic accidents were taking too many lives, the president stated; traffic jams wasted productive hours every day; and the economy was strangled by lack of adequate transport. He asked the Conference of Governors for help in designing a full-scale national interstate system, to be built over 10 years for $50 billion. The cost would be borne by tolls and gas taxes, he suggested, and it would require close federal-state cooperation. The governors remained skeptical, however, and Eisenhower realized he was going to have to generate pressure to get a plan drafted. In August 1954 he turned to one of his closest and most politically experienced friends, Gen. Lucius Clay, to take control of the bureaucratic machinery and get a detailed proposal before Congress.[28]

Clay, an engineer by training who had supervised the American occupation of postwar Germany, also served on the board of General Motors and was an outspoken advocate for the auto industry. Getting roads built, he felt, was a vital economic necessity for the country and for business. Clay took command of the President's Advisory Committee on a National Highway Program and handpicked its members, among them Stephen Bechtel, a titan of the engineering industry. The committee toiled for three months, holding public hearings and consulting widely with engineers, planners, financial experts, trucking companies, auto companies, concrete manufacturers, and labor unions. In January 1955 Clay presented Eisenhower with a plan whose numbers and scale were staggering: 41,000 miles of highway at a total cost of $101 billion, to be built in 10 years. To solve the knotty problem of financing, the Federal Highway Corporation would be chartered by Congress to sell 30-year bonds. These bonds would be paid back over time by the use of the gas tax, a revenue stream that would only increase as car travel, and gas consumption, rose. The corporation could fund the project; no tolls would be imposed on drivers; and the proposal envisioned no increase in federal taxes or debt.[29]

It sounded simple, but Clay's plan, which Eisenhower submitted to Congress in February 1955, met a buzz-saw of resistance from various quarters. The powerful chairman of the Senate Finance Committee, Harry F. Byrd of Virginia, argued that the proposed Federal Highway Corporation represented an infringement of states' rights. (Significantly, Byrd was at that time asserting states' rights to try to block implementation of the Supreme Court's 1954 desegregation decision.) Trucking companies protested the reliance on gas taxes, which cut into their profit margins. Farmers opposed the emphasis on a limited-access road network that would cut off their local routes from the highway system. City and state officials wanted to protect their right to plan local routes based on local needs rather than accept federal directives; they wanted to take gas tax revenues and design their own roads. Many critics thought the bond issuance, which would require the government to pay back $11 billion in interest to bond purchasers, wasted valuable funds that ought to be spent on roads.

Eisenhower tried to cajole congressional leaders into seeing his plan as a sensible, prudent response to a national emergency. He even used the specter of a nuclear attack to justify highway building, pointing out that evacuation of cities in wartime required better roads. Without a crash program of highway building, the economy would suffocate, national defense would be harmed, and "we will have a terrible condition in this country. . . . We must build new roads." Few could disagree with the goal, but many disagreed with the plan to pay for it. Bonds? Tolls? Gas taxes? Some combination of all three? Eisenhower's road plan got tangled up in congressional committees in the summer of 1955, and by the time of the August recess no law had been passed. The president went off to Denver for vacation—a prolonged one, as it turned out—without having a highway bill to sign.[30]

Yet Eisenhower had one ace in the hole: all the major parties to the debate wanted a highway bill, and eventually a compromise was found. It was sketched out by Congressman George Fallon, Democrat of Maryland, who served on the House Public Works Committee. Fallon replaced the bond issue with a proposal to create a Highway Trust Fund supplied by slightly increased taxes on gasoline, diesel oil, tires, trucks, buses, and trailers. The proposal promised to bring in a constant, indeed constantly increasing stream of revenue into the Trust Fund, and it stipulated that money so raised could be used only for highway building and no other public works. The highways would be built without any federal budget appropriations. Only a small user fee in the form of gas and excise taxes was needed to create a self-perpetuating machine: gas taxes would be spent on new roads that would allow greater traffic, which in turn would consume more gasoline, providing more revenue to spend on more roads, leading to more gas consumption and so more tax revenue. In May and June 1956 both houses of Congress passed the legislation, and on June 29 the president signed into law the Interstate Highway Act of 1956. The law reflected Eisenhower's political philosophy: it married government initiative with technocratic expertise in the service of market-enhancing public projects. In return for effective government, the public could be fairly asked to pay a small additional tax to support it.[31]

VI

By the end of his second year in office, Eisenhower had accumulated a number of significant legislative achievements, and more seemed well on the way. In areas such as infrastructure, housing, health care, and social security, his administration had made progress and cut federal spending at the same time. As the midterm elections of November 1954 loomed, Ike hoped this strong record would translate into victories at the congressional level for Republicans. Both chambers were in GOP hands, but the margin of control was razor-thin and Eisenhower wanted to expand it. He and Nixon threw themselves into campaigning. Ike gave 40 political speeches in the fall of 1954 and traveled 10,000 miles on behalf of candidates. Nixon worked tirelessly and in typical fashion slammed the Democrats as the party of communism, cowardice, and corruption. But these efforts could not forestall a significant defeat at the polls. The GOP lost control of both the House (where the Democrats took 17 seats) and the Senate (where the Democrats gained 2). It was a slap in the face for the president. He now had to preside over a divided government.[32]

In a postmortem on the elections, Eisenhower and some of his close advisers drew the conclusion that the Republican Party was in a dangerous position. It could win national elections only when a genuine political phenomenon like Eisenhower stood at the top of the ticket. Without such a known vote-getter pulling everyone else along, GOP candidates struggled. The party remained divided between far-right conservatives and moderates and had no clear vision or platform to offer voters that could contest the Democratic legacy of the New Deal. Ike had been mulling over this problem since coming to Washington and tangling with the Taft wing of his party. From time to time he would vent his feelings in his diary or in letters to friends. As early as April 1953 he speculated about forming a new party under the banner "the Middle Way." It would gather those who were internationalists in foreign policy, fiscal conservatives who wanted a balanced budget, and social liberals who understood the need for a basic safety net to catch those who, "through no fault of their own, suddenly find themselves poverty-stricken." Between those who wanted "socialism" and those who sought "to eliminate everything the Federal government has ever done," there had to be some common ground. Mere hostility to government was not a winning formula.[33]

In the wake of the disastrous midterms Eisenhower decided that the answer to his party's problems was to embrace the middle of the road as a political strategy. It would not be easy. He told a gathering of his close advisers that "the time had come to start the fight against the Old Guard within our party." If the GOP was to have a chance of winning majorities in the future, it first had to reform itself by bringing forward the "progressive moderates" in the party. In his diary he spelled it out clearly: "The Republican Party must be known as a progressive organization or it is sunk."[34]

As 1955 opened, Eisenhower began consciously to shape a political message that would appeal to the nation's moderates and independents. His January 2, 1955, State of the Union address carefully outlined proposals that balanced fiscal restraint against expanded social welfare projects and a robust defense policy. From time to time Eisenhower floated the term "moderate progressive" to describe this platform, but in February 1955, in a speech to the Republican National Committee, he coined a phrase that captured his ambitions: the Republicans must champion "dynamic conservatism." Here was a winning formula that suggested generous and humane solutions to social problems within a framework of fiscal restraint, moral rectitude, and a scrupulous observance of states' rights. The right wing bucked at this: the *Chicago Tribune* whined, "We cannot see what purpose was served by Republicans fighting the New Deal for 20 years if they were going to wind up by embracing the New Deal."[35]

But that sort of carping could not contend with the rousing chorus of approval from Republican activists who understood what a godsend Eisenhower was for their party. At its national meeting, the Republican National Committee (RNC), now under the direction of former New York congressman Leonard Hall, passed a glowing, worshipful resolution praising Eisenhower in language that bordered on a cult of personality: "In Dwight Eisenhower we have a political leader whose vigor, judgment and wisdom have breathed fresh life, energy and determination into our party organization." There was something godly about the man: Ike had become, the party leaders stated, "not only the political leader but the spiritual leader of our times. We thank him and salute him."[36]

No doubt this deeply embarrassed Eisenhower. Yet it revealed the degree to which the party embraced his Middle Way and jettisoned the principles of the more conservative Taft faction. Political analysts caught on to Ike's emphasis on reforming his party and banishing the ghosts of Coolidge and Hoover. *New York Times* columnist Arthur Krock saw that Ike had drawn a key lesson from the November 1954 defeat: "The Republican party must accept the political verities of the second half of the twentieth century instead of indulging in nostalgia for the dead past and continuing to run against Presidents Roosevelt and Truman."[37]

In early August 1955, just as he was preparing to depart for his long-awaited Denver vacation, Eisenhower casually spoke to a group of Republican congressional staff workers and once again stressed the centrist ambitions of Eisenhower Republicanism. "It is idle to say that the Federal

Government can be standoffish" toward the needs of the people, he said in the steaming August heat on the White House lawn. Certainly the Republican Party must identify itself with economic freedom and individualism. But "we must never be a party that is indifferent to the sufferings of a great community where, through some unusual cause, people are out of work, where people can't educate their own children, where through any kind of disaster, natural or economic, people are suffering." Eisenhower thought these ideas formed a "middle way" philosophy that could transform the Republican Party into the majority party in the United States—if only his loyalists would simply follow his advice.[38]

CHAPTER 11

TO THE SUMMIT

*"I believe mankind longs for freedom
from war and rumors of war."*

I

BY THE START OF 1955 EISENHOWER HAD ATTAINED EXTRAOR-
dinary popularity and prestige in American public life. He had tamed the
war in Korea and avoided American entanglement in Indochina. He had
brought fiscal balance back to Washington. He had guided the nation
through a brief recession and ushered in an era of robust economic growth.
His expansion of social security aided millions. His defanging of McCarthy
won him wide respect. Even his tepid support of civil rights for African
Americans aligned with public opinion in much of the nation. And in July
1955 he pulled off yet another success. He traveled to Geneva to meet with
the heads of government of Britain, France, and the Soviet Union in an effort to ease cold war tensions. It was the first time since 1945, when Stalin,
Truman, and Churchill had met at Potsdam, that American and Soviet leaders had convened. The intervening decade had been a time of great anxiety,
political upheaval, war, and an intensified nuclear arms race. The meeting in
Geneva brought a break in the clouds, a moment when world leaders talked
peace and when Great Power war, which had once seemed inevitable, began
at last to look unlikely. Eisenhower basked in what was quickly dubbed "the
spirit of Geneva."

The Geneva summit of 1955 grew principally from the need of the new
post-Stalin leaders in the Kremlin to show the world a moderate face. The
collective leadership that replaced Stalin had stumbled for a while in finding
a strategy for waging the cold war, but by the spring of 1955, when Nikita
Khrushchev emerged as the dominant figure in the Soviet government, a

new look began to take shape. This bellicose, rotund Ukrainian with a bald head and a menacing grin had been one of Stalin's closest associates in the 1930s and during the war years. A belligerent ideologue, he now held the post of first secretary of the Central Committee of the Communist Party of the Soviet Union. Yet he saw that Stalin's foreign policy had failed to win security and stability for his country. Stalin's brutal behavior had triggered a robust Western response, from the infusion of Marshall Plan dollars to the creation of NATO and the rearming of Western Germany. Most worrisome, the United States had developed a massive arsenal of nuclear weapons and the aircraft to deliver them anywhere in the world. Meanwhile the Soviet Union was still poor and relatively weak—its atomic weapons arsenal was a fraction of America's—and its hold on its Eastern European satellites was uncertain, as uprisings in Berlin in 1953 revealed. Soviet interests, Khrushchev believed, would best be served by a period of peaceful coexistence with the West rather than direct confrontation.

To signal his willingness to temper the conflict with the West, Khrushchev took some notable steps. In early 1955 the Soviets acquiesced to the long-standing Western demand to evacuate neutral Austria and end the four-power occupation of that country. He also made a major break with Stalin's policy by traveling to Belgrade to curry favor with Marshal Josip Tito, the Yugoslav communist whom Stalin had declared an apostate and traitor to the Marxist cause. Khrushchev also applauded the meeting in Bandung, Indonesia, of world leaders from 29 African and Asian nations; even though these states declared themselves to be nonaligned in the cold war, they aired their grievances about the capitalist and colonial world order, much to Khrushchev's delight. To cap off this period of activity, Khrushchev put public pressure on the Western powers to convene a major international summit to resolve such issues as the division of Germany, the militarization of Europe, and the nuclear arms race.[1]

Eisenhower initially rebuffed the idea of a summit with the Soviets, even saying in a news conference in April, "I see no reason for that summit meeting." In a private conversation Ike said he perceived no "fundamental changes in Communist motives or objectives," just a shift in tactics. Secretary of State John Foster Dulles agreed, and strongly. Dulles believed that Khrushchev's charm offensive sprang from fundamental weakness. The Soviet economy had failed to meet basic consumer needs; the subventions to satellite states in Eastern Europe and China had become a costly burden; and the Russians were struggling to keep up with the Americans in the arms race. Dulles concluded that the Soviets wanted "a pause" in the geopolitical contest, and he was not inclined to give them one. In fact Dulles feared that a summit would merely give Khrushchev and his front man, the nominal head of state Nikolai Bulganin, a world stage to propose a series of bold ideas about uniting Germany, disarming Europe, and halting the arms race. Such ploys would play well in Europe and in the Third World, and might lead to the weakening of the NATO alliance that Dulles had toiled so long to secure. In short, a summit promised only risk and no reward.[2]

So why agree to meet the Soviets at all? Eisenhower, unlike Dulles, felt he could not appear "senselessly stubborn," as he put it later. If proposals for peace and reconciliation were on the table, America must at least consider them. The public in America and in Europe, so accustomed to bad news about the Great Power rivalry, had been heartened by signs of a softening coming from Moscow. Intransigence now would be bad publicity for the United States.[3]

British leaders felt even more pressure. On April 6, 1955, Anthony Eden took over as prime minister from an ailing Winston Churchill. Eden, the suave, handsome Tory and longtime foreign minister, had toiled for years in Churchill's shadow. Given the top job at long last, he announced a general election so as to strengthen his parliamentary mandate. This was set for May 26; the announcement of a great summit meeting to discuss peace with world leaders would help his campaign against the much more neutralist Labour Party. American officials in London reported to Dulles that "the British are disarmingly frank in acknowledging their proposals [for talks with the Soviets] . . . are aimed at the local electorate." In a personal message Prime Minister Eden pleaded with Eisenhower to agree to a meeting of the Big Four world leaders. Despite Dulles's serious reservations, Ike relented. Privately he told Eden that he feared "raising false hopes" about a break-through in the cold war stalemate. But he understood the political impera-tive of embracing the cause of peace and détente. The date for a meeting with the Soviet, British, French, and American heads of state was set for July 18–23, 1955, in Geneva.[4]

For the next six weeks the national security staff spun itself into a frenzy preparing for the great meeting. One of the major issues they expected the Soviets to press was the reunification and neutralization of Germany, a plan unacceptable to the Americans but appealing to many Germans. Another probable Soviet gambit would concentrate on disarming central Europe—perhaps even creating a demilitarized zone in some or all of Europe—a suggestion that struck at the heart of the large American military presence across Europe and that would weaken NATO. And the Great Powers would likely tangle over the question of nuclear weapons: What if the USSR called for a nuclear arms freeze or even a radical proposal like the abolition of nuclear weapons?

The veteran newsman Joseph Alsop captured the preconference buzz in Washington very nicely when he wrote in his column, "Immense numbers of position papers were laboriously prepared. But essentially the aim was to prevent anything awful happening at the summit, rather than to make anything good happen there. Most of the position papers took the form: 'If the Soviets make move A concerning Germany, then we must make move B to secure a check-mate.'" But on one matter, the arms race, American planners were genuinely torn, and it was here that Eisenhower would play a decisive role in shaping the Geneva meeting.[5]

The issue of nuclear weapons most worried American planners because it was the one that had the greatest influence in the public mind. By 1955, the superpowers had attained the ability to detonate hydrogen bombs of extraordinary power. Nuclear war would certainly mark the end of civilization. It was imperative that in public, at least, American officials recognize the deep desire of the world's people to step back from the brink and impose some reasonable limits on atomic weapons. And yet, as government officials debated the appropriate American position, serious cleavages opened. The Pentagon and its military chiefs held an intransigent point of view: America's nuclear arsenal was the best defense against a Soviet attack; it had already proven effective in limiting Soviet expansion. The limitation of nuclear arms would only help the Soviets in their bid for strategic parity with the United States. The USSR looked weak, and the military chiefs wanted to hold the Soviets' "feet to the fire."[6]

Such inflexibility annoyed Eisenhower. In a tense meeting of the National Security Council at the end of June, the president directly challenged Admiral Radford, the chairman of the Joint Chiefs, calling the arms race "a mounting spiral towards war." If Radford really believed that arms agreements could never be advantageous, then perhaps the United States should "go to war at once with the Soviet Union." Defense Secretary Wilson chimed in, backing up Radford. Atomic weapons were essential to countering the Soviet advantage in military manpower in Europe and Chinese manpower in Asia. Without them the communists would have "an overwhelming advantage."

Eisenhower did not give up, however. While he knew that any serious agreement limiting nuclear arms was unlikely, he did not wish to go to Geneva only to obstruct the meeting. He wanted to put an arms proposal on the table that would at least test the willingness of the Soviets to negotiate. He was, he said, "much intrigued" with an idea of mutual inspection of military installations, even before an arms agreement was reached. This idea had been circulating among his various strategy planners for some time as one of many possible proposals the Americans might make. For Eisenhower, this one seemed to have the most appeal. If both the USSR and the United States agreed to open their arms installations to public inspection, this act alone might serve as a foundation for arms reductions and confidence building. At the very least such mutual inspections might help "penetrate the veil of Soviet intentions." More crucial, Ike believed, his trip to Geneva needed some kind of big positive action on this front. If America emphasized only military solutions to all these great problems, he declared, "it would lose the support of the world."[7]

These ruminations by the president led Foster Dulles to despair. This cautious, rigid, and suspicious man knew that Eisenhower wanted to make a bold gesture of peace and reconciliation, and he was terrified that he would go too far. All the patient work of building up the Western alliance and isolating the Soviet Union might be given away in a flash merely to placate public opinion. Two days before he left for Geneva, Dulles invited a fellow cold war hawk, C. D. Jackson, to his home for dinner and unburdened himself of his fears. Eisenhower, Dulles confessed, "is so inclined to be humanly generous, to accept a superficial tactical smile as evidence of inner warmth, that he might in a personal moment with the Russians accept a promise or a proposition at face value and upset the apple cart." The looming danger was that Ike's behavior might smack of appeasement—a word Dulles used and then retracted, as if it were too poisonous to utter. If that happened, Dulles's career, built upon his ferocious anticommunism, would be in tatters. Dulles felt he could go toe to toe with the Soviets and give up nothing, but Eisenhower always wanted to avoid confrontation and believed a handshake could make a difference. Sighing into his afterdinner drink, Dulles said, "I would hate to see the whole edifice undermined in response to a smile."[8]

II

Just an hour before his departure to Europe on the evening of July 15, 1955, Eisenhower sat down behind his desk in the Oval Office, faced a bank of cameras and microphones, and addressed the nation. His worries about raising public expectations had apparently vanished. He declared that for the first time in American history, a president was traveling overseas "to engage in a conference with the heads of other governments in order to prevent wars, in order to see whether in this time of stress and strain we cannot devise measures that will keep from us this terrible scourge that afflicts mankind." In Geneva he wished "to conciliate, to understand, to be tolerant, to try to see the other fellow's viewpoint." Throwing aside his earlier caution, he now asserted that the Great Powers had a chance to take "the greatest step toward peace, toward future prosperity and tranquility that has ever been taken in the history of mankind." With soaring rhetoric like this crackling across the national airwaves, no wonder Dulles was worried!

To cap this remarkable peroration, Ike asked the people of the nation to pray. "Suppose, on the next Sabbath day observed by each of our religions, Americans, 165 million of us, went to our accustomed places of worship and, crowding those places, asked for help, and by doing so, demonstrated to all the world the sincerity and depth of our aspirations for peace. This would be a mighty force."[9]

Eisenhower's flock obeyed. Clergymen of all denominations offered blessings to the president as he set off to Europe. The World Council of Churches appealed for special prayers. At St. Patrick's Cathedral and at Temple Emanuel in New York, fervent orisons could be heard. Daylong vigils were held across the country, as millions of worshippers asked for divine blessings upon the Big Four peacemakers. Some religious leaders chose to get as close as possible to the action: Billy Graham appeared in Geneva at the opening of the summit, setting up a revival meeting in a public park, where he led prayers for the world leaders. Graham joined in the chorus of heightened expectations, saying, "The next six days may be the most important in the history of the world."[10]

The president, traveling on the presidential aircraft *Columbine* with Mamie and their son Maj. John Eisenhower, who served as Ike's aide for the conference, arrived in Geneva on July 16. They were welcomed at the airport by a small Swiss military band and the Swiss president, Max Petitpierre. Speaking into a microphone on the tarmac, Eisenhower recalled that 11 years earlier he had come to Europe at the head of a great war machine to destroy Nazism. Now he came as an ambassador of peace. The 1,500 reporters far outnumbered the curious civilian onlookers. Mamie, holding an enormous bouquet of dark red roses, followed Ike to a waiting limousine, and they were whisked off through empty streets to a glamorous 18th-century chateau on the shore of icy-blue Lake Geneva.[11]

The next morning, a quiet Sunday, the president and his son escaped from the official residence to attend services at the small American church in Geneva, where an African American singer, Fanni Jones, then studying music in the city, sang the Negro spiritual "Sweet Little Jesus Boy." Billy Graham was in attendance that day and, looking at Eisenhower in church with his head bowed, remarked to a friend, "I believe God is really on the side of that man."[12]

The conference opened on Monday morning, July 18, at the Palais des Nations, a sprawling, white neoclassical behemoth that once housed the ill-fated League of Nations. As the world leaders took their places—Nikolai Bulganin for the USSR, Eden for Britain, Eisenhower for America, and Prime Minister Edgar Faure for France—it became apparent that there would be no private meeting of the minds. James Reston of the *New York Times* wrote, "The four leaders are sitting around four vast tables flanked by hordes of officials and addressing one another as if they were at a public meeting.... Officials are banked around the principals like ringside spectators at a championship prizefight." British foreign minister Harold Macmillan, a friend of Eisenhower's from the war years, confessed that his heart sank as he looked out over the cavernous hall: "The walls were decorated with vast, somewhat confused frescoes depicting the End of the World, or the Battle of the Titans, or the Rape of the Sabines, or a mixture of all three. I could conceive of no arrangement less likely to lead to intimate or useful negotiations."[13]

This formal atmosphere encouraged ponderous moralizing. The four leaders took turns laying out their positions, restating views that were already well known and on which they appeared to be inflexible. Premier Bulganin, a figurehead closely controlled by Khrushchev, mouthed the tired old argument calling for the withdrawal of foreign troops from Europe, an end to NATO, and only then the unification of Germany. The Americans wanted Germany unified and kept in NATO. The British offered a tepid proposal for a European security pact that would include all the major powers; the French, in a reprise of Eisenhower's "atoms for peace" proposal, offered a plan to take all the money the world spent on nuclear arms and place it in a fund for the development of Third World countries. All of these airy ideas fell harmlessly to the marble floors of the great meeting hall.

Yet once the leaders adjourned from their set-piece exercises at the conference table, little ripples of cordiality began to radiate through the meeting rooms. Between breaks the delegations chatted around groaning tables of food and drink, and the quartet of leaders entertained one another at dinners and cocktails throughout the week, allowing some spontaneous discussions. The Soviets were surprisingly warm hosts, Macmillan recalled, offering guests at their evening dinners large tumblers of vodka and giving heartfelt toasts to the memory of the great Second World War alliance. In these informal settings the Eisenhower magic had an opportunity to shine. One observer noted that Eisenhower's "man-from-Abilene" style impressed the Soviets, and his earnest, sincere declarations seemed to disarm their suspicions. Ike showed off his talent as "the great pacifier, the master of the sweeping generalization." He spoke unceasingly about "building a bridge between East and West," prompting one reporter to ask, "How many bridges can he build in one afternoon?" Long on gestures of warmth, Ike was short on detail: "He has shunned specifics like the plague."[14]

Eisenhower put his sincerity to work outside the conference meetings. On July 18 he hosted a dinner at his villa for Khrushchev, Bulganin, and Foreign Minister Vyacheslav Molotov. With Molotov seated on his left and Bulganin on his right, Eisenhower regaled the men with a detailed analysis of his campaign in Normandy, from D-Day to the liberation of France. Bulganin, who had been a lifelong apparatchik in the security services and had served as defense minister before taking over as nominal head of state under Khrushchev's patronage, peppered the president with questions. Evidently he knew little about American military operations in Europe in 1944–45. As the evening wore on, Bulganin, a rotund man with a white goatee and an amiable laugh, frequently expressed "the warmest feelings of friendship for the American people and for the President." The two men returned again and again to the "futility of war in the atomic age." Even Dulles, having received a respectful toast from his old nemesis Molotov, was touched by the change in the Soviets' tone.

Two days later Eisenhower invited Marshal Georgy Zhukov, the great battle commander and conqueror of the German Wehrmacht, for a private luncheon. One of the Second World War's heroes, Zhukov had been sidelined by Stalin as a possible rival and threat, but he had returned to prominence since Stalin's death and now served as defense minister. The two men spoke as friends and seasoned warriors. They had a remarkably open and wide-ranging discussion whose theme was the urgent need to restore good U.S.-Soviet relations despite their differing systems of government. The lunch concluded with a casual discussion of trout fishing, a passion the men shared. In all these exchanges the heads of government agreed to little of substance, but after so many years of frozen hostility, these warm currents of sympathy promoted good feeling and optimism.[15]

By the end of the third day of meetings, however, the atmosphere in the meeting hall had become strained. Bulganin continued to read speeches clearly prepared for him by others. Khrushchev seemed to the Westerners to be the real circus master. Macmillan was amazed: "How can this fat, vulgar man, with his pig eyes and ceaseless flow of talk, really be the head—the aspirant Tsar—of all these millions of people and this vast country?"[16]

The summit began to look like a failure. But then Eisenhower made a move that he had carefully planned ahead of time. He had been drawn to the idea of a mutual weapons-inspection program that would open both American and Soviet military installations to regular monitoring. Given the intense security and secrecy that had always surrounded military bases in both countries, this seemed a quixotic idea at best. Yet the context helps explain Eisenhower's thinking: just a few months earlier, James Killian had made his heart-stopping presentation in the White House about the vulnerabilities of the United States to a surprise attack. In reply the president had ordered a rapid program to get the U-2 spy plane operational. Its first test run would come in August. Eisenhower desperately wanted the information the secret overflights would provide to be sure that the USSR was not preparing a major attack. But how much easier it would be if both sides simply opened their skies to aircraft for approved overflights! Photographs would make plain the size of the arsenals and their state of readiness. In theory, such information, publicly gathered, would raise confidence and ease tensions. Ike hinted at this in Geneva in his very first conversation with his British and French allies. Instead of arguing about how to reduce weapons, why not simply allow inspections of the existing arsenals? "If this were done," the president mused, "what would be left to a potential aggressor? His capability for surprise would be severely limited."[17]

On the evening of July 20 Eisenhower summoned to his villa his chief advisers on the disarmament problem, including Nelson Rockefeller, who had been serving since 1954 as a special assistant on foreign affairs, Harold Stassen, Admiral Radford, and NATO's commander Gen. Alfred Gruenther. Sitting in the library with this powerful cohort, the president made plain his intention to push the idea of mutual inspections of military bases as a preliminary step in a broader disarmament plan. In order to capitalize on the propaganda value of the proposal, the advisers agreed that no word of the plan would be shared beforehand with the British or French. The men also counseled the president to make his announcement "in more or less extemporaneous fashion," as part of his longer speech on disarmament the following day.[18]

And that is just how Ike handled it. When, on the afternoon of July 21, the Big Four met to discuss disarmament, Eisenhower took the floor to present a general statement on the desirability of reducing world armaments; it was platitudinous. Halfway through, he stopped, removed his reading glasses, looked directly at Bulganin, and spoke as if off the cuff. His words were simple and moving, though carefully prepared. He said he had been searching his heart and mind for a suitable demonstration of the good faith of the United States in the search for peace, and he hit upon this: "to give each other a complete blueprint of our military establishments, from beginning to end, from one end of our countries to the other." In this scheme each nation would "provide within our countries facilities for aerial photography to the other country." Each side could take unlimited photographs, study them, and so build certainty that neither side was preparing any "great surprise attack, and so lessening the dangers, [and] relaxing tensions."[19]

The Soviets, experts at making ringing declarations for propaganda purposes, scoffed at Eisenhower's proposal. After the president finished his remarks, Khrushchev sidled up to him and said, "Mr. President, we do not question the motive with which you put forward this proposal, but in effect whom are you trying to fool? In our eyes, this is a very transparent espionage device." With a hint of contempt, Khrushchev added, "You could hardly expect us to take this seriously." Eisenhower stuck to his script. The plan offered to share information equally; neither side would benefit more than the other. We need, Ike insisted, "a departure from established custom." But Khrushchev dismissed the scheme as worthless and a distraction from the real need to reduce weapons. His response was "100 percent negative."[20]

But at a summit starved for signs of real progress, Eisenhower's visionary proposal captivated world opinion—just as he hoped it would. His suggestion was hailed in West German papers as "revolutionary"; the London *Daily Mail* called the speech "the greatest of [Eisenhower's] career"; the British Labour Party paper, the *Daily Herald*, considered the idea "amazing"; even the French communist paper, *L'Humanité*, thought the scheme "sensational." "Its chances of acceptance must be almost nil," noted the British

News-Chronicle, but it was a ringing testament of "the idealism which is prepared to fight for peace at any cost."[21]

When the conference came to an end on July 23, the professional diplomats called it a failure. The U.S. ambassador to the Soviet Union, Charles Bohlen, thought it "the most disappointing and discouraging of all the summit meetings," and he had been present at the great wartime meetings between Stalin and Roosevelt. There was "no real progress" on the major issues, and though the foreign ministers would continue to meet in the following months, they produced no breakthroughs. But for Eisenhower personally, the summit had been a magnificent success. Ike transformed a meeting he initially opposed into a triumph for his style of politics. He won a "moral victory," the *New York Times* asserted, by stressing his desire for peace and making innovative proposals for arms inspections: "He represented what is best in this nation." He persuaded a skeptical world that "the United States is sincerely opposed to war, cold or hot." He also imposed his will over his truculent secretary of state, his chief military advisers, and many on the right in his own party who viewed conciliation toward the Soviets as tantamount to appeasement. These achievements testified to Eisenhower's genuine political prowess.[22]

When he arrived back in Washington, he was met at the airport by 2,000 well-wishers in a summer rainstorm. Much of the cabinet stood in line to greet the returning peacemaker, who beamed through the downpour and happily shook every hand. Then he went directly to church and offered prayerful thanks. The press churned out page after page of glowing reports of Eisenhower's triumph in Geneva. Nothing much had happened, reporters admitted, but even so, Ike had prompted a global sigh of relief. With "instinctive sureness" and the "disarming conviction of his almost boyish manner," he convinced the world's people of his desire for peace. "The big figure of the American president, perfectly tailored, vigorous in action and broad and sweeping in thought, dominated the conference," according to *New York Times* reporter Drew Middleton. Eisenhower, wrote an admiring Stewart Alsop, "has the grandeur and the power, and a curious brand of earnestness as well, which makes him a man remarkably difficult to disbelieve." Ike scored a "signal victory" in the conference and "smashed into smithereens the deeply rooted image of America as inflexible and bent on war."[23]

There was one additional benefit of the summit, as the crafty muckraker Drew Pearson reported: Eisenhower was "now in a mood as never before to run in 1956. The platform would be 'peace in our time.'"[24]

III

Pearson, though, was wrong. The prospect of running for reelection and serving a second term did not appeal much to Eisenhower. For a man in his mid-60s who had been working hard for 40 years since he left West Point in 1915, it was natural that his thoughts frequently turned to retirement. By 1955 the Eisenhower home in Gettysburg was fully remodeled. It was a beautiful, comfortable place, the perfect expression of Ike and Mamie's tastes. There Eisenhower felt fully relaxed. He enjoyed country life, inspecting cattle, talking to farmers, practicing on his own putting green, and entertaining small groups of intimate friends. He had served his country well, and he did not hide his resentment toward those who prodded him to stay on the job for another term. In an August 4 news conference, journalists asked him about his plans to run in 1956. Ike dodged, saying his decision would depend upon how world affairs, domestic affairs, and his own health looked in early 1956, when he would make his decision. Without the "gift of prophecy," he said, he had no idea which way he would lean. Most observers felt certain he would stay in harness, noting that the president "has the vitality of a man of 54 instead of 64."[25]

In his private correspondence, though, Eisenhower voiced much deeper concern about the prospect of reelection. To Swede Hazlett he confided that he did think about the question of age; he would turn 65 in October 1955 and would hit 70 in his last year of a second term. "No man has ever reached his 70th year in the White House," he pointed out, and wondered if that barrier should be broken. After all, "the last person to recognize that a man's mental faculties are fading is the victim himself." He did not want to become one of those men who "hang on too long" while thinking that only they could do the job at hand. Yet he confessed he had not had much success in pushing forward an obvious successor. So far the "able younger men" he favored had been met with "inertia and indifference" by the public.[26]

In early August the Eisenhowers were looking forward to a long summer holiday. The Geneva summit had been grueling, and Ike was ready for a break. On August 6 he left Washington for Gettysburg and on August 15 flew to Lowry Air Force Base in Denver, eager to spend a month in the outdoors, playing golf and fishing. He and Mamie stayed at the Doud home with Mamie's mother, a place they had known since they were newlyweds. Although he attended to government business each day for an hour or two, using the offices at Lowry as a command center, Ike knew how to take a vacation: he played golf almost every day at Cherry Hills Country Club, spent hours working at his oil paintings, and met friends for evening card games at a presidential suite in the Brown Palace Hotel in downtown Denver. He spent many days at the Fraser, Colorado, ranch of an old pal, Aksel Nielsen, where the fishing was especially fruitful. Naturally he kept abreast of the political developments back in Washington. When Roscoe Drummond of the *New York Herald Tribune* described senior officials as "happily confident" that Eisenhower would run again in 1956, Ike shot off a private letter to his brother Milton. "I have done my very best to discourage the thought that automatically I shall be the candidate," he fumed. "Of course you know exactly what that decision would be unless extraordinary circumstances would convince me to the contrary." Indeed Milton steadfastly urged his brother not to run for reelection.[27]

His supporters would not listen to any talk of Eisenhower's stepping aside after one term. In early September, Republican Party state chairmen met in Washington to discuss the elections of 1956 and declared, according to Reston, that "Ike was the answer" to everything. "If he should refuse to stand for reelection next year the confusion would be indescribable," these men told Reston. More than that, they openly loved him. He is "a symbol of the atmosphere of the time: optimistic, prosperous, escapist, pragmatic, friendly, attentive in moments of crisis and comparatively inattentive the rest of the time." Reston asserted that Eisenhower's popularity had "gone beyond the bounds of reason" and had become "a national love affair." Who could blame the public for engaging in constant speculation about a second term?[28]

For the time being Ike avoided all the nonsense. He was having too much fun in Colorado. But his vacation was about to come to an abrupt end. On September 23, during what was now his seventh week away from sultry, humid Washington, he did a few hours of paperwork and then headed out to the golf course. He played 18 holes with the club pro, then wolfed down a late lunch, and returned to the links for nine more holes. As he finished up his game, he complained to his playing partner that the onions on his lunchtime hamburger had given him indigestion and heartburn, and he called it quits. He returned to the Doud home for dinner, picked at his food, and turned in early. At two in the morning he awoke with a searing pain in his chest. Mamie, sleeping in an adjoining room, heard him moving about. She took one look at him and called Gen. Howard Snyder, their physician, who was staying a few miles away at Lowry.[29]

Snyder, a lifelong army doctor who had attended both Eisenhower and Mamie since 1945, had seen the president suffer many bouts of painful indigestion. Ike had a chronic problem of an inflamed small intestine, known as ileitis, which caused bouts of gastrointestinal distress. Knowing that Eisenhower had complained in the evening about heartburn, Snyder assumed the problem was related to his GI tract and administered morphine to ease his discomfort. In the morning Snyder told the staff the president was resting from his "digestive upset" and would not be in the office that day. It was not until 1:15 in the afternoon that Snyder began to fear Ike's illness was more serious. He called Fitzsimons Hospital, the nearby military facility, and summoned a cardiologist to administer an electrocardiogram to the president. As soon as Snyder saw the results, he knew the president had suffered a coronary thrombosis, which had resulted in an "acute massive anterior myocardial infarction"—in layman's terms a blood clot had caused a heart attack. Snyder now ordered Ike to be transferred to Fitzsimons by the Secret Service. There doctors gave him a number of anticoagulants and put him in an oxygen tent to ease his breathing. He slept fitfully through the afternoon and night.[30]

Saturday, September 24, was supposed to be a quiet one for the White House staff, and many of the top assistants had taken a vacation to coincide with Eisenhower's Denver trip. The heart attack shattered that calm. Snyder called press secretary Jim Hagerty, who was at home in Washington taking a nap after a round of golf at Columbia Country Club. Hagerty called key officials, including Nixon, Foster Dulles, and (because Sherman Adams was in Europe on holiday) Jerry Persons, the deputy White House chief of staff. Persons in turn alerted cabinet members to the news. Hagerty's deputy press secretary, Murray Snyder, who was with the team in Denver, released a bulletin to the press at 2:30 p.m. announcing that the president had suffered a "mild" coronary thrombosis. Hagerty hastily arranged to fly to Denver on a military aircraft and brought with him Dr. Thomas Mattingly, the cardiologist at Walter Reed Army Hospital in Washington who had regularly examined Eisenhower and never detected any heart disease. Hagerty arrived at midnight in Denver and immediately imposed order on the scene, ensuring that the press would be regularly informed of the president's condition. He also effectively squelched what might have become serious criticism of Dr. Snyder for waiting 12 hours before transferring a gravely ill president to the hospital.[31]

John Eisenhower arrived from Washington the next morning. "Obviously under sedation," he wrote later, "Dad spoke quietly. 'You know,' he said with an air of wistful detachment, 'these are things that always happen to other people; you never think of their happening to you.'" John and Mamie took rooms in the hospital and slept there for the next few days. Mamie held up extremely well, spending most of her time writing replies to the flood of personal cards she was receiving daily from around the world.[32]

The nation's leading heart expert, Dr. Paul Dudley White of Massachusetts General Hospital, arrived at Fitzsimons later that afternoon and lent the authority and credibility of an independent, nonmilitary physician to the team. After consulting with the medical staff and examining the president, White described the heart attack as "neither mild nor serious" but "moderate" and tried to be reassuring about the president's prognosis. By the afternoon of September 26, White felt comfortable enough to return to Boston, following a detailed and lucid press conference in which he gave the nation a tutorial on heart disease. He expressed his confidence in the "excellent" medical care the president was receiving. These words did little to reassure the financial markets, however; when the New York Stock Exchange opened on Monday morning, it suffered its worst one-day loss since the Crash of 1929. The traders bet that Eisenhower's time in the White House was coming to an end.[33]

IV

In the next few days the news out of Denver improved. Eisenhower signed a few papers on September 30 in a carefully orchestrated demonstration that he was still competent. On October 2 doctors reported that the president had made it halfway through the crucial two-week period when heart attack patients might develop complications. In this period only family members, medical staff, and Sherman Adams were allowed to see him. On October 5 the doctors reported him "cheerful" and making good progress. Hagerty even detailed the president's diet, which on October 7 included grilled trout, vegetable soup, and fresh fruit. The soup was made lovingly by Sergeant Moaney, Ike's valet, who kept busy by preparing a few of the president's favorite dishes in the Doud family kitchen. On October 9 Dr. White returned to examine the patient and reported that while Ike's prognosis was favorable, he would need five more weeks in the hospital before he could be transferred to his home in Gettysburg. White thought it possible the president could be back to work in Washington by the first of January, when Congress was back in session.[34]

Eisenhower had survived a heart attack but could not function fully as chief executive. In principle Nixon ought to have supervised the government while the president recovered. But Nixon later admitted that he was "completely unprepared" for the shocking news of the heart attack, relayed to him in the early afternoon of September 24 by Hagerty. After putting down the receiver, Nixon sat in a stupor in an armchair in his Washington home. After a while he called his close friend and confidant William P. Rogers, the deputy attorney general, and asked him to come to his house. The two men sat together awhile, talking about Nixon's next move. But with news of the president's illness now flooding the airwaves, reporters started to crowd Nixon's front lawn. Only then did Nixon make his first decision: he and Rogers fled out the back door, crossed his neighbor's lawn in darkness, and slipped into a waiting Pontiac driven by Rogers's wife. The vice president then went into seclusion at the Rogers home, staying out of public view until Sunday, when he attended church services with his family. Only then did he speak to reporters. For almost 24 hours after hearing about the heart attack, the president's constitutional successor refused "even to be photographed" by the press.

Why was Nixon suddenly so publicity shy? Surely his role should have been to reassure the public right away about the continuity of government. Instead he weighed the politics. "Every move during this period," he calculated, "had to be made with caution, for even the slightest misstep could be interpreted as an attempt to assume power." Thus, in a moment of grave national crisis, Nixon ran through the political costs to himself of any public statement. When he gave his first press conference, he nonchalantly declared that the Eisenhower "team" would carry on as usual. Any political implications of the president's illness, he said, were "unworthy of consideration." Yet on Monday evening Nixon held a four-hour strategy session with Len Hall, the Republican national chairman, to discuss precisely that subject. Adams, who returned from a fishing vacation in Scotland, sat in on the discussion and refused to speak. Nixon grasped why: "Adams' sole loyalty was to Eisenhower." He would have no part in discussing a future without him.[35]

In fact the senior members of the Eisenhower administration quickly moved to limit Nixon's authority. The vice president did not occupy center stage during the weeks that followed the heart attack. Sherman Adams did. It was Adams who along with Attorney General Brownell (also hastily returned from a European vacation), decided that there was no need to turn power over to the vice president. The president was ill, but still alive and mentally alert. He needed time to convalesce, and the nation needed continuity. Adams and Brownell decided to develop a staff system to shield the president from any burden or worry during what would be a prolonged recovery. In any case, Adams viewed Nixon as far too inexperienced to run the government. The cabinet met on September 30 and, despite Nixon's initial resistance, decided that Adams would go to Denver on October 1 to take command of the president's affairs there and act as the "sole official channel of information between Eisenhower and the world." Nixon stayed behind, and he did not even visit the president until October 9, a day after Eisenhower and Secretary Dulles met in private conference.[36]

For the next two months the Eisenhower administration was managed by a committee consisting of six men: Adams, Nixon, Brownell, Dulles, George Humphrey, and Jerry Persons. Hagerty was the official spokesman and orchestra conductor. Of these, Nixon was the least consequential. He chaired the NSC and cabinet meetings, as he had done occasionally during the first term. But he had no executive power or authority to speak for the administration. Meanwhile Dulles controlled the State Department, Humphrey the Treasury, Brownell the Justice Department. Most important, Adams, seated at Ike's bedside, controlled access to the stricken president.

Eisenhower gradually regained his stamina at Fitzsimons Hospital. Daily announcements marked his progress, which was slow. On October 10 the president sat in the sun in a wheelchair for half an hour; the following day he met with Dulles for 25 minutes. But he did not sit upright in a chair until October 15, the day after his 65th birthday. He stood upright for the first time on October 23, a month after the heart attack, and did not take unassisted steps until October 26—and even then, he merely shuffled across his bedroom. He was in fact a seriously ill man. Yet his handlers carefully managed the flow of information to suggest steady improvement, and on October 25 the president was wheeled out onto the sundeck next to his eighth-floor room, where the press was allowed to photograph him. He smiled broadly, looked a bit thinner, and wore deep red pajamas, a birthday gift from the White House press corps. Above the pocket the words "Much Better, Thanks," had been embroidered in gold thread.[37]

He stayed in Denver until November 11, then flew to Washington. Arriving at National Airport to the ovation of a large crowd, he quipped that he was sorry his trip to Denver had been "a little longer stay than we had planned." His limousine drove him to the White House through cheering throngs. He gingerly resumed a light workload but transferred his life to

Gettysburg until the end of 1955, with occasional trips to Camp David. There, in the Catoctin Mountain retreat, he met the National Security Council on November 21 and December 1; the discussions were substantive. By December he was meeting daily with advisers and cabinet officials. On the doctor's orders he went to Key West, Florida, for the New Year holiday, and it was not until January 9, 1956, that Eisenhower returned to the White House to resume his official duties—almost five months from the time he had left the capital in mid-August, yearning for a break from the pressures of the presidency.[38]

With the president convalescing in the care of attentive doctors, all the talk in Washington turned to the horse race of 1956. A consensus quickly emerged among the insiders: the president was too ill to run again, and without Eisenhower, the Republicans faced a political catastrophe. The 1954 congressional elections had revealed that nationally the GOP remained a minority party. It possessed no leader other than Eisenhower who could unite the country. In fact the Republicans had no one who could even unite their party: the factional disputes between the Old Guard and the moderates had only been masked since 1952.

All the men whose names attracted speculation had serious flaws. Nixon led the pack by virtue of his official position, but most Republican Party elders either did not like him or felt he could not beat Adlai Stevenson in a head-to-head contest (as polls showed). Earl Warren, now happily ensconced at the Supreme Court, steadfastly refused to be drawn into the mix. Senate Minority Leader William Knowland inherited the mantle of Robert Taft but had none of his dignity or intelligence and was loathed by most Eisenhower loyalists, especially Nixon, with whom he had a lifelong rivalry. The president's brother Milton possessed a winning last name but never showed the least interest in stepping into the political limelight, despite the president's constant prodding. Treasury Secretary Humphrey, an able public servant, was six months older than Eisenhower. Senator Everett Dirksen had little national standing. And so it went. Things looked so bad that some insiders resurrected the idea of a Thomas Dewey candidacy. In short, the GOP cupboard was bare.

There was something almost Shakespearean about this political scene. The stricken leader lay hidden away in Denver or Gettysburg, screened from public view by a cloak of doctors, observing the junior officers of the party, vying for position in his absence. He almost seemed to be enjoying his position: no one could pressure him now to run again. As his strength recovered he mused frequently about whether to stay in politics or retire. In a late October letter to Swede Hazlett, he revealed that his decision to run hinged on the issue of a successor: "I am vitally concerned in seeing someone nominated who not only believes in the program I have been so earnestly laboring to have enacted into law, but who also has the best chance of election. This is the tough one." But no one came close to matching his political strength. He had no viable protégé, and he knew it.

When in late November Eisenhower summoned Len Hall to Gettysburg, the GOP chairman desperately hoped he might coax an answer out of the Sphinx of Abilene. But Eisenhower was not yet ready to tip his hand. "Len, you're looking at an old dodo," Eisenhower sighed, seeming discouraged. Leaving the president's side with no clear statement to give to the waiting reporters, Hall improvised. He put on a big smile and told the press that he was "encouraged" by the conversation and thought Eisenhower would indeed run for election. "Ike will run if he is able," Hall told reporters, although the president had said no such thing. But Hall went all in: Ike was looking well and was sharp as ever. "As far as I am concerned, there is no other candidate." Hall wanted to project an air of inevitability about the race, though Ike remained silent.[39]

In private Ike brooded on the problem of running again. Hagerty's diary recounts an intense period of four days in December when he and Ike discussed little else. Eisenhower said he was "appalled" by the low quality of Democratic aspirants Averell Harriman, Adlai Stevenson, and Estes Kefauver, but, he admitted, "we have developed no one on our side within our political ranks who can be elected or run this country." The two men spent hours reviewing possible contenders before discarding every name. Hagerty asked Eisenhower point blank if he would run again. His reply echoed 1952: "I don't want to, but I may have to." A conversation with Dulles in early January yielded a similar result. As the president summarized the discussion in his diary, the world political situation remained so dangerous—"on the verge of an abyss"—that however much he wanted to retire, he "must try to carry on." If lesser men should take over, "individuals of less experience, lesser prestige . . . than Foster and I have," he mused, "what will happen?"[40]

Eisenhower likely made the decision to run again over the New Year holiday, which he spent in Key West, surrounded by his intimate friends and family, including Bill Robinson, the Kentucky liquor entrepreneur Ellis Slater, the Mississippi Democrat and wise-cracking pal George Allen, Al

Gruenther, Mamie, Milton, and his retinue. He returned to Washington on January 9, and on January 13 he held a quiet dinner for his most senior advisers and cabinet members—except, significantly, Nixon. Ike told Nixon that the dinner was to discuss Eisenhower's future, and "since you are going to be so much the object of conversation, it would be embarrassing to you" to be present. What Ike really meant was that the dinner guests would likely say that Nixon certainly could not replace Eisenhower in 1956.[41]

Not surprisingly, his advisers—whose status depended upon Eisenhower remaining in the White House—all urged him to run again. Dulles was particularly effusive, declaring Eisenhower to be the only man "in the world" who could guide humanity through the tempestuous crises of the decade and avoid a possible nuclear war. Len Hall argued that Ike needed to secure his political legacy. He had begun to transform the Republican Party but still had work to do: "If you have four more years, I think you'll make the Republican Party the dominant party in the United States." Milton sat quietly, taking notes, until Eisenhower asked him to sum up. He had already made the case privately for early retirement, and did so again, basing his argument mainly on health concerns. Ike's son John (who also urged Ike to step aside) later reflected, "[I] probably will never know exactly how Dad felt emotionally about a second term. Probably he was ambivalent." But the January dinner "seemed to have the greatest single influence on him." If he did not run, the Democrats would take back the White House. Only he could save the party and the country from that dreaded fate. John nailed it: "His colleagues were telling him what, by that time, he wanted to hear."[42]

As in 1952, Eisenhower chose to run because he had come to believe he was the best man for the job and the consequences of his refusing would be catastrophic for the country. He had the kind of powerful ego that characterizes all men who attain the nation's highest office. The idea of standing aside as a rookie like Nixon went down to defeat against the Democrats tormented him. He had never been a quitter and he was not going to let a weak heart stop him now. Of course he would run. Was there ever any doubt?

On February 29, when he felt he could not keep silent any longer, he announced in a garbled and rambling statement to a press conference that he had finally answered the great question on everyone's mind: "My answer will be positive, that is, affirmative." That evening at 10:00 he went on national television to explain his decision. After much "prayerful consideration" and long discussions with family, friends, and especially his doctors, he had decided to seek reelection. His health was good, he said, although he would do little "barn-storming" during the campaign. More important, his work was not yet done. He remained passionate, he said, about expanding economic freedom, building equal opportunity, and ensuring national security. He would fight on.[43]

CHAPTER 12

A FORMIDABLE INDIFFERENCE

"The Republican Party is the party of the future."

I

EISENHOWER'S DECISION TO RUN FOR REELECTION POSED AN awkward question: Would Nixon remain on the ticket in 1956? The answer was not obvious. While the president's popularity remained high throughout the heart attack crisis—his party and his countrymen fretted anxiously about a future without Eisenhower—Nixon seemed diminished by the whole affair. Instead of acting as a valuable second in command, Nixon had been shunted aside as Adams, Foster Dulles, and Hagerty steered the ship of state during Ike's convalescence. Nixon drew praise in the press for being a good team player during Eisenhower's illness, yet it also became clear that he had no serious role to play in the administration. Nixon was superfluous.

Eisenhower, with his sixth sense for picking winners and losers, understood this. During his long recovery he spent many hours wondering if Nixon could fill his shoes. His conclusion: decidedly not. Nixon was able, loyal, hardworking, devoted, but he was not ready to be president. The only way he could hope to emerge in 1960 as a viable presidential candidate was by gaining greater experience in government. Eisenhower viewed the vice presidency as a ceremonial post, not a place to gain executive skills. Even after four years in the job, Ike knew, Nixon trailed Adlai Stevenson in the Gallup poll in a hypothetical head-to-head match. Eisenhower thought Nixon needed a "crash program" to enhance his visibility and prestige. A top cabinet job, like Defense or Commerce, would serve as better preparation for higher office than another four years of being lost in Eisenhower's shadow. And that is what Ike suggested to Nixon in a conversation in December 1955, the day after Christmas.[1]

The suggestion to step off the ticket and take a cabinet job seemed to Eisenhower a constructive one. But it came as a shattering blow to Nixon and triggered yet another of his famous "crises." Nixon knew that a cabinet post would represent a demotion; worse, it would mean "Nixon had been dumped." Eisenhower asked him "five or six times" to join the cabinet. Each time, Nixon refused; if Eisenhower wanted him "off the ticket," he should say so, and Nixon would step down. Eisenhower thought he was offering Nixon a chance to improve himself; Nixon considered Ike's advice a political cyanide capsule.[2]

While awaiting Nixon's decision in January and February 1956, Eisenhower mused about replacements. One man he considered was Frank Lausche, the Catholic and Democratic governor of Ohio, known for his independence and bipartisanship. Ike thought the GOP would benefit immensely from putting a Catholic on the ticket. But he told Len Hall that his "first choice" was Robert Anderson, a Texan and nominal Democrat who initially served as Ike's secretary of the navy and then as deputy secretary of defense (propping up the increasingly unreliable and gaffe-prone Charles Wilson). Anderson was a businessman, an administrator, a moderate, self-effacing, nonpartisan wise man, just the kind of technocrat Eisenhower wanted in government. (Unbeknownst to Ike, he was also an alcoholic.) In fact Ike briefly discussed with Adams the idea of having two vice presidents, one to handle domestic policy and the other foreign matters, men of substance who could handle the heavy burdens of government and bring to the president only the most crucial decisions. Ike did not have Nixon in mind for either role.[3]

In the early spring of 1956, while Eisenhower relaxed on George Humphrey's Georgia plantation, shooting quail and enjoying the luxurious surroundings with Jock Whitney, Bill Robinson, Bob Woodruff, and their families, Nixon endured a period of "agonizing indecision." Even by the time of Ike's official announcement on the last day of February that he would run again, the two men still had not resolved Nixon's future. The press asked the president directly if he wanted Nixon as his running mate. Eisenhower simply said he would wait to see what the Republican convention would decide. While full of "admiration" for Nixon, he would "say no more about it." The press predictably interpreted this evasive comment as a sign of disapproval; a week later they peppered Eisenhower with more questions. The president replied testily that he had asked Nixon "to chart out his own course, and tell me what he would like to do." But Nixon refused to beg.[4]

The stalemate endured. In mid-March the two men discussed the issue again. Nixon told Eisenhower that the decision to wait until the convention to announce his running mate had created "some misconception in the minds of some people that there is some conflict between the President and himself." Further he said that moving to the cabinet would suggest to the press that "Nixon is afraid to run again, or the president is afraid to have him; therefore it is a way of kicking him upstairs (or downstairs)." Ike replied that the decision was Nixon's to make but continued to make his own preference clear. "The president's concern is," according to the written summary of one conversation, "where is Nixon going to be 4 years from now? . . . What does 8 years in this job do for him? In the long run, he is thought of as the understudy to the star of the team, rather than being a halfback in his own right." Eisenhower kept repeating how much he liked Nixon and that he had his best interests at heart, but Nixon said at least three times in this conversation that he would not move to the cabinet.[5]

Ike did not relent. In early April he again urged Nixon to take a cabinet job but did not order him to do so. Nixon again demurred, waiting for an offer to stay on the ticket that did not come. Privately Eisenhower told RNC chairman Len Hall that Nixon, while having done a fine job as vice president, was "making a mistake" in seeking to stay on the ticket: "I think he would do better by taking a Cabinet post." Even so, Eisenhower would not directly order Nixon off the ticket. Ike did not like confrontation and hated to deliver bad news. He hoped Nixon would interpret the offer of a cabinet job as a presidential command. But Nixon did not comply. On April 25, two full months after Ike had announced his reelection bid, the matter came to a head. In his news conference, journalists asked Eisenhower if Nixon had made a decision yet about his own future, and Ike replied that Nixon hadn't "reported back." This comment cleverly placed the onus for the delay on Nixon and made it impossible for Nixon to remain aloof any longer. The next day Nixon formally asked Eisenhower to be kept on the ticket. Eisenhower pretended to be "delighted," but he then sent Nixon out to meet the press with Jim Hagerty by his side to inform the waiting reporters while Ike stayed out of sight, suggesting that more pressing business needed his attention.[6]

The whole affair would not matter much but for the insight it gives into Eisenhower's style. He could have ended the standoff simply by stating publicly that he wanted Nixon to remain his vice president. He never said this. Instead he made Nixon sweat. The price of rejecting Ike's advice was public humiliation, which duly came and which Nixon never forgot or forgave. With good reason, Nixon concluded years later that Eisenhower "was a far more complex and devious man than most people realized."[7]

Nixon was not alone in drawing this conclusion. Although Eisenhower appeared to the public as a rosy, optimistic, ebullient figure, a genial and avuncular man, those who watched him carefully never could quite understand him. "Four years ago this week," wrote the seasoned newsman James Reston in late May 1956, "Dwight D. Eisenhower arrived in Washington from Paris to seek the presidency. The capital is still trying to figure him out." Reston mused about how Ike governed. Was he a leader or a mediator? Did he make tough decisions or avoid them? Had he merely substituted personality for policy? Other than optimism and pragmatism, what skills did Eisenhower possess that made him such a political phenomenon? Reston concluded simply that Ike looked good to Americans because the previous two decades had been so troubled. "After a generation of contention, of war, of depression, of acrimonious divisions in the nation, he was urged to enter the arena precisely because he was an attractive mediator." He had calmed a turbulent nation, poured soothing balm on its abrasions. His bid for reelection in 1956 rested mainly on a promise to deliver more of the same.[8]

Some commentators delivered a more cutting assessment. Richard Rovere, the acerbic *New Yorker* columnist, described the Eisenhower administration as a non-event in the nation's history: "It has left the country almost exactly as it found it, with nothing added and nothing taken away." Ike governed with reference to a "pastiche of pieties" and seemed content to "subcontract" his job to others. Eisenhower himself was lazy. "The whole operational side of government has bored him," Rovere asserted. "No president since Calvin Coolidge, who was a devotee of the afternoon snooze, has relaxed more or taxed his energies less than Eisenhower." He preferred to be kept out of the loop: "There is a great deal of which Eisenhower has never heard, and he has organized his office staff and his Cabinet into a kind of conspiracy to perpetuate his unawareness." To be sure, he had steered the country away from war and proved able to restrain his hawkish lieutenants. Even so, the dirty work of politics diminished him. He had become merely a "distressed, flustered, put-upon man." If Eisenhower possessed a certain sanity, a quality of decency and maturity that Americans respected and valued, his chief characteristic as president had been his coldness, what Rovere called "a formidable indifference."[9]

This theme of a president missing in action—a leader uninterested in leading—became the leitmotif of the Democratic Party's 1956 campaign. Governor Stevenson, trying to erase the memory of his Hamlet-like hesitations of 1952, had declared his candidacy in November 1955 with a hard-charging speech about the need to avoid confusing "moderation with mediocrity." Following Eisenhower's prolonged absence from Washington as he recovered from his heart attack, Stevenson declared that the presidency "cannot be conducted on a part-time basis." Nor should the president be allowed to forgo a serious national campaign on account of fatigue or infirmity. According to Stevenson, Eisenhower's refusal to campaign vigorously seemed disdainful, more like the behavior of a monarch or corporate CEO than a public servant. Stevenson made every effort to link Eisenhower to the do-nothing presidencies of Harding, Coolidge, and Hoover, Republicans who had failed to use the powers of the presidency and chose simply to "stand pat." He accused Ike of sleepwalking through four years of an inconsequential presidency.[10]

Even some on the right voiced a similar critique. In the pages of the new magazine *National Review*, William F. Buckley and L. Brent Bozell articulated conservatives' deep disappointment with the president's record. The armistice in Korea, the deal to partition Vietnam, the lack of support for Chiang Kai-shek, the cheery embrace of Soviet leaders at the Geneva summit—achievements Eisenhower believed had helped the cause of global peace—all looked like appeasement to hard-line conservatives. Worse, Eisenhower's actions on the home front, from appointing Earl Warren to the Supreme Court to expanding the role of the federal government in civil rights, public housing, and social security while cutting the defense budget, amounted to a betrayal of the conservative principles Eisenhower had embraced as a candidate in 1952.[11]

Soon after Ike announced that he would run for a second term, Buckley cast a vote of no confidence. What were "the objectives of the Eisenhower program?" Buckley asked in a scathing *National Review* editorial. "It is hard to say." Buckley likened Ike to the "housewife next door" who wishes only "to get on with her chores, . . . to like, and to be liked, to be tranquil and serene." Ike's policy vision was "undirected by principle, unchained to any coherent idea as to the nature of man and society, uncommitted to any estimate of the nature or potential of the enemy." The Eisenhower administration "is always emitting a squid-like ink of moral justification," and then hastily darting away through the clouded waters. Eisenhower was self-righteous but hollow, doctrinaire in rhetoric but soft in action; strident in mouthing words like "freedom" and "liberty" but afraid to fight for them. And here for Buckley lay the genuine danger of Eisenhower: to resist "the socialist tidal wave," Americans needed ideas, passions, and beliefs; Ike had given them only "aimless mush-headedness." Eisenhower himself was mostly immune to these kinds of criticisms, but Buckley's critique laid the groundwork for a campaign to push the GOP further to the right once the Age of Eisenhower had run its course.[12]

II

Just as critics on both the left and the right were registering doubts about Eisenhower's competence and energy, the president suffered another health crisis. On June 7, 1956, Eisenhower attended a dinner at the Sheraton Park Hotel to honor the White House news photographers. He enjoyed the elaborate floor show and ate a bland dinner that had been approved beforehand by his personal physician, Howard Snyder. Soon after returning to the White House, Eisenhower went to bed. Around midnight, however, Mamie called Snyder at his home and reported that the president was having terrible stomach pain. Snyder, used to such calls, suggested that Mamie give Ike some Milk of Magnesia. But 20 minutes later she called again and said the pain was worse. Snyder hurried to the president's bedside.[13]

Eisenhower was stricken with an attack of ileitis, the chronic inflammation of the lower portion of the small intestine. For many years he had endured sharp pains in his lower abdomen, at times extremely painful and debilitating. Snyder had examined Eisenhower repeatedly, trying to find the precise source of the problem. But not until he administered a barium x-ray in May 1956 did he find a constriction in the lower ileum. The problem did not incapacitate the president, but Snyder knew it would flare up again. As he examined the president in the early hours of June 8, Snyder realized that this was no mere attack of gas. Eisenhower began to vomit, his blood pressure was 160 over 90, and he was perspiring. The problem demanded immediate operative relief. At 1:30 in the afternoon Snyder ordered an ambulance and had Eisenhower transferred to Walter Reed Hospital.

Unfortunately virtually all the senior medical staff at Walter Reed had left Washington. Gen. Leonard Heaton, the commander of the hospital and its chief surgeon, was on vacation in West Virginia, where the state police tracked him down and put him on an airplane back to Washington. The team of doctors who gathered at Walter Reed were wary of conducting the operation Snyder recommended on a 65-year-old man who had suffered a heart attack only nine months earlier. As Snyder wrote later, "Everyone hesitated to put a knife into his abdomen."

In fact 12 hours passed while the doctors deliberated. After more x-rays they reached agreement that the problem was an acute obstruction of the terminal ileum. In the early morning of June 9, after lengthy debate, Heaton accepted the unenviable task of performing major surgery on a sitting president. At 2:25 a.m. the doctors gave Eisenhower general anesthesia; at 2:59 Heaton made the first incision, and for two hours he snipped away at Eisenhower's innards, searching for, then finding, and then cutting out the constricted portion of the ileum. It was for Heaton a familiar operation, one he had performed "scores of times." But there could be no denying the tension in the room. At 5:00 in the morning Heaton finished his work and deemed the operation a success.[14]

The surgery resolved the physical crisis but inevitably triggered a political one. Above all, reporters wanted to know, who had been in charge while the president was unconscious? The answer seemed to be, as usual, Sherman Adams. Spokesman Jim Hagerty casually told the press corps in the hours after the operation that "no thought had been given to transferring presidential powers" to the vice president. (The Twenty-fifth Amendment, clarifying the procedures for presidential succession, did not become law until 1967.)

The operation posed again the question of whether Eisenhower should go ahead with his plan to run for reelection. He spent three weeks in Walter Reed after the surgery, and his medical reports reveal a difficult recovery. His inflamed bowels caused him distress, and his wound briefly became infected. He stoically endured frequent enemas (one of "milk and molasses," another of olive oil). He had diarrhea and did not eat solid food for a week. His weight dropped to 158 pounds—almost 20 pounds lighter than usual. Two weeks after the operation he continued to endure "moderately severe anorectal pain" and hemorrhoids. After three weeks he moved to his home in Gettysburg to continue his recuperation.[15]

Eisenhower clearly could not endure an arduous national campaign for reelection. For a time, he wrote, he "seriously doubted if I would ever feel like myself again" and was "miserably uncomfortable." He found Gettysburg restful after the constant surveillance of Walter Reed, but not until July 14 could he boast of having "walked all the way to the gate and back, a distance of a mile." He put on a brave face when a group of congressional leaders visited the farm on July 10 and reassured them that he had every intention of keeping his pledge to run for reelection. He told them, "I have had a rough ride. But if I was right on February 29th, I am now in much better condition."

Brave talk. But he had been significantly slowed by his recent surgery. When he returned to Washington on July 16 he looked frail and thin. According to Ann Whitman, his personal secretary, the president had regained some strength but showed signs of "a great physical and psychological depression." And he would have trouble hiding this from the public. The Democrats made it clear Eisenhower's "health and his absences from the White House would be a major issue in the election campaign." After all, in the 11 months since his September 1955 heart attack, Eisenhower had been incapacitated for six of them. With the Republican National Convention set to open on August 20 in San Francisco, it was natural that some might ask: Could he carry on?[16]

III

The issue of Eisenhower's strength and fortitude became urgent in 1956, not only because a presidential reelection campaign loomed but because the country entered into a period of dramatic tumult over the politics of race. If ever there was a time for wise and active presidential leadership on civil rights, the mid-1950s was it, and yet Eisenhower seemed to many observers to have gone missing in action.

By the start of 1956 the white South had developed a political strategy to oppose the Supreme Court ruling in *Brown v. Board of Education.* One influential activist who helped shape this strategy in defense of racial segregation was James J. Kilpatrick, the 35-year-old editor of the *Richmond News Leader* in Virginia. A balding, stocky, humorless Catholic originally from Oklahoma, Kilpatrick used his editorial page to rally southerners to fight the ruling by reviving the doctrine of "interposition." This warmed-over version of the nullification thesis conceived in the 1830s by the pro-slavery senator John C. Calhoun of South Carolina held that the states could interpose themselves between the people and the federal government to block any tyrannical usurpation of power by Washington. The *Brown* decision, according to Kilpatrick and many other white southerners, sought to rob the states of their right to educate children in a manner conducive to southern tastes and values. The Constitution did not give to the federal government the duty to educate children; it left education to the states. This right must now be defended with "massive resistance" to federal demands for racial integration. In Kilpatrick's skilled hands, "interposition" became a way of hiding the ugliness of white supremacy in the legalistic appeal to states' rights.[17]

Kilpatrick's arguments found a warm welcome across the South. On February 1, 1956, Virginia's Senate and House of Delegates passed a resolution denouncing the "illegal" action of the U.S. Supreme Court in ordering desegregation of public schools. (On the same day four large crosses were set alight on the campus of the University of Alabama in protest of the court-ordered enrollment of Autherine Lucy, a black graduate student.) South Carolina's legislature followed Virginia's lead, passing a resolution of interposition that railed against the "illegal encroachment by the central government into the reserved powers of the States." Mississippi did the same on February 29, as did Georgia on March 9. Soon every state of the Confederacy had passed similar resolutions defying the Supreme Court.[18]

And the leading political figures of the South rose with one voice in the halls of the Capitol to denounce federal overreach and the specter of race mixing. On March 12 Senator Walter George read the infamous "Declaration of Constitutional Principles," or "Southern Manifesto," on the floor of the Senate. Nineteen senators and 82 members of the House of Representatives appended their names to the shameful document. Distinguished legislators like Richard Russell of Georgia, Harry Byrd of Virginia, Russell Long of Louisiana, William Fulbright of Arkansas, and even the 1952 Democratic vice-presidential nominee John Sparkman of Alabama, all signed. The manifesto accused the Supreme Court of substituting "naked power for established law," declared the *Brown* decision an "abuse of judicial power," and insisted that the South be allowed to protect its "habits, traditions, and way of life." The Supreme Court's action had triggered racial tumult in the South that was "destroying the amicable relations between white and Negro races." The Court had "planted hatred and suspicion where there has been heretofore friendship and understanding."[19]

Mississippi senator James Eastland lent his Delta-accented voice to the segregationist cause. A Democrat and cotton farmer from Sunflower County, Eastland had earned a reputation as a conspiracy-minded anticommunist who used his Internal Security Subcommittee to probe into politically suspect activities. He offered a simple explanation for the *Brown* decision: the Supreme Court had fallen victim to "left-wing brainwashing." He criticized Eisenhower directly for expressing even tepid support of the Court's decision and asserted that Ike himself would not send his own grandchildren to integrated schools. "Ike is like all interracial politicians," Eastland sneered. "He wants it for the other fellow."[20]

Eastland articulated the view, common among powerful white southerners, that the race problem had been manufactured by outside troublemakers. "There is no discrimination in the South," he declared on NBC's *Meet the Press.* "There are social questions that we think we know more about than others do who don't have those social questions. Segregation is in the best interest of both races. Both races develop their own culture, and develop better when they are separated." In March 1956 this passionate defender of Jim Crow segregation was elevated to the chairmanship of the Senate Judiciary Committee.[21]

Eisenhower, in his usual fashion, tried to pour oil on these troubled waters. In a press conference on March 14 he downplayed the nature of the constitutional challenge from the states. "No one in any responsible position anywhere has talked nullification," he declared disingenuously. He went on to stress that the Supreme Court had recognized the emotional dimension of the subject and had called only for "gradual" desegregation of schools. He hailed "people who are ready to approach this thing with moderation." In a masterful example of double-speak, Ike said that Americans "must be patient without being complacent." While deploring "extremists on either side," he said it seemed perfectly understandable for southerners to "take time to adjust their thinking" to a new legal reality. He concluded in a matter-of-fact way that all he would do was "uphold the Constitution of the United States"—as if that might settle the issue.[22]

Hoping to avoid any personal role in the debate, Eisenhower turned to the nation's white church leaders in search of support. He met with his friend and adviser Billy Graham on March 20 and exchanged letters with Graham in the following days. Ike wanted ministers to talk up the need for "progress in our race relations." He suggested to Graham that southern pastors call for a few modest, concrete measures in order to fend off heavy-handed federal action. Putting black citizens on school boards and city and county commissions, getting blacks into graduate schools, and easing Jim Crow laws in public transportation—such simple steps would help moderate black demands and posed no threat to white authority. Could not church leaders emphasize the need for such actions?[23]

Graham promised to convene leaders of the major southern denominations and urge them to speak out in favor of "moderation, charity, compassion and tolerance toward compliance with the Supreme Court." But Graham advised Eisenhower to stay away from the issue until after the November elections. "You have so wonderfully kept above the controversies that necessarily raged from time to time," he wrote. It would be best "to stay out of this bitter racial situation that is developing." Eisenhower was only too happy to take this advice. "Let's don't try to think of this as a tremendous fight that is going to separate Americans and get ourselves into a nasty mess," he told reporters on March 21. For Eisenhower, civil rights politics should simply be avoided.[24]

As the 1956 presidential campaign approached, Ike adopted what his speechwriter Emmet Hughes called "the most conservative caution" toward the subject of civil rights. Although Max Rabb, the "minorities officer" in the White House, urged Sherman Adams to push Eisenhower on civil rights, the president remained wary. He did not think there was much to be gained politically by drawing attention to the *Brown* decision. On August 8, just before a press conference, Hagerty advised Eisenhower that black voters in the North were likely to fall in line behind the Democrats anyway, and too much pressure on civil rights would alienate white southerners. Ike agreed. When asked by reporters later that day if the GOP platform should explicitly embrace the *Brown* decision, Eisenhower dodged the question. "I don't know how the Republican plank on this particular point is going to be stated," he said.[25]

In fact Ike was working behind the scenes to avoid just such an endorsement of *Brown*. He had grown frustrated by the civil rights issue. He mused privately to Ann Whitman that the "troubles brought about by the Supreme Court decision were the most important problem facing the government domestically today." But he had no desire to attack that problem head-on. Instead he wished the Supreme Court had ordered a much more gradual process of school desegregation, starting with graduate schools and then colleges, and only then integrating high schools and lower grades. He bemoaned the "passionate and inbred attitudes" of white southerners, yet he sought every opportunity to express his sympathy for their position.[26]

In the days before the Republican convention in San Francisco, Eisenhower directly intervened in the drafting of the party platform. On August

19 he called Herbert Brownell to demand a change in the civil rights plank. Ike had seen a draft put together by Senator Prescott Bush of Connecticut, the chairman of the platform committee, which stated that the Eisenhower administration "concurred" with the Supreme Court's *Brown* decision. The president insisted that was untrue: his administration merely "accepted" the ruling and would follow the law; the Court's decision was its own. He expressed his frustration to Brownell at being caught "between the compulsion of duty on the one side, and his firm conviction on the other that because of the Supreme Court's ruling, the whole issue had been set back badly." He felt that any direct link between himself and *Brown* would appear as an affront to the white South. If the platform drafters did not change the language to distance Eisenhower from *Brown*, "he would refuse to go to San Francisco." Needless to say, Bush altered the language of the civil rights plank as directed by Eisenhower.[27]

The president also shaped his acceptance speech, which he delivered to the GOP convention on August 23, to avoid any provocative language on civil rights. Speechwriter Arthur Larson, who worked with Eisenhower throughout July and August on this speech, tried to insert a "strong and unequivocal condemnation of racial discrimination," but the president objected. In a number of conversations with Larson, Eisenhower repeated by-now familiar themes about the need to "understand the Southerners as well as the Negroes." In Larson's account of these discussions, Eisenhower stressed the point that "equality of political and economic opportunity did not mean necessarily that everyone has to mingle socially—'or that a Negro should court my daughter.'" Larson reluctantly drafted a speech that omitted the charged terms *race*, *racial*, and *Negro*, downplayed any notion of a national civil rights crisis, and instead hailed a number of "quietly effective actions conceived in understanding and good will for all." Larson drew a painful and damning conclusion after this experience: "President Eisenhower, during his presidential tenure, was neither emotionally nor intellectually in favor of combatting segregation in general."[28]

Most of Eisenhower's advisers found the president's caution on civil rights profoundly distressing, especially as racial violence spiked in the South with the opening of the new school year in late August. In Mansfield, Texas, where a district court had ordered the integration of the high school in response to a suit filed by the NAACP, 12 black students arrived at school on the morning of August 30 to enroll. They encountered an angry mob of 400 stone-throwing, placard-toting white residents. Three ghastly black effigies hung from ropes strung up over the school entrance and from the school flagpole. *Life* magazine carried photographs of the hand-painted signs that adorned the necks of these blood-smeared dummies: "This Negro tried to enter a white school," one read. The mob gathered in the schoolyard shrieked, "Go home, niggers" at the black teenagers. A few days later an angry mob at Texarkana Junior College blocked black students from enrolling. White students there erected a 14-foot cross on school grounds, and when night came, they set it alight.[29]

In Clinton, Tennessee, local residents staged protests and angry demonstrations to halt the enrollment of black students at the public high school. The mayor feared he could not keep order and asked Governor Frank G. Clement for help. On September 2 the Tennessee National Guard arrived in Clinton in force, bringing with them seven tanks, three armored personnel carriers, and over 100 jeeps and trucks. This show of force dispersed the rioters but also generated considerable press across the country. Newspaper reports about the tanks parked in Clinton's town square showed a national readership that for the South, the struggle against integration was starting to look like a war.[30]

When Eisenhower took questions in his weekly press conference on September 5, Robert Clark of the International News Service pointed out that "Negro children are risking physical injury to attend school" in the South. Was there something the federal government could do to help? Eisenhower said no: "Under the law the Federal Government cannot . . . move into a State until the State is not able to handle the matter." And in any case, "when police power is executed . . . by the Federal Government, we are in a bad way." When another reporter asked him if he had any message about the civil rights crisis for the nation's young people who were just about to start the school year, Eisenhower fell back on his usual platitudes: "It is difficult through law and through force to change a man's heart." He denounced the actions of "extremists on both sides," thus equating the actions of stone-throwing segregationists with the work of black lawyers and church leaders who, he said, "want to have the whole matter settled today."

Pressed once again by reporters to endorse the *Brown* decision—the very thing he had so far refused to do—Ike snapped. "I think it makes no difference whether or not I endorse it. The Constitution is as the Supreme Court interprets it, and I must conform to that." In a narrow, technical sense he was right. But a great chance to side with the forces of justice and history had passed.[31]

Hearing Ike's remarks, a crestfallen Roy Wilkins, executive director of the NAACP, made a public reply: "All the nation is watching in shocked horror at men making war upon children and upon the Supreme Court of the United States . . . and from the White House, not a mumbling word. Here is the one man who without favoring your child or mine or trespassing upon any right of a state, could set a moral tone for the nation in this sorry mess, but he chooses to stand mute." African Americans who had looked with such hope upon the important achievements of Eisenhower's first years in office now felt the president had turned his back on their struggle.[32]

IV

As Republicans gathered for their national convention in San Francisco in late August 1956, the party faithful tried hard to talk up the boom times of the Age of Eisenhower. The crowds that gathered at the Cow Palace on the edge of town—a cavernous concrete exhibition hall—wanted to revel in the near-certainty of Eisenhower's reelection, and they chortled with glee at the prospect of facing Stevenson again, a man Ike had so thoroughly thumped in 1952. The convention itself was described by reporters as "slumberous" and "soporific" because it lacked any drama whatsoever. It was merely a coronation of a leader who received the adulation of his party with good-natured bemusement. Ike put in a sporting effort in delivering his acceptance speech, bellowing from the rostrum, "The Republican Party is the party of the future." But few of the delegates seemed to be thinking too much about the future because the present, at least for them, was so good. "Rarely in American political history," wrote newsman Edward Folliard, "has any man dominated a political convention as President Eisenhower dominates this one. In the eyes of the assembled Republicans he is a soldier-statesman of colossal proportions, and they regard criticism of him as almost sinful."[33]

What a change from four years earlier! Then Ike had barely won the nomination, nimbly snatching it away from Robert Taft and earning the bitter enmity of the Ohioan's devoted supporters. Columnists Joseph and Stewart Alsop recalled that in 1952 Eisenhower had been untried and unpolished as a politician, giving poor speeches and struggling to connect with the voters. "Now, he is a new master of the political art who has stolen or quietly muffled just about every issue the Democrats could possibly use against him. . . . In pure political terms, the performance of the first Eisenhower years has been nothing less than brilliant." According to *Life* magazine, Eisenhower had masterfully pulled together a once-divided party. The Old Guard that had nearly stymied his bid for the nomination in 1952 no longer mattered. Ike had "captured the party and put his progressive stamp on it." Republicans "love and revere their leader" and are "proud to belong to the Eisenhower party. That's something new."[34]

Eisenhower left San Francisco buoyed by the rapturous reception he had received and spent a quiet week playing golf at the Cyprus Point Golf Club in Monterey, California, in the company of old friends Bill Robinson, Ellis Slater, and Bob Woodruff. On September 12, back in Gettysburg, he officially kicked off his 1956 campaign at an informal picnic on his own large lawn. Some 500 GOP operatives gathered under a large circus tent, merrily wolfing down fried chicken and baked beans and enjoying the partisan atmosphere. Nixon spoke to the group first, promising a fighting campaign on behalf of the Republican Party. He insisted he would vigorously "set the record straight" if the Democrats should ever dare to distort Ike's record. He relished his role as attack dog, saying with glee, "You don't win campaigns on a diet of dishwater and milk toast."

The president then addressed the group, and as usual took the high road. His message was somewhat off the cuff, drawing on his usual battery of stories from the war years and homespun yarns about the importance of leadership. But as he wound up, he found his theme. What did the Republican Party really stand for? What was the 1956 election really all about? Unlike 1952, when Eisenhower was a newcomer to the party, he had now earned the right to define the values of the GOP—*his* party.

Republicans, he said, wanted a government that promotes individual liberty and freedom while also protecting each citizen "against falling into the depths of poverty and misery through no fault of his own." Good government must enhance free enterprise but also encourage community values and mutual goodwill so that no American will be left behind. Government must operate with thrift and integrity but "must never pinch pennies where the security of the nation is concerned." Government must arm for war but strive toward world peace through cooperation and diplomacy. Here in a nutshell was the basic message of the Age of Eisenhower: Government must be moderate, efficient, empathetic, responsive, and compassionate. It must govern with restraint, wisdom, and a constant insistence on frugality. Above all, government must adhere to a disciplined policy of limited spending and limited interference in the lives of American citizens.[35]

These themes had appeared in Eisenhower's correspondence and public speeches going back to the 1940s. Yet they had recently been given great precision in a short book called *A Republican Looks at His Party* by Arthur Larson, who at the time was a lawyer working in the Labor Department and had since become one of Eisenhower's chief speechwriters. The book appeared in the spring of 1956, and Eisenhower read it while he was convalescing from his abdominal surgery. Larson argued that during the 1950s the people of the United States had converged toward a common set of principles—a consensus about what constituted the right balance between the federal government, the states, and the free market—and that President Eisenhower expressed this new consensus. While the Democrats were divided between big government New Dealers and conservative southerners, Eisenhower had "established the Authentic American Center in politics." Far from being just a genial caretaker, Eisenhower had engineered a new politics in America. On the campaign trail, Eisenhower called it "modern Republicanism."[36]

Eisenhower could never have espoused such centrist ideas in 1952, when so many Republicans still thrilled to the Taft brand of conservatism. But in his first term in office Eisenhower had governed by these principles, and his popularity in the nation provided all the rebuttal he needed to quiet any critics. Under a flapping white circus tent on his Gettysburg lawn, he casually blended the New Deal ethos with a dose of homespun conservative rhetoric about states' rights and individual liberty. His concoction raised not a single Republican eyebrow amid the picnickers—an indication of his supremacy over a party that had once viewed him as a dangerous outsider.

The 1956 presidential campaign did not tax Eisenhower's stamina. Over six weeks the president made about a dozen appearances across the country. On a typical visit he would fly from Washington to Peoria or Cleveland or Pittsburgh or Denver, allow himself to be driven through adoring crowds and submit to a ticker-tape parade, and then give a speech. Usually he hastened back to the White House on the same day so as to avoid too much time on the road. It was as clinical and streamlined a campaign as possible, designed to avoid too much stress on Eisenhower's health. Since the Stevenson campaign never landed any real blows, there was no need to alter this compact schedule. Indeed Ike found time to attend the opening game of the 1956 World Series, between the New York Yankees and the Brooklyn Dodgers. His son John advised against it, urging Ike to take the election more seriously and do more vigorous campaigning. "Dad sat back and roared with laughter," recalled John. Referring to Stevenson, Ike said,

"This fellow's licked and what's more, he knows it! Let's go to the ball game." Though critics used such nonchalance against him, his supporters admired his confidence. An editorial in *Life* magazine, which favored Ike, captured the spirit of the 1956 election: "This is an era of good feeling. In such an era, it is hard to find much to fight about."[37]

CHAPTER 13

DOUBLE CROSS AT SUEZ

*"I've just never seen great powers make such
a complete mess and botch of things."*

I

ADLAI STEVENSON BUILT HIS 1956 CAMPAIGN ON ONE BASIC
message: that Eisenhower had failed to govern well because he spent too
much of his first term either on the golf course or in a hospital bed, leaving
the nation adrift and in need of firm direction. Eisenhower found this an insulting and infuriating charge; but there was a kernel of truth in Stevenson's
critique. In mid-1956, as he endured his intestinal ailments, Eisenhower
had delegated a crucially important decision to John Foster Dulles that led
directly to one of the biggest crises of his presidency.

The case concerned Egypt and the vital waterway that ran through
its commercial heart: the Suez Canal. On July 26, 1956, Egypt's dashing
38-year-old leader Col. Gamal Abdel Nasser shocked the Western powers
and delighted the Arab world by declaring the nationalization of the canal.
He did not desire to close this crucial sea lane; rather he sought to take ownership of it away from the international consortium—mainly the British and
French governments—that had financed and built the canal and collected
tolls from its waterborne traffic. Nasser, who had led a military coup against
Egypt's monarchy in 1952 and who had only just declared himself Egypt's
president in June, saw the nationalization of the canal as a declaration of
Egypt's independence from the colonial powers. Egypt, not the Europeans,
had a right to control its own sovereign territory, Nasser believed, and that
included the passageway from the Red Sea to the Mediterranean.

Nasser's action struck at the jugular vein of the British Empire. For almost a century Egypt had been a zone of British influence because of its

strategic importance in the eastern Mediterranean. The opening of the canal in 1869 only enhanced Britain's desire to maintain its presence in Egypt, for the canal offered a strategically valuable route to the Red Sea, East Africa, and India. Over the years since, Suez had become a highway of world trade and allowed Britain to project global economic and naval power. A third of the ships that transited the canal each year were British, and the British government held a 44 percent stake in the Suez Canal Company, making it the largest shareholder. Some 70 percent of Western Europe's oil passed through the canal; along with Gibraltar and Malta, Suez formed a chain of outposts that projected British influence across the Mediterranean and into the Middle East.[1]

In light of Nasser's overthrow of the once-pliant Egyptian monarchy, Britain found itself suddenly needing to curry favor with the new regime. In 1954 the British agreed to evacuate their massive military base in the Canal Zone, hoping that this gesture would build up some credit with Nasser's government. Britain also offered loans to Nasser's government for the construction of a new hydroelectric dam along the Nile River at Aswan, a modernization project that Nasser saw as epitomizing his new, technologically ambitious plans for his developing country. However, Britain could not fund the project alone. Anthony Eden, the long-serving foreign secretary who had become prime minister in April 1955, appealed to the United States for help. Eisenhower and Dulles, aware that Nasser was also bidding for Soviet aid, agreed to open discussions to help finance the dam project. Eisenhower understood Nasser's game but concluded that the United States should "go all out for the Dam in Egypt." In December 1955 the United States made a preliminary offer of $56 million to support the massive engineering project.[2]

Britain and America hoped the generous offer would earn Nasser's loyalty to the West. Instead of demonstrating his gratitude for the financing of the dam project, however, Nasser continued to hurl epithets at the British for their colonial pretensions in the Middle East. He championed the cause of Arab unity, pressured the Jordanians to rid themselves of their British military advisers, and worked to sabotage the Baghdad Pact, a regional security arrangement among Britain, Iran, Iraq, Turkey, and Pakistan that Eden saw as essential to his Middle East policy. Egypt offered diplomatic recognition to communist China and, perhaps most damning, signed a deal with Czechoslovakia for the purchase of arms and aircraft.

To Dulles such behavior could not be rewarded with generous financial assistance. In late March 1956 he proposed to Eisenhower that the United States slow the discussions with Egypt over financing the Aswan Dam while awaiting an improvement of Nasser's attitude toward the Western powers. Dulles wanted to make it plain that Nasser "cannot cooperate as he is doing with the Soviet Union and at the same time enjoy most-favored-nation treatment from the United States." Dulles proposed that the Eisenhower administration hold up loans, credits, humanitarian aid, and approvals of export licenses and also start to "tilt" toward Saudi Arabia as a way to isolate Egypt's leadership in the region. Eisenhower, also growing anxious about Nasser's defiance of the West and chumminess toward the Soviets, approved Dulles's proposals.[3]

But Nasser refused to be bullied. He openly courted the USSR, seeking its aid to build his dam should the Western powers renege on their promises of support. Dulles had backed himself into a corner and had no way out. He could hardly restore an American offer of aid without some sign of contrition from Nasser, yet none came. Aware that Congress too was growing increasingly critical of Nasser and would be unlikely to approve an American aid package to such a headstrong nationalist, Dulles now began to contemplate an outright break with the Egyptian leader.

Unfortunately, at the crucial moment of decision, Eisenhower was sidelined by illness. From June 8 to July 16 he was either in Walter Reed Hospital or recovering in Gettysburg from his intestinal surgery. Just three days after returning to the Oval Office—thin, still in pain, and irritable—Eisenhower met with Dulles to discuss the Egyptian issue. On July 19, in a 10-minute conversation, Dulles outlined his proposal to withdraw financing from the Aswan Dam project. Eisenhower, who for two months had been out of touch with this issue, accepted his recommendation. That afternoon Dulles told the Egyptian ambassador that the United States would withdraw its offer of financial support for the project. In his memoirs Eisenhower admitted the matter had been handled poorly. In a rare criticism of Dulles, he wrote, "We might have been undiplomatic in the way the cancellation was handled."[4]

A week later the world heard Nasser's reply: speaking to a crowd of 100,000 in Liberation Square in Alexandria, he announced his decision to nationalize the Suez Canal and use the toll profits to build the Aswan Dam. (In fact Nasser later received enormous amounts of aid from the USSR to fund the project.) "We shall industrialize Egypt and compete with the West. We are marching from strength to strength." The crowds in the street roared their approval.[5]

Political leaders in London, Paris, and Jerusalem reacted with outrage at Nasser's actions. In British eyes, Nasser looked like a small-time thug who dared challenge the might of the British Empire in a region of vital strategic interest. To allow an upstart Arab colonel to place a choke hold on Europe's oil supplies was intolerable. More than that, Nasser struck a very tender nerve in the British psyche. To many Britons, Nasser sounded a good deal like the European dictators of the 1930s, and the memory of Britain's weak-kneed appeasement of those men hung like a shadow over the Suez affair. Indeed in February 1938 the British foreign minister Anthony Eden had resigned in frustration over Neville Chamberlain's appeasement of Hitler. Now Eden was prime minister, and he would show the world that Britain had learned the lessons of appeasement: aggression must be checked early and with firmness.

In drawing this conclusion Eden was supported by the majority of his advisers, who also read the Suez Crisis through the lens of World War II. Harold Macmillan, then chancellor of the Exchequer, referred to Nasser in his diary as "an Asiatic Mussolini." By attaching this stigma to Nasser, the British raised the stakes of the crisis to enormous heights. Eden's colonial secretary, Alan Lennox-Boyd, wrote to the prime minister, "If Nasser wins or even appears to win we might as well as a government (and indeed as a country) go out of business." Eden wasted no time in alerting President Eisenhower: Britain was prepared "to use force to bring Nasser to his senses."[6]

The French government, also a shareholder in the Suez Canal Company, had been equally outraged by Nasser's behavior and just as prone to resort to specious analogies from the 1930s. To France, however, Nasser presented a more concrete and immediate danger. France was in the midst of a bitter colonial war in Algeria, and Nasser's pan-Arab rhetoric had inflamed the Algerian liberation movement. More galling, the Egyptian leader had been sending arms to the Algerian rebels. France wanted Nasser destroyed every bit as much as Britain did. And alongside Britain and France, Israel saw Nasser as a serious threat. Under Nasser's rule, border skirmishes between Israel and Egypt had spiked and Nasser had moved to unite the Arab states of the region into a hostile anti-Israel bloc under his leadership. Thus no sooner had Nasser made his announcement on July 26 than three determined states, Britain, France, and Israel, lined up together in hopes of forcing a confrontation that might weaken and even destroy the defiant Egyptian colonel.

II

The tangle over Suez presented Eisenhower with one of the most complex problems of his eight years in office. Since the spring of 1956 he and his closest advisers had been grappling with the problem of how to win friends among nonaligned nations in the developing world. Eisenhower understood instinctively that in the coming years the world would be shaped by the yearning of millions of people in the Third World to be free of the shackles of colonial rule. Indeed the very term *third world* emerged at just this moment, coined by a French economist in 1952 to describe the great majority of nations that had not yet found their place between the developed "first" world and the socialist bloc "second" world. Eisenhower spent a great deal of time worrying about which way the emerging nations would turn. His national security team felt that the Soviets had been more effective in using offers of technology, development aid, and of course weapons to seduce Asian and African nations to join their cause. The NSC concluded that the United States had not yet created "an affirmative sense of community of interests with the underdeveloped countries." To make matters worse, in the confrontation with Nasser America's closest allies had set a course for war that would inflame the Arab world and turn Nasser into a hero. It would certainly open the door to greater Soviet influence in the region.[7]

In his initial reaction to the canal's nationalization, Eisenhower stressed that Nasser's behavior, while unforgivable, was not strictly speaking illegal. Nasser wanted to assert Egyptian sovereignty but had not threatened to close the canal to shipping traffic. As Eisenhower instructed Dulles over the phone on July 30, the United States would demand that Egypt "operate the Canal efficiently" but would not get "hysterical" over the issue: "We are not going to war over it." Eisenhower understood better than his British and French counterparts that Nasser "embodies the demands of the people of the area for independence and slapping the white man down." Any use of force against Nasser now would "array the [Muslim] world from Dakar to the Philippines against us." When Eisenhower learned from his special envoy Robert Murphy that the British cabinet had already decided to "drive Nasser out of Egypt," he responded by writing immediately to Eden, whom he had known well since the Second World War. But that old friendship did not soften Eisenhower's tone now. The president expressed his "personal conviction . . . as to the unwisdom of even contemplating the use of military force at this moment." Eden could have no doubt: the United States opposed any British military action toward Egypt.[8]

Eisenhower dispatched Dulles to London. There the secretary of state found top British officials in a state of extreme bellicosity. In a discussion with Macmillan, Dulles heard the anguished cry of an injured lion. Macmillan was a thrice-wounded veteran of the Great War, a Conservative member of Parliament throughout the interwar years, and a protégé of Churchill's. During the war, as British minister in Algiers, he was Churchill's man in North Africa and worked closely with American military leaders, especially Eisenhower. He spoke with authority but also a certain end-of-days sentiment about the Suez Crisis. To Dulles, Macmillan prophesied that Nasser's seizure of the canal would trigger successive acts of defiance toward Britain across the Middle East and lead to "the destruction of Great Britain as a first-class power and its reduction to a status similar to that of Holland." Macmillan bitterly declared that it would be better to be "destroyed by Russian bombs now" than to be "reduced to impotence" by Nasser. "No one wanted to see another Munich. They would rather die fighting than slowly bleed to a state of impotence." This was the voice of imperialism on its deathbed.[9]

It is possible that British policy was influenced not just by a romantic attachment to the colonial past but by the poor health of the prime minister. Unbeknownst to the Americans, Eden was an ill man. In April 1953, while undergoing an operation to remove his gallbladder, the surgeons had damaged his bile duct. For years afterward Eden endured recurrent infections and fevers and constant abdominal pain. His doctors prescribed a drug called Drinamyl to treat the pain; it contained both a barbiturate and an amphetamine—rather like taking a sleeping pill with six cups of strong coffee. For three years Eden popped these pills that, after prolonged use, left him a nervous and exhausted wreck, prone to mood swings and outbursts of euphoria followed by depression. Added to his physical ailments, the tension of the Suez Crisis pushed Eden to the brink of collapse.[10]

Only with the greatest effort did Dulles and Eisenhower manage to persuade the British to agree to a series of conferences, first with a large group of maritime nations that used the canal, then with the Egyptians themselves, to try to find a peaceful resolution to the crisis. In August these nations worked out a proposal for the international control of the canal and some sharing of the canal's revenue with Egypt. Nasser had no reason to accept such a plan, however, as any concession would be perceived as a defeat for him. Nor did the British and French really want a negotiated settlement. Instead Eden repeated to Eisenhower his belief that Nasser had become a dangerous pawn of the Soviets, who wished to expel Western influence from the Middle East. "Nasser must not be allowed to get away with it," Eden wrote.[11]

In an exchange of remarkably frank letters with Eden in September, Eisenhower alerted the British prime minister to his firm opposition to war. The use of force against Egypt, he insisted, would rally Arab opinion to Nasser, certainly lead to a cutoff of oil shipments to Europe, and open the door to wider Soviet influence. Yes, Nasser must be deflated, Ike agreed, but Suez was "not the issue on which to do this by force." Eden, however, refused to accept such counsel. He had made up his mind. Writing to Eisenhower on September 6, Eden insisted that Nasser's actions exactly mirrored Hitler's "carefully planned movements" between 1936 and 1940. Hitler's brazen aggression was "tolerated and excused" by the Western governments, leading to catastrophe. Similarly Nasser's seizure of the canal was "an opening gambit" in a plan to expel the West from the Middle East. "Nasser can deny oil to Western Europe and we here shall all be at his mercy." Eden refused to let his country be "held to ransom by Egypt acting at Russia's behest. . . . It would be an ignoble end to our long history."[12]

On the phone with Dulles on the morning of September 7 Eisenhower said Eden's sentimental cries about the end of the British Empire were "strongly reminiscent of Churchill," who was prone to utter equally mawkish prophecies. In any case, the British were "in a box" and were "choosing the wrong place to get tough." Ike spent much of the day drafting a response to Eden that coolly brushed aside the comparison of Nasser to Hitler. "You are making of Nasser a much more important figure than he is," he wrote. Because Nasser thrived on controversy, the Western powers must "let some of the drama go out of the situation." Above all, Britain must avoid war, Ike warned. Any use of force against Nasser would not only fail to solve the immediate problem, but it would also "cause a serious misunderstanding between our two countries." Eisenhower deployed every argument he could to deter Britain from making a fatal mistake.[13]

During October the Great Powers worked through the United Nations to devise a plan acceptable to both Egypt and the Europeans that would restore international control of the canal. Eisenhower stayed fixed on one basic point: the United States would not support the use of force, overt or covert, against Nasser. Such an action would be "dead wrong." Dulles conveyed this message to his British and French counterparts when they met in New York, stressing the damage that a war over Suez would cause. "The

sympathies of all the Middle East, Asian and African peoples would be irre-
vocably lost," and they would rapidly turn to the Soviet Union. "War would
be a disaster." Conversations at the UN continued, but Dulles began to suspect the British and French did not truly desire a negotiated settlement. He
confidentially told his brother, Allen, that he had no idea what the British
and French were up to: "They are deliberately keeping us in the dark."[14]

Tragically Eisenhower could not alter Eden's fixed intent to destroy
Nasser. Even as the British and the French kept up a pretense of negotiations with Egypt through the United Nations, they moved secretly to
prepare an invasion. Meeting at the prime minister's country residence,
Chequers, on October 14, British and French leaders conceived of a devious and illegal scheme to bring about Nasser's downfall. Israel should be
prevailed upon to attack Egypt; Britain and France would intervene, ostensibly to separate the warring sides; in the process the Canal Zone would be
occupied, and the Egyptian Army and Air Force destroyed. Nasser would
be so humbled by the defeat that his ouster would naturally follow. The
French arranged for the Israeli prime minister, David Ben-Gurion, to attend a secret meeting in the Paris suburb of Sèvres with the British foreign
minister Selwyn Lloyd and the French foreign minister Christian Pineau.
There, from October 22 to 24, they worked out the contours of the plan.
Israel would attack Egypt on the evening of October 29. The next morning
the British and French governments would call on Egypt and Israel to stop
military action and withdraw their forces from the Suez Canal Zone, and
Egypt would be told that it must accept an Anglo-French occupation of the
zone so as to ensure freedom of passage through it. The plotters expected
Egypt to refuse this condition, whereupon Anglo-French forces would attack Egypt early the next day.[15]

It is hard to overstate the gravity of the moment. Just days before a U.S.
presidential election, three major American allies agreed to trigger a Middle Eastern war. They kept their actions secret, deliberately lying to their
American colleagues about the plan, even though they knew that a wider
Arab-Israeli war might well draw the United States into direct conflict with
the Soviet Union. Eden's actions were not merely reckless. They amounted
to outright betrayal of Britain's closest ally.

Incredibly, on October 24 the world picture darkened even further, as
appalling news from Budapest, Hungary, flashed across the world's wire services. "The worst week" of the Eisenhower presidency, as Sherman Adams
called it, had begun.[16]

III

On October 24, the same day that the British, French, and Israelis wrapped up their secret meeting outside Paris and initialed their brazen plot to invade Egypt, another invasion of a sovereign nation began, this time in Eastern Europe. Thousands of Soviet troops, backed by hundreds of tanks and trucks, were rolling into Budapest, firing upon anticommunist protesters. The Western world looked on aghast at this dramatic and tragic confrontation in the heart of the Soviet bloc.

The crisis in Hungary formed part of a wider picture of dissent and unrest in Eastern Europe. And Nikita Khrushchev, the dominant figure inside the Soviet leadership, bore much of the blame. On February 25, 1956, in a bid to strengthen his standing in the Soviet political structure, Khrushchev had issued a stunning denunciation of Stalin and his tyrannical era. In a four-hour address to delegates at the 20th Congress of the Soviet Communist Party, Khrushchev bitterly attacked the monstrous legacy of Stalinism, claiming that Stalin had distorted the true purposes of communism and turned the USSR into a police state. Under new leadership, Khrushchev promised, the true principles of communism would be restored. The speech administered a massive shock to the assembled delegates; one leading Polish communist suffered a fatal heart attack moments later.[17]

Khrushchev's risky gamble had been part of a series of actions—including his agreeing to the neutralization of Austria, his openness to meet Eisenhower in Geneva, and his effort to improve ties to Yugoslav leader Josip Tito, whom Stalin had excommunicated for his anti-Soviet sentiments—all designed to send the message that the communist experiment in Eastern Europe would no longer rely upon terror. The world would see a new communist bloc, made up of willing socialist states working in harmony toward a common Marxist future.

Having opened up Pandora's box, however, Khrushchev found himself struggling to contain the demons within. In Poland, long one of the most ardently anti-Soviet nations of Europe, workers called Khrushchev's bluff and began to agitate for improved pay and working conditions. In late June 1956 a wildcat strike erupted into a major uprising in the city of Poznan, as workers rioted against food shortages, inadequate housing, low wages, and the incompetence of their managers. The protestors carried signs declaring "Bread and Freedom" and "Russians Go Home." As the march grew, shots were fired into the crowd by the Polish security forces; over 50 marchers died. In October, Khrushchev traveled to Warsaw to meet with Polish leaders and make it plain that the Soviet Red Army would use force to ensure Poland's continued obedience. Rather than knuckle under, however, Polish leaders insisted that any use of force by the Soviets would trigger a massive uprising, and crowds in the major cities of Lodz, Wroclaw, and Warsaw protested the Soviet threats.[18]

Meanwhile, in Hungary, anti-Soviet feeling surged. On October 22 students, intellectuals, and factory workers gathered at the Technological University in Budapest and adopted a wide-ranging list of demands, including the removal of Soviet troops and the replacement of the pro-Moscow leadership with Imre Nagy, a former prime minister who was identified with liberalization policies. Protesters also demanded multiparty elections, freedom of press and assembly, and the prompt removal of the massive statue of Stalin that still stood in central Budapest. A mass demonstration the next day led to an outpouring of anti-Soviet rhetoric, and spontaneous demonstrations popped up across Budapest. In the evening a group of ironworkers managed to cut through the metal legs of the statue of Stalin, toppling the grotesque memorial. At about 9:00 p.m. on October 23 the Hungarian Security Police fired into the crowd, killing unarmed demonstrators. Hungary was on the brink of revolution.

Eisenhower watched these events with alarm. He knew the satellite nations were too important for Moscow to tolerate their departure from the communist bloc. Any such gamble, he feared, could end only in a wider conflict, and he did not wish to be drawn into a war to liberate Eastern Europe. His reluctance to stir the pot revealed a yawning gap between his and Dulles's rhetoric of 1952, when Republicans lambasted the Democrats for passively accepting Soviet dominion in Eastern Europe and the wait-and-see attitude they now adopted.[19]

Khrushchev, confronted with threats of an uprising in Poland and a full-blown revolt in Hungary, faced the prospect that the entire socialist bloc might be coming unraveled. He was determined not to let Hungary slip away, and almost immediately upon learning of the situation in Budapest decided to use force to crush the rebels. The Soviet Presidium met on the night of October 23 and ordered Soviet troops stationed near Budapest to restore order in the city. These were joined by units from Romania and Ukraine. By early the next morning 30,000 Red Army troops had entered the country, bringing with them over 1,000 tanks. But these invaders only provoked the citizens of Budapest to defend their city. Using Molotov cocktails, as well as thousands of rifles taken from the barracks of army units that had rallied to the side of the rebels, Hungarians defied the Soviet troops, and open combat broke out in the streets.

In Washington the Eisenhower team spent October 24 waiting and watching. The news from Budapest was sporadic and ugly. Dulles wanted to take the matter to the UN Security Council, where he could score points by denouncing the Soviets. He told UN Ambassador Henry Cabot Lodge he feared criticism if he did not act: "It will be said that here are the great moments and when they came, and these fellows [Hungarians] were ready to stand up and die, we were caught napping and doing nothing." The following day Eisenhower issued a short statement deploring the violence in Budapest and adding, "The heart of America goes out to the people of Hungary."

But in private he told Dulles to take things slowly. He was not keen to rush to the Security Council, for fear that it might be perceived as a gesture designed for domestic political purposes. That night, October 25, Eisenhower delivered a major campaign address to 20,000 cheering supporters at Madison Square Garden in New York City. It was a partisan stem-winder, defending his four years in office and lambasting the Democrats. Ike devoted only one line to the events in Eastern Europe. "The people of Poland and Hungary," he declared, "they are men and women whom America has never forgotten and never will." But he did not plan to start a war for them.[20]

On the morning of Friday, October 26, Eisenhower convened a meeting of the National Security Council to review the increasingly troubled picture in Hungary and the Middle East. Allen Dulles gave a chilling account of what had transpired in Budapest. Soviet soldiers had been engaged in heavy fighting in the city, and some units of the Hungarian forces had deserted and joined the rebels. Tanks plowed up the streets with their heavy steel treads. Crowds of protestors had gathered in front of the now bullet-ridden U.S. Embassy begging for American intervention. It was evident, Dulles stated, that "the revolt in Hungary constituted the most serious threat yet" to Soviet control of Eastern Europe.

Eisenhower did not want to add fuel to the fire. He worried that the Soviet leaders might be tempted "to resort to very extreme measures," including "global war." He mused about the final days of the Third Reich: "Hitler had known well, from the first of February 1945 that he was licked. Yet he carried on to the very last and pulled down Europe with him in his defeat.

The Soviets might even develop some desperate mood as this." Any sudden American action designed to profit from Moscow's troubles might bring about greater tragedy.[21]

Later that night Eisenhower spoke with Foster Dulles twice by telephone. He wanted Dulles to include in a speech he was scheduled to give in Dallas a reassuring signal to the Soviets: while the United States desired Hungary's freedom and condemned Soviet repression, it did not seek to enroll Hungary or any Eastern bloc country into the Western sphere. Dulles complied, telling his audience in Dallas that America wanted Eastern European states to reclaim their sovereignty, but "we do not look upon these nations as potential military allies." Eisenhower explicitly directed Ambassador Bohlen in Moscow to convey this message to "the highest Soviet authorities." He wanted them to know the United States would take no active measures to free Hungary from Soviet rule.[22]

IV

As the shocking news from Hungary trickled in to the White House, it joined disturbing reports from the Middle East. CIA sources learned on October 26 that the Israelis were mobilizing their armed forces for war. The Americans did not know the intended target of the Israeli action but suspected it was Jordan. (The Israelis asserted that a hostile Jordanian-Egyptian-Syrian alliance was poised to attack them.) The next day, October 27, Eisenhower gained more detailed intelligence from U-2 overflights. The invaluable spy planes had been running regular flights over the eastern Mediterranean since late summer, using bases in Germany and Turkey. In late October these flights found clear evidence that French jets had been delivered to Israel and that a large British naval buildup was under way in Cyprus. Eisenhower sent a personal message to Prime Minister Ben-Gurion expressing his concern about the Israeli mobilization and calling for "self-restraint." At the same time Secretary Dulles reported that America's key allies, Britain and France, had gone suspiciously quiet, "keeping us completely in the dark as to their intentions" in the Middle East. Dulles's sensitive diplomatic antennae began to sense that something was amiss.[23]

That afternoon Eisenhower entered Walter Reed Hospital for a long-planned medical checkup. The timing could not have been worse, but he wanted to put to rest any lingering public worries about his health. For 24 hours the president submitted to a close inspection of his vitals, especially his heart and gastrointestinal tract, and on Sunday his doctors released to the press a detailed and encouraging report of his fitness. Eisenhower quipped of the uncomfortable hospital visit: "Israel and barium make quite a combination."[24]

The picture that greeted him back at the White House was an ominous one. More detailed intelligence revealed full-scale Israeli mobilization. When the president spoke with Dulles that evening on the telephone, the secretary conveyed his suspicion that the British and French were egging on the Israelis to attack Egypt. Eisenhower resisted this conclusion, saying, "[I] just cannot believe Britain would be dragged into this," especially in light of the firm and repeated warnings he had personally given Eden. Dulles was not so sure. The silence of the British and French ambassadors, he noted, "is almost a sign of a guilty conscience."[25]

The following day, October 29, revealed just how right Dulles had been. The day began with no news of an Israeli attack, and Eisenhower decided to keep his scheduled campaign appearances that day in Florida and Virginia. He left for Miami soon after breakfast. But just after 10:00 a.m. Dulles conferred by phone with his brother, the CIA director, and they both agreed that the evidence was now overwhelming of a French-Israeli plot to trigger a conflict in the Middle East. Not only was that conflict a serious danger in itself, but Foster Dulles feared "a spark in the Middle East could give the Soviets a shield to do things they can't do now," including sending military forces to aid the Egyptians.[26]

After giving his speech in Miami, Eisenhower was heading back to the presidential airplane when he received the dreaded news: Israeli forces had begun an invasion of Egypt's Sinai Peninsula. The president flew to Richmond, Virginia, delivered a brief campaign address at the airport, then hastened back to Washington, reaching the White House, and a distraught Foster Dulles, at 7:15 p.m. A tense meeting began.

The president, Admiral Radford, Allen and Foster Dulles, Defense Secretary Wilson, and Sherman Adams hastily gathered in the Cabinet Room. Allen Dulles and Radford provided a detailed account of the scale and scope of the Israeli invasion. Eisenhower asked if the United States should invoke its obligation under the 1950 Tripartite Declaration, an agreement signed by the United States, Britain, and France that pledged the Great Powers to stop any nation in the Middle East that launched an aggressive attack against its neighbors. That implied supporting Egypt against Israel. Radford, who was personally inclined to support Israel in its attack, laconically said that he guessed the invasion would be "all over in a few days" because of Israel's strategic advantage over a weak Egyptian military.

Secretary Dulles broke in and alerted the group to the larger picture. The Israelis had not acted alone. Dulles now fully grasped that he had been lied to for weeks by America's closest allies. "British and French intervention must be foreseen," he told the group. "They appear to be ready for it and may in fact have concerted their action with the Israelis." It was a bitter pill for Dulles to swallow.

Eisenhower exploded. How would they like it, he asked, if "we were to go in to aid Egypt to fulfil our pledge [under the Tripartite Declaration]. . . . We cannot be bound by our traditional alliances." The British certainly had plenty of reason for complaint against Nasser, but "nothing justifies double-crossing us." America must stand by its word, or else "we are a nation without honor."

As soon as the meeting ended, the British chargé, Sir John Coulson, was ushered into the Oval Office. Eisenhower, his face flushed, told Coulson that the United States was going to take the question of Israeli aggression to the UN Security Council "first thing in the morning—when the doors open—before the USSR gets there." Not knowing yet just how deeply the British had colluded with the Israelis about the invasion, he all but demanded the British pledge their support for a resolution condemning Israel's invasion.[27]

But just over an hour later, at 10:00 p.m., word came to the president from Ambassador Lodge at the UN in New York. He had met with his British counterpart, and endured "one of the most disagreeable and unpleasant experiences" of his career. Sir Pierson Dixon had mocked America's commitment to the Tripartite Declaration, calling the American position "moralistic," and said Britain "would never go along with any move against Israel in the Security Council." The whole picture now came plainly into view: Britain wanted Israel to attack Egypt, knew about it, and would use it as a screen to wage its own war on Nasser. The painful realization set in: the Americans had been duped.[28]

V

Eisenhower arrived in the Oval Office on the morning of October 30, "his face drawn, eyes heavy with fatigue, worry or both," speechwriter Emmet Hughes recalled. He canceled his planned one-day campaign trip to Texas and instead worked with his key advisers on a message to Eden. The president invoked their longtime friendship and asked Eden to explain "exactly what is happening between us and our European allies." The Israeli invasion, he wrote, was a grave matter that ought to be taken up by the UN immediately. Eisenhower described himself as "astonished" to learn that Sir Pierson Dixon refused to join Ambassador Lodge in a common front at the UN. Britain and America now found themselves "in a very sad state of confusion" which, if allowed to continue, could open the door to a general war in the Middle East and Soviet intervention on Egypt's side. "Then the Mid East fat would really be in the fire."[29]

Eisenhower's message was a study in diplomatic finesse. Yet in reply Eden redoubled his duplicity. He claimed that Egypt was responsible for the tensions in the region, having seized the canal and provoked Israel. "And now this has happened," he said of the Israeli invasion, as if he knew nothing about it. Egypt had "brought this attack on herself," Eden argued—an outrageous falsehood, since the attack had been carefully planned by the British, French, and Israelis. Britain, he continued, had urged "restraint" upon the Israelis (another lie). Eden felt "no obligation to come to the aid of Egypt" under the Tripartite Declaration since Egypt had started all the trouble. Britain wanted only to protect the canal and the shipping that passed through it. And to do that would require "decisive action." What did that mean?[30]

Eden gave an answer a few hours later in the House of Commons. Following the script he and his co-conspirators had written, he delivered an ultimatum to Israel and Egypt. Britain and France called upon both states to cease fighting, to withdraw their troops from a 10-mile zone along the Suez Canal, and to accept the stationing there of Anglo-French forces to ensure continued operation of the canal. Egypt and Israel were given 12 hours to respond, and if they refused, the Anglo-French forces would launch an invasion of the Canal Zone. In a phone call with Eisenhower Foster Dulles called the ultimatum "as crude and brutal as anything he had ever seen" and predicted that "by tomorrow they will be in."[31]

Later in the day Dulles met with the British and French ambassadors and tore into them, calling this "the blackest day which has occurred in many years in the relations between England and France and the United States." He declared that their action would damage NATO and the UN and all but accused both nations of collusion with the Israelis. Perhaps most galling, the Anglo-French action "may well obliterate the success we have long awaited in Eastern Europe" by giving the Soviets the cover they needed to crush Hungary. Dulles's words packed months of anger and resentment into a few moments of unadulterated hostility.[32]

Eisenhower shared Dulles's fury. In the afternoon of October 30, while meeting with Arthur Flemming, the director of defense mobilization, to review the global impact of the Israeli invasion upon the world's oil supplies, Eisenhower said he was "extremely angry" at his allies. He expected that world oil markets would be thrown into disarray, that the British and French would soon need to find alternative sources of oil and would find themselves "short of dollars to finance these operations." Anticipating a sudden increase in his leverage over his ill-behaved friends, Eisenhower mused that Britain and France were going to have a rough time of it, and should be left "to boil in their own oil, so to speak."[33]

One week away from a presidential election, Eisenhower had to face the domestic politics of the crisis. In a harsh attack, Adlai Stevenson denounced the "blundering vacillation" of the Eisenhower team toward events in Hungary and the Middle East. He claimed Dulles had appeased the Soviets over Hungary while alienating America's closest friends, including Israel. Adams, in a telephone call with Dulles, confessed his own concerns about how Eisenhower "looks to the country and to the world." The British and the French had "trapped" us, he said, and he implied that the allies had made Eisenhower look weak. He suggested that the president should address the nation and explain America's response to the growing crisis. Dulles agreed.[34]

That evening the UN Security Council debated a resolution calling for Israel to withdraw its forces from Egypt. In an unprecedented development, the United States and the Soviet Union supported the measure, but Britain and France vetoed it. The next day, October 31, with the Egyptians having scorned the Western ultimatum, British and French forces began to bomb Egyptian airfields, ports, railways, and radio towers. They justified these air attacks as a necessary preliminary operation before their troops could land and secure the canal. Eisenhower and the United States had been ignored. The crisis in Suez had cleft the Western alliance in two.[35]

Emmet Hughes described the atmosphere in the White House on October 31 as "thick and heavy with righteous wrath against Britain." The president seemed deflated by the treachery of his wartime allies. "I just don't know what got into those people," he sighed. "It's the damnedest business I ever saw supposedly intelligent governments get themselves into." Eisenhower at last consented to Adams's request that he speak to the nation on television, triggering a whirlwind of activity as the staff now drafted and redrafted the president's remarks. Eisenhower hit golf balls on the White

THE AGE OF EISENHOWER

House lawn while Hughes raced to write a 15-minute speech that recounted the recent events, explained American policy, and avoided too much direct criticism of America's NATO allies. At four minutes before 7:00 p.m. Hughes handed Eisenhower the last page of text, typed in large print, with key passages underlined for emphasis. Dressed in a trim gray suit, seated at his desk in the Oval Office under glaring spotlights, Eisenhower "seemed the most calm man in the room." At 7:00 on the dot the president began to speak.[36]

His remarks aimed above all to reassure the public that the events in Hungary and Suez would not lead to an American war. He spent half his time praising the courageous Hungarians for their devotion to freedom and calling on the Soviets to respect Hungarian independence. He then admonished the British and French for violating Egypt's sovereignty, though he hastened to condemn Egypt's behavior in purchasing Soviet weapons and nationalizing the Suez Canal. The invasion he described as an "error." America, he pointedly said, "was not consulted in any way" beforehand. He insisted that the whole affair be taken to the United Nations and resolved with respect for international law. "There can be no peace without law," he concluded. "And there can be no law if we invoke one code of international conduct for those who oppose us and another for our friends."[37]

The *Los Angeles Times* praised Eisenhower's "calm, mature appeal" for peace and justice and applauded the nation's "competent pilot." But the *Washington Post* editorial page, while admitting that the mess in the Middle East was not Eisenhower's fault, nonetheless stated that "American policy—or lack of policy—has failed." And columnist Walter Lippmann, a reliable critic of the administration, piled on. Eisenhower's criticism of Israel amounted to a "grave mistake." Lippmann saw Nasser as an "implacable enemy" with a plan to "become master of the Arab world," and all Eisenhower seemed to offer was appeasement. The results spoke for themselves: the fires of war now burned across the Middle East, NATO was shattered, the Soviets were running roughshod over Hungary, and Eisenhower's call for peace was ignored. If Eisenhower was going to show leadership, and actually impose order on these sad events, he had waited long enough.[38]

VI

Anyone wishing to make the case for Eisenhower as a master of the arts of politics and diplomacy need only look to the first 10 days of November 1956. In these anxious hours any mistake or miscalculation could have led to global war. Eisenhower demonstrated uncanny discipline, steadfast leadership, and cool judgment. No less than John F. Kennedy during the Cuban Missile Crisis, Eisenhower managed the dispute over Suez with assurance and wisdom that headed off what could easily have become a far more deadly conflagration.

At 9:00 a.m. on November 1 the president convened the National Security Council. The discussion turned first to Eastern Europe. CIA director Dulles informed the group that "a miracle" had occurred in Hungary. In order to ease popular unrest, the Hungarian communist leadership, with Soviet approval, had installed the moderate Imre Nagy as prime minister, hoping he could use his popularity with the people to stem the rebellion. The Soviet troops, which for days had been locked in fierce conflict with the Hungarians, appeared to be withdrawing. Nagy, perhaps inflamed by the intense anti-Soviet emotions in the streets of Budapest, asserted Hungary's independence. On October 30 he announced the end of one-party rule in Hungary and the revival of multiparty democracy. This opened the way to the formation of a coalition government made up of members of the once-outlawed noncommunist parties. On October 31, in his boldest move, Nagy declared the Hungarian government's intention to withdraw from the Warsaw Pact. Astonishingly the Soviets made no move to challenge Nagy's apostasy.[39]

While the NSC cheered this outcome as a defeat of Soviet imperialism in Europe, the apparent Soviet tolerance for Nagy's neutralist actions presented the Western powers with a dilemma. By appearing to respect Hungary's independence, the USSR positioned itself on the moral high ground at the United Nations, from which it could more effectively denounce the invasion of Egypt. Soviet restraint in Hungary therefore only intensified the need for Eisenhower to keep up American criticism of the Anglo-French-Israeli invasion of Suez, lest the United States be seen as condoning aggression at the very moment the Soviets were tolerating Hungarian neutralism.

This concern not to be outfoxed by the Soviets and to avoid being tarnished by the brush of old-fashioned European colonialism preoccupied Eisenhower. "These [colonial] powers were going downhill," he stated emphatically. "How could we possibly support Britain and France if in doing so we lose the whole Arab world?" Nothing would ever induce the United States to "abandon" its oldest allies. Still, he insisted, "if we did not do something to indicate some vigor in the way of asserting our leadership, the Soviets would take over the leadership from us." For this reason he and Foster

Dulles together worked out the language of a fairly mild resolution to be introduced in the General Assembly of the United Nations—where the British and French could not exercise a veto. The resolution called for a cease-fire and the withdrawal of combatant forces from Egypt. At the same time, on Eisenhower's orders, Dulles announced that the United States would suspend all shipments of military supplies to the "area of hostilities." Since the United States had already suspended military sales to Egypt, this effectively meant cutting off military aid to Israel.[40]

This was an unprecedented, even shocking step: one week before the presidential election, Eisenhower announced a cutoff of military aid to Israel at the very moment Israel was fighting an Arab state with clear Soviet sympathies. And his secretary of state strongly agreed with the decision. In response to a vigorous challenge launched in the NSC by Harold Stassen, who argued for accepting the Israeli seizure of Sinai as a fait accompli and backing Israel, Dulles bristled: "We do not approve of murder. We have simply got to refrain from resort to force in settling international disputes." Throughout the crisis Eisenhower consistently held to this position, even though some in his cabinet and many in the press disagreed. He went so far as to record his views in a secret "memorandum for the record." He wrote that Israel should not assume "that winning a domestic election is as important to us as preserving and protecting the interests of the United Nations and other nations of the free world in that region." Eisenhower did not veer from this belief.[41]

Indeed the president personally shaped American policy in these trying days. Following the long and tumultuous debate among the NSC members on November 1, Eisenhower sent a short strategy paper to Dulles so there could be no ambiguity about the policy he wanted. "The United States must lead," he wrote. The first order of business was to secure a cease-fire in Egypt. Eisenhower feared that if the United States did not act quickly, the USSR would introduce a "harshly worded resolution" against Britain, France, and Israel, compelling a U.S. veto and thus "putting us in an acutely embarrassing position." Above all, "the Soviets must be prevented from seizing the mantle of world leadership." In essence Ike wanted to discipline his own side in the cold war so he could sustain the narrative that the Soviet Union, not the Western powers, was the true source of conflict and trouble in the world.[42]

On the afternoon of November 1 Dulles flew to New York to make his case at the UN. He proposed a cease-fire and the withdrawal of all combatant forces and urged all UN members to refrain from sending any military supplies to the conflict zone. In fact Dulles wanted to do more than squelch a brush-fire war in Sinai. Speaking before the General Assembly, on the world stage, Dulles sought to portray America as an impartial adjudicator of world affairs. In a moving and obviously heartfelt address, he told the General Assembly, "The United States finds itself unable to agree with three nations with which it has ties of deep friendship, of admiration and of respect, and two of which constitute our oldest and most trusted and reliable allies." It was a public slap in the face for Britain and France.

Dulles acknowledged that Egypt was hardly blameless in the affair and had aggravated relations with its neighbors. But if, "whenever a nation feels it has been subjected to injustice, it should have the right to resort to force in an attempt to correct that injustice, then I fear that we should be tearing the [UN] Charter into shreds, that the world would again be a world of anarchy, that the great hopes placed in this Organization and in our Charter would vanish." Unlike so many interventions at the UN, Dulles's speech won great acclaim. His resolution garnered 64 votes, with only five nations—Britain, France, and Israel, joined by Australia and New Zealand—voting against. The world had rallied to America's leadership.[43]

That evening Eisenhower used a major speech to reinforce Dulles's message. Though he had canceled all but one of his campaign events because of the world crisis, Ike knew his appearance before 18,000 wildly enthusiastic Republicans in Philadelphia's Convention Hall would draw the nation's attention. Rising above partisan politics, he reminded his listeners of the grave events in the world: "We have heard with deep dismay the crack of rifle fire and the whine of jet bombers over the deserts of Egypt." In such an anxious time, he asked, what does American stand for? "What are the marks of America—and what do they mean to the world?" He gave a clear answer: Americans believed in the rule of law. That principle had won the admiration of so many millions of the world's peoples. America was a land without "class or caste," a country that did not judge a man by his "name or inheritance." It was America's mission to uphold the rule of law around the world. "There can be no second-class nations before the law of the world community."

Eisenhower acknowledged that the crisis in the Middle East posed "a test of our principles" because it asked Americans to choose between friendship with old allies and respect for the law. But America had made its choice and would uphold the integrity of the law of nations. "We cannot proclaim this integrity when the issue is easy—and stifle it when the issue is hard." Law must govern nations just as it must govern free peoples. "We cannot and we will not condone armed aggression, no matter who the attacker and no matter who the victim." More than a campaign speech, Eisenhower's remarks revealed his deep devotion to a world based upon law rather than force.[44]

These dual public speeches by Dulles and Eisenhower put heavy pressure on the British prime minister. Eden, who for so many years had labored in Churchill's shadow, believed that his coup against Nasser would secure his place among the great British leaders of the century. He wanted to show the world that the British Empire endured. But it had all turned to ashes in his mouth. Not only had the U.S. president firmly rebuked the British, but the UN—following America's lead—had spoken almost with one voice to condemn the invasion of Egypt, to denounce the warlike actions of the Anglo-French forces, and to demand the withdrawal of all combatants.

And Eden faced even more terrible news: his actions had placed Britain's oil supply in jeopardy. In retaliation for the invasion of Suez, the Syrians destroyed three pipelines that carried oil from Kirkuk in Iraq to the Mediterranean for shipment to Europe. These pipelines carried 500,000 barrels of oil a day and amounted to a quarter of Europe's Middle East imports. And the Egyptians sank old trawlers and barges in the narrows of the Suez Canal itself to halt all traffic—a sure way to interrupt the flow of oil from the Persian Gulf. In a matter of weeks, British oil supplies would dry up. Eden had brought world opprobrium on Britain and placed his country on the brink of an economic crisis.

When, on November 3, Eden defended his Suez policy in the House of Commons, Labour Party leader Hugh Gaitskell ripped into him, calling on Eden to accept the UN cease-fire or risk shaming Britain in the eyes of the world. In a tumultuous debate Labour members shouted down the government ministers with cries of "Resign!" Huge crowds staged antiwar protests in Trafalgar Square. Even reliably pro-Tory newspapers such as the *Times* of London and the *Observer* denounced Eden's policy as ill-conceived and illegal.

Eden had gone too far to flinch now, however. Late in the evening of November 3, while French and British aircraft continued to bomb Egyptian targets, the pain-wracked but impeccably groomed prime minister appeared on British national television. He confidently explained that the lessons of appeasement from the previous war demanded a confrontation with Nasser. "There are times for courage, times for action, and this is one of them." It was Nasser, not Britain, who threatened world peace with his illegal seizure of the canal and his terroristic border raids against Israel. These actions had in turn triggered the Israeli invasion. Britain and France merely wished to restore order, ensure the smooth functioning of the canal, and separate the warring parties. Nasser's failure to respond to the Anglo-French request to withdraw from the Canal Zone had made the use of force inevitable. It was strong medicine, Eden implied, but Nasser would have to take it until he was cured of his aggressive habits.[45]

Britain and France, then, would move ahead with their plans for a land invasion of the Suez Canal. Hoping to forestall this, the Canadian delegation at the UN, with strong American backing, proposed the creation of a UN peacekeeping force that would enter the Canal Zone and do the job that Britain had arrogated to itself. On the evening of November 3 the UN endorsed this proposal by an overwhelming vote of 57–0. The British and French abstained. But it was a race to see who would get there first: British and French soldiers or the blue-helmeted UN troops.[46]

In the midst of this whirlwind Eisenhower faced more unsettling news. Very late on the night of November 2, Foster Dulles had been taken to Walter Reed Hospital after suffering severe stomach pain. The doctors initially thought he might have appendicitis, but it soon became apparent that the 68-year-old had colon cancer. On November 4 surgeons removed a tumor from his large intestine. Eisenhower visited Dulles soon after the surgery and remarked to Gen. Leonard Heaton, the surgeon who had so recently opened up the president's own abdomen, "Take good care of the boy. I need him."[47]

Dulles remained at Walter Reed for the next two weeks and did not return to full-time work until January. In the meantime Herbert Hoover Jr., son of the former president and an engineer with an extensive background in the oil business, stood in as acting secretary of state. The absence of Dulles did not substantially change U.S. policy, though it left Eisenhower without his most loyal, most reliable lieutenant. Eisenhower and Dulles were not warm friends, although they spoke on the phone almost every day, sometimes two or three times a day, and had developed a close partnership. Dulles served the president like a lawyer serves his most important and valuable client: with tenacity and obsequious devotion. Dulles would take the reins of U.S. foreign policy again, but the cancer never retreated. He had only a little more than two years left to live.

VII

Just as Eisenhower began to despair about the Middle East, terrible news arrived from Hungary. The Soviets were invading again, and this time they meant to win.

The Soviet Union had installed Imre Nagy in power on October 24 with the intention of using this moderate and reform-minded leader to quell the Hungarian uprising. Instead Nagy had been captured by the euphoria of the anti-Soviet rebellion and declared Hungary's intention to leave the communist bloc, setting off a panicked reaction in the Kremlin. Khrushchev and his colleagues worried that if Hungary could slip away from communist control just when Egypt, a potential client state, was being invaded by the Europeans, the West would have delivered a dual blow to Soviet prestige. In a secret meeting on October 31, Khrushchev and the Soviet Presidium ordered the preparation of Operation Whirlwind: the repression of the Hungarian Revolution by over 60,000 Soviet troops.[48]

The blow fell savagely at 4:00 a.m. on November 4. Artillery shells slammed into the center of Budapest. Soviet troops moved swiftly into the city, capturing the radio broadcasting stations and munitions depots. They surrounded the Hungarian Army barracks and disarmed the troops. They occupied all the bridges across the Danube, and then seized the Parliament building. Soviet troops were met with fierce but sporadic and uncoordinated resistance. Prime Minister Nagy went on national radio to declare, "At daybreak Soviet forces started an attack against our capital, obviously with the intention to overthrow the legal Hungarian government. Our troops are fighting. The Government is in its place." But that was not the case, for Nagy himself then fled to the Yugoslav Embassy, leaving his government in disarray. By noon most of the city was under Soviet control. The Hungarian Revolution, which had electrified captive peoples across Europe, lay crushed beneath Soviet tank treads.

These events shocked a confused and anxious world. At the United Nations, Ambassador Lodge rose to denounce the Soviet invasion; he was met with a sneering, dismissive rebuttal from the Soviet ambassador, who asserted that the Western powers merely wanted to divert attention from the fiasco at Suez. The State Department hastily drafted a message for the president to send to the Soviet leadership, declaring his "profound distress" at reports of Soviet brutality in Hungary. The ambassador to Italy Clare Boothe Luce, an outspoken hawk and Eisenhower's friend, wrote Ike a private cable calling for action to rescue the Hungarians: "Let us not ask for whom the bell tolls in Hungary today. It tolls for us if freedom's holy light is extinguished in blood and iron there." But Eisenhower understood there were no measures the United States could take to halt Soviet aggression. Hungary was landlocked and surrounded by Warsaw Pact countries. Any intervention there would certainly lead to a wider war. As he candidly wrote later in his memoirs, "We could do nothing."[49]

On the Suez matter, however, Eisenhower did have some leverage. But had he waited too long to use it? When he arrived at the Oval Office on the morning of November 5, he found on his desk an overnight cable from Eden, offering an unrepentant explanation for the British "police action" in Suez. The message was timed to arrive with the depressing news that at dawn British and French paratroopers had landed in the Suez Canal Zone—just the outcome Eisenhower most wished to avoid. Eden hoped to soften the blow, asserting, "This is the moment to curb Nasser's ambitions. . . . If we draw back now, chaos will not be avoided. Everything will go up in flames in the Middle East." Even as the president met with his advisers, Anglo-French units were fighting in Port Said, taking control of the key access point into the Suez Canal.[50]

The Anglo-French landings stirred the Soviets into action. Their invasion of Hungary had produced an avalanche of global criticism, and they were all too keen to redirect the world's focus to the Suez Crisis. Nikolai Bulganin, the Soviet premier and titular head of state, delivered a barrage of public messages to world capitals. To Israel, Britain, and France came a searing condemnation and direct threat: Withdraw from Egypt or face Soviet military action. "We are fully determined to crush the aggressors and restore peace in the East through the use of force." At 2:00 p.m. the premier's message to Eisenhower clattered out of the telex machine. Bulganin denounced Anglo-French military operations and demanded that the invaders accept the UN cease-fire resolution of November 1. Then came a shocking proposal: that the United States and USSR send a joint task force to Egypt to pull apart the warring nations, impose peace, and restore order. "If this war is not stopped," Bulganin darkly concluded, "it is fraught with danger and can grow into a third world war."[51]

Coming at the very moment the Soviets were slaughtering Hungarians in the streets of Budapest, Bulganin's outrage at Anglo-French aggression in Egypt revealed the worst kind of cynicism. Even so, Ambassador Charles Bohlen in Moscow urged the president not to dismiss the Soviet proposal as mere propaganda. The Soviets might be laying the ground for an intervention in the Middle East on the grounds of resisting imperialist aggression. They probably did not want to start "World War III," Bohlen said, but they no longer seemed content to sit on the sidelines.[52]

Eisenhower had predicted that the USSR would use the crisis in Egypt as an opportunity to spread its own influence in the region. It had been preoccupied with the Hungarian affair; now it seemed ready to exploit the Suez conflict to its advantage. Meeting with Hoover and other senior aides in the afternoon, Eisenhower wanted a reply sent to Bulganin immediately with "a clear warning" to stay out. The Soviets were embarking on "a wild adventure," perhaps because their invasion of Hungary had been such a stain on their public reputation. They were "scared and furious" and therefore liable to make very bad decisions.[53]

Emmet Hughes, who was present at the meeting, recalled that "the lines and pallor of [Eisenhower's] face betrayed fatigue." It had been a dreadful and tense two weeks for the president. During those days he suffered from hypertension, his pulse was erratic, his head ached, his abdominal scar throbbed, and his stomach was bloated with gas. He consulted Dr. Snyder every few hours during these days of crisis.[54]

As he and his advisers crafted a response to Bulganin's challenge, Eisenhower's mind turned to the prospect of war. "He was thinking," Hughes recalled, "with cold realism and as Commander in Chief of the menace that seemed to him implicit in the Bulganin message. 'You know,' he said tautly, 'we may be dealing here with the opening gambit of an ultimatum. We have to be positive and clear in our every word, every step. And if those fellows start something, we may have to hit 'em—and, if necessary, with everything in the bucket.'"[55]

After a somber discussion, Eisenhower issued a statement to the press rejecting the Soviet proposal for a joint task force as "unthinkable." The UN already had agreed to send a peacekeeping force to Suez once a cease-fire had been accepted. That decision must be respected. The United States therefore opposed any "introduction of new forces." The message did not state unequivocally that the United States would use force to oppose a Soviet move to aid Egypt, but, as the *New York Times* noted, "that was the implication." On November 5 the Great Powers seemed closer to a world war than at any time since 1945.[56]

VIII

As Americans went to the polls on Election Day, November 6, they surely carried with them into the voting booths the images from the front pages of their morning newspapers. The Soviet Army had just invaded Budapest, killing as many as 2,000 Hungarians. Premier Bulganin had threatened to intervene in Egypt to halt the Anglo-French-Israeli invasion. British and French paratroopers continued to drop out of the Egyptian sky and were fighting for control of key points along the Suez Canal. Soviet MiG fighter aircraft had been spotted in Egypt. At any moment the "police action" Eden had designed could erupt into a much wider and more deadly war.

For Eisenhower the day began with a worrisome intelligence briefing from Allen Dulles, who reported, "The Soviets told the Egyptians that they will 'do something' in the Middle East hostilities." Just what they planned to do, Dulles could not say, though he suggested the Soviets might move aircraft to Syria in anticipation of a wider conflict. The president ordered Dulles to get U-2 planes over Syria as soon as possible to search for evidence of any such activity. Thinking of the vulnerable British and French planes and ships that were gathered in Cyprus, Eisenhower remarked that "if the Soviets attack the French and British directly, we would be in war."[57]

Shortly after 9:00 a.m. Eisenhower and Mamie got into a car for the two-hour drive to Gettysburg, their official voting district. No sooner had they arrived and cast their ballots than Eisenhower got word from Washington that he needed to return immediately. He boarded a helicopter and was whisked back to the White House, where he landed just after noon. The immediate cause for alarm was a message from Ambassador Bohlen in Moscow, which had arrived while Eisenhower was en route to Pennsylvania. He reported that the Soviet attitude had become "ominous." The USSR seemed poised for some kind of military action to demonstrate its solidarity with the Arab world.[58]

Just after 12:30 p.m. the president went into a conference with his advisers and the Joint Chiefs of Staff. Radford briefed Eisenhower on the steps that he proposed to take to increase America's military readiness in response to the recent Soviet statements. Ike agreed that "we should be in an advanced state of readiness," but he did not want to take any obviously provocative measure, such as calling for a general mobilization of active-duty troops. Radford doubted the likelihood of a direct Soviet military move into the Mediterranean because they had no naval presence in the region. They could use "long range air strikes with nuclear weapons," but he said that seemed "unlikely." Eisenhower approved Radford's suggestion to send two aircraft carriers, the newly minted USS *Forrestal* and the USS *Franklin Roosevelt*, to the eastern Atlantic. He also approved putting the Continental Air Defense Command on increased readiness, thus sending more interceptor aircraft in the sky above the homeland. Eisenhower did not want to be the victim of a surprise Soviet attack.[59]

Midmorning brought hopeful signs that the crisis might ease rather than worsen. The Israeli government told the UN secretary-general that it would agree to a cease-fire. And why not? By that time Israel occupied all of the Sinai Peninsula and had destroyed much of the Egyptian Army and Air Force. Its military aims had been achieved. Egypt, desperate to stem its losses, tentatively agreed to a cease-fire as well.

In London, Eden was running out of time. At 9:45 a.m. the British cabinet convened to consider the news of the Israeli-Egyptian cease-fire. British soldiers had only just gained control of Port Said, at the mouth of the canal; they had days of tough fighting ahead if they wanted to secure the entire Canal Zone. Eden was inclined to keep the invasion going. To halt military activities now would be an admission of failure and make Nasser look like the winner. Foreign Minister Selwyn Lloyd, however, could see the game was up. He reluctantly concluded that Britain must accept the cease-fire, for three powerful reasons. First, the Soviet Union might well join the hostilities in the region, which would be a worldwide calamity. Second, the British had claimed all along that their invasion was mainly a "police action" designed to separate the Israelis and the Egyptians; now that those nations had agreed to a cease-fire, there was no plausible excuse to continue an armed invasion of Suez.

The third and most pressing reason was that Britain had come under terrific economic pressure as a result of the crisis. With the canal blocked and the Iraq pipeline closed, Britain had lost about a quarter of its daily oil supply. The only way it could offset those losses was to purchase oil elsewhere, mainly from the United States or Latin America. That required dollars. And Harold Macmillan, chancellor of the Exchequer, reported that Britain's dollar reserves were evaporating at an alarming rate. Markets do not like war, and Britain had started one. Currency traders and national banks around the world were rapidly cashing in their British pounds for dollars, threatening to wipe out Britain's supply. Dependent on dollars to pay for oil imports,

"It was a good, secure small-town life." Left to right, Milton, a dour David, DDE, the always smiling Ida, Earl, and the family dog Flip in 1910.

"Her long-lashed eyes were the dark blue of a piece of sky reflected in a well." Mamie Eisenhower in 1916, the year she and Ike married.

"The greatest disaster in my life." Doud Dwight Eisenhower, nicknamed Icky, died on January 2, 1921, of scarlet fever.

"No one . . . can understand the intensity of these burdens." Eisenhower observing the invasion forces off the shores of Normandy, France, June 7, 1944, the day after D-Day.

"An easy air of personal authority." DDE, chief of staff of the U.S. Army, enjoying a smoke in Hawaii, May 1946.

"You have summoned me . . . to lead a great crusade." At the Republican National Convention, July 11, 1952.

Senator Robert Taft of Ohio, who narrowly lost the GOP nomination after a bitter convention fight.

Hiding the bitter feelings between them, Eisenhower and President Truman drive to the inauguration ceremony, January 20, 1953.

"I insist on going for a bit of recreation every once in a while." Ike at Augusta just after his election in 1952, with golf greats Byron Nelson and Ben Hogan. His close pal and founder of the Augusta National Golf Club, Clifford Roberts, is at the far right.

"It's pound, pound, pound. Not only is your intellectual capacity taxed to the utmost, but your physical stamina." Eisenhower in 1954.

One of Ike's first major decisions was the appointment of Governor Earl Warren as chief justice of the Supreme Court.

The decade's most powerful pair of brothers: Allen and John Foster Dulles.

13

Iran's Prime Minister Mohammad Mossadeq, who had nationalized Iranian oil production, speaks to the crowd on October 3, 1951.

Senator Joseph McCarthy of Wisconsin, where he liked it best: in front of the microphones.

14

15

Democratic leader in the Senate and Ike's political nemesis, Senator Lyndon Johnson of Texas in 1955.

Premier Nikolai Bulganin of the USSR, Ike, Premier Edgar Faure of France, and Prime Minister Sir Anthony Eden of Great Britain, in Geneva in July 1955.

Herbert Brownell, who as attorney general steered Ike's program on civil rights.

"Tough, self-centered, suspicious, insensitive." Secretary of State John Foster Dulles with Eisenhower, August 14, 1956.

Ike, recovering from his heart attack, meets the press on the sun deck of Fitzsimons Hospital, wearing pajamas.

"He lighted up the sky like a flaming arrow." Adlai Stevenson, right, with his running mate, Senator Estes Kefauver, in 1956.

Gamal Abdel Nasser is cheered by a huge crowd on his arrival back in Cairo from Alexandria in August 1956, where he announced he had taken over the Suez Canal Company.

Hungarians burn a picture of the Soviet leader Josef Stalin during the anticommunist revolution in November 1956.

"A spiritual awakening is taking place throughout the nation." Billy Graham and Eisenhower.

"On the verge of a dangerous racial conflagration." E. Frederic Morrow, the only African American on the White House executive staff, waged a persistent campaign to alert the administration to the civil rights crisis.

Soldiers of the 101st Airborne escort black students into Little Rock High School, September 1957.

Eisenhower reluctantly met with civil rights leaders in June 1958. Left to right, Lester Granger, Martin Luther King Jr., White House adviser Frederic Morrow, DDE, A. Philip Randolph, Attorney General William Rogers, special assistant Rocco Siciliano, and Roy Wilkins.

Ngo Dinh Diem, named premier of South Vietnam in 1954, would go on to rule with an iron hand and lavish support from Washington.

Sukarno, president of Indonesia, during his trip to Washington in May 1956, when he addressed Congress.

Five days after the launch of *Sputnik*, Eisenhower firmly denied accusations that America had fallen behind the Russians in the space race. Jim Hagerty sits on Ike's left.

"Cold steel between us." Nixon and Khrushchev argue in the kitchen debate in Moscow, July 1959.

Francis Gary Powers, whose U-2 spy plane was shot down by the Soviets on May 1, 1960, speaks to the Senate Armed Services Committee on March 6, 1962, after returning home through a prisoner exchange.

"A heroic man." Khrushchev took delight in wooing Fidel Castro when both leaders met in New York in September 1960.

"If you give me a week . . ." Ike campaigning for the Nixon-Lodge ticket, September 12, 1960.

"Good Morning, Mr. President." On December 6, 1960, President-elect John F. Kennedy paid a call on Eisenhower at the White House.

On April 22, 1961, days after the failed invasion of Cuba, President Kennedy sought Eisenhower's counsel at Camp David.

"The man instantly conveyed one quality—strength." President Dwight D. Eisenhower.

Britain could not survive long if its reserves disappeared. The British economy teetered on the brink, and only the Americans could help pull it back.[60]

Yet the Americans showed no inclination to help. The U.S. Treasury kept the pressure on the British government by blocking what in normal times would have been a simple request: the repatriation of dollars that Britain had supplied to the International Monetary Fund. The previous night Macmillan had frantically called American officials to get them to release these British-owned dollars, but Treasury Secretary Humphrey refused to allow the transaction. Although no evidence exists to link Eisenhower to this decision, Humphrey never would have taken such an unfriendly position without the president's approval. Britain had come up against a basic reality: it could not act alone on the world stage without the support of the United States.

Macmillan, who only 10 days earlier had adopted a most bellicose posture and fulminated about the need for Britain to act decisively against the upstart Egyptians, now told the cabinet that Britain was going bankrupt and must cease its military operations. Prime Minister Eden, exhausted, outmaneuvered by his allies, and losing the confidence of his own cabinet, accepted the news stoically. He agreed that Britain must accept the cease-fire and appeal to the United States for immediate economic aid.[61]

Eisenhower, hearing this news from his ambassador in London, put through a call to Eden. "I can't tell you how pleased we are that you found it possible to accept the cease-fire," he said, hiding his feeling of triumph.

Eden, smarting over what he perceived to be American disloyalty, was sullen. "We cease firing tonight," he repeated, unwilling to engage in a conversation. Ike said he was "delighted."

But he was not satisfied with only a cease-fire. Before approving any economic aid to Britain, Eisenhower wanted Eden to withdraw his troops from Egypt. The UN would send in a peacekeeping force now, and that force should have no troops from any of the "big five"—the United States, Britain, France, the USSR, and China. "You people ought to be able to withdraw very quickly."

This hit Eden hard. He had assumed that he would be able to keep his forces in the Canal Zone, thus giving him leverage over the Egyptians if they should not cooperate. Eisenhower foiled him.

"May I think that one over?" Eden said.

Yes, Ike replied. "Call me anytime you please."[62]

IX

At 7:00 p.m. Washington time, the fighting in Egypt stopped—just as the first U.S. election returns began to roll in. The early results looked good. The safe Republican Northeast went solidly for Ike. Then the tallies from border states arrived; Delaware, Maryland, West Virginia, and Kentucky also went into the Republican column. Soon came the news that Eisenhower had broken open the solid Democratic South, winning Virginia, Tennessee, Florida, and Louisiana. "Louisiana?" he exclaimed when Hughes told him he was leading there. "That's as probable as leading in Ethiopia!"[63]

And so it went. By the time he made his way to Washington's Sheraton Park Hotel for the victory party among 6,000 guffawing, backslapping, tipsy Republican celebrants, Eisenhower was on his way to a great reelection victory. He won 41 states to Stevenson's 7, giving him 457 electoral votes to Stevenson's 73. He took 57 percent of the popular vote, the biggest share since FDR's landslide in 1936 over Alf Landon. Even in Stevenson's home state, Illinois, Eisenhower won 60 percent of the vote. Stevenson won only states that had once been part of the Confederacy—the South's sullen response to Eisenhower's moderate proposals on civil rights. Eisenhower became the first Republican in the 20th century to win two consecutive presidential elections.

At 10 p.m. the giant billboard above Times Square in New York City blazed with the news of Eisenhower's triumph. It took Adlai Stevenson, sulking in his hotel room, another four hours to concede. "What in the name of God is the monkey waiting for?" fumed Ike. Not until 1:40 in the morning could the president enter the hotel ballroom to accept the cheers from his fans.[64]

Eisenhower's victory was due to his personal popularity and to the unprecedented prosperity over which he presided. But Americans also wanted an experienced leader at the helm in a time of crisis. "The voting took place under pressure of extraordinary events overseas," James Reston wrote in the *New York Times*. "Not since the election of 1944, when the Second World War was reaching its decisive phase with the American armies deep in Germany, have the American people gone to the polls so preoccupied with alarming foreign policy developments." Americans overwhelmingly agreed: they wanted Eisenhower's steady hand to guide the country in this hour of crisis.[65]

There was still urgent work to be done, however, and no time for celebration. Early on the morning of November 7, as the White House was savoring the election results, Prime Minister Eden called the president and asked if he could come to Washington to consult on the Suez matter—perhaps hoping that the personal touch would persuade Eisenhower to provide oil and financial aid to Britain. Eden obviously thought that since he had accepted the cease-fire, he would be forgiven his trespasses. Eisenhower, pleased by his electoral victory and eager to mend the frayed special relationship, accepted Eden's proposal. Sounding suddenly magnanimous, he said he wanted to clear up this "family spat."[66]

As soon as Ike hung up the phone, his advisers rushed into his office. Sherman Adams, staff secretary Col. Andrew Goodpaster, Herbert Hoover Jr., Treasury Secretary Humphrey—all strongly discouraged a personal visit, fearing that it would give Eden a reprieve before he had accepted the UN demand for withdrawal of all forces from Suez. An Eisenhower-Eden meeting now would send the Arab world into an uproar and forfeit all the gains Ike had made by holding to such a firm line against British policy. Reluctantly Eisenhower accepted the point and phoned Eden back. It was an awkward call, with Ike stumbling to make his excuses. "We will have to postpone it a little bit," he said, pleading a sudden rush of other commitments.

Eisenhower then motored to Walter Reed to visit Foster Dulles, still recovering from his surgery. They chatted about the election results briefly, then turned to Suez. For a man who had just undergone a major operation, Dulles was remarkably lucid. He described the British-French invasion as a "crazy act" and insisted that any meeting with Eden must be contingent upon a withdrawal of troops. As long as those 15,000 British and 4,000 French soldiers sat in Port Said, the Egyptians would not cooperate and the Soviets would very soon take advantage of the disarray, perhaps sending forces of their own into the region. It was essential to get the UN police force, to be made up of 3,000 Scandinavian, Indian, and Indonesian troops, into position in Suez and to get the Anglo-French forces out immediately.[67]

Upon returning to the White House, Eisenhower sent Eden a cable, reinforcing the message he had delivered over the phone. He desired "that the UN Force will promptly begin its work and the Anglo-French Forces will be withdrawn without delay. Once these things are done, the ground will be favorable for our meeting." In short, Eisenhower would not welcome his old friend to the White House until the British had fully conformed to American wishes.[68]

The next day, in a prolonged NSC meeting, Eisenhower and his advisers discussed the acute oil crisis that Britain and Europe now faced. The falloff in oil deliveries due to the blocked canal and the destruction of the Iraq pipelines had been so severe that rationing of gasoline would soon have to start in Europe. The president was told that in the best-case scenario, the United States and Venezuela could ship to Europe at most 800,000 barrels of oil a day—and even that would leave the Europeans 10 to 15 percent short of their daily needs. Furthermore Britain would use up its scarce supply of dollars in paying for these additional imports.

Eisenhower understood the gravity of the problem but decided to use the oil shortage to his advantage. He wanted to get the British and French to withdraw completely from the Suez Canal Zone. To bail them out now, while their invasion forces remained in Suez, would "get the Arabs sore at all of us, and they could embargo all oil." Allen Dulles added that prolonged instability in the region would play into Soviet hands, for they wanted to "keep the pot boiling." Therefore Ike refused to send Eden any reassuring signals. Instead, in a short and terse cable on November 11, he urged Eden to withdraw all British troops from the Canal Zone "with the utmost speed." Only then would there be any Anglo-American reconciliation.[69]

Eisenhower's firmness came as a terrible shock to the British. On November 12 Macmillan told the cabinet that U.K. dollar reserves were dangerously low, and if the hemorrhaging did not stop, Britain would have to devalue its currency, thus delivering a death blow to the sterling area and the entire British Commonwealth. The only way to avoid this dire fate was immediate support from the International Monetary Fund (IMF) to the tune of $1.3 billion. Macmillan privately appealed for help to the U.S. ambassador Winthrop Aldrich. Why must the Americans be so rigid, he wondered? Did Ike not perceive that Britain was suffering? If Britain had to withdraw its forces now, without winning some kind of new international agreement to control the canal, "the loss of prestige and humiliation would be so great that the Government must fall." Macmillan, who was prone to rhetorical flights, told IMF president Eugene Black the next day that they "were probably witnessing the end of western civilization, and that in another 50 years yellow and black men would take over." Such were the apocalyptic sentiments of the British leaders.[70]

The French too continued to stall on withdrawing from the Canal Zone. Prime Minister Guy Mollet spoke heatedly to the U.S. ambassador in Paris, Douglas Dillon, telling him that the Americans had failed to grasp the real problem in the Middle East: the Soviet threat. The Egyptians and Syrians were in cahoots with Moscow, he claimed, and were planning to destroy Israel and take over the Middle East. The American opposition to the Anglo-

French strike against Nasser had prevented what might have been a brilliant coup against Soviet plans in the region. Instead the prestige of the Soviets had been increased and France and Britain faced "a new Munich."[71]

But it was no use. Eisenhower did not budge. Even when the news came from Ambassador Aldrich that Eden had suffered a physical breakdown due to many weeks of sleepless nights and amphetamine use, the president remained firm. He directed Aldrich to let British leaders know that he sympathized with their financial difficulties, but they must leave Egypt: "If we undertook commitments before the UK and French forces are withdrawn, we would be in the position of going back upon a matter of major principle."[72]

On November 23 Eden flew to Jamaica for what became a three-week period of rest and recovery, though it looked as if he was abandoning his post in a crucial hour. Britain was rudderless. That day Churchill, retired now and spending much of his time painting on the French Riviera, wrote the president, begging him to close the rift that had opened up between Britain and America. "If we do not take immediate action in harmony," he solemnly wrote, "it is no exaggeration to say that we must expect to see the Middle East and North African coastline under Soviet control." Still Eisenhower did not bend. In a lengthy reply to the former leader, Ike remarked that it was Eden who had created the problem by ignoring American advice and defying world opinion. "All we have asked," Ike said, is that Britain "conform to the resolutions of the United Nations." Once that was done, he wanted to see the affair "washed off the slate as soon as possible."[73]

With Eden out of the country, Macmillan worked behind the scenes to bring the cabinet into line with American demands. The fall in reserves, he told his colleagues, had become desperate. The Americans would not help until Britain made a clear public statement of its intention to withdraw its troops from Egypt. On November 29 the British cabinet, leaderless, facing an economic catastrophe and knowing that only American aid could save the country, capitulated. On December 3, while Eden swam in the warm, silky waters of the Caribbean, Foreign Minister Lloyd announced to the House of Commons Britain's intention to withdraw its forces from Egypt. The Suez Crisis had ended; the British Empire was not far behind.[74]

X

Reconciliation came quickly. Within hours of Lloyd's announcement, the U.S. government activated plans drawn up by the Office of Defense Mobilization to increase shipments of oil to Europe. Director Arthur Flemming reported that within "48 to 72 hours" the oil would begin to flow. Secretary Humphrey unlocked American dollars for Britain; by Christmas, Britain had received almost $2 billion in U.S.-backed loans. The closed American fist now unclenched and proffered the vital oil and dollars needed to keep Britain alive. A few weeks after his return from Jamaica, a ruined Anthony Eden resigned.[75]

But this was not the end of the story, for at the heart of the Suez Crisis lay a contest between the United States and the European powers about who would guide the future of the Middle East. Eisenhower had definitively answered that question. The invasion had discredited the Europeans, enraged Arab opinion, jeopardized Western access to Middle East oil, and opened the door to Soviet interference. The British and French, in Eisenhower's eyes, had forfeited any claim to influence in the Middle East. They had to leave, and the United States must now replace them.

Ike understood that the Suez Crisis marked the start of a new American order in the Middle East, which would not be organized around colonies and empires. In his vision, the area would be held together by the appeal of American know-how, technology, economic aid, and military assistance, packaged to win the allegiance of conservative, pro-Western Arab leaders who could protect Western interests. Where American offers of largesse were refused, the United States would find ways to punish defiance. Eisenhower asked Herbert Hoover Jr. at the State Department to draw up a study about "what we could and should do for Iraq, Jordan, Saudi Arabia, Libya and even Egypt, by holding out the carrot as well as the stick."[76]

Fears of Soviet interference fueled Eisenhower's anxiety about the need to move fast to replace the discredited Europeans. A telegram from Charles Bohlen in Moscow about a recent meeting of the Central Committee of the Communist Party painted a worrisome picture. According to Bohlen's source, the Soviet leadership concluded that "the Middle East will be the focus of Soviet efforts in the future. [Foreign Minister Dmitri] Shepilov and [Defense Minister Georgy] Zhukov were exponents of the view that the Middle East represents a vital link which can be severed to cut West off from East. Destruction of Western position in Middle East will open Africa to Soviet influence and will permit denial to West of strategic bases, vital communications lines, raw materials, and markets. 'Turn your eyes to the South,' Zhukov is reported to have told his colleagues." And, Bohlen's source added, "Egypt and Syria are considered by Soviet leadership to be reliable instruments of Soviet policy in the Middle East." A military agreement with Syria was already inked and would supply the Syrians with tanks, artillery, armored trucks, and jet aircraft. There was not a moment to lose.[77]

Eisenhower and Dulles decided to make their bid for influence in the Middle East public by seeking a congressional resolution, just as they had done in the Formosa Crisis. The resolution would give them a free hand to distribute the carrots of economic and military aid to friendly regimes in the Middle East while authorizing the president to use the stick of military action against any communist threat. Such a public statement of American ambition in the Middle East might provoke a hostile reply from Moscow, but it was worth the risk. Eisenhower lobbied for the resolution with congressional leaders on New Year's Day 1957. Middle East oil, he argued, was vital to Europe and to the West. If the Soviets seized it, the security of the United States would be directly at risk. He wanted to "put the entire world on notice that we are ready to move instantly if necessary." They had to act quickly. "Should there be a Soviet attack in that area he could see no alternative but that the United States move in immediately to stop it." In the meantime economic and military aid would help build pro-Western sentiment in the area and head off discontent in the region. "The United States just cannot leave a vacuum in the Middle East and assume that Russia will stay out."[78]

By the time the president mounted the rostrum in the House of Representatives on January 5, 1957, to announce before a joint session of Congress what became known as the Eisenhower Doctrine, the restraint and caution that had characterized his actions during the Suez Crisis had vanished. It was as if a curtain had been pulled back on the real American strategy in the region. In his address Eisenhower boldly asserted an American obligation to police the Middle East.

The end of the colonial era, he explained, had opened promising new vistas for the emerging nations, but had also created instability that "international Communism" now sought to exploit. "Russia's rulers have long sought to dominate the Middle East." The United States must frustrate their plans. He asked Congress to approve a program of economic and military aid to friendly Middle East nations. He also asked Congress to permit "the employment of the armed forces of the United States to secure and protect the territorial integrity and political independence of such nations, requesting such aid, against overt armed aggression from any nation controlled by International Communism."

Ike wanted a clear message sent to Moscow that the Middle East now formed part of America's beat in the world, and from now on America would police it. This policy "involves certain burdens and indeed risks for the United States," he solemnly noted. But Americans had already given "billions of dollars and thousands of precious lives" to the cause of freedom in Europe and Asia. The United States would expand its sphere of influence to ensure unfettered access to the black gold beneath the sands of Arabia. In early March Congress overwhelmingly passed the resolution.[79]

The Eisenhower Doctrine was no improvisation. It formed part of Eisenhower's grand strategy for waging and winning the cold war—a contest that would unfold especially in the developing world. European countries under Soviet rule, such as Poland and Hungary, could not be saved by American actions. Referring specifically to Hungary, Ike coldly told the press a week after his reelection that the United States did not advocate "open rebellion by an undefended populace against a force over which they could not possibly prevail." Any kind of "armed revolt" would only bring "disaster." So much for liberating the captive nations.[80]

But the Third World was up for grabs. There the contest must be won. Though later historians often praise Eisenhower for his restraint and his aversion to war, in fact during his first term he had deployed American power again and again in order to counter what he saw as the Soviet danger in the developing world. In Iran in 1953 a coup had dispatched a bombastic nationalist leader. In Guatemala in 1954, U.S.-led subversion ousted a radical left-wing president. In Indochina, Eisenhower had seen off the French colonists; by 1955 Americans were pouring millions of dollars into the client state of South Vietnam. Eisenhower had met Chinese communist threats to Taiwan by appealing to Congress for a free hand to respond to any attack and openly threatened to unleash nuclear weapons. The Seventh Fleet stood on permanent picket duty in the watery channel between the two Chinas.

And in the Middle East in 1956 Eisenhower again expanded the range of American global commitments. Not content to compel his European allies to stand down from their ill-conceived Suez adventure, he now sought to impose an American order on the Middle East. Of course the Eisenhower Doctrine was expressed in the language of self-determination and liberty, but beneath the finery of good intentions lay the cold steel of military power. In January 1957 Eisenhower declared that the United States would fight to protect its interests in the Middle East; more than six decades later it is fighting still.

PART III

RACE, ROCKETS, AND REVOLUTION

CHAPTER 14

THE COLOR LINE

*"There must be respect for the
Constitution . . . or we shall have chaos."*

I

IN THE DARKNESS OF A WARM AND HUMID MIDNIGHT, A FLUT-
tering British Union Jack smartly made its way down a white pole on the
top of the National Assembly building in the city of Accra, the capital of the
Gold Coast. At 12:01 a.m. precisely, March 6, 1957, the symbol of British
rule was replaced by a new standard: a flag bearing three bold stripes of red,
yellow, and green with a black star in the center. The new flag told the world
a story: Gold Coast had become the free nation of Ghana.

Ghana's independence ceremonies captured world attention. Journalists, political delegates from 70 countries, literary and cultural figures, all
traveled to Accra to see the historic transfer of power. Speaking to thousands of guests gathered in the city's polo grounds, the nation's new leader,
Kwame Nkrumah, declared that Ghana's independence marked the start of
a new era of African freedom and the arrival of "an African personality in
international affairs." Nkrumah, educated in Catholic schools in Ghana, had
spent 10 years in the United States in the 1930s, earning academic degrees
in economics and theology from Lincoln University and the University of
Pennsylvania. From 1947 on, he led a political movement in Gold Coast
that gradually wrested political power from the British colonial authorities
and put his country on a path to independence. His assumption of power
marked the beginning of a new era for the continent. To African American
journalists attending the ceremony, it seemed that "the black man of Africa
has taken another giant step forward."[1]

Among the honored guests at the celebrations was Vice President Richard Nixon, sent by Eisenhower to bear America's good wishes to Ghana. Eisenhower believed that by acclaiming the end of the colonial era and the independence of African peoples, the United States could more readily keep these nations out of the clutches of Soviet influence. In the wake of the Suez Crisis, America had a chance to benefit from its public opposition to the European invasion of Egypt by embracing the global anticolonial movement. Just a few weeks after his reelection, on December 16, 1956, Eisenhower had welcomed Indian prime minister Jawaharlal Nehru to Washington and devoted almost three full days to Nehru during his stay. In an unprecedented gesture of welcome, he took Nehru on an overnight trip to Gettysburg, where they spent 14 hours in private discussions, mostly seated on the glassed-in porch of the Eisenhower home. They walked the farm and gazed companionably at Eisenhower's Black Angus bulls. Mamie honored Nehru's daughter and adviser, Indira Gandhi, with an elaborate official luncheon in the White House State Dining Room. Eisenhower understood, he wrote later, that Nehru, as well as many other Asian and African leaders, resented "Western condescension," and above all else they wanted "recognition as equals by the 'white' race." Bringing Nehru to Washington for such personal talks, Ike believed, could help demonstrate America's genuine desire to remain on the best possible terms with India—as long as India resisted the blandishments of Khrushchev and the communists.[2]

And so Eisenhower, sensitive to the desires of Third World leaders for gestures of respect, asked Nixon to lead the American delegation to the independence celebrations in Ghana. Nixon made the most of it. In typical Nixonian overachieving fashion, he planned a trip of 18,000 miles to eight African countries—Ghana, Morocco, Tunisia, Libya, Liberia, Ethiopia, Uganda, and Sudan—bringing his youthful charm, his pretty wife, and his tireless desire to please. His entourage was unusually diverse for the time; it included Congresswoman Frances Bolton of Ohio, a member of the House Foreign Affairs Committee and a specialist on Africa, and a young black Democratic congressman from Michigan, Charles C. Diggs Jr. Nixon also traveled with Frederic Morrow, the only black member of the White House staff. Asked later what impressed him most about Africa, Morrow quipped, "For the first time in my life, I was a member of the majority, and it was a damn nice feeling."[3]

Ghana's historic celebrations attracted other visitors from the United States, notably a delegation of distinguished African Americans, expressly invited by Nkrumah. Ralph Bunche of the United Nations was there, along with A. Philip Randolph, the venerable leader of the Brotherhood of Sleeping Car Porters; Congressman Adam Clayton Powell Jr. of New York; Lester Granger of the National Urban League; and Martin Luther King Jr., the pastor from Montgomery, Alabama, who had so recently led the boycott of segregated buses in that city. All these dignitaries, as well as hundreds of other leading Africans, Asians, and Europeans, gathered on March 5 for a reception at the University College of Ghana. Standing just outside the university's large hall, King and Nixon met for the first time. As they shook hands, Nixon smiling warmly, King did not miss his opportunity. "I'm very glad to meet you here," he said. "But I want you to come visit us down in Alabama where we are seeking the same kind of freedom the Gold Coast is celebrating."[4]

An awkward moment. After a pause, and without breaking his mirthless smile, Nixon casually invited King to meet with him in Washington upon his return. Ethel Payne, the pioneering black journalist, wryly noted, "Eight thousand miles away from Washington and even more from Montgomery, Alabama, Rev. King and Vice-President Nixon met here and agreed to hold a conference in the nation's capital on the crisis in the South."[5]

In the previous months King had become the face of the African American civil rights movement. The boycott of public buses in Montgomery had dragged on for a long, difficult year. But in November 1956 the U.S. Supreme Court upheld the ruling of a federal three-judge panel in *Browder v. Gayle* that declared segregation of public buses unconstitutional. When this decision was implemented just before Christmas 1956, allowing blacks to sit anywhere they chose on buses in Montgomery, white vigilantes unleashed a wave of violence, tossing dynamite into the homes of civil rights leaders and blowing up their churches. King's home was hit by a drive-by shotgun blast. Integrated buses were struck by gunfire; a pregnant woman was grievously injured in both legs while riding in a bus across town. On January 10, 1957, the home of King's fellow minister Ralph Abernathy, as well as three churches, were damaged by bombs.[6]

King had sent open telegrams to Eisenhower, Nixon, and Attorney General Brownell decrying the violence and beseeching the White House for help. "A state of terror prevails" across the South, he declared. He asked the president to use his "immense moral power" by coming to the South, making a major speech, and condemning these acts of violence. King sent a pointed message to Nixon questioning why, having conducted a "fact-finding" mission to Austria to examine the plight of Hungarian refugees fleeing Soviet repression, he would not also come to the South to examine the repression of American citizens there.[7]

These appeals did not receive a sympathetic welcome in the White House. When asked about King's plea in a press conference on February 6 Ike said, "[I have] a pretty good and sizable agenda on my desk every day, and as you know I insist on going for a bit of recreation every once in a while. . . . I have expressed myself on this subject so often in the South, in the North, wherever I have been, that I don't know what another speech would do about the thing right now." In an act of astonishing bad taste, he then departed Washington for 10 days of turkey shooting at the Humphrey plantation in Georgia. Knowing that Eisenhower was in the South, King sent another telegram, asking the president to make a statement denouncing the eruption of violence against blacks. Eisenhower again refused.

But the national press noticed. On February 18, 1957, *Time* magazine put a handsome portrait of King on its cover and published an admiring story about the Montgomery boycott: "Across the South—in Atlanta, Mobile, Birmingham, Tallahassee, Miami, New Orleans—Negro leaders look toward Montgomery, Alabama, the cradle of the Confederacy, for advice and counsel on how to gain the desegration that the U.S. Supreme Court has guaranteed them. The man whose word they seek is not a judge, or a lawyer, or a political strategist or a flaming orator. He is a scholarly, 28-year-old Negro Baptist minister, the Rev. Martin Luther King Jr." There could be no ignoring him now.[8]

On that celebratory day in early March in Ghana, as Nixon shook King's hand, he told the young pastor he had read the *Time* story and enjoyed it. But King represented a serious political challenge to Nixon and Eisenhower. Here was a man who now stood at the head of a powerful social movement, a movement capable of mobilizing millions of people and shining a bright light on America's history of racial segregation and violence. Above all, King's very presence in Ghana revealed the profound hypocrisy of America's policies on race: while the U.S. government acclaimed the birth of freedom in Ghana, it still barred blacks and whites from attending school together, riding buses together, or eating together. Nixon understood all this in a flash and swiftly wriggled away from King's firm handclasp. But Nixon, and his president, could not run from the issue of civil rights any longer. In 1957 civil rights dominated American politics, and the whole world was watching.

II

At the outset of his second term in office Eisenhower remained deeply ambivalent about the role the federal government should play in advancing civil rights. On November 14, 1956, while he was preparing with Jim Hagerty for his first postelection press conference, Eisenhower discussed the implications of the Supreme Court's decision the previous day to uphold the ruling in *Browder v. Gayle* that declared unconstitutional the racial segregation of passengers on public buses. He spoke with some bitterness about the topic. The notes of the meeting, taken by his secretary Ann Whitman, reveal his continuing doubts:

> President said that in some of these things he was more of a "States Righter" than the Supreme Court. He fears that by some steps the country is going to get into trouble, and the problems of the Negroes set back, not advanced. He referred to the schools—said how could the Federal Government inforce a ruling applying to schools supported by state funds. Said could have a general strike in the South. Feels that even the so-called great liberals are going to have to take a second look at the whole thing. He may say that the Supreme Court does not refer its decisions to him for approval or study. . . . President said that eventually a District Court is going to cite someone for contempt, and then we are going to be up against it.[9]

These remarks bear careful consideration, as they open a window into the real Eisenhower. We hear his devotion to the principle of states' rights. We hear his belief that enforcement of the federal antidiscrimination law as enshrined in the Fourteenth Amendment of the Constitution would actually harm black Americans more than it would help them. We hear him distancing himself from the Supreme Court, whose chief justice he had appointed. We find him anxious about a clash he rightly anticipates between federal courts and local customs. Eisenhower remained a social conservative, a man unused to change, wary of challenging hierarchy. These comments tell us much about where he stood on the great social and moral issue of his time as he began his second term in office.

And yet—and here is the real story—Eisenhower overcame his limitations. Despite his deep-seated aversion to social movements and to the increasingly urgent demands for action on civil rights, he presided over two enormously important developments that would shape the history of race in America. He lent support to Attorney General Brownell's strenuous efforts to pass the Civil Rights Act of 1957; and he used the power of his office to enforce court-ordered school desegregation in Little Rock, Arkansas, overcoming the resistance of the demagogic governor, Orval Faubus. Eisenhower may at times have been an unwilling combatant in these struggles, yet in the end he did act, and decisively, to advance the progress of civil rights.[10]

Why did Eisenhower, so wary of the civil rights cause, find himself in the surprising role of abetting it? For one thing, there was the promise of a glittering electoral prize in black votes. Eisenhower received 40 percent of the African American vote in 1956—a higher percentage, by far, than any Republican presidential candidate between 1932 and today. (Nixon would win 32 percent in 1960, but since then Republican presidential aspirants have managed to garner on average only 9.6 percent of the black vote.) While black voters nationally remained sympathetic to the legacy of the New Deal and to the memory of Franklin Roosevelt, Eisenhower started to make inroads into this constituency. He just about doubled his share of the black vote from the election of 1952. More striking than these national numbers, however, were the results in the South. In Atlanta, Ike won 85 percent of the black vote in 1956, whereas in 1952 he had attracted only 30 percent. In Richmond, Virginia, he won 73 percent of the black vote in 1956 against only 22 percent four years earlier. All across the South the swing of black voters away from the Democrats toward Eisenhower's Republican Party was striking: in cities such as Charleston, Raleigh, Memphis, Nashville, New Orleans, Tampa, Houston, Mobile, and Knoxville, African American voters switched parties. Of course the raw totals were tiny: legal chicanery as well as outright intimidation and brutality kept most southern blacks away from the polls. Yet the pattern was clear: those few African Americans who could vote in the South were moving decisively away from the Democratic Party.[11]

Eisenhower attracted these voters not because of his strong stance on civil rights. To be sure, he had accumulated a significant record of progress since 1953, but he did not emphasize it in the 1956 campaign. Rather, black voters in the South turned away from the Democratic Party because of its ferocious hostility to *Brown*. In the two years since the Court's decision, white southern Democrats had openly taken up the cause of white supremacy by signing the Southern Manifesto. In this charged political climate, GOP strategists believed, modest progress on civil rights might win over blacks to the Republican Party for a generation.[12]

Three important Republicans accepted this argument. Senate Minority Leader William Knowland, though an Old Guard conservative, had his eye on the governorship of California, and maybe even the presidency. To attain either post, he needed black votes. Nixon, also thinking about 1960, had heard the laments of black leaders like Clarence Mitchell, head of the NAACP in Washington, D.C., who said that "the Democratic Party has become the party of Eastland," the viciously segregationist senator from Mississippi. Nixon envisioned using black votes to pull southern states out of the Democratic column in the next presidential election. And of course Brownell, the architect of the civil rights program, was determined to get on with the job. He had suffered deep humiliation in the Emmett Till case when he was unable to intervene to rectify a gross miscarriage of justice. So, despite Eisenhower's continuing ambivalence, Brownell picked up the cause again and insisted that civil rights be placed at the top of the administration's legislative agenda. On the last day of December, Eisenhower and Brownell met with key Republican congressional leaders to discuss his domestic priorities, and Brownell—not Eisenhower—made the pitch for civil rights. Knowland agreed to work for it, though he despaired of the "inevitable Southern filibuster."[13]

As a result of these pressures, Eisenhower placed civil rights at the center of his State of the Union address, which he delivered on January 10, 1957. He reiterated the four-point proposal he had submitted to the previous Congress: (1) to create a bipartisan congressional commission to investigate civil rights violations; (2) to create a Civil Rights division in the Department of Justice under a new assistant attorney general; (3) to empower the attorney general to pursue contempt proceedings against anyone who violated civil rights stemming from the Fourteenth Amendment; and (4) to empower the attorney general to do the same in connection with a violation of voting rights as laid out in the Fifteenth Amendment. Brownell had succeeded in leading a reluctant president to embrace civil rights legislation by emphasizing the aim of protecting constitutional rights, especially the right to vote. How could that be controversial?[14]

Even with the backing of a popular president, however, civil rights legislation faced one enormous hurdle: the U.S. Senate. At the start of the 85th Congress in January 1957, the Democratic Party held a slim majority with 49 seats against the Republicans' 47—unchanged from the previous Congress. Twenty-two of those Democratic senators came from the 11 states of the Confederacy, and at least 19 of them were dead-set against any civil rights legislation. Since many of those 19 men enjoyed the privileges of seniority and held committee chairmanships—Eastland ran the Judiciary Committee, for instance—it was an easy matter for the South to use the filibuster rules of the Senate to block any undesirable proposals. The Senate's Rule 22—the cloture rule—required the support of three-fifths of the senators to close off debate and force a vote on a piece of legislation. That meant 38 senators, working together, could ensure that the Senate never even held a vote on a pending bill. Southern Democrats, allied with a handful of arch-conservative Old Guard Republicans and a few uneasy midwestern Democrats could stymie progress on civil rights legislation.

Nor did it seem likely that the leader of the majority party, Senator Lyndon Johnson of Texas, would help pass a civil rights bill. During his previous 20 years in public life, Johnson had opposed all proposals to strengthen civil rights protections. In his youth he had lived with and worked among Texas's migrants, sharecroppers, and bone-weary farm laborers. In 1928 he taught Mexican American students at a local school in Cotilla. He may even have had personal empathy for the plight of minorities. But politically he had always stayed loyal to the abiding principles of the South: that race relations were best handled locally by people who "knew" the South and its ways, and that outsiders from the federal government had no legal right—and certainly no moral right—to compel the South to change. Johnson parroted these nostrums out of expediency: he knew that the way to augment his personal power in the Senate was to lead the southern caucus, and the southern caucus demanded strict adherence to this racial code. Johnson followed the rules.

However, LBJ's political calculations changed after November 1956, for with the second defeat of Adlai Stevenson, the Democratic Party had lost its national leader. Harry Truman and Averell Harriman, the stalwarts of the New Deal and the Fair Deal, were yesterday's men. John Kennedy, the junior senator from Massachusetts whose nomination speech on Stevenson's behalf had electrified the 1956 Democratic Convention, and Hubert Humphrey, the 45-year-old tribune of progressivism from Minnesota—perhaps they were tomorrow's men. But now, today, Johnson saw a vacancy at the head of the table, and he meant to occupy it.

To seize the mantle of party leader, to win the Democratic nomination for president in 1960, and then to transcend his Southern roots and become a truly national candidate, Johnson would have to conjure up a great deal of political magic. He would have to unite his own fractious party, bringing northern liberals and southern conservatives into at least a tolerable working relationship. He would have to lead them to accept compromises they were inclined to reject. And then, having brought about a degree of unity, he would have to pass new laws—starting with civil rights laws—that would earn him the respect of voters from across the nation. If he did all that, then maybe, just maybe, he could dream of taking the White House.

So Johnson's future, if not the country's, depended on passing a civil rights bill. To do that he had to solve two complicated puzzles. First, he had to take the bill that the administration wanted and draw out its teeth without making the surgery too painful for Eisenhower. Then he had to persuade his southern colleagues that a defanged civil rights bill should be allowed to come to the floor of the Senate for a vote. They did not have to vote for it, but they had to voluntarily stand aside and let others—mainly northern Democrats and moderate Republicans—pass the bill and make it the law of the land. His fellow southerners would thereby raise Johnson to such a level of national prominence that they could be assured he would become president—and all the more able to propitiate southerners with patronage from the Oval Office. In one of the great ironies of modern politics, the Texas senator, a longtime stalwart of southern intransigence, now planned to ride civil rights all the way to the White House.[15]

III

Although Eisenhower had announced his intention to submit a civil rights bill to Congress in January, various snares slowed it down. In February and early March, Congress took up the "Eisenhower Doctrine" request, which required congressional approval of military and economic aid to Middle Eastern states fighting communist aggression. That request did not pass until March 5. The president's 1958 budget proposal also became an acrimonious topic in Congress, as Eisenhower sent in a budget asking for $72 billion in spending, including $4 billion for foreign aid—one of his passions. Conservatives in both parties whittled away at these numbers; the administration fought back; and not until the fall did Congress strike a budget deal.

Meanwhile the civil rights bill had to be reintroduced in the House of Representatives, hearings had to be conducted, and a new vote held. That finally occurred on June 18, 1957, when H.R. 6127 passed by a vote of 286–126, almost exactly the same tally that the civil rights bill had won in 1956. That bill contained the four key provisions that Brownell had sought, and it now moved on to the Senate. Normally it would have died there, as it did in

1956. But this time Senate leaders connived to keep the bill out of Eastland's Judiciary Committee. Knowland made a motion to place the bill directly onto the Senate calendar, a preliminary to its being debated. Knowland's motion passed, its path cleared by LBJ who had marshalled just enough votes to ensure the bill would not be derailed into Eastland's graveyard. Knowland and Johnson, though bitter foes, each had reasons to see the bill move forward, and so by the end of June the U.S. Senate looked likely to do something it had not done for the better part of a century: debate a civil rights bill.[16]

But from then on, progress slowed. In a telephone conversation on June 15 Johnson had tried to warn the president of the coming conflict. The majority leader told Ike that he wanted to work mainly on passing appropriations bills because the rest of the summer would be taken up "fighting" on the civil rights bill. "Tempers were already flaring," he said, and "would be worse." The country's business was likely to be suspended while that debate roiled. Eisenhower didn't seem to grasp why the bill would stir up controversy. He had repeatedly declared that his administration's civil rights proposals were "moderate," that they aimed chiefly to protect the right to vote as expressed in the Fifteenth Amendment. During the spring he repeated his view that the civil rights bill threatened no one: "In it is nothing that is inimical to the interests of anyone. It is intended to preserve rights without arousing passions and without disturbing the rights of anyone else." To Johnson's warnings of an impending battle Eisenhower replied that "he devised and approved what he thought was the mildest civil rights bill possible—he stressed that he himself had lived in the South and had no lack of sympathy for the southern position. He said he was a little struck back on his heels when he found the terrific uproar that was created."[17]

If the president did not understand how the South viewed his "moderate" civil rights bill, he found out on July 2, 1957, when Senator Richard Russell of Georgia rose to speak on the floor of the Senate. This deeply respected, indeed venerated senator, a man who for many even in the North embodied the very ideal of the southern gentleman, who poured his heart and soul into his work on behalf of a threatened southern way of life, now stood at his desk and launched a devastating attack on the civil rights bill. So powerful were the volleys, so accurate the fire, so explosive the charges that the bill never recovered from the wounds Russell inflicted that day.

Russell began by crying foul: the president, he said, had told the country he wanted a bill to protect voting rights. But what the attorney general had sent to Congress was something else altogether. It had been "cunningly designed to vest in the Attorney General unprecedented power to bring to bear the whole might of the Federal government, including the armed forces if necessary, to force a commingling of white and Negro children in the state-supported public schools of the South." Not only that, but the bill proposed to give the attorney general such sweeping powers that he could "force the white people of the South at the point of a Federal bayonet to conform to almost any conceivable edict directed at the destruction of local custom, law or practice separating the races, and enforce a commingling of the races throughout the social order of the South."

At first Russell's attack sounded like the kind of apocalyptic fearmongering that one could hear across the South in the 1950s, from tobacco-stained taverns to corporate boardrooms. But Russell was not merely venting racial bile. He went on to dissect, with expert skill, the most threatening part of the bill. Section 3 was somewhat obscure, and Russell meant to shed light on it. It proposed to give the attorney general the power to appeal to a federal court for an injunction against any individual who obstructed, or who was planning to obstruct, a citizen's right to equal protection of the laws. If the injunction was then violated, and a court order ignored, a judge could assess penalties, including fines and imprisonment, without reference to a jury trial. In essence it allowed the Justice Department to use the federal courts to bypass local police forces and municipal and state authorities when a citizen's civil rights were at risk. And those civil rights were not precisely defined in the bill, leaving wide discretion to the attorney general. They could cover school integration, interstate transportation, seating in movie theaters and restaurants, and any number of fields in which the attorney general decided equal protection was being denied.

Russell was right about this: Brownell later admitted in his memoirs that Section 3 "gave the attorney general direct authority to enforce Court orders to desegregate public schools and to enter cases such as the Emmett Till murder." This would have been news to Eisenhower, who understood Brownell's bill to be chiefly an augmentation of voting rights protections. Brownell had tried to slip the real import of the bill past the president and Congress. Russell blew the whistle on him using egregious language: "If you propose to move into the South in this fashion, you may as well prepare your concentration camps now, for there are not enough jails to hold the people of the South who will today oppose the use of raw federal power to forcibly commingle white and Negro children."[18]

The following day Eisenhower regrettably gave credence to the suspicion that he was unfamiliar with the content of his signature piece of legislation. At a news conference the press asked him to comment on Russell's allegations that the bill was a "cunning device" to enforce racial integration. "Naturally, I'm not a lawyer and I don't participate in drawing up the exact language of proposals," he admitted. "I know what the objective was, which was to prevent anybody illegally from interfering with any individual's right to vote." In that case, asked James Reston of the *New York Times*, should the bill be revised to make it more precise? "Well," said Ike, "I would not want to answer this in detail because I was reading part of that bill this morning, and there were certain phrases I didn't completely understand." In essence Russell was right: Ike did not grasp the scope of his own bill.[19]

Eisenhower could not have been pleased that Brownell had left him vulnerable to this charge. He called the attorney general that afternoon, obviously still stinging from Russell's withering criticisms. The notes taken by Ann Whitman reveal that Eisenhower was indeed poorly informed about the purposes of the bill. He insisted to Brownell that for two years he had been seeking legislation to allow the attorney general to halt "interference of the right to vote." But now he found the bill was "somewhat more inclusive," giving the federal government wide powers—perhaps too wide. "If the bill has been expanded to a form so general that it scares people to death, that is something else again." By the end of the day, Ann Whitman noted, the president was "very worried" about civil rights.[20]

Well might he worry. His bill was in trouble. When he met with Republican legislative leaders on July 9, he could see they were wavering. Representative Charles Halleck asked just how important Section 3 was to the administration. Senators Everett Dirksen and Leverett Saltonstall reported that the sentiment in the Senate was running against that part of the bill; compromise was now a "foregone conclusion." The next morning that message was reinforced when Senator Russell met with Eisenhower. No notes were kept of their conversation, but Ann Whitman wrote down a summary afterward. Russell made an "emotional" case against the bill. Eisenhower emerged from the meeting telling his staff "he would be willing to listen to clarifying amendments to the Bill as it stands. He is not at all unsympathetic to the position that people like Senator Russell take." The meeting, according to Mrs. Whitman, had restored "some measure of friendship between the Senator and the President." No wonder Fred Morrow feared a "capitulation to the South."[21]

Johnson too pressured Eisenhower. In a secret meeting, so secret that it was not even recorded in the highly detailed presidential appointment book, Johnson informed the president of the facts of life in the Senate. According to Brownell, "Johnson went directly to the Oval Office" and told Eisenhower "that the entire bill would be defeated on the Senate floor if section three . . . was included. He said he had the votes to do this. The president was convinced and agreed that this provision be dropped." Brownell added, "Eisenhower made this decision without consulting me"—a damning comment from the chief field general for the civil rights bill.[22]

On July 16 Eisenhower tried to change the narrative. Russell had successfully defined the civil rights bill as a case of federal overreach and a return to the evil days of Reconstruction. Eisenhower now issued a White House statement that insisted his bill sought mainly "to protect the constitutional right of all citizens to vote regardless of race or color." To that end, federal courts should be allowed to enforce their orders, and local juries could not be allowed to stand in the way of such federal enforcement. Beyond that, Eisenhower said, all he sought was "assistance in efforts to protect other constitutional rights of our citizens"—as tepid a statement of support for the equal protection clause of the Fourteenth Amendment as one could possibly imagine. In political code words Eisenhower had publicly invited Congress to toss out Section 3 of the bill in hopes of saving Section 4, which focused on voting rights protections.[23]

The normally somnolent Senate began to act. Johnson announced his intention to move the bill to the Senate floor for debate. The Senate passed a procedural vote to make the bill the "business of the Senate," a move that came only because Johnson approved it. He promptly served notice that the bill would be amended, knowing that the Senate would move to kill Section 3.[24]

Eisenhower seemed unperturbed by these developments, saying the next day at his weekly press conference that in the civil rights bill "the voting right is something that should be emphasized." He backed away from the part of the legislation that strengthened the federal government's hand to enforce school integration. And he strongly repudiated the idea that the federal government would ever have to use force to compel obedience to the law. "I can't imagine any set of circumstances that would ever induce me to send Federal troops . . . to enforce the orders of a Federal court." This public retreat disheartened both the Republicans in the Senate who had been working hard to pass the bill and their liberal Democratic colleagues. Senator Richard Neuberger of Oregon, an outspoken liberal, said in exasperation after Eisenhower's press conference that the president "revealed, first, that he is not thoroughly familiar with the contents of his administration's bill, and second, that he is not enthusiastically in favor of what he does believe the bill to contain." It was a harsh indictment, one now widely shared in the Senate. Ike had thrown in the towel on Section 3.[25]

Johnson delivered the coup de grâce a week later, allowing a vote on an amendment to cut the offending section from the bill. It passed, 52–38, in what the *New York Times* called "a heavy defeat for the administration." Brownell's bold proposal to tip the balance of power from the states to the federal government in the struggle to enforce civil rights had been disemboweled on the Senate floor. The federal government's ability to enforce federal law on school desegregation, racial violence, lynching, intimidation, economic retaliation, and job discrimination had been denied to the nation's chief law enforcement officer. The leader of the liberal forces in the Senate, Paul Douglas, a Democrat from Illinois, bitterly remarked that the death of Section 3 would arouse "gleeful pleasure among the advocates of apartheid and white supremacy but deep sadness amongst those who are struggling for men to live together."[26]

IV

Eisenhower had retreated from what he saw as an indefensible position. But he did not leave the field of battle. The position to which he now withdrew, and which he defended with the conspicuous vigor missing so far from the civil rights debate, was the other major part of the bill, the section Eisenhower really did believe in: Section 4, designed to protect the right of African Americans to vote. "No person," the proposed law read, "whether acting under color of law or otherwise, shall intimidate, threaten, coerce, or attempt to intimidate, threaten, or coerce any other person for the purpose of interfering with the right of such other person to vote." If such interference occurred or seemed likely to occur, "the Attorney General may institute for the United States, or in the name of the United States, a civil action or other proper proceeding for preventive relief, including an application for a permanent or temporary injunction, restraining order, or other order." Nothing could be simpler: the attorney general could go to a federal court to get an injunction against any local official who sought to deny black people the privileges of the Fifteenth Amendment.[27]

Eisenhower assumed that because he had shown such solicitude for southern opinion on Section 3, he could now expect a reasonable degree of cooperation on Section 4. He told his congressional allies that he would fight for it. In particular he wanted to block the southerners' effort to attach a "jury trial" amendment to the bill, the purpose of which was to interpose a jury between a judge and a defendant in a contempt case. Typically judges could issue injunctions and assess penalties in cases of contempt—that is, a case of open defiance of a court order—without a jury. The purpose of Section 4 was to extend the powers of federal judges to enforce voting rights laws by opening civil or criminal contempt proceedings against anyone who hampered the rights of American citizens to vote.

The southerners devised a clever strategy to blunt the effectiveness of such powers. They did not wish to publicly oppose the right to vote, so instead they shaped the debate as one of an unwarranted expansion of federal power. They conjured up a fearful image of federal judges throwing southerners in jail without trial. It seemed un-American that a judge could imprison a person without a jury trial, but in fact it was common in contempt cases and entirely legal. No matter: southerners were joined by pro-labor and liberal Senators who were concerned about federal judges overturning workers' rights to strike. There was now a coalition persuaded that the Civil Rights Act would open the door to a dramatic extension of federal judicial power.

The administration denied any such purpose in the voting rights bill and also insisted that a jury trial in a case of contempt would dramatically weaken the ability of federal judges to enforce federal voting rights law in the South since southern juries could hardly be relied upon to convict white people for the crime of denying black voters their rights. But these arguments proved hard to sustain against the wily tandem of Johnson and Russell, who prophesied that federal troops would soon be marching across the South to force racial commingling at the end of a bayonet, while jailing without trial the millions of decent southerners who might be inclined to resist this federal assault on their cherished way of life.[28]

Johnson, needing to keep the bill alive while simultaneously gutting it, went back to work, offering incentives, twisting arms, persuading pro-labor senators that union officials who valued the right to strike would also benefit from certain restraints placed on the attorney general's powers, even appealing to liberal senators that the right to trial by jury was sacrosanct. Whipping together his Democratic forces and winning over a dozen, mostly

Old Guard conservative Republicans as well, on the evening of August 1 Johnson managed to pass the jury trial amendment in a 51–42 vote.[29]

It was a stunning blow to Eisenhower and his team. Not only had they lost the battle for Section 3, but now they had been outmaneuvered on Section 4 as well. In a meeting of his cabinet the next morning, Eisenhower seethed with rage. The vote was "one of the most serious political defeats of the past four years, primarily because it was such a denial of a basic principle of the United States." He issued a public statement to the press, effectively labeling the Senate action an assault on the right to vote. "The result cannot fail to be bitterly disappointing to those many millions of Americans who realized that without the minimum protection that was projected in Section 4 of the bill . . . many fellow Americans will continue, in effect, to be disenfranchised." The jury trial amendment, which hobbled federal judges from enforcing federal law, "would weaken our whole judicial system." In her diary Ann Whitman called August 2 "the blackest of black days." In a meeting of congressional leaders a few days later to survey the damage, Deputy Attorney General William Rogers called the resulting bill "a monstrosity—the most irresponsible act he had seen in his time in Washington." To provide the attorney general with the power to enforce voting rights but then place local juries in his way was like "giving a policeman a gun without bullets." The result would be defiance and mockery of federal power. A few days later Ike wearily wrote to his friend Bob Woodruff, "The week has been a depressing one. I think the country took an awful beating."[30]

It was not only the country but Eisenhower that had been beaten—twice in one week, by Lyndon Johnson. In large part this defeat occurred because Eisenhower fought on unfamiliar ground, namely, Capitol Hill. Nor did his field officers, especially Minority Leader Knowland, prove adequate to the task of besting Johnson, perhaps the most gifted parliamentary tactician of his generation. But the defeat may also have been due to Eisenhower's own absence of zeal. Again and again on civil rights he expressed "moderate" opinions in the face of men whose views were immoderate. He sought gradual change where others sought immediate progress or none at all. He showed dispassionate common sense; his opponents fought with passionate zealotry. It was immensely frustrating for Eisenhower to discover that while his appeal to moderation made him admired in the country as a whole, it disarmed him in Congress. Compromise was the ultimate outcome of most congressional proceedings, but to win even half a loaf, you had to fight fiendishly for a whole one while threatening to burn down the bakery. This was not Eisenhower's style.

What remained to him was a depressing and unpalatable choice between vetoing the civil rights bill—his signature legislative proposal for 1957—or signing a weak and perhaps harmful bill into law. For a few weeks he fulminated. He bitterly resented that Johnson had painted him into a corner; he told Republican congressional leaders on August 13 he "thought it ironic that the Democrats had succeeded in making it appear that any civil rights legislation that might be enacted would be their proposal," while if he vetoed the bill, he would seem to have opposed civil rights. Of course that was just what Johnson had intended. Even so, most senior Republicans believed the president had to sign the bill. Nixon and Knowland both advised accepting the bill and seeking improvements in a later session. Eisenhower was not so sure. He "spoke at length in favor of fighting it out to the end to prevent the pseudo-liberals from getting away with their sudden alliance with the Southerners on a sham bill." But once again the passion he expressed in the Cabinet Room did not appear in the public arena, where it counted.[31]

Fearful that Eisenhower might indeed veto the entire bill because of the odious jury trial amendment, Johnson threw the administration a small crumb. Working with legislative aides in the Justice Department and the White House, he agreed to tweak the amendment ever so slightly. In the revised language a jury trial would be triggered in contempt cases only when a judge desired to impose a fine greater than $300 or 45 days in jail. That is, the small-fry cases of minor harassment could still be handled by a federal judge without a jury present. But in major cases in which a judge sought to punish violators of civil rights with real jail time, the defendant could rely on having a jury of his southern white peers ready at hand to protect him and the ways of the Southland. On August 29 the final version of the bill passed the Senate, 60–15, with only southern Democrats opposed. Eisenhower reluctantly signed the bill into law on September 9.[32]

The Civil Rights Act of 1957 satisfied no one. Segregationists denounced it, of course. The white supremacist Citizens' Councils of America issued a statement declaring the Act "coercive and vicious." Senator Russell railed against the law as heralding a new era of Reconstruction, in which "Negro political leaders will direct the attorneys of the Justice Department" in an all-out attack on the South. Nonetheless he boasted that the fight he waged to cripple the measure had been "the greatest victory of his 25 years in the Senate." Ethel Payne of the *Chicago Defender* called the law "a Confederate victory," and in a way Russell agreed. The *Chicago Defender* editorial page said it did not go nearly far enough, as it left intact a wide array of devices the South had used to disenfranchise black voters, from the poll tax to literacy tests. Signing the bill, Eisenhower expressed little pride. "I think the President's views on the bill are well known," a fatigued Jim Hagerty told the press.[33]

Not everyone saw the act through jaundiced eyes, however. In a letter to Nixon on August 30, Rev. King wrote, "The present bill is far better than no bill at all." It was the first civil rights law in 82 years. It created a Civil Rights Division of the Justice Department, a new assistant attorney general for civil rights, and a bipartisan congressional commission to investigate civil rights abuses. It gave the attorney general powers to seek injunctions in cases of voting rights violations, though the penalty for such violations would likely remain little more than a gentle wrist slap. And it signaled that the Congress had started to take seriously the crisis in the South. Powerful arguments had been made that Eisenhower should veto the bill because of its flaws. "While I sympathize with this point of view," King wrote, "I feel that civil rights legislation is urgent now." King knew the struggle was not going to be won all at once, nor could many centuries of violence be righted by the stroke of a president's pen. Change would come through "a sustained mass movement on the part of Negroes" and would take decades to achieve. Every step toward that goal helped. King thanked Nixon for his efforts on behalf of civil rights, welcoming any sign of progress. "I am sure we will soon emerge from the bleak and desolate midnight of man's inhumanity to man to the bright and glittering daybreak of freedom and justice for all men."[34]

V

The battle over the Civil Rights Act left Eisenhower weary and in need of a break from politics. He looked forward to spending most of September at the Naval Station in Newport, Rhode Island, where he would have peace and quiet and play a great deal of golf at the Newport Country Club. He imagined leaving the subject of civil rights behind for a while, but at his weekly press conference the day before leaving town, he received a question from Merriman Smith of United Press. Would the president comment on the situation in Arkansas, "where the Governor has ordered state troops around a school that a Federal court had ordered integrated"? The school in question was Central High School in Little Rock.

Eisenhower said he first heard of the matter that very morning, and the attorney general was looking into it. Then, in his practiced way, he equivocated. The decision in *Brown v. Board of Education* must be "executed gradually, according to the dictum of the Supreme Court," but everyone must remember "you cannot change people's hearts merely by laws."

Every reporter in the room had heard this sort of doublespeak many times from the president. Anthony Lewis of the *New York Times* pushed a bit harder. Did the president "have any plans to take a personal part in the problem" of school integration, he asked. Did he plan to speak out, to guide, in short, to lead? Ike refused to make any moral judgments on the matter. Certainly, he said, the Supreme Court's decision must be obeyed. "But there are very strong emotions on the other side, people that see a picture of a mongrelization of the race, they call it. There are very strong emotions, and we are going to whip this thing in the long run by Americans being true to themselves, and not merely by law."[35]

Hearing these words, it was impossible to divine Eisenhower's beliefs on the subject of desegregation. He respected the Supreme Court's role in interpreting the Constitution and believed he had a duty to implement the *Brown* decision, but he seemed no less insistent that customs and habits of the South be respected as well. Was there common ground here? Eisenhower did not say. He preferred to reassure everyone that "being American" was enough to solve the country's problems. And with these baffling and contradictory phrases lingering in the air, he departed for a New England vacation. It would not be a restful one.

Few could have predicted that the nation's greatest crisis over school desegregation would break out in Little Rock, Arkansas. Some cities in the state had already started along the road of gradual compliance with the Supreme Court demand to integrate the public schools. The University of Arkansas had admitted black students, and school boards in Fayetteville, Hoxie, Fort Smith, Van Buren, Ozark, and North Little Rock had made modest progress on school desegregation with little public outcry. In 1955 the Little Rock school board adopted a plan to implement a very gradual, indeed token desegregation of Central High School (but not the junior high or elementary schools), starting in fall 1957.

In Little Rock, however, a white segregationist group, the Capital Citizens' Council, was formed in 1956 and put heavy pressure on Governor Orval Faubus to block the integration plan. The group also sponsored the Mothers' League of Central High School, which vocally opposed integration. Faubus, a 47-year-old army veteran from the Ozarks in just his second two-year term, had a record as a moderate on race relations, at least in southern terms. But he was facing a stiff challenge from a rabid race-baiting state legislator named Jim Johnson who planned to use the segregation issue to win the next gubernatorial election. Faubus calculated that his political fortunes would be improved if he openly took sides on the issue. Backed by Faubus, these segregationist groups asked for an injunction from the county court to delay Little Rock's desegregation plan, claiming that the school would erupt with bloody violence if the plan went forward. The governor himself testified that revolvers and knives had been confiscated from students in the preceding days. Even though the school superintendent, Virgil Blossom, disagreed with Faubus's account, the court on August 29 granted the injunction and halted the integration plan.[36]

The next day, however, Judge Ronald N. Davies of the federal Eastern Arkansas District Court overruled the county court. He found the rumors of violence insufficient to warrant a delay and ordered Central High School to open its doors to the dozen or so carefully screened African American students who had been chosen by the school board as the vanguard of integration. Dr. Blossom announced that the school would comply. "I am confident the problem will be resolved in a peaceful manner," he said.[37]

Faubus now confronted a challenge to his authority as governor, and he meant to meet it aggressively. The federal government "is cramming integration down our throats," he told the press, and wants to "make an object lesson out of Arkansas." He chose to fight back. Rejecting the court order, he sent 200 soldiers from the Arkansas National Guard to take up positions around the high school on the evening of September 2. In a televised speech he declared this was necessary to prevent the violence that would surely break out if black children were allowed to enroll in school the following morning. He insisted that he wanted only to maintain peace and order, and since desegregation was a threat to peace and order, it had to be refused. The school board promptly issued a statement asking black children not to come to school and breach the line of soldiers, for fear of violence. A state governor, backed by an armed militia, now stood in defiance of a federal court order. The battle lines were drawn.[38]

On Tuesday morning, September 3, the first day of school, some 500 townspeople converged on the school, some perhaps just curious, some spoiling for a fight. No black students appeared, and the crowd dispersed. But in the chambers of Judge Davies, school board officials were ordered once again to proceed with their plan to enroll the African American students. Davies noted that Governor Faubus had directed the soldiers only to "keep order." He would "take the Governor at his word."[39]

Thus on the morning of September 4, 1957, under the glare of the national spotlight, nine nervous black teenagers, six girls and three boys, set out for school. Eight of the children traveled together under the guidance of Daisy Bates, a prominent black newspaper publisher and the local leader of NAACP. They were joined by four ministers—two black, two white. Jostled and heckled by the crowd, the group made it as far as the cordon of troops at the school's front entrance, where they were turned away. They returned to their cars and drove off, leaving behind a noisy and restive mob. But the one child who came to school alone, Elizabeth Eckford, endured an hour of terror that morning. Immaculate in her handmade cotton dress and white bobby socks, she took the city bus to school, unaccompanied. As she walked toward the school, the mob of hundreds shouted at her. When she too was denied admittance by the National Guard and began to walk back to the bus stop, the abuse grew louder and more horrific. Angry whites, their sneering faces full of hate, shouted "Lynch her!" and "No nigger bitch is going to get into our school!" As Elizabeth sat waiting for the bus, tears running down her cheeks, the crowd moved in closer, the vulgar abuse increased, and it seemed only the arrival of the bus saved her from physical harm.[40]

The next morning the events at Little Rock became a national and indeed global news story. This may have been because of the astonishing photographs taken that day. On the front page of most papers across the country, readers saw a stoic, well-dressed Elizabeth Eckford walking away from a mob of angry hecklers, one petite young white girl in a mint-green dress following closely behind. That was Hazel Bryan, her face twisted into a mask of hatred as she shouted at Elizabeth. These photographs perfectly captured the cruelty that lay behind the practice of Jim Crow segregation. And they traveled across the world, putting on display the most shameful of American customs, contradicting in an instant any American claim to moral superiority.[41]

VI

Between the time Eisenhower left the White House at 9:30 a.m. on September 4 and the time his aircraft landed at Quonset Point Naval Air Station in Newport two hours later, the events in Little Rock had become a national crisis. As Ike met with Rhode Island's governor and other local dignitaries, receiving gifts and shaking hands and getting settled into his Newport head-quarters, a telegram from Orval Faubus was making its way to the president's office. It was a declaration of defiance.

"I was one of the soldiers of your command in World War II," Faubus began. "I spent 300 days of combat with an infantry division defending our country, its people and their rights on the battlefields of five nations." Having established his record of selfless patriotism, Faubus claimed that the issue in Little Rock was not one of integration versus segregation but whether "the head of a sovereign state can exercise his constitutional powers and discretion in maintaining peace and good order within his jurisdiction." Alleging a plot by the FBI to arrest him, Faubus asserted that any interference in his actions at Little Rock would amount to a violation of the "rights and powers of a state." If any challenge were made to his authority, Faubus warned, the situation might soon spiral out of control. In that case "the blood that may be shed will be on the hands of the Federal government." He asked the president to stop federal interference in Little Rock so the townspeople could "again enjoy domestic tranquility and continue in our pursuit of ideal relations between the races."[42]

Faubus's challenge to the president triggered a public statement from Roy Wilkins, executive secretary of the NAACP. Wilkins accused Faubus of "deliberately provoking a test of the authority of the Federal government to enforce the orders of Federal courts." Faubus seemed to think that "states are free to decide whether to abide by the Constitution and the Federal rulings or not." Lester Granger of the National Urban League added his voice, asking Eisenhower to resolve once and for all whether a state could defy the federal government in opposing court-ordered desegregation.[43]

Eisenhower replied to Faubus on September 5 with a brief and elliptical message: "The Federal Constitution will be upheld by me by every legal means at my command." Eisenhower intended this to sound like a thinly veiled threat. Yet no one could be certain how he would act in the face of Faubus's defiance. Nor did his highly publicized rounds of golf lend any sense of urgency to the issue; every day from 9:00 to noon, with national attention riveted on Little Rock, Ike could be found on the fairways of the Newport Country Club, working on his game with the club pro.

On Saturday, September 7, Eisenhower flew to Washington. His trip had been scheduled in advance, for he planned to attend the debutante ball of his niece, Ruth Eisenhower, in Baltimore. But in light of the school crisis, he decided to stop at the White House to consult with the attorney general. According to both Brownell and Sherman Adams, Eisenhower wished to avoid a confrontation with Faubus. He wanted to give the governor a way to save face and conduct "an orderly retreat." Yet the ground for such a backward maneuver had already disappeared, for that day Judge Davies had made headlines when he denied a request from the Little Rock school board to halt the desegregation plan due to the threat of mob violence. Insisting that the integration plan move forward, Davies declared, "There can be nothing but ultimate confusion and chaos if court decrees are flaunted."[44]

On Sunday afternoon, while Eisenhower was back in Newport playing a round of golf, Faubus replied to Judge Davies's order by saying that the National Guard would remain in place and no black students would be allowed to enroll on Monday morning. "I sincerely hope," he said menacingly, "that no one is shot or that violence or harm comes to no one." With the National Guard out in force around the school, there was no chance the African American students would attempt to enter on Monday morning. With the city tense but quiet, Davies asked the Justice Department to issue an injunction against Governor Faubus, and he sent Faubus a summons to appear in his court on September 20 to explain his actions. The stalemate between the federal court and Faubus, backed by his state guard, would last another 10 days.[45]

Here, Eisenhower made a tactical mistake. Sherman Adams's good friend Congressman Brooks Hays, who represented the Little Rock district, had approached Adams suggesting the president meet with Faubus in person in Newport. When Adams proposed this to Eisenhower, saying he thought Faubus "realizes he has made a mistake and is looking for a way out," the president accepted "without a moment of hesitation." Ike believed his personal touch might be able to persuade Faubus to do what a federal court order had failed to accomplish. Brownell advised against the meeting, pointing out that Faubus had no incentive to back down now and that meeting with a governor who was openly defying federal authority was unwise. Ike believed Brownell failed to account for "the seething in the South" and agreed to the meeting anyway.[46]

Faubus arrived at the Newport headquarters at 8:45 a.m. on September 14 and met with the president privately for 20 minutes. Eisenhower later dictated his account of the meeting: "Faubus protested that he was a law abiding citizen, that he was a veteran, fought in the war, and that everyone recognizes that the Federal law is supreme to state law." Eisenhower then gave Faubus a means to save face and end the conflict in Little Rock: simply order the troops in place at the high school to allow the black children to enter the school. The troops could then "preserve order" should there be any trouble. If Faubus did this, Eisenhower would make sure that the Justice Department found a way to revoke Judge Davies's order that Faubus appear in court. Ike saw this as a good deal; he wanted to avoid "a trial of strength between the President and a Governor because . . . there could only be one outcome—that is, the State would lose, and I did not want to see any Governor humiliated." Ike's proposal also squared with his own sensitivity toward states' rights. He thought Faubus seemed "very appreciative" and would go "back to Arkansas to act within a matter of hours to revoke his orders to the Guard."[47]

In fact Faubus did not agree to any kind of deal. After their meeting, Faubus and Eisenhower were joined by Brownell, Adams, Congressman Hays, and Jim Hagerty. The conversation went on for another two hours. Brownell asserted the responsibility of the federal government to carry out the Supreme Court's orders on school desegregation. His message was unambiguous: "The desegregation law did not have to be liked or approved, but it had to be obeyed." Adams recalled that Faubus "listened intently in inscrutable silence." Adams thought Brownell condescending, the Yale man and prominent New York lawyer dictating to the country politician with barely a high school education. When the meeting ended, according to Adams, Faubus was "noncommittal." By 3:00 Ike was back on the links at Newport Country Club.[48]

No one knew just what the meeting signified. Ann Whitman jotted down in her diary that "the meeting had not gone as well as had been hoped" and that Faubus "stirred the whole thing up for his own political advantage." Adams confessed, "We were not sure that anything had been accomplished at the meeting. The President was hopeful and somewhat optimistic. Brownell was quietly skeptical." Hagerty prepared a statement for the press that described the meeting as "constructive" and said that Faubus had given his word he would "respect the decisions of the United States District Court." But when it came time for Faubus to issue his own statement, he refused to cooperate. Rather than abide by the court order, he claimed he was obliged to "harmonize [his] actions under the Constitution of Arkansas with the requirements of the Constitution of the United States"—as if he had a right to choose which document he would obey. When he returned to Little Rock, he did not withdraw the National Guard, nor did he issue them a change of orders. The stalemate endured. Eisenhower called Brownell and admitted, "You were right. Faubus broke his word."[49]

Eisenhower had made a serious miscalculation. He had invited a governor who was in flagrant violation of a federal court order to meet with him without securing his capitulation beforehand. Faubus was a slippery character, as Brownell had warned, and Eisenhower failed to nail him down. As the *New York Times* editorial page described it, Faubus regarded federal court orders "as a matter for horse-trading between a State Governor and a President of the United States," and Eisenhower had participated in the deal-making. A group of influential liberal Democrats termed Eisenhower's handling of the crisis "tragic" and "weak." Black leaders too were restive. Adam Clayton Powell, one of Ike's most prominent black supporters, demanded action. Baseball legend Jackie Robinson called for Eisenhower to meet with black leaders to discuss the problem. Famed band leader Louis Armstrong told the press he would cancel a government-sponsored tour of Europe because the president "lacked guts" and had failed to end the standoff. Eisenhower's patience and moderation now appeared to many in the North to be little more than appeasement of the southern segregationists.[50]

On September 20 the much-anticipated showdown in Judge Davies's courtroom duly unfolded. Spectators and participants gathered early in Room 436 of the federal building in Little Rock. Camera crews mounted bright lights. The nine black students who had sought admission to the high school filed in, perfectly attired in suits and dresses. Just before 10:00 in walked Thurgood Marshall, chief legal counsel for the NAACP and a nationally recognized attorney. Judge Davies took his seat at 10:00 sharp. Governor Faubus did not appear, but his lawyers asked Davies to dismiss the case against him, asserting that the court had no authority over a state governor. This ludicrous assertion was denied by Davies, prompting the governor's lawyers to walk out of the courtroom. After taking testimony from witnesses, Davies issued an injunction, demanding that Faubus halt his obstructionism and allow "the attendance of Negro students at Little Rock High School."

Three hours later Faubus complied. He gave the order for the National Guard to leave the school grounds, but not before making an announcement to the press. He denounced the Court's rulings and its proceedings, claiming them rigged and unconstitutional. He lashed out at his critics. And he concluded by suggesting that since his own powers to keep the peace had been revoked, any violence that followed would be the problem of the federal authorities. Before leaving the state to attend a governors' conference in Georgia, he offered a "fervent prayer" that the mob would not come out to the school on Monday morning, September 23, and instigate any trouble.[51]

VII

But of course there was trouble. On Monday morning Daisy Bates and her nine student charges gathered at her home before setting out for Little Rock High School. They knew there was a crowd of over 1,000 people waiting for them, though the city and state police were also present in a small contingent. As they arrived at the high school, they noticed a great commotion among the large and unruly mob but hastily made their way to a side entrance of the school building and entered. Only then did they discover that the mob was assaulting four black reporters who had arrived at the scene early and had been mistaken for the students. One, L. Alex Wilson of the *Tri-State Defender* in Memphis, was badly beaten. Photographs show a brick-wielding punk kicking him in the face; other hoodlums jumped him from behind and punched and kicked him to the ground amid cheers and hollers. These actions had briefly distracted enough of the angry crowd to allow the black students to enter the school. But within a few minutes, the cry went up: "They're in! The niggers are in!"

Chaos ensued. About 300 white students walked out of the building, chanting "Two, four, six, eight, we ain't gonna integrate!" The increasingly belligerent crowd outside harassed the thin blue line of officers and seemed prepared to storm the school. Fearing for the safety of the black students, who were huddled in the principal's office, the mayor and the superintendent decided to have them removed and taken back to Daisy Bates's home. Bates told reporters she would not send them back to school until "they have the assurance of the President of the United States that they will have protection against the mob." The first day of integration at Little Rock High School had lasted about three hours.[52]

That afternoon Mayor Woodrow Wilson Mann sent off an anxious message to the president, which was intercepted by Brownell. Praising the "valiant effort" of the police to hold off the demonstrators, the mayor accused Governor Faubus of directing the crowd through various intermediaries, and said he would turn over evidence of this claim to the Justice Department. Brownell called the president, who was on his way to the golf course, and filled him in on the details. Eisenhower was profoundly annoyed and aggrieved. He drafted a statement for public release, stating that federal law cannot be "flouted with impunity by any individual or mob of extremists." The president would "use the full power of the United States including whatever force may be necessary to prevent any obstruction of the law." But he was, he told his advisers, "loath to use troops." He hoped that the threat of force would suffice. He issued that night a "proclamation" that ordered "all persons engaged in such obstruction of justice to cease and desist." It was a last effort to compel obedience. But it did not work.[53]

The following day, September 24, 1957, marks one of the most significant dates in the Age of Eisenhower. Although no black students appeared at Little Rock High School that morning, a crowd of angry protestors gathered menacingly. The mayor, fearing that he would not be able to control the mob without a larger police force, sent another and perhaps exaggerated telegram to the president. "The immediate need for federal troops is urgent. . . . Mob is armed and engaging in fisticuffs and other acts of violence. Situation is out of control." Mann fairly begged the president, "in the interest of humanity, law and order," to send federal troops to restore order in the city.

Here was the invitation Brownell needed to complete his legal case that local authorities had asked for federal intervention to halt the actions of mob violence. He recommended that Eisenhower send in federal troops, drawing for authority on Sections 332 and 333 of Title 10 of the U.S. Code, which enshrines the Insurrection Act of 1807. According to the statute, "Whenever the President considers that unlawful obstructions, combinations, or assemblages, or rebellion against the authority of the United States, make it impracticable to enforce the laws of the United States in any State or Territory by the ordinary course of judicial proceedings, he may call into Federal service such of the militia of any State, and use such of the armed forces, as he considers necessary to enforce those laws or to suppress the rebellion." Faubus's defiance presented just such a case of rebellion. Eisenhower reluctantly acknowledged this fact and agreed to use federal troops to enforce the law. According to Adams, this decision was "the most repugnant to him of all his acts in his eight years at the White House."

Repugnant, for it made a prophet of the many Richard Russells of the South who had predicted just this kind of "integration at the end of a bayonet." Nevertheless, once committed, Eisenhower went all in. "If you have to use force," he told Brownell, "use overwhelming force." He ordered the army chief of staff Gen. Maxwell Taylor to send in units of the 101st Airborne and also issued an executive order federalizing the Arkansas National

Guard, thus placing those troops under his command. By 7:00 that evening, the first of over 1,000 army troops rolled into Little Rock and began to deploy around the high school. Eisenhower flew from Newport to the White House, and at 9:00 he spoke to the nation.[54]

Speaking "from the house of Lincoln, of Jackson and of Wilson," he expressed "sadness" for the decision to send troops to the city. He pointed to "demagogic extremists" and "disorderly mobs" who had refused to abide by federal law, and asserted that in such a case, "the President's authority is inescapable." Unless he carried out the orders of federal courts, "anarchy would result." He was fulfilling his oath to defend the Constitution. With a flourish he added, "Mob rule cannot be allowed to override the decisions of our courts."

Predictably he avoided the moral questions at hand. He did not champion the need for equality and fairness in America, nor did he embrace the *Brown* decision or praise the Little Rock Nine as heroes every bit as courageous as the men he had led into battle. He had no interest in engaging the history of race relations in America. He never mentioned Orval Faubus; he did not refer to the Southern Manifesto; he did not quote any of the prolonged declarations in favor of racial segregation made that summer in the U.S. Senate by leading statesmen of the age. In fact he went out of his way to praise the great majority of southerners, who "are of good will, united in their efforts to preserve and respect the law."[55]

In short, he positioned himself not as a champion of civil rights but as a defender of law and order. As he would say again and again to his southern critics, he sent troops to Little Rock to uphold the courts. The country was faced with "open defiance of the Constitution," and if he were to tolerate that, he would invite "anarchy." His decision, he told one southern senator, had nothing to do with "integration, desegregation or segregation": he aimed to uphold the law. To fail in that duty was "to acquiesce in anarchy, mob rule, and incipient rebellion," which would "destroy the Nation."[56]

Eisenhower would later be much criticized for his narrow reading of the nature of the desegregation crisis. His own speechwriter Arthur Larson, looking back on the issue in 1968, criticized Eisenhower for his "failure" to use the presidency to "set a tone of broad presidential concern for racial justice" in the manner that Larson's hero, John Kennedy, later did. Looking at the president's record on civil rights, one prominent biographer asserted that "Eisenhower's refusal to lead was almost criminal." From the perspective of the late 1960s and subsequent decades, Eisenhower's unwillingness to grasp the moral dimension of the issue certainly seems obtuse. But he did not govern in the late 1960s. In 1957 he saw himself acting as Andrew Jackson and Abraham Lincoln did, and it was no accident that he invoked them both in his speech. Jackson, though a champion of states' rights, insisted on the constitutional powers of the federal government to enforce federal law in the face of South Carolina's defiance during the Nullification Crisis of 1832. And in 1861, when confronting the secession of southern states, Lincoln too looked to the Constitution for his authority to preserve the Union. Eisenhower believed he was following the playbook written by his illustrious predecessors.[57]

What is more, *at the time* few Americans spoke of Eisenhower's timidity or weakness in confronting Governor Faubus. As the soldiers of the elite 101st Airborne Division took up positions around the school, holding back the crowd and accompanying the nine black students into school on the morning of September 25, telegrams poured in from around the country. Black leaders praised Ike's decision. Martin Luther King Jr. wired the president, thanking him for his support of "Christian traditions of fair play and brotherhood." Jackie Robinson sent Ike a brief note of thanks. And down in Little Rock, Daisy Bates rose to speak on Sunday morning at the Methodist church, her voice shaking with emotion. Despite the rocks thrown through her windows and the crosses burned in her front yard, she kept up her fight to see that black children in her city were treated fairly. "What happens in Little Rock," she declared, "transcends this city and has serious implications for democracy all over the world."[58]

Eisenhower certainly did not look timid or weak in southern eyes. White southerners interpreted the intervention at Little Rock as a mortal threat to the Jim Crow order and reacted with venomous outrage. Senator Eastland described the intervention as "an attempt by armed force to destroy the social order of the South." Senator Olin Johnston of South Carolina called for armed insurrection against the federal troops. To Harry Byrd of Virginia the president's action would only "intensify existing bitterness and strengthen the resistance of the South to enforced integration." The Jackson, Mississippi, *Clarion-Ledger* called September 24 "the South's darkest day since Reconstruction." A congressman from Arkansas, E. C. Gathings, denounced Eisenhower's use of "inhuman, cruel, and savage brutality inflicted upon a helpless people." A local politician from Georgia wrote to ask the president never to come to that state again for fear of an outburst of "violence and physical injury" against him. The Kentucky White Citizens' Council held a mass meeting to place Eisenhower on trial for "high treason."

The most egregious message came from that paragon of southern gentility, Senator Richard Russell himself, who likened the federal troops in Little Rock to "Hitler's storm troopers." Eisenhower's actions, Russell asserted, would "crush by tank and bayonet the thousands of American citizens who are sincerely convinced that they have an inalienable right to send their children to schools attended by their own race and kind." Later writers who would condemn Eisenhower for half-measures and timidity would do well to consider that to many in the South, Eisenhower's actions amounted to a declaration of war.[59]

VIII

Eisenhower understood perfectly well how extreme his actions appeared to southerners, and it pained him greatly. He sought to defuse the crisis as soon as possible. The soldiers of the 101st Airborne effectively kept the rabble at bay and enabled the Little Rock Nine to enter the high school. Within two weeks half of the army troops were withdrawn, and at the end of November the rest of them departed. However, the federalized National Guard troops remained at Little Rock High School for the duration of the 1957–58 school year, standing watch as a handful of black students dutifully attended classes in an atmosphere of hostility, intimidation, constant scuffles, insults, and jeers. The troops had been assigned to allow the students to enter the school, but they rarely went beyond that narrow remit and were unable or unwilling to create an atmosphere of safety and tolerance within the school itself. And why would they? Eisenhower's conception of the role of federal responsibility limited soldiers to the task of enforcing the court order. "The troops are not there as part of the segregation problem," he told the press on October 3. "They are there to uphold the courts."[60]

On October 23, a month after Eisenhower sent troops to Little Rock, Herbert Brownell resigned. He would be replaced by his deputy, William Rogers. This move had been planned in advance, as Brownell wished to return to his law practice. But some saw the timing as linked to the events in Little Rock. Brownell had been an influential attorney general, much admired by Eisenhower. Yet he had taken risks. Starting with the masterminding of Earl Warren's appointment, followed by the briefs he filed on behalf of the *Brown* case, and then the long struggle to get the Civil Rights Act passed, Brownell pushed the administration further than the president wanted to go. Having laid the groundwork for the intervention decision in Little Rock and helped to construct the rock-solid legal defense of Eisenhower's use of troops, he nonetheless encountered resistance from his colleagues, notably Sherman Adams, who counseled much greater restraint. Governor Faubus publicly identified Brownell as the villain of the Little Rock affair and routinely denounced him as a zealot and latter-day abolitionist. Eisenhower liked and trusted him, but his departure sent a signal of reconciliation to the South.

Although black leaders continued to seek further support from the White House, Eisenhower was unreceptive. The Soviet launch of the *Sputnik* satellite on October 4, 1957, soon dominated the concerns of the administration; interest in civil rights sagged. In November, Martin Luther King Jr. asked if the president would receive a delegation of black leaders to discuss race relations. The request was denied. In January 1958, Eisenhower devoted his entire State of the Union speech to defense matters and the cold war, completely ignoring the extraordinary events in Little Rock.

Yet black activists kept up the pressure, hoping to capture Eisenhower's attention to their cause. In May they invited the president to speak at a national summit of black leaders hosted by the National Newspaper Publishers Association. Eisenhower agreed and accepted an award from the group honoring his commitment to civil rights progress. He then rose to speak before 350 black journalists, church leaders, educators, and public figures, including Daisy Bates, whose hand he warmly shook. In his speech he dutifully invoked the American principles of equality before the law, and his audience responded with warm applause. But then he pivoted, uttering off-the-cuff comments about the "problems" of civil rights that shocked his audience into silence. "I do believe that as long as they are human problems—because they are buried in the human heart rather than ones merely to be solved by a sense of logic and right—we must have patience and forbearance. . . . We must make sure that enforcement will not in itself create injustice." Fred Morrow, who had done so much to arrange Ike's appearance at the event, wrote later, "I could feel life draining from me, and I wished I could escape." A furious Roy Wilkins issued a bitter statement that very night: "We have been patient and we have been moderate and all we get for it is a kick in the teeth." Numerous denunciations followed in the national black press.[61]

In the resulting furor King cabled the president, demanding a face-to-face meeting with black civil rights leaders. A somewhat contrite Eisenhower finally agreed to receive a delegation at the White House. On June

23 King, A. Philip Randolph, Wilkins, and Lester Granger spent 45 minutes with the president. Ike was subdued as these men asked for more federal support in the ongoing school crisis. He told them he was "extremely dismayed to hear that after five and a half years of effort and action in this field, these gentlemen were saying that bitterness on the part of Negro people was at its height." He then said, to the astonishment of his listeners, that "further constructive action" might only "result in more bitterness." Wilkins recalled, "It was a touchy moment." The meeting broke up inconclusively.[62]

That same month the Little Rock school board won approval from a federal district court to delay the city's desegregation plan, citing continuing trouble in the school and hostility in the community. The school board wanted black students to go back to segregated schools for at least two and a half years. The NAACP filed an appeal, and won. The case, *Cooper v. Aaron*, then went to the Supreme Court. On September 12, 1958, the Court upheld the appeals court's ruling: desegregation must continue. But Governor Faubus had one more trick to play. He closed the public schools entirely and tried to set up a private corporation to lease the public school buildings; these would then open only to white students. Not until June 1959, under yet another federal court order, did Little Rock High reopen as an integrated school. And how far the country still had to go! As the 1959 school year opened, five years after *Brown*, only six percent of black students in the South attended desegregated schools.[63]

As white Americans continued to resist desegregation, black leaders grew understandably restive. The continued defiance by state and local authorities, combined with provocations like the September 3, 1958, arrest in Montgomery of Martin Luther King for loitering, led to calls for mass action. Wilkins wrote to Morrow at the White House and asked for help: "Doesn't the White House understand that it cannot remain aloof from this struggle?"[64]

On October 25, King and Randolph initiated the Youth March for Integrated Schools and organized the travel of about 9,000 students from across the East Coast to Washington, D.C. The large group gathered at the Lincoln Memorial and heard speeches that praised the Little Rock Nine and their heroic mentor, Daisy Bates. They heard calls for bolder leadership from the White House. Jackie Robinson, a pioneer in crossing the color line, urged the students to see that the real America was not in Little Rock but right there among the protesters, at the foot of the Lincoln Memorial, peacefully voicing their concerns.

As the gathering broke up, the singer, actor, and activist Harry Belafonte led a small delegation of marchers across the National Mall to the grounds of the White House. Halting at the wrought-iron gates, the students asked the guard for an audience with the president, as they wished to present him with a petition on behalf of "equality in education." The president did not receive them, nor did any administration official. The youthful idealists, their hearts full from an afternoon of prayer and singing before the statue of Abraham Lincoln, stood and waited for a while at the house of Eisenhower. Then they were politely shooed away.[65]

CHAPTER 15

IKE'S MISSILE CRISIS

*"The world must stop the present plunge toward
more and more destructive weapons of war."*

I

THE FIGHT OVER THE CIVIL RIGHTS ACT OF 1957, FOLLOWED
by the bitter clash in Little Rock, left Eisenhower reeling and unsteady. His
political fortunes sagged further when, in August 1957, the nation's economy
slipped into a short, sharp recession. High interest rates, held in place by the
Federal Reserve, began to curtail consumer spending. A falloff in purchases
of durable goods, especially automobiles, and a tight-fisted government approach to spending triggered a contraction of the economy. Unemployment
climbed to 7.5 percent—the highest since 1941—and in auto-dependent
Michigan it topped out at 11.4 percent. Northeastern industrial states were
also hard hit. At the start of 1958 polls showed that Americans were more
anxious about the economy than at any time since the Great Depression.[1]

Eisenhower might have muddled through the racial turmoil and the
economic troubles of the country. But in October 1957, just two weeks after
sending federal troops to Little Rock, he endured a jolt that nearly wrecked
his presidency. On October 4 the Soviet Union successfully put into orbit
the world's first man-made satellite, a 184-pound aluminum sphere named
Sputnik, meaning "fellow traveler." Moving at 18,000 miles per hour and
orbiting the Earth every 96 minutes, the satellite carried a simple radio
transmitter that emitted periodic beeps. "An eerie intermittent croak—it
sounded like a cricket with a cold—was picked up by radio receivers around
the world last week," noted *Life* magazine. Not only was it audible; some
Americans claimed they could see it in the night sky, a bright dot moving
rapidly through the darkness.[2]

After a decade of intense anti-Soviet propaganda, Americans had come to believe that the USSR was a brutish, backward, and totalitarian society in which individual creativity had been extinguished. Yet *Sputnik* demonstrated that a communist nation with a command economy could outperform the free world in scientific achievement. The R-7 rocket that carried the sphere into space produced 220,000 pounds of thrust at liftoff, powerful enough to break free of Earth's gravity and put its cargo into orbit. And the implications were terrifying: if the USSR could accomplish this feat, it could surely place an atomic bomb on a missile and launch it at the United States.

Inside the White House, Eisenhower hastily gathered his military and scientific advisers to discuss the Soviet achievement. He wanted to know why the USSR had beaten the United States into space. Undersecretary of Defense Donald Quarles explained: In 1955 the president had told the defense establishment to put all its energies into building long-range missiles for the purpose of carrying nuclear warheads. The effort to launch a satellite had been considered of secondary importance since its value was scientific rather than military. There was "no doubt," said Quarles, that the United States could have launched a satellite earlier, but there had been no urgency about the matter.

This must have been an awkward moment. The decision to sidetrack satellite development now looked shortsighted. CIA chief Allen Dulles told the president that the USSR had done what the United States had not: it had combined its rocket research with its satellite program and would reap the huge propaganda reward of having put *Sputnik* into orbit. Dulles admitted that in the Middle East and the underdeveloped nations, the Soviet success was getting great play.[3]

The American press now engaged in recrimination and soul-searching. Weekly magazines *Time* and *Newsweek* rushed out articles bemoaning Soviet superiority in science and technology. *Life* magazine called *Sputnik* "an epochal breakthrough into the new age of space exploration" but wondered in a headline, "Why Did the U.S. Lose the Race?" Democrats provided ready answers. Senator George Smathers of Florida blamed "government ineptness and smugness." Senator Henry Jackson of Washington accused Eisenhower of failing to make the missile program a priority. "Russia has dealt a devastating blow to U.S. prestige as the world's technical leader," he declared. Senator Stuart Symington of Missouri, who had served as the first secretary of the air force under Truman and had his eye on the 1960 presidential race, asserted that "ironclad budgets have harmed our defense." Lyndon Johnson claimed, "The Soviets have beaten us at our own game—daring scientific advances in the atomic age."[4]

During a news conference five days after the launch, the first question to the president, from Merriman Smith of United Press, carried a tinge of accusation: "Russia has launched an earth satellite. They also claim to have had a successful firing of an intercontinental ballistic missile, none of which this country has done. I ask you, sir, what are we going to do about it?"

Eisenhower tried to reassure the public. He downplayed the Soviet achievement and said the United States planned to put a satellite into orbit by the end of 1958. Since the satellite was little more than a scientific curiosity, he suggested, there was no need for haste. "Never has it been considered a race," he stated, fooling no one. As to the missile used in launching *Sputnik*, the Soviets had proved "they can hurl an object a considerable distance." But could their rockets hit a target anywhere on Earth? Ike was doubtful. "Until you know something about their accuracy, you know nothing at all about their usefulness in warfare." When asked if the presence of "a Russian satellite whirling about the world" made him anxious about the nation's security, Ike replied firmly, "That does not raise my apprehensions, not one iota."[5]

Eisenhower's nonchalance did nothing to quiet the national outcry. Columnist Arthur Krock, normally an administration supporter, asserted that *Sputnik* had vindicated the critics: on Ike's watch, America had fallen behind. Moreover the USSR had scored an undisputed propaganda victory, one that could pull neutral nations toward the Soviet orbit. The United States would have to rethink its entire defense effort, Krock argued, and the Democrats would be quite right in putting the heat on the administration for its lackluster space effort. There would be political consequences: "Eisenhower's image as the soldier to whom the people can safely entrust every military decision will be permanently damaged."[6]

Walter Lippmann, often a sharp critic of Eisenhower, agreed: *Sputnik* represented a failure of American science, ideas, and daring. American leaders had become complacent and anti-intellectual, nurturing a "popular disrespect for, and even a suspicion of, brains and originality of thought." Low-brow culture had dampened the intellectual firepower of the country. Prosperity had become "a narcotic," while President Eisenhower, dozing in "a kind of partial retirement," let the nation drift. Reflecting these morose sentiments, the stock market took its sharpest plunge in two years.[7]

II

The picture worsened in November. In fact the administration endured a series of hammer blows that badly dented Eisenhower's image. The Soviets sent another satellite into space on November 3, this time with a dog named Laika on board. Immediately labeled "Muttnik" by the jocular press, this satellite weighed six times more than *Sputnik I*. The rocket that carried it into orbit generated over a million pounds of thrust—a major scientific achievement. And in placing a dog on board that survived the launch (but died hours later), the Soviets had taken the first step toward putting humans into space. Laika's craft reached an altitude of over 1,000 miles above the Earth, twice as high as *Sputnik I*. Timed to coincide with the 40th anniversary of the Bolshevik Revolution, the launch prompted enormous pride and self-congratulation in Moscow. Khrushchev taunted the Americans at his anniversary address to a huge Communist Party assembly, with Mao Zedong at his side: the Soviet *Sputniks* "are circling the Earth and are waiting for the Americans and other satellites to join them!"[8]

Americans were once again amazed but rueful about Soviet technical prowess. "We have at last been out-gadgeted," the *Washington Post* editorial page sighed. Stewart Alsop in his column declared that *Sputnik II* "proves beyond serious question that the Western world is in deadly danger." The Democrats moved quickly to capitalize on the political opportunity. The day after the *Sputnik II* launch, the Senate scheduled hearings, to be chaired by Majority Leader Lyndon Johnson, to probe America's lackluster missile program. Congressmen who a few months earlier had railed against government spending now demanded to know why the missile program had been starved for funds.[9]

Just days later, on November 7, the National Security Council met to hear the recommendations of a large blue-ribbon panel that had been commissioned the previous April to examine the state of America's readiness to survive a nuclear attack. Under the chairmanship of H. Rowan Gaither, one of the founders of the RAND Corporation and a former president of the Ford Foundation, some 90 defense experts had come to the depressing conclusion that the United States was woefully unprepared to deter and to survive a large Soviet nuclear "first strike." The United States relied upon a fleet of over 1,600 medium- and long-range nuclear-armed bombers, directed by Gen. Curtis LeMay's Strategic Air Command, as its principal means of deterring a Soviet attack. But with Soviet advances in rocketry, these airplanes could soon be obsolete. "By 1959," the Gaither Report concluded, "the USSR may be able to launch an attack with ICBMs carrying megaton warheads against which SAC will be almost completely vulnerable." The United States had no way to defend against such an attack, nor could it protect enough of its bombers to ensure the delivery of a sufficiently lethal counterattack. The way the Gaither group saw it, America was now more vulnerable to a Soviet nuclear attack than ever.[10]

Eisenhower greeted the Gaither Report like a skunk at a picnic. He did not like its doom-laden tone, and he simply did not believe that the USSR would launch an unprovoked nuclear attack. He had taken the measure of Soviet leaders at Geneva in 1955 and concluded that they were more inclined to avoid war than start one. If anything, the report reinforced Eisenhower's core belief that nuclear war must be avoided at all costs. And the report carried enormous financial implications: the measures it proposed to defend the nation would cost an additional $4 billion per year over the next five years—on top of the $38 billion per year already spent on defense. Miffed that Ike refused to take the report seriously, members of the panel leaked much of its contents to the press, causing further headaches for the president.[11]

Try though he might to dismiss the anxious counsel of the Gaither team, Eisenhower received still more bad news just a few days later from Allen Dulles and the CIA. A long and detailed National Intelligence Estimate titled "Main Trends in Soviet Capabilities and Policies, 1957–1962," presented a sobering picture. This analysis depicted the USSR in the midst of a spurt of economic, technological, and military growth. The testing of two long-range missiles in the summer of 1957, in addition to the *Sputnik* triumph, clearly revealed an advanced Soviet missile program. By 1959, this report concluded, the Soviets would probably have about 10 prototype operational ICBMs that could carry a megaton warhead a distance of 5,500 nautical miles—a capability the Americans did not yet possess. And the USSR had made even more rapid progress with its intermediate-range missiles, which could travel some 1,000 miles—enough to hit Western Europe. Those missiles would be ready for use by 1958. Assessing all this information, a CIA review panel concluded that the U.S. missile program was "lagging by two to three years" behind the Soviets'. "The country is in a period of grave national emergency," the experts concluded. For the first time, intelligence analysts began to fear that a significant gap, soon to be called "the missile gap," had opened up between the two cold war adversaries.[12]

In an effort to calm troubled waters, Eisenhower gave two televised speeches, on November 7 and 13, 1957. Hastily prepared by Arthur Larson, the theorist of "modern Republicanism" who was now running the U.S. Information Agency, the texts had a certain "Father Knows Best" quality to them. Rather than ring the alarm bells, Eisenhower sought to reassure the public. The United States was immensely strong, the president asserted. It was spending an average of $42 billion a year on its defense and was "well ahead of the Soviets in the nuclear field." As evidence of American progress in the missile program, he displayed next to him in the Oval Office the nose cone of a Jupiter missile that had been shot 270 miles into space and then retrieved at sea by the navy. *Sputnik* gave no cause for panic: "Certainly we need to feel a high sense of urgency. But this does not mean that we should mount our charger and try to ride off in all directions at once." He cautioned against rash spending: "There is much more to the matter of security than the mere spending of money." Instead of more money for missiles, he advocated a broad investment in scientific education across the nation's schools and announced that he was bringing James Killian of MIT directly into the White House to lead the President's Science Advisory Committee.[13]

Such parsimony at a moment of nationwide anxiety over *Sputnik* failed to quiet the president's critics. Lippmann panned the performance, saying Ike had sought "to dampen down and to soothe, rather than to awaken and to arouse." Senator John Kennedy was even less charitable. "The people of America," he said in a speech in Topeka, Kansas, "are no longer willing to be lulled by paternalistic reassurances, spoon-fed science fiction predictions, or pious platitudes of faith and hope." He denounced Eisenhower's "complacent miscalculations" and "penny-pinching" as the source of the lag in missile production. The country demanded action.[14]

No doubt the strain of those anxious days weighed on the president. The combined Little Rock and *Sputnik* crises left him exhausted. On November 25 he was in the Oval Office, awaiting the arrival of King Mohammed V of Morocco for a state dinner, when he felt dizzy and found that he was having difficulty reading his official papers. Suddenly he felt cold and his body grew numb. When he tried to speak to his secretary, Ann Whitman, he was able only to mumble. Dr. Snyder arrived within moments and got Eisenhower to bed. Neurologists examined the president and concluded that he had suffered a small stroke—an occlusion of the left middle cerebral artery—but that his condition would be temporary. Richard Nixon took the president's place at the dinner for their royal guest. After two days of bed rest, Ike took Mamie to Gettysburg for a quiet Thanksgiving holiday.[15]

Almost immediately voices in the press called for Eisenhower to resign. Drew Pearson, the influential muckraker, asserted that in view of the high-stakes *Sputnik* crisis, Eisenhower should step down. Stewart Alsop agreed. The president's third illness in two and a half years, coming at a time of "major crisis," raised the question of whether he ought to continue. *Newsweek* polled 20 leading newspaper editors; half of them thought Eisenhower should resign or delegate all power to Nixon until he recovered.[16]

However, Eisenhower improved rapidly and returned to Washington on December 2 for his weekly cabinet meeting, followed the next day by a meeting with top congressional leaders. He looked well enough, but that afternoon, he met with Nixon and the two discussed Ike's health. Eisenhower said he was determined to attend to his duties as president, even if his speech was still a bit troubled. He admitted he had occasional difficulties recalling certain words, giving the example of *thermostat*. Otherwise he felt well, though he told Nixon that if his health prevented him from functioning fully, he would have to do some "very hard and tough thinking about the future."[17]

These had been troubling times for Eisenhower. His son John later wrote that the "fall of 1957 and early part of 1958 constituted probably the lowest point" in his father's presidency. The crisis in the South, the shock of *Sputnik*, the failing economy, and now another health scare. Eisenhower had faced serious crises before, from Indochina and Taiwan to Hungary and Suez, as well as Little Rock. But the *Sputnik* crisis was different from these, for it struck at the fundamental claim of his administration that it was possible to wage the cold war in a patient, disciplined, and fiscally sensible manner. *Sputnik* opened the door to sharp criticism: Had America been sleeping while the Soviets stole a march in the missile race? Had the warrior-statesman failed to keep the nation prepared? Eisenhower's answers to these pointed questions would define the rest of his presidency.[18]

III

That *Sputnik* became a major and enduring political crisis for Eisenhower had everything to do with Lyndon Johnson. On November 25, 1957, the same day that Eisenhower suffered his stroke, Johnson began his promised congressional hearings into the alleged failings of the U.S. missile program.

Johnson had emerged in 1957 as Eisenhower's chief political antagonist, gutting his civil rights bill and controlling the Senate and the Washington press corps with enormous skill. With the president incapacitated, the energetic and forceful Texan sought to take center stage. *Sputnik* offered him an opportunity to keep his name in the headlines by leading a well-publicized investigation into the American failure to beat the Soviets into space. From late November through early January his Preparedness Subcommittee of the Senate Armed Services Committee called in hundreds of scientists, military leaders, and government officials to explain why America had fallen behind and what must be done to catch up to the USSR. Although Johnson theatrically stressed his desire to keep politics out of the hearings and promised not to "wander up any blind alleys of partisanship," his committee brought out into the open a number of critical facts that made Ike look bad and lent support to the perennial theme of a dangerously disengaged chief executive.[19]

The subcommittee's first witness was Edward Teller, the controversial Hungarian-born scientist who designed the hydrogen bomb. Teller had been a leading critic of J. Robert Oppenheimer and was loathed by many in the intellectual and scientific world. But he spoke his mind, as Johnson expected, and delivered a stern rebuke to the idea, recently mooted by Eisenhower, that *Sputnik* posed no military threat. "It has great military significance," Teller countered, because it showed how advanced the Soviets were in rocket propulsion, guidance systems, and fuel technology. The matter was simple: if the Soviets controlled space, they could control the Earth. In a spellbinding two-hour performance to a packed hearing room, Teller detailed the many ways that Soviet science had left the Americans behind and profoundly vulnerable.[20]

Others concurred. Vannevar Bush, the leading science and engineering administrator during the Second World War and now at MIT, stressed the huge advances the Soviets had made. "We have been complacent and we have been smug," he sternly insisted. The persistence of interservice rivalry slowed advances, he said, and the nation had paid insufficient attention to scientific education. All this had to change if the United States was to survive. Gen. James Doolittle, who had helped reorganize the CIA in 1954, suggested the Defense Department be overhauled to strengthen the secretary of defense and impose order on the Joint Chiefs of Staff. "We must develop a sense of urgency," he demanded. Lt. Gen. James Gavin, army deputy chief of staff for research and development, insisted the Soviets were ahead of the

United States in almost every area of weapons and technology. And Wernher von Braun, the man who directed the Nazi V-2 program and who had been designing missiles for the army since the end of the war, gave shocking testimony about the bureaucratic tangles and lack of steady funding that had slowed missile research. Von Braun said the army could have launched a satellite in 1956, but the Pentagon halted his efforts. And so the hearings went, painting the picture of a defense establishment that was badly organized, led by a weak secretary of defense, slowed by endless committees, tangled in red tape, underfunded, and beset by interservice rivalry.[21]

Worse was yet to come, for the most significant and damaging testimony given to Johnson's committee came from a leading member of the administration—none other than Allen Dulles. On November 26, the second day of the hearings, the CIA chief, accompanied by Herbert Scoville, the assistant director for scientific research, gave the committee a top-secret briefing about Soviet military and technological capabilities. Dulles informed the senators that since the *Sputnik* launch, his agency's analysts had grown increasingly worried about the pace of Soviet missile production. There did indeed seem to be a missile gap opening up between the two superpowers. And the danger was growing.

Many historians have claimed that Eisenhower never worried much about the alleged missile gap because he had available to him the top-secret photographs taken by the U-2 spy plane that showed a tiny and unimpressive Soviet missile program. This oft-repeated assertion is misleading. In fact the 13 U-2 flights the CIA conducted over the USSR between June and October 1957 provided no comfort at all. These overflights reaped a bonanza of information, capturing pictures of the Soviet missile testing facilities at Kapustin Yar, near Astrakhan, as well as the nuclear weapons research site at Semipalatinsk in northeast Kazakhstan. The flights also discovered an intercontinental ballistic missile site at Tyuratam in southern Kazakhstan, from which *Sputnik* would soon be launched. The U-2 photographs taken in the month before *Sputnik* revealed a large and growing Soviet nuclear weapons and missile testing program. Exactly how far the Soviet Union's new rockets could travel, how many it planned to build, how accurate they were—all that remained unknown. But the liftoff of the R-7 rocket on October 4, with the *Sputnik* satellite on board, confirmed Americans' worst fears. The Soviets clearly did have an ICBM and were trying to build more.[22]

The U-2 flights provided priceless information, yet because of the extreme risk of the illegal overflights—Ike believed a shoot-down of a U-2 might well trigger a war—he did not persevere with them. From mid-October 1957 until December 1959, a period of more than two years, he approved only two flights into Soviet airspace. The U-2 was all but grounded. Instead of illegal overflights, CIA analysts had to rely on a second means to observe Soviet rocketry. In early 1955 the United States had deployed a sophisticated radar system in eastern Turkey to monitor tests of Soviet missiles. This testing data, far from reassuring the Americans, showed the astonishing frequency of Soviet missile tests—nearly 300 between 1953 and 1957—and the approximate range and altitude of the missiles the Soviets were developing. Although most of the missiles they tested were short- or intermediate-range, it was clear they were trying to achieve long-range ICBM capability. CIA analysts combined the radar data, the U-2 photographs, and their analysis of the rocket that carried *Sputnik* into orbit, and concluded that they had *underestimated* Soviet missile capabilities.[23]

This explains why, when Allen Dulles went before the Preparedness Subcommittee on November 26, he presented such an arresting account of Soviet missile progress—even more dire than the report he had given to the NSC just a few weeks earlier. The USSR, the CIA now claimed, would have an operational ICBM big enough to carry a one-ton nuclear warhead some 5,000 miles as early as 1958—a year sooner than predicted by the Gaither Report. If present trends continued, it could have 100 ICBMs by the middle of 1959 and 500 by the middle of 1960. This information, though classified, was a bombshell. Putting all his authority and credibility on the line, Dulles told a handful of senators that the Soviets were about to take a dangerous lead in the missile race.[24]

Dulles wrote these alarming new figures into a revised intelligence estimate on Soviet missile capabilities, given to the NSC on December 17, 1957. Labeled SNIE 11-10-57, this document asserted that the Soviet ICBM program had "an extremely high priority" and was even running on a "crash basis." In the midst of the *Sputnik* crisis and the Johnson hearings, these initial predictions of an imminent wave of new Soviet ICBMs directly contradicted Eisenhower's public reassurances. Dulles knew exactly what he was doing: a dire report about a Soviet lead in the missile race would prompt congressional outcry and lead to increased dollars for the CIA's espionage capabilities. Dulles therefore gave Johnson and his fellow committee member Stuart Symington a magnificent opportunity to use the still-raw intelligence the CIA had gathered to damage the Eisenhower administration. By the end of the hearings, a bleak picture had emerged: the scientists, the military experts, the engineers, and especially the top intelligence analysts now asserted that America faced mortal danger and that if the nation did not respond immediately, the Soviet Union would turn its mastery of science into domination of the world.[25]

IV

Were things that bad? Was America truly vulnerable? Ike did not think so, and his confidence derived less from his limited knowledge of the Soviet missile program than from his detailed knowledge of the vast American one. Contrary to the claims of his critics, Eisenhower had been pushing hard to prod the Defense Department to develop a new arsenal of nuclear weapons and the means to deliver them. Although he had done a poor job of informing the public and shaping the narrative, by the end of 1958 the United States stood on the threshold of a dramatic breakthrough in the missile and space race.

After World War II, America's missile program evolved slowly, taking a backseat to the development of the Strategic Air Command's fleet of long-range bombers, which remained the chief delivery system of America's nuclear deterrent. Still, missile research quietly went ahead, leavened by the knowledge and experience of German scientists like Wernher von Braun, whose V-2 rocket served as a prototype for the U.S. Army's first ballistic missile, the Redstone. By September 1956 Von Braun's team had developed a rocket called Jupiter-C, an intermediate-range missile that had the potential, its designers believed, to place a satellite in orbit.[26]

But they did not get the chance to prove their claim before the USSR put *Sputnik* into space. The reason for this missed opportunity was simple: Eisenhower had decided in 1955 to make the construction of an intercontinental ballistic missile the overriding priority of the U.S. missile program. He sidetracked satellite research into Project Vanguard, a second-tier program run by the navy. This decision followed the recommendation of the February 1955 Killian Panel, which declared long-range rockets vital to sustain the effectiveness of American deterrence. In late July 1955 Eisenhower received a briefing by air force missile engineers, who insisted that the rapidly shrinking size and weight of thermonuclear weapons combined with increasingly powerful rockets had brought the United States and the Soviet Union to the edge of a new era of missile technology in which the Great Powers could strike devastating and unstoppable blows at one another. After a summer of debate the National Security Council determined that beating the Soviets to the ICBM was "a matter of great urgency" and that building the long-range missile was "a program of the highest priority above all others."[27]

Under direct presidential pressure, missile research made rapid progress. The Department of Defense gave the air force the green light to build two ICBM systems, the Atlas and the Titan. Once operational, each of these behemoths would be able to carry warheads with the explosive power of 1.4 megatons and 4 megatons, respectively, over a distance of 5,500 miles. (By comparison, all the bombs used in World War II amounted to approximately 3 megatons.) A single one of these missiles could obliterate a large city in a flash. The air force planned to have the Atlas missiles operational by 1959 and the Titans by 1960.

ICBMs alone were insufficient, however. The Pentagon also wanted intermediate-range ballistic missiles (IRBMs), designed for deployment in Europe as a counterweight to Soviet pressure on America's NATO allies. At the end of 1955 the Defense Department had added an IRBM program to its high-priority list and divided up the spoils across the services. The air force got funds to proceed with a land-based IRBM called Thor; the army would move ahead with Jupiter; and the navy would develop a sea-based IRBM called Polaris, for use on ships and submarines. Despite the obvious risks of overlapping efforts and interservice rivalries, Eisenhower was determined to press ahead with all of these rocket designs. To his advisers he said "he was absolutely determined not to tolerate any fooling with this thing. We had simply got to achieve such missiles as promptly as possible, if only because of the enormous psychological and political significance of ballistic missiles."[28]

Not since the Manhattan Project of World War II had the United States invested such effort in the production of a weapon system, and the cost was enormous. Spending on the IRBM and ICBM programs together jumped from $161 million in 1955 to $515 million in 1956 and $1.3 billion in 1957. These rockets, built in conjunction with private industry, created an immense web of military procurement. For the Atlas rocket, the Convair Corporation of San Diego built the frame, General Electric built the guidance systems, the Rocketdyne division of North American Aviation built the engines, and Burroughs Corporation of St. Louis built its computers. The Glenn L. Martin Company built the Titan missile, using guidance systems provided by Bell Telephone, engines built by Aerojet, and computers built by Remington Rand. In all, the Atlas, Titan, and Thor projects involved 18 principal contractors, 200 subcontractors, and 200,000 parts suppliers. The major contractors alone employed some 70,000 people. The missile race fueled the dramatic expansion of the military-industrial complex.

Despite the enormous complexity of these missiles and the engineering challenges they presented, American scientists made rapid progress. In September 1956 Von Braun's Redstone missile, Jupiter-C, fired a test rocket a distance of 3,355 miles. In 1957 the Thor missile went through eight flight tests and by October 1957 had proven it could fly on target over 2,000 miles. In June the air force started tests of the Atlas ICBM in a rush to make it operational. Meanwhile the army developed various short-range nuclear-tipped missiles with endearing, folksy names such as Corporal, Little John, Honest John, and Davy Crockett. And the navy pushed ahead with innovative plans for Polaris, a solid-fuel missile (actually built by Lockheed) that promised greater stability on oceangoing vessels than the liquid-fueled IRBMs. The Polaris program started development in late 1956; less than four years later, on July 20, 1960, the submarine USS *George Washington* launched a Polaris missile while submerged—a breakthrough of enormous strategic significance.

Plenty of missteps dogged the missile program. On December 6, 1957, America's first attempt to launch a satellite ended in disaster. At Cape Canaveral, in front of a crowd of media and onlookers, a Vanguard rocket shuddered, rose two feet in the air, then exploded in a fireball. The failure dealt "a stunning new blow to American prestige," the *Los Angeles Times* concluded. Lyndon Johnson called it "one of the best publicized and most humiliating failures in our history." Wags renamed Vanguard "Sputternik."[29]

The engineers learned from their mistakes, as scientists do. On December 17 the air force launched the first fully successful test flight of an American ICBM, the Atlas. Just when *Sputnik* triggered an avalanche of criticism, Defense Secretary Neil McElroy, who had replaced Charles Wilson in the fall, told Eisenhower that December 1957 had been the "most active and successful month to date in the ballistic missile flight test program." Within two years—by the end of 1959—squadrons of Atlas missiles, each 100 times more powerful than the Hiroshima bomb, stood as silent sentinels across the American landscape, ready for liftoff. The still more powerful Titan missile would be available for use by 1960, and a second-generation solid-fuel missile called Minuteman was being rushed into production. Missile bases sprang up in North and South Dakota, Montana, Nebraska, Wyoming, Colorado, Kansas, California, Texas—eventually 19 states in all. Meanwhile the construction of the signature long-range bombers of the cold war, the B-47 and the B-52, proceeded at breakneck speed; hundreds of these monstrous aircraft were kept in the sky 24 hours a day, armed with nuclear weapons and ready to fly to Moscow on the president's order.[30]

Eisenhower pushed forward this huge expansion of the U.S. nuclear deterrent because he had come to accept a basic paradox of the cold war: that the only way to avoid using weapons of mass destruction was to build more of them. He did not do this only as a result of the *Sputnik* crisis. These projects had been in the works for years. By the time *Sputnik* had made its first trip around the Earth in October 1957, the United States was well on its way to building the strategic "triad"—a three-pronged deterrent of bombers and land-based and submarine-based ballistic missiles—that defined America's nuclear arsenal for the entire cold war. The accusation of complacency or smugness thrown at Eisenhower bore no relation to the facts. The nation stood on the threshold of breakthroughs in every conceivable kind of strategic weapon and rocket technology. Perhaps the Americans were slightly behind the Soviets in missile research; perhaps not. As of late 1957 nobody knew for certain. But Eisenhower did know this: in the race to build the next generation of nuclear weapons, the United States planned to win.[31]

V

Eisenhower's response to the *Sputnik* crisis encompassed more than missile construction. In fact he moved decisively on three fronts—diplomatic, institutional, and political—to take control of the problem. In mid-December 1957 he took a much-publicized trip to meet with the heads of state of the NATO countries. It was only three weeks since his stroke, but he knew the world needed to see a vigorous president in command. And he himself viewed the trip as a personal test: he feared that he might end up like Woodrow Wilson, whose severe stroke in late 1919 had left him incapacitated and irrelevant. "I was going to make sure it would not happen in my case," he later wrote.[32]

Eisenhower arrived in Paris on a cold, gray day but found the Parisians in a warm and welcoming mood: his route from the airport was lined with cheering onlookers who seemed to have forgotten the bitter dispute over Suez just a year earlier. Ike and John Foster Dulles—still recovering from his recent surgery—brought with them what they considered an enormously valuable gift. The United States proposed to construct in Europe a stockpile of atomic weapons, held in joint custody between the Americans and Europeans, and the United States would agree to transfer some of its new Thor and Jupiter IRBMs to Europe. These weapons would show America's determination to defend its allies from Soviet nuclear blackmail. The countries hosting such missiles would share with NATO's supreme commander (always an American) any decision about their use. Sending IRBMs to Europe seemed a sensible way to balance the Soviet lead in the missile race. While explaining to the press his enthusiasm for nuclear proliferation, Dulles asked why the Soviets should be allowed to threaten Europe with nuclear weapons while the Europeans could defend themselves only with "weapons from the pre-atomic age." The more nukes on the doorstep of the USSR, the better, as far as Dulles was concerned.[33]

In addition to offering nuclear missiles to European allies, Eisenhower beefed up defense spending. Over the New Year holiday he closeted himself with his advisers at Gettysburg and hammered out the details of the 1959 budget proposal to Congress. He decided to ask Congress for immediate passage of a supplemental spending package of $1.3 billion to accelerate missile production and improve early-warning radar systems. He also asked for a $40 billion defense budget—about $1.5 billion larger than the previous year. Overall his budget request was $74 billion, a substantial increase from the previous year and the largest peacetime budget in U.S. history to that time. After years of fighting the upward trend of government spending, Ike admitted the need to plow more money into defense.

Congress wanted more than spending, though: it clamored for leadership. Given Eisenhower's recent stroke, congressional critics worried about his capacity to lead. "The president himself, after five years of apparent immunity to attack, is now on the hot seat," one *Washington Post* writer claimed. "In the words of the politically sacrilegious, his halo has slipped." The Democratic speaker of the house, Sam Rayburn, opined that Ike had "not shown enough urgency"; he needed to respond to a nation that had been "disturbed and humiliated" by *Sputnik*. "We are in a struggle for survival," he insisted.[34]

Eisenhower knew what the critics were saying, and he planned to answer them in his State of the Union address, scheduled for January 9, 1958. Commentators believed the speech would be "one of the most important of his career." Just after noon on the big day, Ike and Mamie left the White House in a huge Chrysler Imperial, itself a tribute to the rocket age, with its enormous tailfins, rocket-like fenders over each headlight, and taillights formed to look like aircraft gun sights. They drove down Independence Avenue to the south entrance of the Capitol. Mamie, in a natty gray wool suit, mink stole, and blue pillbox hat, proceeded into the Executive Gallery of the House chamber, receiving a thunderous ovation. Eisenhower waited in Speaker Rayburn's office until he was beckoned to the floor of the House. Doorkeeper William "Fishbait" Miller announced the arrival of the president, and the members erupted in hearty applause.[35]

During his relatively short speech, Eisenhower delivered what had been lacking so far since the October 4 *Sputnik* launch: a clear sense of direction for the country in the new missile age. He finally admitted that Americans had been spooked by *Sputnik* and demanded a response. He proposed a series of "imperative" actions to fix the problems that the *Sputnik* crisis had revealed. He wanted a reorganized Defense Department to halt the crippling interservice rivalries that had slowed missile progress. He wanted an immediate infusion of cash to improve radar capability, bomber dispersal, missile production, nuclear submarines, and mobile conventional forces. He wanted to help America's allies by lowering barriers to trade and by sharing nuclear secrets so they could better defend themselves. And he wanted major federal investment in scientific education.

Such actions would ensure that America's military and scientific power, already strong, would never lapse. Such a program would require "sacrifice"—a word he used throughout the speech. The people must know that to counter the Soviet Union's "total cold war" against America, they would have to toil and strive with common purpose. "The world is waiting to see," he declared, "how wisely and decisively a free representative government will now act."[36]

The speech reflected Eisenhower's belief that while arms were certainly expensive and might have seemed wasteful, they provided the foundation for order in a disordered world. He asked Americans to accept the basic unpleasant fact about the cold war: To deter war, America must prepare for it. And that meant investing in science, technology, and education as well as arms manufacturing. For Eisenhower, the purpose of such a titanic effort was not war but peace—an armed and anxious peace, but peace nonetheless. Here lay the basic national security principles of the Age of Eisenhower.

Critics hailed the speech as a success. It was "forceful and incisive in content, spirited and vigorous in delivery," wrote speechwriter Emmet Hughes. Sam Rayburn called it "the strongest, I think, the president has delivered to the Congress." The *Washington Post* described it as among the best speeches of his presidency. "The President Shows His Stuff," was the *Los Angeles Times* headline. It also mattered that Ike *looked* so good. Arthur Krock wrote in the *New York Times* that the speech swept away any lingering doubts about the president's physical vigor. This was no "semi-invalid but a man who seemed to be in excellent physical condition. . . . The sense of relief as to his condition was tangible on the floor and in the galleries."[37]

Perhaps even greater relief flooded across the land on January 31, 1958, when at long last the United States successfully put its own satellite into orbit. Belying his breezy assertion that there was no satellite "race," Eisenhower wanted an American craft in orbit immediately and pressed his scientists to get it done. He no doubt regretted his decision of 1955 to downgrade satellite research, but now he wanted results. When the navy's Vanguard rocket blew up on the launchpad in mid-December, Von Braun's army team in Huntsville saw its chance. They adapted a Jupiter-C rocket with an extra booster stage and strapped on a 30-pound pod of instruments that included a small radio transmitter. They called the satellite *Explorer*, and on the night of January 31 they successfully shot it into space from Cape Canaveral.

The president received word while at the Augusta golf club. "I sure feel a lot better now," he happily sighed on hearing the news. As he put it in his memoirs, "A long and difficult period had ended." Americans cheered this welcome sign of a comeback in the space race. Officials in the nation's capital issued happy statements, and down in Huntsville, Alabama, where the Jupiter-C was made, townsfolk rushed into the streets in celebration. One citizen carried a hastily daubed placard reading "Move Over Sputnik: Space Is Ours!"[38]

VI

As he plotted his post-*Sputnik* strategy, Eisenhower benefited from the guidance of James Killian and the President's Science Advisory Committee. The men who joined PSAC came from leading universities, and many had records of extensive wartime and public service. This group of technocrats offered Eisenhower well-informed judgments about science and technology that he could not find among the military, and they applied cutting-edge research to matters of national security. Killian saw PSAC as "a voice of sense and moderation" in the midst of the *Sputnik* panic. The scientists came to admire Eisenhower enormously. Killian described Eisenhower's deep interest and his "extraordinary capacity to evoke the best from those around him." He was "exceptionally responsive to innovative ideas." Eisenhower in turn felt deeply devoted to the men he called "my scientists." He told Killian much later, "This bunch of scientists was one of the few groups that I encountered in Washington who seemed to be there to help the country and not help themselves."[39]

With PSAC, Eisenhower pressed on with a series of crucial administrative actions. On January 27 he announced a major federal commitment to scientific education. The idea that American schools and universities had fallen behind the Soviets in the fields of engineering, math, and physics had been suggested to him by his science advisers in their first meeting after the *Sputnik* launch. Edwin Land, the genius behind the U-2 plane, spoke to the president eloquently about the failures of American scientific education. The Soviets, he said, "regard science both as an essential tool and as a way of life. They are teaching their young people to enjoy science." The president must inspire the country to embrace scientific inquiry rather than material pursuits.[40]

Eisenhower became a great enthusiast of science education, and in January 1958 he described an ambitious plan to overhaul science teaching, train a new generation of science teachers, provide scholarships and graduate fellowships for work in scientific fields, and promote the study of foreign languages. He wanted to make science a prominent part of American life. He saw his plan as an emergency program to enhance the nation's security; it was going to cost $1 billion over four years—a huge investment. Congress, under the glare of the *Sputnik* crisis, fell in line behind the proposal, and in September 1958 Eisenhower signed the National Defense Education Act (NDEA) into law.[41]

Eisenhower also embraced the idea that the country needed a federal agency to lead nonmilitary research on space, and on April 2 he proposed the creation of the National Aeronautics and Space Agency (NASA). The idea grew in part from Eisenhower's conclusion that to leave space exploration in the hands of the military would stifle innovation and encourage more fighting among the services over money. Most of his scientific advisers agreed, urging him to commit resources to space exploration as a matter of human curiosity rather than warfare. And the best way to attract leading minds to work on space was to separate it from purely military projects. In remarkably rapid fashion Congress passed legislation creating NASA, and Eisenhower signed the bill on July 29, 1958.[42]

Eager to suppress the persistent interservice rivalry inside the defense establishment that had slowed missile development, Eisenhower on April 3 submitted to Congress a plan to strengthen the powers of the secretary of defense over the individual military services. The plan would allow the secretary to channel funds directly into key programs—a change from the usual practice, in which each service went to Congress separately and sought money for itself. After a summer's worth of negotiations, Congress passed, and Eisenhower signed, the Defense Reorganization Act of 1958. It allowed greater concentration of authority in the hands of the secretary over the individual service chiefs and also approved the creation of a new director of defense research and engineering—the "missile czar" that Congress had called for. Defense Secretary McElroy gave the job to Herbert York, a nuclear physicist and Manhattan Project veteran who was running the Lawrence Livermore facility in California.[43]

These three major legislative moves—the NDEA, NASA, and Defense Reorganization Act—marked an extraordinary period of activity for the president and Congress, and they all responded directly to the challenge of *Sputnik*. Combined with his beefed-up defense budget, these actions revealed a shift away from the small-government Republicanism that Eisenhower cherished. The missile race, and for that matter the cold war, required robust military-industrial-scientific collaboration on a nationwide scale, the sort of thing that only the federal government could direct. As the leading historian of the Space Age has said, Eisenhower had to discard "the old verities about limited government, local initiative, balanced budgets, and individualism. The United States had to respond in kind to Soviet technocracy."[44]

Some of the actions Ike took were invisible to the public. On February 10, 1958, just two weeks after the successful launch of the *Explorer* satellite, James Killian and Edwin Land brought Eisenhower a proposal for yet another technological marvel. Ever since the U-2 aircraft had begun to fly missions over the Soviet Union in search of photographic intelligence, Eisenhower had been anxious to avoid violations of Soviet airspace. With the success of *Explorer*, Killian and Land now envisioned a replacement for the spy plane: a satellite that could take photographs and then jettison a recoverable capsule with the film inside. The satellite could be designed to emit no signals so that it would be "completely covert," and either aircraft or naval vessels would recover the dropped film. Because of the scale and complexity of the satellite program, it would need the cooperation of the air force, the CIA, and a new office in the Defense Department created on February 7, 1958, called the Advanced Research Projects Agency. Eisenhower applauded the plan but insisted on absolute secrecy. "Only a handful of people should know about it," he ordered.[45]

In mid-April Eisenhower orally approved what became known as the Corona Project, which planned to use Thor rockets to put camera-equipped satellites into orbit above the USSR, Eastern Europe, and China. It was a long hard road to success: the first 12 Corona satellites malfunctioned. But on August 19, 1960, a Corona satellite that had passed over the communist bloc successfully dropped its payload of film to Earth by parachute, where a waiting air force C-119 snatched it out of the sky using a long grappling hook extending from its fuselage. Six days later Allen Dulles and Eisenhower stared at photographs of the Soviet Union taken from space. "This one satellite mission," said the secret CIA history of the program, "yielded photo coverage of a greater area than the total produced by all of the U-2 missions over the Soviet Union." For the next decade the United States used the top-secret Corona satellites to take detailed photographs of virtually every corner of the globe.[46]

By the summer of 1958 Eisenhower had established his post-*Sputnik* strategy for the space race: he accelerated the ongoing missile programs and channeled $4 billion more into the defense budget; he brought leading scientists into a close working partnership with the White House; he strengthened the powers of the Pentagon to control interservice squabbling; he intensified work on a secret reconnaissance satellite; and he signed key pieces of legislation that reshaped the role of the federal government in space exploration and science education. In doing these things he framed outer space as a new frontier of cold war rivalry, requiring the United States "to be strong and bold in space technology" in order to "enhance the prestige of the United States among the peoples of the world." Above all, in these years he set in motion a great national effort to construct and deploy a sophisticated missile capability with truly awesome destructive power, such that by 1961 the United States could wipe out most of the human beings in the Soviet Union in an instant.[47]

These patterns of action look clear to us now. But in the atmosphere of panic and accusation that *Sputnik* had triggered, Eisenhower's steady policy response to the Soviet missile challenge did not look so clear. And that left an opening for his critics to exploit.

VII

On the morning of July 30, 1958, readers of the *Washington Post* might have choked on their breakfast cereal when they came to Joseph Alsop's column titled "The Gap." Alsop, one of the most well-connected journalists in the capital, claimed to have seen classified materials proving that up through 1963 the United States would be vulnerable to a massive Soviet missile attack. In the coming five years, he claimed, "the American government will flaccidly permit the Kremlin to gain an almost unchallengeable superiority in nuclear striking power." The USSR was racing to put hundreds of ICBMs into action, Alsop asserted, while "our missile programs are pitiable." According to Alsop, the Soviets would have 100 ICBMs ready in 1959 and "should reach an output of 500 per year in 1960." They would have no less than "1,000 ICBMs in place against our seventy by the end of 1961" and as many as "2,000 ICBMs against our 130" by the end of 1963. How did Alsop know about the Soviet missile program? Very likely someone had leaked to him the contents of Allen Dulles's alarming December 1957 Special National Intelligence Report (SNIE 11-10-57), though Alsop inflated even those dubious figures for maximum effect.[48]

Two days later Alsop threw another grenade in a column called "Untruths on Defense," a piece bristling with outrage and high dudgeon. Alsop alleged that "the Eisenhower administration is guilty of gross untruth concerning the national defense of the United States." The president had been "consciously misleading" the people about the state of the nation's defenses. Between 1960 and 1963 the Soviets could strike the United States at will using numerous rockets the likes of which the United States did not possess. "Massive orders for hardware must be placed immediately," he demanded. "The last chance to save ourselves is slipping through our hands." Alsop kept up this barrage all week; on August 3 he declared that the Eisenhower administration deliberately sought "to permit the Kremlin to gain an overwhelming nuclear striking power in the next five years." Once the Soviets achieved that superiority, Alsop warned, they would use it. "Any man who is not intoxicated by official self-delusion must at least expect the Kremlin to threaten to strike the first blow."[49]

Alsop did not limit himself to attacking Ike's nuclear strategy. At the conclusion of this flurry of venomous columns in the first week of August, he went after the president himself. The leitmotif: Ike was washed up. "Anyone whose private Eisenhower image is the vigorously striding, easily smiling, richly self-confident Eisenhower of the past is bound to be a little shocked by the Eisenhower of today." These columns marked the start of the 1960 presidential campaign and contained within them the chief lines of attack that John Kennedy would direct against the legacy of Ike: a failing and aging president had allowed America's enemies to prosper, and only youth, vigor, and boldness could save the country from a fatal slippage.[50]

Alsop's attacks had been previewed in the spring and summer, when congressional critics, most notably Senators Symington and Johnson, had badgered the administration about its lackluster response to *Sputnik*. Symington, a presidential aspirant, lambasted Ike in a heated speech on the Senate floor in late May 1958, denouncing his "ostrich-like state of complacency." In a familiar line of attack, he said, "Our government continues to place soft living and budgetary considerations ahead of national security." The Democrats kept up this drumbeat throughout the summer, as Johnson criticized Ike for spending too little on missiles. The president lacks "a feeling of grim urgency," Johnson insisted and told Defense Secretary McElroy he was "disappointed" at the response to the *Sputnik* challenge.[51]

With powerful critics paving the way, the junior senator from Massachusetts, already considered a leading contender for the presidency, decided to join the battle. Armed with purloined data given to him by his admiring Georgetown neighbor Joe Alsop, John F. Kennedy stood at his desk in the Senate on the evening of August 14, 1958, and delivered what was, up to that moment, the most important speech of his career. In a long and artfully crafted address, Kennedy attacked the cold war doctrines of the Eisenhower administration. Not only had Eisenhower allowed a missile gap to open up, Kennedy asserted; he had also underfunded the conventional military arsenal of American power. The Soviets would now use nuclear blackmail to spread their influence, and America would be powerless to stop them. "Their missile power will be the shield from behind which they will slowly, but surely, advance—through sputnik diplomacy, limited brushfire wars, indirect non-overt aggression, intimidation and subversion, internal revolution, increased prestige or influence, and the vicious blackmail of our allies. The periphery of the free world will slowly be nibbled away."[52]

Eisenhower stood doubly accused: he had failed to build enough missiles, and he had cut conventional forces, thus hobbling America's response to the limited emergencies that burned across the developing world. Worse, his policy had been driven by a shortsighted emphasis on fiscal balance and tight budgets. The Eisenhower budget-cutters had hollowed out America's military power, ceding to the Soviet Union the leadership in the cold war. Kennedy looked to Scripture for the right phrase to hang on the Age of Eisenhower and found it: "the years the locusts have eaten," a tag line he would deploy again and again in the 1960 campaign.

Alsop, who had urged Kennedy to make the speech, now went into print with unstinting praise for the young, "hard-hitting" senator. Kennedy's Senate address, gushed Alsop on August 18, was "one of the most remarkable speeches on American defense and national strategy that this country has heard since the end of the last war." Kennedy spoke candidly in "the authentic voice of America." A star was born, and Alsop was not alone in noticing. James Reston, a wily observer of the political carnival in Washington, recognized that Kennedy's speech had vaulted him into the pole position for the Democratic nomination in 1960. "Senator Kennedy is on the make," Reston wrote; "he makes no pretense about it." The Democratic Party had found its candidate and a winning issue: Ike's insufficient zeal to confront the menace of Soviet power.[53]

Privately Eisenhower fumed about Alsop's "senseless diatribe." He viewed Alsop, a well known bon vivant and irreverent gossip, as a man of "low character" who brought disgrace on his newspaper. To old friend Bill Robinson, who used to be the publisher of the *Herald Tribune*, Ike seethed about Alsop's "garbage." The FBI considered tapping his phone. In his public remarks to the press, however, Eisenhower simply dismissed the idea of a gap of any kind and insisted that American military capabilities "are the most powerful they have ever been in our history."[54]

Eisenhower possessed more knowledge about the case than he let on. Although Ike had grounded U-2 flights over the USSR, his military and intelligence services carefully reviewed the radar data they possessed on Soviet tests of ICBMs and found, to their surprise, that such tests had not been frequent enough to indicate robust missile development. It was a puzzle: If the Soviets were building a fleet of hundreds of ICBMs, why had they tested so few of them? In fact up to May 1958, the CIA could verify only eight Soviet ICBM launches in total, including the *Sputnik III* satellite on May 15. These rockets revealed Soviet technological advances, but were too few to indicate the existence of a major ICBM development program.

Somewhat reluctantly Allen Dulles had to report to the president and the NSC on August 27, that the intelligence services, while still certain of the Soviet desire for a large ICBM fleet, were pushing back by six months, to the end of 1959, their prediction for an operational Soviet nuclear-tipped

ICBM. In their new National Intelligence Estimate, SNIE 11-5-58, they speculated that the USSR could have 100 of these by the end of 1960. It was still an alarming possibility, but not quite so alarming as the picture Dulles had painted for Congress in November 1957.[55]

This proved to be the first of many backward steps by the intelligence community. On October 9, 1958, Dulles initiated another review of the available radar data—still without any help from U-2 flights, and the lengthy report that emerged from an interagency review admitted, "We have no conclusive evidence that a Soviet ICBM production program of the type estimated in NIE 11-5-58 is currently being accomplished." The report hastened to add that because of the restrictions on U-2 overflights, the available intelligence was incomplete, and so a final judgment remained elusive. But so far it was difficult to understand how the USSR could have a big missile program without conducting regular tests. By the start of November the intelligence community again walked back by another six months their estimate of when the Soviet ICBM would be operational. Not until Eisenhower allowed U-2 overflight of the USSR in July 1959 and again in early 1960 did a clearer picture emerge, and it confirmed that the Soviet ICBM program had been significantly slowed down in favor of the production of intermediate-range missiles. But none of this could be communicated to the public for fear of revealing the top-secret overflights. The myth of the missile gap endured, kept alive by those who wanted an easy way to attack Eisenhower for his alleged complacency.[56]

VIII

Ever since *Sputnik* went into orbit in October 1957, Eisenhower had endured insulting complaints about his "flaccid" leadership (to use Alsop's term). Quite possibly this context explains his uncharacteristic decision in mid-July 1958 to send a division of American soldiers to Lebanon to offer political and diplomatic protection to an ally, the Lebanese president Camille Chamoun. The origins of this decision lay in the ever-wider reach of Gamal Abdel Nasser in the Middle East. Since his triumph in 1956 over the Europeans, Nasser had meddled in the region, strengthening his ties to Syria and backing a coup in Iraq. Chamoun, a Maronite Christian in a multiethnic nation, feared that Nasser had his sights set on Lebanon as well. The link between Nasserism and communism lived mainly in the minds of American strategists, but even the chance of losing a pro-Western ally in the Middle East made Eisenhower and Foster Dulles deeply anxious. They viewed the Lebanon problem as a matter of prestige: if Lebanon were to collapse and be swept up in a Nasserite-communist web of influence, Nasser's prestige would soar, America's would sag, and the Eisenhower Doctrine would be seen as meaningless. "We must act, or get out of the Middle East," Eisenhower told his advisers.[57]

Applying the logic of credibility and prestige, which his successors would do later in Vietnam, Ike saw Lebanon as another theater in which the United States was fighting the USSR. In a televised address to the nation, he invoked a doom-laden catalogue of cold war horrors, conjuring up the communist efforts to subvert Greece, Turkey, Czechoslovakia, China, Korea, and Indochina. Lebanon could be next, he warned. (He sounded much like Anthony Eden on the eve of the Suez invasion, a fact Prime Minister Harold Macmillan gently pointed out. "You're doing a Suez on me," he chuckled to Ike over the phone.) On July 15, 14,000 American soldiers (army and marines) splashed down on the beaches of Beirut in pleasant sunshine, where they were welcomed by sunbathing locals. The threat that these soldiers were supposed to guard against never materialized; no shots were fired or soldiers killed; within three months the troops were withdrawn.[58]

The Lebanon action, though, came at a cost. Eisenhower and Dulles forfeited whatever credit they had accumulated during the Suez Crisis and now appeared in Arab eyes to be acting like a colonial power. Instead of cultivating nationalist leaders in the region, they alienated them. Rather than enhance American prestige, the intervention gave the Russians the opportunity to denounce American imperialism. And it did little to bolster Ike's reputation at home. Most Americans seemed puzzled by the action and anxious lest the United States get caught in a briar patch. The headline in the *Los Angeles Times* caught the national sentiment: "What Are We Doing, Anyway?"[59]

If the Lebanon affair had something of the comic about it, the events in the Far East in the autumn of 1958 looked far more dangerous. What became the Second Taiwan Straits Crisis opened on August 23 with a massive artillery barrage from communist Chinese batteries onto Quemoy, the small island held by Chiang Kai-shek's Nationalists just a mile or so off the coast of mainland China, athwart the approaches to the city of Xiamen. Just why Mao chose this moment to restart the shelling of Quemoy remains a subject of dispute among historians. Most likely he had domestic political purposes in mind, as he had just initiated the Great Leap Forward, a tumultuous period of collectivization and social upheaval. Generating an air of crisis through conflict with the Americans might help to inflame the people's revolutionary ardor. Mao also knew that U.S. prestige was at a low ebb in the non-Western world due to its alleged failures to keep pace with the Soviets in the missile race and because of its intervention in Lebanon.[60]

Whatever Mao's motives, this second artillery bombardment of Quemoy came at an awful time for Eisenhower. Precisely because he had been the subject of so much criticism for his alleged indecisiveness and complacency in confronting the Soviets on the world stage, Eisenhower felt that he must demonstrate resolve and firmness—those baleful keywords of cold war strategy. Privately he admitted that the islands had no value in the defense of Taiwan itself, which was 100 miles away across the rough and stormy Taiwan Strait and defended by the U.S. Seventh Fleet. Nonetheless the ill-conceived Formosa Resolution of 1955 had pledged the United States to defend Taiwan and related Nationalist possessions and seemed to imply that Quemoy fell under this umbrella of protection.

Chiang meant to hold the United States to its word. By 1958 he had placed 130,000 Nationalist soldiers on Quemoy. When Mao commenced his artillery barrage, Chiang could say that if Quemoy was taken by the communists, Taiwan would have lost one-third of its army and would be vulnerable to a direct Chinese attack on Taiwan itself. Chiang argued that if the United States was serious about containing the menace of communist China, it must commit itself to protect Quemoy, even if that meant attacking mainland China itself. Once again Chiang put on a master class of how the tail wags the dog.

Eisenhower and Dulles faced a nasty dilemma. Either they could declare solidarity with Chiang and commit American forces to the defense of Quemoy, risking all-out war with China or they could declare Quemoy to be outside the sphere of American interest and leave it to its fate.

The first choice—defend Chiang and his islands at all costs—likely meant war, and even the use of nuclear weapons. That outcome did not seem hypothetical. In the spring of 1957 the United States had sent 40 Matador nuclear-tipped cruise missiles to Taiwan. As recently as June 1958 American military leaders had accepted a policy paper stating that the only way the United States, so far from its own bases of support, could fight against China, even in a limited war to protect Taiwan, would be by using nuclear weapons.

In the first week of the communist artillery attack, Foster Dulles and the

Joint Chiefs of Staff met to consider their military plans. They all agreed if the communist Chinese attacked Quemoy in an amphibious landing, the United States would drop several "small atomic weapons," which they defined as 7- to 10-kiloton bombs, on Chinese airfields and military staging grounds. (A 10-kiloton bomb would create about two-thirds the explosive power of the bomb dropped on Hiroshima.) The chief of staff of the U.S. Army, Gen. Maxwell Taylor, said such nuclear weapons were "the only way to do the job" in order to avoid a "protracted Korea-type conflict." The chairman of the Joint Chiefs, Gen. Nathan Twining, agreed, casually admitting he "could not understand the public horror at the idea of using nuclear weapons." The military chiefs knew that some Asian countries, like Japan, would recoil at the use of atomic bombs on China, but they insisted that the loss of influence among such allies was a smaller price to pay than the huge loss of world prestige that would occur if America failed to live up to its word and crumpled under communist pressure. Dulles, evidently much enthused by the iron-fisted determination of the military chiefs, advised the president that the Chinese assault on Quemoy was part of a broader plan to liquidate Chiang's Nationalists on Taiwan and that the United States must be prepared to use nuclear weapons in a war with China: "If we will not use them when the chips are down because of adverse world opinion, we must revise our defense set-up."[61]

The second choice—leaving Quemoy to its fate—struck Dulles as far more dangerous than hitting China with atom bombs. He argued, "If we do give up the islands, Chiang is finished." He would be militarily weakened and possibly overthrown by neutralist elements inside Taiwan. Very soon the Pacific would become a communist lake, and all the wobbly Asian nations, such as the Philippines and Japan, would make their peace with their new communist masters in Beijing. Those allies had become symbols of American resolve to wage the cold war. "The problem is primarily one of psychology," Dulles explained to Prime Minister Macmillan, "and what would look like a retreat before the new, tough and arrogant probing of the Communists. If the United States seems afraid, and loses 'face' in any way, the consequences will be far reaching, extending from Vietnam in the south to Japan and Korea in the north." The domino theory never had a clearer explanation.[62]

Eisenhower has often been criticized for indecision and a tendency to postpone and prevaricate. But never was there a more suitable moment for his particular kind of strategic patience than in the Second Taiwan Straits

Crisis of September 1958. He refused to accept the problem as Dulles and his military advisers framed it. He rejected the stark choice between nuclear war and appeasement. There had to be a third choice, even if it meant making no choice at all. And so he waited.

Eisenhower did not want to overreact to Mao's dangerous gamesmanship. He instructed his advisers that unless a much bigger and direct threat to Taiwan emerged, they "should probably hold back on nuclear measures." The offshore islands were unnecessary to defend Taiwan, he reiterated, and he would be happy to cut a deal in which Chiang left them altogether, in exchange for some kind of acceptance by Mao of the status quo in Taiwan. Ike told his secretary of defense, Neil McElroy, that Dulles "tends to take a somewhat stiffer view" of things, but Eisenhower had no use for such inflexibility. "It is not adequate simply to say that we will stand on Quemoy and Matsu. We must move beyond that." He would not allow the offshore islands to draw America into war.[63]

Instead he made a few carefully calculated moves. He reinforced Taiwan's supply of fighter aircraft and provided them with new Sidewinder missiles. He transferred a regiment of Nike anti-aircraft missiles to Taiwan and gave the Nationalists powerful artillery pieces. He ordered the Seventh Fleet to provide convoy cover so that supply ships from Taiwan could reach Quemoy and resupply the besieged garrison there. This proved tricky and dangerous, as there were many soldiers and civilians to feed on Quemoy. But the navy accomplished the task. At the same time, Eisenhower insisted that Chiang do nothing to trigger a full-scale war, like bombing airfields on the mainland of China. In short, Ike figured he could wait out the communist provocation, resupply the soldiers on Quemoy, and avoid either war or retreat.[64]

It was a gamble, and it worked. On October 6, after six weeks of intensive shelling, Mao announced a one-week moratorium on the artillery attacks, a pause that stretched on for a few more weeks, until the crisis had passed. Quemoy remained under Taiwan's control (as it does today). No "small" atomic bombs were dropped. America did not lose face in Asia. Chiang did not attack the mainland, though he continued to fume about insufficiently firm American support. Eisenhower's strategy of patience paid off. He restrained his generals and his secretary of state, calmed his allies, and showed that the United States would not be bullied. It was a quiet and terribly important victory for the president.

But of course it was not the kind of victory that played well on the home stage. The press attacked Eisenhower and Dulles mercilessly, first for allowing the United States to be manipulated by Chiang into such a dangerous predicament, and then for being insufficiently bold in standing by the Nationalist leader in his hour of need. Walter Lippmann wrote a dozen columns during the six-week-long crisis in which he flayed the administration for strategic incoherence and incompetence. "There is no policy" on the offshore islands, he asserted, only a "wager" that the Chinese won't do anything too rash. He described the administration as "paralyzed," at a "dead end," and "embarrassing." Joseph Alsop, not to be outdone, actually rushed to Taiwan in the midst of the crisis and published no fewer than 17 smoldering essays of invective against the Eisenhower administration. He used the crisis to bash Ike for failing to keep a sufficiently robust naval and military presence in Asia and for hesitating in the face of communist aggression. Such was the verdict of the pundits.[65]

The domestic politics of the Second Taiwan Straits Crisis were indeed disastrous for the president. Democrats repackaged Eisenhower's policy of restraint and patience as incoherence and indecision. "We have teetered consistently on the brink of foreign wars no American wants or could even explain," commented Senator Kennedy, a future architect of America's war in Vietnam. Presidential aspirants Averell Harriman and Hubert Humphrey, as well as leading Senate Democrats Mike Mansfield, William Fulbright, and Theodore Francis Green, excoriated Eisenhower's brinkmanship. Little did they know that Eisenhower was the one firmly pulling on the reins of restraint, guiding the horses of war away from the abyss.[66]

IX

What a year it had been! Since September 1957, when the bitter confrontation erupted in Little Rock and the recession began, Eisenhower had known nothing but trouble: the launch of *Sputnik* in October, a stroke in November, the embarrassing congressional probe into the missile programs that ran until January 1958, the much-publicized failures of American test rockets on their launching pads contrasting with the success of the Soviets' *Sputnik III* in May 1958, and now in July and August two foreign entanglements that seemed to many Americans as ill-conceived as they were dangerous. Throw into that depressing litany the most damaging, and least truthful, criticism of all, namely, the opening up of a vast and threatening "missile gap," the result of Ike's supposedly complacent leadership. Without a doubt the period from September 1957 to November 1958 marks Eisenhower's most troubled year in office.

Two personal losses added anguish to the year. His longtime chief of staff, Sherman Adams, resigned in September 1958. Adams had been with Eisenhower from the first snowy days in New Hampshire in 1952 and served the president with tenacity and ferocious loyalty. He was respected and feared in Washington, and little liked, earning the nickname "the Abominable 'No' Man." Eisenhower relied on him enormously. But in June the House of Representatives began an inquiry into accusations that Adams had accepted gifts from a Boston rug merchant named Bernard Goldfine, who was under investigation by the Federal Trade Commission. Adams had indeed accepted an expensive vicuña coat, an Oriental carpet, and free hotel accommodations from Goldfine, though he denied exerting any pressure on the FTC on Goldfine's behalf. The scandal grew and became a threat to the administration's record of incorruptibility. Adams resigned on September 22 and returned to his native New Hampshire. Eisenhower felt Adams had been wronged. "Nothing that has occurred has had a more depressive effect on my normal buoyancy and optimism than has the virulent, sustained, demagogic attacks made upon him," he wrote to a mutual friend.[67]

In that difficult autumn Eisenhower also lost one of his oldest friends. On November 2, 1958, following a long illness, Swede Hazlett died. They had known each other since their school days, when Eisenhower, strong and athletic, had stood up for Swede on the playground against a neighborhood tough. "Why don't you try that on me," he said to the bully, who skulked away. They were fast friends from that day on. Hazlett had kept up an extraordinary correspondence with Eisenhower, writing to him regularly in what might be called the unadorned voice of the everyman. In dozens upon dozens of letters Hazlett expressed opinions on matters from the Supreme Court to race relations, foreign policy, and taxes. Eisenhower often responded at length, and his letters form a crucial body of material for historians. "I can never quite tell you what Swede meant to me," Eisenhower wrote to Swede's wife, Ibby. "While I am glad for his sake that he suffers no longer, his passing leaves a permanent void in my life."[68]

The coup de grâce in this troubled year came on November 4, 1958, just two years after Eisenhower's triumphant reelection. On that day the midterm congressional elections delivered a huge defeat to the Republicans and implicitly to the president himself. The Democrats already controlled both houses of Congress, but they dramatically widened their lead. In the Senate, which the Democrats had held by a narrow margin for the previous four years, the Republicans lost a whopping 13 seats, giving Democrats a 30-seat advantage. In the House 48 Republicans lost their reelection bids, and the Democrats now enjoyed a 130-seat cushion. It was an unmitigated rout. Nixon, who had given speeches across the country during the campaign, recalled it as "one of the most depressing election nights I have ever known."[69]

What explains this decisive rebuke from the voters? Eisenhower blamed "the seeming desire of the people of our country to depend more and more upon government—they do not seem to understand that more governmental assistance inevitably means more governmental control." But the problems went deeper than that. The main explanation lay in the economic troubles the country faced. Most of the losses came in states with high unemployment; people were hurting, and they sent a message. More broadly, Eisenhower in 1958 lost control of the political narrative of his own presidency. Peace, prosperity, security, and small government—these had been the watchwords of "Eisenhower's Modern Republicanism." By late 1958 these looked like hollow phrases. The horizon was clouded by threats of war; the economy sputtered; claims of a missile gap suggested a weak national defense; and both taxes and spending remained high.[70]

In retrospect we can see that Eisenhower governed wisely and well in 1958. He responded thoughtfully to the *Sputnik* crisis and once again stamped out the flames of war in Asia. But his opponents described him as a failure. They painted a portrait of an America that had faltered economically, had fallen behind in the missile race, had let its military might wane, had stumbled over the racial crisis in the South, and had surrendered the mantle of leadership on the world stage. To his critics Eisenhower looked out of touch, indecisive, and adrift. In the final two years of his presidency Eisenhower would have to find an effective way to rebut this criticism. The stakes were enormous: his place in history was at risk.

CHAPTER 16

CONTENDING WITH KHRUSHCHEV

"We don't escape war by surrendering on the installment plan."

I

SOON AFTER THE DISASTROUS MIDTERM ELECTIONS OF 1958, Eisenhower retreated to Augusta and the cocoon of his favorite golf club. He played golf every day for two weeks, usually scoring about 90 and betting with his playing partners on every game. He also huddled with his advisers and staff to discuss the future. He and his party had suffered a bad beating at the polls, a defeat that followed a rough two years for the administration. How could Eisenhower revive his flagging presidency?[1]

As he surveyed the domestic political scene and considered the 2–1 advantage the Democrats enjoyed over Republicans in Congress, Eisenhower knew that he could not count on any major legislative victories. In fact he expected nothing but trouble from Congress. In his first postelection press conference he pledged to fight "as hard as I know how" any proposals from the Democrats for greater spending—not exactly a message of conciliation. But simply halting Democratic activity and wielding a veto was no way for the president to recover his momentum. If he was going to restore luster and sparkle to his tarnished second term, he needed something that would fire up the national imagination.[2]

Eisenhower had hoped he might be able to deliver a major agreement with the Soviets on the matter of nuclear weapons testing. Anxieties about nuclear "fallout"—a new word in the American vocabulary—reached a crescendo in 1958, as scientific studies began to show the dangerous health effects of radioactivity on humans. In February 1958 Edward Teller and the

Nobel laureate Linus Pauling held a televised debate on the consequences of fallout, with Teller pooh-poohing the matter and Pauling calling for an end to nuclear tests. In August a United Nations scientific committee released a damning report on the effects of nuclear weapons testing, stirring a public debate about the presence of the radioactive isotope strontium-90 in the nation's food supply.[3]

The public had reason to worry. In 1957 and 1958 the Defense Department had been setting off nuclear weapons in the Nevada desert at an unprecedented rate: 28 tests in July 1957 and 36 more in October 1958. Many of the test bombs were carried into the atmosphere by balloons, thus ensuring wide broadcasting of radioactive particles. The United States and the USSR began exploratory talks in summer 1958 about an atmospheric test ban treaty, and in response to growing public pressure Eisenhower announced a one-year moratorium on such tests on October 31. But by the end of the year talks with the Soviets had bogged down and no progress seemed likely.[4]

What other initiatives might bring Eisenhower a victory? As he left for Augusta on November 20, he wrote a letter to his former speechwriter Emmet Hughes with an idea that might spark national enthusiasm. He wanted "to center greater attention in our country, and so far as possible in the free world, on the predominant influence of spiritual values in our lives." He yearned to transcend the stale arguments in the "freedom-communist struggle," as he called it. "We have been tending too much toward the material. We have too much thought of bombs and machines and gadgets as the arsenal of our national and cultural strength." He wondered if there was some way to reach out to heads of state around the world and persuade them to join in a great affirmation of the importance of religion and faith in world affairs.[5]

Hughes was skeptical. Although he couched his criticism elegantly, he asserted that mere "rhetoric and exhortation" would do little to impact world affairs; if Eisenhower wanted results, he would have to take action. "A good way to damage a principle or ideal is to affirm it passionately, then fail to give it true testimony in deed." Besides, Hughes wondered, what would Secretary Dulles say about a religious and pacific appeal to the world? Not surprisingly, the stern and cagey Dulles snuffed out the idea. He had no interest in a heartfelt but vague call to spiritual uplift. That would only suggest irresolution and weakness in the cold war contest.[6]

Yet Eisenhower needed something bold to restore public faith in his leadership. In Augusta he held long discussions with Jim Hagerty, his press secretary and confidant. Eager that Ike should avoid looking like a "lame duck" in his last years in office, Hagerty urged Eisenhower to adopt the role of "Tribune of the People," going over the head of the partisan Congress and speaking out on matters of national and global importance. In addition to holding the line on spending and denouncing the "sheer nonsense" about American failures in the missile race, Ike had a unique opportunity to reestablish his prestige by undertaking visible and constructive measures on the world stage. It was time for a globe-trotting campaign of personal diplomacy.

"Americans know," Hagerty asserted in a long memo to Eisenhower, "that if anyone in our nation can keep the world at peace, it is you. They, like all the peoples of the world, look to the President as the one individual who can contribute the most to keeping the peace." It was time to push aside the State Department and make Eisenhower the spokesman of American interests on the world stage. The president should appear more frequently at the United Nations and speak the language of goodwill. He should launch a major program of international travel to raise his profile and spread the gospel of peace and understanding in the developing world. India, Pakistan, Southeast Asia, Latin America, Europe, Africa, maybe even the USSR—Eisenhower should set out to visit all of them and wave high the flag of peace. And he should seek out direct contact with the Soviet leaders through international summits, where global crises could be settled. Hagerty felt much good could come from meeting with Khrushchev and that the initiative should come from Eisenhower. "Why not propose it ourselves, on our terms, rather than end up eventually as reluctant participants in a meeting which the Soviets will herald as a meeting for peace?"

These personal gestures, which could not be constrained by a feisty, partisan Congress, might generate enthusiasm for the president and his party at home, and might also open the way to a genuine East-West peace agreement before Eisenhower left office. Accompanied by monthly radio and television speeches by the president, these trips and summits would once again place Eisenhower in the forefront of world affairs. If he could ease or even end the cold war in his final years, Eisenhower's place in history as a champion of peace would be forever secure. Hagerty urged him to seize the moment and turn the coming two years "to advantage for the President, the United States—indeed for the entire world."[7]

II

As he mused about these various initiatives, however, Ike got some disturbing news that seemed sure to dash his hopes for a new beginning in U.S.-Soviet relations. On November 27, 1958, sitting in rumpled golf togs in a small office above the pro shop at Augusta National, Eisenhower heard a report from his son and aide, Maj. John Eisenhower, who had just flown in from Washington to brief him. Khrushchev had decided to pick a fight over the city of Berlin, thus triggering a crisis that would loom over the rest of Eisenhower's presidency and shape the cold war for decades.[8]

At the close of World War II, Germany was divided into four zones of occupation. The United States, Britain, France, and the Soviet Union each acted as the sovereign authority in their zone. The arrangement was supposed to be temporary, but it soon became permanent. In 1949 the Western powers merged their zones into a single entity that became the Federal Republic of Germany, or West Germany; the Soviets transformed their occupation zone into the German Democratic Republic, or East Germany. Because the four occupying powers never signed a peace treaty with Germany, these two successors to Hitler's Reich were not legally sovereign (and would not be until 1990), yet they looked and acted like fully functioning states. West Germany, led by the staunchly anticommunist Christian Democrat Konrad Adenauer, joined NATO in 1955; East Germany became a member of the communist bloc alliance, the Warsaw Pact. Odd though it seemed, dividing Germany in two proved a Solomonic solution: it was far better than fighting another war.

One major irritant remained: Berlin. Located deep inside East Germany, the former capital of the Reich was also subdivided into four occupation zones. By international agreement, U.S., British, and French soldiers and diplomats lived and worked in Berlin and could move freely across the city. Furthermore they could travel to Berlin across East German territory by road, rail, and airplane from West Germany, and the Western powers scrupulously insisted that their access into the occupied capital city never be impeded. Stalin in 1948 had tested Western resolve by imposing a blockade of Berlin, halting all road and rail travel into the city. Loath to shoot down allied airplanes, which would have been an act of war, Stalin left the "air bridge" open, and the Western states broke the yearlong blockade by airlifting millions of tons of supplies into Berlin. It was an enormous propaganda victory for the West and only heightened their determination never to leave Berlin under duress.

To the East Germans the presence of a large and distinctly capital-ist foreign occupation force inside their own territory became intolerable. They declared Berlin the capital city of the German Democratic Repub-lic. But what kind of nation would allow its capital city to be occupied by foreigners—and foreign soldiers, no less? The East Germans put constant pressure on the Soviets to resolve the nagging and embarrassing problem of Berlin. They wanted to control the city and expel the Western powers. Would Moscow help them? Khrushchev gave his answer in a formal ultima-tum on November 27, 1958. He demanded the Western powers sign a peace treaty with East Germany, acknowledge its full sovereignty, and leave Berlin. If they did not do so in six months—that is, by May 27, 1959—the Soviet Union would turn over its occupation zone in Berlin to the East Germans, forcing the Western powers to negotiate directly with the East Germans over access to the isolated city.[9]

Khrushchev's ultimatum pointed a threatening dagger right at one of the most sensitive spots of the cold war. Why did he do it? The explana-tion lies in Khrushchev's personality and his peculiar way of thinking about world politics. Khrushchev was a true believer in the ideology of commu-nism. He gloried in its muscular, forward-looking optimism, its promises of rapid industrialization and perfect equality among workers. He felt cer-tain that the USSR and the world communist movement, with its vast sup-ply of manpower and natural resources, could outproduce and outlast the crooked, rotten capitalist world in an open competition. This belief inspired his famous taunt to a roomful of Western ambassadors at a meeting in 1956: "Whether you like it or not, history is on our side. We will bury you!" An aggressive, garrulous, argumentative man, Khrushchev relished these kinds of verbal provocations. He operated on bluff, bluster, and biting tirades. He boasted of Soviet military power, hoping to intimidate his enemies. With the October 1957 launch of *Sputnik*, his rhetorical boasts reached new heights. He bragged about cranking out missiles "like sausages" and threatened to strike any nation that blocked the Soviet Union's path.

For all his bravado, Khrushchev did not want war. Though his tactics were clumsy and counterproductive, he hoped for a period of stability in world affairs so that Soviet industry and science could continue their re-markable progress, demonstrating the superiority of the communist system. At the same time he could never appear complacent. He was the leader, after all, not just of the Soviet Union but of the entire communist world, and for the world's radicals, the anticolonial nationalists, the rebel fighters and leftist prophets in Latin America, Africa, and Asia, he needed to demonstrate his zeal for global revolution. Thus his dilemma: he wanted to ease the cold war with America and lower its cost, yet he also wanted to benefit from the prestige of leading an assault on the capitalist-imperialist West. Khrushchev was caught in a contradiction of his own making.

His ultimatum on Berlin in November 1958 sprang from these competing pressures. He hoped to gain prestige within the communist bloc by standing up for his East German ally, poking his finger in the chest of Western leaders and wresting full control of Berlin from the capitalists. Yet he privately hoped that his move would open up a round of high-level negotiations with the United States that might lead to a broad settlement of the German problem and even of the cold war. It was a terrific gamble: if it worked, he would secure his place as the great leader who built a firm foundation for Soviet success, but if Eisenhower felt directly threatened by this move on Berlin, Khrushchev might trigger World War III.[10]

Eisenhower reacted to Khrushchev's declaration on Berlin with circumspection. He understood that this defiant outpost of Western power deep inside the communist bloc irritated the Soviets. He also knew the city could not be defended militarily if communist forces chose to seize it. He described the West Berliners as little more than "a group of hostages in the hands of the Soviets," and he privately regretted that the United States had pledged its honor to defend them. He had advised against a joint international occupation of the city in 1945, and he now felt vindicated. Discussing the matter with his advisers, he called the Western position in Berlin "untenable" and "illogical." He compared the predicament to Quemoy, where the United States had committed itself to defend a strategically useless and vulnerable citadel. Nonetheless there was no question of retreating under pressure. The United States would "stand firm," he said simply. "If the Russians want war over Berlin, they can have it."[11]

That is not, however, what the Soviets wanted, as Eisenhower soon learned. On December 1 Khrushchev met with Senator Hubert Humphrey, who was on a congressional visit to Moscow. Khrushchev devoted a full day to the senator, eager for him to return home with a clear message. In a session lasting over eight hours, Khrushchev's emotions as usual swung between bellicose and cordial. Humphrey recalled that the Soviet leader "tried to frighten me" with talk of Soviet missile strength, but insisted later, "There will never be a war." Khrushchev struck Humphrey as sincere but impulsive, "a man with no time to waste." Humphrey observed Khrushchev's mixture of pride, aggression, and insecurity, and reported to the State Department what he had learned. Khrushchev described Berlin as a "thorn," a "cancer," and "a bone in my throat." If it could be removed, peace could soon follow. Berlin, he suggested, should be turned into a "free city" and perhaps turned over to the United Nations. It could be neutralized, as Austria had been. He also tossed out ideas for the prompt reunification of East and West Germany as one neutral nation. Spluttering and angry one moment, congenial the next, Khrushchev told Humphrey, "I like President Eisenhower. We want no evil to the U.S. or to free Berlin. You must assure the president of this." Only a "madman or a fool," Khrushchev insisted, would think of war between the superpowers.[12]

These observations clearly influenced Eisenhower, since they squared with his own belief that the USSR did not want to fight over Berlin. In sessions with his advisers in December and January, Eisenhower developed the strategy he would adopt toward Khrushchev. He would make it absolutely clear that the United States would not leave Berlin or allow any part of Berlin to come under the control of the East Germans. Using a poker analogy, he said there should be no ambiguity about America's position: "In order to avoid beginning with the white chips and working our way up to the blue, we should place them on notice that our whole stack is in play." The United States would respond "in a friendly tone," however, and encourage negotiations. Eisenhower thought the foreign ministers of the four occupying powers should meet and discuss German matters, giving Khrushchev a means to save face and quietly back down.

Vice President Nixon, prophetically as it turned out, thought that perhaps what Khrushchev really wanted was a summit meeting with Eisenhower as a way to bolster his own prestige. If so, saber rattling over Berlin seemed an awkward way to ask for it. Ike called the Berlin problem a "can of worms," but his usual inclination toward patience and moderation paid dividends here. He rejected the kind of provocative actions that the Joint Chiefs of Staff seemed to favor, such as driving a heavily armed convoy down the Autobahn and daring the Russians to stop it. Ike would have none of that. He resented Soviet tactics, but he would much prefer talking to fighting.[13]

Arranging a meeting of the foreign ministers took a great deal of haggling and delicate maneuvering, and it fell to Harold Macmillan to speed things up. Macmillan had risen to prime minister in early 1957, taking over from the disgraced Anthony Eden. The Conservative Party had been badly tarnished by the Suez debacle, and Macmillan needed to notch a success to restore public confidence in the Tories. He hoped that he could improve his standing at home by playing the honest broker, a man who could ease the Berlin crisis first by getting a foreign ministers' conference under way and then by arranging a great summit meeting of Khrushchev, Eisenhower, the newly installed French president Charles de Gaulle, and himself. A high-visibility summit that eased the anxieties of the cold war could deliver a great political boost to Macmillan and his Conservatives and pave the way to a general election victory in the fall of 1959.

In late February 1959 Macmillan, full of hope, traveled to Moscow to sound out the Soviets. The trip began well enough, as Khrushchev plied his British guests with caviar, salmon, excellent vodka, Russian brandy, ballet performances, and long late-night suppers. But then Macmillan discovered what all the other Westerners who engaged with Khrushchev learned: there were two Nikitas. The first was a rational statesman, ready to talk about peace, arms control, and coexistence. The other was the communist zealot, the prosecutor, the brawler who threw angry punches in every direction. After three inconsequential days of easy conversations and liquid lunches, Khrushchev gave a menacing speech, denouncing the Western powers for blocking progress on unifying Germany and resolving the Berlin matter. The idea of a foreign ministers' meeting was a stalling tactic, he said, a sign that the Western states had no desire to solve their differences. He wanted action and demanded the Great Powers respond to his demands.

Macmillan, deeply shocked by this mercurial behavior, told Khrushchev at the tail end of a long and alcohol-fueled luncheon, "If you try to threaten us in any way, you will create the Third World War. Because we shall not give in, nor will the Americans." At this Khrushchev leaped to his feet and shouted, "You have insulted me!," and stormed out. That evening Khrushchev mocked the failed British invasion of Egypt and bullied Macmillan. He meant to have his way over Berlin, he said, whatever the Western nations did. Khrushchev then abandoned his guest, letting him visit the country like a wayward tourist and paying him little heed. Macmillan's mission looked like an epic failure. At one point he collapsed physically and had to be hauled off to bed by his staff. This rebuff from the ever-unpredictable Khrushchev highlighted the real risks of personal diplomacy.[14]

And then, true to his nature, Khrushchev tried to salve the wounds he had inflicted on the British prime minister. At the very end of Macmillan's visit, Khrushchev quite suddenly agreed to the foreign ministers' meeting as a stepping-stone to a summit of world leaders. He also withdrew his six-month "clock" for the Berlin ultimatum he had issued in November. Macmillan could go back to London with some good news: the Soviets would negotiate a way out of the Berlin crisis. Having battered and bullied Macmillan and demonstrated his willingness to fight, Khrushchev now seemed happy to offer an olive branch. He had displayed his unique if crude negotiating style, which began with shouting and verbal assaults and proceeded toward compromise.[15]

III

Eisenhower and Foster Dulles observed Macmillan's Soviet diplomacy with growing dismay. They were appalled at the Englishman's willingness to put up with Khrushchev's bullying, a cardinal sin in the prestige-centered cold war. Eisenhower wondered "how long Britain needs to be slapped in the face" before it stood up to this sneering, ill-mannered man. Ike told his chief advisers and congressional leaders that he would never tolerate that kind of treatment. The Soviets respected only firmness and strength. Resorting again to a poker analogy, he said the communists always bluffed big, but then backed off. "The question is whether we have the nerve to push our chips into the pot." Eisenhower had no hesitation, since "appeasement means disaster." But "if we stand firm . . . the Soviets will back down." A world-class poker player, Ike knew how to read his opponents.[16]

This determination to defy Soviet bullying and never tolerate the slightest sign of disrespect explains the very tense and emotional argument between Eisenhower and Macmillan in late March, when the prime minister came to Washington for private consultations. Macmillan arrived expecting congratulations for having gotten Khrushchev to agree to negotiation instead of war over Berlin. Instead he found his American friends cool indeed.

Eisenhower took Macmillan to Camp David for the weekend of March 20–21, and in the brisk spring air of the Catoctin Mountains the two men had a serious and tough exchange. Macmillan believed he was on the cusp of winning a great coup: a summit meeting of leaders to discuss Germany. But he found that Eisenhower deeply resented Macmillan's effort to manipulate the United States into agreeing to talks in response to Soviet threats. Ike told Macmillan that "he would not go to a meeting under circumstances which made it appear that he had his hat in his hand." If the foreign ministers met first and made serious progress on the issues of Berlin, German unification, disarmament, and so on, then a summit could be arranged. But until the

Soviets showed good faith and a willingness to compromise, he would hear no talk of a summit.[17]

Ike's stubborn attitude shattered Macmillan. All the work he had done appeared to be in jeopardy. He said that World War I broke out in 1914 because of the failures of the leaders of that era to meet and talk; Britain had then paid a terrible price and lost a million young men. (Macmillan himself had fought in France and been wounded three times.) To that Eisenhower gave a sharp rejoinder: on the eve of World War II the world leaders had met at Munich, and those discussions had done nothing to avoid war. Invoking the dreaded legacy of appeasement, Eisenhower would not be associated with any deal that came as a result of a threat. Macmillan said surely negotiation was better than nuclear war. Eisenhower replied that he would not surrender to blackmail. He would not be "dragooned" by Soviet threats and compelled to parley. "We don't escape war by surrendering on the installment plan," said the president. Though under pressure, he refused to bend. Macmillan, deflated and mournful, retreated to his woodsy cabin for the night.[18]

Eisenhower had made his point, and the next morning Macmillan joined the president in writing a letter to Khrushchev that made the Western position plain: if the foreign ministers, meeting in the summer of 1959, made enough progress on the thorny questions of German policy, then a summit meeting might be held in the fall of 1959. On March 30 Khrushchev accepted the deal. It was a victory for Eisenhower. He would make any future meeting of heads of state dependent upon Soviet good behavior. Both Macmillan and Khrushchev, who wanted to hold a high-level meeting right away, would have to be patient. Ike had reestablished his dominance over world affairs and found a way to defuse the Berlin crisis without showing any sign of bending under pressure. He insisted on America's rights in Berlin while leaving open the door to diplomatic discussions. Khrushchev backed down; Ike held firm. Negotiations on Berlin and Germany could move ahead, but on Eisenhower's timetable.[19]

This success in lowering the heat over Berlin was clouded by unsettling news. John Foster Dulles was dying. In February he had gone to Walter Reed for another operation on his cancerous intestines. Ann Whitman noted in her diary that the postoperation report was "not good": "The doctors feel there is no use attempting another operation—they are going to give him radiation every other day." The president, who, Whitman wrote, "did not dwell on death" and was rarely shaken by the loss of friends, was "hard hit."

He even mused about dying and seemed in a funk at the prospect of losing his closest adviser.[20]

Eisenhower visited Dulles regularly at Walter Reed, spoke to him on the telephone, and continued to rely on his advice. But Dulles's condition grew steadily worse. On April 11, 1959, his brother, Allen, told Eisenhower the end seemed near. He was in "severe pain," despite heavy use of sedatives, and "his spirits have also been declining." Allen then produced a letter for the president containing the secretary of state's resignation. Foster recommended that he be replaced by Christian A. Herter, his undersecretary. A well-heeled, moderate Republican who had served 10 years in Congress and five years as governor of Massachusetts, Herter had been acting secretary during the last stages of Dulles's illness. He was a mild-mannered gentleman, almost crippled by severe arthritis, and not nearly as hawkish as Dulles. Ike seemed reluctant to face the fact that Dulles was dying and said he would not "rush to a decision in the matter" of replacing him. But Dulles had made up his mind. On April 15 Eisenhower announced to the press that Dulles would resign his post. On May 24 he died.

Eisenhower took the loss hard, for although he often had to restrain the secretary's more aggressive instincts, he relied on and trusted Dulles and knew that Dulles's loyalty was complete and unbending. The two men formed a powerful team, and they could be found together commiserating over a drink at the end of each workday. Without Dulles, and now without Sherman Adams, George Humphrey, Herbert Brownell, Robert Cutler—the whole team that had so cheerfully and optimistically joined Eisenhower in Washington in January 1953—Ike felt alone, his time in office running out.[21]

IV

Having eased tensions over Berlin, Eisenhower began quietly to revive his earlier idea about a rapprochement with Moscow, perhaps even involving a trip to the Soviet Union. Naturally such a trip had to be carefully prepared. It could never appear that Eisenhower was asking to be received by the Soviets, as Macmillan had done. But if Eisenhower played his cards right, he might get an opportunity to launch his own gesture of personal diplomacy and end his presidency on a high note.

Fortunately a test case soon presented itself. For some time Nixon too had been hoping to make a trip to the Soviet Union. He had already done a great deal of international travel. Much of it was arduous and demanding, as when he traveled 18,000 miles across Africa in the spring of 1957. Some of his travels caused embarrassment, especially his ill-fated eight-nation tour of Latin America in 1958. In most of the nations he visited on that trip, Nixon met with loud opposition, placards, and stone-throwing protestors. In Caracas, Venezuela, his motorcade was attacked by an angry mob wielding lead pipes and stones. Nonetheless such journeys raised Nixon's international profile. Burnishing his credentials for his 1960 presidential run, he thought a trip to Moscow could help him look like a world statesman.[22]

The opening of the American National Exhibition in Sokolniki Park in Moscow, slated for midsummer 1959, provided the perfect occasion for Nixon to visit. A common feature of international cultural diplomacy of the 1950s, such exhibitions served as public advertisements for the commercial and technical achievements of the given nation. The Soviet Union was set to open a major display of its own scientific prowess in June in New York City. Nixon saw his opportunity. On April 4, 1959, he discussed the idea of going to Moscow with Foster Dulles as he sat by his bedside in Walter Reed. Dulles gave the trip his blessing, and the president approved as well. Two weeks later Eisenhower announced that Nixon would lead a delegation to the USSR to cut the ribbon of the American exhibition. Nixon spent the spring and summer preparing for his trip, devouring briefing books, meeting with officials across Washington, seeking insight from men like Hubert Humphrey, Averell Harriman, and Harold Macmillan, all of whom had recently met with Khrushchev. He was determined to make his encounter with Khrushchev a personal success.[23]

It soon became clear, though, that Eisenhower did not want to delegate the role of globe-trotting statesman to his vice president. Well before Nixon left for his trip, Eisenhower began to plan an exchange of visits with Khrushchev. Dulles had long opposed any such personal diplomacy, on the grounds that a meeting with Khrushchev would help the Soviets more than the United States. But Dulles was no longer by Ike's side, cautioning him about the perils of appeasement. In mid-June Eisenhower discussed with his advisers, and with the British ambassador, the tendering of an invitation to Khrushchev to come to the United States. On July 8 Ike told Christian Herter that "if we are ever to break the log jam" with the Soviets, an exchange of visits might do the trick. "We would like to negotiate" with the USSR, Ike insisted, but not "with a gun pointed at our head." Herter, less cautious and suspicious than Dulles, cheered the plan. "There is a feeling worldwide," he stated, "that no one in the world other than President Eisenhower would have so much influence" in reaching for world peace.[24]

At the president's direction the senior staff now prepared a confidential invitation to Khrushchev. Robert Murphy, the veteran diplomat, approached Frol Kozlov, the Soviet deputy prime minister, who was in New York to preside over the Soviet exhibition, and asked him to convey a message to Khrushchev "in the strictest confidence." Murphy passed Kozlov a sealed envelope containing an invitation from Eisenhower. The visit, Eisenhower wrote, would be merely a personal discussion—not a negotiation—at the presidential retreat, Camp David, and could include a tour of the United States. The president expressed his hope that such a meeting would breathe new life into the ongoing discussions over Germany and arms control and pave the way to a larger summit of world leaders. Khrushchev received the invitation with "joy," according to his son Sergei. He was flattered; he also saw the political advantages of being treated as an equal of the United States.[25]

On July 21, the day before Nixon departed on his journey to Moscow, the Soviet ambassador brought to the White House Khrushchev's eager reply. He accepted the invitation and returned the compliment by asking Eisenhower to be his guest in the Soviet Union. They agreed to keep the invitations quiet until after Nixon had completed his trip. Eisenhower and Khrushchev, each in his own way, needed this high-profile meeting of Great Power leaders. It would augment their personal prestige, ease the cold war, and quite possibly cement their respective legacies. By the time Nixon landed in Moscow on July 23, 1959, for his tour of the USSR, his trip had become little more than a curtain-raiser for the historic Khrushchev-Eisenhower encounter.[26]

Nixon made the most of his moment on the world stage. He first met with Khrushchev in the Kremlin on July 24, where the Soviet leader began their conversation by vehemently criticizing the passage by Congress of a law proclaiming the third week in July "Captive Nations Week," a piece of cold war posturing that denounced the Soviet subjugation of Eastern Europe and the suppression of religious and political freedom. Nixon tried to explain that Congress was independent of the Executive, but Khrushchev saw the resolution as provocative propaganda. Khrushchev remained in an argumentative mood for most of the 10-day visit. When Nixon toured the American exhibit in Moscow with Khrushchev at his side, the two men held an impromptu exchange in front of a new American video camera that caught the leaders on tape. They also engaged in a boastful "debate" about the standard of living in their two countries as they stood in front of a model American kitchen, assessing the latest appliances. On a memorable trip down the Moscow River on a 25-foot motor launch, Khrushchev mocked Nixon's assertion that the people of the communist bloc lived under slavery by shouting to startled picnickers and bathers, "Are you captives? Are you slaves?" He roared with laughter as they replied "Nyet, nyet!" Nixon duly reported back to Eisenhower the details of his visit, which, he wrote with Nixonian embellishment, "can only be described as an extraordinary experience."[27]

In his 1962 book, *Six Crises*, Nixon sought to heighten the significance of the trip. He depicted his long one-on-one sessions with Khrushchev as monumental clashes of will between two tough and unforgiving combatants. Khrushchev, he wrote, was always "on the offensive," always "aggressive, rude, and forceful," always probing for weaknesses. Nixon described himself as "on edge," "keyed up," and "ready for battle." But since he was the guest, he had to avoid making any rude remarks in reply to Khrushchev's provocations. "I had to counter him like a fighter with one hand tied behind his back." Nixon fought by "Marquis of Queensberry rules," while Khrushchev punched like a "bare-knuckle slugger." The two men went "toe-to-toe"; it was "cold steel between us"; it was "hand-to-hand combat." And so on. Khrushchev would later refer to Nixon as a "son-of-a-bitch," a "puppet of McCarthy," and "an unprincipled puppet—which is the most dangerous kind." So perhaps Nixon did manage to rattle the Soviet leader.[28]

Nixon's trip served him well. He received praise from the press for his handling of Khrushchev. According to James Reston, the trip "enhanced Mr. Nixon's chances of nomination" for president by the Republican Party in 1960. In Russia, Nixon had found a more complex and dynamic society than he had expected. He had effectively spoken out about American freedom of religion and the press, and done so in a manner that was firm but respectful. Reston concluded that Nixon had "handled a delicate political assignment . . . with considerable skill." Even Walter Lippmann praised him for demonstrating that personal diplomacy could be far more effective in lowering world tensions than meetings of professional diplomats. Voters too took notice: in August and September the Gallup poll showed Nixon leading both Adlai Stevenson and John Kennedy in a presidential contest by 2 points.[29]

Eisenhower approved of Nixon's performance, but he did not wish to let the spotlight linger on his junior partner. On August 3, while Nixon was concluding his tour with a brief stop in Poland (and basking in the adulation of large crowds in Warsaw), Eisenhower made even bigger news. In a hastily prepared press conference, Eisenhower announced that he would welcome Khrushchev to the United States within a matter of weeks and would travel to the USSR by the end of the year. Giant headlines filled the world's newspapers. The exchange of visits was the biggest news story since *Sputnik*. The Soviet Union remained for many Americans a frightening and menacing country. Stalin had been dead for only six years, and memories of Soviet tanks in Budapest and Khrushchev's nuclear saber-rattling over Suez still burned. Yet Ike put out a hand of peace and invited the Soviets to grasp it.

The announcement marked a turning point for Eisenhower. The doldrums of the postelection defeat lifted; new air filled the sails of the ship of state. His approval rating, which had slumped to 52 percent in November 1958, now hit 64 percent, according to the Gallup poll. The *Wall Street Journal* hailed Ike's new "personal diplomacy" as a "sharp turn in the conduct of foreign affairs." Reston wrote that Eisenhower seemed reborn, "a man of action again, moving and planning and speaking out with a new serenity. . . . He has moved out of the shadows and into the center of the stage." With the restraining figures of Sherman Adams and John Foster Dulles gone, Eisenhower seemed more flexible, dynamic, determined to secure his legacy. "He sees the light at the end of the tunnel," Reston observed, "and some of the old sparkle has returned."

Ann Whitman, who saw the president every day and knew his moods well, described him as "happy as a lad" about the news that he and Khrushchev would exchange visits. Instead of frosty, tense arguments over Berlin and nuclear weapons, carried out by tired, faceless bureaucrats in Geneva, Eisenhower proposed "to melt a little bit of the ice that seems to freeze our relationship," as he said in his news conference. Americans overwhelmingly approved. If anyone had the prestige and stature to thaw the cold war, it was Eisenhower.[30]

V

Planning for Khrushchev's visit began immediately. On August 5 Eisenhower debriefed Nixon, who provided some churlish comments. Khrushchev, he said, had a "closed mind" and was "primitive" and "polemical." Nixon suggested that the State Department arrange long meetings with Khrushchev to tire him out and "ferret out his main points" before he met with Eisenhower, so as to put him at a disadvantage—precisely the tactic to which Nixon had been subjected. From the U.S. Embassy in Moscow, Ambassador Llewellyn "Tommy" Thompson, who had replaced Chip Bohlen in 1957, cabled Eisenhower with more thoughtful advice. Khrushchev, he reminded Ike, was a true believer in communism and in the inevitable collapse of capitalism. If organized correctly, the trip might "shake his convictions" that America was a feeble, rotten society. The trip should demonstrate the "long-term prospects for growth" of the vast American economy. If Khrushchev was forced to confront the reality of American power and industry, he might prove more amenable at the conference table.[31]

Eisenhower reiterated to his advisers that while he did not anticipate any major breakthrough with Khrushchev, he wanted "to bring about some lessening of tension" and "some measure of confidence and relief to the minds of our people." In a revealing phrase, he told Staff Secretary Andrew Goodpaster that he thought "he personally might make an appeal to Khrushchev in terms of his place in history" by taking steps to ease the cold war. He planned to warm him up by hosting him both at Gettysburg and at Camp David in an informal setting where the two could try to move beyond stale ideological arguments.[32]

One crucial preliminary task awaited before Ike met with the Soviet leader. He had to reassure his NATO allies that the United States did not intend to negotiate any grand bargain in the cold war or sell out West Germany by agreeing to Khrushchev's demands. To make his point, in late summer Eisenhower conducted a hasty tour of three key capital cities: Bonn, London, and Paris. On August 26 he set off for West Germany and was met by Chancellor Konrad Adenauer and by an enormous crowd lining the streets of the capital city—a heartwarming welcome for the man who, only 14 years earlier, had arrived in Germany as a conqueror. Now Eisenhower came as a symbol of America's commitment to defend Germany from Soviet pressure. A day of discussion with Adenauer left the Germans reassured: the allies would stay in Berlin and never cede their rights there under duress.[33]

A short hop to London followed. In the late afternoon of August 27 Eisenhower and Prime Minister Macmillan rode together from the airport to the American Embassy in an open car past great crowds of well-wishers, gathered in the lingering sunshine to get a peek at the man so beloved in Britain. The car moved, Macmillan recalled, "at a snail's pace," with no security or police protection. This was a reunion of friends. Eisenhower was the guest of Queen Elizabeth II for the weekend at Balmoral, the Scottish home of the royal family. The 33-year-old queen drove Eisenhower around the vast parklands in her station wagon, across moors and rutted roads, and served him tea and scones in a remote stone cottage looking out over the Caledonian heather.

Back in London, Macmillan again tried to press Eisenhower to agree to a summit of the Big Four powers. Ike remained noncommittal, stressing that he did not want to look as if he had been bullied by Khrushchev into a negotiation. He would wait and see how the Khrushchev visit unfolded. This stubbornness frustrated Macmillan, but he bit his tongue because the joint appearance with the American president on a live television broadcast, direct from 10 Downing Street on the evening of August 31, did wonders for the prime minister's political popularity. Just a few days after Eisenhower's departure, Macmillan seized the opportunity to announce the dissolution of Parliament and called a general election. The Eisenhower magic, it seemed, even rubbed off on Macmillan.[34]

On September 1, his last night in London, the president hosted an extraordinary dinner at Winfield House, the American ambassador's residence. It was a gathering of wartime compatriots that served to remind the world, if anyone had forgotten, that Eisenhower stood at the center of a transatlantic fellowship of great warriors and leaders. To dine with the president came former prime minister Winston Churchill, now almost 85, as well as the great British generals whom Ike had fought alongside, including Field Marshals Alanbrooke and Montgomery. A passage from Shakespeare's *Henry V* sprang to Eisenhower's mind:

> *Old men forget: yet all shall be forgot,*
> *But he'll remember with advantages*
> *What feats he did that day: then shall our names . . .*
> *Be in their flowing cups freshly remember'd.*[35]

From London, Eisenhower headed to Paris for what John Eisenhower called "the stickiest part of the trip": a meeting with President Charles de Gaulle. Eisenhower had not seen de Gaulle since the war. A tall, humorless nationalist, a man acutely sensitive to any slight or condescension from the Anglo-Americans, de Gaulle had been a difficult, inflexible ally during the war. In office since 1958, he still crossed swords with the Americans on a variety of matters. But on one important issue Eisenhower and de Gaulle strongly agreed: Berlin. The Allied powers were there by right and would not be pushed out by Soviet threats. The USSR, de Gaulle insisted, must never conclude that it could intimidate the West. Eisenhower came away from the Paris trip heartened by the stalwart support of France. As an old soldier, Eisenhower admired de Gaulle's "mystical self-confidence and his unswerving dedication to the restoration of French prestige." The two great war leaders stood shoulder to shoulder before enormous crowds on the balcony of the Hôtel de Ville and in a somber ceremony placed a wreath at the tomb of the unknown soldier at the Arc de Triomphe.[36]

VI

With his allies squarely behind him, Eisenhower braced for the arrival of the Soviet leader. On the eve of the big event, Ike received an irksome piece of news. On September 12 the Soviets had fired a new rocket, *Lunik II*, into space, and the next day the spacecraft plunked down on the moon, becoming the first man-made object to land there. Eisenhower called the moonshot "poor behavior" by the USSR. He snappishly said he was trying to "make one big effort to see if the Soviets will loosen up and adopt a cooperative approach to world problems." Why would they now launch another rocket to tweak the Americans? He had perhaps forgotten the impact on the Soviets of the congressional "Captive Nations" declaration on the eve of Nixon's trip. The Americans too were capable of poor behavior: the day before Khrushchev's arrival, Nixon delivered a dinner speech to 2,500 dentists at the New York Waldorf Astoria in which he called the Soviet leader "cold, calculating, and tough-minded" and said that showing any signs of compromise toward the USSR "would be a grave mistake." Keen to protect his anticommunist credentials, Nixon seemed to be distancing himself from Eisenhower's charm offensive.[37]

Khrushchev, the chairman of the Council of Ministers and first secretary of the Central Committee of the Communist Party of the USSR, arrived in Washington on September 15, 1959, accompanied by an entourage of over 100 officials. In his memoirs he admitted he was "worried" about the trip. "This was America!" he recalled. "It was necessary to represent the USSR in a worthy manner." He felt pressure to "argue for our position and defend it in a worthy way so as not to humiliate ourselves." As his son later recounted, Khrushchev fretted over "every trivial detail," feeling certain that the "capitalists and aristocrats" would look on him as an inferior. For example, he thought holding meetings at Camp David might be some kind of slight, as if he was not important enough to be welcomed to the White House. He had insisted on traveling to Washington in the world's largest passenger plane, the huge new Tupolev 114, despite the engineering flaws and cracks that its designers had recently discovered. Khrushchev was delighted that the plane was too big to land at National Airport and had to be rerouted to Andrews Air Force Base, with its longer runways.[38]

If he was nervous, Khrushchev hid it well. Wiley Buchanan, the White House chief of protocol, remembered the scene: "He came down the stairs [of the plane] with a springy stride, a chunky little bald-headed man who looked more like a teddy-bear than a monster." He carried a black homburg hat and sported two Hero of Socialist Labor medals on his left lapel and a Lenin Peace Prize on his right. "He was smiling broadly, but his sharp little eyes were shrewd and appraising." Before him spooled out an immense red carpet along which stood a glittering honor guard. Eisenhower "looked grim," perhaps because as he stood at attention for the national anthems, he faced directly into the sun and had to squint. But he also took umbrage at Khrushchev's short speech, in which he bragged about the Soviet space program. The president and his guest strode past the handsomely arrayed soldiers of the 3rd Infantry and got into an open limousine for the 15-mile drive into Washington. Along the route they sped past hundreds of Secret Service officers and police and thousands of curious but silent onlookers.[39]

Khrushchev, his wife, Nina Petrovna, their two grown daughters, Rada and Julia, and a small party of top officials were driven to Blair House, the guest residence for official visitors. Shortly after his arrival, Khrushchev met with Eisenhower in the Oval Office for 90 minutes, during which the two men reiterated their shared desire for peace and a new beginning in their relations. But they did not limit themselves to pleasantries. Khrushchev presented Eisenhower with a copy of the small hammer-and-sickle pennant that the *Lunik* rocket had just speared into the moon—an ill-mannered reminder of Soviet scientific prowess. He also presented him with a shotgun, a highly polished box containing special wines and vodkas, 12 jars of caviar, and a collection of records of Russian folk songs. Ike moved directly to the main subject of contention, Berlin, stressing that while the whole situation was "abnormal" and "irritating," America would never surrender its rights there nor respond to ultimatums. Khrushchev insisted that he wanted peaceful ties and pointed to Nixon's provocative speech of the day before, suggesting that the Americans had shown a lack of respect to their guest. All in all, it was an awkward beginning.[40]

Eisenhower, not wishing to start the visit on the wrong foot, dismissed all the senior staff and advisers from the Oval Office, keeping only two translators. In a 10-minute tête-à-tête Ike delivered his planned personal appeal to the Soviet leader, saying that Khrushchev "had an opportunity to become the greatest political figure in history" by taking up the cause of peace and changing the direction of Soviet policy. But the gesture fell flat. Khrushchev firmly replied that both sides must compromise. And with that, the president walked his guest onto the South Lawn for an impromptu helicopter tour of Washington. They slowly lifted off, then veered out across the city at rush hour, gazing down at the Washington Monument, the Lincoln Memorial, and the Potomac River, its waters rippling in the fading sunlight.[41]

The visit never settled into a comfortable rhythm. Khrushchev managed to find small ways to upset his hosts, whether refusing to dress appropriately for the large formal state dinner at the White House that night, or raising his glass with a toast to a future in which the USSR would soon outproduce America, or sitting grimly through an evening performance by Fred Waring and his Pennsylvanians as they played "The Battle Hymn of the Republic" and other patriotic tunes. American journalists at the National Press Club angered Khrushchev the next day by asking him embarrassing questions such as "What were you doing while Stalin was committing his crimes?" and "[How do you] justify armed intervention in Hungary?" According to Wiley Buchanan, as Khrushchev listened to these questions, "a tide of red crept up his bull neck; his little eyes glared with a ferocity that reminded me of a wild boar." But that night he hosted Eisenhower at the grand Soviet Embassy (a Beaux-Arts mansion built by the sleeping-car tycoon George Pullman) for a lavish dinner of caviar, black bread, vodka, borscht, stuffed partridges, and shashlik. Khrushchev even echoed Eisenhower's words when he said in his toast, "The ice of the cold war . . . has started to crumble."[42]

After a train ride to New York on September 17, the Soviet delegation was installed at the Commodore Hotel and given lunch by the mayor, Robert Wagner. More awkwardness ensued. Khrushchev addressed a dinner that night at the Economic Club of New York and was openly heckled by drunken members of the audience, eliciting an apology from the club's president. The next day he made a hasty trip to Hyde Park to pay his respects to Eleanor Roosevelt and lay a wreath at the grave of the former president. He toured the Roosevelt home but seemed uninterested and disengaged.

"I'm not getting through to him!" Mrs. Roosevelt sighed. He skipped a lavish buffet lunch that she had arranged and sped back to New York. At the United Nations that afternoon he delivered an address calling for total world disarmament and the banning of atomic weapons—a disheartening speech that contained shopworn phrases and empty rhetoric. By the end of his East Coast trip, Americans had begun to grow disappointed with the "tough, high-tempered, chip-on-the-shoulder Khrushchev," as Chalmers Roberts of the *Washington Post* described him.[43]

Then the trip, already going wobbly, took a turn for the worse. In New York, Henry Cabot Lodge Jr., ambassador to the United Nations, joined the party as Eisenhower's personal representative and accompanied the visitors on a cross-country flight to Los Angeles. There they were greeted by what Lodge recalled as a "smoldering, Sahara-like heat," as well as a tomato thrown by a youth at the chairman as he left the airport. (It missed.) Inexplicably the first item on the itinerary was a visit to the studios of Twentieth Century Fox, where a cast of Hollywood stars awaited. At that moment Fox was filming *Can Can*, a vapid song-and-dance picture starring Frank Sinatra, Shirley MacLaine, Maurice Chevalier, and Louis Jourdan—all of whom were present to greet the Soviet leader, along with dozens of curious onlookers, including David Niven, Bob Hope, Gary Cooper, Charlton Heston, and Marilyn Monroe. The plot of the movie centered on the performance of a dance routine in the nightclubs of Paris, so the studio was crawling with dance girls in French ruffled skirts "exposing plenty of bare things and black garters," according to Lodge. The foreign guests were treated to a chorus number, which featured, to the horror of the American hosts, "a brassy, sexy dance scene." When a photographer tried to get the dancers to do a high kick while posing alongside Khrushchev, the Soviets put a halt to the risqué performance.

That night, at a huge dinner at the Ambassador Hotel, Khrushchev had the feeling that the wealthy dinner guests mainly wanted "to have a look at the strange guest as a kind of exotic bear from Russia." The mayor of Los Angeles, Norris Poulson, delivered the last straw with a bellicose, sneering speech, asserting, "We shall fight to the death to preserve our way of life." Khrushchev asked for the microphone and replied in a violent outburst that he was President Eisenhower's guest and he would not tolerate "any disparagement, any humiliation" against the Soviet Union. As he put it later, "It was necessary to let this anti-Soviet person have it in the teeth." By midnight the delegation had lodged a formal protest and threatened to pack their bags and return home. Lodge feared the trip had become "a horrible failure." Freeman Gosden, a radio personality and Ike's golf pal, told Ann Whitman, "Everyone in Los Angeles has decided that their town is going to be the first one the Russians aim a missile at!"[44]

VII

As they left Los Angeles by train to San Francisco, cooler weather seemed to soothe the visiting dignitaries. On the ride north, Khrushchev delighted in getting off the train at local stops to shake hands and engage with ordinary people, who cheerfully greeted him. The city by the bay charmed him with its beauty and demeanor; it was the most beautiful place in the country, Khrushchev declared. Triumphantly he said to Lodge, "The plain people of America like me. It's just those bastards around Eisenhower that don't." Next came a stop in Iowa to visit a corn farm and meatpacking plant, a day in Pittsburgh, and then back to Washington and a huge reception at the Soviet Embassy, where the 24-year-old piano prodigy Van Cliburn, who had recently won the prestigious Tchaikovsky piano competition in Moscow, entertained the guests.[45]

Now at long last Khrushchev and Eisenhower met for their two days of personal talks at Camp David. Just after 5:00 p.m. on September 25, the two men departed from the White House by helicopter for a 35-minute ride to the Maryland mountain retreat. Eisenhower had been told by Lodge, who spent a week in close contact with Khrushchev, that the Soviet leader "wants peace . . . and needs peace." He had been "deeply impressed" by what he had seen on the trip and privately had acknowledged to Lodge that the Soviet Union was still far behind America in its economic development. Yet Eisenhower approached the weekend at Camp David warily, as if fearing he might lower his guard and give away too much.[46]

He need not have worried. The meetings at Camp David produced little, other than the remarkable fact that they happened at all. In their first meeting, over breakfast on September 26—a foggy, damp morning—the two men talked mostly about the Second World War and Khrushchev's relations with Stalin in those years. Khrushchev seemed relaxed, wearing a loose embroidered shirt, but picked at his food. According to John Eisenhower, he seemed intent on establishing an "old-soldier rapport" with the president and passed on the news that Stalin had always praised the fighting qualities of General Ike. The two men even strolled around the grounds together companionably. But when the discussions moved on to Berlin, there was no room for compromise. Eisenhower said the ultimatum on Berlin was unacceptable to the Americans; Khrushchev insisted the status quo in the divided city was unacceptable to the Soviets. The two leaders were earnest, frank, and unmovable. And there the matter rested.

Hoping at least to keep up the cordial atmosphere, Eisenhower called for his helicopter. At 4:30 p.m. they took off for Gettysburg, to tour the family farm. They looked over the grazing cattle, admired the freshly scrubbed Eisenhower grandchildren, and sat for an hour on the glass porch. John Eisenhower recalled that these were the moments when Khrushchev was at his best, posing as a "beneficent grandfather," admiring the children and giving them trinkets. Back at Camp David the leaders dined on strip steak, creamed broccoli, and Pol Roger 1952 Champagne, then gathered in the film room to watch a few recent westerns—*Shane, Gunfight at the O.K. Corral*, and *High Noon*. Khrushchev remarked that Stalin too enjoyed watching westerns, and though he loudly denounced their reactionary political content, he was always eager for more.[47]

Khrushchev admired Eisenhower and found him "a very good-hearted man and a good conversationalist." But they made no progress on substantive issues. Berlin, disarmament, trade relations, and the nuclear test ban questions—nothing moved. "We knew their position and they knew ours," Khrushchev recalled. Both men were cordial but inflexible. Neither seemed too concerned. In fact they had not come to negotiate a real resolution of concrete points but simply to demystify one another, to humanize the U.S.-Soviet relationship. In the course of a long weekend, over meals, movies, walks in the woods, helicopter rides, and the swapping of war stories, this is exactly what happened. The only specific result of the conversations was that Khrushchev agreed to announce that he had withdrawn his ultimatum over Berlin and Eisenhower agreed to keep discussing future solutions to the German problem. He also signaled his willingness to attend a summit meeting of the Big Four in the spring of 1960, followed by a visit to the Soviet Union.[48]

By the time of Khrushchev's departure, at 11:00 p.m. on September 27, the cold war had shifted from a bitter rivalry into something else, a competition to be sure, but one that could be disputed with words and ideas rather than nuclear weapons. The two leaders had engaged with one another on a personal, human level as never before. Khrushchev's visit had been at times tense and awkward, at times comic and downright goofy. But it had sparked curiosity and even some goodwill. Ike told a press conference that the "threat" of war over Berlin had been lifted. In his last act in the United States, Khrushchev delivered a televised address to the American public—a remarkable occurrence in a country that only five years earlier had been gripped by the anticommunist hysteria of the McCarthy hearings. Khrushchev praised "the beautiful cities, wonderful roads, but most of all your amiable and kind-hearted people." He spoke of the "common understanding on many points" that he and Eisenhower reached. The press inevitably hailed the "spirit of Camp David."[49]

Back in the Soviet Union Khrushchev received a tumultuous welcome. According to biographer William Taubman, Khrushchev was "elated" by the trip, by the prestige it gave him as an equal of Eisenhower's, and as a vindication of his policy of détente toward the United States. In a staged tribute to the returning leader, adoring party functionaries hailed Khrushchev for "crushing the ice of the cold war with the strength of an ice-breaker." He promised a "new era" of peace and praised Eisenhower's "wise statesmanship." And he took particular delight that Eisenhower now agreed to visit the Soviet Union the following spring to show his respect and to continue their rapprochement. Khrushchev believed that he had pulled off his great gamble: he had moderated the cold war, won the support of the American president, and fended off hard-liners and militarists in the Soviet system. He all but promised his people an end to the cold war as a result of his American overtures.[50]

Back in the United States, there were two chief winners of the "spirit of Camp David." One was Nixon. Russell Baker of the *New York Times* wrote that Nixon could now run in 1960 as the candidate best qualified to maintain Eisenhower's personal diplomacy and his "peace policy," since he had helped to launch it. Nixon could, and did, claim that he had shown his talent for toe-to-toe combat with the Soviet leader, yet he also knew how to keep the USSR at the negotiating table. He described himself as the man who could "straighten out" the Soviets while avoiding war.[51]

But the real winner was Eisenhower. His personal diplomacy had restored his aura of world statesman, moving boldly and leaving tawdry partisan quarrels behind him. And he kept up the momentum. In December 1959 he departed on a 20,000-mile trip to India, Pakistan, Afghanistan, Iran, Turkey, and Europe to continue his global goodwill tour, just as Hagerty had advised a year earlier. In 1959 Eisenhower built a legacy as a man of peace who was also a man of firm principle where America's rights were concerned. Of course there were those who feared the president had appeased Khrushchev by agreeing to negotiate about Berlin. Joseph Alsop, in a column that infuriated Eisenhower, considered Ike the new Neville Chamberlain. (Eisenhower privately called Alsop a "bastard" in return.)[52]

But the public looked on Eisenhower's personal diplomacy enthusiastically. Just six years earlier America had been at war in Korea against the forces of "international Communism." In his first term Ike stressed that the nation was "in peril" as a result of the communist threat. The frenzy of the McCarthy era remained white hot through 1954, and in 1956 the invasion of Hungary made the Soviets look like ruthless beasts. The early phase of the space race alarmed Americans and drew their eyes upward to search the nighttime skies for Soviet rockets. Yet now, at the close of 1959, Eisenhower, at his paternal and unruffled best, assured his people that the cold war could be managed, eased, and perhaps even defrosted through the power of his ice-melting charm. All that remained was to put Ike's warm words of peace into action.

CHAPTER 17

SECRET WARS IN THE THIRD WORLD

"Our hand should not show in anything that is done."

I

ON NOVEMBER 3, 1959, EISENHOWER'S LIMOUSINE PULLED OUT of the White House gates just after 11:00 a.m. and headed west, toward the Arlington Memorial Bridge and the Potomac River. Crossing into Virginia, the car eased onto the George Washington Parkway, a scenic road that carried the president northeast, along the Virginia bank of the river. After just a few miles the president got out to cut a ribbon to celebrate the opening of a stretch of the road that had been specially constructed for the employees of a federal agency whose new offices were being built in the quiet, woodsy hills nearby. The ceremonial act completed, Ike got back into the car and drove the remaining few miles to his destination: a leafy, 140-acre parcel of land that had been named two centuries earlier by Sir Thomas Lee, a prosperous 18th-century Englishman, after his ancestral home in Shropshire: Langley.

On this private and secluded spot, nine miles from the White House, construction crews had been busy for months laying the foundations of a sprawling new complex. They halted their noisy work on this warm autumn day to observe a solemn and significant occasion. President Eisenhower had arrived to lay the cornerstone of the new headquarters of the Central Intelligence Agency.

Building a new home for America's spy agency had become an obsession of its director Allen Dulles. In 1955 Dulles won a whopping $45 million congressional appropriation to construct a building on a secluded "campus" in Virginia in order to gather in one place the many pieces of his clandestine service that had previously been scattered around Washington. Some CIA employees were still holed up in World War II–era temporary shacks along the National Mall. It was a sign of the growing importance of the CIA that it should be so richly rewarded with a gleaming new headquarters. Designed by the firm of Harrison and Abramovitz, the concrete and glass office looked like a huge H, but with two horizontal connecting bars. A perfect midcentury modern office block, it would feature air-conditioning throughout the building, self-operated elevators, an airy cafeteria, and a 3,000-car parking lot.

In the bright fall sunshine, standing in front of a large marble plinth, Eisenhower used a small silver trowel to dab some mortar onto a ceremonial stone. Then Dulles spoke. The CIA, he said, was one of the great agencies tasked with protecting the nation's security. It had grown so large because "our vital interests are at stake in places as distant as Korea, and Laos, and Central Africa, and in the islands of the Pacific as well as in this hemisphere and Europe." He praised the "high purpose and dedication" of the employees who strove "fearlessly" to protect the nation. And he solemnly declared that the CIA must be guided by truth and facts rather than wedded to "causes and theories." Ideologies had no place in the intelligence business. With that he unveiled the marble slab on which was engraved a verse from the Gospel of John: "Ye shall know the truth, and the truth shall make you free."

Eisenhower echoed these sentiments. The secret work of the CIA, he said, demanded "dedication, ability, trustworthiness," and "the finest type of courage." The successes of the CIA "cannot be advertised, failure cannot be explained. In the work of intelligence, heroes are undecorated and unsung." Their reward came from knowing that they were performing "an indispensable service for their country."[1]

With his trowel of cement, Eisenhower laid the foundations of a secret global empire dedicated to using any means necessary to advance American interests in the perilous cold war struggle. Beyond collecting intelligence through aerial overflights and other forms of electronic eavesdropping, Eisenhower's CIA also undertook an astonishing range of covert actions against various enemies who were thought to pose a threat to the United States and its friends. Eisenhower condoned those secret wars with the argument that the ends justify the means. In facing an insidious global enemy, the United States had to use every tool at its disposal to fight back. It is a powerful argument that has held sway in every presidency since then.

Unfortunately Eisenhower's CIA did far more harm than good to American interests. Rather than enhancing national security, Eisenhower's secret wars created great human suffering, propped up awful dictatorships, left the U.S. government vulnerable to exposure and public humiliation, and alienated millions of people who otherwise had reason to like and admire the United States. Over the course of the 1950s the CIA engaged in sabotage, arms smuggling, destabilizing of governments, widespread radio and print propaganda, and the arming of insurgencies. It supplied arms, intelligence, and training to certain friendly regimes that were engaged in repression, summary arrests, torture, and murder. And it plotted the ouster and in a few cases the assassination of foreign leaders, violating American law and tarnishing America's reputation.

Why did Eisenhower order such brutal and ultimately damaging secret operations, especially at a time when he was attempting to improve relations with the USSR? The simplest answer points to a failure of moral imagination. Eisenhower's cold war strategy rested on these basic principles: To deter the USSR from attacking the United States, Ike invested heavily in nuclear weapons and air defense. To contain the USSR, he built global alliances and positioned American troops overseas. To surpass the Soviet system, he encouraged economic growth at home and demanded prudent stewardship of the domestic economy. And to foil the global design of communist expansion, he willingly embraced covert operations to weaken the ability of threatening nations, leaders, and movements to harm American interests. That made a kind of sense.

The failure lay in misunderstanding the long-term consequences of such policies for the billions of people just emerging from centuries of repressive European colonial rule. When Asians and Africans shook off colonial despotism, they often embraced revolutionary nationalism, radical socialism, and communism, not because they wished to become the lackeys of the Soviet Union but because they desired economic justice, distribution of wealth, agrarian reform, and the breakup of foreign economic control of their natural resources. Such demands sounded threatening to American ears. And when threatened, American officials in the Age of Eisenhower tended to retreat to the well-defended ramparts of anticommunism. Eisenhower and his advisers refused to put themselves in the shoes of the struggling rebels, wild-eyed radicals, and utopian dreamers who populated the nationalist movements of the Third World. And that lack of empathy too often led to policies that earned the United States the enduring hostility of newly independent nations.[2]

Having embraced the rationale for an active program of covert operations, Eisenhower compounded the problem by giving Allen Dulles free rein. He had known since the 1954 Doolittle Report that Dulles was a poor manager, but he continued to rely on him, perhaps out of respect for his experience and his brother. He did try to create better supervision of the CIA. At the end of 1955 Eisenhower ordered the creation of an interdepartmental committee to monitor covert operations and report back to him. The group became known as the Special Group, or the 5412 Committee, because it had been called into being by NSC 5412/2 on December 28, 1955. At the 5412 Committee meetings representatives from the State Department, Defense, and the White House met with the director of the CIA, ostensibly to review ongoing operations.

The real purpose of the committee, though, was to allow Eisenhower to stay in the loop while sustaining the principle of "plausible deniability." As long as the president did not formally chair discussions of such secret activities, he could always claim that he did not know about them. Dulles chafed at even this weak oversight. He faithfully informed Eisenhower about covert operations but sidetracked the bureaucracy. Until the end of the Eisenhower years, and indeed beyond, the initiative for designing and implementing covert operations remained with Dulles, who answered only to the president.[3]

A little more than a month after meeting with Khrushchev and insisting on his desire for world peace, Eisenhower had no difficulty pivoting back to the dirty business of waging the cold war. He ardently believed communism to be a misguided ideology nourished by false hopes and empty promises. Above all, he considered it a mortal threat to the United States. So no matter how earnestly and frequently he spoke the language of peace in public, behind closed doors he remained a determined and ruthless cold warrior. He saw no contradiction between his aspirations as a statesman of peace and his persistent reliance on subversion and deceit in the secret wars of the 1950s.

II

In 1957 the CIA implemented the largest covert military operation it had ever attempted in its decade-long history. That year had been a tumultuous one in Indonesia, the oil-rich archipelago of 17,000 islands stretching along the strategic sea lanes between the Indian and Pacific oceans. It was then that President Sukarno, the country's first post-independence leader, established a new ruling order that he termed "guided democracy" in order to distinguish it from the chaotic experiment in parliamentary democracy he had led since 1950. Sukarno's model offered a kind of multiparty dictatorship, in cooperation with the Communist Party of Indonesia (PKI) and the army, which declared martial law in March 1957. In the eyes of U.S. observers, these moves, which seemed to trample democracy, embrace military rule, and appease the communists, looked extremely dangerous. Not surprisingly CIA analysts rang the alarm bells.

Sukarno had been on a CIA watch list ever since he hosted the 1955 Bandung Conference in April 1955. The conference had gathered representatives from 29 Asian and African nations in an effort to oppose the cold war division of the world into two blocs. The gathering gave voice to the powerful anticolonial sentiments of the Third World and pledged the delegates to an agenda of anticolonial solidarity. Naturally the conference served to heighten suspicions in Washington about Sukarno's left-leaning ideology, and he was ever after a marked man.

When in 1957 Sukarno seemed inclined to welcome communists into his government, Washington lost little time in acting against him. In August the CIA put together a study group to make recommendations, which were duly presented to the National Security Council in September. The CIA jumped to the worst-case scenario: a loss of Indonesia to communist forces would allow the Soviet bloc to "threaten directly Malaya, Singapore, British Borneo, the Philippines, New Guinea, and Australia. . . . The U.S. strategic posture in Southeast Asia and the Southwest Pacific would be jeopardized." And U.S. military supply operations in support of friendly governments in Laos, Cambodia, Thailand, Vietnam, and Malaya would be hampered. "Furthermore," the memo asserted, "the Communist bloc would benefit from the exploitation of Indonesia's oil, rubber, and tin." Guided by the powerful paradigm of the domino theory, CIA analysts concluded that communist influence in Indonesia constituted a direct threat to the United States.[4]

Allen Dulles reached into his Guatemala playbook and proposed creating a force of disaffected army officers and rebellious right-wingers who would build a base of operations on the Indonesian island of Sumatra. Deploying "all feasible covert means" to build up this rebel army, the United States would then use this force to exert pressure on Sukarno if he should move any further to the left. If the communists seized the central government, the forces in Sumatra would become "a rallying point" to launch a military counterattack. U.S. arms deliveries began in October 1957 and carried on for months, some coming by air drops, others by ship and submarine. These arms shipments had to remain secret, for the United States continued to pose publicly as a friend, albeit a concerned one, to Indonesia, urging Sukarno through diplomatic channels to crack down on the PKI. Privately, however, John Foster Dulles described Sukarno as "dangerous and untrustworthy" and "susceptible to the Communist way of thinking." Coming from Dulles, that amounted to a death sentence.[5]

On February 10, 1958, these CIA-supplied rebels in Sumatra issued an ultimatum to Sukarno to fire his cabinet, ban the communists from positions of influence, and hold national elections. Following a defiant reply from Sukarno, they declared the formation of a provisional government. Allen Dulles egged them on, hoping for "widespread guerilla warfare on Java," the central island and home to the capital city, Jakarta. However, the uprising proved premature. The Indonesian Army and Air Force, largely loyal to Sukarno, launched successful raids against the rebel strongholds on Sumatra in February and March, causing Allen Dulles to wonder if perhaps the United States should shed its mask of neutrality and intervene directly. "If this dissident movement now went down the drain," he told Eisenhower, "Indonesia would go over to the Communists." The president was inclined to agree, replying, "We would have to go in if a Communist take-over really threatened."[6]

But did it? Having routed the rebels in Sumatra, Sukarno tried to assure the United States that, as he put it to the new U.S. ambassador, Howard P. Jones, "he was no Communist." Sukarno said he wanted a neutral and independent Indonesia: "Nationalism is the fire that is sweeping Asia. . . . I am a nationalist but no Communist." It was extremely difficult for the Americans to accept this self-portrait. In Allen Dulles's mind, any leader who allowed communists into his cabinet or who failed to see communists as a mortal threat was at least a stooge and a knave, and more likely a secret Red. Along with many other Afro-Asian leaders, Sukarno insisted on a middle ground: that communism, if balanced by other factions in a plural system, could be contained and tolerated. Sukarno proposed simply to keep his friends close and his enemies closer.[7]

As the Indonesian Air Force pummeled the rebel positions on Sumatra, the CIA refused to give up, rushing more guns, ammunition, and supplies to the rebels, even at the risk of discovery. The American press got wind of these operations in April and began to pepper Foster Dulles with questions about American support for the rebel force. Dulles denied any knowledge. On April 15 Eisenhower, growing wary, told Secretary Dulles that he "did not want any U.S. government personnel or persons . . . taking part in any operations partaking of a military character in Indonesia." But, he went on, "private persons operating on their own," or "soldiers of fortune," could still be deployed. This was vintage circumlocution to insist that the CIA carefully cover its tracks and obscure its airborne assistance to the rebels. Predictably this is just where things went wrong.[8]

The CIA, anxious to put some spine into the besieged rebels, cobbled together a few surplus B-26 bombers and P-51 fighter aircraft from Clark Air Base in the Philippines and put CIA-trained "civilian" pilots in them. In late April and early May these planes bombed oil installations, tankers, and Indonesian Navy gunboats, in operations designed to make it appear that the rebels were regrouping and had hidden reserves of air power. But on May 18 a B-26 was shot down, and its pilot, an American named Allen Lawrence Pope, was captured alive and in possession of incriminating papers. The involvement of the United States had been revealed, and Allen Dulles immediately canceled all further operations in support of the rebels. But it was too late. On May 27 Pope was placed in front of cameras at a news conference in Djakarta. Ambassador Jones "expressed regret that a private American citizen was involved as a paid soldier of fortune serving with the rebel forces." Not for the last time Eisenhower and the CIA had been caught with their hands in the cookie jar.[9]

III

The CIA did not limit itself to destabilizing unfriendly governments; sometimes it expended its resources to prop up friendly ones. On May 8, 1957, Eisenhower welcomed to Washington one of the most prominent recipients of American military and economic aid: the president of South Vietnam, Ngo Dinh Diem. Eisenhower viewed Diem as so important to America's grand strategy in Asia that he personally appeared at National Airport to greet the visiting leader, an honor Ike bestowed only once before, when King Saud of Saudi Arabia came to town just a few months earlier. And no wonder. While prominent Asian leaders like Indonesia's Sukarno and India's Nehru had proclaimed neutrality in the cold war, Diem had fought relentlessly since 1954 against communists inside South Vietnam and transformed his nation into a pro-American bastion.[10]

Diem did not see himself as an American puppet. Born into a prominent Catholic family of administrators and clerks, this devout, lifelong celibate was groomed for a career as a colonial bureaucrat. But his pride and nationalism led him to reject the path laid out for him. Refusing to work for either the French colonists or the Vietnamese administration that served the French, in 1933 he resigned his post as a regional functionary and spent the better part of two decades quietly laying the foundations of a nationalist, noncommunist opposition to French rule. In the early 1950s he spent more than three years in the United States, living chiefly at a Maryknoll seminary in New Jersey and cultivating ties to many American politicians, including Senators John Kennedy and Mike Mansfield (both Catholic), publisher Henry Luce, and Cardinal Spellman, the archbishop of New York. Though he had no official role, these contacts would prove invaluable to him later in gaining American support.

In June 1954, as the French and Vietnamese communists hammered out the Geneva accords that partitioned Vietnam at the 17th parallel, Diem saw his chance. At the request of Emperor Bao Dai, Diem returned to Vietnam to form a government that would usher out the hated French and open the way to the creation of an independent and noncommunist South Vietnam. A short, stocky man with heavily oiled hair who always seemed to be drowning in the folds of his double-breasted sharkskin suits, Diem became the face of a new experiment in Asian self-rule.[11]

Although Diem was a Catholic in a Buddhist country; although his extended family, the Ngo clan, had a notorious reputation for corruption, criminality, and connections to reactionary military circles; and although he had little popular appeal or legitimacy, he seemed to the Americans the perfect man to build a free and democratic South Vietnam. He was ferociously anticommunist. His Catholicism marked him as Western in American eyes. And he already had close friends in Washington. In fact his brother, Ngo Dinh Nhu, had been working with the CIA since 1952 and would maintain that link for the rest of the decade. As Diem consolidated power, he relied upon American support to fend off a military coup attempt in 1954 as well as uprisings launched by sects and gangs in Saigon in 1955. The CIA sent an experienced hand to help him: Edward Lansdale, an air force officer and former operative in the Office of Strategic Services (OSS) who had spent years in the Philippines assisting in the repression of a communist insurgency there. From the start of his regime Diem relied upon the CIA for intelligence, training, and counterinsurgency activity. In October 1955 he staged a bogus referendum that proposed to abolish the monarchy and approve a new constitution giving the president sweeping powers. On the eve of the referendum, Lansdale urged Diem to limit himself to only modest vote-rigging; Diem instead announced a vote total of 98 percent in favor of his new regime.[12]

As Diem's power grew, his relationship with the United States became more troubled. He was an authoritarian man with a messiah complex. He relied upon his brother, who ran the secret police, to wage a relentless war upon communist sympathizers and subversives. By itself that did not displease Washington, but the methods used—mass arrests, torture, wanton murder—did upset the narrative that Washington wished to write of Diem as a model Asian leader. Even the CIA station in Saigon urged Diem to adopt land reform and political liberalization so as to develop some degree of popular support and legitimacy. Diem refused, citing the constant threat of internal subversion as a reason to focus on building up the South Vietnamese Army and deploying harsh tactics against any dissidents.

Diem understood that he could manipulate the Americans. In return for his anticommunism, he sought and received enormous amounts of aid, totaling $2 billion between 1954 and 1961. Not only did the United States supply the South Vietnamese Army and security police, but it gave vast sums in the form of development aid and loans, allowing South Vietnam to purchase huge quantities of American cars, trucks, household goods, and food. The United States built roads, bridges, schools, railways, canals, and airports; set up a national telecommunications network; supplied civil aviation aircraft; and implemented nationwide English-language education. South Vietnam rapidly became the showcase for the American way of modernization and militarization in the Third World. And all the while hopes for democratization withered.[13]

American officials consoled themselves that, for all his shortcomings, Diem nevertheless shared America's aims in Asia. A briefing book prepared for Eisenhower on the eve of Diem's visit declared that Diem "feels that Vietnam in its present situation and given its own heritage is not yet ready for a democratic government. . . . His concept is one of benevolent authoritarianism." Diem "believes that the Vietnamese people are not the best judges of what is good for them." While these attitudes prompted some discomfort in Washington, Diem's anticommunism inoculated him from serious American criticism.[14]

When Diem met with Eisenhower at the White House on May 9, 1957, Ike praised him for "the excellent achievements he has brought about" and barely registered any protest when Diem insisted that he needed more military aid. Given the honor of addressing a joint session of Congress, Diem declared that his country had used its annual subvention of $250 million to wage war on communism. The budget-conscious representatives gave him a standing ovation. In New York City, Diem received a ticker-tape parade. Mayor Robert Wagner hailed the Vietnamese "miracle" and described Diem as "a man to whom freedom is the very breath of life itself." The press hailed him as "Vietnam's man of iron" and a "symbol of a free new Asia."[15]

Privately, though, American officials expressed grave concern about Diem's autocratic tendencies. At the end of 1957 the U.S. ambassador in Saigon, Elbridge Durbrow, sent to the State Department a very pessimistic report on Diem's regime, painting the president as obsessed with internal enemies and uninterested in creating the foundations for long-term economic growth and political reform. Diem's authoritarianism, his reliance on his powerful clan to run the secret police, and his lack of interest in the welfare of his people had alienated educated elites, businessmen, villagers, and peasants. He ruled harshly, squashed dissent, and erected a cult of personality. And though he willingly took American money, he refused to take American advice.[16]

Durbrow's assessment was, if anything, too gentle. In 1958 and 1959 Diem transformed South Vietnam into a regime of terror, corruption, and repression in his campaign to wipe out communist subversion. He was tactically successful in hunting down and cracking communist cells, but his methods were so brutal that they alienated his own people. More significant, his methods persuaded North Vietnam to escalate its support for the rebellion inside South Vietnam. In January 1959 the North Vietnamese decided to launch a major campaign of subversion in the South to overthrow Diem's regime and attempt to reunite the country. A new Indochina War was about to begin.[17]

As communist attacks increased in South Vietnam, Diem responded in kind. His government herded hundreds of thousands of peasants into concentrated villages ("agrovilles") so they could be better policed and blocked from offering support to the rebellion. Diem also expanded even further his security apparatus, channeling American aid into the secret police and diverting the army into internal security duties. In May 1959 he forced through a new decree that gave the government extraordinary emergency powers to arrest, try, and execute suspected communist guerrillas. In an appalling act of barbarism, the government sent guillotines to all the provinces. Those people found guilty of subversion met their death strapped to a horizontal plank beneath a slashing blade. Predictably such policies stimulated massive hostility throughout the South. A CIA analysis in May 1959 candidly admitted that Diem's regime was on the brink of disaster, yet in Washington Eisenhower called for no change in policy. Despite billions in U.S. aid and an unrelenting war on internal enemies, Diem had failed to defeat the communist insurgency or build any legitimacy for himself. By the start of 1960 Diem's regime, once held up as a model of Asian freedom and democracy, had become a brutal police state standing watch over a restive and seething people.[18]

None of these problems led to a reconsideration of America's strategy in Vietnam. Eisenhower remained firm: the Diem regime must be given the tools to win its fight for freedom against communism. Since the start of his administration, Eisenhower had styled Vietnam as a domino that must not be allowed to fall. To wage and win the cold war in Asia required resolute support for leaders such as Diem of South Vietnam, Chiang Kai-shek of Taiwan, and Syngman Rhee of South Korea. Of course an Orientalist and patronizing discourse underpinned these geopolitical arguments: since Asians were not yet ready for the complexities of self-government, the United States had an obligation to train and guide their Asian protégés. Sometimes their immaturity led to tension with the paternal Americans. Nonetheless communism could be beaten, Eisenhower and his advisers believed, by the steadfast application of generous economic and military aid as well as political leadership. To lure Asian minds away from utopian communism, Americans offered their own dreamscape of democracy, prosperity, and freedom, engineered by the proper application of American know-how.[19]

These were noble aspirations, and Eisenhower believed in them firmly. Yet they were consistently betrayed in their implementation. Instead of building freedom and democracy, the Eisenhower administration militarized "free" Indochina. It propped up Diem's dictatorial government and provided enormous sums of money that allowed Diem to strengthen his hold on power even as he was driving his people into the arms of the communist insurgency. By the start of 1960, while Ike looked forward to his meeting with Khrushchev in hopes of resolving many cold war tensions, his administration was fanning the flames of anger and resentment across Indochina. That fire would soon engulf not just Southeast Asia but America as well.

IV

To most Americans in the 1950s, Indonesia and Vietnam remained distant, dimly understood places. Cuba, by contrast, occupied a bright and sun-drenched corner of the American imagination. A short plane ride from the United States, Cuba had long been a lucrative target for American business. The island's sugar plantations, mining enterprises, utilities, and large-scale farms were almost entirely owned by American companies, while the tourist industry, boosted by the advent of cheap commercial flights, opened up Cuba's gambling casinos, dance halls, and beaches to thousands of Americans searching for a taste of tropical nightlife. The luxurious Hotel Nacional, built in 1930 overlooking Havana Harbor, epitomized the new era of elegant excess and indulgence. All the famous actors and singers of the era flocked there for the sun, the fun, and the gaiety, performing for adoring audiences. And they gambled in casinos that were run by the American crime bosses Meyer Lansky and Lucky Luciano.

Since 1952 the president of Cuba, a former army sergeant named Fulgencio Batista, gladly abetted the exploitation of his country by American corporate, entertainment, and gambling interests because he got rich in the process. Batista had held power either in a junta or by himself for most of the years since 1933. He aligned himself with wealthy landowners and the military and allowed American companies to squeeze hefty profits out of the sugar industry. To maintain the allure of his vacation paradise for wealthy American tourists, and to generate handsome kickbacks and bribes, he enabled a flourishing underground traffic in drugs and prostitution. The U.S. government supported Batista with military aid and assisted in the expansion of Cuba's intelligence services and secret police. As a pro-American, anticommunist, moneymaking tropical den of iniquity, Batista's Cuba found plenty of sympathetic supporters in the corridors of power in Washington.[20]

Inside Cuba, however, Batista faced a growing insurrection. On July 26, 1953, a small band of rebels attacked an army barracks in Santiago, signaling the start of the Cuban Revolution. The leadership of the July 26 Movement included a young and dynamic law student named Fidel Castro and his hard-line brother Raúl, sons of a well-to-do plantation owner. For the next five years Castro and his group plotted and fought against Batista, hiding in the forested uplands of the Sierra Maestra region of southeastern Cuba and enduring the ruthless repression, torture, and murder by government forces of many of their brother revolutionaries.

Because of the well-known barbarism of Batista's dictatorship, Castro's revolutionary movement won sympathetic coverage in the American press. *Life* magazine, published by that noted cold warrior Henry Luce, styled Castro "a kind of Cuban Robin Hood" in one 1957 issue, while denouncing Batista's "strong-arm rule." *New York Times* reporter Herbert L. Matthews scored the scoop of the decade when he interviewed Castro in his mountain hideout in February 1957. Matthews depicted Castro as a youthful idealist fighting for a democratic Cuba: "It was easy to see that his men adored him and also to see why he has caught the imagination of the youth of Cuba all over the island. Here was an educated, dedicated fanatic, a man of ideals, of courage and of remarkable qualities of leadership." And, Matthews insisted, "there is no communism to speak of in Fidel Castro's July 26 Movement." Instead "the best elements in Cuba—the unspoiled youth, the honest businessman, the politician of integrity, the patriotic Army officer," sympathized with Castro and hated Batista's thuggish regime.[21]

In the spring and summer of 1958 *Life* reporters who trekked into the jungle to seek out the dynamic Fidel wrote of the charismatic leader as "soft-spoken but confident," a man more interested in building hospitals than becoming president. His brother raised suspicions, however, for he seemed doctrinaire and brutal in his methods. A rail-thin 27-year-old, Raúl sported "a cowboy hat, mustache and shoulder-length hair" and toted a machine gun everywhere he went. He seemed "partly heroic, partly melodramatic and partly sinister." Yet both Fidel and Raúl denied any communist affiliation. "If we were Communist dominated," Raúl asked a journalist, "don't you think they would supply us with all the arms and ammunition we need to defeat Batista?"[22]

In contrast to these admiring reports about the rebels, Batista's counterinsurgency tactics drew condemnation. His police routinely kidnapped suspects, tortured them to death, and threw their mutilated bodies into the streets to instill fear across the country. They set off bombs in public places and blamed the rebels, hoping to turn public opinion against the uprising. More worrisome for American officials, Batista used the tanks, aircraft, and artillery the United States sold to him against his own people— an embarrassing violation of the terms of the arms sales. Under increasing congressional criticism, the State Department announced the end of arms shipments to Cuba in March 1958, signaling a sharp change in the once-friendly attitude toward Batista. That same month U.S. officials began to consider how to ease Batista out of power.[23]

As elites and business owners in Cuba turned against Batista's rule, the CIA tried and failed to establish contacts with political groups that might take control of the country in the wake of Batista's removal. This failure frustrated Eisenhower and his top advisers. Discussing Castro, they all agreed that the Cuban rebel represented "extremely radical elements," as Allen Dulles put it, and that Cuba could soon be in the hands of the communists. But the United States could not continue to prop up Batista. Acting Secretary of State Herter explained that Batista had lost the confidence of his people, suppressed basic democratic freedoms, and alienated "some 80 percent of the Cuban people," as well as public opinion across Latin America and in the U.S. Congress. Batista had created "a very difficult public relations problem" and had to go. Despite their grave worries about Castro, the Americans now pressured Batista to resign. On the last day of December 1958 he flew out of Cuba and into exile in the Dominican Republic.[24]

A week later, on January 8, 1959, to the roar of enormous crowds, Fidel Castro and his victorious rebel army swept into the capital city and took power. *Life* reported that the crowds in Havana "screamed *Viva!*, thundered applause and flung torrents of flowers when Castro and his *barbudos* (bearded ones) appeared." The crowds greeted Fidel "not as a dutifully honored conqueror but as a man ecstatically acclaimed by the people he had liberated." American reporters flocked to Havana to cover the rebel leader. Ed Sullivan, the host of one of America's most-watched television programs, conducted a hasty and admiring interview with Castro at 2:00 a.m. on January 11 from a television studio jammed with armed guards; later that day CBS News conducted an improvised episode of *Face the Nation* with Castro from Havana, giving Cuba's new leader an unprecedented chance to explain his revolutionary movement to the American public.

Not only the press treated him gingerly; even Foster Dulles, mortally ill and nearing the end of his long service to Eisenhower, proposed to the president that the United States officially recognize the new regime. It is ironic that the era's greatest anticommunist crusader should have advised Eisenhower to reach out to Castro, yet there was reason to be cautiously optimistic. Castro had named a moderate lawyer, Manuel Urrutia, as the provisional head of state, and despite Castro's fulminations against America, his movement appeared "free from Communist taint," Dulles claimed. Dulles probably did not really believe that. He simply knew that the United States had lost an ally in Batista and now had no choice but to try to work with, and guide, the youthful rebel. Tacitly admitting failure, the United

States recognized Castro's new government and proffered a cautious hand of friendship.[25]

V

Very quickly that caution changed to alarm. Just days after Castro's triumphant arrival into Havana, Eisenhower received a report that Castro had ties to "Communist-front groups." While there was "no present firm indication that Castro is a Communist-sympathizer," the new Cuban leader did seem "nationalistic and somewhat socialistic." Castro appointed a number of well-known moderates to the new government and remained undeniably popular across the country, but he also allowed a period of bloodletting and vulgar show trials of former Batista officials. *Life*, which had so recently published flattering essays about the rebel leader, now reported "an ugly tide of blood vengeance" across Cuba. Lurid photos showed the execution of alleged "war criminals" following summary trials. "After seven years of rage, Cubans are now going to make the sadists pay," one article breathlessly concluded, and indeed several hundred former regime supporters were executed. Castro, once styled a cheery Robin Hood in the American press, now earned a more sinister nickname: "the whiskery messiah of Sierra Maestra."[26]

U.S. officials, perhaps reluctant to admit that a communist revolution had just taken power in a country only 90 miles from American shores, told themselves that Castro could be controlled with the proper tutelage. In their conversations officials portrayed Castro as a wayward child, a headstrong youngster who needed some discipline. Foster Dulles established this paternalist framework in remarks he made in mid-1958 to his colleagues. "Throughout much of the world and certainly in Latin America," he opined, "there had been in recent years a tremendous surge in the direction of popular government by peoples who have practically no capacity for self-government and indeed are like children in facing this problem." Allen Dulles used similar terms: Cuban officials "really had to be treated more or less like children," he believed. "They had to be led rather than rebuffed. If they were rebuffed, like children, they were capable of doing almost anything." The U.S. Embassy in Cuba urged Washington to show "patience, goodwill, and cooperation toward Cuba," while tolerating the unruly behavior of these Caribbean toddlers.[27]

Yet a creeping unease began to settle on Washington as Castro and his revolution took hold. One of Castro's first acts was to legalize the Popular Socialist Party, Cuba's communist party that had been banned since 1952. The State Department worried about reports that Castro's fellow revolutionary Ernesto "Che" Guevara had outlined a plan to export Cuba's revolution to Nicaragua, Haiti, the Dominican Republic, and Paraguay. Che was labeled "an extreme leftist" who had been "acting like a Communist since the fall of the Batista regime." Raúl Castro was thought to be even more radical. In late March 1959 Allen Dulles reported to the president that he was "disturbed" by Raúl's "demagoguery" and his "wild statements." Though the regime was not "Communist-dominated," Dulles stated, it was clear that "Communists were now operating openly and legally in Cuba" and that Fidel "was moving toward a dictatorship." Far from a Cuban George Washington, Fidel Castro began to look to Americans like "a Nasser of the Caribbean."[28]

Hoping to dispel the darkening clouds that had formed over Cuban-American relations, Castro seized upon an invitation from the American Society of Newspaper Editors to address their annual convention in mid-April in Washington, D.C. The trip was unofficial, and Eisenhower chose not to meet Castro, hastening to Augusta to avoid him. But the State Department arranged for a packed 11-day tour that included a meeting with Vice President Nixon, Secretary of State Herter, and congressional leaders, as well as a trip to New York and Boston. Castro arrived at National Airport on April 15, 1959, to the hearty cheers of some 1,500 onlookers and a crowd of reporters who were amazed to find him still wearing his trademark green battle fatigues. After meeting with the Cuban leader the next day, Secretary Herter reported to Eisenhower that he found Castro "a most interesting individual, very much like a child in many ways, quite immature regarding the practical problems of government." Castro tended to become "voluble, excited, and somewhat 'wild,'" but Herter thought he was sincere in his desire to work with the United States.[29]

In his April 17 speech to the newspaper editors at the Statler Hotel, Castro launched a full-scale charm offensive. Speaking in English for over two hours in a packed ballroom under the glare of a thousand flashbulbs, he insisted that his revolution was not communist, that Cuba wanted good relations with America, that investors were welcome to do business in Cuba, and that the United States naval base at Guantanamo would remain untouched. "Our revolution is a humanistic one," he assured his hosts. At the end of his performance, the hard-bitten newspapermen gave him a prolonged ovation.[30]

Nixon, however, painted a darker picture after his encounter with Castro. In a private meeting in the vice president's office in the Capitol on Sunday evening, April 19, the two men talked for almost three hours. Nixon adopted the paternalist tone so popular with the Dulles brothers and tried to coach Castro on how to soften his revolution and open Cuba up to democratic reforms and private American investment. In Nixon's account of the discussion, Castro defended his decision to postpone national elections in Cuba for a period of four years. "The people did not want elections," Castro said, "because elections in the past had produced bad government." Nixon described this as "slavish subservience to . . . the voice of the mob" and found the Cuban "incredibly naïve with regard to the Communist threat." Castro "sounded almost exactly like Sukarno" in his assertion that the communists would never be able to infiltrate his government. Nixon ended his report by saying that Castro "has those indefinable qualities which make him a leader of men. . . . He is either incredibly naïve about Communism or under Communist discipline—my guess is the former." Yet because of Castro's popularity, the United States could not oppose him directly. "We have no choice," Nixon felt, "but at least to try to orient him in the right direction."[31]

Castro's visit electrified the American public. After leaving Washington he traveled to Princeton University and then to New York City, where enormous crowds greeted him amid cries of "Viva Fidel!" and "Viva el Liberador!" The tall, bearded rebel in his olive-drab fatigues repeatedly broke free of his bodyguards to plunge into the crowds and shake hands. In Cambridge, Massachusetts, he addressed a crowd of 10,000 admirers outside Dillon Field House on the Harvard campus. Still, some reporters had their doubts. Roscoe Drummond of the *Washington Post* admitted that Castro possessed a friendly, outgoing, "almost mesmeric personality," but his hostility to elections hinted at a future tyranny. The *Wall Street Journal* editorial page likewise worried about Castro's lack of "maturity" and his emphasis on melodrama rather than substance. The Cuban government looked like "a band of very young men who, having fought hard, were a little intoxicated by their sudden success."[32]

Inside the State Department, Herter's staff tried to assess the new Cuban strongman. Castro's power to sway world opinion, they thought, was not charming but dangerous. His personal magnetism might blind the public to the true radicalism of his regime. Far from being a child or ingénue, Castro was "a strong personality and a born leader of great personal courage and conviction." With such enormous political gifts, Castro spelled trouble. "It would be a serious mistake to underestimate this man."[33]

VI

Few did. Yet the attention of the administration in the summer of 1959 was drawn elsewhere. The Berlin crisis, Nixon's trip to the USSR in July, followed by Khrushchev's passage across the country in September and Eisenhower's personal hopes for a thaw in U.S.-Soviet relations—these issues preoccupied the White House. Eisenhower pushed Cuba to the back burner.

Even so, the temperature continued to climb. Reports out of Cuba painted an alarming picture of Castro's postrevolution purges. "Civil Prisoners Jam Cuban Jails," was a headline in the *New York Times* in February 1959; "Reds' Alleged Role in Castro's Regime Alarming Havana," blared another in April. Castro's constant public criticism of the United States and the "whipping up of extreme nationalist spirit" had left the middle classes "uneasy," the papers reported.[34]

In May the Castro government announced an ambitious program of land reform, proposing to nationalize utilities (many owned by American companies) and seize the large agricultural estates that produced Cuba's lucrative sugar crop. The government promised compensation, but American landowners and industrialists sent outraged envoys to Washington, demanding Eisenhower suspend the purchase of Cuban sugar as retaliation. Secretary Herter now considered Cuba a danger to all of Latin America and told the National Security Council "the fire would spread very fast" if they did not act. In June, Che Guevara launched a heavily publicized world tour to curry favor with nonaligned nations from Yugoslavia to Egypt, India, and Indonesia. Meanwhile the U.S. Embassy in Havana, which initially had adopted a friendly and tolerant view of Castro, acknowledged that though not a communist himself, Castro had allowed the Communist Party to flourish. His government was following "a course which we believe favors Communist objectives."[35]

Domestic politics also played a role in keeping pressure on Eisenhower. In the summer of 1959 Senator Eastland, the Democratic chairman of the Judiciary Committee, opened hearings on what he called "the communist threat to the United States through the Caribbean." Designed to embarrass the administration for its lax attitude to communism in the region, Eastland's committee gave a platform to various exiles and disgruntled anti-Castro figures. One hearing featured the testimony of Maj. Pedro Luis Díaz Lanz, the former head of the Cuban Air Force. Having fled Cuba two weeks earlier under threat of arrest, Díaz Lanz vividly described the grip of communism upon Castro's government and especially on Raúl Castro and Che Guevara. He pointed to the penetration of communists into all facets of Cuban politics and society. His testimony was made even more dramatic because it was interrupted by a bomb scare, forcing Eastland to clear the room.

These revelations by a former Cuban insider embarrassed the administration, and Eisenhower tried to deflect the matter at his July 15 news conference. As to accusations that Castro's regime was communist, Ike said, "the United States has made no such charges." Eisenhower's political rivals took note of his slowness to ring the alarm. Just three days later Eastland invited Spruille Braden to testify before his committee. Braden, a former U.S. ambassador to Cuba, Colombia, and Argentina and a man who nourished McCarthy-like conspiracy theories about communists in the State Department, announced that "unless eradicated," Castro's regime "will convert the Caribbean into a Red lake." By midsummer Eisenhower was starting to feel the political heat from Cuba.[36]

Castro gave his critics in the United States plenty of ammunition. On July 18 he forced the moderate president Urrutia to resign after he mildly criticized communist activities in Cuba. More shocking to American observers, Castro replaced Urrutia with Osvaldo Dorticós Torrado, a longtime leader of the Cuban communists. The U.S. press howled. *Life*, once so enamored of Castro, now asserted that he had "clobbered democracy" and "by his violent and irresponsible attacks against a moderate anti-Communist like Urrutia had served the Kremlin beautifully." Castro seemed set on a confrontation with the United States.[37]

The breaking point came in late October 1959. On October 21, in an act of defiance and desperation, Major Díaz Lanz, who had denounced Castro before the Senate Judiciary Committee, commandeered a B-25 aircraft from an airfield at Pompano, Florida, flew it to Havana, and dropped thousands of anti-Castro leaflets over the city. (How he pulled this off, with no evident U.S. government support, remains a mystery.) Cuban anti-aircraft fire from the ground missed Díaz Lanz's plane but fell onto the crowded streets below, killing three people. The leaflet-dropping, which embarrassed American officials, gave Castro more fuel for his anti-American campaign. He denounced this "bombing" of Havana and alleged that a conspiracy was afoot in the United States to overthrow the Cuban government.

On October 26 Castro staged a mass "loyalty rally" in Havana. Before hundreds of thousands of listeners, he mocked the official denials from Washington. "How is it possible," he wondered aloud, "that the authorities of a nation so powerful, with so many economic and military resources, with radar systems which are said to be able to intercept even guided missiles, should admit before the world that they are unable to prevent aircraft from leaving their territory in order to bomb a defenseless country like Cuba?" Hailing his own reforms and likening the "attack" to that on Pearl Harbor, Castro incited roars of anti-American hatred among his adoring audience. The once-sympathetic American ambassador, Philip Bonsal, found Castro's foaming, screeching performance "reminiscent of Hitler at his most hysterical and most odious."[38]

The events of that week in October marked a decisive turning point. American officials now irreversibly shifted against Castro and his government. Allen Dulles asserted in an NSC meeting on October 29 that "the threat of extremist control is worse than ever," that Raúl Castro had taken over the armed forces and all moderate voices had been snuffed out. In early November, Secretary Herter summarized the state of U.S.-Cuban relations in a memo for Eisenhower. He claimed that while Washington had shown great "restraint in the face of provocations," Castro had gone too far. He fomented anti-American sentiment across the Caribbean, allowed the infiltration of communists into his government, imposed statist economic doctrines on the country, and held out a model of defiance toward the United States that could inflame other Latin American countries. Herter proposed a new "basic policy" toward Cuba: the encouragement of an anti-Castro opposition that could in due course unseat the Cuban strongman. Eisenhower approved the plan on November 9, 1959.[39]

The wheels now began to turn quite rapidly within the CIA. On December 11, Allen Dulles received a memo from J. C. King, his chief of the Western Hemisphere Division, describing a plan to bring about "the overthrow of Castro within one year, and his replacement by a junta friendly to the United States." The program would rely on clandestine radio propaganda, the jamming of Cuba's own radio broadcast capabilities, and the formation of anti-Castro groups that would "establish by force a controlled area within Cuba." King went one step further, asking that "thorough consideration be given to the elimination of Fidel Castro." Allen Dulles personally edited this memo, deleting the word *elimination* and inserting "removal from Cuba." The modification is significant, but the conclusion remains the same: by

December 1959 the United States had settled on a plan to oust Castro by covert means.[40]

On January 8, 1960, Allen Dulles directed Richard Bissell to organize a special task force to implement the Castro operation. Bissell, the well-heeled Yale man who had earned plaudits for successfully directing the U-2 spy plane operation, had recently been named deputy director for plans—the director, in effect, of all the covert activities around the globe. To mount the Cuba operation, Bissell created Branch 4 of the Western Hemisphere Division and tapped Jacob D. Esterline, an OSS veteran and a leading player in the 1954 Guatemala coup, to run it. As they hammered out the details, the plotters focused on infiltrating specially trained Cuban exiles into Cuba, where they would set up underground networks along the lines of those in Europe during World War II, Bissell later recalled. They wanted to establish safe houses, supply depots, and a reliable network of operatives to sustain the budding resistance movement. Initially the CIA thought they could make this work with 100 to 200 trained operatives who could in turn teach sympathetic Cubans the necessary techniques of subversion and sabotage.[41]

How much did Eisenhower know about these plans? It is tempting to assume that Allen Dulles and Richard Bissell were pushing ahead on their own, hoping to shape the Cuba operation and present it more or less fully formed to the president at the appropriate moment. But the recently de-classified minutes of the 5412 Committee suggest that Ike was in the know all the way. The regular meetings of the 5412 Committee obliged Dulles to update Gordon Gray, Eisenhower's national security adviser, about ongo-ing covert plans. Gray then informed the president. Gray frequently told the members of the committee that he had spoken to his "associate" about the topics the group had covered, careful never to mention the president by name. This created a protective buffer around Eisenhower, allowing him to deny direct knowledge of the committee's discussions while remaining firmly in control.

Eisenhower knew, then, that the group had discussed the start of an anti-Castro radio propaganda operation, using transmitters that would be installed on the American-controlled Swan Island in the Caribbean Sea. Eisenhower also knew that in January 1960 the anti-Castro programs picked up speed, moving from propaganda to coup plotting. On January 13 Dulles announced to the 5412 Committee that "over the long run the U.S. will not be able to tolerate the Castro regime in Cuba, and suggested that covert contingency planning to accomplish the fall of the Castro regime government might be in order." (In fact this planning was already under way.) Dulles said he did not have in mind "a quick elimination" of Castro; he wanted to "enable responsible opposition leaders to get a foothold." The 5412 Committee approved and the planning went into high gear.[42]

This scheme to promote opposition to Castro, and eventually to oust him from power, met with Eisenhower's approval. Speaking privately with Herter on January 23, Eisenhower said Castro was "going wild and harming the whole [Latin] American structure." Perhaps a blockade of the island might be needed. He went on to say, "Dictators devoted to fomenting disorder can have a terrible influence on our affairs." If it were not for the sensitivity of other Latin American states to U.S. intervention, Ike said, he would like to begin "building up our forces at Guantanamo." Such remarks indicate Eisenhower's eagerness for a confrontation with Castro. Two days later, in a conversation with Ambassador Bonsal, who had been recalled from Havana, Eisenhower responded to the litany of Castro's anti-American actions by saying "Castro begins to look like a madman."[43]

In February the CIA planners tried to give more precise detail to their plans to destabilize Cuba. They proposed intensified radio broadcasts, sabotage of sugar mills by Cuban "assets," the interruption of Cuba's oil supply, and additional U.S. forces at Guantanamo in case the president ordered direct intervention to save American lives and property. Gordon Gray reported these measures to Eisenhower, who "wondered why we were thinking of something on such a narrow basis. He said he wondered why we weren't trying to identify assets for this and other things as well across the board, including things that might be drastic." Eisenhower wanted a bolder plan for Cuba—and he wanted to approve it personally. Before any plans were launched, he said, the 5412 Committee had to fully approve and he himself "would like to be involved." Far from delegating these matters, Eisenhower had taken a personal interest in the Cuba operation.[44]

At the end of February 1960 Eisenhower undertook a two-week tour of Latin America, with visits to Brazil, Argentina, Chile, and Uruguay. This trip formed part of the Hagerty plan for exposing Eisenhower to the world and demonstrating his global prestige. Ike came bearing promises of increased American aid, and he quietly stressed to his hosts his displeasure with trends in Cuba. In Rio he met with a roaring welcome, but his heart sank when he saw a placard reading "We Like Ike! We Like Fidel Too!" Wherever he went, crowds swelled as people strained to get a glimpse of him. But he also sensed "the seething unrest not far beneath the surface." In

Montevideo, Uruguay, his motorcade drove down a main avenue whose air was filled with tear gas that had been used to chase away unruly protesters.[45]

During his trip Eisenhower insisted to his hosts that the United States "would not intervene in their local affairs." As he put it in his 1965 autobiography, he knew that memories of such interventions in the era of "gunboat diplomacy" still burned red-hot, and he asserted that since the 1930s, "intervention as an American policy had gone into the discard, replaced by the policy of the Good Neighbor." This statement is wholly false. The Guatemala intervention against Arbenz in 1954 contradicted Ike's claim; so too did his Cuba policy, whose details were being hammered out at the very moment he was on his tour of Latin America.[46]

Three days after his trip he met with the National Security Council to review the Cuba planning. Once again Allen Dulles went through a long list of Fidel's anti-American activities, concluding that the United States could never hope to work with a Cuba "dominated by Castro and his associates." Douglas Dillon, the undersecretary of state, chimed in: "Our objective is to bring another government to power in Cuba." However, Dillon cautioned the group that an overt U.S. intervention in Cuba would help the Soviets and be held up as a "counterpart of Soviet intervention in Hungary." The implication was clear: America's role in the anti-Castro plot had to remain invisible.[47]

One week later the president gave formal approval to a CIA plan to oust Castro from power and replace him with a pliant pro-American junta. At a meeting at 2:30 p.m. on March 17, 1960, following a briefing by Allen Dulles, Eisenhower approved "A Program of Covert Action against the Castro Regime," a policy memorandum dated March 16 that had been drafted and vetted in the CIA and in the 5412 Committee while the president was on his Latin American trip. The memo was not lengthy. It outlined four parts of the anti-Castro program: to create a popular Cuban opposition as an alternative to Castro; to develop an extensive broadcasting capability within Cuba so the opposition could communicate with the Cuban people; to build a covert network inside Cuba to assist in destabilizing the regime; and to prepare a paramilitary force, assembled outside Cuba, "to be available for immediate deployment into Cuba to organize, train and lead resistance forces recruited there both before and after the establishment of one or more active centers of resistance." Ike approved the plan, saying "he [knew] of no better plan for dealing with the situation." He demanded the strictest security: "Everyone must be prepared to swear that he has not heard of it." He wanted to be kept informed of every detail, but he insisted, "Our hand should not show in anything that is done."[48]

This was a fateful moment. The plan marked the start, and only the start, of a long campaign of deception and subversion in an effort to destroy Castro and his regime. Certainly the plan did not yet envision an amphibious landing on Cuban beaches of the kind that was eventually attempted at the Bay of Pigs in April 1961 in Kennedy's first months in office. However, it put into motion a planning structure that led directly to that botched and tragic event. Eisenhower failed to anticipate that covert operations, once started, have a curious way of expanding until they take on a life and momentum of their own. Under pressure of world events, the small-scale infiltration operation sketched out in March 1960 soon grew into something bigger—and altogether more dangerous.

CHAPTER 18

U-2

"The embarrassment to us will be so great if one crashes."

I

EISENHOWER HAD COME TO RELY HEAVILY ON THE CIA TO IM-
plement actions that he believed would serve American interests. Arming
friends and destroying enemies: that is what the CIA could and did do, and
Eisenhower fully supported these actions. Signing off on the ambitious
Cuba operation, he demonstrated his confidence in his spies and saboteurs.
As it turned out, this confidence was misplaced, for in the spring of 1960,
just as Eisenhower approved the Cuba plan, he received another CIA request: to launch a series of overflights of Soviet territory by a U-2 spy plane.
Against his better judgment, and under intense and sustained pressure from
his intelligence and military advisers, he allowed the flights. It was a disastrous decision, perhaps the worst of his presidency, and it requires a careful
explanation.

Ever since he took office, Eisenhower had accepted, but never resolved,
the fundamental tension between his covert operations and his foreign policy. He wanted to pursue a bold public agenda of peacemaking and détente
with the USSR. He and his advisers had made great efforts in laying the
groundwork for a summit meeting of the four Great Powers that was scheduled for May 16, 1960, at which he hoped to win agreements on the thorny
issues of disarmament, nuclear weapons testing, and Berlin. He wanted to
"thaw out the rigidity between the two sides," he told his defense officials
in February, "or there would be a disaster in the world." Khrushchev's visit
to America set the stage, and Ike had traveled across the globe in 1959 and
early 1960, to Asia, India, the Near East, and Latin America, spreading
the gospel of peace and understanding. His own trip to the Soviet Union

had now been scheduled for June 10, and it would surely be the crowning achievement of his presidency.

At the same time Eisenhower built a huge nuclear deterrent, ordered hundreds of nuclear-armed bombers into production, approved aggressive covert actions across the world, and allowed numerous overflights of the USSR that violated Soviet airspace—a defiant intrusion that he himself had said was tantamount to an act of war. How could Eisenhower square these two sets of policies? Was he a man of peace or a man of war? He refused to settle the question, and on May 1, 1960, he paid the terrible price.[1]

While Eisenhower actively supported the use of aggressive covert operations to destabilize unfriendly governments around the world, he had always been deeply cautious about the use of the U-2 airplane over Soviet territory. From its first flight over Russia on July 4, 1956, Eisenhower recognized that the U-2 flights were intrusive and illegal. If ever one of the aircraft was intercepted and shot down, the cold war might take a sudden, sharp turn for the worse, possibly even toward war.

Yet the U-2 flights supplied invaluable and extraordinary intelligence about Soviet military capabilities. In the era of intercontinental ballistic missiles, Eisenhower feared the possibility of a surprise attack, a nuclear Pearl Harbor that could wipe out the country in a single strike. The U-2 provided the best available means to learn about Soviet missile and bomber production, and to gauge the Soviet ability to harm the United States. Eisenhower accepted overflights of the USSR because he believed the benefits of having detailed knowledge of Soviet missile capabilities outweighed the risks. And so in 1956 he permitted six U-2 flights over Russia. In 1957, as the Soviets were making their great breakthroughs in missile technology, he approved 13 more U-2 flights there—flights that yielded a trove of data proving that the Soviets had not yet developed an operational ICBM. Through 1957, then, the U-2 had been a huge success. In fact it was the greatest American intelligence achievement since the cracking of the Japanese codes on the eve of the Battle of Midway in 1942.

Even so, Eisenhower grew increasingly anxious about the overflights. Although the planes flew too high to be intercepted by Soviet missiles or fighter planes, Soviet radar did locate and track each of these flights. The Soviet government privately protested these overflights each time they occurred, making it impossible for the Americans to pretend these were simply off-course weather aircraft. Eisenhower knew that each flight provoked deep resentment in the Kremlin and surely egged on the Soviets to improve their air defenses. It was a matter of time, he knew, before something went wrong.

At the start of 1958 Eisenhower therefore put the brakes on U-2 over-flights of Soviet territory. (The air force continued to fly regular missions just off the Soviet border, gathering electronic intelligence.) In January he told Foster Dulles and the chairman of the Joint Chiefs, Gen. Nathan Twining, that he was worried overflights could lead to a serious and justifiable Soviet reaction, perhaps an attack on Berlin. Eisenhower approved one flight in March 1958, and then refused to allow any further flights for a full year. Meeting with his board of consultants on foreign intelligence activities in December, at the start of the Berlin Crisis, he said he doubted that the "intelligence which we receive from this source is worth the exacerbation of international tensions which results." By late 1958 the United States knew a great deal about Soviet missiles—enough to rebut the panicky congressional claims of a "missile gap." Ike concluded that there should be "a re-evaluation of the U-2 program."[2]

In 1959 his advisers continued to press for more flights, but Ike continued to refuse. In February, Defense Secretary McElroy, his deputy Donald Quarles, and General Twining asked the president to reconsider his opposition. They insisted that without hard facts, the congressional outrage over the alleged missile gap would continue, and demands for greater defense spending would soon follow. In any case, they said, the military had provided assurances that no U-2 would be shot down. Ike held his ground. He preferred to wait until the Corona satellite had become operational. The U-2 planes constituted "an undue provocation," he said. Putting himself in Khrushchev's shoes, he thought "nothing would make him request authority to declare war more quickly than the violation of our air space by Soviet aircraft."[3]

His intelligence advisers kept up their campaign. On April 3, 1959, Allen Dulles, accompanied by McElroy, Quarles, and Twining, again asked for a round of U-2 overflights. Dulles called the data the U-2 provided "about as high in importance as any intelligence we can get." Eisenhower stressed the risks involved: "The psychological impact on Khrushchev of our flying such a mission at this time would be very serious. We are currently in a state of negotiation over the Berlin crisis which threatens to be the most serious of our crises to date." The State Department was optimistic, he said, about negotiations on Berlin; putting a U-2 plane over the Soviet Union now would be "needling Khrushchev." The gathered advisers insisted that the Soviets did not have the aircraft or the surface-to-air missiles to intercept the U-2. The plane was "relatively safe," they said, and produced test results showing that even the best American jet fighters could not catch a U-2.[4]

Eisenhower agreed to think about it, but four days later, on April 7, he called McElroy and CIA deputy director Bissell to the Oval Office and told them, once again, he would not approve. The U-2 flights would jeopardize any hope of a negotiated settlement with the USSR on Berlin. "We cannot in the present circumstances afford the revulsion of world opinion against the United States that might occur." Eisenhower admitted that he wanted information on Soviet missiles, not least to counter the "demagoguery" of certain U.S. senators who asserted that America had fallen behind in the missile race. But he kept coming back to the damage if a plane should be shot down. There would be "terrible propaganda" if the Soviets caught the United States in the act of spying.[5]

Yet under repeated assault by his top staff, Eisenhower finally approved one more overflight of the USSR, which took place on July 9, 1959. That flight yielded excellent results, photographing the Tyuratam missile range and showing how much that site had expanded in the year since it had last been examined. But in light of the upcoming Khrushchev visit in September, the president refused to approve further flights. Allen Dulles, increasingly frustrated that he had to testify before Congress with inadequate data on Soviet missile production, empaneled an ad hoc committee of senior advisers under the chairmanship of Lawrence A. Hyland, a leading electrical engineer and general manager of Hughes Aircraft, to review the state of intelligence on Soviet missiles. Although the Hyland panel concluded that the Soviet program was not as large as many in Congress claimed, it nonetheless demanded more U-2 flights to settle the matter. "Positive evidence," the panel concluded, "continues to be missing." The panel pointedly called the lack of data "alarming." Bissell felt the panel's conclusion would "add fuel to the fire" in his campaign to get more U-2 flights approved.[6]

As long as "the spirit of Camp David" hung in the air after Khrushchev's visit, Eisenhower continued to steer clear of the U-2, lest he return the cold war to the deep freeze. But in January 1960 the CIA's campaign to get Eisenhower's approval for more U-2 overflights intensified. On January 14 Khrushchev gave a speech to the Supreme Soviet announcing heavy troop reductions for the Red Army, to be compensated for by corresponding increases in Soviet missiles. Astonished at Khrushchev's claims of a huge nuclear arsenal that could replace the need for airplanes, submarines, and infantry, CIA analysts sounded the alarm. They saw it as a matter of great urgency to verify or disprove these boasts. Robert Amory, the deputy director for intelligence, shot off a heated memo to Allen Dulles, calling for more overflights "on a most urgent basis," declaring, "The identification of Soviet operational ICBM sites is the highest priority national intelligence objective."[7]

Adding fuel to the fire, Joseph Alsop launched a blistering six-part series of columns on the missile gap "crisis," prophesying that Soviet nukes could wipe out all American missile sites in a blitzkrieg strike and the United States could do nothing to defend itself—all because of Eisenhower's failure to take "serious emergency measures." America was courting disaster, Alsop shrieked. "Pearl Harbor was the result the last time the American Government based its defense posture on what it believed a hostile power would probably do, and not on what the hostile power was capable of doing." Eisenhower was running "a hair-raising risk."[8]

Eisenhower received a more sedate version of this message on February 2, from members of his board of consultants on foreign intelligence affairs. On this board served two men of impeccable national security credentials and vast experience: Gen. James Doolittle, the heroic aviator and the man who had chaired Ike's review panel of the CIA in 1954, and Gen. John Hull, a three-star general and former deputy chief of staff of the U.S. Army. These distinguished soldiers now pressed Eisenhower to authorize more overflights of Soviet missile sites, stressing that the window on the U-2 was closing, as Soviet interceptor aircraft and missiles were getting more sophisticated every day. Ike responded in a manner that reveals the heavy weight of the burden he carried: "Such a decision is one of the most soul-searching questions to come before a president."

By now the State Department had settled on the date of May 16 for a full-scale summit meeting with the Soviets, French, and British in Paris. The agenda would include Berlin, nuclear testing, and disarmament. For Ike the stakes were high, as a breakthrough in Paris could cement his legacy as a peacemaker. Under pressure from his intelligence advisers to launch a new round of U-2 flights, he resisted, knowing "he ha[d] one tremendous asset in a summit meeting. . . . That is his reputation for honesty. If one of these aircraft were lost when we are engaged in apparently sincere deliberations, it could be put on display in Moscow and ruin the president's effectiveness." He concluded, "The embarrassment to us will be so great if one crashes." This proved a remarkably prophetic statement.[9]

Despite his reservations, Eisenhower buckled under the intense pressure placed on him by the intelligence community and approved a U-2 flight for February 10, 1960. The constant demands had worn him down. And just days after the February 10 flight, Dulles was at it again, asking for four more flights. The CIA was a hungry beast whose appetite grew with eating. The president approved one more. Dulles complained, and eventually he got two flights approved. Because of problems with weather and with the Pakistani government, which had to approve the use of its airfield in Peshawar, the flights were pushed back to April 9 and May 1.[10]

Richard Bissell later admitted that by the start of 1960 the CIA knew that Soviet surface-to-air missiles were improving and might be able to reach the high-flying U-2, especially if the USSR knew in advance where the U-2 was going to fly. The April 9 flight, which brought back more detailed photographs of the missile sites at Semipalatinsk and Tyuratam, was tracked even before it entered Soviet airspace. Although Soviet aircraft and missiles failed to intercept the plane, its exact course and point of origin were well-known to the Soviets, putting them on guard for aircraft entering their airspace from Pakistan. Bissell should have alerted the president to this fact. He didn't.[11]

Why did Eisenhower approve these two overflights, the second of which would take place just two weeks before the summit meeting in Paris, scheduled for May 16? Clearly the long and intensive campaign by the intelligence community and the military put significant pressure on him. Dulles and Bissell had allies in Joint Chiefs Chairman Twining, Secretary of Defense McElroy and his successor Thomas S. Gates Jr., Secretary of State Herter, the analysts within the CIA, the independent board of consultants on foreign intelligence affairs, even Ike's most trusted wingman, Gen. Andrew Goodpaster; all had at various times urged Ike to use the U-2 more aggressively. They told him that the nation's security depended upon the intelligence these flights yielded and that the planes were all but invulnerable to Soviet interception. It would have taken superhuman rigidity to resist this kind of pressure.

Then too domestic politics played a significant role. Congress repeatedly hauled in Allen Dulles to testify on the Soviet missile program. Because he could not reveal the source of his information, he was often evasive. His lack of clarity and specificity enraged key Democratic senators Stuart Symington and John Kennedy, who alleged that the administration had become "soft" on defense and had failed to keep up with the USSR. If Ike could prove the missile gap was phony, he could stifle partisan criticism.[12]

Finally, Eisenhower liked to gamble, and he especially liked to gamble when he knew what cards his opponent was holding. The U-2 promised to give him priceless knowledge about the true state of Soviet missile and bomber capabilities. Going into the summit meeting in Paris, where Ike would confront a confident and blustering Khrushchev, such knowledge would give him an enormous edge. It was just too tempting to resist. On May 1 a U-2 plane, piloted by a highly experienced veteran of the program named Francis Gary Powers, took off from Peshawar on a course that would take him over some of the most sensitive and secret sites inside the Soviet Union en route to Norway. It was the 26th U-2 penetration of Soviet airspace, and it would be the last.

II

Just a few minutes before 9:00 a.m., Moscow time, a Soviet SA-2 surface-to-air missile exploded just behind Powers's aircraft as it passed over the city of Sverdlovsk. The force of the blast violently shook the fragile U-2, and Powers lost control of the plane, which began to break up and then went into a death spiral. Powers hastily ejected, opened his parachute, but failed to initiate the explosives that were designed to destroy the aircraft. Instead both he and large chunks of his shattered plane fell to the ground. There local farmers and curious onlookers surrounded Powers. Within hours he was on his way to Moscow and the notorious Lubyanka prison. It was May Day, the day commemorating the international labor movement, and a national holiday. As Khrushchev stood on a reviewing platform, watching the enormous May Day Parade, the commander of Soviet air defenses hurriedly approached and informed him that an American aircraft had been shot down.[13]

At noon on May 1 telephones across Washington started ringing. The CIA team in Norway alerted headquarters that the plane was long overdue. The duty officer informed Bissell, Defense Secretary Gates, the State Department intelligence bureau, and the chiefs of staffs of each of the armed services. The news of the plane's downing crackled across Washington, hampering the ability of the White House to control the story. The CIA also contacted General Goodpaster, who had the unenviable job of calling Eisenhower at Camp David to inform him that a U-2 plane was missing and likely downed over the USSR. Eisenhower immediately boarded a helicopter for the flight back to Washington.[14]

Bissell convened a meeting that afternoon at the project headquarters on H Street in Washington. He said later he "felt a sense of disaster about the entire affair," as well he might. By his own admission, the CIA was "not well-prepared for what happened." Bissell hastily dusted off the cover plan he had prepared in the event of a lost U-2 plane. NASA would announce that a high-altitude weather craft, flying out of Adana, Turkey, had gone missing. Such a thin cover story could work only if the pilot died in the crash and if the plane's self-destruct mechanism had been triggered. On May 3 this cover story was sent out to the press, which did not express much interest in the lost weather plane.[15]

In Moscow, Khrushchev savored the moment. His son recalled that he "was extraordinarily pleased. . . . He had finally gotten his revenge on the people who had been offending him for such a long time." In his memoir Khrushchev described how irritated the Soviets had been by the overflights, despite repeated protests. "[The Americans] gloated over our impotence and continued to violate the sovereignty of the USSR." Khrushchev stayed quiet while the interrogation of the pilot continued. He planned to lay a trap while the Americans "tied their own hands by repeating these false-hoods." At the right moment he would reveal the plane, and the pilot, to the world.[16]

Eisenhower had surrounded himself with talented, dedicated staff who served him well across many trying hours. But during the U-2 crisis they performed poorly. "The handling of that critical international situation," Goodpaster confessed many years later, "was about as clumsy in my opinion as anything our government has ever done." The mistakes derived from a failure to anticipate answers to obvious questions: What if a plane was shot down? What if the pilot survived? What if the film was recovered by the Russians? Who would control the public response to these questions? Most important, should the president become involved? None of these things had been thought through because it was assumed that Soviet missiles could not hit the high-flying aircraft, and even if by some miracle they did, the pilot could never survive the destruction of his plane at 70,000 feet. All these assumptions proved false.[17]

The Soviets stayed quiet until May 5, when Khrushchev, taking the podium in a packed Kremlin hall before a meeting of the Supreme Soviet, made his stunning announcement. A U.S. aircraft had violated Soviet airspace and been shot down. The deputies received this news with thunderous applause and cries of "Shame! Shame!" Khrushchev undertook a lengthy harangue against the "Pentagon militarists" who had sent the plane on the eve of the great summit. Someone inside the U.S. government, he asserted, wanted the summit to fail.[18]

Ambassador Tommy Thompson, who was present in the hall to hear Khrushchev's speech, cabled Washington that in his view, Khrushchev had deliberately left open a back door through which Eisenhower could, if he wished, conduct a dignified retreat. By pointing the finger at alleged and unnamed militarists, or mere incompetence on America's part, Khrushchev signaled that he did not want to "slam any doors," Thompson believed. If Eisenhower offered his regrets for the incident and found a suitable scapegoat to take the blame, Khrushchev might allow the summit to proceed unhindered. That is what he seemed to signal in saying "I do not doubt President Eisenhower's desire for peace." Indeed, according to his son, Khrushchev truly believed the "flight came from unauthorized military officers and the CIA, not from the president." He hoped Eisenhower would apologize and the summit could continue.[19]

But the Soviet leader had inadvertently forced Eisenhower into a corner. Either the president had to admit he had sent the spy plane two weeks before his long-planned summit, or he had to apologize for the overflight while acknowledging that he did not control his own government. As Eisenhower stalled, his staff badly bungled the job of working out a reply to Khrushchev's allegations. On May 5, in an inexplicable moment of confusion, both the State Department and NASA issued separate statements. The State Department stuck with the original cover story, but NASA provided quite a bit of additional phony information: that the U-2 was one of 10 "flying weather laboratories" that NASA operated out of Europe, Turkey, Pakistan, Japan, and the Philippines; that it contained no reconnaissance cameras; that it was a civilian aircraft flown by a civilian scientist; that it was conducting routine weather research and had not intended to stray across the Soviet border; and more. All of this was information the Soviets could easily disprove.[20]

And so they did. Khrushchev, with his flair for propaganda, announced on May 7, in another dramatic speech to the Supreme Soviet, that not only did the Soviets possess the plane, its cameras and film, but that the pilot, Gary Powers, was "alive and kicking." Khrushchev took pleasure in rebutting the flimsy cover story, brandishing photographs that the U-2 had taken. He also reported that the pilot had readily confessed that he was no civilian weather analyst. Powers admitted that he was a former air force pilot who worked for the CIA. The United States had been caught in a very public lie.[21]

III

When you are in a hole, the saying goes, the first thing to do is stop digging. This simple adage might have helped Eisenhower's staff, but they failed to heed it. On May 7, in reply to Khrushchev's astounding announcement that Powers had survived the crash and was in custody, the president approved yet another press release. This one was drafted by Herter, who had just arrived home from a trip to the Near East. The statement acknowledged that "in endeavoring to obtain information now concealed behind the Iron Curtain, a flight over Soviet territory was probably taken by an unarmed civilian U-2 plane." Straining credulity, the statement also said that "there was no authorization for any such flight." Instead the flight had been restricted to the "frontiers" of the USSR. Perhaps, Herter reasoned, this clumsy fudging might appease Khrushchev while protecting the president.[22]

The statement was a disaster. It admitted that the United States had been spying on the Soviets for years using a spy plane, yet it also claimed that no one in high authority had ordered the plane to fly into Soviet airspace. While confessing to an egregious act of espionage, the wording of the statement supported the cartoonish allegation that Eisenhower was a detached, golf-playing absentee president. The national press was aghast. "This was a sad and depressed capital tonight," James Reston wrote from Washington. "It was depressed and humiliated by the United States' having been caught spying over the Soviet Union and trying to cover up its activities in a series of misleading official announcements." Eisenhower's fond hopes for a great breakthrough in Paris were overshadowed by "a swirl of charges of clumsy administration, bad judgment, and bad faith."[23]

Even now, with all the American fumbling, Khrushchev had not yet settled on how to react. At a reception on May 9 at the Czech Embassy in Moscow for the diplomatic corps, Khrushchev pulled aside Ambassador Thompson and greeted him "warmly." Khrushchev said he "could not help but suspect that someone had launched this operation with the deliberate intent of spoiling the summit meeting." He seemed to think it quite possible that Eisenhower really did not know about the U-2 flight and that Allen Dulles was responsible. Khrushchev had a great deal riding on the summit and did not want it to fail. He clung to the faint hope that a scapegoat could be found.[24]

Yet none appeared. Instead Eisenhower decided, about a week too late, to assert some personal control over the mess his team had created. Instead of firing Dulles, putting the blame on an overzealous subordinate, announcing an inquiry and assuring the Soviets that he would not allow such overflights in the future, Eisenhower decided to take the path of personal honor. On May 9 he ordered yet another press release, the fourth on the U-2 affair in just five days, and finally admitted that the United States had conducted extensive spying on the Soviets, including periodic overflights of their territory. The statement adopted a defiant tone, insisting that the U.S. government would be "derelict" if it did not try to ascertain Soviet intentions and capabilities, given the enormous power of new missile technology to destroy the world.[25]

If Khrushchev had left open an escape hatch for Eisenhower, the president soon nailed it shut. On May 11, at his weekly press conference, Eisenhower came clean. In a prepared statement, he described spying as "a distasteful but vital necessity." He coolly invoked the world war: "No one wants another Pearl Harbor. This means that we must have knowledge of military forces and preparations around the world, especially those capable of massive surprise attacks. Secrecy in the Soviet Union makes this essential. In most of the world no large-scale attack could be prepared in secret, but in the Soviet Union there is a fetish of secrecy and concealment. This is a major cause of international tension and uneasiness today." Far from apologizing, Eisenhower remained defiant: If you would agree to open your country to weapons inspections and sign disarmament agreements, we would not have to spy on you.[26]

The May 11 press conference marked an important moment in Ike's presidency and in the history of the cold war. Rather than leave things vague or heap blame on a subordinate or offer a muted apology and a reassurance that such things would not happen in the future, Eisenhower embraced spying as a professional obligation and threw a cloak of invulnerability around all his subordinates who had worked on the U-2 program. He would not offer a head on a platter. He would not apologize. On the contrary, he would blame the Soviets for their obsessive secrecy and militarism. Eisenhower's actions on this day won him everlasting praise from intelligence professionals and many subsequent biographers who have seen in this moment the true character of a great leader. When things go wrong, the president must take the blame. And having cleared the air in this manner, Eisenhower saw no reason why the summit in Paris could not go ahead as planned.[27]

Some critics, though, wondered if Eisenhower had acted wisely. Allen Dulles and Richard Bissell had given the president faulty advice about the

U-2 plane's vulnerability. They had pushed for a flight just two weeks before the summit, and then bungled the cover-up. Eisenhower could have found a diplomatic way to deflect responsibility onto these risk-taking subordinates, as Khrushchev wanted him to do. Eisenhower's decision to take the blame may have pleased his staff, but it destroyed the Paris summit. As Walter Lippmann wrote in his column, Eisenhower "locked the door which Mr. Khrushchev had opened." In his press conference Eisenhower "transform[ed] the embarrassment of being caught in a spying operation into a direct challenge to the sovereignty of the Soviet Union." Lippmann believed that Eisenhower's "refusal to use the convention of diplomacy was a fatal mistake." For Khrushchev to accept without protest Eisenhower's statement and continue with the summit would be a terrible blow to Soviet prestige and sovereignty. Even a leader less sensitive to personal slights than Khrushchev would never have done that. Eisenhower chose an honorable path, one that kept his reputation for decency and integrity intact. Yet the price of that noble act was a dramatic worsening of the cold war. It is fair to ask if the price was too high.[28]

At almost the same time Eisenhower was speaking to the press, Khrushchev paid an emotional and stormy visit to the exhibition hall in Gorky Park in Moscow to inspect the wreckage of the U-2 plane that was put on public display. Before a gaggle of journalists, he gave vent to his fury and indignation. "Impudence, sheer impudence!" he cried, inspecting the bent and scorched metal of the plane. "Only countries which are at war with each other can act this way!" Asked about his opinion of Eisenhower, he sadly replied that he was "horrified" to learn the president did in fact authorize the overflight. "I had high hopes, and they were betrayed." Ambassador Thompson, hearing these remarks, cabled Washington in despair: "The Cold War is back on again."[29]

Certainly Eisenhower met with a chilly reception when he arrived in Paris on May 15. Gathering with the host of the summit, President Charles de Gaulle, and Prime Minister Harold Macmillan at 6:00 that evening, Eisenhower learned that Khrushchev had the day before presented to de Gaulle three demands that must be met for the conference to proceed: Eisenhower must apologize for the U-2 flight; he must ban all future overflights; and he must punish those responsible for the U-2 incident. Hearing this, Eisenhower reacted sharply. The USSR had spies throughout the United States, he said, and he would be "damned" if he was going to renounce or apologize for a practice everyone else carried on.[30]

Khrushchev knew perfectly well that Eisenhower would not agree to his demands. He had decided during his flight to Paris on May 14 to sabotage the summit. Later he explained his thinking: "We had to present an ultimatum to the United States. They would have to apologize for the insult and injury done to our country. We would have to demand that the president take back his statement asserting the right of the United States to make spy flights over foreign territory, something no sovereign state could permit." America's behavior had been an affront, Khrushchev felt, and "if we simply sat down at the table as though nothing had happened and began negotiating in the usual way . . . such behavior would do great harm to our authority in the eyes of world public opinion, especially among our friends, the Communist parties, and countries that were fighting for independence." Khrushchev quite rightly thought the whole world was watching, and he could not buckle.[31]

When the summit opened on May 16 at 11:00 a.m. in the Élysée Palace, Khrushchev demanded the floor and attacked the U-2 overflight, Eisenhower, and America's unwillingness to recognize the provocative and illegal character of such espionage. Unless Eisenhower condemned the overflight and promised future flights would cease, the Soviet government would leave the summit meeting. What's more, Eisenhower would not be welcome to visit the USSR under such circumstances. Eisenhower responded briefly and calmly: he had already put a stop to future overflights, and he reiterated that the U-2 flight had no aggressive intent. Its purpose was only to gather intelligence.

Khrushchev refused to accept this gracious reply since he had already decided to scuttle the meeting. The combative premier insisted that Eisenhower apologize and that his apology be immediately given to the press. At this Eisenhower went silent. The minutes indicate that he never said another word. His son John explains: Ike was struggling to keep his temper during Khrushchev's insulting monologue. Herter correctly concluded, "It was clear that Khrushchev had been determined even before arriving to torpedo the meeting." Two days later the leaders departed Paris. A mere 48 hours after it began, the Big Four summit that might have altered the course of the cold war had collapsed.[32]

It was easy enough to blame Khrushchev for the summit's failure, but Eisenhower too bore responsibility, which he refused to accept. Upon returning to Washington, he wrote letters to two dozen friendly heads of state, casting Khrushchev as the villain for his "calculated campaign . . . to insure the failure of the conference." The United States had done nothing that justified Khrushchev's "polemics and abuse" in Paris. In his memoirs Eisenhower insisted that the only "big error" the United States had made had been to release an "erroneous cover story." As for his role in approving the overflight at such a critical moment, he expressed no regret. "I know of no decision that I would make differently," he wrote. Given his numerous, well-documented reservations about the overflights before May 1, this statement is difficult to accept. Once again Eisenhower protected his underlings, even at the expense of the truth.[33]

Though Eisenhower treated the U-2 affair with nonchalance in his memoirs, the downing of the spy plane had a huge impact on his presidency and on the cold war itself. It shattered his hopes to bring about a thaw in the war, thereby robbing him of a brilliant achievement in his last months in office. It led to a sharp intensification of cold war hostilities. It undermined all of his efforts to establish himself as a man of peace and goodwill in the eyes of the world's peoples. And it provided his domestic political rivals with powerful ammunition to use against him and his handling of the cold war. In retrospect his decision to approve the U-2 overflights in the spring of 1960 was the biggest mistake he ever made.

IV

The collapse of the summit became a source of domestic political controversy. In the spring of 1960 both political parties had started weighing candidates to nominate for president in the November elections. The Republicans leaned heavily toward Vice President Nixon and a platform of "peace and prosperity," the winning formula of 1956. But immediately after the Paris failure, the Democrats hit Ike hard. Adlai Stevenson declared the presidential campaign would now "be waged under the darkest shadows that ever hovered over the world—the mushroom clouds of a nuclear war." Stevenson, speaking to an audience of 3,000 Democrats at a fund-raiser in Chicago, summarized the affair in a memorable turn of phrase: "Khrushchev wrecked the conference," but Eisenhower "handed Khrushchev the crowbar and sledgehammer." It was America's "series of blunders" that gave the Soviet leader the pretext to walk out. Eisenhower and his administration "have helped make successful negotiations with the Russians—negotiations that are vital to our survival—impossible."[34]

John Kennedy, the Democratic hopeful who had amassed nine primary victories since March, was campaigning in the Oregon Democratic primary on May 19 when he too weighed in. He said in a brief campaign speech that if he had been president, he would have found a way to keep the summit going by "expressing regret" to Khrushchev; he initially used the word *apologize* but then corrected himself. Senator Stuart Symington called for a new foreign policy built on the "ruins of the summit conference." The Democratic Advisory Council, made up of leading liberals, declared that "the fiasco in Paris" had done "incalculable harm to the cause of peace." The Democrats ripped the administration: "The integrity of the word of the United States has been put into doubt. The danger of an all-out destructive nuclear war has been increased." The GOP revealed its "fundamental lack of purpose" in its foreign policy, they said.[35]

The Republicans did not take these attacks lightly. The Republican National Committee smelled appeasement in the air. Stevenson, it said, "fell like a ton of bricks for the Khrushchev line." His "wishy-washy 'let's not anger the Russians' position" looked weak next to Ike's stalwart defense of America's cold war strategy. On the floor of the Senate on May 24, Hugh Scott, Republican of Pennsylvania, declared that Kennedy and Stevenson must now be asked to "relieve themselves of the gross suspicion of appeasement" for the suggestion that they might have apologized to Khrushchev. Six hours later Kennedy strode into the Senate chamber and fairly shouted, "I do not have to purge myself of the suspicion of being an appeaser," and demanded a retraction.

Now the fat was in the fire. The Republican National Committee chairman, Senator Thruston Morton of Kentucky, added more fuel, calling the Democrats "soft on Communism" and asserting that Kennedy "would have bowed to the Khrushchev bluster and expressed regret" for the U-2 flight. Mike Mansfield, the assistant Democratic leader in the Senate, struck back: "We are not the ones who are soft on Communism. . . . We did not invite Khrushchev over here, and he has never invited a Democratic presidential candidate to visit him." The fight for the White House was on, and it would take place on a well-trodden patch of ground: determining which party was tougher on communism.[36]

In late May, Senator William Fulbright, the Democratic chairman of the Senate Foreign Relations Committee, opened an inquiry into the U-2 and Paris events. Leading figures of the administration were invited to testify, thus keeping the pressure on the Republicans to explain their mishandling of the affair. The investigations centered on the decision to order the U-2 into Soviet airspace as well as the failure to handle the cover story adequately. The committee finally concluded that because of the enormous stakes of the Paris summit, the U-2 flight should not have been sent.[37]

In a speech to the Senate, Fulbright delivered a harsh verdict: "The prestige and influence of our country on the affairs of nations has reached a new low" as a result of the administration's "blunders." Sending the plane on May 1 was "a serious error of judgment." More than that, Fulbright indicted Eisenhower personally on a key matter of presidential leadership. Echoing Lippmann, Fulbright insisted that Eisenhower made a mistake when he took the blame for the U-2 in a "self-righteous" manner that was "unbearably provocative to the Soviet Government and contributed substantially to the violence and intemperate bad manners of Mr. Khrushchev." Fulbright asserted, "It is unprecedented among civilized nations for a chief of state to assume personal responsibility for covert intelligence operations." Doing so all but forced Khrushchev to demand a personal apology that could not be delivered.

There is some irony to savor here. While Democrats typically blasted Eisenhower as a detached, disengaged golf-obsessed president, Fulbright blamed him for being too closely involved in the handling of the U-2 affair and for taking personal responsibility for the actions of his administration. Had he only floated above the dirty business of spycraft, feigned a lack of awareness of the CIA's program, and offered up Allen Dulles as a "whipping boy" (Fulbright's term), Eisenhower could have saved the summit. Never was there such an effective if unintentional rebuttal of the thesis that Eisenhower "didn't run the store."[38]

Kennedy, by June the clear front-runner for the Democratic presidential nomination, knew that the events in Paris presented him with a golden political opportunity. Since he began his run for the nomination, Kennedy had been hitting the Eisenhower administration for its alleged weakness and confusion. He depicted American foreign policy as rudderless, failing, and reactive. The country was on "a slide downhill into dust, dullness, languor and decay," he claimed. Eisenhower offered only "soft sentimentalism" when America needed "tough-minded plans and operations."[39]

Now, after the Paris fiasco, Kennedy pressed his case. In a speech in the Senate on June 14, 1960, before a packed gallery of admirers and autograph seekers, the handsome 43-year-old legislator delivered a scathing assessment of Eisenhower's cold war strategy. It had all been based on an "illusion," Kennedy argued, "the illusion that platitudes and slogans are a substitute for strength and planning . . . the illusion that good intentions and pious principles are a substitute for strong creative leadership." The collapse of the summit revealed America's "lack of coherent and purposeful national strategy backed by strength." Eisenhower offered only "eleventh-hour responses to Soviet-created crises." To counter Eisenhower's "confusion and indecision," America needed "a comprehensive set of carefully prepared, long-term policies."[40]

This portrait of a befuddled, ill-prepared Eisenhower out of his depth in a dangerous world became the leitmotif of Kennedy's campaign. Of course the charges were hollow. Indeed when Kennedy went on in his Senate speech to itemize all the things he proposed to do, he cribbed shamelessly from Eisenhower's own agenda. Kennedy demanded a stronger nuclear deterrent; beefed-up conventional armed forces; a stronger NATO; more foreign aid; better relations with governments in Latin America, the Middle East, and Africa; a lasting solution in Berlin; and a serious effort at arms control—precisely the policies Eisenhower had pursued. RNC chairman Morton responded by saying that Kennedy seemed to have "endorsed the administration's policies but said they should be carried out with brighter, nicer people."[41]

Yet the Paris fiasco—Khrushchev's sneering, Eisenhower's fumbling, the sense of dashed hopes—irked Americans all across the political spectrum. Just as Kennedy attacked Eisenhower from the left, another powerful assault hit Eisenhower from the right. It came from an Arizona Republican named Barry Goldwater. Like Kennedy, Goldwater was a handsome World War II veteran, and also like Kennedy he came to the Senate in 1953. But unlike Kennedy, Goldwater did not want simply a better version of Ike's policies. He demanded a clean break from the Ike years. His indictment came in a short, powerful book titled *The Conscience of a Conservative* that hit the bookstores on April 15, 1960.

In the 15 years since 1945, Goldwater argued, America had failed to maintain the dominant global position it had earned as a result of its great victory over Hitler. The country's leaders had stood by and watched as the Soviet Union gained power, territory, and followers around the world. American leaders had been complacent. "Our leaders have not made victory the goal of American policy." Instead they sought "peace" or "settlements." "We have tried to pacify the world," Goldwater stated. "The Communists mean to own it." For Goldwater, the sole objective of American foreign policy must be not to end the cold war but to *win* it.

Goldwater scorned Ike's foreign policy, with its reliance on defensive alliances, foreign aid, negotiations, disarmament, and the United Nations. He wanted the United States to defeat the Soviet Union and communism by taking the offensive, carrying the conflict into the enemy camp, subduing any and all challenges to American interests around the world, pressuring the USSR to withdraw and retreat. The risk of global nuclear war was real, he recognized, but such risks were better than accepting half-measures and compromise. "War may be the price of freedom." The militant tone of Goldwater's short book (in fact ghost-written by *National Review* writer Brent Bozell) echoed across the country. It became a best-seller within weeks; by November it had sold half a million copies.

On July 15, 1960, Kennedy accepted the presidential nomination of the Democratic Party. In his acceptance speech in Memorial Coliseum in Los Angeles, he laid out the essential themes of his campaign: the Republican leaders had let America decline, and it was time for a new and younger generation to revive the nation. "The old era is ending. The old ways will not do." America had lost its stature on the world stage. "The balance of power is shifting," he declared. "Communist influence has penetrated further into Asia, stood astride the Middle East and now festers some ninety miles off the coast of Florida. Friends have slipped into neutrality—and neutrals into hostility." The Republicans had allowed "dry rot" to set in; "seven lean years of drought and famine have withered the field of ideas."

Kennedy, facing west and staring into the setting sun in the huge (and half-empty) sports arena, challenged the voters to choose between "national greatness and national decline; between the fresh air of progress and the stale, dank atmosphere of 'normalcy'; between determined dedication and creeping mediocrity." Too many Americans "have lost their way, their will and their sense of historic purpose." The mere pursuit of creature comforts and an easy prosperity cannot animate a great nation. Leaders must articulate larger goals and ask the people to "sacrifice" in order to achieve them. He conjured up a vision of a "New Frontier" in which Americans once again took risks like the pioneers of old and set out to renew the promise of America.[42]

Whether the denunciations came from Democrats or Republicans, Eisenhower's reputation as a masterful statesman suffered in the spring of 1960. On the cusp of achieving what he hoped might be a real breakthrough in the cold war, Eisenhower stumbled and missed his great chance, just when eager would-be presidents sought to take his place. Inevitably his spirits sagged. His chief science adviser, George Kistiakowsky, recalled that sometime after the Paris summit, he found himself alone with the president in the White House. Eisenhower "began to talk with much feeling about how he had concentrated his efforts the last few years on ending the cold war, how he felt that he was making big progress, and how the stupid U-2 mess had ruined all his efforts. He ended very sadly that he saw nothing worthwhile left for him to do now until the end of his presidency."[43]

A touching portrait, but perhaps misleading. For Eisenhower did not spend the last few months of his presidency as a weepy, self-pitying recluse. Rather, stung by the critics, angered by Khrushchev's rejection of his peace overtures, and driven to shore up his legacy as an effective leader, Eisenhower set out in his final months to reassert American power across the globe. Kennedy and the critics demanded more action, more aggression, more boldness—and Eisenhower meant to give it to them.

CHAPTER 19

FIGHTING TO THE FINISH

"The past eight years have been the brightest of our history."

I

REPUBLICANS OF THE 1950s KNEW HOW TO SELL A PRODUCT. They pioneered the use of television advertising in politics, and at their national conventions in 1952 and 1956, they mobilized actors, dancers, acrobats, sports figures, crooners, jugglers, and sword-swallowers to infuse their rather dull message of "peace and prosperity" with some pizzazz. In mid-July 1960, though, as the GOP faithful gathered in Chicago at the International Amphitheater, the same hall in which Ike and Dick had formed their political tandem eight years earlier, the convention planners were running out of ideas. A giant elephant named Koa, on loan from Louisiana, proved to be too big to amble down the aisles of the hall and had to be returned. The torchlight parade of 500 young Republicans had to be canceled due to the fire hazard of their kerosene-soaked rags. Plans to get Henry Fonda into costume as Abraham Lincoln—a role he had played woodenly in the 1939 film *Young Mr. Lincoln*—were scotched when Fonda turned out to be a Democrat. Half the hotel rooms in Chicago remained empty a few days before the convention.[1]

Besides an absence of hoopla the top Republican leaders had serious worries. A Gallup poll on the eve of the convention showed that since 1952, the Republicans had lost support among business and professional voters, white-collar workers, and farmers—three key demographic groups. And they had made no inroads among skilled and unskilled laborers, who favored the Democratic Party by a ratio of 4 to 1. President Eisenhower's personal popularity had masked serious weaknesses in the Republican Party.

As the Republicans gathered in Chicago, John Kennedy, a junior senator with little national name recognition, led Nixon in the polls by 4 points.[2]

The press corps, bored to tears by the lack of drama in Republican ranks, worked hard to breathe life into the candidacies of New York governor Nelson Rockefeller and Arizona senator Barry Goldwater, who might, they earnestly hoped, challenge Nixon for the GOP nomination from the left and the right. The *Washington Post* editorial page noted that both parties inclined toward "moderate" nominees like Kennedy, Lyndon Johnson, and Nixon, but cautioned that "an excess of moderation can yield a pudding devoid of flavor or shape" and hoped that Goldwater would add a dash of "pepper to the otherwise Bland Old Party's Chicago solemnities." Indeed Old Guard supporters of the dear departed Bob Taft now had a new champion in the ruggedly handsome conservative from the desert West.[3]

It was not to be. Goldwater did not seek the nomination and backed Nixon. Rockefeller, whom most veteran Republicans distrusted for his ideological elasticity and his vanity, pressured Nixon to adopt a number of Kennedy-like platform planks on issues such as defense spending, civil rights, health insurance, and housing. Nixon, terrified that a Rockefeller boomlet might snatch away his long-sought prize, caved in to these demands after meeting with Rocky in New York on July 22, three days before the convention opened. Rockefeller in turn threw his support to Nixon in a feeble gesture of party unity. In extracting concessions from Nixon on the GOP platform, though, Rockefeller managed to weaken Nixon's case that he and he alone had the toughness to confront Khrushchev on the world stage.[4]

The real challenge Nixon faced in taking the leadership of the Republican Party did not come from Goldwater or Rockefeller. It came from Eisenhower. Of course Ike supported Nixon's presidential bid since Nixon offered the best hope of extending the Eisenhower legacy. But the distance between the two men, which had always been great, never seemed wider than in 1960. Eisenhower had become the world's most respected, most recognized, and most liked man. For all of his apparent political weaknesses and occasional lapses, and his mishandling of the U-2 affair, he occupied an unassailable place in the pantheon of great figures of his time. His war service alone would have placed him on history's pedestal, but he followed that with eight years of dignified leadership of a country whose global power had reached unprecedented dimensions.

When Eisenhower arrived in Chicago on July 26 to address the Republican Convention, over one million Chicagoans lined the streets along his route to the Sheraton Blackstone Hotel. Shouts of joy rang through the miles of well-wishers. "We Like Ike" signs dotted the scene, along with hand-painted expressions of thanks to the old warrior. Confetti, so dense that it stuck to Ike's moist and beaming face, poured from the rooftops. Banners and flags draped every storefront and lamppost in a blaze of red, white, and blue. Seated behind him in the open-top presidential Lincoln, Illinois governor William G. Stratton and Senator Everett Dirksen seemed like supernumeraries. It was Ike the crowd wanted. A loudspeaker in a truck following the motorcade blared out a popular tune by the Four Knights, "I Love the Sunshine of Your Smile." The president, visibly moved, told reporters outside the hotel, "It is one of the finest crowds I've ever seen."[5]

On Tuesday evening Senator Dirksen, a famously orotund speaker in a profession known for producing magnificent windbags, came to the podium in the Amphitheater to introduce the president. Few recalled that eight years earlier Dirksen had nominated Senator Taft and worked against Ike. Now Dirksen likened Eisenhower to Abraham Lincoln, the Illinois Republican whose gaunt visage hung on a huge poster above the convention speakers. During his presidency Lincoln was "excoriated and pilloried, criticized and maligned, caricatured and cursed, but with humility, determination, and firm resolve, he held the course and the union was saved." Eisenhower too, Dirksen asserted, "has been assailed and impugned. He too has been mocked and castigated." But Eisenhower's simple political credo of peace through strength, devotion to individual freedom, limited and prudent government, and a spirit of compassion had healed the nation and brought it unprecedented prosperity.[6]

At 9:30 p.m., as Ike and Mamie stepped onto the stage, the crowd in the hall burst into riotous applause that endured for a full eight minutes. Eisenhower then gave a powerful speech that showed how much fight remained in the old warrior. Nearing 70, a survivor of a serious heart attack, a major intestinal operation, and a small stroke, Eisenhower delivered a blistering defense of his eight-year record. The crowd, delighted by this demonstration of vigor, interrupted the speech 77 times with applause, shouts, and demonstrations of affection.[7]

In triumphant tones Eisenhower struck sharply at those—especially Kennedy—who dared to doubt the power of the United States. "I glory in the moral, economic and military strength of this nation," he said with an imperial flourish. "I bring no words of despair or doubt about my country—no doleful prediction of impending disaster." The United States "is enjoying an unprecedented prosperity"; he gleefully rattled off the economic results of his years in office. Compared to the Truman years, America enjoyed lower unemployment, higher wages, less inflation, a staggering rate of growth of the nation's productive capacity, higher rates of homeownership, greater investment in research and engineering education, and an expansion of social security. And Ike had done it while balancing the federal budget.

To those who had criticized him for letting America fall behind in the arms race, Eisenhower delivered an especially defiant blast: "In the sum of our capabilities we have become the strongest military power on Earth. But just as the Biblical Job had his boils, so we have a cult of professional pessimists who . . . continually mouth the allegation that America has become a second-rate military power." This claim infuriated him, and he savored the opportunity to deflate it. He enumerated the new aircraft, the vast web of radar alert systems, the arsenal of ballistic missiles, the nuclear-powered naval vessels, the technologically stunning Polaris submarine, the globe-circling space satellites, the newly equipped army—a breathtaking catalogue of accomplishment on his watch. Giving due credit to the scientists, engineers, and armed forces who had built these weapons, he spoke with steel and fire in his voice: "To belittle this might, prestige, pride and capabilities of these groups does such violence to my sense of what is right that I have difficulty in restraining my feelings of indignation." Bedlam in the hall. James Reston, who had covered Eisenhower closely during his eight years in office, wrote that the president "has never been more appealing or more effective politically than he has been this week in Chicago." The "old magic" was working again.[8]

Did anyone notice that during his long convention speech, Eisenhower never mentioned the name of Richard Nixon? No doubt Nixon noticed. He also observed the hero worship Ike received and must have gloomily wondered how he could compete with the president for the adulation of the country. Nixon and his running mate, Henry Cabot Lodge Jr., faced the awkward challenge of running both on and against the Eisenhower record. Nixon wanted to benefit from Ike's successes while implying that he could fix the problems Ike had left unresolved. Playing against his natural instinct for political knife-fighting, Nixon posed as a moderate, tempered, and decent fellow, full of bromides and Boy Scout nostrums—in short, another Eisenhower. But the 47-year-old Californian possessed none of Eisenhower's authenticity. Eisenhower had a gift for making the cornpone vocabulary of American politics sound decent and truthful. When Nixon tried it, he sounded artless and insincere.

Nixon arrived at the Amphitheater on July 27, accompanied by his wife, Pat, and their daughters, Julie and Tricia. He received a warm welcome, though nothing like the delirium Ike prompted. His acceptance speech was wordy and lawyerly and lacked spark. Nixon told his fellow Republicans that 1960 was "a time of greatness," but his bland comportment left them wondering if he was really the man for the job. Many in the hall looked wistfully at the brawny and uncompromising Goldwater. Nixon ticked off the usual list of domestic projects that needed attention: health care, education, wages, more defense spending, more prosperity, more spirituality, and less government. Unlike the partisan, energetic, and heartfelt address by Eisenhower, Nixon's speech seemed engineered to tranquilize the convention and to reassure the television viewers that Nixon was a younger, technocratic version of the beloved incumbent. The crowds cheered dutifully, and the band played "California Here I Come" over and over again. But something about Nixon's uneasy, labored performance hinted at a difficult road ahead.[9]

And Eisenhower did not exactly smooth the path. In his first post-convention press conference, he seemed to suggest that the business of getting Nixon elected would not occupy much of his time. Yes, he said in reply to a question, he would "promote" the Nixon-Lodge ticket, but "this doesn't mean I possibly should be out on the hustings and making partisan speeches." After all, "I've got a lot of other responsibilities and I've got a lot of other commitments around the country. But I think these two fellows can take care of themselves pretty well and they are tops." A week later, prodded by the press, Ike called the GOP ticket "fine" but considered himself "just a spectator" since he was no longer running.

It got worse. In a press conference on August 24 Eisenhower again distanced himself from the political campaign—and perhaps from Nixon himself. Asked what "big decisions" Nixon had shaped while vice president, Eisenhower snappishly replied, "I don't see why people can't understand this: no one can make a decision except me if it is in the national executive area." He went out of his way to stress *no one* three times when explaining who helped make his decisions. A few minutes later, when a reporter returned to the issue, Ike again insisted that he and he alone made the decisions in his administration. Of course Nixon took part in the "discussions," but not in the decisions.

Eisenhower was on a slippery slope, and the veteran press corps sensed an imminent stumble. So they pushed him. "I just wondered," said Charles Mohr of *Time* magazine, "if you could give us an example of a major idea of his [Nixon's] that you had adopted in that role." It was the last question of the press conference, and Ike was already preparing to depart the podium. Hastily—too hastily—he replied with a wry grin, "If you give me a week, I might think of one. I don't know."[10]

Pow. Had Nixon been there, he would have dropped to his knees as if poleaxed. Although Eisenhower knew he'd blundered and called Nixon right away to try to reassure the candidate, the remark completely undid all of Nixon's own claims about his vast experience in government, on which he had premised his entire campaign. With this unguarded remark, Eisenhower confirmed the widespread suspicion that Nixon did not enjoy the confidence or trust of the president. In retrospect it seems plain that Eisenhower simply was not yet ready to share the stage with anyone, least of all Dick Nixon.[11]

II

Though staying aloof from the campaign, Eisenhower nonetheless felt the sting of Kennedy's attacks on his record. Kennedy blamed Ike for America's "slippage" in the cold war. He questioned Ike's stewardship of the national defense and accused him of "losing" Cuba to the communists. He also asserted that the newly independent nations in Asia and Africa now looked to Moscow for inspiration rather than Washington. The Soviets were advancing, Kennedy charged, while America stood still.

If Eisenhower wanted to rebut such Democratic accusations of drift, a crisis in central Africa gave him an opportunity to do so. On June 30, 1960, the former Belgian colony of Congo declared its independence; its new prime minister was Patrice Lumumba, a charismatic leftist whose political party had won the most seats in the newly formed Parliament. Wealthy in cobalt, bauxite, iron, manganese, zinc, and gold, Congo had been ruthlessly exploited by European mining interests for decades, while the Belgians shamefully deprived the Congolese of any social or institutional advancement. In 1960 the country was not well-prepared for the trials of self-government. With independence, the nation's security forces fell to pieces, as Congolese soldiers mutinied against their white Belgian officers and threatened the safety of some 100,000 Europeans still living in the country. In the midst of this chaos the mineral-rich province of Katanga in southeastern Congo, where many of the leading industrial firms had headquarters, declared its own independence and also called for Belgian military protection. The Belgians promptly sent paratroops to the breakaway province, thus aiding and abetting the breakup of Congo while seizing the richest part of the country.

Prime Minister Lumumba, angered by the Belgian military intervention, appealed to the United Nations to send peacekeeping soldiers to replace the Belgian troops. Locked in a global propaganda battle with the Soviets to win the allegiance of newly independent Third World nations, the United States had to support a peaceful resolution of the Congo crisis and duly helped pass a UN resolution to send in peacekeepers to restore order and to keep the country from splitting apart. By the end of July some 11,000 UN troops had arrived in Congo to replace the Belgians. But the UN secretary general Dag Hammarskjöld insisted that these UN soldiers could not be used by Lumumba to compel the Katanga province to remain in Congo. Lumumba began to suspect that the UN forces had a secret agenda to provide cover to the secessionist province. In a very unwise move, Lumumba publicly denounced Hammarskjöld and demanded the UN withdraw from Congo. In mid-August he turned to the Soviet Union with a request for military assistance with which to invade the rebellious province of Katanga and seize its secessionist government.[12]

Allen Dulles offered a simple explanation for the seesaw events in Congo. "In Lumumba, we were faced with a person who was a Castro or even worse," he told the National Security Council on July 21. Lumumba, Dulles claimed, was "in the pay of the Soviets." To Dulles, one Third World nationalist was like another: Lumumba was like Castro, Castro was like Nasser, Nasser was like Sukarno. They were all Soviet-inspired threats to American interests and had to be stopped.[13]

On August 18 an alarming cable from Larry Devlin, the CIA station chief in Congo, landed at CIA headquarters. It seemed to confirm the worst predictions. With telegraphic brevity, Devlin wrote, "Congo experiencing classic Communist effort takeover government. . . . Whether or not Lumumba actually Commie or just playing Commie game to assist his solidifying power, anti-West forces increasing power Congo and there may be little time left in which take action to avoid another Cuba." Ike's advisers gathered at 9:00 that morning to discuss the problem. Undersecretary of State Douglas Dillon said that if the UN was forced to withdraw from Congo, the USSR would intervene at Lumumba's invitation and the United States would be faced with a "disaster." Dulles again insisted that Lumumba was "in Soviet pay." Eisenhower said the "possibility that the UN would be forced out was simply inconceivable." Ike spoke with real heat: "we were talking of one man forcing us out of the Congo; of Lumumba supported by the Soviets."[14]

According to the note-taker at this meeting, Robert H. Johnson, Eisenhower said even more than this. In testimony given in 1975 to a Senate investigation under the chairmanship of Frank Church, Johnson reported that Eisenhower "said something—I can no longer remember his words—that came across to me as an order for the assassination of Lumumba." Johnson then went on to say that he could not be certain of Eisenhower's words or his intentions: "I have come to wonder whether what I really heard was only an order for some such political action." But his testimony implicated Eisenhower in the murder of a foreign leader.[15]

Other officials who were present at the meeting recalled it differently. Douglas Dillon and Gordon Gray gave testimony to Senator Church's committee denying that Eisenhower gave any such order, though they admitted that Dulles might have interpreted a strong statement by the president against Lumumba as an order for his assassination. General Goodpaster, in an interview given in 1975, firmly denied that Eisenhower ever discussed the assassination of Lumumba or anyone else. Precisely what Ike said at the August 18 meeting cannot be known with certainty. Yet his subordinates, all very careful and loyal men, acted as if the president had approved their course of action.[16]

Just a week after the August 18 meeting, Gray chaired a meeting of the 5412 Committee during which he reported on Eisenhower's state of mind regarding Lumumba. "His associate," Gray said, using the code-word for the president, "had expressed extremely strong feelings on the necessity for very straightforward action in this situation." Dulles affirmed that he "had every intention of proceeding as vigorously as the situation permits or requires." Both men insisted that "planning for the Congo would not necessarily rule out consideration of any particular kind of activity which might contribute to getting rid of Lumumba." Cloaked in a fog of euphemism, these senior U.S. government officials were planning to oust and possibly murder Patrice Lumumba. This conclusion is supported by Dulles's own telegram to Devlin on August 26: "We conclude that [Lumumba's] removal must be an urgent and prime objective and that under existing conditions this should be a high priority of our covert action."[17]

In his memoirs Richard Bissell, Dulles's deputy and the man tasked with overseeing these various plots, explained how such matters worked in the halls of government. In official settings the president did not speak of assassination. Instead his colleagues interpreted certain phrases as approval for their extreme plans. "If you had asked Eisenhower what he was thinking at that moment he probably would have said, 'I sure as hell would rather get rid of Lumumba without killing him, but if that's the only way, then it's got to be that way.'" Bissell clearly admired Eisenhower for his cold-bloodedness: "Eisenhower was a tough man behind that smile."[18]

Bissell wished to implicate Eisenhower in the Lumumba plot to show that what followed had presidential approval. In late August, aware of the high priority Eisenhower gave to the Congo operation and the elimination of Lumumba, Bissell turned to his special assistant for scientific matters, Joseph Scheider, also known as Sidney Gottlieb. A graduate of Cal Tech with an advanced degree in chemistry, Scheider joined the CIA's Technical Services Staff in 1951 and had been the leading person behind the CIA's experimental use of psychotropic drugs in human subjects. Bissell ordered Scheider to deliver toxic biological materials to CIA station chief Devlin in Congo's capital, Leopoldville. In late September Scheider traveled to Congo with the vials of toxins in his luggage, carefully disguised as innocuous drugs, along with rubber gloves, a syringe, and a gauze mask; these he handed over to Devlin. Scheider told Devlin that the operation had been approved by the president. Just how the poison might be delivered to Lumumba—by food or drink or toothpaste tube—would be up to Devlin and his agents.[19]

Devlin had the good sense to see the murder-by-poison plot as zany and dangerous. Had the CIA carried it out and been discovered, it might have triggered an outburst of anti-Western sentiment across Africa at a terribly delicate moment. Devlin therefore locked the vials in his office safe and stalled. However, events moved so rapidly that Devlin did not need to carry out the poison operation. On September 14 a coup d'état led by Col. Joseph Mobutu toppled Lumumba from power; the deposed prime minister holed up in his residence under the protection of UN troops, with Mobutu's police also standing watch. Even under house arrest, though, Lumumba still remained a powerful symbol; Eisenhower quipped that he wished "Lumumba would fall into a river full of crocodiles." Two days later Dulles expressed esteem for Mobutu, "the only man in the Congo able to act with firmness," and said that Lumumba "remained a grave danger as long as he was not disposed of." Indeed Dulles now termed Lumumba "insane," making his elimination appear urgent.[20]

In late November, Lumumba fled his home to join his sympathizers in

Stanleyville. But he was captured, imprisoned by Mobutu, and slated for trial. However, Mobutu had no desire to offer Lumumba a public platform. Instead Mobutu handed Lumumba over to his political enemies in Katanga province, where Belgian and Katangan soldiers beat and tortured him; on January 17, 1961, they shot him to death and boiled his body in a vat of sulfuric acid.[21]

In the end, then, Lumumba did not die at the hands of the CIA or its agents. Yet the dismal tale of his fate in no way absolves the CIA or the U.S. government of responsibility. Colonel Mobutu's coup against Lumumba was undertaken with direct CIA knowledge and support. Lumumba's arrest by Mobutu's police served American interests, since both Mobutu and the CIA shared a desire to eliminate the former leader. And the CIA station chief knew that Lumumba was to be delivered to his political foes in Katanga, where he was certain to be murdered. In short, the CIA did everything possible to ensure Lumumba's death. In the process they formed an alliance with Joseph Mobutu, who became a loyal ally of the United States and one of history's most repellent dictators. For three decades Mobutu ruthlessly governed his renamed country, Zaire, casually murdering political opponents and amassing a personal fortune in one of the world's poorest nations. This too is a legacy of the Age of Eisenhower.[22]

III

Coming in the middle of a high-spirited presidential campaign, the tumult in central Africa did not attract much national attention from the American press. Cuba mattered far more to Americans, and the "loss" of the Caribbean island to communism became one of Kennedy's most potent themes in the 1960 campaign. Kennedy argued that the loss of Cuba revealed a broader failure of American verve and determination in waging the cold war. The United States, he asserted, had fallen behind, while the communist bloc had surged ahead. "There is no disputing the fact," he said in Portland, Oregon, brimming with confidence, "that our prestige, our stature and our influence have all declined" during the 1950s. There was "a lack of respect" around the world for America. The country had entered a period of decline and needed to "move with vigor" to restore its flagging influence.[23]

Cuba offered a painful example of the consequences of inaction. "Communism has expanded to within 90 miles of the coast of the United States, eight minutes by jet from the coast of Florida," Kennedy charged in Harrisburg, Pennsylvania. Yet Eisenhower had done nothing. In Raleigh, North Carolina, Kennedy denounced the "drift and complacency" of the administration. "We talked tough when the people of Hungary revolted, but [Khrushchev] crushed the revolt. We talked tough when communism began to grow in Cuba—but Cuba is a communist satellite today." Kennedy's muscular anticommunist rhetoric might well have come from the lips of Barry Goldwater.[24]

Eisenhower greeted these accusations with sardonic reserve. Far from tolerating communism in Cuba, his administration had been preparing since March 1960 a major covert operation to infiltrate guerrilla fighters into Cuba to destabilize Castro's regime. In the spring the CIA had started training Cuban guerrillas in Guatemala and had set up the Revolutionary Democratic Front, a coalition of anticommunist factions that would replace Castro. In April the navy began construction of a medium-wave radio station on Swan Island for broadcasting anti-Castro news into Cuba; it went live in May. In July the United States announced a halt to purchases of Cuban sugar, a massive blow to the island's economy designed to put more pressure on Castro. And in August, Bissell enlisted key leaders of the American Mafia in a plot to assassinate Castro in conjunction with the guerrilla infiltration plan. Far from doing nothing about Castro, the Eisenhower White House devoted immense energy to developing ways of destroying him.[25]

And Eisenhower pushed the pace. On August 18, the same day that he allegedly called for the murder of Lumumba, Eisenhower met with Dulles, Bissell, Gray, and other top security advisers, and approved a significant increase in the budget for the anti-Castro plan. Initial funds for the operation amounted to $2.5 million; Bissell now asked for an additional $10.75 million. This dramatic increase reveals the growing ambition of the project. Originally designed to place small teams of saboteurs and guerrillas into Cuba, Bissell's scheme had grown dramatically. It now envisioned a paramilitary strike force, placed on Cuban shores by an amphibious landing, equipped with air power and heavy weapons, that would provide more muscle to the infiltrated guerrilla fighters once their subversion efforts got under way. Gray supported Bissell's expansive ideas, and Eisenhower approved both the funds and the backup force. The minutes of the meeting show that Eisenhower spoke firmly about his eagerness to move ahead: he said "he would defend this kind of action against all comers and that if we were sure of freeing the Cubans from this incubus, $25 million might be a small price to pay."[26]

During the fall of 1960 the Cuba issue came right to Ike's doorstep. On September 20 the United Nations General Assembly convened in New York City. This gathering possessed special significance, as the UN planned to admit no fewer than 14 new nations, all former colonies of Western empires. The world body was quite literally changing its complexion, and by 1960 it stood ready to become the tribune of the nonwhite world, an amplifier of the grievances of millions of newly independent peoples. Held under the glare of intense media attention, this UN meeting offered a priceless opportunity to the great rivals in the cold war to court the new member states. Soviet premier Khrushchev arrived in New York at the head of a large delegation to make his pitch. In contrast to his visit a year earlier, when he was Eisenhower's guest, Khrushchev's arrival on September 19 was met with jeers and insults from thousands of protesters, mostly people of Eastern European heritage who denounced Soviet domination of their homelands. Khrushchev did not seem to mind: still bitter about the U-2 affair in May, he came to New York to turn up the heat in the cold war, inflame the sedate halls of the United Nations, and woo the Third World.[27]

Khrushchev, though, had to share the spotlight. Thrilled at the chance to grab his own share of world publicity, Fidel Castro arrived in New York on September 18 amid a flurry of demonstrations and counterdemonstrations. A natural propagandist, Castro milked the trip for all it was worth. From the opening hour of his visit he caused commotion. Taken to a bourgeois midtown hotel, he and his entourage refused the demand of hotel management that they post a $10,000 deposit against any damages or expenses that his bearded, fatigue-wearing revolutionaries might incur. Instead he stalked out and moved his delegation to the Hotel Theresa on 125th Street and Seventh Avenue, in the heart of Harlem.

This location, a well-known hub of black cultural life in New York, offered Castro a perfect stage from which to denounce the segregation and racism of American society. Holding court at the Theresa, Castro gleefully reached out to Harlem's African American residents, who, he suggested, shared more with Cubans than they did with white Americans. Malcolm X, a prominent leader of the Nation of Islam, met with him briefly, after which Castro professed solidarity with the black struggle in America and around the world. "We are all brothers," he declared in accented English. Cuban officials, strolling through the neighborhood, praised Harlem for its "democratic atmosphere" and said, "It's like Havana."[28]

Not to be outdone in the pursuit of press coverage, Khrushchev decided to pay Castro an unannounced visit on September 20, racing his black limousine and large police escort all the way uptown to Castro's hotel. Thousands of spectators had crowded the hotel's entrance, which was guarded by a ring of steely blue-clad New York City police. Inside, Khrushchev met Castro in a ninth-floor suite, emerging after 20 minutes with a grin, declaring Castro a "heroic man." Savvy observers of the Castro-Khrushchev encounter at the Hotel Theresa understood its significance. Jackie Robinson, the former baseball star and civil rights leader, said the meeting of the two communist leaders "shows the concern they both have regarding the new African countries and of segregation and discrimination in the United States." Robinson called on the U.S. government to send more aid to Africa and to dismantle Jim Crow at home. James L. Hicks, editor of the venerable black newspaper *Amsterdam News*, phrased the issue more pointedly: "Fidel Castro stuck a knife into the heart of America's race problem Monday night, and Nikita Khrushchev broke it off at the hilt Tuesday morning." Later in the day, when both men arrived at the UN headquarters in midtown Manhattan, they embraced in a bear hug in front of dozens of popping flashbulbs. Pictures of this *abrazo* appeared in all the world's newspapers the next day. It was a particularly delicious moment for Khrushchev, who believed he had drawn the charismatic revolutionary into his orbit and successfully poked President Eisenhower in the eye.[29]

Eisenhower meanwhile conducted a rather more sedate and regal charm offensive of his own during this extraordinary week in New York. On September 22 he gave a solemn speech to the General Assembly praising the human yearning for self-determination, stating America's desire for peaceful relations with all nations, and calling on the Great Powers to commit far more money to the economic development of the newly independent African nations. He invited the heads of 18 Latin American countries for lunch, deliberately leaving Castro out. In the afternoon, in a counterpoint to Castro's outreach efforts, he welcomed leading figures of the nonaligned movement to his suite at the Waldorf Astoria, then one of the world's most glamorous hotels and a far cry from Castro's digs in Harlem. He met with Kwame Nkrumah of Ghana and Josip Tito of Yugoslavia; later in the week he hosted President Nasser of Egypt, and also met with Prime Minister Nehru. The conversations were not substantial, but the symbolism mattered enormously. Ike understood, no less than Castro and Khrushchev, that the United States needed friends among the emerging nations of the Third World. By appealing to these moderate and influential men of the nonaligned movement, Eisenhower hoped to limit the propaganda value to the communist bloc of the Castro-Khrushchev embrace.

But for all of Ike's efforts, the week surely belonged to Castro. In his extraordinary three-hour address to the General Assembly on September 26, Castro gave the world a history lesson of the kind that Americans had rarely heard. He spoke about American colonization and exploitation of Cuba. He thundered about the degradation and suffering of the Cuban people at the hands of the U.S.-backed Batista dictatorship. He pointed an accusing finger at the U.S. government for its radio propaganda station based in Swan Island—an embarrassing revelation—and invoked the fate of Guatemala to remind his listeners of the consequences of agrarian reforms that threaten U.S. business interests. And he held out Cuba as an example to the world of how to throw off the shackles of colonial servitude. To the delegations from Asia and Africa, Castro's words seemed like lightning bolts in a dark sky.[30]

IV

The extraordinary events at the United Nations formed the backdrop to the first of the Nixon-Kennedy televised debates. Senator Kennedy understood how to exploit the anxiety that Khrushchev and Castro had provoked. Although the first debate, on the evening of September 26, focused on domestic issues, Kennedy's opening remarks invoked Khrushchev's menacing presence in New York and spoke darkly of a communist offensive going on around the world. The great question of the age, Kennedy suggested, was whether America was strong enough to counter that offensive. Nixon did a poor job that evening in rebutting these charges. He had recently been ill, had lost weight, and looked tired; his makeup streaked, and his stubbly chin glistened with sweat. All agreed that Kennedy won the first round going away.

Kennedy kept up the pressure. On the eve of the second debate, in a speech in Cincinnati, he called Eisenhower's Cuba policy a "glaring failure." America had backed the dictator Batista, he said, prompting such despair among the Cuban people that they fell for the seduction of a communist revolutionary. Now Castro "threatens the security of the whole Western Hemisphere." When the second debate opened on October 7, Kennedy beat the drum of American decline, alleging that the United States had been standing still while the communists surged. Nixon, more poised, better prepared, and less sickly-looking than in his debut, replied sharply. He scolded

Kennedy for such "defeatist" talk and for running down the great republic. He pointed to the advances the communist bloc made under Truman, when "600 million people went behind the Iron Curtain," and asserted that Eisenhower had turned back the Red tide. "We have stopped them at Quemoy and Matsu, we have stopped them in Indochina, we have stopped them in Lebanon," Nixon crowed.

Nixon's boasts about the defense of Quemoy during the second debate drew Kennedy into an attack on Eisenhower's handling of the defense of Taiwan. Kennedy alleged that American policy there was fuzzy and confused and had therefore invited Chinese provocation. He preferred to draw a line, stating clearly that America would not risk war over Quemoy and Matsu. "I think it is unwise," he said in a memorable blunder, "to take the chance of being dragged into a war which may lead to a world war over two islands which are not strategically defensible" or essential to the defense of Taiwan. This sounded like Kennedy was advocating retreat under communist pressure, and Nixon pounced. In the third debate, on October 13, Nixon painted Kennedy as an advocate of appeasement toward communist China.[31]

Sensing that he had been hurt by Nixon's attacks on the Quemoy issue, Kennedy tried to change the subject. On October 18 he gave a blistering speech at the American Legion convention in Miami Beach on the "steady erosion of American power." In an address filled with factual inaccuracies and distortions, Kennedy damned the Eisenhower administration for cutting back on missile development, slowing the modernization of the armed forces, failing to develop jet airlift capacity, failing to prepare for conflict abroad. "We have been slipping, and we are moving into a period of danger." The United States needed to show the world that it had the guts "for a long, long hard fight" against the "Communist advance in the 1960s." The day before the final debate Kennedy struck again, this time on Cuba. He issued a statement that denounced the administration for "doing nothing for six years" and called for the arming of "non-Batista democratic anti-Castro forces in exile, and in Cuba itself, who offer eventual hope of overthrowing Castro." He asserted, "Thus far, these fighters for freedom have had virtually no support from our government."[32]

Did Kennedy know that the United States was in the midst of planning just such a covert operation to overthrow Castro? And if so, did he use this highly secret knowledge to score a debating point and make himself look stronger than Nixon in his desire to oust Castro? Nixon certainly thought so, and wrote with bitterness about the episode in his memoirs. Kennedy had indeed been briefed by Allen Dulles on July 23 and September 19 on a wide range of intelligence matters, as part of the normal routine of giving major presidential candidates a review of ongoing policies. Nixon assumed that Dulles had filled Kennedy in on the Cuba plans, and that JFK then used this sensitive information to embarrass the administration. It has never been clear, nor is it fully demonstrable, that Dulles gave Kennedy a detailed brief on the Cuba operation, which was still evolving. The two Dulles-Kennedy meetings covered many issues, Cuba being only one. Even so, given Kennedy's excellent contacts on Capitol Hill, in the Defense Department, and in the CIA itself, it seems likely that he had a general idea that the CIA was plotting Castro's ouster by using Cuban exiles. Yet he recklessly attacked the administration for doing nothing to help anti-Castro forces, knowing that Nixon could not affirm the existence of the covert operation. At the very least it was a cynical move.[33]

The issue took a bizarre twist in the fourth debate, on October 21, when Nixon denounced Kennedy for his "dangerously irresponsible" proposal of arming Cuban exiles and promoting the overthrow of Castro—the very plan that his own administration was pursuing! Nixon believed he had to differentiate himself from Kennedy, so he argued *against* the policies he himself had long favored. Ironically, his case against a covert operation to overthrow Castro was so skillful and well-delivered he seemed actually to have carried the point. Intervention in Cuba would alienate world opinion completely, he said, and it would be "an open invitation to Khrushchev to come into Latin America." Nixon did as well as he could to develop a sensible, reasoned argument for "quarantining" Cuba rather than invading it. Yet every word he spoke undermined Eisenhower's own secret plans to disable Castro.[34]

As the debates were coming to a close, Nixon suffered yet another blow, this one self-inflicted. On October 19 Rev. Martin Luther King Jr. was arrested while conducting a peaceful sit-in at a segregated restaurant in Atlanta. A local judge, eager to settle the score with the civil rights leader, sentenced King to four months of hard labor in the state penitentiary. Numerous African American leaders sought Nixon's help, and White House aide Fred Morrow rushed to write a statement for Nixon to use, calling for King's immediate release. Inexplicably Nixon stalled and his press spokesman issued a "no comment" to the media. By contrast, Kennedy moved quickly. He telephoned Coretta Scott King and expressed his sympathies. His campaign manager and brother, Robert Kennedy, interceded with the judge and got King sprung from jail. It was a stunning sequence of events, one Nixon badly fumbled. In the following days hundreds of thousands of black voters deserted the GOP, and they never went back.[35]

As the campaign reached its final week, Nixon, who had struggled to overtake Kennedy in the polls, at last deployed his most powerful weapon, one he had been deeply reluctant to unleash: Dwight Eisenhower. The two men had done a curious dance on the question of Ike's role in the campaign. Just a few days after the Republican Convention in July, they had met in Newport to discuss strategy, and Ike said he'd do whatever Nixon asked of him during the campaign. But throughout the fall of 1960 Nixon didn't ask. He wished to win on his own terms and to campaign in his own voice. Eisenhower watched from the sidelines, increasingly frustrated over Nixon's inability to rebut effectively Kennedy's charges of drift and decline. He told one Oval Office visitor, "Listen, dammit, I'm going to do everything possible to keep that Jack Kennedy from sitting in this chair." He wrote to Nixon after the first debate that his campaign needed more "zip" and "should be more hard-hitting." But Nixon never found the right way to cut Kennedy down to size. As Ike's staffer William Ewald explained it, Nixon built his campaign on a negative: "America has not been standing still." With statistics at the ready, Nixon could prove it—but he was fighting on ground chosen by Kennedy, always counterpunching, always defending, while failing to lay out his own vision for the future. With a week to go, and the polls very close, Nixon finally turned to Eisenhower, a 70-year-old man of unsteady health, to sprint the final mile and bring home victory.[36]

The reunion began awkwardly. On October 31 Nixon and Eisenhower met at the White House for lunch, along with Len Hall, Nixon's campaign manager. They planned to discuss an ambitious series of appearances by Eisenhower in the coming days. But according to Nixon, the night before the lunch, Mamie Eisenhower called Pat Nixon to beg that the vice president not ask Eisenhower to do any campaigning. In the previous few weeks he had been showing signs of strain, with high blood pressure and heart palpitations. Mamie feared that a week of strenuous speechifying might trigger another heart attack. With Mamie's tearful plea in mind, Nixon declined Eisenhower's offer to undertake a big swing to Illinois, Michigan, and upstate New York. "Mr. President, you've done enough," Nixon responded when Ike asked how he could help. Eisenhower looked "like somebody had thrown cold water over him," according to Hall. Nixon recalled Ike was "hurt, and then he was angry." Eisenhower did not know about Mamie's personal request, and according to Nixon, he seemed "puzzled and frustrated by my conduct." So he was. Ike called Hall after the lunch and asked, "What the hell's the matter with that guy?"[37]

Eisenhower nonetheless carried out his long-planned appearances in New York City, Cleveland, and Pittsburgh in the first week of November, and once again demonstrated the effect of his personal magnetism. On November 2 he arrived in New York City for a ticker-tape parade down Broadway with Nixon at his side. Perhaps two million people lined the avenues as the caravan made its way to the New York Coliseum, where Ike spoke to thousands of delirious supporters. He gave the kind of speech Nixon could not: an appeal that drew on his own deep experience, his life of public service, and his sheer mastery of the complex issues that he had faced as president. With his distinctive style of humility mixed with confidence, he pointed to the successes of his administration, which had ended the Korean War, avoided further conflicts, strengthened the armed forces, halted communism's advance, built up alliances, and expanded the U.S. economy while carefully husbanding the nation's money. "The past eight years have been the brightest of our history," he insisted, and he defied anyone to match that record.[38]

Two days later, in Cleveland, before more adoring crowds, Eisenhower denounced Kennedy's criticism of America's achievements and mocked the claims of "this young genius" to know better than the Joint Chiefs of Staff how to run the military establishment. To the crowd of Buckeye faithful, he likened Kennedy to an Ohio State football player who spent the season on the bench running down the team and saying "You are a second-rate bunch of muckers," but then asked to be made head coach. In Pittsburgh the same day, Eisenhower depicted Kennedy as immature, untested, and unreliable. It was time, he said sternly, for some "woodshed honesty." Promising more programs and more government would cost too much money and trigger "catastrophic" inflation. "These wizards in fiscal shell games," Ike declared, "are idolatrous worshippers of bigness—especially of big government." Furthermore the nation's security could not be entrusted to a neophyte who needed on-the-job training. In times of crisis the president alone must make the decisions. He cannot turn to a "brains trust" or a "warehouse of trick phrases."[39]

To journalist Theodore White, Eisenhower's speeches seemed "crisp, fresh and dramatic," especially after Nixon's corny, saccharine style. According to White, Ike had the most sought-after and yet rarest of qualities in politics: "He makes people happy. No cavalcade I have followed in the entourage of any other political figure in this country has ever left so many smiling, glowing people behind as an Eisenhower tour." The 70-year-old hero, with his "cherubic pink face," drew from the crowds "a yearning burst of cheers" of the kind Nixon never received. James Reston noted the same phenomenon: "Pinch-hitting for Mr. Nixon, [Eisenhower] is now the central figure in one of America's favorite scenes: the old pro coming off the bench and swinging for the fences for the last time."[40]

V

But the hero struck out. When the results of the vote on November 8 were finally tallied, Nixon had lost by 112,000 votes, the narrowest loss of the 20th century and still one of the closest elections in American history. On the morning of November 9 Ike and his son sat silently in the Oval Office, the president slumped in his chair staring vacantly out the window. "I rarely saw him so depressed," John wrote later. "'All I've been trying to do for eight years,' he finally said, 'has gone down the drain.'" John insisted he get out of Washington and down to Augusta as quickly as possible, and "almost physically" shoved him into his car for the ride to the airport.[41]

Instead of greeting Nixon on his return to Washington from California, Eisenhower left behind a personal note. Explaining his hasty departure, he said he was "feeling a great need to get some sunshine, recreation and rest." He tried to find a silver lining in the election results by suggesting that Nixon would undoubtedly "have a happier life during these next four years" since he would not have to handle the difficulties of being president—a statement that anyone who knew Nixon could never believe. The letter could not hide the deep pain Ike felt at that moment. As soon as he reached his presidential airplane and sat down in the company of his specially invited golf and bridge pals Cliff Roberts, Bill Robinson, and Ellis Slater, he blurted out his real feelings: "Well, this is the biggest defeat of my life." Even five years later, as he wrote in his memoirs, Eisenhower called Nixon's defeat the "principal political disappointment" of his presidency.[42]

What went wrong? Above all, Kennedy proved a gifted presidential candidate. He won voters with his charisma, his youth, and his style, combined with his intelligence and his central argument: that wise and active government could better serve the needs of the people than the penny-pinching, restrained policies of the Ike age. His choice of Lyndon Johnson as his running mate helped him win across the South (though the margin in Texas was only 46,000 votes). Kennedy also persuaded voters that America under Eisenhower had become stagnant and needed a new cause and clear direction to realize its great potential. His adviser and friend Arthur Schlesinger Jr. believed that Kennedy's relentless emphasis on the gap between America's achievements and its promise worked: "He wisely decided to concentrate on a single theme and to hammer that theme home until everyone in America understood it—understood his sense of the decline of our national power and influence and his determination to arrest and reverse this course. He did this with such brilliant success that, even in a time of apparent prosperity and apparent peace, and even as a Catholic, he was able to command a majority (though such a slim majority) of voters." Kennedy made the election about the future, about dreams and possibilities, and about greatness, and Americans thrilled to his dynamic vision.[43]

And yet the margin was so close that Nixon would be tormented for years by what Theodore White called "an interminable series of ifs." If he had worked harder to court African Americans, could he have swung Illinois to his camp? If he had abandoned the black vote altogether and courted the white South (as Goldwater would do in 1964) could he have won South Carolina, Texas, Missouri, or Arkansas? What if he had not done so poorly in the first debate? What if he had used Eisenhower earlier? What if he had done better in framing a vision of the future rather than offering to continue the Age of Eisenhower without Eisenhower? What if he had been a warm, personable man of exuberance and charm instead of a brooding, paranoid introvert? The questions cannot be answered.[44]

Although the defeat belonged to Nixon, Eisenhower must bear some responsibility. Eisenhower's principal weakness as president lay in his failure to transfer his personal popularity to his party. His effortless and massive victories in 1952 and 1956 allowed him to believe that the country had ratified his ideas, when in fact they had chiefly welcomed his personal qualities of optimism, decency, and experience. During his time in office, his party imploded. In the elections of 1954, 1956, and 1958, Republicans lost a total of 68 seats in the House and 17 seats in the Senate—a devastating verdict from the electorate. In 1960, with Nixon as the standard-bearer, the Republicans clawed back one Senate seat and 22 House seats, but Democrats still enjoyed huge majorities in both chambers. Eisenhower never found the new young leaders who could rebuild the party on a solid foundation. He mused about forming a Modern Republican Party but never threw himself into the task. In 1960 the Republican cupboard was bare, in part through Ike's neglect.[45]

Then too there was Eisenhower's mistrust of Nixon. The infamous remark in the news conference—"If you give me a week, I might think of one"—may have been a lapse, but it told a deep truth about the relationship. William Ewald explained the problem well: "Eisenhower did not so much wish victory for Nixon [as] he wished defeat for Kennedy." When he went into battle in the last week of the campaign, Eisenhower fought to defend his own record, not to clear a path for Nixon as his successor. Ike never believed in Nixon and did not particularly like him, and he was unable to keep his feelings hidden.[46]

Nixon's loss stung. For two weeks after election day, Eisenhower played a great deal of golf and bridge and engaged in "lugubrious post-mortem discussions" with his friends at Augusta. Even after this long rest the defeat still felt bitter. "I felt like I had been hit in the solar plexus with a ball bat, especially in the first few days," he wrote a friend. "But now my normal optimism has taken command."[47]

Not quite. He stewed over the election results. On November 30 he called Attorney General William Rogers to say that he was "very much disturbed about continuing allegations of fraud in the election." According to Ann Whitman's notes of the call, Ike said "he wanted the Federal government to exercise whatever rights and responsibilities were inherent in the situation. He admitted that the election was a closed issue, but he felt we owed it to the people of the United States to assure them . . . that the Federal government did not shirk its duty." Rogers, a close confidant of Nixon's, replied that the FBI "was working" on the matter.[48]

Rumors and accusations of fraud began on election night and emerged chiefly from Chicago. One local Republican election official announced that 10,000 Republican voters had been wrongfully purged from the voter rolls there. Right after the election, Senator Morton, national chairman of the GOP, called for a recount in 11 states where the vote had been extremely close. Nixon dissociated himself from the effort in a press release on November 11. But two days later the chairman of the Cook County Republican Party, Francis X. O'Connell, asserted that "professional vote thieves" had stuffed ballot boxes and stolen votes, swinging Illinois to Kennedy. Since the official tally gave Kennedy the edge there by only 8,858 votes, the issue looked serious indeed. On November 15 the vote counting in California finally concluded, and Nixon narrowly won the state, making the margin in the Electoral College even closer. If Illinois and Texas had switched columns from Kennedy to Nixon, the vice president would have won the election. On November 19 the Justice Department announced that it had ordered the FBI to investigate complaints of voter fraud. Attorney General Rogers seemed willing to use his authority to launch grand jury probes and hold up the voting in the Electoral College, scheduled for December 19.[49]

Nixon discouraged Rogers when the two met at Nixon's hotel in Key Biscayne, Florida, on November 20. Nixon did not show any zeal for a prolonged legal wrangle. Even if he could have reversed the election, it would come at a high cost of personal and partisan acrimony and might well have crippled his presidency. More likely, Nixon knew, he would lose any challenge to the election results and only mar his reputation. He would look like a sore loser and damage his future political prospects. Even though Eisenhower lent his support to Senator Morton's continuing efforts to "expose irregularities," as Morton put it, Nixon dropped the matter. But he never forgot. William Ewald recalled vividly Nixon welcoming staffers to his Washington home just before Christmas with these words: "We won, but they stole it from us."[50]

CHAPTER 20

A NEW GENERATION

*"We must guard against the acquisition of
unwarranted influence, whether sought or
unsought, by the military-industrial complex."*

I

TWO MINUTES BEFORE 9:00 ON THE MORNING OF DECEMBER 6, 1960, Eisenhower strode out onto the north portico of the White House, stopped at the top of the stairs, and stood rigid in a brown suit and brown felt hat, as if at a funeral. The 70-year-old president bore a dignified countenance, grave and preoccupied. An honor guard drawn from the army, navy, air force, and marines lined the driveway to the White House, and a marine band stood at the ready. The White House gleamed under a fresh coat of paint; the newly blackened wrought-iron railings and lampposts sparkled. Across Pennsylvania Avenue the president could hear the hammering of carpenters who were erecting a large reviewing stand. The nation's leading officials and public servants would gather there to watch the Inaugural Parade on January 20. The president remarked, "I feel like the fellow in jail who is watching his scaffold being built."

At 8:59 precisely, a cream-colored limousine arrived at the northwest gate of the White House, bearing the man on whom the world's attention had been intensely focused since the morning of November 9, when his election victory was announced. As the car slowed to a stop, the door precipitately opened. President-elect John F. Kennedy, lean and tanned, holding a gray hat in his hand, leaped from the door of the still-moving vehicle, his momentum carrying him swiftly up the stairs in a few athletic bounds. "Good Morning, Mr. President," he cheerfully exclaimed. The glow of victory, youth, and destiny radiated from the 43-year-old. Eisenhower, caught off guard by this rush of vitality, reached out, shook the proffered hand, and mumbled, "Senator." The two men paused for the photographers, then turned and walked into the White House together, a somber Eisenhower and a smiling Kennedy.[1]

This could have been a difficult, tense encounter. On the campaign trail Kennedy had laid it on thick, accusing Eisenhower of failing to meet the global communist threat with sufficient zeal. In accepting the Democratic nomination for president in July 1960, Kennedy had painted the Eisenhower years as a lost era. "There has been a change—a slippage—in our intellectual and moral strength," Kennedy said. He called on Americans to leave behind men of Eisenhower's generation who sought only "the safe mediocrity of the past." To JFK the Age of Eisenhower had been bland, unimaginative, and sclerotic. Privately Kennedy jeered at Eisenhower, calling him "the old asshole" to members of his entourage. Kennedy told Arthur Schlesinger Jr. that Eisenhower was "a terribly cold man. In fact, he is a shit."[2]

Kennedy may in fact have believed some of the caricature he drew of the president. But if, as he arrived at the White House on December 6, he expected to find Eisenhower dim-witted and distant, out of touch with the realities of governing, he was deeply mistaken. Eisenhower brought the president-elect into the Oval Office and over two hours treated him to an astonishing tutorial that ranged across domestic policy, economics, the governing structure of the National Security Council and cabinet, military security, and world affairs. In a far-reaching briefing, Eisenhower pulled back the curtain on the powers, and preoccupations, of the presidency.

He took control of the meeting from the outset, spending some time on the structure of the National Security Council, the setting for "the most important weekly meeting of the government," as well as the Defense Department. Kennedy, eager to show that he was well-briefed, referred to a recent Senate proposal to reorganize the Pentagon. Eisenhower urged Kennedy to avoid any decisions on reorganization until he had studied carefully the activities of the defense establishment. Eight years of "patient study and long drawn out negotiations with Congress and the Armed Services" had made major changes to national defense; Eisenhower wanted Kennedy to take time to assess these changes before making alterations. Eisenhower's call for patience applied also to the cabinet and White House staff: both bodies were carefully designed to serve the needs and interests of the president, so he could make decisions based on the best information possible. Eisenhower told Kennedy that it was vital to have a chief of staff who could coordinate the flow of information to the president.

Kennedy would later show himself allergic to this sort of hierarchy and careful structure: he believed in a loose flow of information, people, and ideas; his watchwords would be "flexibility" and "improvisation." He would have no chief of staff. In fact Kennedy seemed uninterested in structure and pressed Eisenhower for details about personalities like French president Charles de Gaulle, British prime minister Harold Macmillan, German chancellor Konrad Adenauer. Eisenhower knew them all, of course. He had worked closely with the first two during the war, while Lieutenant Kennedy was skippering a torpedo boat in the Pacific. Eisenhower was cautious in characterizing these men; he knew Kennedy would have to take their measure one by one, on his own terms. He did allow that de Gaulle was a difficult ally at times, but insisted that NATO was crucial to American "security and prosperity." He urged Kennedy to think through the possibility of sharing nuclear weapons technologies with American allies.

Then he shifted terrain and spoke for 20 minutes on the growing problem of America's unfavorable balance of payments, an issue close to his heart. The United States was spending too many dollars overseas, partly the result of a large U.S. troop presence in Europe. Since the dollar was still pegged to a fixed exchange rate for gold, these dollars could be cashed in for U.S. gold by European banks, so the United States was facing a drain on its gold reserves. Eisenhower suggested that the balance of payments problem had to be addressed by asking the NATO allies to pay a greater share of their own defense. He spoke freely, without notes.

The meeting between the two men ended after one hour and 45 minutes. They then walked to the Cabinet Room, where Secretary of State Christian Herter, Secretary of Defense Thomas S. Gates Jr., and Secretary of the Treasury Robert B. Anderson, along with Eisenhower's chief of staff Gen. Wilton B. Persons and Kennedy's transition director, Clark Clifford, joined them for an additional hour and 15 minutes of briefings on foreign affairs, national security matters, and economic issues.[3]

President-elect Kennedy was obviously impressed by what he found in the Eisenhower White House. He spoke to reporters afterward and was gracious in his thanks to the president for his effort to assure an easy transfer of power to the new administration. But privately Kennedy said even more than that. "Eisenhower was better than I had thought," he later confided to his brother Robert. Ike had a "strong personality," and JFK "could understand, talking to him, why he was President of the United States."[4]

Of course the Kennedys—like many later historians—would never truly respect Eisenhower. They viewed him as belonging to another age, without the imagination to grapple with the dawning world of the 1960s. John Kennedy "felt Eisenhower was a 'non-President,'" according to Clark Clifford, because he did not effectively use the powers of the office. Clifford also admitted that all of Kennedy's staff looked on Eisenhower "with something bordering contempt."[5]

Yet on this day, as Kennedy sat with the outgoing president, he could see that the old general was more than just a numbskull, a pachyderm, a dinosaur. He demonstrated his mastery of detail and could effortlessly conduct a briefing on a wide array of complex issues before a sparkling, supremely confident Kennedy, who had been devouring briefing books for a week in preparation for this meeting. The two men were worlds apart in their personalities, their styles, and their political philosophies. There was little warmth between them; they offered one another simply the dignified respect due to the office of the presidency. But at this meeting, though Kennedy's star was shining and Eisenhower was now yesterday's man, Eisenhower dominated the proceedings. He showed, and Kennedy perceived in him, the attributes that had made him such an effective leader for the previous two decades: assurance, careful accumulation of detailed knowledge, and above all a habit of command.

II

Foreign crises preoccupied Eisenhower during his final weeks in office, and while he dutifully kept Kennedy informed, he still made key decisions that would shape the choices available to his successor. One problem, the source of later headaches for President Kennedy, was Laos, a small Southeast Asian nation that mattered to the United States because of its geography: it shared a long, sinuous border with Vietnam. Laos had been declared neutral by international agreement at Geneva in July 1954, and an uneasy standoff prevailed between the Royal Laotian government and a communist movement called the Pathet Lao, which was loosely aligned with the North Vietnamese.

The Eisenhower team had been watching Laos carefully for years, nervous that its government was too "soft" in its handling of the communist threat in its midst. They saw Laos as a vital buffer state; were it to fall under

North Vietnamese influence, South Vietnam as well as Cambodia and Thailand might be imperiled. The Americans opened up an economic aid mission in the capital, Vientiane, and sent significant military aid there in hopes this would embolden the government to take firmer steps. The CIA also set up a program to arm and train the Hmong tribes in northern Laos, who were ardently anti-Vietnamese. In 1959, though, as the North Vietnamese stepped up their infiltration of South Vietnam, Laos became a dangerous zone of Great Power conflict.

The Americans, desperate to halt the slippage of Laos into the communist camp, supported a right-wing coup in December 1959 that brought Brig. Gen. Phoumi Nosavan to power. Phoumi's position was always weak, and during 1960 he fought against dissident factions in the army as well as Pathet Lao communists. In November and December 1960, much to Eisenhower's alarm, the Soviet Union launched a major airlift of supplies via Hanoi to the Pathet Lao. Ike sent U.S. Air Force bombers from Taiwan to Thailand in case they were needed to support Phoumi. In mid-December Phoumi began a major campaign against the neutralist and communist forces around Vientiane and secured control of the capital. Eisenhower personally ordered that a bonus of one month's pay be doled out to Phoumi's soldiers "to maintain morale."[6]

A new pro-Western government now held a tentative grip on power and immediately sent out a request for American military aid. The Pathet Lao was licking its wounds and gaining more supplies from North Vietnam and seemed poised to reopen a push to take Vientiane and perhaps seize control of the country. When Allen Dulles reported to the NSC on December 20, he predicted a "strong Communist reaction" to Phoumi's victory, and said "the present anti-Communist government in Laos would require extensive outside assistance to survive." To openly aid the government, however, would invite an equally vigorous Soviet response.[7]

On the last day of 1960 Eisenhower had a somber and anxious meeting about Laos with key members of his security team. CIA reports suggested that Pathet Lao forces were on the move out of North Vietnam and appeared to be planning to seize control of the country. Eisenhower stated simply, "We cannot afford to stand by and allow Laos to fall to the Communists." He was prepared to deploy the Seventh Fleet and the marines to forestall a communist attack. The Joint Chiefs declared their readiness, with the aircraft carrier *Lexington* in the Gulf of Tonkin, airborne troops at the ready in Okinawa, and a fleet of C-130 transport planes ready in Bangkok.

Eisenhower, the man who had built a reputation on avoiding entangling conflicts, seemed prepared to commit U.S. troops to battle in Southeast Asia. He directed Ambassador Tommy Thompson to tell Khrushchev that the United States viewed the threat to Laos very seriously and that, "in the event of a major war, we will not be caught napping." Eisenhower reiterated his position: "We must not allow Laos to fall to the Communists, even if it involves war in which the U.S. acts with allies or unilaterally." Invoking the domino theory a few days later, he insisted, "If the Communists establish a strong position in Laos, the West is finished in the whole Southeast Asian area."[8]

The day before Kennedy took the oath of office, he came to the White House again, chiefly to discuss Laos. Eisenhower seemed to relish the opportunity to show Kennedy just how much power the commander in chief possessed. He walked Kennedy through the procedures to launch a nuclear attack, drawing on "the satchel filled with orders applicable to an emergency and carried by an unobtrusive man who would shadow the President for all his days in office." He also went into a detailed discussion about the acute Laos crisis with Secretary Herter. The Soviets had launched an airlift to supply communist fighters in Laos; the North Vietnamese were helping. Kennedy asked Herter directly if the United States should intervene if invited to do so by the Laotian government, and Herter unequivocally said yes. Some 12,000 U.S. troops could be transported into Laos in two weeks from Okinawa. "It was the cork in the bottle. If Laos fell, then Thailand, the Philippines, and of course Chiang Kai-shek would go." Eisenhower concurred. Kennedy dictated a memorandum of the meeting showing the impact of the discussion on him. "I came away from that meeting feeling that the Eisenhower administration would support intervention—they felt it was preferable to a communist success in Laos."[9]

Clark Clifford believed the discussion had enormous significance. Eisenhower, with his vast experience in military affairs, firmly invoked the domino principle and insisted that this tiny backwater nation suddenly held the key to America's position in Asia. The mood was grim, Clifford remembered, and the conversation marked "a real turning point." Eisenhower's portentous tone "had a powerful effect on Kennedy" and all others in the room and "cast a shadow over the early decisions on the next administration." The dark assessment of the Laos problem, and Ike's clear support for a military intervention there to counter a communist offensive, influenced

Kennedy's early thinking not just toward Laos and Vietnam, but also—most immediately—toward Cuba.[10]

III

If Eisenhower was prepared to fight a war in faraway Laos in the waning hours of his presidency, it is not hard to imagine how strongly he felt about the Cuba problem festering just off the coast of Florida. The centrality of Cuba to the 1960 election only fed the fires of his impatience. Indeed the evidence shows that in his final weeks in office, Eisenhower dramatically increased the scope and tempo of the covert operation against Castro. As of the fall of 1960, the subversion plan, which focused on infiltration of small sabotage teams, seemed bogged down. Small groups of guerrillas had been sent in, but most were rounded up by Castro's militia. Air drops went astray, radio communication with the infiltrated teams was nonexistent, and there was no hope that such small-scale efforts would trigger internal uprisings against Castro. At the start of November, CIA planners concluded that a strike force of as many as 3,000 armed and trained fighters would be needed to stage an invasion of Cuba, seize and hold a lodgment area, and begin military operations in conjunction with guerrilla warfare teams. Such a force would require air and naval support on a substantial scale.[11]

On November 3 the 5412 Committee convened for a wide-ranging review of the Cuba operation, led by National Security Adviser Gordon Gray. "Covert operations of the type originally envisaged," they agreed, "would not be effective." Castro had tightened his grip, a popular uprising against him was unlikely, and "time was actually working on Castro's side." Gray now took the unprecedented position that the only way to "clean up" the situation in Cuba was with an overt invasion of the island "by U.S. military forces." He even floated the idea of using Cuban exiles to launch a fake attack on American forces in the Guantanamo base, which would create a pretext for a U.S. invasion. This idea was quickly shot down, but Livingston Merchant, the State Department representative on the 5412 Committee, inquired whether the CIA had plans for "direct positive action against Fidel, Raul, and Che Guevara." Without these three, he said, the government would be "leaderless and probably brainless." Gen. Charles Cabell, the deputy director of the CIA, reared up against such talk, saying such operations were "highly dangerous" and "beyond our capabilities." Either he did not know that Richard Bissell was deeply engaged in a series of plans to assassinate Fidel, or he lied to his colleagues. The discussion reveals the frustration senior planners felt about the lack of results of the CIA's efforts against Castro.[12]

In the midst of this reevaluation of the anti-Castro plan, Dulles and Bissell traveled to Florida on November 18 to meet with President-elect Kennedy and brief him on the operation. In Dulles's account, Kennedy said that "if Mr. Dulles believed it to be in the U.S. interest to proceed with the project, he had no objection." But what was Kennedy assenting to? The project was in flux, expanding from an infiltration and sabotage operation into a full-scale invasion. Kennedy's presidency would clearly be shaped by Eisenhower's decision on Cuba.[13]

Eisenhower began to assert more personal command over the operation in a meeting with his top national security team on November 29. He expressed his "unhappiness about the general situation" and thought the Castro threat to the Caribbean and Latin America looked like it was "beginning to get out of hand." He went to the heart of the matter: "Are we being sufficiently imaginative and bold, subject to not letting our hand appear?" He wanted results. "We should be prepared to take more chances and be more aggressive." According to Bissell, Eisenhower made it clear that "he wanted all done that could be done with all possible urgency, and nothing less." Coming just three weeks after the bitter election in which Eisenhower had been caricatured as inactive and timid in his handling of Cuba, these words reveal the degree to which he wanted to make a lasting mark in his final few days in office. He had something to prove.[14]

Eisenhower's message moved quickly down the chain. On December 8 the 5412 Committee convened a meeting to review the beefed-up operation against Cuba. Around the table that day sat Gen. Edward Lansdale, now seconded to the Defense Department to work on Cuba; Tracy Barnes, one of the key men behind the 1954 Guatemala coup and now Bissell's deputy at CIA; Jacob Esterline, chief of the special CIA branch WH/4 that was running the Cuba plan; and Marine Col. Jack Hawkins, a World War II and Korean War veteran with extensive guerrilla warfare experience. Over the course of the morning the men laid out the details of the ever-expanding plan. Their plan called for an invasion force, spearheaded by a well-armed brigade of Cuban exiles, trained by the CIA at their Guatemala base camp. The plan initially envisioned "an amphibious force of 600–750 men," but that number nearly doubled as the date drew near. They would be accompanied by an air bombardment of "extraordinarily heavy firepower. Preliminary strikes would be launched from Nicaragua against military targets. The strikes, plus supply flights, would continue after the landing." This assault force would seize a landing area, "draw dissident elements to our own force," and quickly "trigger off a general uprising."

This scheme looked nothing like the infiltration plan of March 1960, with its small teams of guerrillas and use of anti-Castro radio broadcasts. The CIA now envisioned an amphibious landing of hundreds of armed Cubans, arriving on American-supplied ships and landing craft and supported by significant air power. The Eisenhower administration had not worked out the details yet, but the CIA had its marching orders and was putting into place a much bolder scheme to topple Castro than anything so far considered. The only fly in the ointment was "plausible deniability." Could the CIA hide its role in such a visible invasion effort? That seemed, frankly, unlikely. As the meeting broke up, General Lansdale laconically observed, "Everyone in Latin America knows about this U.S.-backed force of Cubans." The one condition that Eisenhower insisted upon—not showing America's hand—had been casually tossed aside.[15]

Eisenhower knew the invasion of Cuba would not commence on his watch; the inauguration was only a few weeks off and there was still much planning to be done. But he could take one decision that would bind Kennedy's hands and make it difficult for him to back away from the plan: he could break off diplomatic relations with Cuba, a move widely understood as a harbinger of armed conflict. He told Livingston Merchant on December 29 that he wanted this done "before January 20," when he left office. He pointedly said he wanted the State Department "to work quickly." And it did. On January 3, 1961, following a provocative act by Castro that demanded the United States reduce its embassy staff in Havana, the United States broke off relations with Cuba. This move had the effect of putting Cuba on notice of America's hostile intent, but it also intensified the pressure on the incoming Kennedy administration. John Kennedy would find it extremely difficult to resist the momentum behind the Cuba operation.[16]

IV

In his last week in the White House, President Eisenhower had one more formal task to undertake: his last State of the Union address to the Congress. He chose to send it in writing rather than deliver it in person. He knew that his time in the spotlight was over and that on January 30, 1961, President-elect Kennedy would come before the Congress to deliver his own address and lay out his own agenda. Yet in the text he submitted to Congress, and which was duly read by the clerk to a mostly empty House of Representatives on January 12, Eisenhower took a victory lap of sorts. "We have carried America to unprecedented heights," he wrote. And in retrospect it is hard to disagree.

He took credit for ending the war in Korea, stamping out the fires of war over Suez and Lebanon, halting Chinese threats to Quemoy, and keeping West Berlin free. America had built global alliances in Europe, the Middle East, and Asia and enhanced the role of the United Nations as the world's parliament. The national defenses had been built up to a state of high readiness "sufficient to deter and if need be destroy" any enemy. The age of the ballistic missile and the space satellite had dawned. The Polaris missile, housed in submarines that silently knifed through the ocean depths, stood ready to strike anywhere in the world at a moment's notice. A fleet of nuclear-powered warships cruised the oceans, while thousands of jet-propelled bombers and fighters could strike at targets around the world. The Age of Eisenhower had shaped and implemented a warfare state of unprecedented size and lethality.

The nation's gross national product had passed the half-trillion mark, and the average American family enjoyed an income 15 percent higher than it did in 1952. Wages of factory workers had risen 20 percent over the life of the administration, while inflation averaged only 1.8 percent for the decade of the 1950s. The strikes that so crippled the nation in the Truman years had been reduced by half. Unemployment insurance and social security had been expanded, and builders had erected more than a million new houses a year for the previous eight years—a record—and the government offered more home mortgages than ever. New highways were spooling out across the land. And yet the government had passed tax cuts and kept careful control of the federal budget. The Union itself grew too, as Alaska and Hawaii became the 49th and 50th states.

Democrats dismissed Ike's speech as "far-fetched" and "an extravagant misstatement of the actual conditions" the country faced. Congress was, after all, hostile territory, dominated by Democrats in both chambers. And when Kennedy came before these members just 18 days later, he heaped abuse on the outgoing administration for its failures to meet "the grave perils" abroad and the economic problems at home. Kennedy declared the very existence of the Union was in jeopardy, and Americans would "have to test anew whether a nation organized and governed such as ours can endure." To invoke Abraham Lincoln and the crisis of the Civil War might have been a trifle high-handed in the bountiful year 1961, but it was Kennedy's first State of the Union address, and he enjoyed rhetorical flourishes. In any case, the huge surplus of Democrats in the House that day gave Kennedy a thunderous ovation and interrupted his speech 37 times.[17]

The real reason Eisenhower did not read his message to Congress is that he was working on a personal statement of farewell to the American public, which he planned to give in a televised address on January 17. It was not a spur-of-the-moment idea. Eisenhower had been thinking about it since the middle of 1959, when he told speechwriter Malcolm Moos, who had joined the staff in mid-1958 to replace Arthur Larson, that he wanted to give a farewell address recalling the envoi delivered by his role model, George Washington. He wanted to avoid any partisan statement, and initially he had in mind that he would "emphasize a few homely truths" about governing in a democracy, as he put it in a letter to his brother Milton.[18]

Eisenhower's staff pored over Washington's 1796 send-off and circulated it around the White House. They noted especially its tone of warning against partisanship and sectionalism that might "disturb our Union," followed by an admonition to avoid the European tendency to erect "those overgrown military establishments which, under any form of government, are inauspicious to liberty." Obviously Ike, who had so recently adumbrated to Congress the immense growth of America's national defense under his peacetime government, could hardly now call for its undoing. But he could put the nation on guard about its significance.

In the fall of 1960, Moos and his assistant Capt. Ralph E. Williams sketched out some ideas about the place of militarism in American life. The United States for the first time in its history, they noted, possessed a "permanent war-based industry" and a "war-based industrial complex" that inevitably shaped governmental decisions. "This creates a danger," Williams wrote, "that what the Communists have always said about us may become true. We must be very careful to insure that the merchants of death do not come to dictate national policy." Over the course of the late fall, Eisenhower worked with his staff to hone the speech, the core of which had become a warning not about the military-industrial complex itself but about *limiting* its power over democratic government.[19]

At 8:30 p.m. on January 17 Eisenhower spoke to the nation from the

Oval Office, seated at his desk, reading from notes and wearing his glasses, which tended to make his eyes look rather tortoise-like. He wore, as always, a three-piece suit. He looked old, and he was. But his voice was the same clear mid-American baritone, and he delivered a stern warning to the 70 million Americans who tuned in. "America is today the strongest, the most influential and most productive nation in the world," he began. But a "hostile ideology" of "infinite duration" had compelled the United States to build "a permanent armaments industry of vast proportions." This new development would have "grave implications" for the country's democracy. Thinking perhaps of the recent calls from Democrats for still more defense spending, more missiles, more aircraft and combat forces, and thinking too of the inexperience in managing such forces of the president-elect, Eisenhower warned, "In the councils of government, we must guard against the acquisition of unwarranted influence, whether sought or unsought, by the military-industrial complex. The potential for the disastrous rise of misplaced power exists and will persist. We must never let the weight of this combination endanger our liberties or democratic processes."

It was in a way a paradoxical send-off. Eisenhower had worked so hard to build this massive warfare state, even as he worried about its cost. He never hesitated to use the military power of the United States, whether covertly, in various coups and subterfuges, or overtly, as when he rattled nuclear missiles at communist China. Yet now, after eight years of frenetic expansion of America's arsenal, Eisenhower sounded the alarm. Why now? Undoubtedly he had in mind the youth and inexperience of his successor. For Eisenhower there was only one way to meet the challenge of the military-industrial complex: strong and prudent leadership: "It is the task of statesmanship to mold, to balance, and to integrate these and other forces, new and old, within the principles of our democratic system." Eisenhower had shown he could provide that leadership; it would be Kennedy's task to follow in the general's footsteps.

As he closed the speech, he made a characteristic gesture. Just as he had begun his inaugural address in 1953 with a prayer, so he ended his last presidential message by beseeching Providence for peace, freedom, charity, and well-being and a wish that "all peoples will come together in a peace guaranteed by the binding force of mutual respect and love." Taking off his glasses, looking into the camera, he said he now looked forward to becoming a private citizen, and bade his audience good night.[20]

V

John F. Kennedy took the oath of office on January 20, 1961, as the 35th president. The youngest man elected president, he took over the reins of government from the oldest man to serve as chief executive up to that time. Kennedy understood the importance of this generational divide, and his remarks on that cold January morning stressed a new beginning and a New Frontier, a break with the ways of the past. "The torch has been passed to a new generation of Americans—born in this century," he said, consigning Eisenhower (born in 1890) to the dustbin of history. After Kennedy's swearing-in, Ike and Mamie attended a farewell lunch with former cabinet officials, then quietly slipped out of Washington by car, driving through the snow-blanketed Maryland countryside to Gettysburg, and home at last.[21]

Yet the Age of Eisenhower did not come to an abrupt and decisive end in January 1961; it endured. Presidential transitions feature more continuity than rupture, and that was certainly true of the Eisenhower-Kennedy handoff. Consider the men Kennedy drew into his administration. The new president reached out to Douglas Dillon, a wealthy establishment Republican who had been Ike's ambassador to France and undersecretary of state, to run the Treasury. Kennedy's defense secretary, Robert McNamara, was also a Republican, and like Eisenhower's first Pentagon chief, he was a businessman; Charles Wilson had run General Motors, and McNamara had been president of Ford. As his national security adviser Eisenhower had appointed Robert Cutler, a Harvard-educated Bostonian with a career in banking and the military. JFK's national security adviser was McGeorge Bundy, also a resident of Boston, who attended Yale before pursuing graduate studies at Harvard, where he became dean of the college. Bundy, a Republican before 1960, counted Allen Dulles, Richard Bissell, and George Kennan among his friends. Like Ike, Kennedy kept his brother close at hand, though JFK gave Robert, whom he appointed attorney general, far more power than Milton ever enjoyed. Perhaps the most striking illustration of continuity came with the decision to leave both Allen Dulles and J. Edgar Hoover in place running the CIA and the FBI, respectively. Kennedy's team might have been younger and smarter than Eisenhower's cabinet, but these men were cut from the same cloth.

Even Kennedy's famous inaugural address bore a striking resemblance in substance, though not in style, to the rhetoric of Eisenhower. Kennedy insisted, as Ike had before him, that what distinguished the free world from the communist bloc was a belief that the "rights of man" derived from God and not from the state. Kennedy, like Ike, pledged to "bear any burden" to defend liberty around the world. Kennedy said that nations newly emerging from colonial rule would have a friend in Washington and that America would champion the United Nations as the place to settle international disputes. These too had been Eisenhower's hopes. And when Kennedy pointed woefully to the looming threat of the nuclear arms race, he echoed Eisenhower's 1953 "Chance for Peace" address. In fact the central theme of Kennedy's unforgettable speech—America's unbending and tireless commitment to human freedom around the world—had been hammered out, shaped, and polished in the Age of Eisenhower.

Continuities abounded. On the burning issue of civil rights, on which Kennedy had campaigned so boldly, progress crept forward at about the same rate as it had under Eisenhower. Knowing that Congress would not pass meaningful civil rights legislation, Kennedy took some executive actions to combat discrimination in federal hiring, building on the measures of his predecessor. Like Eisenhower, Kennedy encountered furious southern intransigence to desegregation, and like Eisenhower, he used federal troops to assert his authority. At the University of Mississippi rioters and school officials blocked the enrollment of James Meredith, an African American student, in September 1962; Kennedy responded much as Ike had in Little Rock. In June 1963 Kennedy intervened to compel the University of Alabama to enroll black students, despite the defiance of the segregationist governor George Wallace. Only then, two and a half years into his administration, did President Kennedy break with Eisenhower's approach. On June 11, 1963, he spoke to the nation, and for the first time framed the civil rights struggle as a moral issue, not just a legal matter. Announcing new legislation to address the enduring problem of segregation in the United States, Kennedy finally departed from the cautious incrementalism of the Eisenhower years.

In his management of the cold war, however, Kennedy picked up right where Eisenhower left off. As biographer Robert Dallek noted, "no foreign policy issue commanded as much attention during the first two months of his presidency" as did Laos, the seemingly insignificant nation in Indochina. The Soviets appeared to be backing a communist seizure of power there, in a move that would jeopardize America's ally, South Vietnam. Kennedy reluctantly prepared to airlift U.S. troops. "The security of all Southeast Asia will be endangered if Laos loses its neutral independence," he said in a late March 1961 news conference, sounding much like his predecessor.[22]

But it was in Cuba where Kennedy most tragically ensnared himself in the threads of continuity. In his January 19 meeting with the outgoing president, Kennedy heard Eisenhower state unequivocally, "In the long run the United States cannot allow the Castro Government to continue to exist in Cuba." Ike told him the plan to overthrow Castro should be "continued and accelerated." On January 25 President Kennedy met with his military advisers, and Gen. Lyman Lemnitzer, the chairman of the Joint Chiefs of Staff, urged him not to delay. "Time is working against us," warned the general, because Castro was rapidly strengthening his defenses in preparation for an invasion. And on January 28, just a week after taking office, Kennedy received his first full briefing on the Cuba plan. Although the military cautioned that the landing forces were not sufficiently large to defeat Castro's militia, CIA director Dulles spoke optimistically, claiming that the invasion force was adequate to bring down the regime. Kennedy showed no inclination to shelve the plan. In fact he ordered that the planning go forward and that the military do a careful evaluation of the CIA's proposal. This review was duly undertaken, and at the start of February the military chiefs signed off on it. Bundy told Kennedy that Defense and the CIA were "quite enthusiastic" about the invasion.[23]

The pressure on the new president was enormous. Here was a young, untested, and overconfident leader who, as a candidate, had stridently called for action against the communist menace in Cuba. Taking office, he found a large, complex plan already in place, endorsed by the greatest soldier of the era, and now backed by the Joint Chiefs and the CIA. The plan had been in the making for a year, and thousands of people were waiting for a signal to set it in motion—not least the Cuban fighters at their Guatemalan training grounds, straining at the leash. In these circumstances, backing off the invasion was almost unthinkable. Politically it would have made him look "soft." And what an enormous victory it would be for the new team if it worked!

During the month of March, Kennedy became, as even his loyal and devoted chronicler Arthur Schlesinger Jr. admitted, "a prisoner of events." The invasion plan had a momentum of its own, and the bureaucratic forces pushing for it would have been hard to resist. On March 11 Kennedy told his senior advisers that he was "willing to take the chance of going ahead," though he asked that the plan be modified to mask the role of the United States. Dulles assured him the plan would work just as smoothly as the daring coup in Guatemala that Dulles had orchestrated in 1954—another sign of the powerful continuities at work in this drama. Kennedy continued to feel uneasy about the invasion plan, but he did not stop it. He allowed himself to be carried toward disaster.[24]

On April 15 the misguided and ill-conceived affair began. A few aging B-26 aircraft, flown by Cuban pilots from airfields in Nicaragua, bombed three Cuban airfields, doing only moderate damage to Castro's tiny fleet of combat aircraft but alerting the Cuban government that the invasion was imminent. Castro accused the United States of fomenting the attack and raised the alarm at the United Nations, spooking the Kennedy administration into canceling further air support, lest the U.S. connection be discovered. Meanwhile, late at night on April 16, the invasion force of some 1,400 Cuban exiles jumped into their landing craft and headed toward their target: a swampy inlet on Cuba's southern coast called Bahía de Cochinos, or Bay of Pigs. The landings were immediately discovered by local militia, and at dawn Cuban aircraft began to fire on the invaders. Their ships were hit, sinking much of their ammunition and equipment, while Cuban forces swarmed into the landing zone, bringing with them heavy tanks. With no air support, the invaders were sitting ducks. Castro's forces mounted sustained attacks and by the end of the day on April 17 had effectively crippled the invasion. Kennedy, under pressure to authorize American air strikes from the nearby carrier *Essex*, refused. On the afternoon of April 18 the invasion force surrendered, having lost over 100 men killed and nearly 400 wounded. Kennedy was shattered by the fiasco. "How could I have been so stupid?" he repeatedly asked his advisers.[25]

Kennedy drew as his chief lesson from the Bay of Pigs affair never to trust the experts, especially the generals and the CIA planners who had all but promised success. But this lesson he could have learned by heeding Ike's warning, proffered just weeks before, that "in the councils of government, we must guard against the acquisition of unwarranted influence, whether sought or unsought, by the military-industrial complex." Kennedy had mocked the old asshole then; he was not laughing now.

In order to protect himself politically from Republican attacks, Kennedy invited Eisenhower to confer with him at Camp David on April 22. It must have been an absolutely delicious moment for Ike, though he was too much of a patriot to take any pleasure in seeing Kennedy in trouble. Eisenhower choppered in from Gettysburg, and the two men wandered the grounds of the woodsy retreat, side by side, a father figure tutoring the younger man. Over lunch Ike peppered Kennedy with the kind of questions Kennedy ought to have asked the military brass: about the logistics, the air support, the timing of the landings, just the kind of thing Eisenhower had spent his life mastering. Eisenhower questioned Kennedy's decision-making process, again stressing the need for an orderly and disciplined approach to national security policy. Kennedy, mournful and chagrined, could only say that he had asked Gen. Maxwell Taylor to prepare a full review. "No one knows how tough this job is until he has been in it a few months," Kennedy sighed. Ike could not resist a small moment of triumph: "Mr. President, if you will forgive me, I think I mentioned that to you three months ago."

Publicly Ike backed Kennedy and told the waiting press that all Americans must stand together when the chips were down. But privately he was appalled at the poor planning and management of the invasion, especially Kennedy's lack of resolve in sending in additional air power once the fight had started. In his diary Ike jotted down his real feelings: "This story could be called a 'Profile in Timidity and Indecision.'"[26]

Kennedy might have agreed with that brutal assessment. He *had* been timid, but he would not make that mistake again. Although he dismissed Dulles and Bissell from their posts, he moved quickly to recommit the country to the basic cold war maxims so frequently invoked during the Age of Eisenhower. Even as the pathetic Cuban exiles were being marched into Castro's jails on April 20, Kennedy gave a speech to the American Society of Newspaper Editors in which he expressed no regret for his audacious failure in Cuba. "The message of Cuba, of Laos, of the rising din of Communist voices in Asia and Latin America—these messages are all the same. The complacent, the self-indulgent, the soft societies are about to be swept away with the debris of history. Only the strong, only the industrious, only the determined . . . can possibly survive." A week later, sending the message that he would not falter in waging the cold war, he approved an increase of U.S. military personnel and military aid to South Vietnam. He then ordered Vice President Lyndon Johnson to deliver personally a letter to South Vietnamese president Ngo Dinh Diem, pledging greater American support to meet the communist threat in Southeast Asia.[27]

Nor did Kennedy forget about Cuba. In the fall of 1961 he authorized an expanded covert operation against Castro, to be led by none other than Gen. Edward Lansdale, the man so closely identified with the botched Bay of Pigs operation. Relying on propaganda, economic sabotage, and guerrilla operations inside Cuba, the CIA aimed to destabilize Castro's regime and foment conditions that might open the way to an American invasion of the embattled island. The specter of the disgraced Allen Dulles hung over it all.[28]

Thus Kennedy could not escape the Age of Eisenhower. During his short time in office, Kennedy confronted the problems of Cuba, Laos, Vietnam, Berlin, nuclear weapons, the space race, and civil rights—all issues that had taken shape during Ike's years. Though a gifted leader, Kennedy found these tangled troubles no easier to resolve than Eisenhower had, and many of his proposed solutions drew from the tool kit of his predecessor. Far from charting a new course for the country, Kennedy steered the ship of state through the same shoals and eddies that Ike had navigated. No wonder Schlesinger, looking back over Kennedy's first 18 months in office, would confide in his diary this downcast assessment: "In area after area, we have behaved exactly as the Eisenhower administration would have behaved—in spite of everything we said in the campaign. . . . The old continuities, the Eisenhower-Dulles continuities, are beginning to reassert themselves."[29]

VI

On November 22, 1963, with the unspeakable murder of President Kennedy in Dallas, Texas, the country changed forever, and the Age of Eisenhower slipped into the past. The United States soon entered a decade of civil strife, racial unrest, antiwar protests generated by a misguided war in Vietnam, and still more violence, punctuated by the murders of Martin Luther King Jr. and Robert Kennedy in 1968. From the vantage point of such a troubled era, Americans inevitably looked back to the period from the end of World War II until that awful day in Dallas with reverence and nostalgia. Those seemingly charmed years would be forever invoked as a time of peace, prosperity, security, and confidence. The ugly realities of the 1950s—the war in Korea, the shame of McCarthyism, the persistence of Jim Crow, the deadly CIA plots, the nuclear fears—drifted out of focus. Instead popular memory dwelled happily on kitschy ephemera like *Father Knows Best*, Elvis Presley, Marilyn Monroe, and men in fedoras. We know the 1950s were never so happy, so innocent, so magical, but they were certainly *different* from what came after, and Americans have never ceased to think and dream about the "glad, confident morning" of those years.

Ike himself lived through the upheavals of the 1960s, through Kennedy's death, through the worst of the Vietnam War, the student protests, and the racial violence. He and Mamie retreated to Gettysburg and, in the winter months, to the lavish Eldorado Country Club in Indian Wells, California, a sparkling oasis in the arid desert just on the border of Joshua Tree National

Park. He devoted considerable time to his ponderous two-volume memoir, an earnest if uninspiring defense of his presidential record. He also published a far more lighthearted and revealing book titled *At Ease: Stories I Tell to Friends*, which recounts his family history, his life in the army, and his wartime career. He stayed abreast of Republican Party politics and opposed Goldwater's ascendancy in 1964, seeing the Arizona senator as too far right and dismissive of the modern Republicanism that Ike had championed. Goldwater's catastrophic defeat at the polls seemed a partial vindication of Eisenhower's moderate views.[30]

As the years passed, the great leaders of the age disappeared. On January 24, 1965, Churchill died. President Johnson chose not to attend the funeral, but Eisenhower did, and gave a memorable eulogy. Ike recalled the great Englishman as the "embodiment of British defiance" before Hitler's onslaught and warmly praised Churchill's leadership during the cold war years. With an elegant flourish, he ended simply, "Here was a champion of freedom." It was another sign of the passing of that generation of war leaders who had won the great struggle against fascism and shaped the strategy to contain and finally defeat communism.

In late 1965 Eisenhower suffered another heart attack. He lost weight and spent more time secluded at Gettysburg and his winter retreat in California. At the end of April 1968 he collapsed after a golf game at Eldorado and was transferred to Walter Reed Hospital, where he spent the last year of his life. He delighted in seeing his old sidekick, Dick Nixon, finally elevated to the presidency in November 1968; it was a moment of enormous relief for both men, and Nixon rushed to Ike's bedside the day after his victory to receive the benediction of the man whose esteem he most craved and had never fully won. On March 28, 1969, a bright spring day, Eisenhower died, while his faithful doctor, Leonard Heaton, his son John, and his grandson, David, stood at attention at his bedside.[31]

Although Eisenhower remained among the most popular men in America at the time of his death, contemporary journalists and analysts could not bring themselves to see his true worth. The obituaries praised his war leadership but discounted his presidency. *Time* magazine polled a number of prominent intellectuals—the kind of people who never quite understood Ike's appeal—and their assessment of his presidency reflected the by-now familiar condescension of academia. One leading scholar of the presidency, Clinton Rossiter of Cornell University, said Eisenhower "didn't believe in the exercise of presidential power" and so failed to grapple with the great problems of the country. James Banner of Princeton termed the Eisenhower era "a period of drift rather than mastery." Arthur Link, the longtime student of Woodrow Wilson, concluded that Eisenhower was "hemmed in, hobbled by a lifetime of experience in the Army," and so failed to understand and apply the powers of the presidency. At best, he achieved "a healing of wounds" in the country following the partisanship of the Truman era.[32]

Looking back at Eisenhower now, however, across a half-century of war, presidential scandals, resignations, impeachments, Oval Office calumnies, and bitter partisanship, we see him in a new light. In 2017 a poll of over 100 historians ranked Eisenhower among the five greatest presidents in the nation's history, behind only the true titans, George Washington, Abraham Lincoln, Franklin Roosevelt, and Theodore Roosevelt. It was a judgment that would have stunned his contemporaries but seems eminently sensible now. According to the poll, historians gave Ike particularly high marks for his handling of international affairs, his management of the economy, and his moral authority.[33]

These are sound judgments. Eisenhower's approach to international affairs was masterful. In 1953 he used his considerable political capital to bring about an armistice in the Korean War, ending an unpopular conflict that had taken the lives of over 36,000 Americans. He declined to bail out France in its doomed colonial war in Indochina, refusing to send American troops there in 1954 despite immense pressure from his military advisers to do so. He used American economic pressure to compel Britain and France to halt their ill-conceived invasion of Egypt in 1956, following Egypt's nationalization of the Suez Canal. In 1957, in response to the launch of *Sputnik*, Eisenhower initiated a massive program to build a new generation of rocket and space technology that positioned the United States to dominate the celestial arena for the rest of the century. And he was always willing to talk to his Soviet adversaries, going so far as to welcome Khrushchev for a memorable visit to Camp David in 1959. His foreign and security policies combined restraint and vigilance in equal measure.

Eisenhower showed less restraint in his use of covert operations. In Guatemala, Iran, Vietnam, Laos, Indonesia, Cuba, and Congo, Eisenhower gave CIA director Dulles carte blanche to cause havoc. The CIA in the 1950s triggered coups, plotted assassinations, and shipped arms and cash to authoritarian regimes. Dulles also urged upon Ike an aggressive use of the U-2 spy plane, which led to the disastrous events of May 1960. Eisenhower was a cold warrior, and there was brutality in the means he adopted to wage that ideological conflict. To be fair, all the postwar presidents have succumbed to the temptations of shadow warfare. Historians will continue to debate the consequences of Eisenhower's use of the CIA, but they will have to balance that story against the remarkable record of Great Power stability and the absence of large-scale conflict that marked his presidency.

Evaluating his stewardship of the economy, historians gave Eisenhower high marks, and with good reason. The GDP of the United States increased by an astonishing 60 percent during his administration. Because of his antipathy toward budget deficits and inflation, Eisenhower kept a tight hold on the federal purse strings. He balanced three budgets and came close on five others. Fewer federal dollars in the economy translated into sharp recessions in 1953–54 and 1958, with unemployment spiking significantly in 1958. Still, Ike demonstrated real creativity: he found a way to expand defense spending, boost the minimum wage, widen social security, and invest in infrastructure—especially highways, school construction, and public housing—all while maintaining tight fiscal policies. He rightly deserves to be known as one of the shrewdest managers of the nation's economy.

Finally, the historians gave Eisenhower superlative marks for his moral authority. And no wonder: Americans viewed Eisenhower as a legendary hero even before he entered politics, and his time in the White House strengthened his reputation as a man of integrity. He gave his life to public service in war and in peace, and his administration was remarkably free of scandal. Eisenhower possessed great dignity, and he held himself to the highest standard of personal conduct befitting the most honored office in the country. He could do no less.

Between 1915, when he left West Point, and 1961, when he finally laid down the cares of office, Eisenhower worked wholeheartedly and passionately for the good of his country. Americans looked to him during the 1950s as a model of loyalty, dignity, and decency. For a period of nearly two decades, from the cataclysms of the Second World War, through the prosperous if anxious days of the early cold war, until the transfer of power to a younger generation, Eisenhower lent his name to the age. And his people knew they had lived in the presence of greatness.

ACKNOWLEDGMENTS

I have lived with Dwight Eisenhower for some eight years—as long as he served the country as president, and far longer than I had anticipated when I first began this book. During this journey I have relied on and learned from friends, scholars, archivists, and public audiences who share my fascination with the decade of the 1950s and with Ike himself.

The idea for the book came from the wise old head of my editor Marty Beiser, who thought this might be a good time to return to the Age of Eisenhower. I thank him for nudging me forward when I was rather hesitant. Before I dug in I spoke to my then-colleague at Temple University, Richard Immerman, one of the most important and authoritative historians of the Eisenhower years, to ask for his blessing, which he kindly gave. He also read the final manuscript with his usual care and attentiveness, pressing me on some of my ideas and saving me from a few gaffes.

For many years I have visited Abilene, Kansas, to work in the pleasant setting of the Eisenhower Library. The collections there are wonderfully rich, and the kind and generous staff helped me find my way through mountains of crucial documents. To Tim Rives, Valoise Armstrong, Kathy Struss, and Chalsea Millner, I want to express my deep gratitude for your professionalism and all-around decency.

This book is very much a product of the University of Virginia and in particular the Miller Center for Public Affairs. At Mr. Jefferson's university nobody doubts that presidents are worthy of scholarly attention, and the Miller Center has been for 40 years one of the nation's most important centers of inquiry into the history of the presidency. I am grateful to the former director, Governor Gerald Baliles, who brought me into the Miller Center family, and to the current director, Bill Antholis, who has enthusiastically encouraged my work on Eisenhower and given me those invaluable commodities: time, space, and moral support. Gene Fife and Claire Gargalli have helped lead the Miller Center with wisdom and grace and have been kind friends and mentors to me.

The Miller Center is home to a group of smart and dedicated presidential scholars who have become friends and cherished colleagues. Heartfelt thanks to Barbra Perry, Marc Selverstone, Russell Riley, Guian McKee, Niki Hemmer, Stefanie Georgakis Abbott, Ken Hughes, and Sheila Blackford for everything they have done to help me find my way through the Age of Eisenhower. Marc shared his deep knowledge of the Kennedy years with me, and Guian gave me some insightful advice about 1950s social policy. I'm grateful to have enjoyed many hours with Doug Blackmon and Doug Trout at some of Charlottesville's abundant diners and dives. And to Andrew Chancey for paying the bills: Thank you.

During 2013 I spent a productive semester at the Kluge Center of the Library of Congress as the Henry A. Kissinger chair. That fellowship allowed me access to the greatest library in the world, and I owe a great debt to the former director Carolyn Brown for her support. I also spent a memorable month of quiet work in Oslo in 2013 as a fellow at the Nobel Institute; my thanks to Geir Lundestad and Asle Toje for their warm welcome.

A number of scholars read portions of the manuscript and gave me immensely valuable advice about how to improve it. Sidney Milkis, Kenneth Osgood, and Kathryn Brownell participated in a roundtable review of the first half of the book at the Miller Center. And at the Lyndon Johnson School of Public Affairs at the University of Texas, Eugene Gholz and Joshua Rovner orchestrated a high-powered scholarly review of a few chapters that led me to rethink some key passages. Sharon Weiner's comments there were especially useful. My thanks also to old friends and presidential historians Jeremi Suri, Jeffrey Engel, and Tim Naftali, and to Michael De Groot and Lauren Turek for research and web help. Beth Bailey and David Farber put me up in their beautiful Kansas home during my trips to Abilene. To the Poker Guys, who shall remain anonymous: Thank you for your friendship, laughter, and occasional mockery.

A few friends went beyond the call of duty. David Farber, Richard Immerman, Hal Brands, and Fred Logevall read and commented on the entire manuscript, graciously taking time away from their own pressing obligations to give me immensely helpful comments. I can't thank them enough for sharing with me their knowledge and insight. To Brian Balogh and Melvyn Leffler, my colleagues and dear friends in the History Department at the University of Virginia, I owe an incalculable debt of gratitude. Brian has been a friend, an advocate, a cheerleader, a critic, a mentor, and an inspiration ever since I arrived at Virginia. He read the whole manuscript and helped me improve it. And Mel Leffler, whom I met when I was in graduate school, has been an academic role model for me for over two decades. He is a generous reader, an insightful critic, a kindhearted scholar, and a true professional in every sense of the word. I am honored to have him as a colleague and friend.

I have relied upon the smarts and savvy of my agent, Susan Rabiner, for many years, and I am very lucky that she steered this book into the hands of Bob Bender, my editor, who has made the book immeasurably better. Johanna Li carefully guided the book through production and Judith Hoover did a truly miraculous job of copy editing. Any errors that remain are entirely my fault.

Over the years that I have been tangled up in Ike, my dear family has been there to straighten me out. My children, Ben and Emma, kept me fortified with goofy drawings of "President Ike" and gave me immense joy as they grew from little kids into inspiring adults. My wife, Elizabeth Varon, a great historian, is also the funniest lady I know. "Ike was a badass!" she once declared, brilliantly summarizing a long and ponderous story I was trying to tell. She has kept me chuckling for almost a quarter of a century.

I dedicate the book to my father, David I. Hitchcock, Jr. He lived through these years as a keen and wide-eyed young man, working as a legislative aide to Senator H. Alexander Smith, a moderate New Jersey Republican. In the mid-1950s Dad had a front-row seat in the U.S. Senate, and he observed the titans of the age as they strutted and fretted their hour upon the stage. From Richard Russell to Lyndon Johnson, Margaret Chase Smith, Everett Dirksen, Hubert Humphrey, Paul Douglas, William Knowland, and even the reptilian Joe McCarthy, Dad got to see them all in their element, in the rough and tumble of American democracy. Then, in 1957, he went overseas as a young foreign service officer—to Vietnam, as it happened, beginning his long and distinguished career in public diplomacy. Never cynical, always optimistic, ever curious, and fundamentally decent, he has throughout his life reflected the best of America. I offer him this book as a small token of thanks for all he has given me.

A NOTE ON EISENHOWER SCHOLARSHIP

The documentary sources held at the Eisenhower Library in Abilene, along with the 21 volumes of private letters and papers published by Johns Hopkins University Press, form the foundation for any serious study of Ike's life. There is also an abundant scholarly literature on Eisenhower and his times. Some of the earlier surveys of his life and presidency have not aged well. Peter Lyon, *Eisenhower: Portrait of the Hero*, and Herbert Parmet, *Eisenhower and the American Crusades*, are quite out of date. Others skim along the surface, such as Michael Beschloss, *Eisenhower: A Centennial Life*; Geoffrey Perret, *Eisenhower*; and Piers Brendon, *Ike: Life and Times of Dwight D. Eisenhower*. Stephen Ambrose's two-volume life contains much of value but is crippled by the author's use of dubious evidence. More substantial and well-researched is Jean Edward Smith, *Eisenhower in War and Peace*, which gives more attention to war than to peace. Jim Newton, *Eisenhower: The White House Years*, is concise and even-handed, while Evan Thomas, *Ike's Bluff*, provides a loose jumble of revealing vignettes. An excellent short synthesis is Chester Pach and Elmo Richardson, *The Presidency of Dwight D. Eisenhower*. Ike produced a two-volume presidential memoir, *The White House Years*, whose subtitles are *Mandate for Change* and *Waging Peace*. Stolid and mostly reliable, they are guarded and buttoned up, revealing little of the man himself. None of these authors effectively captures the acidic contempt with which the intellectuals of the era viewed Eisenhower. For a contemporary example of that, see Richard Rovere, *The Eisenhower Years*.

The most useful sources on Eisenhower's pre-presidential life include his own memoir, *At Ease: Stories I Tell to Friends*, and Kenneth Davis, *Soldier of Democracy*, a book full of purple prose and many small mistakes but that treats in detail the early family life in Abilene. Ike's prewar diaries and letters are now available in a collection edited by Dan Holt. Six volumes of Eisenhower's papers from the war years have been published in the Johns

Hopkins series. Ike's own memoir of the war, *Crusade in Europe*, is diplomatic to a fault and ought to be read alongside his diary, as well as the candid, and controversial, diary kept by his naval aide, Harry Butcher, published as *My Three Years with Eisenhower*. For key details of Eisenhower's personal and social life during the war, Kay Summersby's admiring (and discreet) account is valuable: *Eisenhower Was My Boss*. Her rather less discreet memoir, published 30 years later, is *Past Forgetting: My Love Affair with Dwight D. Eisenhower*. John Gunther, the journalist who covered Ike in the war and after, wrote a short but revealing biography in 1952 titled *Eisenhower: The Man and the Symbol*. Among the better treatments of Eisenhower's war leadership are the study written by his grandson, David Eisenhower, *Eisenhower at War, 1943–45*; Carlo d'Este, *Eisenhower: A Soldier's Life*; and Merle Miller, *Ike the Soldier: As They Knew Him*.

Eisenhower was an avid letter writer and diarist, and these written materials are a boon to scholars. Robert Ferrell published selected highlights in *The Eisenhower Diaries*. Ike's *Letters to Mamie* and his correspondence with Swede Hazlett, edited by Robert Griffith and published as *Ike's Letters to a Friend*, are especially valuable. His son John's observations of the president, titled *Strictly Personal*, are also revealing. Two books written by White House aides shed light on Eisenhower's leadership style: William Ewald, *Eisenhower the President*, and Arthur Larson, *Eisenhower: The President Nobody Knew*.

Among the most useful sources on the election of 1952 are the memoirs of key advisers: Sherman Adams, *Firsthand Report*; Herbert Brownell, *Advising Ike*; Robert Cutler, *No Time for Rest*; and Emmet Hughes, *The Ordeal of Power*. William B. Pickett, *Eisenhower Decides to Run*, gives a detailed narrative. Eisenhower's own version in *Mandate for Change* is somewhat sterile. James Patterson, *Mr. Republican*, expertly covers the contest with Taft. On Nixon in 1952, William Costello, *The Facts about Nixon*, provides a critical view; Earl Mazo, *Richard Nixon*, is far more positive. Both are essential, but the authoritative work on the young Nixon is Roger Morris, *Richard Milhous Nixon*. On the crisis over Nixon's campaign fund, the most revealing account of all is surely Nixon's own in *Six Crises*, next to which must be placed *Nixon Agonistes* by Garry Wills, although it overstates Eisenhower's political genius in handling the issue. For a fresh look at Nixon, see John Farrell, *Richard Nixon: The Life*. Two new books assess the Ike-Nixon relationship: Jeffrey Frank's *Ike and Dick* is a masterwork of elegance and concision; a more detailed portrait, quite favorable to Nixon, is Irwin Gellman, *The President and the Apprentice*.

The "New Look"—Eisenhower's cold war grand strategy—has received sustained and detailed attention from many historians over the years. Among the most valuable works are Richard Immerman and Robert Bowie, *Waging Peace*; John Gaddis, *Strategies of Containment*; Melvyn Leffler, *For the Soul of Mankind*; Campbell Craig, *Destroying the Village*; Richard Hewlett and Jack Holl, *Atoms for Peace and War*; McGeorge Bundy, *Danger and Survival*; Richard Leighton, *Strategy, Money and the New Look*; and Michael Hogan, *A Cross of Iron*. Immerman's book *John Foster Dulles* is an excellent portrait of Ike's wingman, and the essays in *John Foster Dulles and the Diplomacy of the Cold War*, edited by Immerman, are excellent.

For Eisenhower's approach to McCarthy and the Red Scare in general, see Jeff Broadwater, *Eisenhower and the Anti-Communist Crusade*; David Oshinsky, *A Conspiracy So Immense*; Robert Griffith, *The Politics of Fear: Joseph R. McCarthy and the Senate*; and a highly critical contemporary account, Richard Rovere, *Senator Joe McCarthy*. William Ewald wrote a well-researched study on Eisenhower's role in undermining the Red-baiting senator: *Who Killed Joe McCarthy?* Fred Greenstein's classic study, *The Hidden-Hand Presidency*, rests mainly upon the McCarthy case as evidence of Ike's governing style. David Nichols follows Greenstein in *Ike and McCarthy*, making a somewhat overstated case for Eisenhower as the genius behind the effort to bring down McCarthy. For Oppenheimer, see the excellent study by Kai Bird and Martin Sherwin, *American Prometheus*. Two important works that reveal the gendered nature of McCarthyism are Robert Dean, *Imperial Brotherhood*, and David Johnson, *The Lavender Scare*.

Historians of the CIA and its associated secret agencies owe an enormous debt of gratitude to the National Security Archive at George Washington University for its efforts to pry out of the U.S. government many of its most closely guarded secrets. One of their scholars, John Prados, has written many books studded with new revelations, including his masterful if somewhat droll account of America's obsession with covert operations, *Safe for Democracy: The Secret Wars of the CIA*. Stephen Ambrose wrote an early survey of these matters called *Ike's Spies* that suffers from lack of access to much declassified material. On Allen Dulles, Peter Grose, *Gentleman Spy*, should be supplemented by the CIA's once-secret study *Allen Welsh Dulles as Director of Central Intelligence*, written by Wayne Jackson in 1973. Stephen Kinzer's work is uniformly critical and polemical; see *The Brothers* and *All the Shah's Men*. A similar accusatory tone infuses Tim Weiner, *Legacy of Ashes*. The most up-to-date book on events in Iran in 1953 is Mark J.

Gasiorowski and Malcolm Byrne, *Mohammad Mossadeq and the 1953 Coup in Iran*. On Guatemala, Nick Cullather added enormously to our knowledge with *Secret History*, a book that has a complex history of its own. Piero Gleijeses, *Shattered Hope*, is an essential book, the product of deep archival and oral history research in Guatemala. One of the first and still best books on the topic is Richard Immerman, *The CIA in Guatemala*. The CIA itself has at long last started to release large troves of secret materials from the 1950s. See the CIA Reading Room at https://www.cia.gov/library/readingroom.

Amid a sea of controversial and contentious works on America's early involvement in Vietnam up to 1960, a few stand out for balance and good sense. Fredrik Logevall's Pulitzer Prize–winning survey of the transition between the French and the American wars, *Embers of War*, brilliantly narrates this often misunderstood moment, though Logevall's Eisenhower appears far more eager for war in 1954 than the portrait sketched in these pages. See as well William Conrad Gibbons, *The U.S. Government and the Vietnam War*; Ronald Spector, *Advice and Support*; David Anderson, *Trapped by Success*; and William J. Duiker, *U.S. Containment Policy and the Conflict in Indochina*. For the decision not to go to war in 1954, see the important 1984 article by George Herring and Richard Immerman, "Eisenhower, Dulles, and Dienbienphu: 'The Day We Didn't Go to War' Revisited," as well as Melanie Billings-Yun, *Decision against War*. In 2011 the National Archives released the full text of the Pentagon Papers; this once-secret report can be read at https://www.archives.gov/research/pentagon-papers/. On the Taiwan crisis, see Gordon Chang, *Friends and Enemies*; a critical assessment by Appu Soman, *Double-Edged Sword*; and for China's point of view, Chen Jian, *Mao's China and the Cold War*.

The writing on the advent of the civil rights movement is vast. The most accessible treatment of the whole scene is Taylor Branch, *Parting the Waters*, which covers the period 1954–63. On the role of the Eisenhower administration in advancing civil rights legislation, David Nichols has published an excellent study, *A Matter of Justice*, which might be a trifle too fulsome in its praise for Eisenhower. Nichols's work has superseded two earlier works that were based on only limited access to sources from the Eisenhower Library: Richard Kluger, *Simple Justice*, a monumental study of the *Brown* decision that gives little attention to Eisenhower and Brownell, and Robert Burk, *The Eisenhower Administration and Black Civil Rights*, which is especially strong on the desegregation of Washington, D.C., and the military but less good on the *Brown* case. James T. Patterson, *Brown v. Board of Education* is superb.

Herbert Brownell's memoir *Advising Ike* should be consulted as a crucial source for civil rights policy, especially the passage of the 1957 Civil Rights Act. Important documents have been published in a 20-volume series, Michal R. Belknap, ed., *Civil Rights, the White House and the Justice Department, 1945–1968* and in *The Papers of Martin Luther King, Jr.* On the role of LBJ in the passage of the Civil Rights Act, see Rowland Evans and Robert Novak, *Lyndon B. Johnson*, and Robert Caro's monumental study, *Master of the Senate*. On Little Rock, see Elizabeth Jacoway, *Turn Away Thy Son*. Frederic Morrow, who worked in the Eisenhower White House on minority affairs, wrote two poignant memoirs; *Black Man in the White House* and *Forty Years a Guinea Pig* offer frank, and often bitter, commentary on the racial attitudes of the Eisenhower team. The global ramifications of America's racial problems are illuminated by Thomas Borstelmann, *The Cold War and the Color Line*, and Mary Dudziak, *Cold War Civil Rights*. The African American press, especially the *Baltimore Afro-American*, the *Chicago Defender*, the *Norfolk Journal and Guide*, and the *Pittsburgh Courier*, covered civil rights politics with particular skill.

Among the excellent new scholarship on the confluence of American ideals, commerce, and religion in the 1950s, see Darren Dochuk, *From Bible Belt to Sunbelt*; Kim Phillips-Fein, *Invisible Hands*; Kevin Kruse, *One Nation under God*; and Wendy Wall, *Inventing the "American Way."* One of the best essays on Eisenhower's pro-business ideology is Robert Griffith, "Dwight Eisenhower and the Corporate Commonwealth." On the rise of the new right in the 1950s, see David Farber, *The Rise and Fall of Modern American Conservatism*; Sam Tanenhaus, *The Death of Conservatism*; and Geoffrey Kabaservice, *Rule and Ruin*. Arthur Larson, Ike's speechwriter, tried to summarize the chief themes of moderate Republicanism in *A Republican Looks at His Party*. Carl Bogus recounts William F. Buckley's scorn for Eisenhower's centrism in *Buckley*.

The twin crises of 1956, Suez and Hungary, have been extensively studied. The best attempt to knot the story together and see it as Eisenhower experienced that year is David Nichols, *Eisenhower 1956*; see also Alex von Tunzelmann, *Blood and Sand*. Eisenhower's handling of Suez and the rise of the Eisenhower doctrine are expertly evaluated in Salim Yaqub, *Containing Arab Nationalism*, and Ray Takeyh, *The Origins of the Eisenhower Doctrine*. Michael Doran, in a tendentious work titled *Ike's Gamble*, criticizes Eisenhower for failing to back up the Anglo-French-Israeli invasion. Eisenhower's relationship with Anthony Eden is best viewed through the documents:

see Peter Boyle, *The Eden-Eisenhower Correspondence*. Eden's mendacious memoir, *Full Circle*, should be supplemented by the more candid diary of his private secretary Evelyn Shuckburgh, *Descent to Suez*. The best single volume on the crisis is Keith Kyle, *Suez*.

The most useful and well-researched monographs on the *Sputnik* effect are Robert Divine, *The Sputnik Challenge*, and Yanek Mieczkowski, *Eisenhower's Sputnik Moment*. The best history of the space race remains Walter McDougall, *The Heavens and the Earth*. For an elegant and brilliant analysis of nuclear history, see McGeorge Bundy, *Danger and Survival*. Fred Kaplan captured the world of the nuclear theorists and intellectuals of the 1950s in *Wizards of Armageddon*. David Alan Rosenberg gives a superbly detailed analysis of nuclear strategy in "The Origins of Overkill: Nuclear Weapons and American Strategy, 1945–1960." For a lively narrative about the making of the ICBM, see Neil Sheehan, *A Fiery Peace in a Cold War*. Two fine studies of the missile gap debate are Peter Roman, *Eisenhower and the Missile Gap*, and Christopher Preble, *John F. Kennedy and the Missile Gap*. James Killian's memoir, *Sputnik, Scientists, and Eisenhower*, is a crucial insider's view of how Ike used science. For hair-raising factual data on nuclear weapons, see the extraordinary book edited by Stephen Schwartz, *Atomic Audit*.

The most useful works on Khrushchev are William Taubman, *Khrushchev*; Aleksandr Fursenko and Timothy Naftali, *Khrushchev's Cold War*; and Sergei Khrushchev, *Nikita Khrushchev and the Creation of a Superpower*. Also very revealing are Khrushchev's own memoirs. Harold Macmillan's memoir of this period, *Riding the Storm*, is essential to see the European perspective. Henry Cabot Lodge's account of Khrushchev's visit in *The Storm Has Many Eyes* is quite dull compared to the real-time reports he sent back to Washington as the trip unfolded. For behind-the-scenes details on the Khrushchev visit, see Wiley Buchanan, *Red Carpet at the White House*. A lively account of U.S.-Soviet relations in this period is Michael Beschloss, *Mayday*.

An excellent place to start for a critical assessment of Eisenhower's policies in the Third World is Robert J. McMahon, "Eisenhower and Third World Nationalism: A Critique of the Revisionists." See also the fine essays in Kathryn C. Statler and Andrew L. Johns, *The Eisenhower Administration, the Third World, and the Globalization of the Cold War*. On Indonesia, two well-researched studies give a detailed account: Kenneth Conboy and James Morrison, *Feet to the Fire*, and Audrey Kahin and George Kahin, *Subversion as Foreign Policy*. Among the many excellent books on the Diem years in

Vietnam, see especially Fredrik Logevall, *Embers of War*; Seth Jacobs, *America's Miracle Man in Vietnam*; and Edward Miller, *Misalliance*. America's reaction to Castro's revolution is expertly chronicled in Thomas Paterson, *Contesting Castro*. For the origins of the March 16, 1960, plan, the CIA's own secret internal history by Wayne Jackson is extremely useful and should be supplemented with the sources in Peter Kornbluh, *Bay of Pigs Declassified*. To follow the evolution of the anti-Castro operation, Richard Bissell's memoir, *Reflections of a Cold Warrior*, remains useful if self-serving. Peter Wyden, *Bay of Pigs*, contains important interviews, and Jim Rasenberger in *The Brilliant Disaster* has updated the story with new research in once-classified documents. On Congo, we now have detailed studies, most notably Emmanuel Gerard and Bruce Kuklick, *Death in the Congo*, which draws on newly released Belgian materials. Larry Devlin's hair-raising memoir, *Chief of Station, Congo*, can be combined with the Church Committee report, *Alleged Assassination Plots*, to complete the sorry picture.

On John F. Kennedy generally, Theodore Sorensen, *Kennedy*, and Arthur Schlesinger Jr., *A Thousand Days*, benefit from their inside knowledge of Camelot but suffer from hero worship. Biographies by Robert Dallek, *An Unfinished Life*, and Thomas Reeves, *President Kennedy*, are more circumspect. For the election of 1960, it is hard to top Theodore White, *The Making of the President, 1960*, though White fell in love with Jack Kennedy and it shows throughout the book. A more recent and well-researched assessment is Edmund F. Kallina Jr., *Kennedy v. Nixon*. Nixon gives his own somewhat pathetic account in *Six Crises*. Eisenhower's reaction to the election, his departure from Washington, and his post-presidential years are lovingly and insightfully recounted in David Eisenhower, *Going Home to Glory*.

NOTES

ABBREVIATIONS USED IN THE NOTES

DDEL   Dwight D. Eisenhower Library
DDO   U.S. Declassified Documents Online (Gale, Cengage Learning)
FRUS   U.S. Department of State, *Foreign Relations of the United States*
PDDE   *Papers of Dwight D. Eisenhower*
PPP   *Public Papers of the Presidents*

PROLOGUE

1. Quoted in a short essay in *Ike: A Pictorial Biography*, 138. Beach was a decorated naval officer with a storied career, including combat at Midway. His 1955 novel, *Run Silent, Run Deep*, became a hit movie in 1958.

2. Stevenson in *New York Times*, September 12 and 20, 1952; Truman quoted in speeches delivered on September 29 and October 30, 1952, *PPP: Harry S. Truman*, 612 and 1001; Stone, *The Haunted Fifties*, 6; McCullough, *Truman*, 914.

3. Shannon, "Eisenhower as President."

4. Mailer, "Superman Comes to the Supermarket."

5. *New York Times*, January 19, 1961; Graebner, "Eisenhower's Popular Leadership"; Schlesinger Sr., "Our Presidents." Harrison and Garfield were omitted from the poll due to their short terms in office. On JFK's reaction, Schlesinger Jr., *Journals*, 162, 178.

6. Arthur Schlesinger Jr., *A Thousand Days*, 165, 206, 210.

7. *New York Times*, March 29, 1969; "A First Verdict" and "Eisenhower: Soldier of Peace"; *Time*, cover story, April 4, 1969.

8. Kempton, "The Underestimation of Dwight D. Eisenhower."

9. Wills, *Nixon Agonistes*, 117, 118, 131.

10. Greenstein, *The Hidden-Hand Presidency*, 5. Robert Divine in *Eisenhower and the Cold War* also argues that restraint was a strategy of governance that applied to the foreign policy realm as well.

11. For a discussion of the way Eisenhower's reputation was revised in the 1980s, see Immerman, "Confessions of an Eisenhower Revisionist"; McMahon, "Eisenhower and Third World Nationalism"; Rabe, "Eisenhower Revisionism."

12. For a comprehensive thematic bibliography, see Boyle, *Eisenhower*, 183–93.

13. Speaking with Field Marshall Bernard Montgomery, November 24, 1954, Papers as President, Ann Whitman File, Ann Whitman Diary Series, box 3, DDEL.

14. In 1984 Stephen Ambrose published the first major biography that exploited the vast documentary sources available in Abilene. However, in 2010 the Eisenhower Library reported that Ambrose had apparently fabricated a number of interviews with the former president and inserted unsubstantiated quotations in his text. Ambrose's work has been clouded by controversy ever since. On the Ambrose controversy, see Rives, "Ambrose and Eisenhower"; Rayner, "Channeling Ike." Earlier accounts include Lyon, *Eisenhower*; Parmet, *Eisenhower and the American Crusades*; Beschloss, *Eisenhower*; Perret, *Eisenhower*; Brendon, *Ike*. The most recent biographical studies include Smith, *Eisenhower in War and Peace*; Newton, *Eisenhower*; and Thomas, *Ike's Bluff*. An excellent synthesis is offered by Pach and Richardson, *The Presidency of Dwight D. Eisenhower*, which is probably the best short book on the 34th president, along with Boyle's concise and well-informed study, *Eisenhower*.

15. "Remarks at the National Defense Executive Reserve Conference November 14, 1957," American Presidency Project, http://www.presidency.ucsb.edu/ws/?pid=10951. For numerical tally of Ike's attendance at NSC meetings, see NSC meeting, minutes, January 12, 1961, Papers as President, Ann Whitman File, NSC Series, box 13, DDEL.

16. I am indebted to Farber, *The Rise and Fall of Modern Conservatism*, for the idea of discipline as a distinctive feature of conservative ideals.

17. Jeffrey M. Jones, "Obama's Fourth Year in Office Ties as Most Polarized Ever," *Gallup*, January 24, 2013, http://www.gallup.com/poll/160097/obama-fourth-year-office-ties-polarized-ever.aspx.

CHAPTER 1: ASCENT

Epigraph: DDE, *Mandate for Change*, 107.

1. Childs, *Eisenhower*, 160.

2. Wills, *Nixon Agonistes*, 119.

3. Diary entry, January 21, 1953, in Ferrell, *The Eisenhower Diaries*, 225.

4. Eisenhower's mother always called him Dwight. Eisenhower reversed the order of his names upon his entry into West Point.

5. Davis, *Soldier of Democracy*, 7–45; Smith, *Eisenhower in War and Peace*, 5–11.

6. DDE, *At Ease*, 31, 68, 305–6. For further details on religion in the Eisenhower home, see Milton Eisenhower, *The President Is Calling*, 186–88.

7. DDE, *Mandate for Change*, 32.

8. Davis, *Soldier of Democracy*, 100–101. See Ambrose and Immerman, *Milton S. Eisenhower*, 8–30, for a portrait of Abilene in these years.

9. DDE, *At Ease*, 5, 7, 12, 16. For details on his West Point days, Davis, *Soldier of Democracy*, 135–50.

10. DDE, *At Ease*, 138, 147–51, 155. Carlo D'Este covered these years very thoroughly in *Eisenhower: A Soldier's Life*, 109–37.

11. DDE, *At Ease*, 185–87. "I can never adequately express my gratitude to this gentle-

man, for it took years before I fully realized the value of what he had led me through."

12. Susan Eisenhower, *Mrs. Ike*, 33–43; quotation from Hatch, *Red Carpet for Mamie*, 3.

13. DDE, *At Ease*, 181.

14. Neal, *The Eisenhowers*, 64; Susan Eisenhower, *Mrs. Ike*, 66–72. Eisenhower spelled the nickname "Icky," but Mamie spelled it "Ikkie," and Susan Eisenhower uses "Ikky." On the roses, see D'Este, *Eisenhower*, 156.

15. "Gruber-Eisenhower Diary," August 28–September 5, 1929, Holt, *Eisenhower: The Prewar Diaries*, 84–96.

16. Diary entry, November 9, 1929, Holt, *Eisenhower: The Prewar Diaries*, November 9, 1929, 110–11.

17. "Fundamentals of Industrial Mobilization," June 16, 1930, Holt, *Eisenhower: The Prewar Diaries*, 139. This paper appeared in *Army Ordnance* 11 (July–August 1930): 7–8. Eisenhower's "Brief History of Planning for Procurement and Industrial Mobilization" of October 1931 is a masterly synthesis of the relationship between industrial production and government procurement for the armed services. His depth of knowledge and growing sophistication is evident in these reports. Holt, *The Prewar Diaries*, 176–88.

18. DDE, *At Ease*, 213–14.

19. DDE, *At Ease*, 216–17.

20. Eisenhower's frustration in his Philippines post is evident in his diary. See diary entries, April 5 and April 17, 1939, Holt, *The Prewar Diaries*, 429–31. Further evidence of his deteriorating view of MacArthur can be seen in Ferrell, *The Eisenhower Diaries*, 7–26. The two men were temperamentally opposite; only Eisenhower's self-control kept the friction from surfacing. More details on Eisenhower's period in the Philippines can be found in Holland, *Eisenhower between the Wars*, 187–203; Lyon, *Eisenhower*, 68–80.

21. DDE, *At Ease*, 230–32.

22. *New York Times*, February 20, 1942.

23. Pogue, *George C. Marshall: Ordeal and Hope*, 339.

24. Diary entry, January 22, 1942, Ferrell, *The Eisenhower Diaries*, 44. On Marshall and Eisenhower at this moment, see D'Este, *Eisenhower*, 284–98.

25. Diary entry, June 8, 1942, Ferrell, *The Eisenhower Diaries*, 62.

26. *New York Times*, June 26, 1942.

27. Hastings, *Winston's War*, 241–44.

28. Diary entry, June 25, 1942, Ferrell, *The Eisenhower Diaries*, 64.

29. Churchill, *The Second World War: The Hinge of Fate*, 374–85, 432–51; diary entries, July–September 1942, Ferrell, *The Eisenhower Diaries*, 70–78.

30. Raymond Daniell, "He Is Our 'Eisen' and This Is Our Hour," *New York Times*, November 1, 1942.

31. Atkinson, *An Army at Dawn*, 198–99. Churchill supported the deal on the grounds of military necessity, even if it came at a high political cost at home. The episode is portrayed in Churchill, *The Second World War: The Hinge of Fate*, 629–47; Miller, *Ike the Soldier*, 417–432.

32. Danchev and Todman eds., *War Diaries, 1939–1945*, 343, 351.

33. Butcher, *My Three Years with Eisenhower*, 245, 247.

34. Butcher, *My Three Years with Eisenhower*, 388.

35. Letter, April 7, 1943, Griffith, *Ike's Letters to a Friend*, 19.

36. Butcher, *My Three Years with Eisenhower*, 116. For an equally glowing assessment by a war correspondent who spent years covering Eisenhower, see Gunther, *Eisenhower*, 19–24. General Brooke desperately wanted to command Overlord but was denied it; Eisenhower expected that Marshall or perhaps Brooke would be given the job and seemed both resigned and perhaps even relieved that others would carry the burden for a while. It is hard to imagine that he would have felt the despair that Brooke experienced upon being told that Overlord would not be his assignment. See Butcher, *My Three Years with Eisenhower*, 421; Roberts, *Masters and Commanders*, 395–98. For FDR's informing Eisenhower about the command, see David Eisenhower, *Eisenhower at War*, 42–46.

37. Roberts, *Masters and Commanders*, 386–88; diary entry, June 3, 1944, Ferrell, *The Eisenhower Diaries*, 118.

38. For details about life in Telegraph Cottage, see Summersby, *Eisenhower Was My Boss*, 25–32.

39. Butcher, *My Three Years with Eisenhower*, 730.

40. Butcher, *My Three Years with Eisenhower*, 792; letter, July 9, 1945, Griffith, *Ike's Letters to a Friend*, 26.

41. Butcher, *My Three Years with Eisenhower*, 834.

CHAPTER 2: STAR POWER

Epigraph: DDE quoted in *New York Times*, July 5, 1947.

1. John Eisenhower, *Letters to Mamie*, 224.

2. Letter, Marshall to DDE, *PDDE*, 6:14–15.

3. Churchill quotation and text of speech in *New York Times*, June 13, 1945; Danchev and Todman, *Lord Alanbrooke*, 697; coverage in *The Times* (London), June 13, 1945.

4. *New York Times*, June 20, 1945. On La Guardia's declaration, *New York Times*, June 18, 1945.

5. Ferrell, *Off the Record*, 47.

6. The Truman offer is recounted in DDE, *Crusade in Europe*, 444. Truman later denied the episode. Letters to Neill Edwards Bailey, August 1, 1945, and George Marshall, August 27, 1945, *PDDE*, 6:239, and 309–10.

7. Letters, May 12 and 18, 1945, John Eisenhower, *Letters to Mamie*, 253–54.

8. For press criticism, see letter to Marshall, June 1, 1945, *PDDE*, 6:114–17; John Eisenhower, *Strictly Personal*, 113.

9. DDE, *Crusade in Europe*, 459.

10. DDE, *Crusade in Europe*, 463; John Eisenhower, *Strictly Personal*, 102–4.

11. John Eisenhower, *Strictly Personal*, 106–9; DDE, *Crusade in Europe*, 475.

12. Letter to Marshall, August 27, 1945, *PDDE*, 6:309–10; letters, August 31 and September 4, 1945, John Eisenhower, *Letters to Mamie*, 269–70.

13. DDE, *At Ease*, 316. Coverage of demobilization crisis in *New York Times*, January 5, 8, 10, 11, 13, 1947; *Washington Post*, January 10 and 16, 1946.

14. Eisenhower statement to Congress in *New York Times*, January 16, 1947; ban on demonstrations, *New York Times*, January 18, 1946; letter to Douglas MacArthur, January 28, 1946, *PDDE*, 7:797–99.

15. Letter to Bernard Baruch, January 5, 1946, *PDDE*, 7:735–36; Griffith, *Ike's Letters to a Friend*, 80.

16. DDE, *At Ease*, 319.

17. For Eisenhower's report on military readiness, *New York Times*, March 6 and 7, 1946; for speech to American Newspaper Publishers Association, *New York Times*, April 26, 1946.

18. Letter, March 13, 1946, Griffith, *Ike's Letter's to a Friend*, 34; letter to John Sheldon Doud Eisenhower, March 3, 1946, *PDDE*, 7:881–82.

19. Patterson, *Grand Expectations*, 39–52.

20. *New York Times*, November 10, 1946.

21. Arthur Krock, "Taboo against Soldiers May Die in the '48 Race," *New York Times*, September 29, 1946.

22. *New York Times*, September 29, 1946; "Eisenhower for President Talk Grows Louder," *New York Times*, December 8, 1946; diary entries, November 12 and December 7, 1946, Ferrell, *The Eisenhower Diaries*, 138–39.

23. *New York Times*, November 11, 1946; letter to John Sheldon Doud, January 31, 1947, *PDDE*, 8:1470–72.

24. Letter to Walter Bedell Smith, April 18, 1946, *PDDE*, 8:1648–49.

25. DDE, *At Ease*, 337; letter to Thomas I. Parkinson, June 23, 1947, *PDDE*, 8:1775–76.

26. "The appointment [to Columbia] immediately revived talk of Eisenhower entering politics, possibly as a '48 or '52 White House candidate," reported the *Washington Post*, June 25, 1947. Joseph and Stewart Alsop declared that the Columbia appointment triggered a "sheep-like stampede" among Republicans to Ike (*Washington Post*, August 20, 1947). On the Draft Eisenhower group and Ike's repudiation of it, see *New York Times*, August 29, September 11, September 12, October 12, 1947; *Washington Post*, September 11, 1947.

27. He made these remarks to reporters in Vicksburg on July 4, 1947 (*New York Times*, July 5, 1947). Letter to Walter Bedell Smith, September 18, 1947, *PDDE*, 9:1933–35. He wrote in a similar vein to Milton (October 16, 1947, *PDDE*, 9:1986–88).

28. *New York Times*, January 10, 1948; correspondence between Finder and Eisenhower in *PDDE*, 9:2191–93, 2202–3; Leonard Finder Papers, box 1, DDEL. Finder had written to Eisenhower on January 12 telling him of the paper's endorsement of the draft movement in New Hampshire. Eisenhower told Finder a week later that the public refusal had been "a difficult letter to write." Finder papers, box 1, letter to Finder, January 27, 1948, DDEL.

29. Letter to James Forrestal, September 27, 1948, *PDDE*, 10:230–31.

30. Diary entry and footnote, December 13, 1948, *PDDE*, 10:365–68.

31. On the frequency of his speaking engagements, letter to Helen Rogers Reid, September 24, 1948, *PDDE*, 10:224.

32. Columbia University inaugural speech, text in *New York Times*, October 13, 1948.

33. Diary entry, January 14, 1949, *PDDE*, 10:430–32; letter to Professor Benjamin Wood, May 6, 1949, *PDDE*, 10:570–72; *New York Times*, January 30, 1949.

34. Letter to Amon G. Carter, June 27, 1949, *PDDE*, 10:665–69.

35. Diary entry, September 27, 1949, *PDDE*, 10:755–57. For press comment on Ike's renewed presidential fortunes, see *New York Times*, September 11 and 18, 1949; *Washington Post*, September 8, 1949; diary entry, November 25, 1949, *PDDE*, 10:839–41.

36. On the best-dressed poll, *Los Angeles Times*, February 9, 1950.

37. Hughes, *The Ordeal of Power*, 19–20; on Ike "moving young," see C. D. Jackson, "Notes on Ike," C.D. Jackson Papers, box 50, DDEL; Susan Eisenhower, *Mrs. Ike*, 34; Kenneth Davis, *Soldier of Democracy*, 135–36; Krock, *Memoirs*, 280; Cutler, *No Time for Rest*, 262.

38. Cleveland *Plain Dealer*, April 6, 1950.

39. Robinson on Eisenhower's energy is in Robinson notes on meeting of October 17, 1947, Robinson Papers, box 9, DDEL; obituary of William E. Robinson, *New York Times*, June 8, 1969; Samuel T. Williamson, "Cokes All Around," *New York Times*, January 17, 1960.

40. Sampson, *The Masters*.

41. *New York Times*, March 2, 1962, and August 26, 1952.

42. *New York Times*, March 9, 1985; *Washington Post*, March 9, 1985.

43. Profile of Woodruff in *Wall Street Journal*, January 9, 1981; *New York Times*, December 20, 1982; "Robert Woodruff (1889–1985)," in *New Georgia Encyclopedia* at newgeorgiaencyclopedia.org.

CHAPTER 3: CALL TO DUTY

Epigraph: Diary entry, October 4, 1951, *PDDE*, 12:609.

1. Diary entry, January 1, 1950, *PDDE*, 11: 882–89.

2. Gallup poll conducted February 26–March 3, 1950, www.ropercenter.uconn.edu; Richard Rovere, *Harper's*, May 1950; Dewey in *New York Times*, June 19, 1950.

3. *New York Times*, March 24, March 28, March 30, March 31, 1950.

4. Marshall to Rose Page Wilson, July 24, 1950, *Papers of George C. Marshall*, 7:146.

5. For a brilliant summary of U.S. strategic thinking in this period, see Leffler, *A Preponderance of Power*, 361–74.

6. Eisenhower's notes on his meeting with President Truman, diary entry, October 28, 1950, *PDDE*, 11:1388–92; letter to Swede Hazlett, November 1, 1950, *PDDE*, 11:1396–98.

7. Diary entries, July 6, 1950, November 6, 1950, and December 5, 1950, *PDDE*, 11:1211–12, 1408–11, 1459–60; letter to Gen. Al Gruenther, November 30, 1950, *PDDE*, 11: 1450–51.

8. "Table 3.1—Outlays by Superfunction and Function: 1940–2017," *White House*,

http://www.whitehouse.gov/omb/budget/Historicals; Leffler, *A Preponderance of Power*, 372–74.

9. Hoover speech, *New York Times*, December 21, 1950; Taft speech in Senate, *Los Angeles Times*, January 6, 1951; *New York Times*, January 6, 1951. The full text of the January 5 speech is in *Papers of Robert A. Taft*, 4:230–52.

10. Text of the speech in *New York Times*, February 2, 1951.

11. *New York Times*, February 2, 1951.

12. DDE, *Mandate for Change*, 14; DDE, *At Ease*, 369–72. Eisenhower related the details of this encounter to his brother. See Milton Eisenhower, *The President Is Calling*, 243–45).

13. *Washington Post*, February 2, 1951; *New York Times*, March 4, 1951.

14. Diary entry, March 13, 1951, *PDDE*, 12:124. German attitudes in Vigers, "The German People and Rearmament."

15. Letter to Edward J. Bermingham, February 28, 1951, *PDDE*, 12:74–78. A few days later Eisenhower forwarded this letter to his pal Bill Robinson with an accompanying note recalling how he had been "violently opposed" to many of the Truman administration's policies and that only a sense of "military duty" compelled him to take up the NATO position. Letter to Bill Robinson, March 6, 1951, *PDDE*, 12:97–99; Robinson Papers, box 1, DDEL.

16. Rovere and Schlesinger, *The General and the President*, 168–72; *Hartford Courant*, March 24, 1951; *New York Times*, March 25, 1951; *Christian Science Monitor*, March 26, 1951; *Boston Globe*, April 6, 1951.

17. Rovere and Schlesinger, *The General and President*, 5; *Boston Globe*, April 11, 1951.

18. Address by General MacArthur to Congress, April 19, 1951, reproduced in Rovere and Schlesinger, *The General and the President*, 270–77. Parade details: *New York Times*, April 21, 1951.

19. Clay to Eisenhower, April 13, 1951, Robinson Papers, box 1, DDEL; Clay to Eisenhower, May 18, 1951, Pre-Presidential Papers, Principal File, box 24, DDEL. According to Herbert Brownell, Clay was "the key man." He said "it would have been impossible for any other individual to convince him to run." Brownell Oral History, OH-362, DDEL. Cliff Roberts and Bill Robinson both sent similar analyses of the MacArthur issue to Ike: Roberts to Eisenhower, April 18, 1951, and Robinson to Eisenhower, April 20, 1951, Robinson Papers, box 1, DDEL.

20. Letters to Clay, April 16 and May 30, 1951, *PDDE*, 12:306–7.

21. William Robinson, "Paris Diary," June 21–July 8, 1951, Robinson Papers, box 1, DDEL.

22. Lodge, *The Storm Has Many Eyes*, 77–79.

23. Clay to Eisenhower, August 22, 1951, Pre-Presidential Papers, Principal File, box 24, DDEL; letter to Ed Birmingham, September 24, 1951, *PDDE*, 12: note 2, 564; diary entry, October 4, 1951, *PDDE*, 12:608–9.

24. The details of Clark's visit and the text of the letter are in Clark's lengthy manuscript "Eisenhower for President," Edwin N. Clark Papers, box 4, DDEL. The actual letter

was discovered only in 1993 by Eisenhower scholar William Bragg Ewald Jr. and was published in the *New York Times Magazine*, November 14, 1993. For the Clark mission, see Ewald's book, *Eisenhower the President*, 40–41. For a profile of Duff, see William S. White, "Senator Duff of the Eisenhower Team," *New York Times*, November 11, 1951.

25. *New York Times*, November 3, 1951. The poll was done in mid-October 1951 and can be seen at http://www.ropercenter.uconn.edu/. The Gallup poll showed Eisenhower with a lead over Truman from February 1950 right through the spring of 1952. Ike's lead in these polls was never smaller than 30 points. The press coverage can be seen in *Christian Science Monitor*, November 5 and 7, *Washington Post*, November 5 and 7, *New York Times*, November 6 and 7, and *Boston Globe*, November 7, 1951. Arthur Krock reported the detailed political exchange in the *New York Times* on November 8, 1951, which was promptly denied by the participants. Krock elaborated on the controversy in his memoirs, where he stuck to the story and revealed that Associate Justice William O. Douglas of the Supreme Court was his source for the Truman-Eisenhower conversation (*Memoirs*, 268–69). Truman admitted this in passing when he referred to the political content of their lunch conversation in a later letter to Eisenhower. Letter to Truman, January 1, 1952, *PDDE*, 12:830–31, note 1.

26. Letter to William Robinson, November 8, 1951, *PDDE*, 12: note 2, 691.

27. *New York Times*, November 18, 1951.

28. On Lodge's efforts, see Lodge, *The Storm Has Many Eyes*, 83–87; letter to Robinson, November 24, 1951, *PDDE*, 12:731.

29. William Robinson memo, December 29, 1951, Robinson Papers, box 1, DDEL. "The Case for Ike," *Life*, January 7, 1952.

30. Lodge, *The Storm Has Many Eyes*, 94–98. In correspondence with Ed Bermingham, Eisenhower said that it had finally become necessary "to acknowledge the existence of a factual record that establishes a party allegiance coinciding with that of so many of my warm friends." Letter to Bermingham, January 7, 1952, Eisenhower-Bermingham Correspondence, box 1, DDEL.

31. McCrary obituary, *New York Times*, July 30, 2003.

32. Extensive press coverage of the event was carried in the February 9 and 10, 1952, editions of the *New York Times, Boston Globe, Los Angeles Times*, and *Washington Post*. *Life* magazine carried many photographs of the evening's festivities in the February 18, 1952, issue.

33. Letter to Philip Young, February 11, 1952, *PDDE*, 13:970.

34. Jacqueline Cochran Oral History, OH-42, DDEL; diary entry, February 12, 1952, *PDDE*, 13:971. Eisenhower gives a less dramatic account in *Mandate for Change*, 20.

35. Lucius Clay Oral History, OH-56, DDEL.

36. Letter to Clay, February 20, 1952, *PDDE*, 13:997–99.

37. Taft campaign speeches covered in *Boston Globe*, March 7, *Christian Science Monitor*, March 8, *New York Times*, March 8, 1952.

38. James Reston, "New Hampshire Stages a Politician's Circus," *New York Times*, March 9, 1952.

39. *Manchester Union Leader*, June 18 and 24, 1952. For an excellent analysis of the campaign, see Robert B. Dishman, "How It All Began: The Eisenhower Pre-Convention Campaign in New Hampshire, 1952," *New England Quarterly*, March 1953, 3–26; Walter Lippmann, *Boston Globe*, March 13, 1952; Pickett, *Eisenhower Decides to Run*, 182.

40. Brownell, *Advising Ike*, 89–103.

41. See the essay in *Time*, April 7, 1952. Arthur M. Schlesinger Jr., who was present that night, recalled that some Democrats in the audience, eager for a new leader, were pleased by the news (*Journals*, 3–4). Truman later claimed he had decided not to run two years earlier, but this seems dubious given his correspondence with Eisenhower in late 1951. Had Ike stayed out and Taft been nominated by the Republicans, it seems highly likely Truman would have run for reelection. See Truman, *Memoirs: Years of Trial and Hope*, 488.

42. Letter to Truman, April 2, 1952, and Truman's reply of April 6, *PDDE*, 13:1154–56.

CHAPTER 4: CRUSADE

Epigraph: "Address Accepting the Presidential Nomination at the Republican National Convention in Chicago," July 11, 1952, American Presidency Project, http://www.presidency.ucsb.edu/ws/index.php?pid=75626.

1. *New York Times*, June 5, 1952.

2. Herbert Brownell Oral History, OH-157, DDEL.

3. *New York Times*, June 5, 1952. "Eisenhower's First Campaign Speech," *Boston Globe*, June 5, 1952; *Atlanta Daily World*, June 5, 1952; *Hartford Courant*, June 5, 1952. For details on the Truman-era scandals, see Dunar, *The Truman Scandals*, chapters 5–6.

4. *Washington Post*, June 6, 1952.

5. Stewart Alsop, *New York Herald Tribune*, June 6, 1952. See also *Christian Science Monitor*, June 6, 1952, and the praise of the *Washington Post* editorial page, June 6, 1952.

6. *New York Times*, June 1, 1952.

7. Staff Files, Citizens for Eisenhower Files of Young and Rubicam, "The Texas Steal," box 5, DDEL. On Eisenhower's Texas speech, see *Boston Globe, New York Times, Baltimore Sun*, and *Washington Post*, all June 22, 1952.

8. Brownell, *Advising Ike*, 117. His chapter 6 provides an excellent summary of the technical issues at stake at the convention, as does Lodge, *The Storm Has Many Eyes*, 105–25. See also Patterson, *Mr. Republican*, 547–58. A smart account of the whole affair by a close observer is Moos, *The Republicans*, 449–84. For the full text of the Fair Play amendment, see Brownell Papers, box 128, DDEL.

9. The detailed vote tabulations are in *Official Report of the Proceedings of the Twenty-Fifth Republican National Convention*, 405–6. See also Parmet, *Eisenhower and the American Crusades*, 83–101.

10. Rovere, *Affairs of State*, 26–27, 32. For the enduring bitterness, see Moos, *The Republicans*, 482–83. Robert Taft died a year later, in August 1953. Had he been nominated,

he probably would have selected Douglas MacArthur as his running mate. Had Taft been elected, MacArthur would have been president at least from 1953 to 1956.

11. *New York Times*, May 22, 1952, reporting the result of a *Newsweek* poll.

12. Brownell quoted in Mazo, *Richard Nixon*, 89; Adams, *Firsthand Report*, 34. Adams put it this way, some years later: "Nixon's activity against the Communist conspiracy in this country had well categorized him as a buoyant, active, aggressive and I guess you could say reasonably intelligent politician, and they accepted him on the basis of his accomplishments, rather than his immaturity" (Sherman Adams Oral History, OH-162, DDEL). Jim Hagerty recalled it much the same way. The key factors were "his Congressional record" and "the Alger Hiss incident" (James Hagerty Oral History, OH-91, DDEL).

13. *New York Times*, May 9, 1952; Nixon, *Six Crises*, 299; Mazo, *Richard Nixon*, 90; Morris, *Richard Milhous Nixon*, 683–84.

14. Smith, *Thomas E. Dewey and His Times*, 596–97; Adams, *Firsthand Report*, 34–36; Brownell, *Advising Ike*, 120–21; Morris, *Richard Milhous Nixon*, 731–33. In 1970 Dewey sent Brownell a memorandum detailing the Nixon selection of 1952, emphasizing that Nixon's role in getting Hiss was the principal argument in his favor. Dewey to Brownell, March 17, 1970, Herbert Brownell Papers, box 108, DDEL.

15. Nixon, *Six Crises*, 75; Nixon, *RN*, 80, 87.

16. Speech of July 11, 1952, *Official Report of the Proceedings of the Twenty-Fifth Republican National Convention*, 432–34.

17. Johnson, *The Papers of Adlai Stevenson*, 4:11–14; Mary McGrory in Doyle, *As We Knew Adlai*, 170; Schlesinger, *Journals*, 10; George Ball in Doyle, *As We Knew Adlai*, 148.

18. Rovere, *Affairs of State*, 38.

19. An excellent portrait of the campaign may be found in Hughes, *The Ordeal of Power*, 17–44. For colorful anecdotes about the campaign train, see Howard, *With My Shoes Off*, 179–224; Cutler, *No Time for Rest*, 275–92.

20. On McCarthy's attack on Marshall, see Rovere, *Senator Joe McCarthy*, 170–79.

21. *Christian Science Monitor*, August 23, 1952; *New York Times*, August 23, 1952.

22. Marquis Childs, *Boston Globe*, September 16, 1952; "Campaign Statements of Dwight D. Eisenhower," unpublished collection available in Reading Room, DDEL.

23. Cutler, *No Time for Rest*, 280–81; *New York Times*, September 16, 1952; Roscoe Drummond in *Christian Science Monitor*, September 16, 1952.

24. The political fund crisis has been carefully annotated by various authors, most exhaustively by Morris, *Richard Milhous Nixon*, 757–866. See also Costello, *The Facts about Nixon*, 103–14; Mazo, *Richard Nixon*, 98–124; Wills, *Nixon Agonistes*, 91–114; Greenberg, *Nixon's Shadow*, 50–54; Perlstein, *Nixonland*, 37–43. Most intriguing are Nixon's own accounts, in *Six Crises*, 73–129 and *RN*, 92–110.

25. Letter to Robinson, September 20, 1952, *PDDE*, 13:1360, note 3. According to Brownell, General Clay "was livid and thought Eisenhower should remove him from the ticket as soon as possible" (*Advising Ike*, 124).

26. Letter to Nixon, September 19, 1952, *PDDE*, 13:1358–59; letter to William Robinson,

September 20, 1952, *PDDE*, 13:1360; *New York Times*, September 20, 1952.

27. The text of the address was printed in *New York Times*, September 24, 1952.

28. *Christian Science Monitor*, September 24, 1952; James Reston, *New York Times*, September 24, 1952; *Boston Globe*, September 24, 1952.

29. *New York Times*, September 25, 1952.

30. The "you're my boy" comment was reported in *Chicago Daily Tribune*, September 25, 1952.

31. An early sense of the rift the fund issue caused was picked up by reporters traveling with the Eisenhower and Nixon campaign teams. "Inside Account of Nixon Affair," *New York Times*, September 26, 1952; William A. Clark, "Veep Tactics," *Wall Street Journal*, September 26, 1952.

32. "Kohler Lifts Finger for McCarthy," *Christian Science Monitor*, September 5, 1952.

33. On McCarthy's criticism of Eisenhower during his own reelection campaign, see Joseph Alsop, *Washington Post*, September 7, 1952. For context, see Broadwater, *Eisenhower and the Anti-Communist Crusade*, 26–53. The proposed speech went through many alterations. See Stephen Benedict Papers, box 4, DDEL; Hughes, *The Ordeal of Power*, 42.

34. Adams, *Firsthand Report*, 30–32; Sherman Adams Oral History, OH-162, DDEL.

35. That Ike was deliberately courting the right was emphasized by Joseph Alsop, "Ike's Strategy Explained," *Washington Post*, October 10, 1952.

36. Speech text in Benedict Papers, box 4, DDEL. Speech was covered in *New York Times*, October 4, 1952.

37. Truman speaking on October 4, 1952, at the Palace Hotel in San Francisco. "Public Papers: Harry S. Truman, 1945–1953," Harry S. Truman Library and Museum, http://www.trumanlibrary.org/publicpapers/index.php. Also see *New York Times*, October 5, 1952; *Christian Science Monitor*, October 6, 1952.

38. *New York Times*, October 8, 1952; *Washington Post*, October 8, 1952; *Boston Globe*, October 8, 1952; Truman, *Memoirs. Years of Trial and Hope*, 501; Bernard Shanley diaries, typescript, p. 527, DDEL.

39. Hughes, *The Ordeal of Power*, 31–35; Adams, *Firsthand Report*, 42–44; Truman, *Memoirs: Years of Trial and Hope*, 501–2. There is some dispute about who came up with the idea. Hughes claims authorship in his memoir. Adams suggests C. D. Jackson may have been behind it (Sherman Adams Oral History, OH-162, DDEL). But in an interview in 1967, James Hagerty suggests Eisenhower himself had had the idea long before. On the golf course two days after he was nominated, he told Hagerty he would "go to Korea" but to "just keep that quiet" (James Hagerty Oral History, OH-91, DDEL).

CHAPTER 5: SCORPIONS IN A BOTTLE

Epigraph: Inaugural address, January 20, 1953, Dwight D. Eisenhower Presidential Library, Museum and Boyhood Home, http://www.eisenhower.archives.gov/all_about_ike/speeches/1953_inaugural_address.pdf.

1. Hughes, *The Ordeal of Power*, 48. The role of Clay and Brownell in picking cabinet officers is confirmed by Maxwell Rabb, the assistant to Sherman Adams, in Maxwell Rabb Oral History, OH-309, DDEL. The National Security Council met weekly, normally on Thursday mornings. Created in 1947, the NSC was mostly ignored by Truman. Eisenhower, by contrast, thought of it rather like the Combined Chiefs of Staff during the war: the leading officers of government thrashed out problems of policy, and the commander in chief made the final decisions. Eisenhower's national security adviser, first Robert Cutler, then Dillon Anderson, and then Gordon Gray, kept the decision-making process moving. Ideas and proposals would come to the NSC from the Planning Board; if approved, they would be handed off to the Operations Coordinating Board, which supervised implementation. To follow up on policy decisions, Ike relied on a staff secretary, first Pete Carroll and then, from 1954 on, the estimable Col. (later Gen.) Andrew Goodpaster. See Nelson, "The Top of Policy Hill."

2. Hoopes, *The Devil and John Foster Dulles*, 6, 142. On Eisenhower's private assessment of Dulles, see diary entry, May 14, 1953, *PDDE*, 14:224. For a nuanced assessment of the relationship, see Immerman, "Eisenhower and Dulles."

3. Gen. Alfred Gruenther urged Eisenhower to consider McCloy or Dewey. Eisenhower told Gruenther that while Dewey might be ideal, he had accumulated too many "bitter political enemies" to be effective in the post. Letter to Alfred Gruenther, November 26, 1952, *PDDE*, 13:1436–37. On Wilson, see Hughes, *The Ordeal of Power*, 50; Ike's comment in diary entry, May 14, 1953, *PDDE*, 14:225.

4. Goldman, *The Crucial Decade and After*, 241.

5. Killian, *Sputnik, Scientists, and Eisenhower*, 51.

6. *New York Times*, November 19, 1952.

7. Truman, *Memoirs: Years of Trial and Hope*, 520–21.

8. Details on the trip can be followed in a special report filed by Don Whitehead of the Associated Press, published in a booklet as "The Great Deception." Jim Hagerty also left detailed notes on the planning of the trip (Hagerty Papers, box 11, DDEL).

9. Hagerty letters, December 2 and 6, 1952, Hagerty Papers, box 11, DDEL; *Boston Globe*, December 6, 1952; *Manchester (U.K.) Guardian*, December 6, 1952; *New York Times*, December 6, 1952.

10. Rhee quoted in *New York Times*, December 7, 1952; DDE, *Mandate for Change*, 95.

11. Hughes, *The Ordeal of Power*, 49–50; Hagerty Papers, box 11, DDEL.

12. Text of Eisenhower's statement in *Boston Globe*, December 15, 1952; *Christian Science Monitor*, December 15, 1952; Truman comments in *New York Times*, December 12, 1952. For Ike's personal fury with Truman, see Drew Pearson, "Ike Was Ready to Blast Truman," *Washington Post*, December 20, 1952.

13. Hughes, *The Ordeal of Power*, 53–54; diary entry, January 16, 1953, *PDDE*, 13:1506; DDE, *Mandate for Change*, 100; "Inaugural Address," January 20, 1953, American Presidency Project, http://www.presidency.ucsb.edu/ws/?pid=9600.

14. Hewlett and Holl, *Atoms for Peace and War and War*, 1–3.

15. NSC 141, "Report to the NSC by the Secretaries of State and Defense and Director of Mutual Security," January 19, 1953, *FRUS 1952–54*, 2: pt. 1, 214.

16. Oppenheimer, "Atomic Weapons and American Policy," 529. The report by the panel, submitted in January 1953 to the secretary of state, was published by its principal author, McGeorge Bundy, as "Early Thoughts on Controlling the Nuclear Arms Race."

17. John Foster Dulles, "A Policy of Boldness," *Life*, May 19, 1952, 146–57. These ideas had been given longer and more nuanced expression in his book *War or Peace*, and he had proposed a policy along these lines to Eisenhower in April 1952, during the presidential campaign. For judicious analysis, see Immerman, *John Foster Dulles: Piety*, 39–41.

18. Dulles opposed any bold appeal to the Soviets, as he told the cabinet at the March 4 meeting (NSC meeting, March 4, 1953, *FRUS 1952–54*, 8:1091–95). This cautious approach was reiterated by the counselor of the Department of State Charles Bohlen on March 10 and repeated by Dulles at a meeting of the NSC on March 11, 1953 (*FRUS 1952–54*, 8:1108–11, 1117–25). CIA memo, "Probable Consequences of the Death of Stalin," March 10, 1953, White House Office, Office of the Special Assistant for National Security Affairs, NSC Series, Subject Subseries, box 5, DDEL.

19. Session of USSR Supreme Soviet, March 15, 1953, in *Current Digest of the Russian Press* 8, no. 5 (April 4, 1953): 3–5. One crucial ally was deeply skeptical about Soviet good intentions: German chancellor Konrad Adenauer, meeting with Dulles on April 7, scoffed at the idea of a serious change inside the USSR. "While it was true that the Soviet Union might extend a peace offer which could be acceptable to the West," he told the secretary, "the West must not relax its vigilance, but instead should continue to build its strength since the only way to negotiate with a totalitarian country was to negotiate from strength. Although the Federal Republic had no desire for war, the danger of war would increase if the West relaxed its build-up efforts" (U.S. Delegation minutes of the first general meeting of Chancellor Adenauer and Secretary Dulles, April 7, 1953, *FRUS 1952–54*, 7: pt. 1, 433).

20. Meeting of the NSC, March 11, 1953, *FRUS 1952–54*, 8:1122; Hughes, *The Ordeal of Power*, 103; Meeting of the NSC, March 25, 1953, *FRUS 1952–54*, 2: pt. 1, 261–62.

21. C. D. Jackson letter to John Foster Dulles, March 10, 1953, and accompanying memo, "Notes for a Draft Outline of a U.S. Political Warfare Plan," in C. D. Jackson Papers, box 104, DDEL. Jackson worked closely with Walt W. Rostow of MIT to draft these proposals. Rostow wrote a book about the origins of the speech, *Europe after Stalin*, and included many relevant documents.

22. "The Chance for Peace," delivered to the American Society of Newspaper Editors, April 16, 1953, American Presidency Project, http://www.presidency.ucsb.edu/ws /index.php?pid=9819. For a masterful account of the "Chance for Peace" speech and its failure to alter the cold war, see Leffler, *For the Soul of Mankind*, 84–150.

23. Adams, *Firsthand Report*, 97. For details on the dissemination see "Foreign Policy Speech," June 4, 1953, C. D. Jackson Papers, box 104, DDEL.

24. The power struggle among the Soviet collective leadership after Stalin's death, and its connection with the June 1953 uprising, is ably recounted in Knight, *Beria*, 176–94.

25. John Foster Dulles, "The Eisenhower Foreign Policy," April 18, 1953, reprinted in Rostow, *Europe after Stalin*, 122–31.

26. Figures from "Review of the 1954 Budget," by Joseph Dodge, August 27, 1953, Office Files, Administration Series, microfilm, reel 10, DDEL. Also see figures in Morgan, *Eisenhower versus "The Spenders,"* 49–53; NSC minutes, March 25 and March 31, 1953, *FRUS, 1952–54*, 2: pt. 1, 258–64.

27. A careful analysis of these debates can be found in Leighton, *Strategy, Money and the New Look*, volume 3 of the official *History of the Office of the Secretary of Defense*, 88–113; Hogan, *A Cross of Iron*, 387–99.

28. Diary entry, May 1, 1953, *PDDE*, 14:195–97; for further details, see *FRUS, 1952–54*, 2: pt. 1, 316.

29. Historical Tables, Office of Management and Budget, Table 3.1, https://obamawhitehouse.archives.gov/omb/budget/Historicals.

30. Press conference, April 30, 1953, *PPP: Dwight D. Eisenhower*, 242.

31. Radio address, May 19, 1953, *PPP: Dwight D. Eisenhower*, 317. For similar comments to the National Security Council, March 25, 1953, *FRUS 1952–54*, 2: pt. 1, 261. See also his letter to Al Gruenther, May 4, 1953, *PDDE*, 14:203. For careful analysis of Ike's defense budget policy, see Bowie and Immerman, *Waging Peace*, 96–108. In a letter to an old friend, Brig. Gen. Benjamin F. Caffey Jr., Eisenhower expressed his philosophy about taxes clearly: "The federal deficit must be eliminated in order that tax reduction can begin. Reverse this order and you will *never* have tax reduction" (July 27, 1953, *PDDE*, 14:429).

32. NSC 147, "Possible Courses of Action in Korea," April 2, 1953, *FRUS 1952–54*, 15:842; DDE, *Mandate for Change*, 171, 181.

33. James Shepley, "How Dulles Averted War," *Life*, January 16, 1956, 70–80. A similar accounting was given by Adams, *Firsthand Report*, 98–99. This view was also enshrined by journalist Robert Donovan in his admiring account of the first years of the administration, *Eisenhower: The Inside Story*, 115–16. Fred Greenstein repeated this uncritically in *The Hidden-Hand Presidency*, 61–62. For historians retelling the Dulles story, see Ambrose, *Eisenhower: The President*, 106; Divine, *Eisenhower and the Cold War*, 29–31; Smith, *Eisenhower in War and Peace*, 574. See also Newton, *Eisenhower*, 99–101; Thomas, *Ike's Bluff*, 74–81.

34. For a careful discussion of the alleged nuclear threat in the armistice negotiations, see Dingman, "Atomic Diplomacy during the Korean War." On Ike's discussions about using nuclear weapons, NSC meeting, February 11, 1953; memo of conversation with Robert Cutler, March 21, 1953; NSC meeting, March 31, 1953, all in *FRUS 1952–54*, 15:769–70, 815, 825–27.

35. Documents collected by the Woodrow Wilson Center make it possible to analyze the Soviet, Chinese, and North Korean attitude toward the armistice. See in particular USSR Council of Ministers resolution of March 19, 1953; memorandum of the So-

NOTES   545

viet representative in Korea, Vasilii Kuznetsov, to Moscow, March 29, 1953; Molotov statement on Korea at the Presidium of the USSR Council of Ministers, March 31, 1953; and a Soviet Foreign Ministry report on the history of the war, August 9, 1966, all at "Korean War Armistice," *Wilson Center Digital Archive*, http://digitalarchive .wilsoncenter.org/collection/169/korean-war-armistice. For a thoughtful review of this evidence, see Gaddis, *We Now Know*, 107–10.

36. NSC 147, "Possible Courses of Action in Korea," April 2, 1953, *FRUS 1952–54*, 15:839–57.

37. Commander in chief, UN Command, Gen. Mark Clark, to Joint Chiefs, April 11, 1953; Rhee to Eisenhower, April 9, 1953; Eisenhower to Rhee, April 23, 1953; Clark to JSC, May 8, 1953, all in *FRUS 1952–54*, 15: 903–4, 902–3, 929–30, 987.

38. NSC meetings, May 7 and May 13, 1953, and Joint Chiefs memorandum, May 19, 1953, *FRUS 1952–54*, 15:977, 1012–17, 1059–64.

39. Memorandum of conversation between Nehru and Dulles, May 21, 1953, *FRUS 1952–54*, 15:1068–69; Dingman, "Atomic Diplomacy during the Korean War"; Foot, "Nuclear Coercion and the Ending of the Korean Conflict"; Jones, "Targeting China."

40. DDE, *Mandate for Change*, 185–87; NSC meeting, June 18, 1953, *FRUS 1952–54*, 15: pt. 2, 1200–1205.

41. Bowie and Immerman, *Waging Peace*, chapter 8, provides an excellent analysis of each task force. The Solarium documents are quite extensive. The final reports of each task force can be seen in White House Office, Office of the Special Assistant for National Security Affairs, NSC Series, Subject Subseries, box 9, DDEL. Draft materials are in White House Office, NSC Staff Papers, 1948–1961, Executive Secretary's Subject File Series, boxes 11, 15, and 17, DDEL. See also "Notes taken at first plenary session of Project Solarium," June 26, 1953, and "Summaries prepared by NSC Staff of Project Solarium Presentations," July 22, 1953, *FRUS 1952–54*, 2: pt. 1, 388–93, 399–434.

42. Papers as President, Ann Whitman File, NSC Series, box 4, NSC summaries of discussion, July 16, 1953, DDEL. George Kennan, who shaped the policy of containment, enjoyed the delicious moment when he was able to lecture Dulles, in front of the president, about the reasons for continuity instead of the more reckless alternatives Dulles had favored (Kennan, *Memoirs, 1950–1963*, 181–82). The shrewd observer was Andrew Goodpaster. See Goodpaster Oral History, OH-477, DDEL.

43. A complete text of NSC 162/2 has been put online by the Federation of American Scientists at http://fas.org/irp/offdocs/nsc-hst/nsc-162-2.pdf. For a lucid discussion of this strategy document and its links to NSC 68, see Gaddis, *Strategies of Containment*, 149–63.

44. Churchill had been thinking of this even before Ike was elected. In June 1952 he told his private secretary John Colville that "if Eisenhower were elected president, he would have another shot at making peace by means of a meeting of the Big Three." This was before Stalin died (Colville, *The Fringes of Power*, 650).

45. Colville, *The Fringes of Power*, 683. The American minutes present a slightly more

delicate version of Eisenhower's language. First Plenary Session, December 4, 1953, *FRUS 1952–54*, 5:1761.

46. On Eisenhower's atomic pool idea, see Young, *Documentary History of the Dwight D. Eisenhower Presidency*, vol. 3, memorandum for Admiral Strauss from Robert Cutler, September 10, 1953, document 53; on Strauss's evaluation, memorandum for the president, September 17, 1953, document 59; correspondence between Jackson and Strauss, September 27, 1953, document 62; Jackson memorandum for the president, October 2, 1953, document 66.

47. Memorandum of conversation, December 4, 1953, Papers as President, International Meetings Series, box 1, DDEL.

48. Churchill's reaction to Eisenhower's remark was redacted from the official record and declassified only in 2003. For the complete text, see Minutes, meeting of December 5, 1953, Papers as President, International Meetings Series, box 1, DDEL. Also Colville, *The Fringes of Power*, 685.

49. Dulles notes, December 5, 1953, and Eisenhower diary entry, December 6, 1953, reproduced in Young, *Documentary History of the Dwight D. Eisenhower Presidency*, vol. 3, document 90. Eisenhower developed these ideas further in a meeting three weeks later with his senior advisers. "The President said that the U.S. had come to a point where it could not back off from atomic weapons. Both the U.S. and the other side are in too deep." The minutes of this meeting have been only partially declassified. "Notes on conference in President's office," minutes taken by Robert Cutler, December 22, 1953, NSC Staff Papers, Executive Secretary's Subject File Series, box 5, DDEL.

50. Donovan, *Eisenhower*, 190; "Atoms for Peace," December 8, 1953, speech before the U.N. General Assembly, *Voices of Democracy*, www.voicesofdemocracy.umd.edu /eisenhower-atoms-for-peace-speech-text.

51. Reactions to the speech in *New York Times*, December 9, 1953, both on the editorial page and in a piece by Hanson Baldwin; *Washington Post*, December 9, 1953, and December 11, 1953, editorial page.

52. For evidence that the UN speech was not at all a disarmament proposal, see Memorandum by the special assistant to the president (C. D. Jackson) to the Operations Coordinating Board, December 9, 1953, *FRUS 1952–54*, 2: pt. 2, 1293; Jackson to Eisenhower, December 29, 1953, reproduced in Young, *Documentary History of the Dwight D. Eisenhower Presidency*, vol. 3, document 119.

53. The text of Dulles's speech is in *New York Times*, January 13, 1953. Hanson Baldwin penned a withering attack on it in the *Times* on January 24, 1953.

54. Dulles, "Policy for Security and Peace."

CHAPTER 6: CONFRONTING MCCARTHY

Epigraph: Press conference, November 18, 1953, *PPP: Dwight D. Eisenhower*, 781–89.

1. West, *Upstairs at the White House*, 129–30. A comprehensive and well-researched account of Mamie's role as first lady is provided by Holt, *Mamie Doud Eisenhower*. See also Brandon, *Mamie Doud Eisenhower*; Susan Eisenhower, *Mrs. Ike*, 275–87.

2. West, *Upstairs at the White House*, 130.

3. "Ike and Mamie in the White House," *U.S. News and World Report*, January 23, 1953. An excellent analysis of the decline of the intellectual in politics, and especially the problems faced by Stevenson in 1952 on this score, is in Hofstadter, *Anti-Intellectualism in American Life*, 221–29. "Now business is in power again; and with it will inevitably come the vulgarization which has been the almost invariable consequence of business supremacy," wrote Schlesinger in "The Highbrow in Politics," 162.

4. Andrew Tully, "Ike and Mamie at Home," *Collier's*, June 20, 1953; "When It's Tea-Time in Washington," *U.S. News and World Report*, March 6, 1953.

5. "What Goes On at Ike's Dinners," *U.S. News and World Report*, February 4, 1955.

6. A superb assessment of Eisenhower's religious attitudes is provided by Inboden, *Religion and American Foreign Policy*, 257–309; and see Preston, *Sword of the Spirit, Shield of Faith*, 440–50; Herzog, *The Spiritual-Industrial Complex*, 99–108; Holmes, *Faiths of the Postwar Presidents*, 24–44.

7. Greenstein uses the word *strategy* repeatedly to impart an overall coherence and consistency to Eisenhower's handling of the McCarthy problem (*The Hidden-Hand Presidency*, chapter 5, especially 157, 169).

8. An excellent synthesis is Fried, *Nightmare in Red*, 53–113.

9. Essential works on McCarthyism include Oshinsky, *A Conspiracy So Immense*; Griffith, *The Politics of Fear*. A brilliant contemporary analysis is Rovere, *Senator Joe McCarthy*.

10. "Veto of the Internal Security Bill," September 22, 1950, Harry S. Truman Library and Museum, http://trumanlibrary.org/publicpapers/viewpapers.php?pid=883.

11. Memorandum on Rosenberg case in European press, January 14, 1953, NSC Staff Papers, PSB Central Files, box 26, DDEL. For details on the French reaction, see Kuisel, *Seducing the French*, 48–52.

12. Press release, February 11, 1953, NSC Staff Papers, PSB Central Files, box 26, DDEL; cabinet minutes, February 12, 1952, Papers as President, Cabinet Series, box 1, DDEL.

13. Douglas Dillon to secretary of state, May 15, 1953; *New York Times*, June 15, 1953; flyer with Michael Rosenberg letter, all in Papers as President, Administration Series, box 32, DDEL; Sophie Rosenberg telegram, June 16, 1953, DDE White House Central Files, Alphabetical File, box 2672, DDEL.

14. Herbert Brownell Oral History, OH-157, May 5, 1967, DDEL; C. D. Jackson to Herbert Brownell, February 23, 1953, C. D. Jackson Papers, box 2, DDEL.

15. Letter to Clyde Miller, June 10, 1953, and letter to John Eisenhower, June 16, 1953, *PDDE*, 14:289–91, 298–300.

16. *New York Times*, June 20, 1953.

17. McCarthy to Eisenhower, February 3, 1953, Papers as President, box 22, DDEL. For the substance of the criticisms against Smith and Conant, whose appointments were approved by the Senate, see *New York Times*, February 7, 1953.

18. *New York Times*, March 3, 14, 15, and 16, 1953; press conference, March 26, 1953,

PPP: Dwight D. Eisenhower, 37. Bohlen's memoir provides a detailed account of the debate on Yalta at the hearings (*Witness to History*, 309–36).

19. *New York Times*, March 19, 1953; *Washington Post*, March 21 and 23, 1953. The headline of James Reston's piece in the March 24 *New York Times* captured the battle well: "Main Issue in Bohlen Case: Who May See FBI Files?" For details on the file contents, see Ruddy, *The Cautious Diplomat*, 120–21. Eisenhower was fully informed; Dulles spoke to him on March 16 to report that all his information indicated that Bohlen had "a normal family life." On constitutional grounds, though, Eisenhower sided with Brownell's position that Congress should not have free access to an FBI file. See minutes of Dulles-Eisenhower telephone conversation, March 16, 1953, and memorandum of conversation with Eisenhower, Brownell, and Dulles, March 22, 1953, Dulles Papers, White House Memoranda Series, box 8, DDEL.

20. *Employment of Homosexuals and Other Sex Perverts in Government, Interim Report Submitted to the Committee on Expenditures in the Executive Departments*, 81st Congress, December 15, 1950, Washington, D.C., GPO, 1950.

21. *New York Times*, March 26, 1953. Taft and Dulles colluded to produce this outcome, as is clear from their telephone call on March 23, 1953. Minutes of the call are in Dulles Papers, White House Memoranda Series, box 8, DDEL.

22. Letter to Edgar Eisenhower, April 1, 1953, and diary entry, April 1, 1953, *PDDE*, 14:141–42, 136–37.

23. Johnson, "The Eisenhower Personnel Security Program."

24. "Television Report to the American People," June 3, 1953, *PPP: Dwight D. Eisenhower*, 374–75.

25. "Remarks at the Dartmouth College Commencement Exercises, Hanover, New Hampshire," June 14, 1953, American Presidency Project, http://www.presidency.ucsb.edu/ws/?pid=9606. See also Oshinsky, *A Conspiracy So Immense*, 276–80. Cohn and Schine did not engage in book burning. In fact it was the libraries themselves that were compelled to destroy some volumes that had to be removed from the shelves.

26. Letter from Philip Reed, June 8, 1953, and reply, June 17, 1953, DDE Office Files, Administration Series, microfilm, reel 24, DDEL; letter to Swede Hazlett, July 21, 1953, *PDDE*, 14:404–7. In the same vein, see his letter to Milton Eisenhower, October 9, 1953, 576–79.

27. *New York Times*, October 24, 1953; *Washington Post*, October 24, 1953.

28. Text of Brownell's remarks in Chicago, *New York Times*, November 7, 1953.

29. *New York Times*, November 8, 1953; Adams, *Firsthand Report*, 137; Marquis Childs, *Washington Post*, November 11, 1953; Walter Lippmann, "Brownell and McCarthy," *Washington Post*, December 15, 1953.

30. Press conference, November 11, 1953, *PPP: Dwight D. Eisenhower*, 757–65; James Reston, *New York Times*, November 11 and 12, 1953; see also comments of Arthur Krock, *New York Times*, November 14, 1953.

31. *New York Times*, November 17, 1953.

32. Press conference, November 18, 1953, *PPP: Dwight D. Eisenhower*, 781–82, 788–89.

33. Text of McCarthy's speech, *New York Times*, November 25, 1953.

34. Stewart Alsop, "The McCarthy Challenge," *Washington Post*, November 27, 1953. Hagerty comment in Papers as President, Ann Whitman File, Ann Whitman Diary Series, November 27, 1953, box 1, DDEL.

35. C. D. Jackson notes, November 27 and 30, December 2, 1953, C. D. Jackson Papers, box 68, DDEL; Dulles-Jackson telephone conversation, December 1, 1953, Dulles Papers, Chronological Series, box 6, DDEL; *New York Times*, December 2, 1953; press conference, December 2, 1953, *PPP: Dwight D. Eisenhower*, 800–803. For reaction to Eisenhower's message, *New York Times, Washington Post, Wall Street Journal*, December 3, 1953.

36. For deft portraits of some key senators from the era, see McPherson, *A Political Education*, 27–84, Knowland remark on 74. On the tragedy of Senator Lester Hunt, see Abell, *Drew Pearson Diaries*, 321–25; Johnson, *The Lavender Scare*, 141.

37. For details, see Tananbaum, *The Bricker Amendment Controversy*.

38. Nixon, *RN*, 140; Mazo, *Richard Nixon*, 132–33.

39. Memorandum for the NSC, December 28, 1953, "Review of Internal Security Legislation," in Young, *Documentary History of the Dwight D. Eisenhower Presidency*, vol. 6, document 4, pp. 25–44.

40. Ferrell, *The Diary of James C. Hagerty*, 20, 24; DDE Diary, Legislative Leadership Meeting, March 1, 1954, microfilm, reel 3, DDEL.

41. *New York Times*, March 4, 1954; press conference, March 4, 1954, *PPP: Dwight D. Eisenhower*, 288–97.

42. *Los Angeles Times*, March 4, 1954. For insightful analysis of the Eisenhower-McCarthy exchange, see James Reston, "Other Cheek Is Struck," *New York Times*, March 4, 1954.

43. Notes on Eisenhower phone call with Knowland, Diary, March 10, 1954, microfilm, reel 3, DDEL; Stevenson speech text, *Washington Post*, March 7, 1954; Walter Lippmann, "The Unappeaseable Aggressor," *Washington Post*, March 11, 1954. Adviser C. D. Jackson was driven to despair by McCarthy's behavior and the failure of the Senate leaders to curb him. He wrote to Nixon, with whom he had a close relationship, that McCarthy's antics "had done more fundamental harm" to the president than anything yet in his term in office and that Eisenhower had lost all the momentum he had gained in December 1953 with his "Atoms for Peace" speech. Unless the president took command and disciplined his party, he could expect certain defeat in the November 1954 congressional elections and lose any hope of pushing a Republican agenda through Congress. C. D. Jackson to Vice President Nixon, March 9, 1954, C. D. Jackson Papers, box 80, DDEL.

44. Leviero in *New York Times*, March 11, 1954; press conference March 10, 1954, *PPP: Dwight D. Eisenhower*, 299–309; Ferrell, *The Diary of James C. Hagerty*, 28.

45. Nixon text in *New York Times*, March 14, 1954. For Nixon's account of the speech and its impact, see *RN*, 144–47.

46. The Adams report can be seen in manuscript in Fred Seaton Papers, box 5, DDEL.

The text that was leaked to the press had been heavily altered and cleaned up by Seaton, who was assistant secretary of defense and was acting in coordination with the White House, especially Sherman Adams, Herbert Brownell, and Assistant Attorney General William Rogers. See Joseph and Stewart Alsop, "McCarthy-Cohn-Schine Tale Was Half-Told," *Washington Post*, March 15, 1954.

47. Adams, *Firsthand Report*, 145. Brownell confirms the direct role the White House played in compiling and leaking the report (*Advising Ike*, 257–59). The version the press received can be seen in *Washington Post*, March 13, 1954. The release of the report was seen as part of a "full-scale attack" by the White House on McCarthy: *New York Times*, March 14, 1954.

48. Letter to Bill Robinson, March 12, 1954, and to Swede Hazlett, April 27, 1954, *PDDE*, 15:949–50, 1042–45; press conference, May 12, 1954, *PPP: Dwight D. Eisenhower*, 467.

49. "Letter to the Secretary of Defense Directing Him to Withhold Certain Information from the Senate Committee on Government Operations," May 17, 1954, *PPP: Dwight D. Eisenhower*, 483–84; Ferrell, *The Diary of James C. Hagerty*, 53. For Eisenhower's preparation on the issue of executive privilege, see notes of phone call with Rogers, March 2, 1954; letter from Paul Hoffman, March 25, 1954; phone call with Herbert Brownell, May 5, 1954, all in DDE Diary, microfilm reel 3, DDEL. Also see exchange of letters with Henry Cabot Lodge, May 7 and 10, 1954, *PDDE*, 15:1062–63; Brownell, *Advising Ike*, 251–61.

50. Press conference, May 19, 1954, *PPP: Dwight D. Eisenhower*, 490.

51. "Address at the Columbia University National Bicentennial Dinner," May 31, 1954, *PPP: Dwight D. Eisenhower*, 517–25; on applause, Ferrell, *The Diary of James C. Hagerty*, 59.

52. *New York Times*, June 2, 1954.

53. For a geographical breakdown of the senators who voted on the censure resolution, see Griffith, *The Politics of Fear*, 312–13.

54. Ferrell, *The Diary of James C. Hagerty*, 43.

55. Ferrell, *The Diary of James C. Hagerty*, 81. For the transcript of the investigation, see *In the Matter of J. Robert Oppenheimer*.

56. "The President's News Conference," June 2, 1954, American Presidency Project, http://www.presidency.ucsb.edu/ws/index.php?pid=9907; "Statement by the President upon Signing the Communist Control Act of 1954," August 24, 1954, *American Presidency Project*, http://www.presidency.ucsb.edu/ws/?pid=9998.

CHAPTER 7: DARK ARTS FOR A COLD WAR

Epigraph: Papers as President, DDE Diaries Series, October 8, 1953, box 4, DDEL.

1. Tim Weiner's best-selling history of the CIA, for example, asserted that Eisenhower's entire cold war strategy was based on nothing more than "nuclear bombs and covert action"; his book also places heavy emphasis on the Iran and Guatemala coups

(*Legacy of Ashes*, 84). Numerous other writers on the 1950s have also succumbed to the temptation of caricature. Blanche Wiesen Cook's analysis of Eisenhower's presidency, she confessed, was so clouded by the evidence she discovered of "covert operations, secrecy, dirty tricks and counterinsurgency" in his administration that she had trouble seeing any other dimension of his leadership. "Eisenhower's legacy is counterinsurgency and political warfare," she regretfully concluded (*The Declassified Eisenhower*, xvi, xix). Stephen Kinzer, an able journalist and chronicler of the dark side of American foreign policy, asserted that "Eisenhower wished to wage a new kind of war," based on secrecy and subversion. "With the Dulles brothers as his right and left arms, he led the United States into a secret global conflict that raged throughout his presidency" (*The Brothers*, 114). Tom Wicker's brief portrait of Eisenhower was deeply colored by the fact that Eisenhower "encouraged infamy in Iran and outrage in Guatemala" (*Dwight D. Eisenhower*, 133).

2. For details on Dulles's wartime life, see Grose, *Gentleman Spy*, chapters 7–10. Dulles provides his own biographical sketch in *The Craft of Intelligence*, 1–5. The richness of Dulles's reports from Bern can be sampled in Petersen, *From Hitler's Doorstep*. A mostly admiring account of Dulles was penned by Wayne G. Jackson in 1973 as part of a CIA secret internal history, *Allen Welsh Dulles as Director of Central Intelligence*.

3. NSC 10/2, June 18, 1948, *FRUS 1945–50, Emergence of the National Intelligence Establishment*: 713–15; Rudgers, *Creating the Secret State*, 19–46.

4. CIA, "Office of Policy Coordination, 1948–1952," DDO, tinyurl.galegroup.com/tinyurl/4mTQx9. On Frank Wisner, see "Address by CIA Director Richard Helms, at Memorial for Frank Gardiner Wisner," January 29, 1971, Langley, Virginia, in DDO, tinyurl.galegroup.com/tinyurl/4mTVr7; Powers, *The Man Who Kept the Secrets*, 24, 32, 48–51, 73–77. Wisner suffered health problems in the mid-1950s and had a breakdown in the mid-1960s. In 1965 he took his own life.

5. The Central Intelligence Agency Act of 1949, Public Law 81–110, *Legis Works*, http://www.legisworks.org/congress/81/publaw-110.pdf.

6. CIA, "DCI Historical Series: Organizational History of the Central Intelligence Agency, 1950–1953," available by subscription at Digital National Security Archive.

7. NSC 10/5, October 23, 1951, and Walter Bedell Smith to the NSC, April 23, 1952, *FRUS, 1950–55: The Intelligence Community*, 206–8, 250–54.

8. CIA memo for the president, March 1, 1953, and NSC Minutes, March 4, 1953, *FRUS 1952–54*, 10:689–701.

9. CIA, "Analysis of Iranian Political Situation," October 12, 1951, DDO, tinyurl.galegroup.com/tinyurl/4mTXg6.

10. William Roger Louis, "Britain and the Overthrow of the Mossadeq Government," in Gasiorowski and Byrne, *Mohammad Mossadeq*, 126–77.

11. CIA, "National Intelligence Estimate 75: Probable Developments in Iran through 1953," November 13, 1952, DDO, tinyurl.galegroup.com/tinyurl/4mTZp3. See also CIA, "Prospects for Survival of Mossadeq Regime in Iran," October 14, 1952, DDO,

tinyurl.galegroup.com/tinyurl/4mTbg4; National Security Council, NSC 136/1, "United States Policy regarding the Present Situation in Iran," Top Secret Report, November 20, 1952, National Security Archive, http://www2.gwu.edu/~nsarchiv /NSAEBB/NSAEBB126/iran521120.pdf.

12. CIA History Staff, "The Battle for Iran," a secret internal study of the coup prepared in 1974, declassified in 2014, National Security Archive, http://www2.gwu .edu/~nsarchiv/NSAEBB/NSAEBB476/. See also the secret CIA report prepared in 1954 by Dr. Donald Wilber, which confirmed Bedell Smith's role in first authorizing initial planning, "Clandestine Service History: Overthrow of Premier Mossadeq of Iran," March 1954, revealed and published by the *New York Times* in 2000, http://www .nytimes.com/library/world/mideast/041600iran-cia-index.html. See also Woodhouse, *Something Ventured*, 120–35.

13. "National Intelligence Estimate 76," January 15, 1953, *FRUS 1952–54*, 9: pt. 1, document 114.

14. CIA History Staff, "The Battle for Iran," 26; date of official approval given in CIA, "Clandestine Service History," 18. Kermit Roosevelt's memoir *Countercoup* provides an unreliable and self-centered account of the Iran coup and should be supplemented by the far more revealing and candid CIA assessments.

15. CIA, "Clandestine Service History." One example of the propaganda the CIA circulated has been published by the National Security Archive. It denounces Mossadeq's use of spies and internal repression to create an authoritarian dictatorship in Iran. "Mossadeq's Spy Service," undated, http://www2.gwu.edu/~nsarchiv/NSAEBB /NSAEBB435/docs/Doc%2021%20-%201953-00-00%20144%20propaganda%20 -%20spy%20service.pdf.

16. The American ambassador in Baghdad, Burton Y. Berry, met with the shah on August 17 and found him "worn from three sleepless nights" and puzzled as to why the plan to oust Mossadeq had failed. Berry to State Department, August 17, 1953, National Security Archive, http://www2.gwu.edu/~nsarchiv/NSAEBB/NSAEBB477/docs /Doc%206%20—%201953-08-17%20Baghdad%20cable%2092%20re%20Shah%20 meeting%20with%20Berry.pdf.

17. For a controversial account that discounts the CIA role in stirring up the anti-Mossadeq crowd, see Takeyh, "What Really Happened in Iran."

18. Eisenhower received updates from General Cabell describing the situation in Tehran as it was unfolding. Gen. Charles Cabell to the president, "To Stevens for the President: Comment on the Iranian Situation," undated (probably August 19, 1953), Papers as President, Ann Whitman File, International Series, box 29, DDEL; minutes of the NSC meeting, August 27, 1953, Papers as President, Ann Whitman File, NSC Series, box 4, DDEL. An excellent account of the coup is Mark J. Gasiorowski, "The 1953 Coup d'État against Mossadeq," in Gasiorowski and Byrne, *Mohammad Mossadeq*, 227–60.

19. NSC Planning Board, "U.S. Policy toward Iran," December 21, 1953, White House Office, Office of the Special Assistant for National Security Affairs, Records, NSC

Series, Policy Papers Subseries, box 8, DDEL; Nixon in the NSC, December 24, 1953, Papers as President, Ann Whitman File, NSC Series, box 5, DDEL.

20. Ike's public remark in a speech on October 28, 1954, in *PPP: Dwight D. Eisenhower*, 981; Papers as President, DDE Diaries Series, October 8, 1953, box 4, DDEL (passage redacted in DDE published papers); letter to Edgar Eisenhower, November 8, 1954, *PDDE*, 15:1387. Eisenhower's 1963 memoir gives an utterly misleading account of events in Iran in the 1951–53 period (*Mandate for Change*, 159–66).

21. Two essential studies provide the foundation for these pages: Gleijeses, *Shattered Hope*, and Cullather, *Secret History*. Cullather's book was written as a classified internal CIA history and released to the public—with many passages redacted by CIA censors—five years later.

22. *New York Times*, May 21, 1952. The degree to which Arbenz aligned himself with the goals of the communists is a subject of debate. Richard Immerman's pioneering history, published in 1982, refutes the Eisenhower administration's argument that Arbenz was a communist fellow traveler (*The CIA in Guatemala*, 183). Piero Gleijeses, drawing on a much wider array of sources, argues that Arbenz was in fact imbued with socialist ideas and sympathetic to the goals of the Guatemalan communists. (*Shattered Hope*, 134–48).

23. Cullather, *Secret History*, 28–32.

24. "Communism in the Free World: Capabilities of the Communist Party, Guatemala," January 1, 1953, *FRUS, Guatemala*, 56–66; letter from Schoenfeld to Armstrong, February 13, 1953, *FRUS, Guatemala*, 67–70; NSC 144/1, "United States Objectives and Courses of Action with Respect to Latin America," *FRUS, 1952–54*, 4:6–10.

25. "NSC Guatemala," draft policy paper prepared in the Bureau of the Inter-American Affairs, August 19, 1953, *FRUS 1952–54*, 4:1077–86; *New York Times*, August 1 and 14, 1953.

26. George Morgan, "Memorandum for the Record," August 12, 1953; "Memorandum," J. C. King to Allen Dulles, August 17, 1953; "Memorandum," King to Wisner, August 27, 1953; "Memorandum for the Record," September 1, 1953; "Memorandum for the Record," September 11, 1953, all in *FRUS, Guatemala*, 86–89, 91–94, 102–9.

27. Wisner's September 11 memorandum and minutes of his September 15 conversation with Dulles, *FRUS, Guatemala*, 102–10.

28. "Draft Memorandum for the Record, November 12, 1953, and "Contact Report," November 16, 1953, *FRUS, Guatemala*, 141–36. Wiley quoted in *New York Times*, October 17, 1953. Dulles to Wisner, December 9, 1953, *FRUS, Guatemala*, 155–56.

29. Wisner to PBSUCCESS Headquarters, June 30, 1954, *FRUS, Guatemala*, 409.

30. Discussion in NSC, July 2, 1954, Papers as President, Ann Whitman File, NSC Series, box 5, DDEL.

31. NSC 5412, March 15, 1954, *FRUS, 1950–55: The Intelligence Community*, 475–78. Compare to NSC 10/2, June 18, 1948, *FRUS, 1945–50: Emergence of the Intelligence Establishment*, 713–15.

32. NSC 5408, "Draft Policy of Continental Defense," *FRUS 1952–54*, 2: pt. 1, 609–24.

This anxiety about the increase in Soviet weapons capabilities dominated NSC discussions in mid-1954. See NSC 5422/1, August 7, 1954, *FRUS 1952–54*, 2: pt. 1, 715–31.

33. The first inquiry to Doolittle was on July 2, 1954, in a letter from the White House to Gen. Lauris Norstad, supreme commander of allied powers, Europe, in DDO, tinyurl.galegroup.com/tinyurl/4mdYi0. Eisenhower's approval, July 13, 1954 in DDO, tinyurl.galegroup.com/tinyurl/4mddo4; Eisenhower's directive to Allen Dulles, July 26, 1954, in DDO, tinyurl.galegroup.com/tinyurl/4mdfxX. "Report on the Covert Activities of the CIA," September 30, 1954, CIA Reading Room, http://www.foia.cia .gov/sites/default/files/document_conversions/45/doolittle_report.pdf.

34. Conversation notes, Doolittle and Eisenhower, October 19, 1954, DDO, tinyurl.gale group.com/tinyurl/4mdot7.

35. Killian, *Sputnik, Scientists and Eisenhower*, 68–69, 71. On the purpose and members of the Killian committee, see James Killian to Donald Quarles, September 2, 1954, White House Office, Office of the Special Assistant for National Security Affairs: Records, 1952–61, Special Assistant Series, Subject Subseries, box 7, DDEL. For a useful review, see Damms, "James Killian, the Technological Capabilities Panel, and the Emergence of Eisenhower's 'Scientific-Technological Elite.'"

36. "The Report to the President of the Technological Capabilities Panel of the Science Advisory Committee: Meeting the Threat of a Surprise Attack," February 14, 1955, and NSC memorandum, "Characteristics of the Timetable of Change in Our Military Position Relative to Russia," November 2, 1955, White House Office, Office of the Special Assistant for National Security Affairs: Records, 1952–61, Special Assistant Series, Subject Subseries, box 16, DDEL; Killian, *Sputnik, Scientists, and Eisenhower*, 71–76.

37. "Report of the TCP," February 14, 1955, and memorandum of discussion, NSC, March 17, 1955, *FRUS, 1955–57, 19: National Security*: 41–56, 63–68. On the ICBM program and the sudden surge in that research effort, see Gainor, "The Atlas and the Air Force."

38. R. Cargill Hall, the emeritus chief historian of the National Reconnaissance Office, has written extensively on overflights. See especially "Clandestine Victory: Eisenhower and Overhead Reconnaissance in the Cold War," in Showalter, *Forging the Shield*; Hall and Laurie, "Denied Territory"; Hall and Laurie, *Early Cold War Overflights*. In that collection, see in particular the paper by Gen. Andrew J. Goodpaster, "Cold War Overflights: A View from the White House," 37–46. A lively and well-informed survey of the U-2 is Beschloss, *Mayday*. For the mostly fruitless experiments with drifting high-altitude reconnaissance balloons set off over the USSR, see Peebles, *The Moby Dick Project*.

39. Brugioni, *Eyes in the Sky*, 87.

40. Pedlow and Welzenbach, *The Central Intelligence Agency and Overhead Reconnaissance*, chapter 1; Killian, *Sputnik, Scientists, and Eisenhower*, 82; Edwin Land to Allen Dulles, November 5, 1954, *FRUS, 1950–55, Intelligence Community*, 563–68; memo-

randum by the DCI, November 24, 1954, and notes on a meeting with the president and Allen Dulles, November 24, 1954, in *FRUS, 1950–55: Intelligence Community*, 571–74; memorandum of conference with the president by Andrew Goodpaster, November 24, 1954 and memorandum of conversation with Senator Knowland, November 24, 1954 (in which Ike spoke of "knowing so many things"), Papers as President, Ann Whitman Diary Series, box 3, DDEL.

41. Eisenhower comments in NSC meeting, December 1, 1955, *FRUS 1955–57*, 19:166–70.

CHAPTER 8: ASIAN DOMINOES

Epigraph: Press conference, February 10, 1954, *FRUS, 1952–54*, 13: pt. 1, 1035.

1. *Los Angeles Times*, November 3, 1953.

2. *Chicago Tribune*, November 1, 1953. Nixon's account of his trip is in *RN*, 119–37. See also Gellman, *The President and the Apprentice*, 170–92.

3. Nixon, *RN*, 136.

4. "U.S. Policy toward Communist China," NSC 166/1, and discussion by the NSC on November 5, 1954, *FRUS, 1952–54*, 14: pt. 1, 265–306.

5. For the idea of Asia as a single zone of conflict, see the remarks of Gen. Walter Bedell Smith to the Senate Foreign Relations Committee. "I have always visualized Asia as one theater," he said, where Korea and Indochina were the two "flanks" and Taiwan formed the "central area." Walter Bedell Smith testimony, February 16, 1954, U.S. Senate, *Executive Sessions of the Senate Foreign Relations Committee*, vol. VI, 130.

6. Divine, *Eisenhower and the Cold War*, 51. For accounts that stress Ike's reluctance to use military force in Indochina in 1954, see Herring and Immerman, "Eisenhower, Dulles, and Dien Bien Phu"; Ambrose, *Eisenhower: The President*, 173–85; Gibbons, *The U.S. Government and the Vietnam War*, 174–227. One scholar, Melanie Billings-Yun, *Decision against War*, asserts that Eisenhower wanted to avoid intervention but did not wish to bear the political burden of appearing weak in the global fight against communism. So he prevaricated and delayed, avoiding a decision on the matter while claiming that congressional reluctance tied his hands.

7. Logevall, *Embers of War*, 473. Logevall's chapter on the crucial debate about intervention is "America Wants In," 454–80. For a similar argument, see Prados, *The Sky Would Fall*.

8. For an articulate expression of this view of Eisenhower's long-term responsibility for the Vietnam War, see Anderson, *Trapped by Success*.

9. Dulles speech, January 27, 1953, *New York Times*, January 28, 1953.

10. Joint Chiefs paper, "Current Situation in Indochina," December 5, 1952, and memo by John M. Allison for Dulles, January 28, 1953, *FRUS 1952–54*, 13: pt. 1, 311–12, 366–71.

11. Radford remark in memorandum by Allison, February 4, 1953, *FRUS 1952–54*, 13: pt. 1, 384–86.

12. Memorandum of conversation, March 24, 1953, and Saigon embassy to State Department, May 20, 1953, *FRUS 1952–54*, 13: pt. 1, 419–20, 571–75.

13. Ambassador Dillon in Paris to Dulles, May 23, 1953, *FRUS 1952–54*, 13: pt. 1, 579–81, note 1, 590.

14. *Los Angeles Times*, June 23, 1953. Ike reached out to GOP hawks through Nixon to assure them of the president's opposition to communist China's entry into the United Nations. See Eisenhower letter to Richard Nixon, June 2, 1953, Papers as President, Ann Whitman File, International Series, box 10, DDEL.

15. State-JCS discussions, July 17, 1953, *FRUS 1952–54*, 13: pt. 1, 683–89.

16. Dillon to Dulles, July 29, 1953, *FRUS 1952–54*, 13: pt. 1, 701–3.

17. Memo by Robert Bowie, August 5, 1953; report to the NSC, August 5, 1953; NSC discussion, August 6, 1953, all in *FRUS 1952–54*, 13: pt. 1, 713–14, 714–17, 718–19. For Eisenhower's later approval, NSC discussion, September 9, 1953, *FRUS 1952–54*, 13: pt. 1, 780–89.

18. Dulles at September 9, 1953, NSC discussion, *FRUS 1952–54*, 13: pt. 1, 781, 783.

19. *New York Times*, August 5, 1953. After the speech, in a most delicious act of foreshadowing, Ike went to visit the Boeing aircraft plant in Seattle and watched in awe as a new B-52 Stratofortress made three low-altitude passes over the airfield. Powered by eight turbojet engines and designed to fly at 50,000 feet, beyond the reach of enemy fighters, the B-52 would become the dreadful symbol of American airpower in Vietnam, where it was deployed with lethal effect from the mid-1960s on.

20. Speech of September 2, 1953, *FRUS 1952–54*, 13: pt. 1, 747.

21. "National Intelligence Estimate," December 1, 1953, *FRUS 1952–54*, 13: pt. 1, 894–95; Spector, *The United States Army in Vietnam*, 182–90. For an excellent discussion of French motives in seizing and fortifying Dien Bien Phu, see Logevall, *Embers of War*, 381–86.

22. NSC meeting, December 23, 1953, Papers as President, NSC Series, box 5, DDEL.

23. NSC meeting, January 8, 1954, *FRUS 1952–54*, 13: pt. 1, 947–54; Spector, *The United States Army in Vietnam*, 195.

24. Notes of meeting with legislative leaders, February 8, 1954, and press conference, February 10, 1954, *FRUS 1952–54*, 13: pt. 1, 1023–25, 1034–35.

25. Memorandum by Macarthur, January 27, 1954; Dulles to Eisenhower, February 9, 1954; Dulles memo, February 18, 1954; NSC meeting, February 26, 1954, all in *FRUS 1952–54*, 13: pt. 1, 998–1000, 1025, 1057, 1079–81.

26. Consul in Hanoi to State Department, January 15, 1954; Ambassador Heath to State, February 22, 1954; NSC meeting, March 4, 1954, all in *FRUS, 1952–54*, 13: pt. 1, 964–66, 1064–67, 1093–97.

27. For a superb account of these anxious weeks, see Logevall, *Embers of War*, 445–53; also see Roy, *The Battle of Dien Bien Phu*; Fall, *Hell in a Very Small Place*; Morgan, *Valley of Death*; Simpson, *Dien Bien Phu*.

28. Heath to State, March 16, 1954; NSC meeting, March 18, 1953; Heath to State, March 20, 1954, all in *FRUS 1952–54*, 13: pt. 1, 1125–26, 1132–33, 1135.

29. Memorandum, March 21, 1954, *FRUS 1952–54*, 13: pt. 1, 1137–40.

30. The memoirs of the two protagonists differ somewhat on the nature of their March 26 conversation. "This was a proposition whose importance did not escape me," Ély wrote drolly (*Mémoires*, 76). Radford thought Ély overstated the case (Jurika, *From Pearl Harbor to Vietnam*, 390–97).

31. Memorandum, Eisenhower-Dulles conversation, March 24, 1954, Dulles Papers, White House Memorandum Series, box 1, DDEL.

32. NSC meeting, March 25, 1954, *FRUS 1952–54*, 13: pt. 1, 1163–68.

33. Memorandum by C. D. Jackson, January 18, 1954, *FRUS 1952–54*, 13: pt. 1, 981–82; Memorandum for the president by Walter Bedell Smith, January 18, 1954, Papers as President, Ann Whitman Diary Series, box 2, DDEL; Walter Bedell Smith testimony, February 16, 1954, U.S. Senate, *Executive Sessions of the Senate Foreign Relations Committee*, vol. VI, 113–16.

34. Text of March 29 speech in *New York Times*, March 30, 1954. Privately Dulles described the speech as necessary "to puncture the sentiment for appeasement before Geneva" (Dulles telephone conversation with Senator William Knowland, March 30, 1954, Dulles Papers, Chronological Series, box 7, DDEL).

35. "The President's News Conference," March 31, 1954, American Presidency Project, http://www.presidency.ucsb.edu/ws/index.php?pid=10196. Historian Fredrik Logevall contends that the Dulles speech was a call to arms: "It's hard to avoid the conclusion that the two men had made up their minds: all of Indochina would have to be held, with direct American intervention if necessary" (*Embers of War*, 463). By contrast, Billings-Yun argues that the Dulles speech in fact hugely overstated American willingness to use force and undermined Eisenhower's more moderate policy (*Decision against War*, 60).

36. Dulles-DDE telephone conversation, and Dulles-Radford telephone conversation, April 1, 1954, Dulles Papers, Chronological Series, box 7, DDEL.

37. Memorandum, Eisenhower-Dulles conversation, April 2, 1954, *FRUS 1952–54*, 13: pt. 1, 1210–11; also in Dulles Papers, White House Memorandum Series, box 1, DDEL. Ike liked deception and wanted to keep his enemies guessing about just how far he might go to protect noncommunist states in Asia. His close adviser Gen. Walter Bedell Smith admitted to the Senate Foreign Relations Committee in February 1954 that the administration had "no intention of putting ground soldiers into Indochina," but he hated having to say so in public; he would rather keep the Chinese guessing. "I wish to God that we could leave that suspicion or that fear in their minds." Walter Bedell Smith testimony, February 16, 1954, U.S. Senate, *Executive Sessions of the Senate Foreign Relations Committee*, vol. VI, 111.

38. Memorandum for the Secretary's File on meeting of April 3 with congressional leaders, April 5, 1954, Dulles Papers, Subject Series, box 9, DDEL.

39. Chalmers Roberts, *Washington Post*, June 7, 1954, and *Reporter*, September 14, 1954. Roberts later admitted that McCormack was playing politics with the issue: he wanted the Democrats to look responsible and he wanted to discredit Dulles and the Republicans. Gibbons, *The U.S. Government and the Vietnam War*, 189–95.

40. Dulles-DDE telephone conversation, April 3, 1954, Dulles Papers, Chronological Series, box 7, DDEL.

41. Eisenhower to Churchill, April 4, 1954, *FRUS 1952–54*, 13: pt. 1, 1238–41.

42. Dillon to Dulles, April 5, 1954, *FRUS 1952–54*, 13: pt. 1, 1236–38.

43. Dulles-DDE telephone conversation, April 5, 1954, Dulles Papers, Chronological Series, box 7, DDEL.

44. NSC meeting, April 6, 1954, *FRUS 1952–54*, 13: pt. 1, 1250–65.

45. NSC meeting, April 6, 1954, *FRUS 1952–54*, 13: pt. 1, 1257; Cutler memo of conversation with Smith, Radford, and Allen Dulles, April 8, 1954, White House Office, NSC Staff: Papers, Executive Secretary's Subject File, box 17, DDEL.

46. Press conference, April 7, 1954, *FRUS 1952–54*, 13: pt. 1, 1280–81.

47. For the outcry about the H-bomb test, see *Washington Post*, March 26 and 27, 1954; *Los Angeles Times*, March 14, 1954; Jones, *After Hiroshima*, 199–234.

48. Memorandum by MacArthur, April 11, 1954, *FRUS 1952–54*, 13: pt. 1, 1307–9. For a vivid account of the Dulles-Eden conversations in London, see Logevall, *Embers of War*, 484–91.

49. Eden, *Full Circle*, 92–93; Jones, *After Hiroshima*, 194–95.

50. Dulles telegrams, April 23, 1954, and Dulles and Radford meeting with Eden, April 24, 1954, *FRUS, 1952–54*, 13: pt. 1, 1374, 1375, 1386–91. Undersecretary Bedell Smith kept Ike informed: see his notes of his telephone calls to the president, April 24 and April 26, 1954, Papers as President, DDE Diary Series, box 5, DDEL.

51. Eden, *Full Circle*, 99–106. The detailed to-and-fro of British diplomacy in this period is memorably captured in the diary of Eden's private secretary: Shuckburgh, *Descent to Suez*, esp. 161–79; and see Logevall, *Embers of War*, 501–7.

52. Letter to Al Gruenther, April 26, 1954, and diary entry, April 27, 1954, Papers as President, DDE Diary Series, box 4, DDEL; letter to Swede Hazlett, April 27, 1954; Hagerty diary extract, April 26, 1954; meeting with legislative leaders, April 26, 1954, all in *FRUS 1952–54*, 13: pt. 2, 1426–27, 1410–12, 1412–14; Robert Cutler memorandum of conversation between Eisenhower, Dulles, Cutler, and Douglas MacArthur II, May 5, 1954, White House Office, Office of Special Assistant for National Security Affairs, Records, NSC Series, Briefing Notes Subseries, box 11, DDEL. In this discussion Dulles described the British as "scared to death" and "beguiled by the soft talk of the Russians."

53. NSC meeting, April 29, 1954, *FRUS 1952–54*, 13: pt. 2, 1431–45.

54. Joseph and Stewart Alsop, "Dien Bien Phu: Another Yorktown?," *Washington Post*, April 30, 1954; see their equally strident column, *Washington Post*, May 9, 1954. "For an Indochina Settlement," editorial, *Washington Post*, May 2, 1954; Knowland quoted in *New York Times*, May 5, 1954.

55. *New York Times* and *Washington Post*, May 7, 1954.

56. Editorial, *Washington Post*, May 4, 1954.

57. Text of Dulles address, *New York Times*, May 8, 1954. The speech received sharp criticism from the Alsops in their column, *Washington Post*, May 9, 1954.

58. Dulles press conference transcript, May 11, *New York Times*, May 12, 1954; Dulles testimony, May 12, 1954, U.S. Senate, *Executive Sessions of the Senate Foreign Relations Committee*, vol. VI, 257–81.

59. Chen, *Mao's China and the Cold War*, 138–44; Zhang, *Deng Xiaoping's Long War*, 17–18; Zhai, *China and the Vietnam Wars*, 57–64. For an account that stresses the North Vietnamese interest in accepting the deal on offer at Geneva, see Asselin, "The Democratic Republic of Vietnam and the 1954 Geneva Conference."

60. On Franco-American contacts about a renewed intervention scheme, see memorandum of conversation between Dulles and French ambassador Bonnet, May 8, 1954, Dulles Papers, Subject Series, box 9, DDEL. Memorandum of conversation between Dulles and Eisenhower, May 19, 1954, Dulles Papers, White House Memorandum series, box 1, DDEL; "Conference in the President's Office" between Eisenhower, Dulles, Robert Anderson, Admiral Radford, Douglas MacArthur II, and Robert Cutler, June 2, 1954, White House Office, Office of Special Assistant for National Security Affairs, Records, NSC Series, Briefing Notes Subseries, box 11, DDEL; "Talking Paper," June 4, 1954, Dulles Papers, Subject Series, box 9, DDEL. Dulles made such threats public in a speech on June 11 in the Los Angeles Biltmore Hotel. See *New York Times*, June 12, 1954. His remark to Smith is in a telegram dated June 14, 1954, Dulles Papers, Subject Series, box 9, DDEL.

61. Meetings with legislative leaders, June 23, 1954, in Papers as President, Legislative Meetings Series, box 1, DDEL. (See also the similar message Dulles delivered in the June 28 meeting with Knowland, minutes also in box 1). At the meeting Eisenhower rebutted the "Far Eastern Munich" charge: "Munich was giving away something without war. These people are giving up something as a result of defeat in war, which is quite a different thing." The press picked up the shift in policy, noting that the administration "is thinking largely of salvage, or a policy of limited loss," in Indochina. *New York Times*, June 24, 1954.

62. Dulles statement, July 23, 1954, Dulles Papers, Subject Series, box 9, DDEL.

63. NSC 5429, "Review of U.S. Policy in the Far East," August 4, 1954, and NSC meeting to discuss this policy, August 12, 1954, both in *FRUS 1952–54*, 12: pt. 1, 699–703, 724–33.

64. Chen, *Mao's China and the Cold War*, 167–70; Zhang, *Deterrence and Strategic Culture*, 189–99.

65. NSC meeting, September 12, 1954, *FRUS 1952–54*, 14: pt. 1, 613–24.

66. NSC meeting, September 9, 1954; Dulles memorandum for the president, September 12, 1954; NSC meeting, October 6, 1954, all in *FRUS, 1952–54*, 14: pt. 1, 583–95, 611–13, 689–701.

67. NSC meeting, September 12, 1954, *FRUS, 1952–54*, 14: pt. 1, 613–24.

68. Dulles memo, October 18, 1954, and NSC meeting, October 28, 1954, *FRUS 1952–54*, 14: pt. 1, 770–71, 803–9.

69. Memo of conversation, Dulles and Dr. George Yeh, Chinese foreign minister, January 19, 1955, and NSC meeting minutes, January 20, 1955, *FRUS 1955–57*, 2:49, 69–82.

70. NSC meeting minutes, January 20, 1955, *FRUS 1955–57*, 2:69–82.

71. Text of message to Congress, *FRUS 1955–57*, 2:115–19. The resolution was passed by the House on January 25 by 410 votes to 3; the Senate acted on January 28, voting 85–3 in favor.

72. Dulles speech, *Washington Post*, March 9, 1955; "The President's News Conference," March 16, 1955, American Presidency Project, http://www.presidency.ucsb.edu/ws /index.php?pid=10434; Nixon in *New York Times*, March 18, 1955. See also detailed analysis by Chang, *Friends and Enemies*, 116–42; Soman, *Double-Edged Sword*, 124–53.

73. See the careful analysis of Ike's nuclear brinkmanship in Sechser and Fuhrmann, *Nuclear Weapons and Coercive Diplomacy*, 188–94. For an especially critical assessment of Ike's handling of the Quemoy crisis, see Soman, *Double-Edged Sword*, 145–53.

74. DDE, *Mandate for Change*, 483.

CHAPTER 9: TAKING ON JIM CROW

Epigraph: Eisenhower letter to Adam Clayton Powell, June 6, 1953, in White House Central File, Official File, box 614, DDEL.

1. On Mrs. Bryant's changing story, see Sheila Weller, "The Missing Woman: How Author Timothy Tyson Found the Woman at the Center of the Emmett Till Case," *Vanity Fair*, January 26, 2017; Tyson, *The Blood of Emmett Till*.

2. *Chicago Tribune*, September 2, 1955; *Washington Post* and *Chicago Tribune*, September 4, 1955; *Chicago Defender*, September 10 and 17, 1955; *Jet*, September 15, 1955. The details of the case are very ably laid out in Metress, *The Lynching of Emmett Till*.

3. *Washington Post* and *Chicago Tribune*, September 4, 1955; *New York Times*, September 8, 1955.

4. A perceptive contemporary commentary was written by journalist John Popham, "Racial Issues Stirred by Mississippi Killing," *New York Times*, September 18, 1955. The confession was published in *Look*, January 24, 1956.

5. *Universal Military Training: Hearings before the Committee on Armed Services, United States Senate*, 80th Congress, Second Session, April 3, 1948. The testimony is on 985–1013; the key passages on segregation are on 995–98.

6. Lawson, *To Secure These Rights*.

7. These quotations come from various digests of speeches on civil rights that Eisenhower made in the 1952 campaign. See Maxwell Rabb Papers, boxes 5, 6, and 44, DDEL.

8. "Annual Message to Congress on the State of the Union," February 2, 1953, Dwight D. Eisenhower Presidential Library, Museum and Boyhood Home, http://www.eisen hower.archives.gov/all_about_ike/speeches/1953_state_of_the_union.pdf.

9. Brownell, *Advising Ike*, 186–87. The Supreme Court case was *District of Columbia v. John R. Thompson Co., Inc.*, 346 U.S. 100 (1953). On the Justice Department brief, see *New York Times*, March 11, 1953; on Thurgood Marshall's praise, *New York Times*, March 12, 1953; on the decision, *New York Times*, June 9, 1953. A report from Samuel

Spencer, president of the Board of Commissioners of the District of Columbia, summarized subsequent progress made in the capital. Spencer to Eisenhower, November 25, 1953, White House Central File, Official File, box 239, DDEL.

10. Press conference, March 19, 1953, *PPP: Dwight D. Eisenhower*, 108.

11. Stevens to Hagerty, March 20, 1953, Young, *Documentary History of the Dwight D. Eisenhower Presidency*, 1:4–7.

12. Powell's public letter of June 3, 1953, White House Central File, Official File, box 614, DDEL.

13. Eisenhower's reply to Powell, June 6, 1953, and Powell's reply to Eisenhower, June 10, 1953, White House Central File, Official File, box 614, DDEL. The African American press also gave wide coverage to the exchange: see *Norfolk (VA) Journal and Guide*, June 6, 1953; *New York Amsterdam News*, June 13, 1953; *Chicago Defender*, June 20, 1953; *Pittsburgh Courier*, June 27, 1953. On Rabb's role, see Donovan, *Eisenhower*, 154–58.

14. Charles C. Thomas, undersecretary of the navy, "Segregation in Naval Activities," June 23, 1953; Navy Secretary Robert Anderson to Eisenhower, n.d., [November 1953]; statement by Eisenhower, November 11, 1953, all in White House Central File, Official File, box 614, DDEL. These matters can be followed more fully in MacGregor, *Integration of the Armed Forces*, 473–500.

15. Eisenhower to Nixon, August 15, 1953, Papers as President, Ann Whitman File, DDE Diary Series, box 3, DDEL.

16. Eisenhower to Nixon, September 4, 1953, Papers as President, Ann Whitman File, Administration Series, box 28, DDEL; Walter White in *New York Amsterdam News*, August 22, 1953, and *Chicago Defender*, September 12, 1953.

17. Diary entry, July 24, 1953, *PDDE*, 14:418. In an effort to explain his moderate position to Byrnes, the president wrote the governor a letter arguing that in desegregating military bases and setting up the Government Contracts Committee, the president was fulfilling his "oath of office." But Ike signaled that he had no desire to trespass on states' rights. Byrnes would not be mollified. He replied that while no one could doubt the supremacy of federal power in a military installation such as the Charleston Navy Yard, "there will be differences of opinion as to the wisdom of your decision," which went further than anything Truman had proposed. But Byrnes directly rebutted Eisenhower's claim that the Government Contracts Committee was merely an advisory board. "The Federal government purchases about one-fourth of our national product," Byrnes wrote. If the government now mandates certain practices of all its contractors that are not mandated by the states, then clearly "the executive would be usurping the powers of the Congress." Byrnes declared that this new government overreach left him "frightened." This exchange was only the start of a long, angry conflict between Eisenhower and the leading men of the South. Eisenhower to Byrnes, August 14, 1953, and Byrnes to Eisenhower, August 27, 1953, Papers as President, Ann Whitman File, Name Series, box 3, DDEL.

18. *Plessy v. Ferguson*, 163 U.S. 538 (1896).

19. *McLaurin v. Oklahoma State Regents*, 339 U.S. 637 (1950), decided June 5, 1950. The second case, decided the same day, compelled the University of Texas Law School to admit a black plaintiff. *Sweatt v. Painter*, 339 U.S. 629 (1950).

20. On Marshall's decision to challenge segregation in public schools, see Patterson, *Brown v. Board of Education*, 21–45.

21. Nichols, *A Matter of Justice*, 52, shows the depth of concern within the Court; see also Kluger, *Simple Justice*, 617. Chalmers M. Roberts article in *Washington Post*, June 9, 1953, suggested a divided and uncertain Court. A careful account of the internal debates on shaping the Eisenhower position on *Brown* is Mayer, "With Much Deliberation and Some Speed." Brownell suggests in his memoir that the Court did indeed want to know where the new president stood on the matter of *Plessy* (*Advising Ike*, 189).

22. "Memorandum for the Record," August 19, 1953, Papers as President, Ann Whitman File, Administration Series, box 8, DDEL; Brownell, *Advising Ike*, 189–90.

23. *Washington Post*, November 28, 1953. Selections from many of the key documents can be consulted in Martin, *Brown v. Board of Education*, including Brownell's brief, 165–68.

24. Warren, *Memoirs*, 260; Brownell, *Advising Ike*, 119, 165.

25. Eisenhower spelled out his thinking in a long diary entry and in a letter to his brother Milton. See diary entry, October 8, 1953, and letter to Milton Eisenhower, October 9, 1953, *PDDE*, 14:567–68, 576–77.

26. Brownell, *Advising Ike*, 165–68.

27. Telephone call notes, November 16, 1953, Ann Whitman File, DDE Diary Series, box 5, DDEL.

28. Robert F. Kennon to Eisenhower, November 20, 1953, and James Byrnes to Eisenhower, November 20, 1953, White House Central Files, Official File, box 614, DDEL.

29. *Pittsburgh Courier*, December 5, 1953; *New York Times*, November 28, 1953.

30. Eisenhower phone call with Brownell, December 2, 1953, Ann Whitman File, DDE Diary Series, box 5, DDEL; Eisenhower to Byrnes, letter backdated December 1, 1953, Ann Whitman File, Name Series, box 3, DDEL.

31. *Brown v. Board of Education of Topeka*, 347 U.S. 483 (1954). The inside account of how the Court arrived at this decision is carefully detailed by Kluger, *Simple Justice*, 660–702.

32. The assertion made by Tom Wicker that Warren had "received no help at all from" the Eisenhower administration in helping prepare the *Brown* opinion is demonstrably false (*Dwight D. Eisenhower*, 52).

33. Wilkins and Mathews, *Standing Fast*, 214–15.

34. "Let's Give Thanks," *Pittsburgh Courier*, May 29, 1954.

35. Ferrell, *The Diary of James C. Hagerty*, 54.

36. Press conference, May 19, 1954, *PPP: Dwight D. Eisenhower*, 489–97.

37. Ambrose, *Eisenhower: Soldier and President*, 542. These critical comments do not appear in the earlier edition of Ambrose's biography, published in 1984. Pach and

Richardson, *The Presidency of Dwight D. Eisenhower*, 142, argue that Eisenhower "declined to endorse" the ruling and "tried to divorce himself" from the decision. Patterson argues that Eisenhower's failure to speak out in favor of *Brown* was "morally obtuse and it allowed southern intransigence . . . to go unchallenged" (Patterson, *Brown v. Board of Education*, 82).

38. Herbert Brownell Oral History, February 24, 1977, DDEL; diary entry, June 16, 1954, Ferrell, *The Diary of James C. Hagerty, 67*. Letter to Hazlett, October 23, 1954, Griffith, *Ike's Letters to a Friend*, 135.

39. *Washington Post*, May 18, 1954, two articles surveying southern opinion; *New York Times*, May 18 and 19, 1954; *Washington Post*, May 19, 1954.

40. Hughes, *The Ordeal of Power*, 200–201.

41. Warren, *Memoirs*, 291; Edwin Lahey, "Byrnes on Integration," *Washington Post*, May 22, 1954.

42. Swede Hazlet to Eisenhower, January 23, 1955, Papers as President, Ann Whitman File, Name Series, box 18, DDEL.

43. Nine Democrats, all southerners, opposed Harlan's nomination: James Eastland and John Stennis (Mississippi), Sam Ervin (North Carolina), Lister Hill (Alabama), Olin Johnston and Strom Thurmond (South Carolina), John McClellan (Arkansas), George Smathers (Florida), and Richard Russell (Georgia). On Harlan, Kluger, *Simple Justice*, 718–19. Harlan's confirmation hearings revealed the depth of Eastland's opposition to Harlan. See Baltimore *Afro-American*, March 5, 1955.

44. *New York Times*, April 13, 1955.

45. *New York Times*, April 13 and 14, 1955.

46. *Washington Post*, November 25, 1954; Mayer, "With Much Deliberation and Some Speed," 69.

47. *Washington Post*, April 14, 1955; *New York Times*, April 14, 1955; *Chicago Tribune*, April 15, 1955; *New York Times*, April 15, 1955.

48. *Brown v. Board of Education of Topeka II*, 349 U.S. 294 (1955); *Washington Post*, June 1, 1955. For the oral arguments before the Court, as well as the internal hammering out of the *Brown II* decision, see Kluger, *Simple Justice*, 731–50, Marshall quote on 750.

49. "The Republican Party and the Negro," and cover letter from Val Washington, director for minorities at the National Republican Committee, July 28, 1955, and Eisenhower to Washington, August 1, 1955, Records as President, Official File, box 614, DDEL; *Pittsburgh Courier*, June 25 and August 20, 1955; *Norfolk (VA) Journal and Guide*, July 2, 1955; *New York Times* and *Los Angeles Times*, August 9, 1955; *Baltimore Afro-American*, August 20, 1955.

50. *Chicago Tribune*, June 2, 1955; *Washington Post*, June 2 and 23, 1955; *New York Times*, June 3, 5, 8, 25, 26, and 27, 1955. A good summary of the southern reaction is in Bartley, *The Rise of Massive Resistance*, 67–81.

51. Bartley, *The Rise of Massive Resistance*, 121.

52. Morrow, *Forty Years a Guinea Pig*, 61.

53. Roy Wilkins to Eisenhower, September 16, 1955, Papers of Maxwell Rabb, box 51, DDEL; *New York Times*, October 3, 1955.

54. Frederic Morrow to Maxwell Rabb, November 30, 1955, Maxwell Rabb Papers, box 51, DDEL.

55. J. Edgar Hoover to Dillon Anderson, special assistant to the president, September 6 and 13, 1955, October 11, 1955, November 22, 1955, December 14, 1955, January 3, 1956, White House Office, Office of the Special Assistant for National Security Affairs, Records, FBI Series, box 3, DDEL. Quotations taken from the reports of September 13, 1955, January 3, 1956, and December 14, 1955, respectively.

56. Morris, *The Origins of the Civil Rights Movement*, 51–54.

57. Morrow to Sherman Adams, December 16, 1955, Rabb Papers, box 43, DDEL.

58. "Annual Message to Congress on the State of the Union," January 5, 1956, Dwight D. Eisenhower Presidential Library, Museum and Boyhood Home, http://www.eisen hower.archives.gov/all_about_ike/speeches/1956_state_of_the_union.pdf.

59. Kirk, *Martin Luther King, Jr.*, 27–28; Branch, *Parting the Waters*, 159–68.

60. James B. Kaetz, "Autherine Lucy," *Encyclopedia of Alabama*, http://www.encyclopedia ofalabama.org/article/h-2489.

61. "Pre-press conference briefing," February 29, 1956, Ann Whitman File, DDE Diary Series, box 13, DDEL; press conference, February 8, 1956, *PPP: Dwight D. Eisenhower*, 234.

62. *Pittsburgh Courier*, February 4, 1956; *New York Times*, February 22, 24, and 26, 1956; *Washington Post*, February 26, 1956.

63. Max Rabb to Sherman Adams, February 27, 1956, Rabb Papers, box 43, DDEL. Rabb also pleaded with Adams in a March 1, 1956, memo that the White House set up a meeting between Ike's senior advisers and "top Negro leaders" such as Roy Wilkins, Thurgood Marshall, and A. Philip Randolph. But Adams threw cold water on this idea, writing in the margin of the memo, "We should talk about this. I am uncertain." Gerald Morgan Records, box 6, DDEL.

64. Brownell, *Advising Ike*, 218–19.

65. "Racial Tension and Civil Rights," March 1, 1956, paper prepared by J. Edgar Hoover for the March 9 cabinet meeting, Papers as President, Ann Whitman File, Cabinet Series, box 6, DDEL. The FBI's obsession with communist activity among African American citizens is plain in a monograph on the topic sent by Hoover to the White House. See J. Edgar Hoover to William H. Jackson, October 24, 1956, and "The Communist Party and the Negro," October 1956, Office of the Special Assistant for National Security Affairs, FBI Series, box 10, DDEL.

66. Maxwell Rabb, the secretary to the cabinet, produced two sets of notes from this extraordinary meeting: "Minutes of Cabinet Meeting: March 9, 1956," which is a short summary of issues discussed, and an informal set of notes that tried to recapture verbatim what Eisenhower had said on civil rights. This was then sent to Brownell after the meeting. "Memorandum for the Attorney General: The President's Views on the Proposed Civil Rights Program," Papers as President, Ann Whitman File, Cabinet

Series, box 6, DDEL. For Rabb's handwritten notes of the meeting, see Rabb Papers, box 16, DDEL.

67. "Southern Manifesto on Integration," March 12, 1956, *Supreme Court*, http://www.pbs.org/wnet/supremecourt/rights/sources_document2.html.

68. Morrow, *Black Man in the White House*, 47.

69. "Minutes of Cabinet Meeting," March 23, 1956, Ann Whitman File, Cabinet Series, box 7, DDEL; notes on conversation with Billy Graham, March 21, 1956, Papers as President, Ann Whitman Diary Series, box 8, DDEL.

70. Brownell, *Advising Ike*, 219. Gerald Morgan penned a one-page "Memorandum for Mrs. Ann Whitman," dated March 24, 1956, that describes Eisenhower showing a good deal of ambivalence in the cabinet meeting about what to do with Brownell's bill. Morgan wrote that after Brownell's private meeting with Eisenhower, "the Attorney General came out, he reported that the President had given the proposed statement a complete okay"—a sign of how clever Brownell could be in handling Eisenhower. Ann Whitman File, DDE Diary Series, box 14, DDEL.

71. The text that Brownell sent to the House and Senate is in "The Civil Rights Program: Letter and Statement by the Attorney General," April 10, 1956, circulated to the cabinet, Maxwell Rabb Papers, box 43, DDEL; also printed in the *Los Angeles Times*, April 10, 1956. Press coverage in *New York Times*, April 11 and May 3, 1956; *Pittsburgh Courier*, April 14, 1956; *Baltimore Afro-American*, April 21, 1956; Anthony Lewis in *New York Times*, June 6, 1956.

72. Martin Luther King Jr., E. D. Nixon, E. H. Mason, and Rufus Lewis, joint letter to President Eisenhower, August 27, 1956, Records as President, General File, box 909, DDEL.

CHAPTER 10: GOD, GOVERNMENT, AND THE MIDDLE WAY

Epigraph: Diary entry, November 20, 1954, *PDDE*, 15:1402.

1. *Washington Post*, January 31, 1951; *Los Angeles Times*, December 28, 1952; *Washington Post*, December 27, 1953; *Washington Post*, December 26, 1954; *Washington Post*, December 30, 1955; *Los Angeles Times*, December 30, 1956; *Los Angeles Times*, January 17, 1958; *Washington Post*, December 28, 1958; *Washington Post*, December 26, 1959; *Washington Post*, December 25, 1960.

2. "Presidential Approval Ratings: Gallup Historical Statistics and Trends," *Gallup*, www.gallup.com/poll//116677/presidential-approval-ratings-gallup-historical-statistics-trends.aspx.

3. William Lee Miller, "The Liking of Ike," in *Piety along the Potomac*, 3–29. The essay was originally published in *The Reporter* on October 16, 1958.

4. Remarks broadcast as part of the American Legion "Back to God" program, February 7, 1954, *PPP: Dwight D. Eisenhower*, 243–44. *Los Angeles Times, New York Times*, and *Washington Post*, February 8, 1954. Correspondence concerning the event can be seen in Central Files, President's Personal File, box 786, DDEL.

5. Peale, *Inspired Messages for Daily Living*, 3, 35, 195–96. See also his *A Guide to Confident Living, The Art of Real Happiness*, and *Stay Alive All Your Life*.

6. Edward Elson, *America's Spiritual Recovery*, 15–29, 33, 35, 53, 59, 83.

7. Graham to Sid Richardson, October 20, 1951, *PDDE*, 12:696–97, note 3.

8. Billy Graham, *Just As I Am*, 188–92; Gibbs and Duffy, *The Preacher and the Presidents*, 31–40. Eisenhower's religious views received wide press attention: *Washington Post*, September 16, 1952; *Chicago Tribune*, September 15, 1952.

9. Billy Graham to Eisenhower, June 29 and September 28, 1953, Central Files, President's Personal File, box 966, DDEL.

10. *Washington Post*, November 4, 1953. Eisenhower thanked Graham for the book in a personal letter dated November 3, 1953, Central Files, President's Personal File, box 966, DDEL.

11. Billy Graham speech and Eisenhower message to the International Christian Leadership prayer breakfast, *Washington Post*, February 4, 1955; Eisenhower speech at the 1955 American Legion "Back to God" radio broadcast, *New York Times* and *Chicago Tribune*, February 21, 1955.

12. *Washington Post* and *New York Times*, March 7, 1955; Reinhold Niebuhr, "Varieties of Religious Revival," *New Republic*, June 6, 1955. Niebuhr kept after Graham in a number of barbed essays. See his editorial in *Christianity and Crisis*, March 5, 1956; "Literalism, Individualism and Billy Graham," *Christian Century*, May 23, 1956; "Proposal to Billy Graham," *Christian Century*, August 8, 1956, which chastises Graham for ignoring racial intolerance.

13. State of the Union address, January 7, 1954, *PPP: Dwight D. Eisenhower*, 6–23; speech at U.S. Chamber of Congress meeting, May 2, 1955, in *Los Angeles Times*, May 3, 1955.

14. These numbers come from the Bureau of Labor Statistics, reports on "100 Years of U.S. Consumer Spending," http://www.bls.gov/opub/uscs/1950.pdf (1950) and http://www.bls.gov/opub/uscs/1960-61.pdf (1960–61). For further indices of prosperity, see Dunar, *America in the Fifties*, 167–203; Oakley, *God's Country*, 228–48.

15. Annual Budget Message to Congress, January 17, 1955, *PPP: Dwight D. Eisenhower*, 89.

16. DDE, *Mandate for Change*, 304; see also Griffith, "Dwight Eisenhower and the Corporate Commonwealth"; Sloan, *Eisenhower and the Management of Prosperity*, 12–20; Eisenhower quote from Annual Budget Message, January 21, 1954, *PPP: Dwight D. Eisenhower*, 89.

17. Address on the Tax Program, March 15, 1954, *PPP: Dwight D. Eisenhower*, 313–18. For a detailed analysis of tax policy in this period, see Joseph Thorndike, "Soak-the-Rich Republicans? The Persistence of High Tax Rates in the 1950s," George W. Bush Institute, http://www.bushcenter.org/sites/default/files/The%20Persistence%20of%20High%20Tax%20Rates%20in%20the%201950s.pdf.

18. Witte, *The Politics and Development of the Federal Income Tax*, 144–50; Gupta, "Revisiting the High Tax Rates of the 1950s"; letter to Harry Bullis, March 18, 1954, and letter to Swede Hazlett, March 18, 1954, *PDDE*, 15:961, 962–64.

19. State of the Union Address, February 2, 1953, *PPP: Dwight D. Eisenhower*, 31; "State-

ment by the President Concerning the Need for a Presidential Commission on Federal-State Relations," February 26, 1953, *PPP: Dwight D. Eisenhower*, 17.

20. "Special Message to the Congress Transmitting Proposed Changes in the Social Security Program," August 1, 1953, *PPP: Dwight D. Eisenhower*, 534.

21. "Annual Budget Message to Congress: Fiscal Year 1955," January 21, 1954, *PPP: Dwight D. Eisenhower*, 140–41.

22. For the changed rules, see "Extension of Old Age and Survivors Insurance," *Social Security Bulletin*, September 1953, 3–7; details on the evolution of the program available at www.ssa.gov/history/1950.html; letter to Edgar Eisenhower, November 8, 1954, *PDDE*, 15:1386–89.

23. DDE, *Mandate for Change*, 295.

24. State of the Union address, January 7, 1954, *PPP: Dwight D. Eisenhower*, 20; *Washington Post*, March 12, 1954.

25. *Washington Post*, July 14 and 15, 1954; press conference, July 14, 1954, *PPP: Dwight D. Eisenhower*, 633; *Chicago Tribune*, July 16, 1954. Ike fumed to Jim Hagerty, "How in the hell is the American Medical Association going to stop socialized medicine if they oppose such bills as this?" (diary entry, July 14, 1954, Ferrell, *The Diary of James C. Hagerty*, 90).

26. Flanagan, "The Housing Act of 1954"; Hunt, "How Did Public Housing Survive the 1950s?"; *Washington Post*, June 13, 1954; *New York Times*, August 3, 1954.

27. DDE, *At Ease*, 157–66; DDE, *Mandate for Change*, 548; Wells, "Fueling the Boom."

28. Message for the Governors' Conference, July 12, 1954, *PPP: Dwight D. Eisenhower*, 628–29; press conference, July 14, 1954, *PPP: Dwight D. Eisenhower*, 629–39; *New York Times*, July 13, 1954; *Washington Post*, July 13, 1954.

29. Lewis, *Divided Highways*, 105–12; Rose, *Interstate*, 69–78; *New York Times*, January 12, 1955; *Washington Post*, January 12, 1955.

30. Rose, *Interstate*, 77–84; Byrd's objections in *New York Times*, January 16, 1955; Ferrell, *The Diary of James C. Hagerty*, February 16, 1955, 195; Eisenhower's message to Congress, *Los Angeles Times*, February 23, 1955, and *Washington Post*, February 23, 1954; reaction to the plan, *Wall Street Journal*, February 23, 1955, and *New York Times*, February 27, 1955.

31. Lewis, *Divided Highways*, 112–23; Rose, *Interstate*, 85–94; Wells, "Fueling the Boom."

32. DDE, *Mandate for Change*, 428–42. A detailed account of Nixon's grotesque stump speeches during the 1954 congressional campaign is in Costello, *The Facts about Nixon*, 119–34.

33. Diary entry, April 1, 1953, *PDDE*, 14:136–39; letters to Bradford Chynoweth, July 13 and 20, 1954, *PDDE*, 15:1185–87, 1202–4.

34. Diary entries, December 8 and 20, 1954, Ferrell, *The Diary of James Hagerty*, 130–31, 145; diary entry, November 20, 1954, *PDDE*, 15:1402–5.

35. *New York Times*, January 2 and 16, 1955; *Wall Street Journal*, January 31, 1955; *Los Angeles Times*, February 18, 1955; *Chicago Tribune*, February 19, 1955.

36. *New York Times*, February 18, 1955.

37. Arthur Krock in *New York Times*, March 20, 1955.

38. Eisenhower spoke at a gathering of the Bull Elephants Club (GOP congressional staff) on the South Lawn, August 2, 1955, *PPP: Dwight D. Eisenhower*, 748–53; *Washington Post*, August 3, 1955.

CHAPTER 11: TO THE SUMMIT

Epigraph: DDE, closing statement, Geneva Conference, July 23, 1955, as reported in *New York Times*, July 24, 1955.

1. A useful assessment of Khrushchev's early moves is Fursenko and Naftali, *Khrushchev's Cold War*, 15–47. For insight into Khrushchev's reasoning and his attack on Molotov's previous policies, see "Central Committee Plenum of the CPSU Ninth Session, Concluding Word by Com. N. S. Khrushchev, 12 July 1955," July 12, 1955, History and Public Policy Program Digital Archive, *Wilson Center Digital Archive*, http://digitalarchive.wilsoncenter.org/document/110452.

2. Press conference, April 27, 1955, *PPP: Dwight D. Eisenhower*, 432; Eisenhower comment reported in telegram from Undersecretary of State Herbert Hoover Jr. to Dulles, May 8, 1955; Dulles telegram to Eisenhower, May 9, 1955; Dulles remarks in NSC meeting, May 19, 1955; Dulles conversation with German chancellor Konrad Adenauer, June 13, 1955, all in *FRUS 1955–57*, 5:172–73, 174–75, 182–89, 224–28.

3. DDE, *Mandate for Change*, 506.

4. Telegram from London to Department of State, April 30, 1955; Eden to Eisenhower, May 6, 1955; Dulles to Eisenhower, May 9, 1955, all in *FRUS 1955–57*, 5:160–61, 164–65, 174–75; letter to Eden, May 31, 1955, *PDDE*, 16:1720–21. Eisenhower knew how important the summit was for European public opinion. See his comments in the NSC meeting of July 7, *FRUS 1955–57*, 5:268–83. Harold Macmillan confirmed the significance of the summit for reasons of domestic politics (Macmillan, *Tides of Fortune*, 584–85).

5. Joseph Alsop, "Ike at the Summit," *Washington Post*, July 18, 1955.

6. Memorandum from the Joint Chiefs of Staff, June 16, 1955, *FRUS 1955–57*, 20:121–25; NSC meeting, July 7, 1955, *FRUS 1955–57*, 5:268–83.

7. NSC meeting, June 30, 1955, *FRUS 1955–57*, 20:144–55. Nelson Rockefeller, Ike's special assistant on cold war affairs, advised the president to "capture the political and psychological imagination of the world" by making a series of new proposals on a wide array of security issues (*FRUS, 1955–57*, 5:298–301). Rockefeller's ideas were drawn from the work of a panel he chaired in early June at the Quantico base in northern Virginia. For the full declassified report, see "Quantico Vulnerabilities Panel," June 10, 1955, DDO, tinyurl.galegroup.com/tinyurl/4mgtm5. Some of the planning documents have been collected and analyzed in Rostow, *Open Skies*. For discussion of Eisenhower's differences with Dulles and the JCS, see Richard Immerman, "'Trust in the Lord and Keep Your Powder Dry': American Policy Aims at Geneva," in Bischof and Dockrill, *Cold War Respite*, 35–54.

8. C. D. Jackson log entry, July 11, 1955, *FRUS 1955–57*, 5:301–5.

9. Radio and television address, July 15, 1955, *PPP: Dwight D. Eisenhower*, 701–5.

10. *Los Angeles Times*, July 17, 1955; *New York Times*, July 18, 1955.

11. *New York Times*, July 17, 1955; description of Ike's villa, *New York Times*, July 11, 1955.

12. *Wall Street Journal*, July 18, 1955; DDE, *Mandate for Change*, 512; *Los Angeles Times*, August 4, 1955.

13. James Reston, *New York Times*, July 20, 1955; Macmillan, *Tides of Fortune*, 616–17.

14. *Los Angeles Times*, July 21, 1955; James Reston, *New York Times*, July 21, 1955.

15. Minutes of the U.S.-Soviet dinner, July 18, 1955, and minutes of conversation with Zhukov, *FRUS 1955–57*, 5:372–82, 408–18.

16. Macmillan, *Tides of Fortune*, 622.

17. Tripartite meeting, July 17, 1955, and lunch with Zhukov, July 20, 1955, *FRUS 1955–57*, 5:350, 412. Eisenhower's deep concern about a surprise attack drove his Open Skies proposal, as he made clear in a private letter to Gen. Alfred Gruenther, July 25, 1955, *PDDE*, 16:1790–91. For the linkage between the U-2 and the Open Skies proposal, see John Prados, "Open Skies and Closed Minds: American Disarmament Policy at the Geneva Summit," in Bischof and Dockrill, *Cold War Respite*, 215–33.

18. Two sets of minutes of this meeting exist, and they bear careful comparison. One suggests unanimity about the idea, the other suggests some dissent. Meeting of July 20, 1955, *FRUS 1955–57*, 5:425–29.

19. Minutes of the fifth meeting of heads of government, July 21, 1955, *FRUS 1955–57*, 5:452–53.

20. Ambassador Charles Bohlen memorandum, July 21, 1955, *FRUS 1955–57*, 5:456–57; Bohlen, *Witness to History*, 384–85.

21. *Los Angeles Times*, July 23, 1955; *New York Times*, July 23, 1955.

22. Bohlen, *Witness to History*, 386; *New York Times*, July 25, 1955.

23. Dana Adams Schmidt, *New York Times*, July 31, 1955; Drew Middleton, *New York Times*, July 24, 1955; Stewart Alsop, *Washington Post*, July 24, 1955.

24. Drew Pearson, *Washington Post*, July 27, 1955.

25. *Washington Post*, August 5, 1955.

26. Letters to Swede Hazlett, June 4 and August 15, 1955, *PDDE*, 16:1729–31, 1820–23.

27. Letter to Milton Eisenhower, September 12, 1955, *PDDE*, 16:1850–52.

28. James Reston, *New York Times*, September 11, 1955.

29. Eisenhower gave a fairly complete account of his heart attack and subsequent events in *Mandate for Change*, 535–46. Dr. Snyder wrote a narrative account after the fact, in an unpublished draft of a memoir. Snyder Papers, box 11, DDEL.

30. The essential book on the topic is Lasby, *Eisenhower's Heart Attack*, which presents remarkable research and analysis showing that Snyder initially misdiagnosed the heart attack and tried to cover up this fact for years afterward. There are detailed hourly accounts of Eisenhower's condition from his admission on September 24 at Fitzsimons Army Hospital until his release on November 11 in the Howard Snyder Papers, box 4, DDEL. Note also the brief summary of the illness by Dr. Paul White,

dated November 10, 1955, Snyder Papers, box 4, DDEL. Snyder, anticipating the criticism, wrote numerous letters to Ike's close friends and associates explaining his decision to put the president to bed under sedation rather than transfer him to the hospital immediately. Snyder claimed his action "limited the heart damage to a minimum." See, for example, Snyder to George Allen, September 29, 1955, Snyder Papers, box 10, DDEL. He wrote dozens of similar letters in the weeks after the attack.

31. September 24, 1955, Ferrell, *The Diary of James C. Hagerty*, 233–36; narrative of events surrounding heart attack, Hagerty diary, James Hagerty Papers, box 1a, DDEL. According to Hagerty, Snyder was an emotional wreck by the time Hagerty got to Denver. "Howard was visibly upset. He was under a great strain and his hands were shaking badly. Almost tearfully he told me he was glad to see me out there."

32. John Eisenhower, *Strictly Personal*, 180–82.

33. An example of the first press reports from Denver is *Los Angeles Times*, September 25, 1955, which reported that the president was in "good condition" and was "resting well." Dr. White's comment, *Los Angeles Times*, September 26, 1955. White's lengthy press conference is transcribed in *New York Times*, September 27, 1955. On stocks, *Wall Street Journal* and *New York Times*, September 27, 1955.

34. *Chicago Tribune*, October 1, 1955; *New York Times*, October 1, 2, 6, 9, 10, 1955; *Washington Post*, October 8, 1955. Eisenhower's appointment calendar is available in Snyder Papers, box 7, DDEL.

35. Nixon, *Six Crises*, 132, 134, 147. For the press reaction to Nixon's disappearance, see *Los Angeles Times*, September 26, 1955.

36. Adams, *Firsthand Report*, 180–87.

37. *Chicago Tribune*, October 11, 12, 1955; *New York Times*, October 16, 26, 1955; *Washington Post*, October 27, 1955. Daily details are in the clinical record prepared by Col. Byron Pollock, dated November 8, 1955, Snyder Papers, box 4, DDEL.

38. *New York Times*, November 12, 1955. Partial minutes of the two Camp David NSC meetings are in *FRUS 1955–57*, 19:150–53, 166–70.

39. Len Hall's account is in his unpublished memoir, typescript pages 92–103, Henry W. Hoagland Papers, box 5, DDEL.

40. *Washington Post*, November 29, 1955; *Los Angeles Times*, November 29, 1955; diary entry, December 12, 1955, Ferrell, *The Diary of James C. Hagerty*, 241; diary entry, January 10, 1956, *PDDE*, 16:1947–49.

41. Whitman diary notes, January 11, 1956, Papers as President, Ann Whitman Diary Series, box 8, DDEL.

42. John Eisenhower, *Strictly Personal*, 184–85; notes by Dulles in Dulles Papers, White House Memoranda Series, box 8, DDEL; Len Hall manuscript, 100, Hoagland Papers, box 5, DDEL; Milton Eisenhower Oral History, OH-292, DDEL.

43. Press conference and address to the nation, February 29, 1955, *PPP: Dwight D. Eisenhower*, 263–79.

CHAPTER 12: A FORMIDABLE INDIFFERENCE

Epigraph: "Address at the Cow Palace on Accepting the Nomination of the Republican National Convention," August 23, 1956, American Presidency Project, http://www.presidency.ucsb.edu/ws/?pid=10583.

1. Nixon, *Six Crises*, 159–60. This episode in the Eisenhower-Nixon relationship has been expertly covered in Frank, *Ike and Dick*, 120–33; Malsberger, *The General and the Politician*, 86–98; Gellman, *The President and the Apprentice*, 298–308.

2. Nixon, *Six Crises*, 160–61. Nixon always thought Eisenhower's move was the result of advice from Sherman Adams, Lucius Clay, and some of the president's friends who wanted Nixon out. "It was hard not to feel that I was being set up," he wrote (*RN*, 167). Milton Eisenhower claimed that the president genuinely wanted to help Nixon and thought the Defense job would strengthen him. The job offer was an "expression of confidence" in Nixon rather than a disparagement of his vice president (Milton Eisenhower Oral History, OH-292, DDEL).

3. Ann Whitman diary, February 9 and March 19, 1956, Papers as President, Ann Whitman Diary Series, box 8, DDEL. Ann Whitman noted that Eisenhower told Len Hall he would run for reelection on February 6. See her entry for February 13, 1956.

4. Press conferences, February 29, 1956, and March 7, 1956, *PPP: Dwight D. Eisenhower*, 266–67, 287. Eisenhower told Foster Dulles on February 27 that he had doubts about Nixon. Nixon "had not gained the popular support he [Eisenhower] thought he deserved, and the polls indicated that he would be defeated" if he ran for president now in Ike's place. Eisenhower "doubted that eight years as Vice President would really help him to become President." Memorandum of conversation, February 27, 1956, Dulles Papers, White House Memoranda Series, box 8, DDEL.

5. Diary entry, March 13, 1956, Papers as President, DDE Diary Series, box 9, DDEL.

6. Press conference, April 25, 1956, *PPP: Dwight D. Eisenhower*, 431–32; Ann Whitman diary, April 9 and April 26, 1956, Papers as President, Ann Whitman Diary Series, box 8, DDEL; *Los Angeles Times*, April 27, 1956; *New York Times*, April 27, 1956.

7. Nixon, *Six Crises*, 161.

8. James Reston, "The Eisenhower Touch," *New York Times*, May 28, 1956.

9. Richard Rovere, "Trial Balances," *New Yorker*, December 1955, reprinted in *Affairs of State*, 337–73.

10. Stevenson's announcement speech is in *New York Times*, November 16, 1955; for his remark about mediocrity, see *New York Times*, November 20, 1955. For later attacks, see *New York Times*, March 4 and 11, April 23, May 9, 1956; *Los Angeles Times*, March 3 and 11; and *Washington Post*, March 7, 1956.

11. L. Brent Bozell, "National Trends," *National Review*, January 11, 1956, 14.

12. William F. Buckley, "Mr. Eisenhower's Decision and the Eisenhower Program," *National Review*, March 21, 1956, 9–10.

13. This account comes from Snyder's typescript memoir, Howard Snyder Papers, box 11, DDEL.

14. A detailed chronology was printed in the *New York Times* on June 9, 1956. General Heaton gave a post-op press conference, covered in *New York Times*, June 10, 1956.

15. James Reston, *New York Times*, June 10, 1956; Clinical record, narrative summary by General Heaton, August 10, 1956, Snyder Papers, box 4, DDEL.

16. Letters to Paul Helms, June 15, 1956, to Floyd Odlum and Jackie Cochran, June 21, 1956, and to David Eisenhower, July 14, 1956, *PDDE*, 17:2188, 2191, 2203. Ann Whitman notes, June 8, 1956, and June 8–July 16 summary, and notes on legislative meeting, July 10, 1956, Papers as President, Ann Whitman File, Ann Whitman Diary, box 8, DDEL. For Democratic critics, *New York Times*, July 23, 1956.

17. On Kilpatrick, Anthony Lewis, *New York Times*, January 22, 1956; Kilpatrick interviewed by Jim Bishop, *Washington Post*, March 31, 1956. Also Joseph Thorndike, "'The Sometimes Sordid Level of Race and Segregation': James J. Kilpatrick and the Virginia Campaign against *Brown*," in Lassiter and Lewis, *The Moderates' Dilemma*, 51–71.

18. Copies of the state resolutions may be seen in Records as President, General File, box 918, DDEL. On Alabama, see *New York Times*, February 2, 1956. A useful survey is Bartley, *A History of the South*, 187–222.

19. "The Southern Manifesto," Strom Thurmond Institute, Clemson University, http://sti.clemson.edu/component/content/article/192-general-info/790-1956-qsouthern-manifestoq.

20. *Washington Post*, January 28, 1956. Eastland's charge was in fact false: Susan Eisenhower attended an integrated preschool kindergarten at Fort Belvoir, where Maj. John Eisenhower was stationed.

21. *New York Times*, January 30, 1956; *New Journal and Guide*, Norfolk, Va., February 18, 1956.

22. Press conference, March 14, 1956, *PPP: Dwight D. Eisenhower*, 304–5.

23. Eisenhower to Billy Graham, March 22, 1956, Papers as President, Name Series, box 16, DDEL.

24. Billy Graham letter, March 27, 1956, Papers as President, Name Series, box 16, DDEL; press conference, March 21, 1956, *PPP: Dwight D. Eisenhower*, 340.

25. Hughes, *The Ordeal of Power*, 200; Rabb memo to Sherman Adams, August 8, 1956, Gerald Morgan Records, box 23, DDEL; Pre-press conference briefing, August 8, 1956, Papers as President, Ann Whitman Diary, box 8, DDEL.

26. Diary entry, August 14, 1956, Papers as President, Ann Whitman Diary, box 8, DDEL.

27. Diary entry, August 19, 1956, Papers as President, Ann Whitman Diary, box 8, DDEL. Text of GOP platform in *New York Times*, August 22, 1956.

28. For press coverage of the controversy over the civil rights plank, see *New York Times*, August 19, 1956; *Los Angeles Times*, August 20, 1956; *Washington Post*, August 22, 1956. Larson, *Eisenhower*, 124–28. For acceptance speech text, *Washington Post*, August 24, 1956. For an equally critical assessment of Ike's evasion of civil rights in 1956, see Morrow, *Forty Years a Guinea Pig*, 103–6.

29. *New York Times*, September 4, 6, and 11, 1956; *New Journal and Guide*, Norfolk, Va.,

September 8, 1956; *Chicago Tribune*, September 8, 1956; *Life*, September 17, 1956, 34–35.

30. For a detailed account of these events, see "A Tentative Description and Analysis of the School Desegregation Crisis in Clinton, TN," typescript, written by researchers from the Anti-Defamation League of B'nai B'rith, December 1, 1956, in Records as President, General File, box 916, DDEL. For national press, see *New York Times*, September 2, 3, and 4, 1956; and a longer magazine essay by George Barrett, "Study in Desegregation: The Clinton Story," *New York Times*, September 16, 1956. Also *Chicago Tribune*, August 31, 1956; *Los Angeles Times*, September 2, 1956; and *Washington Post*, September 2, 1956.

31. Press conference, September 5, 1956, *PPP: Dwight D. Eisenhower*, 732–45.

32. *Washington Post*, September 8, 1956.

33. "Address at the Cow Palace on Accepting the Nomination of the Republican National Convention," August 23, 1956, http://www.presidency.ucsb.edu/ws/?pid=10583; *New York Times*, August 19, 1956; Folliard in *Washington Post*, August 22, 1956.

34. Joseph and Stewart Alsop, "Today and Tomorrow," *Washington Post*, August 24, 1956; *Life*, September 3, 1956, 32.

35. Speech at kickoff picnic, September 12, 1956, White House Central Files, Official File, box 599, DDEL. For details on the picnic, see Ann Whitman notes, September 12, 1956, Papers as President, Ann Whitman File, Ann Whitman Diary, box 8, DDEL. For further efforts to refine the core of "modern Republicanism," see Eisenhower's statement of November 14, 1956, White House Central File, Official File, box 602, DDEL.

36. Larson, *A Republican Looks at His Party*; Stebenne, *Modern Republican*, 151–75.

37. For details on the campaign's travel itinerary, see Additional Papers of Thomas Stephens, box 27, DDEL; Young and Rubicam, Records of Citizens for Eisenhower, box 5, DDEL. John Eisenhower, *Strictly Personal*, 189; *Life*, September 17, 1956.

CHAPTER 13: DOUBLE CROSS AT SUEZ

Epigraph: Eisenhower quoted in Hughes, *The Ordeal of Power*, 217.

1. The British cabinet took the threat to the canal and the oil supply very seriously. See, for example, a cabinet memo of October 13, 1955, "Middle East Oil," in which the cabinet agreed that Britain's dependence on oil required a long-term strategic commitment to the region and a larger amount of aid for friendly regimes there (Porter and Stockwell, *British Imperial Policy and Decolonization*, 385–92).

2. Eisenhower telephone call with Dulles, September 23, 1955; call with Herbert Hoover Jr., November 28, 1955; call with Dulles, November 29, 1955, in Dulles Papers, Telephone Calls Series, box 11, DDEL. A lucid and detailed account of the overlapping crises of 1956 can be found in Nichols, *Eisenhower 1956*.

3. Memorandum from Dulles to Eisenhower, March 28, 1956, and approval by Eisenhower, *FRUS 1955–57*, 15:419–24. For Ike's growing qualms about Nasser, see diary entry, March 8, 1956, *FRUS 1955–57*, 15:326–27.

4. Dulles and Eisenhower conversation, July 19, 1956, and Dulles meeting with Ahmed Hussein of Egypt, July 19, 1956, *FRUS 1955–57*, 15:861–62, 867–73. DDE, *Waging Peace*, 33.

5. *Washington Post*, July 27, 1956.

6. Horne, *Harold Macmillan*, 1:395; Eden to Eisenhower, July 27, 1956, *FRUS 1955–57*, 16:9–11.

7. Memorandum by NSC Planning Board on NSC 5602, and NSC 5602/1, "Basic National Security Policy," *FRUS 1955–57*, 16:194–95, 242–68. For an excellent collection of essays on Eisenhower's engagement with these issues, see Statler and Johns, *The Eisenhower Administration, the Third World, and the Globalization of the Cold War.*

8. Dulles-Eisenhower phone call, July 30, 1956; Murphy to Dulles, July 31, 1956; Eisenhower meeting with Dulles and other leading advisers, July 31, 1956; Eisenhower to Eden, July 31, 1956, all in *FRUS 1955–57*, 16:46–47, 60–62, 62–68, 69–71.

9. Dulles-Macmillan meeting, August 1, 1956, *FRUS 1955–57*, 16:108–9.

10. Owen, "The Effect of Prime Minister Anthony Eden's Illness on His Decision-making during the Suez Crisis."

11. Eden to Eisenhower, August 27, 1956, *FRUS 1955–57*, 16:304–5.

12. Eisenhower to Eden, September 2, 1956, and Eden to Eisenhower, September 6, 1956, *FRUS 1955–57*, 16:355–58, 400–403. Eisenhower and Dulles worked closely together in formulating these messages. See memoranda of conversation, August 29 and 30, 1956, Dulles Papers, White House Memoranda, box 4, DDEL.

13. Eisenhower-Dulles phone call, September 7, 1956, Dulles Papers, Telephone Calls Series, box 11, DDEL; Eisenhower to Eden, September 8, 1956, *FRUS 1955–57*, 16:431–33.

14. Eisenhower-Dulles conversation, October 2, 1956; NSC meeting, October 4, 1956; Dulles conversation with Selwyn Lloyd and Christian Pineau, October 5, 1956; editorial note, Dulles brothers conversation, October 18, 1956, all in *FRUS 1955–57*, 16:625–26, 632–34, 639–45, 745–46.

15. For fully documented and superbly written histories of the Suez affair, see Kyle, *Suez*; Lucas, *Divided We Stand*. American policy is well covered in Hahn, *Caught in the Middle East*. On the specifics of the deal, see Avi Shlaim, "The Protocol of Sèvres, 1956: Anatomy of a War Plot," *International Affairs* 73, no. 3 (1997): 509–30.

16. Adams, *Firsthand Report*, 256.

17. On the origins and impact of the speech, see Taubman, *Khrushchev*, 270–89.

18. These events can be followed in Hitchcock, *The Struggle for Europe*, 206–13.

19. Analysts in Washington closely followed the impact of the speech, though it took time to get details on the exact contents. Ambassador Bohlen reported the thrust of the speech to Washington in early March, and by April the CIA had secured a full text through Israeli intelligence. See NSC discussion, March 22, 1956; State Department analysis, March 30, 1956; report on briefing by Ambassador Bohlen, April 11, 1956, all in *FRUS 1955–57*, 24:72–75, 75–82, 93–95. Bohlen's own account is in *Witness to History*, 393–404. On June 4 the State Department publicly released the text they

had procured. The cautious American position emerged over the summer and fall of 1956. See, for example, NSC 5608, July 3, 1956, and meeting of the Policy Planning Staff, October 23, 1956, *FRUS 1955–57*, 25:190–94, 259–60.

20. *New York Times*, October 26, 1956.

21. NSC meeting, October 26, 1956, *FRUS 1955–57*, 25:295–99.

22. Eisenhower-Dulles phone calls, October 26, 1956, and address by John Foster Dulles to Dallas Council on World Affairs, October 27, 1956, *FRUS 1955–57*, 25:305–7, 317–18; Dulles telegram to Bohlen, October 29, 1956, Dulles Papers, Telephone Calls Series, box 11, DDEL.

23. On the U-2, see Pedlow and Welzenbach, *The CIA and the U-2 Program*, 112–21. Telegram from embassy in Israel, October 26, 1956; intelligence reports on Israeli activity, October 26 and 28, 1956; Dulles comment in telegram to embassy in London, October 26, 1956; Eisenhower message to Ben-Gurion, October 27, 1956, all in *FRUS 1955–57*, 16:785, 787–88, 798–800, 790, 795.

24. "Report of Examination" by Drs. Howard Snyder and Leonard Heaton, Hagerty Papers, box 7, DDEL; Hughes, *The Ordeal of Power of Power*, 212.

25. Eisenhower-Dulles Telephone Conversation, October 28, 1956, *FRUS 1955–57*, 16:807.

26. Dulles telegram to embassy in Paris, October 29, 1956, especially note 1, *FRUS 1955–57*, 16:815–16.

27. Conference with the president, October 29, 1956, *FRUS 1955–57*, 16:833–40.

28. Editorial note, *FRUS 1955–57*, 16:840–42.

29. On Eisenhower's appearance, Hughes, *The Ordeal of Power*, 215; letter to Eden, October 30, 1956, *FRUS 1955–57*, 16:848–50.

30. Eden to Eisenhower, October 30, 1956, *FRUS 1955–57*, 16:856–57.

31. Eisenhower-Dulles phone call, October 30, 1956, *FRUS 1955–57*, 16:863. For the text of the ultimatum, *Washington Post*, October 31, 1956.

32. Dulles meetings with Hervé Alphand, French ambassador, and Sir John Coulson, British chargé, October 30, 1956, *FRUS 1955–57*, 16:867–68, 874–75.

33. Meeting with the president, October 30, 1956, *FRUS 1955–57*, 16:873.

34. Text of Stevenson speech, *Washington Post*, October 24, 1956; Adams-Dulles telephone call, Dulles Papers, Telephone Conversation Series, box 11, DDEL.

35. Editorial note, *FRUS 1955–57*, 16:881–82.

36. Hughes, *The Ordeal of Power*, 218–21.

37. *New York Times*, November 1, 1956.

38. *Los Angeles Times*, November 1, 1956; Walter Lippmann, "Disaster in the Middle East," *Washington Post*, November 1, 1956; editorial, *Washington Post*, November 3, 1956.

39. There is much new evidence on the 1956 revolution in Hungary. See in particular Kramer, "The Soviet Union and the 1956 Crises in Hungary and Poland." For an important collection of material on Soviet actions, there is Gyorkei and Horvath, *1956: Soviet Military Intervention in Hungary*.

40. NSC meeting, November 1, 1956, *FRUS 1955–57*, 16:902–16; *FRUS 1955–57*, 25:358–59.

41. "Memorandum for the Record," October 15, 1956, *PDDE*, 17:2328–29. He wrote to Swede Hazlett the next day, "I gave strict orders to the State Department that they should inform Israel that we would handle our affairs exactly as though we didn't have a Jew in America" (November 2, 1956, *FRUS 1955–57*, 16:943–45).

42. Memorandum by the president, November 1, 1956, *FRUS 1955–57*, 16:924–25.

43. United Nations General Assembly, *Official Records, First Emergency Special Session*, Plenary Meeting 561, Thursday, November 1, 1956, 10–12. New York: General Assembly of the United Nations, 1956.

44. Address at Convention Hall, Philadelphia, November 1, 1956, *PPP: Dwight D. Eisenhower*, 1066–74.

45. Kyle, *Suez*, 428–32; Eden's reply to the UN resolution, November 3, 1956, *FRUS 1955–57*, 16:946.

46. The resolution text is in editorial note, *FRUS 1955–57*, 16:960–64.

47. *New York Times*, November 5, 1956.

48. Khrushchev's thinking can be followed in Kramer, "The Malin Notes on the Crises in Hungary and Poland," 393–94.

49. DDE, *Waging Peace*, 89; editorial note, *FRUS 1955–57*, 25:392–93; Luce to Eisenhower via telegram from Dillon, November 4, 1956, Records as President, White House Central Files, Subject Series, box 32, DDEL.

50. Eden message, November 5, 1956, and memorandum of conversation, November 5, 1956, *FRUS 1955–57*, 16:984–86, 986–88.

51. The messages were printed in *New York Times*, November 6, 1956. See Bulganin's message to Eisenhower, November 5, 1956, *FRUS 1955–57*, 16:993–94.

52. Bohlen telegram, November 5, 1956, *FRUS 1955–57*, 16:995–96.

53. Memorandum of conference, November 5, 1956, *FRUS 1955–57*, 16:1000–1001.

54. Lasby, *Eisenhower's Heart Attack*, 238.

55. Hughes, *The Ordeal of Power*, 223.

56. *New York Times*, November 6, 1956; White House news release, November 5, 1956, *FRUS 1955–57*, 16:1007–8.

57. Memorandum of conference, November 6, 1956, *FRUS 1955–57*, 16:1014.

58. Bohlen telegram, November 6, 1956, *FRUS 1955–57*, 16:1016–17.

59. Memorandum summarizing the November 6, 1956, meeting, written by Col. Andrew Goodpaster, Ann Whitman File, DDE Diary Series, Staff Memos, box 19, DDEL; telegram from Joint Chiefs of Staff, November 6, 1956, *FRUS 1955–57*, 16:1035–36.

60. For the economic dimension of the story see Kunz, *The Economic Consequences of the Suez Crisis*, esp. chapter 6.

61. Lucas, *Divided We Stand*, 292–93; Kyle, *Suez*, 464–68.

62. Transcript of telephone conversation, November 6, 1956, *FRUS 1955–57*, 16:1025–26. Eisenhower put this in writing to Eden a few hours later (Eisenhower to Eden, November 6, 1956, *FRUS 1955–57*, 16:1028–29).

63. Hughes, *The Ordeal of Power*, 227.

64. Hughes, *The Ordeal of Power*, 228.

65. *New York Times*, November 7, 1956.

66. Phone call from Eden, November 7, 1956, *FRUS 1955–57*, 16:1040.

67. Goodpaster memo, November 7, 1956; Eisenhower call to Eden, November 7, 1956; Eisenhower meeting with Dulles, November 7, 1956, all in *FRUS 1955–57*, 16:1043–44, 1045–46, 1049–53.

68. Eisenhower to Eden, November 7, 1956, *FRUS 1955–57*, 16:1056; Eisenhower discussion with Dulles, November 7, 1956, Dulles Papers, White House Memorandum Series, box 4, DDEL.

69. NSC meeting, November 8, 1956, and message to Eden, November 11, 1956, *FRUS 1955–57*, 16:1070–86, 1110–11.

70. Aldrich to Hoover, November 19, 1956, *FRUS 1955–57*, 16:1150–52; Aldrich to Hoover, November 20, 1956, Papers as President, Ann Whitman Files, Dulles-Herter Series, box 8, DDEL.

71. Dillon telegram, November 12, 1956, *FRUS 1955–57*, 16:1117–20.

72. Aldrich telegram, November 19, 1956, and Hoover to Aldrich, November 20, 1956, *FRUS 1955–57*, 16:1163, 1169–70.

73. Letter to Winston Churchill, November 27, 1956, *PDDE*, 17:2412–15.

74. Lucas, *Divided We Stand*, 316–17; Aldrich telegram, November 29, 1956, *FRUS 1955–57*, 16:1210–11.

75. Lucas, *Divided We Stand*, 322–23; Hoover telegram to diplomatic missions, November 29, 1956, and NSC meeting, November 30, 1956, *FRUS 1955–57*, 16:1214–15, 1218–29.

76. Memorandum by the president, November 8, 1956, and Eisenhower telephone call with Hoover, November 13, 1956, *FRUS 1955–57*, 16:1088–89, 1122.

77. Bohlen to State Department, November 14, 1956, Papers as President, Ann Whitman Files, Dulles-Herter Series, box 8, DDEL.

78. Draft resolution by Dulles, December 18, 1956, and meeting with congressional leaders, January 1, 1957, *FRUS 1955–57*, 12:413, 432–37; strategy session with Dulles, December 22, 1956, Dulles Papers, White House Memoranda, box 4, DDEL.

79. "Eisenhower Doctrine," January 5, 1957, *Miller Center Presidential Speeches*, https://millercenter.org/the-presidency/presidential-speeches/january-5-1957-eisenhower-doctrine. The essential scholarly study is Yaqub, *Containing Arab Nationalism*.

80. Press conference, November 14, 1956, *PPP: Dwight D. Eisenhower*, 1096.

CHAPTER 14: THE COLOR LINE

Epigraph: Letter to Swede Hazlett, July 22, 1957, *PDDE*, 18:322.

1. *Washington Post*, March 6, 1957; *Chicago Defender*, March 6, 1957; *New York Amsterdam News*, March 2, 1957.

2. *New York Times*, December 18, 1956; *Washington Post*, December 18, 1956; Eisenhower-Nehru discussions, December 19, 1956, *FRUS 1955–57*, 8:331–40; DDE, *Waging Peace*, 114.

3. Memorandum for Nixon, February 18, 1957, *FRUS 1955–57*, 18:372–74; Morrow, *Forty Years a Guinea Pig*, 133.

4. *Papers of Martin Luther King, Jr.*, 4:145.

5. *Chicago Defender*, March 6, 1957.

6. The court case was *Browder v. Gayle*, 142 F. Supp. 707 (M.D. Ala. 1956). On the bombing, see Branch, *Parting the Waters*, 196–203.

7. Telegrams to Eisenhower and Nixon, January 11, 1957, *Papers of Martin Luther King, Jr.*, 4:99–103.

8. Press conference, February 6, 1957, *PPP: Dwight D. Eisenhower*, 131; King telegram to Eisenhower, February 14, 1957, *Papers of Martin Luther King, Jr.*, 4:132–34; *Time*, February 18, 1957.

9. Pre-press conference briefing, November 14, 1956, Papers as President, Ann Whitman Diary Series, box 8, DDEL; Burk, *The Eisenhower Administration and Black Civil Rights*, 204–6.

10. Some scholars have recently tried to make Eisenhower into a hero of the civil rights movement, an argument that surely overstates the case. See especially Nichols, *A Matter of Justice*. A far more restrained assessment can be found in Burk, *The Eisenhower Administration and Black Civil Rights*, which points to a record of "hesitancy and extreme political caution in defending black legal rights" (263). For a wholly negative and dismissive assessment, see Borstelmann, *The Cold War and the Color Line*, 85–134.

11. Moon, "The Negro Vote in the Presidential Election of 1956." On results in 1952 and 1956, see http://www.gallup.com/poll/9451/election-polls-vote-groups-19521956 .aspx. Rigeur, *The Loneliness of the Black Republican*, 11, 29–31.

12. Klarman, "How Brown Changed Race Relations."

13. *New York Times*, January 1, 1957; and see Legislative Leadership Meeting notes, December 31, 1956, Belknap, *Civil Rights, the White House, and the Justice Department*, 93–106.

14. For Brownell's public statements on voting rights, see *New York Times*, January 25, 1957; *Washington Post*, January 28, 1957.

15. Evans and Novak, *Lyndon Johnson*, 119–40.

16. Caro, *The Years of Lyndon Johnson*, 3: 904–5.

17. Telephone call with Johnson, June 15, 1957, Papers as President, Ann Whitman File, DDE Diary Series, box 25, DDEL; press conferences, February 6 and May 15, 1957, *PPP: Dwight D. Eisenhower*, 122–35, 352–66. For similar words, see press conference, June 19, 1957, *PPP: Dwight D. Eisenhower*, 468–80.

18. Brownell, *Advising Ike*, 219; Russell's speech reported in *New York Times*, July 3, 1957.

19. Press conference, July 3, 1957, *PPP: Dwight D. Eisenhower*, 515–27.

20. Telephone call to Brownell, July 3, 1957, Papers as President, Ann Whitman File, DDE Diary Series, box 25, DDEL; diary entry, July 3, 1957, Ann Whitman Diary Series, box 9, DDEL.

21. Legislative leaders meeting, July 9, 1957, Papers as President, Ann Whitman File,

DDE Diary Series, box 25, DDEL; diary entry, July 10, 1957, Ann Whitman Diary Series, box 9, DDEL; Morrow letter to Adams, July 12, 1957, Morrow Papers, box 9, DDEL.

22. Brownell, *Advising Ike*, 223–25; Caro, *The Years of Lyndon Johnson*, 3:926–27; *New York Times*, July 11, 1957.

23. "Statement by the President on the Objectives of the Civil Rights Bill," July 16, 1957, *PPP: Dwight D. Eisenhower*, 545.

24. *New York Times*, July 12 and 17, 1957; *Washington Post*, July 14, 1957.

25. Press conference, July 17, 1957, *PPP: Dwight D. Eisenhower*, 546–58; *New York Times*, July 21, 1957.

26. *Washington Post*, July 25, 1957.

27. H.R. 6127 (85th): An Act to Provide Means of Further Securing and Protecting the Civil Rights of Persons within the Jurisdiction of the United States, September 9, 1957, *Govtrack*, https://www.govtrack.us/congress/bills/85/hr6127/text.

28. The legal complexities in the debate were notorious. For a lucid contemporary evaluation of the debate, see *New York Times* articles by Robert Phillips and William S. White, July 28 and August 1, 1957; as well as Caro, *The Years of Lyndon Johnson*, 3:944–53.

29. On LBJ's arm-twisting, see James Reston, *New York Times*, August 3, 1957; Caro, *The Years of Lyndon Johnson*, 3:953–89.

30. Statement by the president, August 2, 1957, *PPP: Dwight D. Eisenhower*, 587; diary entry, August 2, 1957, Ann Whitman Diary Series, box 9, DDEL; legislative leaders meeting, supplemental notes, August 6, 1957, Papers as President, Ann Whitman File, DDE Diary Series, box 26, DDEL; letter to Bob Woodruff, August 6, 1957, *PDDE*, 18:354–56.

31. Legislative leaders meeting, August 13, 1957, Papers as President, Ann Whitman File, DDE Diary Series, box 26, DDEL.

32. Memo, August 16, 1957, Gerald Morgan Papers, box 6, DDEL; telephone call with Lyndon Johnson, August 23, 1957, Papers as President, Ann Whitman File, DDE Diary Series Diary, box 26, DDEL.

33. *Chicago Defender*, August 10 and September 4, 1957; *Washington Post*, August 31, 1957; *New York Amsterdam News*, September 14, 1957; *New Journal and Guide*, Norfolk, Va., September 7, 1957; *Los Angeles Times*, September 10, 1957; Citizens' Councils of America press release, September 2, 1957, Records as President, General File, box 918, DDEL.

34. Martin Luther King Jr. to Richard Nixon, August 30, 1957, William Rogers Papers, box 50, DDEL.

35. Press conference, September 3, 1957, *PPP: Dwight D. Eisenhower*, 639–50.

36. Reed, *Faubus*, 175–81; Nichols, *A Matter of Justice*, 170–71; Burk, *The Eisenhower Administration and Black Civil Rights*, 174–77.

37. *New York Times*, August 31 and September 1, 1957.

38. *Washington Post*, September 1, 1957; *Chicago Daily Tribune*, September 3, 1957; *New York Times*, September 3, 1957.

39. *New York Times*, September 4, 1957.

40. The details of these events have been reported by many witnesses and subsequent accounts. See Jacoway, *Turn Away Thy Son*, 1–8; Kirk, *Redefining the Color Line*, 106–38.

41. *New York Times*, September 5, 1957; *Los Angeles Times*, September 5, 1957.

42. Faubus to Eisenhower, September 4, 1957, Records as President, Official File, box 615, DDEL.

43. Wilkins to Eisenhower, September 5, 1957, Records as President, Official File, box 615, DDEL; Granger message in *Chicago Tribune*, September 5, 1957.

44. *Los Angeles Times*, September 8, 1957; *Washington Post*, September 8, 1956; *Chicago Tribune*, September 9, 1957; Adams, *Firsthand Report*, 346; Brownell, *Advising Ike*, 208.

45. Faubus interview, *Los Angeles Times*, September 9, 1957; Davies order, *New York Times*, September 11, 1957.

46. Notes of telephone call with Adams, September 11, 1957, Papers as President, Ann Whitman File, DDE Diary Series, box 27, DDEL; Adams, *Firsthand Report*, 348; Brownell, *Advising Ike*, 209; Nichols, *A Matter of Justice*, 176–79; Burk, *The Eisenhower Administration and Black Civil Rights*, 178–81.

47. "Notes dictated by the President on October 8, 1957, concerning visit of Gov. Orval Faubus," Papers as President, Ann Whitman File, Ann Whitman Diary Series, box 9, DDEL.

48. Adams, *Firsthand Report*, 351; Nichols, *A Matter of Justice*, 179–83.

49. Ann Whitman notes, September 14, 1957, Papers as President, Ann Whitman File, Ann Whitman Diary Series, box 9, DDEL; press release, September 14, 1957, *PPP: Dwight D. Eisenhower*, 674–5; Adams, *Firsthand Report*, 352–53; Brownell, *Advising Ike*, 210.

50. *New York Times*, September 15, 16, 19, and 20, 1957.

51. Faubus address, *Washington Post*, September 21, 1957; details on courtroom in *Washington Post* and *New York Times*, September 21, 1957.

52. Jacoway, *Turn Away Thy Son*, 163–72; Kirk, *Redefining the Color Line*, 118–19; *New York Times*, September 24, 1957, carried shocking pictures of the gang beating of Wilson; Nichols, *A Matter of Justice*, 189–91.

53. Telegram from Mayor Mann to Eisenhower, September 23, 1957, Records as President, Official File, box 615, DDEL; Ann Whitman notes, September 20, 1957, Papers as President, Ann Whitman File, DDE Diary Series, box 27, DDEL; Brownell, *Advising Ike*, 211; Adams, *Firsthand Report*, 354; "Statement by the President," September 23, 1957, *PPP: Dwight D. Eisenhower*, 689.

54. Telegram from Mayor Mann to Eisenhower, September 24, 1957, Records as President, Official File, box 615, DDEL; Ann Whitman notes of phone calls with Brownell, September 24, 1957, Papers as President, Ann Whitman File, DDE Diary Series, box 27, DDEL; Adams, *Firsthand Report*, 355; Brownell, *Advising Ike*, 211. Brownell's detailed legal opinion on which he based his advice is in a memorandum to the president, November 7, 1957, Papers as President, Ann Whitman File, Administration

Series, box 8, DDEL. The text of the law is 10 USC 332: Use of Militia and Armed Forces to Enforce Federal Authority, Government Publishing Office, https://www.gpo.gov/fdsys/granule/USCODE-2011-title10/USCODE-2011-title10-subtitleA-partI-chap15-sec332.

55. "Radio and Television Address to the Nation," September 24, 1957, *PPP: Dwight D. Eisenhower*, 689–94.

56. Eisenhower letter to Senator John Stennis of Mississippi, October 7, 1957, Records as President, Official File, box 615, DDEL; Eisenhower letter to Walter T. Forbes of Chattanooga, Tennessee, October 8, 1957, Papers as President, Ann Whitman File, DDE Diary Series, box 28, DDEL.

57. Larson, *Eisenhower*, 132–33; Ambrose, *Eisenhower: Soldier and President*, 542.

58. King to Eisenhower, September 25, 1957, *Papers of Martin Luther King, Jr.*, 4:278; letter from Jackie Robinson, September 25, 1957, Records as President, Official File, box 615, DDEL; Bates quoted in *Chicago Defender*, September 30, 1957.

59. Roundup of southern opinion in *Washington Post*, September 25 and 26, 1957; Gathings to Eisenhower, September 29, 1957, Records as President, Official File, box 615, DDEL; Talmage B. Echols to Eisenhower, October 21, 1957, Records as President, General File, box 921, DDEL; Kentucky Citizens' Council, FBI report, October 1, 1957, White House Office, OSANSA Records, FBI Series, box 2, DDEL; Russell telegram to Eisenhower, September 27, 1957, Papers as President, Ann Whitman File, Administration Series, box 23, DDEL.

60. Press conference, October 3, 1957, *PPP: Dwight D. Eisenhower*, 704–16.

61. Morrow, *Forty Years a Guinea Pig*, 164; *New York Times*, May 13, 1958; *Washington Post*, May 13, 1958. See for reaction *Chicago Daily Defender*, May 15, 1958; *New York Amsterdam News*, May 17, 1958; *Baltimore Afro-American*, May 24, 1958.

62. Summary of meeting of June 23 (dated June 24), 1957, Papers as President, Ann Whitman File, DDE Diary Series, box 33, DDEL; Wilkins and Mathews, *Standing Fast*, 258. For an inside account, see Morrow, *Forty Years a Guinea Pig*, 164–78.

63. Burk, *The Eisenhower Administration and Black Civil Rights*, 193–96, 201; Nichols, *A Matter of Justice*, 223–29.

64. Roy Wilkins to Fred Morrow, September 4, 1958, Morrow Papers, box 10, DDEL.

65. The FBI reported extensively on the event, duly turning over reports to the White House. FBI Report, October 27, 1958, White House Office, Office of the Special Assistant for National Security Affairs, FBI Series, box 2, DDEL. Also *New York Times*, October 26, 1958.

CHAPTER 15: IKE'S MISSILE CRISIS

Epigraph: State of the Union address, January 9, 1958, *PPP: Dwight D. Eisenhower*, 2–15.

1. Morgan, *Eisenhower versus "The Spenders,"* 99–102.

2. *Life*, October 14, 1957. Viewers on Earth probably saw the large booster rocket in orbit rather than the tiny *Sputnik* craft itself.

3. Memorandum of October 8, 1957, conversation with the president, October 9, 1957, Papers as President, DDE Diary Series, box 27, DDEL; NSC meeting, October 10, 1957, minutes, Papers as President, NSC Series, box 9, DDEL.

4. *Newsweek*, October 21, 1957; *Time*, December 16, 1957; *Life*, October 14 and 21, and November 4, 1957; *New York Times*, October 19, 1957.

5. Press conference, October 9, 1957, *PPP: Dwight D. Eisenhower*, 719–32.

6. Arthur Krock, "The Effects of Sputnik Thus Far," *New York Times*, October 10, 1957; "GOP on the Defensive," *New York Times*, October 13, 1957.

7. Edwin Dale Jr., "Are We Americans Going Soft?," *New York Times*, December 1, 1957; Walter Lippmann, "Analysis by Light of the Sputnik," *Los Angeles Times*, October 11, 1957. Further details on the media reaction in Mieczkowski, *Eisenhower's Sputnik Moment*, 11–33.

8. *New York Times*, November 7, 1957.

9. *Chicago Tribune, Los Angeles Times*, and *New York Times*, November 4, 1957; *Washington Post*, November 5 and 6, 1957; *New York Times*, November 10, 1957.

10. The report was written chiefly by Paul Nitze, who had also written the frightening NSC 68 paper. See Herken, *Counsels of War*, 111–21; Kaplan, *The Wizards of Armageddon*, 144–54.

11. NSC meeting, November 7, 1957, and "Report to the President by the Security Resources Panel of the ODM Science Advisory Committee on Deterrence and Survival in the Nuclear Age," November 7, 1957, *FRUS 1955–57*, 19:630–35, 638–61.

12. The CIA's NIE 11-4-57 (dated November 12, 1957) has been fully declassified and is available at CIA Reading Room, https://www.cia.gov/library/readingroom/docs/DOC_0000267692.pdf. The CIA consultants gave their assessment to Allen Dulles, who passed it to Eisenhower's staff secretary, General Goodpaster. Dulles to Goodpaster, October 28, 1957, DDO, http://tinyurl.galegroup.com/tinyurl/3eqUC0.

13. *New York Times* and *Washington Post*, November 8, 1957; "Address to the American People," November 7, 1957, *PPP: Dwight D. Eisenhower*, 789–99; "Our Future Security," Oklahoma City, November 13, 1957, *PPP: Dwight D. Eisenhower*, 807–17. See also Larson, *Eisenhower*, 154–58.

14. Walter Lippmann, *Washington Post*, November 12, 1957; Kennedy in *New York Times*, November 15, 1957.

15. Adams, *Firsthand Report*, 195–97.

16. *Washington Post*, December 5, 1957; *Wall Street Journal*, November 29, 1957; Stewart Alsop, *Washington Post*, November 29, 1957; Drew Pearson, *Washington Post*, November 30, 1957.

17. Memo by Richard Nixon, December 3, 1957, William Rogers Papers, box 50, DDEL.

18. John Eisenhower, *Strictly Personal*, 199; Lasby, *Eisenhower's Heart Attack*, 239–46; DDE, *Waging Peace*, 227–30.

19. U.S. Senate, *Hearings before the Preparedness Investigating Subcommittee of the Committee on Armed Services*, 2.

20. U.S. Senate, *Hearings before the Preparedness Investigating Subcommittee of the Committee on Armed Services*, 7–8; *New York Times*, November 26, 1957.

21. U.S. Senate, *Hearings before the Preparedness Investigating Subcommittee of the Committee on Armed Services*, Bush quoted on, 60, Doolittle on 113 and 119, Gavin on 485–512, von Braun on 579–89.

22. Pedlow and Welzenbach, *The CIA and the U-2 Program*, 122–43; Peebles, *Shadow Flights*, 164–94; Bissell, *Reflections of a Cold Warrior*, 119. The amount of material the CIA gained on Soviet ICBM progress from the U-2 flights can be seen in documents declassified in 2011 and available at the CIA FOIA Electronic Reading Room, https://www.cia.gov/library/readingroom/collection/what-was-missile-gap. See especially "Photographic Intelligence Briefing," August 23, 1957; joint photographic intelligence memorandum "The Tyurtam Missile Test Facility," September 12, 1957; SNIE 11-8-57, "Evaluation of Evidence Concerning Soviet ICBM Flight Tests," September 18, 1957. For a complete list of U-2 flights over the USSR, see Allen Dulles to Andrew Goodpaster, "U-2 Overflights of Soviet Bloc," August 18, 1960, DDO, http://tinyurl.galegroup.com/tinyurl/3oXNV4. Eisenhower biographers tend to muddle the U-2 story. According to Jean Edward Smith, Eisenhower remained calm and unperturbed because of "iron-clad evidence provided by extensive CIA surveillance flights over the Soviet Union." Smith says the U-2 photographs provided "convincing evidence that there was no missile gap" (*Eisenhower in War and Peace*, 733–43). Evan Thomas too insists that the missile gap was always known to be a falsehood: "The U-2 spy plane had found nothing to suggest that Russia was building a great nuclear strike force" (*Ike's Bluff*, 259). And biographer Jim Newton writes that Eisenhower "had some good reason for nonchalance," namely, the comforting U-2 overflights (*Eisenhower*, 254).

23. Some of the internal discussion in the CIA on how to interpret the reconnaissance data can be seen in the CIA FOIA Electronic Reading Room collection, "ORR Contribution to CIA Proposed Draft of SNIE 11-10-57," November 6, 1957, and "Addendum to CIA Proposed Draft of SNIE 11-10-57," November 8, 1957 https://www.cia.gov/library/readingroom/docs/CIA-RDP79T01049A00 170044001-4.pdf.

24. "Briefing for Senate Preparedness Subcommittee on Soviet Guided Missiles," November 26 and 27, 1957, DDO, http://tinyurl.galegroup.com/tinyurl/3erMD7.

25. SNIE 11-10-57, "The Soviet ICBM Program," December 17, 1957, CIA FOIA Electronic Briefing Room collection. For the problems with these estimates, see Roman, *Eisenhower and the Missile Gap*, 30–47.

26. For a detailed picture, see "Chronology of Significant Events in the U.S. Intermediate and Intercontinental Ballistic Missile Programs," November 8, 1957, White House Office, Office of the Special Assistant for National Security Affairs: Records, 1952–61, Special Assistant Series, Subject Subseries, box 7, DDEL.

27. NSC meeting, September 8, 1955, *FRUS 1955–57*, 19:111–22; "Guided Missiles Summary," April 18, 1957, DDO, http://tinyurl.galegroup.com/tinyurl/3fxDo4. On the July 1955 briefing, see Sheehan, *A Fiery Peace in a Cold War*, 287–302.

28. State Department memorandum, November 30, 1955, and NSC meeting, December 1, 1955, *FRUS 1955–57*, 19:154–61, 166–70. The key presidential decisions on the missile program were tabulated in NSC 6021, "Missiles and Military Space Programs," December 14, 1960, White House Office, Office of the Special Assistant for National Security Affairs: Records, 1952–61, NSC Series, Policy Papers Subseries, box 29, DDEL.

29. *Los Angeles Times*, December 7, 1957; *New York Times*, December 7, 1957.

30. "Monthly Report on Progress of ICBM and IRBM Programs," Department of Defense, December 31, 1957, Digital National Security Archive, Nuclear History I, 1955–68. For a statement on the value of failure in missile research, see memorandum for President Eisenhower from James Killian, December 28, 1957, Papers as President, Administration Series, box 23, DDEL.

31. "Chronology of Significant Events in the U.S. Intermediate and Intercontinental Ballistic Missile Programs," November 8, 1957, White House Office, Office of the Special Assistant for National Security Affairs: Records, 1952–61, Special Assistant Series, Subject Subseries, box 7, DDEL. For summary of the air force and army missile programs, Converse, *Rearming for the Cold War*, 490–506, 592–634. For figures on aircraft, see Schwartz, *Atomic Audit*, 113, and on the missile deployments, 126–39.

32. DDE, *Waging Peace*, 230.

33. Dulles remarks in *Los Angeles Times*, December 24, 1957; coverage of NATO summit, *New York Times*, December 16, 1957; Gaddis, *We Now Know*, 240–41.

34. *New York Times*, January 1 and 8, 1958; *Wall Street Journal*, January 2, 3, and 6, 1958; *Los Angeles Times*, January 3 and 6, 1958; *Washington Post*, January 3, 4, 5, 6, 8, 1958.

35. *Washington Post*, January 10, 1958.

36. Annual message to Congress, January 9, 1958, *PPP: Dwight D. Eisenhower*, 2–15.

37. Hughes, *The Ordeal of Power*, 259; *Washington Post*, January 10 and 11, 1958; *Los Angeles Times*, January 10, 1958; *Wall Street Journal*, January 10, 1958; *New York Times*, January 12, 1958.

38. DDE, *Waging Peace*, 256; Mieczkowski, *Eisenhower's Sputnik Moment*, 127–29; *New York Times*, February 1, 1958.

39. Killian, *Sputnik, Scientists, and Eisenhower*, 219, 239, 241. See also Skolnikoff, *Science, Technology, and American Foreign Policy*, 227–31; York, *Race to Oblivion*, 113–16. See Eisenhower's personal note to Killian, July 16, 1959, Papers as President, Ann Whitman File, DDE Diary Series, box 43, DDEL: "I shall never cease to be grateful for the patience with which you initiated me into the rudiments of this new science."

40. Conversation with the president, October 15, 1957, *FRUS 1955–57*, 19:607–10.

41. Urban, *More Than Science and Sputnik*.

42. McDougall, *The Heavens and the Earth*, 157–76.

43. "Annual Budget Message to Congress," January 13, 1958, *PPP: Dwight D. Eisenhower*, 17–74; Department of Defense Directive 5105.15, February 7, 1958, which created ARPA (semanticvoid.com/docs/darpa_directive.pdf); Defense Act of 1958, Public Law 85-599 www.govinfo.gov/content/pkg/STATUTE-72/pdf/STATUTE-72-Pg514

.pdf; Duchin, "'The Most Spectacular Legislative Battle of that Year'"; Divine, *The Sputnik Challenge*, 128–43.

44. McDougall, *The Heavens and the Earth*, 227.

45. Memorandum of conversation, Killian, Land, Goodpaster, and Eisenhower, February 10, 1958, White House Office, Office of the Staff Secretary, Subject Series, Alphabetical Subseries, Intelligence Matters, box 14, DDEL; ARPA, "Military Reconnaissance Satellite Program," progress report ending March 31, 1958, White House Office, Office of the Special Assistant for National Security Affairs: Records, 1952–61, NSC Series, Briefing Notes Subseries, box 13, DDEL.

46. Ruffner, *Corona*, 24. Valuable documents on the planning, design, and testing, as well as the cover plan for the Corona satellite program, are available at DDO. Corona was discussed and approved at the NSC meeting of July 31, 1958. See the briefing notes by General Goodpaster, http://tinyurl.galegroup.com/tinyurl/3izRsX and the NSC minutes, http://tinyurl.galegroup.com/tinyurl/3izSRX.

47. NSC 5814, "Preliminary U.S. Policy on Outer Space," August 18, 1958, White House Office, Office of the Special Assistant for National Security Affairs: Records, 1952–61, NSC Series, Policy Papers Subseries, box 25, DDEL.

48. Joseph Alsop, "The Gap," *Washington Post*, July 30, 1958; "Untruths on Defense," *Washington Post*, August 1, 1958. Historians have not confirmed the source of Alsop's information, but it is likely either Senator Symington, who had access to classified briefings from Allen Dulles, or persons within the air force who were eager to see an expanded missile production program.

49. Joseph Alsop, "Calculations on the First Blow," *Washington Post*, August 3, 1958.

50. Joseph Alsop, "Eisenhower, 1958," *Washington Post*, August 8, 1958. See also his equally nasty and personal assessment of the failings of Charles Wilson, "Letter to Engine Charlie," *Washington Post*, August 4, 1958.

51. *New York Times*, May 30 and July 25, 1958.

52. "Remarks of Senator John F. Kennedy, in the Senate, August 14, 1958," John F. Kennedy Presidential Library and Museum, https://www.jfklibrary.org/Research/Research-Aids/JFK-Speeches/United-States-Senate-Military-Power_19580814.aspx.

53. Joseph Alsop, "An Authentic Voice of America," *Washington Post*, August 17, 1958; James Reston, "Honors for Kennedy," *New York Times*, August 18, 1958.

54. Letters to Charlie Wilson, August 4, 1958, and to Bill Robinson, August 4, 1958, *PDDE*, 19:1043–45; press conferences, August 20 and August 27, 1958, *PPP: Dwight D. Eisenhower*, 621–31, 639–50. On Alsop, the missile gap, and the whispering campaign against him, see Herken, *The Georgetown Set*, 241–45.

55. Guided Missile Intelligence Committee, "First Operational Availability Date for Soviet ICBM," May 15, 1958; "Soviet ICBM Test," May 27, 1958; National Intelligence Estimate 11-5-58, August 19, 1958, all in CIA FOIA Electronic Reading Room; editorial note on the NSC briefing by Allen Dulles, August 27, 1958, *FRUS 1958–60*, 3:135–36.

56. "Memorandum for Chairman, Guided Missile Intelligence Committee," October

9, 1958, https://www.cia.gov/library/readingroom/docs/1958-10-09.pdf; Quotation from "Re-examination of Soviet ICBM Production," October 24, 1958, https://www.cia.gov/library/readingroom/docs/DOC_0000969848.pdf; "Status of Soviet ICBM Program," November 10, 1958, https://www.cia.gov/library/readingroom/docs/1958-11-10.pdf; "Report of the Ad Hoc Panel on Status of Soviet ICBM Program," November 14, 1958, www.cia.gov/library/readingroom/docs/CIA-RDP61S00750A000500040042-5.pdf, all available in CIA FOIA Electronic Reading Room.

57. Memorandum of conference, July 14, 1958, *FRUS 1958–60*, 11:211–15.

58. "Statement by the President," July 15, 1958, *PPP: Dwight D. Eisenhower*, 553–56; Little, *American Orientalism*, 135.

59. *Los Angeles Times*, July 17, 1958; Yaqub, *Containing Arab Nationalism*, 205–36.

60. Chen, *Mao's China and the Cold War*, 175–204.

61. "JCS Views on the Taiwan Straits Issue," September 2, 1958, DDO, http://tinyurl.galegroup.com/tinyurl/3jpoM5; Joint Chiefs of Staff report, "U.S. and Allied Capabilities for Limited Military Operations to 1 July 1961," June 17, 1958, DDO, http://tinyurl.galegroup.com/tinyurl/3jq6e8; memorandum of conversation, John Foster Dulles and Chiefs of Staff, September 2, 1958, and Eisenhower-Dulles conversation, September 4, 1958, *FRUS 1958–60*, 19:115–22, 130–31. On the Matador missiles in Taiwan, see "Deployment of MATADOR Tactical Missile Unit Taiwan," March 20, 1957, DDO, http://tinyurl.galegroup.com/tinyurl/3jvZQ1.

62. Memorandum of conversation, John Foster Dulles and Policy Planning Staff director Gerard Smith, September 2, 1958, DDO, http://tinyurl.galegroup.com/tinyurl/3jqWXX; Dulles letter to Harold Macmillan, September 12, 1958, *FRUS 1958–60*, 19:175–77. See also Dulles conversation with Sherman Adams, September 5, 1958, DDO, http://tinyurl.galegroup.com/tinyurl/3jt7y2.

63. Meeting at the White House, August 29, 1958, and Eisenhower discussion with McElroy, September 11, 1958, *FRUS 1958–60*, 19:96–99, 161.

64. Zhang, *Deterrence and Strategic Culture*, 225–67. See also a classified RAND study of the crisis prepared in 1966 by M. H. Halperin, "The 1958 Taiwan Straits Crisis: A Documented History," DDO, http://tinyurl.galegroup.com/tinyurl/3okPK5.

65. Walter Lippmann columns in *Washington Post*, September 2, 9, 11, 18, and 30, 1958. For the flavor of the Joseph Alsop columns, see *Washington Post*, September 12, 1958.

66. *New York Times*, September 11 and 13, 1958; *Los Angeles Times*, September 14, 1958; *Washington Post*, September 16 and 26, 1958.

67. Letter to Paul Hoffman, June 23, 1958, *PDDE*, 19:957; Adams obituary, *New York Times*, October 28, 1986.

68. Letter to Elizabeth Hazlett, November 3, 1958, *PDDE*, 19:1187. For the Swede Hazlett story, Papers as President, Ann Whitman Diary Series, December 12, 1958, box 10, DDEL.

69. Nixon, *RN*, 200.

70. Letter to Harold Macmillan, November 11, 1958, *PDDE*, 19:1193.

CHAPTER 16: CONTENDING WITH KHRUSHCHEV

Epigraph: Eisenhower in conversation with Harold Macmillan on March 20, 1959, *FRUS 1958–60*, 8:521.

1. For his golf scores and bets, see one-page memo, "The President's Scores, November 20 to December 2, 1958," Papers as President, Ann Whitman Diary Series, box 10, DDEL.

2. Press conference, November 5, 1958, *PPP: Dwight D. Eisenhower*, 827–38.

3. *New York Times*, February 21 and August 11, 1958.

4. For a brief summary of the state of play of these talks, see memorandum of conference with Eisenhower, Killian, Goodpaster, August 4, 1958, and Eisenhower's conversation with Christian Herter, February 17, 1959, *FRUS 1958–60*, 3:617–18, 707–8. Data on tests, U.S. Department of Energy, "U.S. Nuclear Tests, 1945–1992," (December 2000) nnsa.energy.gov/sites/default/files/nnsa/inlinefiles/doe_nv_2000e.pdf. For an excellent summary with documents, see William Burr and Hector L. Montford, eds., "The Making of the Limited Test Ban Treaty, 1958–1963," August 8, 2003, National Security Archive, http://nsarchive.gwu.edu/NSAEBB/NSAEBB94/.

5. Letter to Hughes, November 20, 1958, *PDDE*, 19:1210–11.

6. Letter to Dulles, December 12, 1958, *PDDE*, 19:1249, note 2; Hughes, *The Ordeal of Power*, 276–82.

7. Jim Hagerty memorandum to Eisenhower, December 9, 1958, Papers as President, Name Series, box 26, DDEL.

8. John Eisenhower, *Strictly Personal*, 212.

9. The essential account of the East German-Soviet relationship in this period is Harrison, *Driving the Soviets up the Wall*. The Soviet note is in Department of State, *Bulletin*, January 19, 1959, 81–89.

10. This analysis of Khrushchev relies upon the work of William Taubman's magnificent biography, *Khrushchev*; the brilliantly researched study by Aleksandr Fursenko and Timothy Naftali, *Khrushchev's Cold War*; and the excellent article by Vojtech Mastny, "Soviet Foreign Policy, 1953–1962," in Leffler and Westad, *The Cambridge History of the Cold War*, 1:312–33.

11. Conversation with Dulles, November 18, 1958; conversation with Christian Herter, November 22, 1958; conversation with Dulles, November 30, 1958; Conference with the president, December 11, 1958, all in *FRUS, 1958–60*, 8:84–85, 113–14, 142–43, 174.

12. Hubert Humphrey, "My Marathon Talk with Russia's Boss," *Life*, January 12, 1959, 80–86, 91. Humphrey's conversation reported in telegram from Ambassador Thompson to State Department, December 3, 1958, *FRUS, 1958–60*, 8:148–52.

13. Conference with the president, December 11, 1958, *FRUS 1958–60*, 8:172–77; see John Eisenhower, *Strictly Personal*, 216. For the more hawkish views of the military, see General Nathan Twining's recommendations, memorandum of conversation, November 21 and December 13, 1958, *FRUS 1958–60*, 8:99–103, 193–96. "We must

ignore the fear of general war," he said. "It is coming anyway. Therefore, we should force the issue." For the final strategy, see the discussions of January 29, 1959, and the summary prepared by Dulles, *FRUS 1958–60*, 8:299–306; DDE, *Waging Peace*, 340–42.

14. Aldous, *Macmillan, Eisenhower, and the Cold War*, 53–57; Macmillan's own account of the trip is in *Riding the Storm*, 592–634.

15. Aldous, *Macmillan, Eisenhower, and the Cold War*, 62–66.

16. Memorandum of conference, March 6, 1959; memorandum for the record, March 14, 1959; Memorandum of conference, March 17, 1959; memorandum of conversation, March 19, 1959, all in *FRUS 1958–60*, 8:428–37, 486–87, 492–95, 507–9.

17. Macmillan-Eisenhower talks, 3:00–4:40 p.m., March 20, 1959, *FRUS 1958–60*, 8:516–18.

18. Macmillan-Eisenhower talks, 6:30–7:30 p.m., March 20, 1959, *FRUS 1958–60*, 8:520–21.

19. Macmillan-Eisenhower talks, March 21, 1959, *FRUS 1958–60*, 8:522–23.

20. Note by Ann Whitman, February 13 and 14, 1959, Papers as President, Ann Whitman Diary Series, box 10, DDEL.

21. DDE, *Waging Peace*, 357–60; Hoopes, *The Devil and John Foster Dulles*, 480–86; memoranda on these events by Joseph Greene, Dulles's special assistant, dated April 11 and 13, Dulles Papers, Special Assistant's Chronological Series, box 14, DDEL.

22. Nixon wrote at length about his Caracas and his Russia trips in *Six Crises*, 183–291.

23. *PPP: Dwight D. Eisenhower, 1959*, 330; Nixon-Dulles conversation, April 4, 1959, Dulles Papers, Special Assistant's Chronological Series, box 14, DDEL.

24. Memorandum of conference, June 19, 1959, Papers as President, Ann Whitman File, DDE Diary Series, box 42, DDEL; Eisenhower-Herter telephone conversation, July 8, 1959, *FRUS 1958–60*, 10: pt. 1, 307–8; Eisenhower-Herter discussion, July 9, 1959, *FRUS 1958–60*, 8:971–73.

25. Robert Murphy meeting with Kozlov, July 12, 1959, and message text from Eisenhower to Khrushchev, *FRUS 1958–60*, 10: pt. 1, 316–19. Khrushchev's reply, July 21, 1959, *FRUS 1958–60*, 10: pt. 1, 324–25; Sergei Khrushchev, *Nikita Khrushchev and the Creation of a Superpower*, 319–20.

26. Staff notes, July 21, 1959, Papers as President, Ann Whitman File, DDE Diary Series, box 43, DDEL.

27. Nixon's reports to Eisenhower of July 26, July 28 (two telegrams), and July 31, 1959, Papers as President, Ann Whitman File, Administration Series, box 28, DDEL.

28. Nixon, *Six Crises*, 245, 250, 252, 254, 257, 258, 265, 271; Talbot, *Khrushchev Remembers*, 458.

29. James Reston, *New York Times*, August 1 and 2, 1959; Walter Lippmann, *Los Angeles Times*, August 5, 1959; polls in *Washington Post*, August 5 and September 18, 1959.

30. *Los Angeles Times, New York Times*, and *Wall Street Journal*, August 4, 1959; poll in *Los Angeles Times*, September 16, 1959; James Reston, *New York Times*, August 13, 1959; Ann Whitman note, August 7–15, 1959, Papers as President, Ann Whitman Papers, Ann Whitman Diary Series, box 11, DDEL.

31. Meeting with Eisenhower and Nixon, August 5, 1959, Papers as President, Ann

Whitman File, DDE Diary Series, box 43, DDEL; Thompson telegram, August 8, 1959, White House Office, Office of the Staff Secretary: Records, 1952–61, International Trips and Meetings Series, box 8, DDEL. The briefing books prepared for the visit echoed Thompson's advice. Papers as President, Ann Whitman File, International Series, box 52, DDEL.

32. Memo of conversation, August 24, 1959, Papers as President, Ann Whitman File, DDE Diary Series, box 43, DDEL.

33. John Eisenhower, *Strictly Personal*, 240–42; DDE, *Waging Peace*, 416–18.

34. Macmillan, *Riding the Storm*, 747–50.

35. Macmillan, *Riding the Storm*, 749; John Eisenhower, *Strictly Personal*, 248 and for the Shakespeare reference, 252.

36. DDE, *Waging Peace*, 426.

37. Memo of conversation, September 14, 1959, and report on *Lunik II*, September 14, 1959, in Papers as President, Ann Whitman File, DDE Diary Series, box 44, DDEL; *Washington Post*, September 15, 1959. Nixon's speech covered in *Los Angeles Times*, *New York Times*, and *Washington Post*, September 15, 1959.

38. Sergei Khrushchev, *Nikita Khrushchev and the Creation of a Superpower*, 326–30; Nikita Khrushchev, *Memoirs*, 3:100.

39. Buchanan, *Red Carpet at the White House*, 19–20; *Los Angeles Times, New York Times*, September 16, 1959.

40. "Gifts Mr. Khrushchev brought to the President," September 23, 1959, Papers as President, Ann Whitman File, International Series, box 52, DDEL.

41. Summaries on the Eisenhower-Khrushchev talks, September 15, 1959, *FRUS 1958–60*, 10:392–402, 409–10.

42. Buchanan, *Red Carpet at the White House*, 26–29; *New York Times*, September 17, 1959.

43. Buchanan, *Red Carpet at the White House*, 31–34; *New York Times*, September 18 and 19, 1959; *Washington Post*, September 20, 1959.

44. Lodge, *The Storm Has Many Eyes*, 163–68; Buchanan, *Red Carpet at the White House*, 36–41; Khrushchev, *Memoirs*, 111–12; Gosden comment, September 21, 1959, Papers as President, Ann Whitman File, International Series, box 52, DDEL. Lodge wrote reports on each day's events for the president and the State Department. See especially a summary of the Los Angeles fiasco, "Talking Paper for Report to the President," September 25, 1959. All the reports are in Papers as President, Ann Whitman File, DDE Diary Series, box 44, DDEL.

45. Buchanan, *Red Carpet at the White House*, 42–50; Lodge, *The Storm Has Many Eyes*, 169–76.

46. DDE conversation with Lodge, September 25, 1959, *FRUS 1958–60*, 10:454–59.

47. Details on menus and films as well as all the logistics are in Edward Beach and Evan Aurand [naval aide] Papers, box 17, DDEL. Khrushchev, *Memoirs*, 166–67.

48. Khrushchev, *Memoirs*, 169; DDE, *Waging Peace*, 446–47.

49. *Washington Post*, September 28, 1959; *New York Times* and *Washington Post*, September 29, 1959.

50. Taubman, *Khrushchev*, 439–41.

51. Russell Baker, *New York Times*, October 8, 1959; see also Arthur Krock, *New York Times*, September 27, 1959.

52. Joseph Alsop, *Washington Post*, September 30, 1959. The Alsop column made Ike "unusually angry," noted Whitman (Papers as President, Ann Whitman File, DDE Diary Series, box 45, DDEL).

CHAPTER 17: SECRET WARS IN THE THIRD WORLD

Epigraph: Memorandum of conversation, March 17, 1960, *FRUS 1958–60*, 6:861–63.

1. *Washington Post* and *New York Times*, November 4, 1959; earlier debate about funding the new CIA headquarters in *New York Times*, December 12, 1955, and *Washington Post*, May 11, 1957. Dulles typed out his remarks ahead of time and sent them to the president. Dulles letter to Eisenhower, October 29, 1959, Papers as President, Ann Whitman File, Administration Series, box 13, DDEL.

2. For excellent essays on this problem, see Statler and Johns, *The Eisenhower Administration, the Third World, and the Globalization of the Cold War*.

3. NSC 5412/2, December 28, 1955, *FRUS 1950–55: The Intelligence Community*, 747–49; "Historical Background of the Functioning of the NSC 5412/2 Special Group and Its Predecessors," memo by Allen Dulles, January 19, 1959, DDO, http://tinyurl .galegroup.com/tinyurl/3xWYZ0; Prados, *Safe for Democracy*, 160–61; Ambrose and Immerman, *Ike's Spies*, 240–44.

4. "Report Prepared by the Ad Hoc Interdepartmental Committee on Indonesia for the National Security Council," September 3, 1957, and Minutes of NSC meeting, September 23, 1957, *FRUS 1955–57*, 22:436–40, 450–53.

5. Memorandum for John Foster Dulles, "U.S. Policy towards Indonesia," January 2, 1958, and memorandum of conversation, January 2, 1958, *FRUS 1958–60*, 17:1–3, 4–6.

6. Memo by Allen Dulles, "Probable Developments in Indonesia," January 31, 1957, and NSC discussion, February 27, 1958, in "Editorial Note," *FRUS 1958–60*, 17:19–24, 49–50.

7. Telegram from Jones to State Department, March 19, 1958, *FRUS 1958–60*, 17:74–80.

8. Memorandum of conversation with the president, April 15, 1958, *FRUS 1958–60*, 17:109–10.

9. Prados, *Safe for Democracy*, 175–79; *Washington Post*, May 29, 1958. Pope was tried and condemned to death but released in 1962 on Sukarno's orders.

10. *Washington Post*, May 3, 1957.

11. On Diem's rise to power and appointment, see Miller, *Misalliance*, 19–53; Jacobs, *America's Miracle Man in Vietnam*, 26–59; Logevall, *Embers of War*, 588–93.

12. On the close ties between Diem and the CIA, see the recently declassified CIA history by Thomas Ahern, *The CIA and the House of Ngo*.

13. Spector, *The United States Army in Vietnam*, 303–27; Gibbons, *The U.S. Government and the Vietnam War*, 305–16.

14. "Briefing Book of May 1957 Visit of Ngo Dinh Diem," DDO, http://tinyurl.galegroup
    .com/tinyurl/429Hi9.

15. Memorandum of conversation between Eisenhower and Diem, May 9, 1957, *FRUS
    1955–57, Vietnam*, 1:799–801; *New York Times*, May 10 and 14, 1957; Jacobs, *America's Miracle Man in Vietnam*, 255.

16. Durbrow to State Department, December 5, 1957, *FRUS 1955–57, Vietnam*, 1:869–84.

17. Logevall, *Embers of War*, 687–91.

18. CIA, National Intelligence Estimate 63–59, "Prospects for North and South Vietnam," May 26, 1959, CIA Vietnam Collection, CIA Reading Room, https://www.cia
    .gov/library/readingroom/collection/vietnam-collection; Ahern, *The CIA and the House of Ngo*, 113–36. On the guillotine, see Richard Ehrlich, "When Heads Rolled in Vietnam," *Asia Times*, September 15, 2010, http://www.atimes.com/atimes/South
    east_Asia/LI15Ae01.html. A guillotine is still on display at the war museum in Ho Chi Minh City.

19. Among the many official documents that reveal this line of thinking, a useful summary statement is in Ambassador Durbrow's year-end telegram to the State Department on December 7, 1959, *FRUS 1958–60, Vietnam*, 1:255–71.

20. Schoultz, *That Infernal Little Cuban Republic*, 52–63.

21. Matthews wrote a three-part portrait of Castro in the *New York Times*, February 24, 25, 26, 1957; see also *Life*, March 25, 1957.

22. *Life*, April 14 and July 21, 1958.

23. Dulles to embassy in Cuba, February 28, 1958; Herter to embassy in Cuba, March 12, 1958; embassy in Cuba to State Department, March 14, 1958, all in *FRUS 1958–60*, 6:42–43, 55–56, 57–59.

24. NSC meeting, December 23, 1958, and Herter to Eisenhower, December 23, 1958, *FRUS 1958–60*, 6:302–3, 304–7. The 5412 Group discussed third force efforts on December 31, 1958. See "Memorandum for the Record," U.S. National Security Council Presidential Records, Intelligence Files, 1953–61, box 1, DDEL. For efforts to find a third force between Batista and Castro, see Paterson, *Contesting Castro*, 216–25.

25. *Life*, January 19, 1959; Dulles to Eisenhower, January 7, 1959, *FRUS 1958–60*, 6:347.

26. White House staff note, January 13, 1959, *FRUS 1958–60*, 6:356; *Life*, January 26 and February 2, 1959.

27. John Foster Dulles remarks in memorandum of discussion, NSC meeting, June 19, 1958, *FRUS 1958–60*, 5:27–32; Allen Dulles remarks in NSC meeting, February 12, 1959, *FRUS 1958–60*, 6:397–98.

28. "Briefing Memorandum—Cuba," February 6, 1959; "Political Conditions in Cuba," February 25, 1959; memorandum of conversation, March 12, 1959; NSC meeting, March 26, 1959, all in *FRUS 1958–60*, 6:395–96, 410–20, 424–28, 440–42; Nasser parallel made by Karl Meyer in *Washington Post*, April 5, 1959.

29. *Washington Post*, April 16, 1959; memorandum of conversation, Eisenhower-Herter, April 18, 1959, *FRUS 1958–60*, 6:475.

30. *Chicago Tribune, New York Times*, and *Washington Post*, April 18, 1959.

31. Nixon's memorandum was reproduced in Safford, "The Nixon-Castro Meeting of 19 April 1959." See also Nixon, *RN*, 201–3.

32. *New York Times*, April 21 and 22, 1959; *Washington Post*, April 26 and 27, 1959; *Wall Street Journal*, April 23, 1959.

33. Memorandum from Herter to Eisenhower, April 23, 1959, *FRUS 1958–60*, 6:482–83.

34. *New York Times*, February 20, April 5, April 24, 1959.

35. Schoultz, *That Infernal Little Cuban Republic*, 93–97; State Department to embassy in Havana, May 22, 1959; Herter comment in NSC meeting, June 25, 1959; Ambassador Philip Bonsal to State Department, August 2, 1959; on Che's world tour, CIA memo to State Department, August 19, 1959, all in *FRUS 1958–60*, 6:510–11, 541–43, 580–82, 589–91.

36. *New York Times*, July 14 and 16, 1959; *Wall Street Journal*, July 15, 1959; testimony of Pedro Luis Díaz Lanz, July 10, 13, and 14, 1959, and testimony of Spruille Braden, July 17, 1959, in U.S. Senate, *Communist Threat to the U.S. through the Caribbean*.

37. *Life*, July 27, 1959.

38. LeoGrande, "Anger, Anti-Americanism, and the Break in U.S.-Cuban Relations"; Fidel Castro, "Speech to the People of Cuba at Loyalty Rally," October 26, 1959, http://lanic.utexas.edu/project/castro/db/1959/19591026.html; Bonsal, *Cuba, Castro, and the United States*, 106.

39. NSC meeting, October 29, 1959; Herter to Eisenhower, November 5, 1959; "Basic Policy toward Cuba," all in *FRUS 1958–60*, 6:646, 656–58, 638–39. Eisenhower read and initialed Herter's November 5 memo. See White House Office, Office of the Staff Secretary, International Series, box 4, DDEL.

40. CIA, *Official History of the Bay of Pigs Operation*, vol. 3 (December 1979), 28–29.

41. Bissell, *Reflections of a Cold Warrior*, 154. On the January 8, 1960, meeting see CIA, *Official History of the Bay of Pigs Operation*, 3:30–34.

42. Minutes of 5412 Special Group meetings, October 28, November 4, November 18, December 9, 1959 and January 13, 1960, U.S. National Security Council Presidential Records, Intelligence Files, 1953–61, box 1, DDEL.

43. Memoranda of meetings on January 23 and 25, 1960, White House Office, Office of the Staff Secretary, International Series, box 4, DDEL.

44. CIA, *Official History of the Bay of Pigs Operation*, 3:47–50; 5412 Group meetings, February 3 and 17, 1960, White House Office, Office of the Staff Secretary, International Series, box 4, DDEL; Gray's report to the president, February 17, 1960, *FRUS 1958–60*, 6:789–90.

45. DDE, *Waging Peace*, 525–31.

46. DDE, *Waging Peace*, 532–33.

47. NSC meeting, *FRUS 1958–60*, 6:832–37.

48. The process of drafting the March 16, 1960, policy memo is covered in detail in CIA, *Official History of the Bay of Pigs Operation*, 3:57–75. A redacted version of the memo is in *FRUS 1958–60*, 6:850–51; the full text, declassified in 1998, can be

seen in White House Office, Office of the Staff Secretary, International Series, box 4, DDEL. Eisenhower quoted in memorandum of conversation, March 17, 1960, *FRUS 1958–60*, 6:861–63.

CHAPTER 18: U-2

Epigraph: Minutes of meeting of Foreign Intelligence Advisory Board, February 2, 1960, White House Office, Office of the Staff Secretary, Records, 1952–61, Subject Series, Alphabetical Subseries, Box 15, DDEL.

1. NSC meeting, February 18, 1960, *FRUS 1958–60*, 3:842–43.

2. Memorandum of conversation, Eisenhower, Dulles, Twining, January 22, 1958, DDO, http://tinyurl.galegroup.com/tinyurl/45Vr28; memorandum of conversation with the president and the President's Board of Consultants on Foreign Intelligence Activities, December 22, 1958, White House Office, Office of the Staff Secretary, Subject Series, Alphabetical Subseries, box 15, DDEL.

3. Memorandum for the record, February 12, 1959, DDO, http://tinyurl.galegroup .com/tinyurl/45Vwp7. On congressional pressures, see Pedlow and Welzenbach, "The CIA and the U-2 Program," 161.

4. Memorandum of conversation, April 3, 1959, DDO, http://tinyurl.galegroup.com /tinyurl/45VdN3; "U-2 Vulnerability Tests," DDO, http://tinyurl.galegroup.com /tinyurl/45VxY8.

5. Memorandum of conference, April 11, 1959, DDO, http://tinyurl.galegroup.com /tinyurl/45VeG3.

6. "Report of the CIA Ad Hoc Panel on Status of the Soviet ICBM Program," August 25, 1959, CIA Reading Room, https://www.cia.gov/library/readingroom/docs/1959-08 -25a.pdf; Bissell to acting chief, Development Projects Division, August 28, 1959, CIA Reading Room, https://www.cia.gov/library/readingroom/docs/1959-08-28.pdf.

7. Robert Amory to Allen Dulles, "Operational ICBM Sites," January 27, 1960, CIA Reading Room, https://www.cia.gov/library/readingroom/docs/1960-01-27a.pdf.

8. Columns in the *Washington Post*, January 25, 26, 27, 28, 29, 30, 1960.

9. There are two sets of notes taken by General Goodpaster of the February 2 meeting, one written on February 5 and one on February 8, 1960. They can be seen at DDO, http://tinyurl.galegroup.com/tinyurl/45WFx8 and http://tinyurl.galegroup.com/tiny url/45Vyy2.

10. Pedlow and Welzenbach, "The CIA and the U-2 Program," 167–70.

11. Bissell, *Reflections of a Cold Warrior*, 123.

12. Bissell stresses the pressure from Congress (*Reflections of a Cold Warrior*, 124–25).

13. Michael Beschloss has written a thoroughly researched and lively account of these events, *Mayday*, and chapters 1, 2, 9, and 10 deal superbly with the shoot-down and the immediate U.S. response. See also Brugioni, *Eyes in the Sky*, chapter 13; Pedlow and Welzenbach, "The CIA and the U-2 Program," 174–81.

14. "Chronological Account of Handling of U-2 Incident," White House Office, Office of the Staff Secretary, Subject Series, Alphabetical Subseries, box 25, DDEL.

15. Bissell, *Reflections of a Cold Warrior*, 128–29.

16. Sergei Khrushchev, *Nikita Khrushchev and the Creation of a Superpower*, 380; Nikita Khrushchev, *Memoirs*, 3:239–40.

17. Andrew Goodpaster, "Cold War Overflights: A View from the White House," in Hall and Laurie, *Early Cold War Overflights*, 44.

18. Beschloss, *Mayday*, 43–44.

19. Thompson telegram, May 5, 1959, White House Office, Office of the Staff Secretary, Subject Series, Alphabetical Subseries, box 25, DDEL; Sergei Khrushchev, *Nikita Khrushchev and the Creation of a Superpower*, 380.

20. The NASA and State Department press releases of May 5, 1959, are in White House Office, Office of the Staff Secretary, Subject Series, Alphabetical Subseries, box 25, DDEL.

21. Beschloss, *Mayday*, 58–59.

22. State Department press release, May 7, 1960, White House Office, Office of the Staff Secretary, Subject Series, Alphabetical Subseries, box 25, DDEL.

23. James Reston, *New York Times*, May 9, 1960.

24. Thompson telegrams to State Department, May 9, 1960, *FRUS 1958–60*, 10:519–21.

25. *New York Times*, May 10, 1960.

26. "The President's News Conference," May 11, 1960, American Presidency Project, http://www.presidency.ucsb.edu/ws/index.php?pid=11778.

27. Certainly Bissell hailed Ike's manly decision (*Reflections of a Cold Warrior*, 128); Brugioni, *Eyes in the Sky*, 345–57. Ike told a group of Republican senators on the morning of May 11 that the summit would be held without any problem and that "the U.S. would not be encumbered by the U-2 incident" (memorandum for Ann Whitman, May 11, 1960, Papers as President, Ann Whitman File, DDE Diary, box 50, DDEL).

28. Walter Lippmann, "The U-2 in Paris," *Washington Post*, May 17, 1960. Eisenhower's brother Milton also thought the president should not have accepted personal blame (Milton Eisenhower Oral History, OH-345, DDEL).

29. Beschloss, *Mayday*, 262–66. Details on Khrushchev's remarks in embassy to State Department, May 11, 1960, White House Office, Office of the Staff Secretary, Subject Series, Alphabetical Subseries, box 25, DDEL.

30. Memorandum, May 15, 1960, 4:30 p.m., Papers as President, Ann Whitman File, DDE Diary, box 50, DDEL; meeting of heads of state, May 15, 1960, 6 p.m., *FRUS 1958–60*, 9:426–35.

31. Khrushchev, *Memoirs*, 3:243–44.

32. Meetings of heads of state, May 16, 1960, and Herter to State Department, *FRUS 1958–60*, 9:438–52, 453–54; John Eisenhower, *Strictly Personal*, 274.

33. Eisenhower to various allies, May 19, 1960, Papers as President, Ann Whitman File, DDE Diary, box 49, DDEL; DDE, *Waging Peace*, 558.

34. Text in *New York Times*, May 20, 1960.

35. Kennedy quoted in *Los Angeles Times*, May 20, 1960; other Democratic critics quoted in *New York Times*, May 21, 22, and 23, 1960.

36. *Washington Post*, May 22, 24, and 29, 1960; *Los Angeles Times*, May 24, 1960; *New York Times*, May 24 and 28, 1960.

37. U.S. Senate, *Executive Sessions of the Senate Foreign Relations Committee*, vol. 12.

38. Excerpts from Fulbright speech in *New York Times*, June 29, 1960.

39. See Kennedy's essay, dated January 1, 1960, published as the foreword to a book of JFK's speeches edited by Allan Nevins, *The Strategy of Peace*, 3–8.

40. Text of speech in *New York Times*, June 15, 1960.

41. *New York Times*, June 15, 1960.

42. "Address of Senator John F. Kennedy Accepting the Democratic Party Nomination for the Presidency, July 15, 1960," American Presidency Project, www.presidency .ucsb.edu/ws/index.php?pid=25966.

43. Kistiakowsky, *A Scientist at the White House*, 375.

CHAPTER 19: FIGHTING TO THE FINISH

Epigraph: Speech at New York Coliseum, November 2, 1960, *PPP: Dwight D. Eisenhower*, 832.

1. *Wall Street Journal*, July 22, 1960.

2. *Los Angeles Times* and *Washington Post*, July 22, 1960; Rowse, "Political Polls."

3. *Washington Post*, July 22, 1960.

4. *New York Times*, July 23 and 24, 1960; *Los Angeles Times*, July 24, 1960.

5. *New York Times*, July 27, 1960.

6. *Chicago Tribune*, July 27, 1960.

7. *New York Times*, July 27, 1960; *Washington Post*, July 27, 1960.

8. "Address at the Republican National Convention," July 26, 1960, *PPP: Dwight D. Eisenhower*, 589–601; James Reston, *New York Times*, July 28, 1960.

9. Richard Nixon, "Address Accepting the Presidential Nomination at the Republican National Convention in Chicago," July 28, 1960, American Presidency Project, http:// www.presidency.ucsb.edu/ws/?pid=25974.

10. Press conferences, August 10, 17, and 24, 1960, *PPP: Dwight D. Eisenhower*, 619–29, 633–43, 647–58.

11. For a careful analysis of the remark, see Frank, *Ike and Dick*, 204–9. Nixon wrote later that the comment "hurt" him (*RN*, 219).

12. Charles C. Cogan and Ernest May, "The Congo, 1960–1963," in May and Zelikow, *Dealing with Dictators*, 49–66.

13. NSC meeting, July 21, 1960, *FRUS 1958–60*, 14:338–42.

14. Devlin cable to CIA, August 18, 1960, in U.S. Senate, *Alleged Assassination Plots Involving Foreign Leaders*, 14; NSC meeting, August 18, 1960, *FRUS 1958–60*, 14:421–24.

15. U.S. Senate, *Alleged Assassination Plots Involving Foreign Leaders*, 55. The minutes that Johnson took appear in *FRUS 1958–60*, 14:421–42; Papers as President, Ann Whitman File, NSC Series, box 13, DDEL.

16. Dillon and Gray remarks in U.S. Senate, *Alleged Assassination Plots Involving Foreign Leaders*, 58–60. Goodpaster said, "My very firm belief and my very strong and clear

recollection is that there was nothing whatsoever of that kind during that period either involving the President or any member of his staff of which I was aware" (Goodpaster Oral History OH-378, DDEL). In 1976 Gray, Dillon, Goodpaster, and Marion Boggs, another NSC note taker, wrote a joint letter to Senator Church to condemn the Church Committee's inference that Eisenhower knew about the plot to kill Lumumba (Gordon Gray Papers, box 2, DDEL).

17. Special Group minutes, and Dulles telegram to Congo station, August 26, 1960, U.S. Senate, *Alleged Assassination Plots Involving Foreign Leaders*, 60, 15. See also Dulles telegram, September 27, 1960, to Station in Congo *FRUS 1964–1968*, 23: 22–23.

18. Bissell, *Reflections of a Cold Warrior*, 144. Bissell said much the same to the Church Committee (U.S. Senate, *Alleged Assassination Plots Involving Foreign Leaders*, 61).

19. U.S. Senate, *Alleged Assassination Plots Involving Foreign Leaders*, 19–70; Devlin, *Chief of Station, Congo*, 94–97.

20. Eisenhower comment made on September 19, 1960; Dulles remark on Mobutu in NSC meeting, September 21, 1960; Dulles on Lumumba as insane, NSC meeting, September 15, 1960, all in *FRUS 1958–60*, 14:495, 497, 490.

21. For the most detailed account of Lumumba's story, based on a careful analysis of all the available evidence, see Gerard and Kuklick, *Death in the Congo*.

22. Larry Devlin met with Mobutu before the coup and offered American support for it (Devlin, *Chief of Station, Congo*, 76–83).

23. Portland speech on September 7, 1960, *Chicago Tribune and Washington Post*, September 8, 1960.

24. *Chicago Tribune*, September 15 and 18, 1960; *New York Times* and *Los Angeles Times*, September 21, 1960.

25. Kornbluh, *Bay of Pigs Declassified*, chronology, 267–74.

26. CIA, *Official History of the Bay of Pigs Operation*, 3:103–9; "Memorandum of Meeting with the President," August 18, 1960, DDO, tinyurl.galegroup.com/tinyurl/4ARK50. The argument that Eisenhower was "unenthusiastic" about the Cuba plan, asserted by Peter Wyden, is clearly incorrect. See his *Bay of Pigs*, 30.

27. *New York Times* and *Washington Post*, September 20, 1960.

28. For the fuss about the hotel, see *Chicago Daily Defender*, September 21, 1960; a profile of the Hotel Theresa in *New York Times*, September 21, 1960. Coverage of the Castro-Malcolm X meeting, which occurred late on September 19, is in *New York Amsterdam News*, September 24, 1960. See also *New Journal and Guide*, Norfolk, Va., September 24, 1960. Khrushchev's meeting with Castro is covered in *Washington Post*, September 21, 1960.

29. *New York Amsterdam News*, September 24, 1960; *New York Times* and *Washington Post*, September 21, 1960; Sergei Khrushchev, *Nikita Khrushchev and the Creation of a Superpower*, 411.

30. Address to the General Assembly, September 22, 1960, *PPP: Dwight D. Eisenhower*, 707–20. Coverage of the events in New York, *Los Angeles Times*, September 23, 1960;

Washington Post, September 22 and 23, 1960; *New York Times*, September 22 and 27, 1960; *Chicago Tribune*, September 22, 1960.

31. Kennedy speech covered in *New York Times*, October 7, 1960. Texts of second and third debates, *Washington Post*, October 8 and 14, 1960.

32. *New York Times*, October 19 and 21, 1960.

33. For a recent effort to get to the bottom of what Dulles told Kennedy, see Helgerson, *Getting to Know the President*, 29–59. Nixon's account is in *Six Crises*, 351–56.

34. Text of fourth debate and commentary in *Washington Post*, October 22, 1960.

35. Morrow, *Forty Years a Guinea Pig*, 205–6; Lawson, *Black Ballots*, 255–58; Sorensen, *Kennedy*, 215–16; White, *The Making of the President*, 321–23; Schlesinger, *A Thousand Days*, 73–74; Nixon, *Six Crises*, 362–63; Burk, *The Eisenhower Administration and Black Civil Rights*, 259–60.

36. Eisenhower quoted in "Biggest Gun," *Time*, October 10, 1960; letter to Nixon, October 1, 1960, *PDDE*, 21:2109–10; Ewald, *Eisenhower the President*, 301–9.

37. Nixon, *RN*, 222; Frank, *Ike and Dick*, 211.

38. Speech at New York Coliseum, November 2, 1960, *PPP: Dwight D. Eisenhower*, 832.

39. Cleveland and Pittsburgh speeches, November 4, 1960, *PPP: Dwight D. Eisenhower*, 836–41, 846–51.

40. White, *The Making of the President*, 309–10; James Reston, *New York Times*, November 2, 1960.

41. John Eisenhower, *Strictly Personal*, 285. Ike expressed similar sentiments to Ann Whitman (Papers as President, Ann Whitman File, DDE Diary Series, box 54, DDEL).

42. Letter to Richard Nixon, November 9, 1960, *PDDE*, 21:2156; Slater, *The Ike I Knew*, 230; DDE, *Waging Peace*, 652.

43. Schlesinger, *Journals*, 93.

44. White, *The Making of the President*, 353.

45. For a nuanced assessment of Eisenhower's party-building efforts that gives Ike more credit than previous scholars, see Galvin, *Presidential Party Building*, 41–69.

46. Ewald, *Eisenhower the President*, 310–11; James Reston, *New York Times*, November 2, 1960; Frank, *Ike and Dick*, 208–9.

47. Letter to George Murphy, November 20, 1960, *PDDE*, 21:2165–66.

48. Papers as President, Ann Whitman File, DDE Diary Series, box 54, DDEL.

49. The affair can be followed in *New York Times*, November 11, 12, 19, 22, 24, 26, 29, and December 2, 1960; *Los Angeles Times*, November 20, 22, 27, 30, 1960; *Washington Post*, November 19, 23, 24, 25, and December 2, 1960. Also see Kallina, *Kennedy v. Nixon*, 183–87, for a careful assessment.

50. Ewald, *Eisenhower the President*, 313. Nixon's account is in *Six Crises*, 411–13. Eisenhower's support for Morton reported in *Washington Post*, December 2, 1960.

CHAPTER 20: A NEW GENERATION

Epigraph: Farewell address, January 17, 1961, *PPP: Dwight D. Eisenhower*, 1035–40.

1. *New York Times*, December 4, 6 and 7, 1960.

2. Schlesinger, *Journals*, 58; White, *The Making of the President*, 177, 329; "Address of Senator John F. Kennedy Accepting the Democratic Party Nomination for the Presidency of the United States," July 15, 1960, American Presidency Project, http://www.presidency.ucsb.edu/ws/?pid=25966.

3. Account of meeting with Kennedy on December 6, 1960, *PDDE*, 21:2189–95; Papers as President, Ann Whitman File, DDE Diary Series, box 54, DDEL.

4. Sorensen, *Kennedy*, 231; Reeves, *President Kennedy*, 23; Guthman and Shulman, *Robert Kennedy in His Own Words*, 55.

5. Clifford, *Counsel to the President*, 334, 342.

6. National Intelligence Estimate, "The Outlook for Laos," May 19, 1959, and "The Situation in Laos," September 18, 1959, CIA Vietnam Collection, CIA Reading Room, https://www.cia.gov/library/readingroom/collection/vietnam-collection; NSC meeting, December 1, 1960; memorandum for the president, December 12, 1960; memorandum of telephone conversation with president, December 14, 1960, all in *FRUS 1958–60*, 16: 982, 1003–4, 1008–9.

7. NSC meeting, December 20, 1960, *FRUS 1958–60*, 16:1014–16.

8. Memorandum of conference with the president, December 31, 1960, and minutes of meeting on January 7, 1961, White House Office, Office of the Staff Secretary, International Series, box 9, DDEL.

9. Notes dictated by John Kennedy of a meeting with Eisenhower, January 19, 1961, *FRUS 1961–63*, 24:19–20. Gen. Wilton Persons also prepared a summary of the discussion, as did Secretary Herter (*FRUS 1961–63*, 24:20–25). See also DDE, *Waging Peace*, 618–19, Greenstein and Immerman, "What Did Eisenhower Tell Kennedy About Indochina?"

10. Clifford, *Counsel to the President*, 342–44.

11. "Support for Covert Paramilitary Operations," November 2, 1960, U.S. National Security Council Presidential Records, Intelligence Files, box 2, DDEL. See also Gleijeses, "Ships in the Night," on the evolution of the plan.

12. Minutes of Special Group (5412 Committee), November 3, 1960, U.S. National Security Council Presidential Records, Intelligence Files, box 1, DDEL.

13. Minutes of Special Group (5412 Committee), November 19, 1960, U.S. National Security Council Presidential Records, Intelligence Files, box 1, DDEL.

14. Memorandum of a meeting with the president, November 29, 1960, *FRUS 1958–60*, 6:1126–31; CIA, *Official History of the Bay of Pigs Operation*, 3:165–73.

15. Minutes of Special Group (5412 Committee), December 8, 1960, U.S. National Security Council Presidential Records, Intelligence Files, box 1, DDEL. Lansdale was right. The *New York Times* printed a front-page story on January 10, 1961, breaking the news about the band of Cuban exiles training in Guatemala.

16. Memorandum of conversation, December 29, 1960, *FRUS 1958–60*, 6:1188–89. For discussion of the decisions yet to be made, see Hawkins to Esterline, January 4, 1961, *FRUS 1961–63*, 10:10–16.

17. *New York Times*, January 31, 1961.

18. Moos, memorandum for the record, May 20, 1959, Arthur Larson and Malcolm Moos Records, box 16, DDEL; Eisenhower letter to Milton, May 25, 1959, Arthur Larson and Malcolm Moos Records, box 17, DDEL.

19. Frederic Fox to Malcolm Moos, April 5, 1960, Arthur Larson and Malcolm Moos Records, box 16, DDEL; memorandum by Williams, October 31, 1960, Ralph E. Williams Papers, box 1, DDEL. For details about the origins of the speech, see Griffin, "New Light on Eisenhower's Farewell Address"; Newton, *Eisenhower*, 336–45; and the oral histories of Ralph E. Williams, OH-503, and Malcolm Moos, OH-260, DDEL.

20. Farewell address, January 17, 1961, *PPP: Dwight D. Eisenhower*, 1035–40.

21. David Eisenhower, *Going Home to Glory*, 3–4.

22. Dallek, *An Unfinished Life*, 351–52.

23. Editorial note; memorandum of conversation, January 25, 1961; "Memorandum of Discussion on Cuba," January 28, 1961; Bundy to Kennedy, February 8, 1961, all in *FRUS 1961–63*, 10:44, 54–55, 61–62, 89.

24. Editorial note, *FRUS 1961–63*, 10:143; Dallek, *An Unfinished Life*, 358–62; Schlesinger, *A Thousand Days*, 256; Reeves, *President Kennedy*, 73. Eisenhower later insisted that the Cuba plan was still in its infancy when Kennedy took office and that Kennedy could have canceled it if he wanted. The attempts of Sorensen and Schlesinger to saddle Ike with the failed planned rankled, as it seemed to suggest Kennedy was imprisoned by Eisenhower's plan. "At no time did I put before anybody anything that could be called a plan," Eisenhower told journalist Earl Mazo in 1965—a remarkable untruth. Earl Mazo, "Ike Speaks Out: Bay of Pigs Was All JFK's," *Newsday*, September 10, 1965.

25. The details are in the excellent chronology in Kornbluh, *Bay of Pigs Declassified*; Dallek, *An Unfinished Life*, 363–72; Schlesinger, *A Thousand Days*, 267–96.

26. David Eisenhower, *Going Home to Glory*, 31. The exchange with Kennedy was reported by Eisenhower in an interview later conducted by Malcolm Moos. Ike also made a record of the meeting in his diary (Ferrell, *The Eisenhower Diaries*, 386–89, and for the acid remark about indecision, see 390).

27. Reeves, *President Kennedy*, 98–99, 116–18.

28. General Lansdale, "Review of Operation Mongoose," July 25, 1962, National Security Archive, http://nsarchive.gwu.edu/nsa/cuba_mis_cri/620725%20Review%20of%20 Op.%20Mongoose.pdf.

29. Schlesinger, *Journals*, July 13 and August 23, 1962, 161, 164.

30. David Eisenhower, *Going Home to Glory*, 57–99.

31. On Nixon visiting Ike, see Nixon, *RN*, 335, and see his portrait of Eisenhower in his final days, 375–80; David Eisenhower, *Going Home to Glory*, 276.

32. *New York Times*, March 29, 1969; *Time*, cover story, April 4 1969: "A First Verdict" and "Eisenhower: Soldier of Peace."

33. CSPAN, "Presidential Historians Survey 2017," https://www.c-span.org/presidentsur vey2017/?page=overall.

BIBLIOGRAPHY

Abell, Tyler, ed. *Drew Pearson Diaries, 1949–1959.* New York: Holt, Rinehart, and Winston, 1974.

Adams, Sherman. *Firsthand Report: The Story of the Eisenhower Administration.* New York: Harper and Brothers, 1961.

Ahern, Thomas. *The CIA and the House of Ngo: Covert Action in South Vietnam, 1954–1963.* Washington, D.C.: CIA, Center for the Study of Intelligence, 2000.

Aldous, Richard. *Macmillan, Eisenhower, and the Cold War.* Portland, OR: Four Courts Press, 2005.

Alexander, Charles C. *Holding the Line: The Eisenhower Era, 1952–1961.* Bloomington: Indiana University Press, 1975.

Alsop, Stewart. *Nixon and Rockefeller: A Double Portrait.* New York: Doubleday, 1960.

Ambrose, Stephen. *Eisenhower: The President.* New York: Simon & Schuster, 1984.

———. *Eisenhower: Soldier and President.* New York: Simon & Schuster, 1990.

———. *Eisenhower: Soldier, General of the Army, President-Elect, 1890–1952.* New York: Simon & Schuster, 1983.

Ambrose, Stephen, and Richard Immerman. *Ike's Spies: Eisenhower and the Espionage Establishment.* New York: Anchor Books, 1981.

———. *Milton S. Eisenhower: Educational Statesman.* Baltimore: Johns Hopkins University Press, 1983.

Anders, Roger M., ed. *Forging the Atomic Shield: Excerpts from the Office Diary of Gordon E. Dean.* Chapel Hill: University of North Carolina Press, 1987.

Anderson, David L. *Trapped by Success: The Eisenhower Administration and Vietnam, 1953–1961.* New York: Columbia University Press, 1991.

Anderson, J. W. *Eisenhower, Brownell, and the Congress: The Tangled Origins of the Civil Rights Bill of 1956–1957.* Tuscaloosa: University of Alabama Press, 1964.

Asselin, Pierre. "The Democratic Republic of Vietnam and the 1954 Geneva Conference: A Revisionist Critique." *Cold War History* 11, no. 2 (2011): 155–95.

Atkinson, Rick. *An Army at Dawn: The War in North Africa, 1942–1943.* New York: Henry Holt, 2002.

Bartley, Numan V. *A History of the South: The New South, 1945–1980.* Baton Rouge: Louisiana State University Press, 1995.

———. *The Rise of Massive Resistance: Race and Politics in the South during the 1950's.* Baton Rouge: Louisiana State University Press, 1997.

Belknap, Michal R., ed. *Civil Rights, the White House, and the Justice Department, 1945–1968.* 20 vols. New York: Garland, 1991.

Bell, Daniel, ed. *The Radical Right.* New York: Criterion, 1955.

Benson, Ezra Taft. *Cross Fire: Eight Years with Eisenhower.* New York: Doubleday, 1962.

Beschloss, Michael R. *Eisenhower: A Centennial Life.* New York: HarperCollins, 1990.

———. *Mayday: Eisenhower, Khrushchev and the U-2 Affair.* New York: Harper & Row, 1986.

Billings-Yun, Melanie. *Decision against War: Eisenhower and Dien Bien Phu, 1954.* New York: Columbia University Press, 1988.

Bird, Kai, and Martin J. Sherman. *American Prometheus: The Triumph and Tragedy of J. Robert Oppenheimer.* New York: Vintage Books, 2005.

Bischof, Günter, and Saki Dockrill, eds. *Cold War Respite: The Geneva Summit of 1955.* Baton Rouge: Louisiana State University Press, 2000.

Bissell, Richard M., Jr. *Reflections of a Cold Warrior: From Yalta to the Bay of Pigs.* New Haven, CT: Yale University Press, 1996.

Bogus, Carl T. *Buckley: William F. Buckley Jr. and the Rise of Modern Conservatism.* New York: Bloomsbury Press, 2011.

Bohlen, Charles E. *Witness to History, 1929–1969.* New York: Norton, 1973.

Bonsal, Philip. *Cuba, Castro and the United States.* Pittsburgh, PA: University of Pittsburgh Press, 1971.

Borgiasz, William S. *The Strategic Air Command: Evolution and Consolidation of Nuclear Forces, 1945–1955.* Westport, CT: Praeger, 1996.

Borstelmann, Thomas. *The Cold War and the Color Line.* Cambridge, MA: Harvard University Press, 2001.

Bose, Meena. *Shaping and Signaling Presidential Policy: The National Security Decision Making of Eisenhower and Kennedy.* College Station: Texas A&M University Press, 1998.

Bowen, Michael. *The Roots of Modern Conservatism: Dewey, Taft, and the Battle for the Soul of the Republican Party.* Chapel Hill: University of North Carolina Press, 2011.

Bowie, Robert R., and Richard H. Immerman. *Waging Peace: How Eisenhower Shaped an Enduring Cold War Strategy.* New York: Oxford University Press, 1998.

Boyle, Peter, ed. *The Eden-Eisenhower Correspondence, 1955–57.* Chapel Hill: University of North Carolina Press, 2005.

———. *Eisenhower.* Harlow, UK: Pearson Education, 2005.

Branch, Taylor. *Parting the Waters: America in the King Years, 1954–63.* New York: Simon and Schuster, 1988.

Brandon, Dorothy. *Mamie Doud Eisenhower: Portrait of a First Lady.* New York: Scribner's, 1954.

Brands, H. W., Jr. *Cold Warriors: Eisenhower's Generation and American Foreign Policy.* New York: Columbia University Press, 1988.

Branyan, Robert L., and Lawrence H. Larsen. *The Eisenhower Administration, 1953–1961: A Documentary History.* New York: Random House, 1971.

Brendon, Piers. *Ike: Life and Times of Dwight D. Eisenhower.* London: Martin, Secker and Warburg, 1987.

Bright, Christopher. *Continental Defense in the Eisenhower Era: Nuclear Antiaircraft Arms and the Cold War.* New York: Palgrave Macmillan, 2011.

Broadwater, Jeff. *Eisenhower and the Anti-Communist Crusade.* Chapel Hill: University of North Carolina Press, 1992.

Brodie, Fawn M. *Richard Nixon: The Shaping of His Character.* New York: Norton, 1981.

Brown, Michael E. *Flying Blind: The Politics of the U.S. Strategic Bomber Program.* Ithaca, NY: Cornell University Press, 1992.

Brown, Stuart Gerry. *Conscience in Politics: Adlai Stevenson in the 1950's.* Syracuse, NY: Syracuse University Press, 1961.

Brownell, Herbert. *Advising Ike: The Memoirs of Attorney General Herbert Brownell.* Lawrence: University Press of Kansas, 1993.

Brugioni, Dino A. *Eyes in the Sky: Eisenhower, the CIA, and Cold War Aerial Espionage.* Annapolis, MD: Naval Institute Press, 2010.

Buchanan, Wiley T. *Red Carpet at the White House.* New York: Dutton, 1964.

Buckley, William F., Jr. *God and Man at Yale: The Superstitions of "Academic Freedom."* South Bend, IN: Gateway Editions, 1951.

———, ed. *Odyssey of a Friend: Whittaker Chambers' Letters to William F. Buckley, Jr., 1954–1961.* New York: G. P. Putnam's Sons, 1969.

Bundy, McGeorge. *Danger and Survival: Choices about the Bomb in the First Fifty Years.* New York: Vintage Books, 1988.

———. "Early Thoughts on Controlling the Nuclear Arms Race: A Report to the Secretary of States, January 1953." *International Security* 7, no. 2 (1982): 3–27.

Burk, Robert Fredrick. *The Eisenhower Administration and Black Civil Rights.* Knoxville: University of Tennessee Press, 1984.

Burrows, William E. *By Any Means Necessary: America's Secret Air War in the Cold War.* New York: Farrar, Straus and Giroux, 2001.

Butcher, Harry C. *My Three Years with Eisenhower: The Personal Diary of Captain Harry C. Butcher, USNR, Naval Aide to General Eisenhower, 1942 to 1945.* New York: Simon & Schuster, 1946.

Callanan, James. *Covert Action in the Cold War: US Policy, Intelligence and CIA Operations.* London: I. B. Tauris, 2010.

Cardwell, Curt. *NSC 68 and the Political Economy of the Early Cold War.* Cambridge, UK: Cambridge University Press, 2011.

Caro, Robert A. *The Years of Lyndon Johnson.* Vols. 1–4. New York: Knopf, 1982–2012.

Carroll, Richard J. *The President as Economist: Scoring Economic Performance from Harry Truman to Barack Obama.* Denver, CO: Praeger, 2012.

Central Intelligence Agency. *Official History of the Bay of Pigs Operation.* 5 vols. CIA Online Reading Room. Updated October 31, 2016. https://www.cia.gov/library/reading room/collection/bay-pigs-release.

Chang, Gordon H. *Friends and Enemies: The United States, China, and the Soviet Union, 1948–1972.* Stanford: Stanford University Press, 1990.

Chapman, Jessica. *Cauldron of Resistance: Ngo Dinh Diem, the United States, and 1950s Southern Vietnam.* Ithaca, NY: Cornell University Press, 2013.

Chen Jian. *Mao's China and the Cold War.* Chapel Hill: University of North Carolina Press, 2001.

Chernus, Ira. *Apocalypse Management: Eisenhower and the Discourse of National Insecurity.* Stanford: Stanford University Press, 2008.

———. *Eisenhower's Atoms for Peace.* College Station: Texas A&M University Press, 2002.

———. *General Eisenhower: Ideology and Discourse.* East Lansing: Michigan State University Press, 2002.

Childs, Marquis. *Eisenhower: Captive Hero. A Critical Study of the General and the President.* New York: Harcourt, Brace, 1958.

Churchill, Winston S. *The Second World War.* 6 vols. Boston: Houghton Mifflin, 1948–53.

Clifford, Clark. *Counsel to the President.* New York: Random House, 1991.

Cohen, Warren I. *America's Response to China: A History of Sino-American Relations.* New York: Columbia University Press, 2000.

Colville, John. *The Fringes of Power.* New York: Norton, 1985.

Conboy, Kenneth, and James Morrison. *Feet to the Fire: CIA Covert Operations in Indonesia, 1957–58.* Annapolis, MD: Naval Institute Press, 1999.

Converse, Elliott V. *Rearming for the Cold War, 1945–1960.* Washington, D.C.: Office of the Secretary of Defense, 2012.

Cook, Blanche Wiesen. *The Declassified Eisenhower: A Startling Reappraisal of the Eisenhower Presidency.* New York: Penguin Books, 1981.

Costello, William. *The Facts about Nixon: An Unauthorized Biography.* New York: Viking Press, 1960.

Craig, Campbell. *Destroying the Village: Eisenhower and Thermonuclear War.* New York: Columbia University Press, 1998.

Crespino, Joseph. *Strom Thurmond's America.* New York: Hill and Wang, 2012.

Cullather, Nick. *Secret History: The CIA's Classified Account of Its Operations in Guatemala, 1952–1954.* Stanford: Stanford University Press, 1999.

Cumings, Bruce. *The Korean War: A History.* New York: Random House, 2010.

Cuordileone, K. A. *Manhood and American Political Culture in the Cold War.* New York: Routledge, 2005.

Cutler, Robert. *No Time for Rest.* Boston: Little, Brown, 1965.

Dallek, Robert. *Harry S. Truman.* New York: Henry Holt and Times Books, 2008.

———. *An Unfinished Life: John F. Kennedy, 1917–1963.* Boston: Little, Brown, 2003.

Damms, Richard V. "James Killian, the Technological Capabilities Panel, and the Emergence of Eisenhower's 'Scientific-Technological Elite.'" *Diplomatic History* 24, no. 1 (2000): 57–78.

Danchev, Alex, and Daniel Todman, eds. *Lord Alanbrooke: War Diaries, 1939–1945.* London: Weidenfeld and Nicolson, 2001.

David, Paul, Malcolm Moos, and Ralph Goldman, eds. *Presidential Nominating Politics in 1952: The National Story.* Baltimore: Johns Hopkins University Press, 1954.

Davis, Kenneth S. *A Prophet in His Own Country: The Triumphs and Defeats of Adlai E. Stevenson.* Garden City, NY: Doubleday, 1957.

———. *Soldier of Democracy.* Garden City, NY: Doubleday, 1945.

Dean, Robert D. *Imperial Brotherhood: Gender and the Making of Cold War Foreign Policy.* Amherst: University of Massachusetts Press, 2001.

De Bellaigue, Christopher. *Patriot of Persia: Muhammad Mossadegh and a Tragic Anglo-American Coup.* New York: Harper Perennial, 2012.

Delton, Jennifer A. *Rethinking the 1950s: How Anticommunism and the Cold War Made America Liberal.* New York: Cambridge University Press, 2013.

D'Este, Carlo. *Eisenhower: A Soldier's Life.* New York: Henry Holt, 2002.

De Toledano, Ralph, and Karl Hess, eds. *The Conservative Papers.* New York: Anchor Books, 1964.

Devlin, Larry. *Chief of Station, Congo: Fighting the Cold War in a Hot Zone.* New York: Public Affairs, 2007.

Dingman, Roger. "Atomic Diplomacy during the Korean War." *International Security* 13, no. 3 (1988–89): 50–91.

Divine, Robert A. *Eisenhower and the Cold War.* New York: Oxford University Press, 1981.

———. *The Sputnik Challenge.* New York: Oxford University Press, 1993.

Dochuk, Darren. *From Bible Belt to Sunbelt.* New York: Norton, 2011.

Donovan, Robert J. *Confidential Secretary: Ann Whitman's 20 Years with Eisenhower and Rockefeller.* New York: E. P. Dutton, 1988.

———. *Eisenhower: The Inside Story.* New York: Harper, 1956.

Doran, Michael. *Ike's Gamble: America's Rise to Dominance in the Middle East.* New York: Free Press, 2016.

Doyle, Edward P., ed. *As We Knew Adlai: The Stevenson Story by Twenty-Two Friends.* New York: Harper & Row, 1966.

Duchin, Brian. "'The Most Spectacular Legislative Battle of That Year': President Eisenhower and the 1958 Reorganization of the Department of Defense." *Presidential Studies Quarterly* 24, no. 2 (1994): 243–62.

Dudziak, Mary. *Cold War Civil Rights: Race and the Image of American Democracy.* Princeton, NJ: Princeton University Press, 2000.

Duiker, William J. *U.S. Containment Policy and the Conflict in Indochina.* Stanford: Stanford University Press, 1994.

Dulles, Allen. *The Craft of Intelligence.* Westport, CT: Greenwood Press, 1977.

Dulles, John Foster. "Policy for Security and Peace." *Foreign Affairs,* April 1954, 353–64.

———. *War or Peace.* New York: Macmillan, 1950.

Dunar, Andrew J. *America in the Fifties.* Syracuse, NY: Syracuse University Press, 2006.

——. *The Truman Scandals and the Politics of Morality.* Columbia: University of Missouri Press, 1984.

Eden, Anthony. *Full Circle: The Memoirs of Sir Anthony Eden.* London: Cassell, 1960.

Eisenhower, David. *Eisenhower at War, 1943–1945.* New York: Random House, 1986.

——. *Going Home to Glory: A Memoir of Life with Dwight D. Eisenhower, 1961–1969.* New York: Simon & Schuster, 2010.

Eisenhower, Dwight D. *At Ease: Stories I Tell Friends.* Garden City, NY: Doubleday, 1967.

——. *Crusade in Europe.* Garden City, NY: Doubleday, 1948.

——. *Mandate for Change, 1953–1956.* New York: Doubleday, 1963.

——. *Waging Peace, 1956–1961.* New York: Doubleday, 1965.

Eisenhower, John S. D., ed. *Letters to Mamie.* Garden City, NY: Doubleday, 1977.

——. *Strictly Personal.* Garden City, NY: Doubleday, 1974.

Eisenhower, Milton S. *The President Is Calling.* New York: Doubleday, 1974.

Eisenhower, Susan. *Mrs. Ike: Memories and Reflections on the Life of Mamie Eisenhower.* New York: Farrar, Straus and Giroux, 1996.

Elson, Edward. *America's Spiritual Recovery.* Westwood, NJ: Fleming Revell, 1954.

Ély, Paul. *Mémoires: L'Indochine dans la tourmente.* Paris: Plon, 1964.

Evans, Rowland, and Robert Novak. *Lyndon B. Johnson: The Exercise of Power.* New York: New American Library, 1966.

Ewald, William Bragg, Jr. *Eisenhower the President: Crucial Days, 1951–1960.* Englewood Cliffs, NJ: Prentice-Hall, 1981.

——. *Who Killed Joe McCarthy?* New York: Simon & Schuster, 1984.

Fall, Bernard. *Hell in a Very Small Place: The Siege of Dien Bien Phu.* Philadelphia: Lippincott, 1967.

Farber, David. *The Rise and Fall of Modern American Conservatism: A Short History.* Princeton, NJ: Princeton University Press, 2010.

Farrell, John A. *Richard Nixon: The Life.* New York: Doubleday, 2017.

Feldman, Glenn, ed. *Before Brown: Civil Rights and White Backlash in the Modern South.* Tuscaloosa: University of Alabama Press, 2004.

Ferrell, Robert H., ed. *The Diary of James C. Hagerty: Eisenhower in Mid-course, 1954–1955.* Bloomington: Indiana University Press, 1983.

——, ed. *The Eisenhower Diaries.* New York: Norton, 1981.

——, ed. *Off the Record: The Private Papers of Harry S. Truman.* New York: Harper and Row, 1980.

Fitzgerald, David. *Learning to Forget: US Army Counterinsurgency Doctrine and Practice from Vietnam to Iraq.* Stanford: Stanford University Press, 2013.

——, ed. *Painting Dixie Red: When, Where, Why, and How the South Became Republican.* Gainesville: University Press of Florida, 2011.

Flanagan, Richard M. "The Housing Act of 1954: The Sea Change in National Urban Policy." *Urban Affairs Review* 33, no. 2 (1997): 265–86.

Foot, Rosemary. "Nuclear Coercion and the Ending of the Korean Conflict." *International Security* 13, no. 3 (1988): 92–112.

Frank, Jeffrey. *Ike and Dick: Portrait of a Strange Political Marriage*. New York: Simon & Schuster, 2013.

Freedman, Lawrence. *Kennedy's Wars: Berlin, Cuba, Laos, and Vietnam*. New York: Oxford University Press, 2000.

Fried, Richard M. *Nightmare in Red: The McCarthy Era in Perspective*. New York: Oxford University Press, 1990.

Friedberg, Aaron L. *In the Shadow of the Garrison State: America's Anti-Statism and Its Cold War Grand Strategy*. Princeton, NJ: Princeton University Press, 2000.

Friedman, Milton. *Capitalism and Freedom*. Chicago: University of Chicago Press, 2002.

Fursenko, Aleksandr, and Timothy Naftali. *Khrushchev's Cold War: The Inside Story of an American Adversary*. New York: Norton, 2006.

Gaddis, John Lewis. *Strategies of Containment: A Critical Appraisal of Postwar American National Security Policy*. New York: Oxford University Press, 1982.

——. *We Now Know: Rethinking Cold War History*. New York: Oxford University Press, 1997.

Gainor, Christopher. "The Atlas and the Air Force: Reassessing the Beginnings of America's First Intercontinental Ballistic Missile." *Technology and Culture* 54 (April 2013): 346–70.

Galbraith, John Kenneth. *The Affluent Society*. Boston: Houghton Mifflin, 1958.

Galvin, Daniel J. *Presidential Party Building*. Princeton, NJ: Princeton University Press, 2010.

Gasiorowski, Mark J., and Malcolm Byrne. *Mohammad Mossadeq and the 1953 Coup in Iran*. Syracuse, NY: Syracuse University Press, 2004.

Gellman, Irwin F. *The Contender: Richard Nixon: The Congress Years, 1946–1952*. New York: Simon & Schuster, 1999.

——. *The President and the Apprentice: Eisenhower and Nixon, 1952–1961*. New Haven, CT: Yale University Press, 2015.

Gerard, Emmanuel, and Bruce Kuklick. *Death in the Congo: Murdering Patrice Lumumba*. Cambridge, MA: Harvard University Press, 2015.

Gibbons, William C. *The U.S. Government and the War in Vietnam*. Part 1: *1945–1960*. Princeton, NJ: Princeton University Press, 1986.

Gibbs, Nancy, and Michael Duffy. *The Preacher and the Presidents: Billy Graham and the Presidents*. New York: Center Street, 2007.

——. *The President's Club: Inside the World's Most Exclusive Fraternity*. New York: Simon & Schuster, 2012.

Gleijeses, Piero. *Shattered Hope: The Guatemalan Revolution and the United States, 1944–1954*. Princeton, NJ: Princeton University Press, 1991.

——. "Ships in the Night: The CIA, the White House and the Bay of Pigs." *Journal of Latin American Studies* 27, no. 1 (1995): 1–42.

Goldman, Eric. *The Crucial Decade and After: America, 1945–1960*. New York: Knopf, 1975.

Goldwater, Barry. *The Conscience of a Conservative*. Princeton, NJ: Princeton University Press, 1960.

Goodman, Melvin A. *National Insecurity: The Cost of American Militarism*. San Francisco: City Lights Books, 2013.

Graebner, Norman A. "Eisenhower's Popular Leadership." *Current History* 39 (October 1960): 230–44.

Graham, Billy. *Just As I Am*. New York: HarperSanFrancisco, 1997.

Gray, Robert Keith. *Eighteen Acres under Glass*. New York: Doubleday, 1962.

Greenberg, David. *Nixon's Shadow: The History of an Image*. New York: Norton, 2003.

Greene, John Robert. *The Crusade: The Presidential Election of 1952*. New York: University Press of America, 1985.

Greenstein, Fred I. *The Hidden-Hand Presidency: Eisenhower as Leader*. New York: Basic Books, 1982.

Greenstein, Fred I., and Richard Immerman. "Effective National Security Advising: Recovering the Eisenhower Legacy," *Political Science Quarterly* 115, no. 3 (2000): 335–45.

———. "What Did Eisenhower Tell Kennedy About Indochina?" *Journal of American History* 79, no. 2 (September 1992): 568–87.

Griffin, Charles J. G. "New Light on Eisenhower's Farewell Address." *Presidential Studies Quarterly* 22, no. 3 (1992): 469–79.

Griffith, Robert. "Dwight Eisenhower and the Corporate Commonwealth." *American Historical Review* 87, no. 1 (1982): 87–122.

———, ed. *Ike's Letters to a Friend, 1941–1958*. Lawrence: University Press of Kansas, 1984.

———. *The Politics of Fear: Joseph R. McCarthy and the Senate*. Rochelle Park, NJ: Hayden, 1970.

Grose, Peter. *Gentleman Spy: The Life of Allen Dulles*. New York: Houghton Mifflin, 1994.

Gunther, John. *Eisenhower: The Man and the Symbol*. New York: Harper & Brothers, 1952.

Gupta, Arpit. "Revisiting the High Tax Rates of the 1950s." Issue Brief no. 19. Manhattan Institute for Policy Research, April 2013.

Guthman, Edwin O., and Jeffrey Shulman, eds. *Robert Kennedy in His Own Words*. New York: Bantam, 1988.

Gyorkei, Jeno, and Miklos Horvath, eds. *1956: Soviet Military Intervention in Hungary*. Budapest: CEU Press, 1999.

Hahn, Peter. *Caught in the Middle East: U.S. Policy toward the Arab-Israeli Conflict, 1945–1961*. Chapel Hill: University of North Carolina Press, 2004.

Halberstam, David. *The Fifties*. New York: Random House, 1993.

Hall, R. Cargill, and Clayton D. Laurie. "Denied Territory: Eisenhower's Policy of Peacetime Aerial Overflight." *Air Power History* (Winter 2009): 4–9.

———. *Early Cold War Overflights, 1950–1956: Symposium Proceedings*. Washington, D.C.: Office of the Historian, National Reconnaissance Office, 2003.

Hamilton-Merritt, Jane. *Tragic Mountains: The Hmong, the Americans, and the Secret Wars for Laos, 1942–1992*. Bloomington: Indiana University Press, 1993.

Harding, Harry, and Yuan Ming, eds. *Sino-American Relations 1945–1955*. Wilmington, DE: Scholarly Resources, 1989.

Harrison, Hope M. *Driving the Soviets up the Wall: Soviet-East German Relations, 1953–1961.* Princeton, NJ: Princeton University Press, 2003.

Hart, Jeffrey. *The Making of the American Conservative Mind.* Wilmington, DE: ISI Books, 2005.

Hastings, Max. *Winston's War.* New York: Knopf, 2010.

Hatch, Alden. *Red Carpet for Mamie.* New York: Holt, 1954.

Helgerson, John L. *Getting to Know the President: Intelligence Briefings of Presidential Candidates, 1952–2004.* Washington, D.C.: CIA, Center for the Studies of Intelligence, 2012.

Herken, Gregg. *Counsels of War.* New York: Knopf, 1985.

———. *The Georgetown Set: Friends and Rivals in Cold War Washington.* New York: Knopf, 2014.

Hermes, Walter G. *Truce Tent and Fighting Front: The United States Army in the Korean War.* Washington, D.C.: Office of the Chief of Military History, United States Army, 1966.

Herring, George C., and Richard Immerman. "Eisenhower, Dulles, and Dienbienphu: 'The Day We Didn't Go to War' Revisited." *Journal of American History* 71, no. 2 (1984): 343–63.

Herzog, Jonathan P. *The Spiritual-Industrial Complex: America's Religious Battle against Communism in the Early Cold War.* New York: Oxford University Press, 2011.

Hewlett, Richard G., and Francis Duncan. *A History of the United States Atomic Energy Commission: Atomic Shield, 1947–1952.* Vol. 2. University Park: Pennsylvania State University Press, 1969.

Hewlett, Richard G., and Jack M. Holl. *Atoms for Peace and War, 1953–1961: Eisenhower and the Atomic Energy Commission.* Berkeley: University of California Press, 1989.

Hitchcock, William I. *The Struggle for Europe: The Troubled History of a Divided Continent, 1945–present.* New York: Doubleday, 2002.

Hodgson, Godfrey. *JFK and LBJ: The Last Two Great Presidents.* New Haven, CT: Yale University Press, 2015.

Hofstadter, Richard. *Anti-Intellectualism in American Life.* New York: Knopf, 1966.

Hogan, Michael J. *A Cross of Iron: Harry Truman and the Origins of the National Security State, 1945–1954.* Cambridge, UK: Cambridge University Press, 1998.

Holland, Matthew F. *Eisenhower between the Wars: The Making of a General and Statesman.* Westport, CT: Praeger, 2001.

Holmes, David L. *Faiths of the Postwar Presidents: From Truman to Obama.* Athens: University of Georgia Press, 2012.

Holt, Daniel D., ed. *Eisenhower: The Prewar Diaries and Selected Papers, 1905–1941.* Baltimore: Johns Hopkins University Press, 1998.

Holt, Marilyn Irvin. *Mamie Doud Eisenhower: The General's First Lady.* Lawrence: University Press of Kansas, 2007.

Hoopes, Townsend. *The Devil and John Foster Dulles.* Boston: Little, Brown, 1973.

Horne, Alistair. *Harold Macmillan, 1894–1956.* New York: Viking, 1988.

Howard, Katherine G. *With My Shoes Off.* New York: Vantage, 1977.

Hughes, Emmet John. *The Ordeal of Power: A Political Memoir of the Eisenhower Years.* New York: Atheneum, 1963.

Hunt, D. Bradford. "How Did Public Housing Survive the 1950s?" *Journal of Policy History* 17, no. 2 (2005): 193–216.

Hutcheson, Richard G., Jr. *God in the White House: How Religion Has Changed the Modern Presidency.* New York: Macmillan, 1988.

Ike: A Pictorial Biography. New York: Time-Life Books, 1969.

Immerman, Richard H. *The CIA in Guatemala: The Foreign Policy of Intervention.* Austin: University of Texas Press, 1982.

———. "Confessions of an Eisenhower Revisionist: An Agonizing Reappraisal." *Diplomatic History* 14, no. 3 (1990): 319–43.

———. "Eisenhower and Dulles: Who Made the Decisions?" *Political Psychology* 1, no. 2 (1979): 21–38.

———, ed. *John Foster Dulles and the Diplomacy of the Cold War.* Princeton, NJ: Princeton University Press, 1990.

———. *John Foster Dulles: Piety, Pragmatism, and Power in U.S. Foreign Policy.* Wilmington, DE: Scholarly Resources, 1999.

Inboden, William. *Religion and American Foreign Policy, 1945–1960.* New York: Cambridge University Press, 2008.

In the Matter of J. Robert Oppenheimer: Transcript of Hearing before Personnel Security Board. Washington, D.C.: GPO, 1954.

Jackson, Wayne G. *Allen Welsh Dulles as Director of Central Intelligence.* Washington, D.C.: CIA Historical Office, 1973.

Jacobs, Seth. *America's Miracle Man in Vietnam: Ngo Dinh Diem, Religion, Race and U.S. Intervention in Southeast Asia, 1950–57.* Durham, NC: Duke University Press, 2004.

Jacoway, Elizabeth. *Turn Away Thy Son: Little Rock, the Crisis That Shocked the Nation.* New York: Free Press, 2007.

Jager, Sheila Miyoshi. *Brothers at War: The Unending Conflict in Korea.* New York: Norton, 2013.

Johnson, David K. *The Lavender Scare: The Cold War Persecution of Gays and Lesbians in the Federal Government.* Chicago: University of Chicago Press, 2004.

Johnson, Robert N. "The Eisenhower Personnel Security Program." *Journal of Politics* 18, no. 4 (1965): 625–50.

Johnson, Walter, ed. *The Papers of Adlai E. Stevenson.* Vol. 4: *Let's Talk Sense to the American People, 1952–1955.* Boston: Little, Brown, 1974.

Jones, Matthew. *After Hiroshima: The United States, Race and Nuclear Weapons in Asia, 1945–1965.* New York: Cambridge University Press, 2010.

———. "Targeting China: U.S. Nuclear Planning and 'Massive Retaliation' in East Asia, 1953–1955." *Journal of Cold War Studies* 10, no. 4 (2008): 37–65.

Jurika, Stephen, Jr., ed. *From Pearl Harbor to Vietnam: The Memoirs of Admiral Arthur W. Radford.* Stanford, CA: Hoover Institution Press, 1980.

Kabaservice, Geoffrey. *Rule and Ruin: The Downfall of Moderation and the Destruction of the Republican Party from Eisenhower to the Tea Party*. New York: Oxford University Press, 2012.

Kahin, Audrey R., and George McT. Kahin. *Subversion as Foreign Policy: The Secret Eisenhower and Dulles Debacle in Indonesia*. New York: New Press, 1995.

Kallina, Edmund F., Jr. *Kennedy v. Nixon: The Presidential Election of 1960*. Gainesville: University Press of Florida, 2010.

Kaplan, Fred. *The Wizards of Armageddon*. Stanford: Stanford University Press, 1983.

Karabell, Zachary. *Architects of Intervention: The United States, the Third World, and the Cold War, 1946–1962*. Baton Rouge: Louisiana State University Press, 1999.

Kempton, Murray. "The Underestimation of Dwight D. Eisenhower." *Esquire*, September 1967.

Kennan, George F. *Memoirs, 1925–1950*. Boston: Little, Brown, 1967.

———. *Memoirs, 1950–1963*. Boston: Little, Brown, 1972.

Khrushchev, Nikita. *Memoirs of Nikita Khrushchev*. Vol. 3: *Statesman*. University Park: Pennsylvania State University Press, 2007.

Khrushchev, Sergei. *Nikita Khrushchev and the Creation of a Superpower*. Translated by Shirley Benson. University Park: Pennsylvania State University Press, 2000.

Killian, James R., Jr. *Sputnik, Scientists, and Eisenhower*. Cambridge, MA: MIT Press, 1977.

Kingson, Eric R., and James H. Schulz, eds. *Social Security in the 21st Century*. New York: Oxford University Press, 1997.

Kinzer, Stephen. *All the Shah's Men: An American Coup and the Roots of Middle East Terror*. Hoboken, NJ: John Wiley and Sons, 2008.

———. *The Brothers: John Foster Dulles, Allen Dulles, and Their Secret World War*. New York: Times Books, 2013.

Kirk, John A. *Martin Luther King, Jr.* New York: Pearson Education, 2005.

———. *Redefining the Color Line: Black Activism in Little Rock, Arkansas, 1940–1970*. Gainesville: University Press of Florida, 2002.

Kirk, Russell, and James McClellan. *The Political Principles of Robert A. Taft*. New York: Fleet Press, 1967.

Kistiakowsky, George B. *A Scientist at the White House*. Cambridge, MA: Harvard University Press, 1976.

Klarman, Michael J. "How Brown Changed Race Relations: The Backlash Thesis." *Journal of American History* 81, no. 1 (1994): 81–118.

Klein, Maury. *A Call to Arms: Mobilizing America for World War II*. New York: Bloomsbury Press, 2013.

Kluger, Richard. *Simple Justice: The History of Brown v. Board of Education and Black America's Struggle for Equality*. New York: Vintage Books, 2004.

Knight, Amy. *Beria: Stalin's First Lieutenant*. Princeton, NJ: Princeton University Press, 1993.

Kornbluh, Peter, ed. *Bay of Pigs Declassified*. New York: New Press, 1998.

Kramer, Mark, ed. "The Malin Notes on the Crises in Hungary and Poland, 1956." *Cold War International History Project Bulletin* 8–9 (Winter 1996): 385–410.

———. "The Soviet Union and the 1956 Crises in Hungary and Poland: Reassessments and New Findings." *Journal of Contemporary History* 33, no. 2 (1998): 163–214.

Krock, Arthur. *Memoirs.* New York: Funk and Wagnalls, 1968.

Kruse, Kevin M. *One Nation under God: How Corporate America Invented Christian America.* New York: Basic Books, 2015.

Kuisel, Richard. *Seducing the French: The Dilemma of Americanization.* Berkeley: University of California Press, 1993.

Kunz, Diane. *The Economic Consequences of the Suez Crisis.* Chapel Hill: University of North Carolina Press, 1991.

Kyle, Keith. *Suez.* New York: St. Martin's Press, 1991.

Larres, Klaus, and Kenneth Osgood, eds. *The Cold War after Stalin's Death: A Missed Opportunity for Peace?* New York: Rowman and Littlefield, 2006.

Larson, Arthur. *Eisenhower: The President Nobody Knew.* New York: Scribner's, 1968.

———. *A Republican Looks at His Party.* New York: Harper and Brothers, 1956.

———. *A Twentieth-Century Life: The Memoirs of Arthur Larson.* Sioux Falls, SD: Center for Western Studies, 1997.

Lasby, Clarence G. *Eisenhower's Heart Attack.* Lawrence: University Press of Kansas, 1997.

Lassiter, Matthew, and Andrew B. Lewis, eds. *The Moderates' Dilemma: Massive Resistance to School Desegregation in Virginia.* Charlottesville: University of Virginia Press, 1988.

Lawson, Steven F. *Black Ballots: Voting Rights in the South, 1944–1969.* New York: Columbia University Press, 1976.

———, ed. *To Secure These Rights: The Report of Harry S Truman's Committee on Civil Rights.* New York: Bedford/St. Martin's Press, 2004.

Layne, Christopher. *The Peace of Illusions: American Grand Strategy from 1940 to the Present.* Ithaca, NY: Cornell University Press, 2006.

Ledbetter, James. *Unwarranted Influence: Dwight D. Eisenhower and the Military-Industrial Complex.* New Haven, CT: Yale University Press, 2011.

Leffler, Melvyn P. *For the Soul of Mankind: The United States, the Soviet Union, and the Cold War.* New York: Hill and Wang, 2007.

———. *A Preponderance of Power: National Security, the Truman Administration, and the Cold War.* Stanford: Stanford University Press, 1992.

Leffler, Melvyn P., and Odd Arne Westad, eds. *The Cambridge History of the Cold War.* 3 vols. New York: Cambridge University Press, 2010.

Leighton, Richard M. *History of the Office of the Secretary of Defense: Strategy, Money, and the New Look, 1953–1956.* Vol. 3. Washington, D.C.: GPO, 2001.

LeoGrande, William M. "Anger, Anti-Americanism, and the Break in U.S.-Cuban Relations." *Diplomatic History* 41, no. 1 (2017): 104–27.

Lewis, Tom. *Divided Highways: Building the Interstate Highways, Transforming American Life.* New York: Viking, 1997.

Lilienthal, David E. *The Journals of David E. Lilienthal.* Vol. 3: *Venturesome Years, 1950–1955.* New York: Harper & Row, 1966.

Little, Douglas. *American Orientalism: The United States and the Middle East since 1945.* Chapel Hill: University of North Carolina Press, 2008.

Lodge, Henry Cabot. *As It Was.* New York: Norton, 1976.

———. *The Storm Has Many Eyes.* New York: Norton, 1973.

Loeber, Charles R. *Building the Bombs: A History of the Nuclear Weapons Complex.* Albuquerque, NM: Sandia National Laboratories, 2002.

Logevall, Fredrik. *Embers of War: The Fall of an Empire and the Making of America's Vietnam.* New York: Random House, 2012.

Long, Michael G, ed. *The Legacy of Billy Graham: Critical Reflections on America's Greatest Evangelist.* Louisville, KY: Westminster John Knox Press, 2008.

Lowe, Peter. *The Korean War.* London: Macmillan, 2000.

Lubell, Samuel. *Revolt of the Moderates.* New York: Harper, 1956.

Lucas, W. Scott. *Divided We Stand: Britain, the U.S. and the Suez Crisis.* London: Hodder and Stoughton, 1991.

Lyon, Peter. *Eisenhower: Portrait of the Hero.* Boston: Little, Brown, 1974.

MacArthur, Douglas. *Reminiscences.* New York: McGraw-Hill, 1964.

MacGregor, Morris J., Jr. *Integration of the Armed Forces, 1940–1965.* Washington, D.C.: Center for Military History, 1981.

Macmillan, Harold. *Riding the Storm, 1956–59.* London: Macmillan, 1971.

———. *Tides of Fortune, 1945–1955.* New York: Harper & Row, 1969.

Mailer, Norman. "Superman Comes to the Supermarket." *Esquire,* November 1960.

Malsberger, John W. *The General and the Politician.* New York: Rowman & Littlefield, 2014.

Marling, Karal Ann. *As Seen on TV: The Visual Culture of Everyday Life in the 1950s.* Cambridge, MA: Harvard University Press, 1994.

Martin, John Bartlow. *Adlai Stevenson of Illinois.* Garden City, NY: Anchor Books, 1977.

Martin, Waldo E., Jr., ed. *Brown v. Board of Education: A Brief History with Documents.* New York: Bedford/St. Martin's Press, 1998.

May, Ernest R., ed. *American Cold War Strategy: Interpreting NSC 68.* New York: Bedford/St. Martin's Press, 1993.

May, Ernest R., and Philip Zelikow, eds. *Dealing with Dictators: Dilemmas of U.S. Diplomacy and Intelligence Analysis, 1945–1990.* Cambridge, MA: MIT Press, 2006.

Mayer, Michael S. "With Much Deliberation and Some Speed: Eisenhower and the Brown Decision." *Journal of Southern History* 52, no. 1 (1986): 43–76.

Mazo, Earl. *Richard Nixon: A Political and Personal Portrait.* New York: Harper and Brothers, 1959.

McCullough, David. *Truman.* New York: Simon & Schuster, 1992.

McDougall, Walter A. *The Heavens and the Earth: A Political History of the Space Age.* Baltimore: Johns Hopkins University Press, 1985.

McMahon, Robert. "Eisenhower and Third World Nationalism: A Critique of the Revisionists." *Political Science Quarterly* 101, no. 3 (1986): 453–73.

McPherson, Harry. *A Political Education.* Austin: University of Texas Press, 1988.

Medhurst, Martin J., ed. *Eisenhower's War of Words: Rhetoric and Leadership*. East Lansing: Michigan State University Press, 1994.

Metress, Christopher, ed. *The Lynching of Emmett Till: A Documentary Narrative*. Charlottesville: University of Virginia Press, 2002.

Mieczkowski, Yanek. *Eisenhower's Sputnik Moment: The Race for Space and World Prestige*. Ithaca, NY: Cornell University Press, 2013.

Miller, Edward. *Misalliance: Ngo Dinh Diem, the United States, and the Fate of South Vietnam*. Cambridge, MA: Harvard University Press, 2013.

Miller, Merle. *Ike the Soldier: As They Knew Him*. New York: Putnam's Sons, 1987.

Miller, Merle. *Plain Speaking: An Oral Biography of Harry S. Truman*. New York: Berkley, 1974.

Miller, William Lee. *Piety along the Potomac: Notes on Politics and Moral in the '50s*. Boston: Houghton Mifflin, 1964.

Mills, C. Wright. *Dwight D. Eisenhower*. New York: Random House, 1964.

———. *The Power Elite*. New York: Oxford University Press, 1956.

Moon, Henry Lee. "The Negro Vote in the Presidential Election of 1956." *Journal of Negro Education* 26, no. 3 (1957): 219–30.

Moos, Malcolm. *The Republicans: A History of Their Party*. New York: Random House, 1956.

Monk, Ray. *Robert Oppenheimer: A Life inside the Center*. New York: Anchor Books, 2012.

Morgan, Iwan W. *Eisenhower versus "The Spenders": The Eisenhower Administration, the Democrats and the Budget, 1953–60*. New York: St. Martin's Press, 1990.

Morgan, Ted. *Valley of Death: The Tragedy at Dien Bien Phu That Led America into the Vietnam War*. New York: Random House, 2010.

Morris, Aldon D. *The Origins of the Civil Rights Movement: Black Communities Organizing for Change*. New York: Free Press, 1984.

Morris, Roger. *Richard Milhous Nixon: The Rise of an American Politician*. New York: Henry Holt, 1990.

Morrow, E. Frederic. *Black Man in the White House: A Diary of the Eisenhower Years*. New York: Coward-McCann, 1963.

———. *Forty Years a Guinea Pig*. New York: Pilgrim Press, 1980.

Neal, Steve. *The Eisenhowers*. Lawrence: University Press of Kansas, 1984.

Neiberg, Michael. *Potsdam: The End of World War II and the Remaking of Europe*. New York: Basic Books, 2015.

Nelson, Anna Kasten. "The Top of Policy Hill: President Eisenhower and the NSC." *Diplomatic History* 7, no. 4 (1983): 307–26.

Nevins, Allan, ed. *The Strategy of Peace: Speeches of John F. Kennedy*, New York: Harper, 1960.

Newton, Jim. *Eisenhower: The White House Years*. New York: Doubleday, 2011.

Nichols, David A. *Eisenhower 1956: The President's Year of Crisis*. New York: Simon & Schuster, 2011.

———. *Ike and McCarthy: Dwight Eisenhower's Secret Campaign against Joseph McCarthy*. New York: Simon & Schuster, 2017.

——. *A Matter of Justice: Eisenhower and the Beginning of the Civil-Rights Revolution.* New York: Simon & Schuster, 2007.

Nixon, Richard. *RN: The Memoirs of Richard Nixon.* New York: Simon & Schuster, 1990.

——. *Six Crises.* New York: Simon & Schuster, 1962.

Oakley, J. Ronald. *God's Country: America in the Fifties.* New York: Dembner Books, 1986.

Official Report of the Proceedings of the Twenty-Fifth Republican National Convention, Chicago, Illinois, July 7–11, 1952. Washington, D.C.: Republican National Committee, 1952.

O'Neill, William L. *American High: The Years of Confidence, 1945–1960.* New York: Free Press, 1986.

Oppenheimer, J. Robert. "Atomic Weapons and American Policy." *Foreign Affairs,* July 1953.

Oshinsky, David M. *A Conspiracy So Immense: The World of Joe McCarthy.* New York: Free Press, 1983.

Owen, David. "The Effect of Prime Minister Anthony Eden's Illness on His Decision-making during the Suez Crisis," *QJM: An International Journal of Medicine* 98, no. 6 (2005): 387–402.

Pach, Chester J., Jr., and Elmo Richardson. *The Presidency of Dwight D. Eisenhower.* Lawrence: University Press of Kansas, 1991.

Papers of Dwight D. Eisenhower (1941–1961). 21 vols. Baltimore: Johns Hopkins University Press, 1970–2001.

Papers of Martin Luther King, Jr. 6 vols. Berkeley: University of California Press, 1992–2000.

Papers of George C. Marshall. 7 vols. Edited by Larry I. Bland. Baltimore: Johns Hopkins University Press, 1981–2016.

Papers of Robert A. Taft. 4 vols. Edited by Clarence E. Wunderlin. Kent, OH: Kent State University Press, 2006.

Parmet, Herbert S. *Eisenhower and the American Crusades.* New York: Macmillan, 1972.

Paterson, Thomas. *Contesting Castro: The United States and the Triumph of the Cuban Revolution.* New York: Oxford University Press, 1994.

Patterson, James T. *Brown v. Board of Education: A Civil Rights Milestone and Its Troubled Legacy.* New York: Oxford University Press, 2001.

——. *Grand Expectations: The United States, 1945–1974.* New York: Oxford University Press, 1996.

——. *Mr. Republican: A Biography of Robert A. Taft.* Boston: Houghton Mifflin, 1972.

Peale, Norman Vincent. *The Art of Real Happiness.* Englewood Cliffs, NJ: Prentice-Hall, 1950.

——. *A Guide to Confident Living.* Englewood Cliffs, NJ: Prentice-Hall, 1948.

——. *Inspired Messages for Daily Living.* Englewood Cliffs, NJ: Prentice-Hall, 1950.

——. *Stay Alive All Your Life.* Englewood Cliffs, NJ: Prentice-Hall, 1957.

Pedlow, Gregory W., and Donald E. Welzenbach. *The Central Intelligence Agency and Overhead Reconnaissance.* Washington, D.C.: CIA History Staff, 1992.

——. *The CIA and the U-2 Program, 1954–1974.* Washington, D.C.: CIA History Staff, 1998.

Peebles, Curtis. *The Moby Dick Project: Reconnaissance Balloons over Russia*. Washington, D.C.: Smithsonian Institution Press, 1991.

———. *Shadow Flights: America's Secret Air War Against the Soviet Union*. Navato, CA: Presidio Press, 2000.

Perlstein, Ricl. *Before the Storm*. New York: Hill and Wang, 2001.

———. *Nixonland: The Rise of a President and the Fracturing of America*. New York: Scribner, 2008.

———, ed. *Richard Nixon: Speeches, Writings, Documents*. Princeton, NJ: Princeton University Press, 2008.

Perret, Geoffrey. *Eisenhower*. New York: Random House, 1999.

Petersen, Neal H., ed. *From Hitler's Doorstep: The Wartime Intelligence Reports of Allen Dulles, 1942–1945*. University Park: Pennsylvania State University Press, 1996.

Petigny, Alan. *The Permissive Society: America, 1941–1965*. New York: Cambridge University Press, 2009.

Phillips-Fein, Kim. *Invisible Hands: The Making of the Conservative Movement from the New Deal to Reagan*. New York: Norton, 2009.

Phillips-Fein, Kim, and Julian Zelizer, eds. *What's Good for Business: Business and American Politics since World War II*. New York: Oxford University Press, 2012.

Pickett, William B. *Eisenhower Decides to Run*. Chicago: Ivan Dee, 2000.

Pierard, Richard V., and Robert D. Linder. *Civil Religion and the Presidency*. Grand Rapids, MI: Academie Books, 1988.

Pogue, Forrest C. *George C. Marshall*. Vol. 1: *Education of a General, 1880–1939*; Vol. 2: *Ordeal and Hope, 1939–1942*; Vol. 3: *Organizer of Victory, 1943–1945*; Vol. 4: *Statesman, 1945–1959*. New York, Viking Press, 1963–87.

Polenberg, Richard, ed. *In the Matter of J. Robert Oppenheimer: The Security Clearance Hearing*. Ithaca, NY: Cornell University Press, 2002.

Porter, A. N., and A. J. Stockwell, eds. *British Imperial Policy and Decolonization, 1938–1964*. Vol. 2. London: Macmillan, 1989.

Powers, Thomas. *The Man Who Kept the Secrets: Richard Helms and the CIA*. New York: Knopf, 1979.

Prados, John. *Safe for Democracy: The Secret Wars of the CIA*. Chicago: Ivan R. Dee, 2006.

———. *The Sky Would Fall: Operation Vulture, the U.S. Bombing Mission in Indochina, 1954*. New York: Dial Press, 1983.

Preble, Christopher. *John F. Kennedy and the Missile Gap*. DeKalb: Northern Illinois University Press, 2004.

Preston, Andrew. *Sword of the Spirit, Shield of Faith: Religion in American War and Diplomacy*. New York: Anchor Books, 2012.

Public Papers of the Presidents: Harry S. Truman, 1945–1953. Washington, D.C., 1961–66.

Public Papers of the Presidents: Dwight D. Eisenhower, 1953–1961. Washington, D.C., 1960–61.

Rabe, Stephen G. "Eisenhower Revisionism: A Decade of Scholarship." *Diplomatic History* 17, no. 1 (1993): 97–115.

Rasenberger, Jim. *The Brilliant Disaster: JFK, Castro, and America's Doomed Invasion of Cuba's Bay of Pigs.* New York: Scribner, 2012.

Rayner, Richard. "Channeling Ike." *New Yorker*, April 26, 2010.

Reed, Roy. *Faubus: The Life and Times of an American Prodigal.* Fayetteville: University of Arkansas Press, 1997.

Reeves, Richard. *President Kennedy: Profile of Power.* New York: Simon & Schuster, 1993.

Rigeur, Leah Wright. *The Loneliness of the Black Republican: Pragmatic Politics and the Pursuit of Power.* Princeton, NJ: Princeton University Press, 2015.

Rives, Timothy D. "Ambrose and Eisenhower: A View from the Stacks at Abilene." History News Network, May 16, 2010. http://historynewsnetwork.org/article/126705.

Roberts, Andrew. *Masters and Commanders.* New York: Harper, 2009.

Rogers, Daniel T. *Age of Fracture.* Cambridge, MA: Harvard University Press, 2011.

Roman, Peter. *Eisenhower and the Missile Gap.* Ithaca, NY: Cornell University Press, 1995.

Roosevelt, Kermit. *Countercoup: The Struggle for the Control of Iran.* New York: McGraw-Hill, 1979.

Rose, Gideon, ed. "What Really Happened: Solving the Cold War's Cold Cases." *Foreign Affairs* 93, no. 4 (2014).

Rose, Mark. *Interstate: Express Highway Politics, 1941–1956.* Lawrence: University Press of Kansas, 1979.

Rosenau, James N. *The Nomination of "Chip" Bohlen.* New York: Henry Holt, 1958.

Rosenberg, David Alan. "The Origins of Overkill: Nuclear Weapons and American Strategy, 1945–1960." *International Security* 7, no. 4 (1983): 3–71.

Rostow, W. W. *Europe after Stalin: Eisenhower's Three Decisions of March 11, 1953.* Austin: University of Texas Press, 1982.

———. *Open Skies: Eisenhower's Proposal of July 21, 1955.* Austin: University of Texas Press, 1982.

Rovere, Richard. *Affairs of State: The Eisenhower Years.* New York: Farrar, Straus and Cudahy, 1956.

———. *Senator Joe McCarthy.* Los Angeles: University of California Press, 1959.

Rovere, Richard, and Arthur M. Schlesinger Jr. *The General and the President.* New York: Farrar, Straus and Giroux, 1951.

Rowse, A. E. "Political Polls." In *Editorial Research Reports 1960.* Vol. 2. Washington, D.C.: CQ Press, 1960.

Roy, Jules. *The Battle of Dien Bien Phu.* New York: Harper & Row, 1965.

Ruddy, T. Michael. *The Cautious Diplomat: Charles E. Bohlen and the Soviet Union, 1929–1969.* Kent, OH: Kent State University Press, 1986.

Rudgers, David F. *Creating the Secret State: The Origins of the Central Intelligence Agency, 1943–1947.* Lawrence: University Press of Kansas, 2000.

Ruffner, Kevin, ed. *Corona: America's First Satellite Program.* Washington, D.C.: CIA Center for the Study of Intelligence, 1995.

Ryan, Yvonne. *Roy Wilkins: The Quiet Revolutionary and the NAACP.* Lexington: University Press of Kentucky, 2014.

Safford, Jeffrey J. "The Nixon-Castro Meeting of 19 April 1959." *Diplomatic History* 4, no. 4 (1980): 425–31.

Sampson, Curt. *The Masters: Golf, Money and Power in Augusta, Georgia.* New York: Villard, 1999.

Schlesinger, Andrew, and Stephen Schlesinger, eds. *The Letters of Arthur Schlesinger, Jr.* New York: Random House, 2013.

Schlesinger, Arthur M., Jr. "The Highbrow in Politics." *Partisan Review* 20, no. 2 (1953): 157–65.

———. *The Imperial Presidency.* New York: Houghton Mifflin, 1973.

———. *Journals: 1952–2000.* New York: Penguin Books, 2007.

———. *A Thousand Days: John F. Kennedy in the White House.* Boston: Houghton Mifflin, 1965.

———. *The Vital Center: The Politics of Freedom.* Boston: Da Capo Press, 1949.

Schlesinger, Arthur M., Sr. "Our Presidents: A Rating by 75 Historians." *New York Times Magazine,* July 29, 1962.

Schlesinger, Stephen, and Stephen Kinzer. *Bitter Fruit: The Untold Story of the American Coup in Guatemala.* Garden City, NY: Anchor Books, 1983.

Schoultz, Lars. *That Infernal Little Cuban Republic: The United States and the Cuban Revolution.* Chapel Hill: University of North Carolina Press, 2009.

Schwartz, Stephen I., ed. *Atomic Audit: The Costs and Consequences of U.S. Nuclear Weapons Since 1940.* Washington, D.C.: Brookings Institution Press, 1998.

Sechser, Todd S., and Matthew Fuhrmann. *Nuclear Weapons and Coercive Diplomacy.* New York: Cambridge University Press, 2017.

Shannon, William V. "Eisenhower as President." *Commentary* 26, no. 5 (1958): 390–98.

Sheehan, Neil. *A Fiery Peace in a Cold War: Bernard Schriever and the Ultimate Weapon.* New York: Vintage, 2009.

Sherry, Michael S. *In the Shadow of War: The United States since the 1930s.* New Haven, CT: Yale University Press, 1995.

Showalter, Dennis E., ed. *Forging the Shield: Eisenhower and National Security for the 21st Century.* Chicago: Imprint, 2005.

Shuckburgh, Evelyn. *Descent to Suez: Diaries 1951–56.* Norton: New York, 1986.

Simpson, Howard. *Dien Bien Phu: The Epic Battle America Forgot.* Washington, D.C.: Brassey's, 1994.

Skolnikoff, Eugene B. *Science, Technology, and American Foreign Policy.* Cambridge, MA: MIT Press, 1967.

Slater, Ellis D. *The Ike I Knew.* Edited by Ernestine Durr and Elsie Maki. Ellis D. Slater Trust, 1980.

Sloan, John W. *Eisenhower and the Management of Prosperity.* Lawrence: University Press of Kansas, 1991.

Smith, Jean Edward. *Eisenhower in War and Peace.* New York: Random House, 2012.

Smith, Richard Norton. *Thomas E. Dewey and His Times.* New York: Simon & Schuster, 1982.

Snead, David L. *The Gaither Committee, Eisenhower, and the Cold War.* Columbus: Ohio State University Press, 1999.

Soman, Appu K. *Double-Edged Sword: Nuclear Diplomacy in Unequal Conflicts. The United States and China, 1950–1958.* Westport, CT: Praeger, 2000.

Sorensen, Theodore C. *Kennedy.* New York: Harper & Row, 1965.

Spector, Ronald H. *The United States Army in Vietnam: Advice and Support. The Early Years, 1941–1960.* Washington, D.C.: Center of Military History, 1983.

Statler, Kathryn C., and Andrew L. Johns. *The Eisenhower Administration, the Third World, and the Globalization of the Cold War.* Lanham, MD: Rowman and Littlefield, 2006.

Stebenne, David L. *Modern Republican: Arthur Larson and the Eisenhower Years.* Indianapolis: Indiana University Press, 2006.

Stone, I. F. *The Haunted Fifties.* New York: Random House, 1963.

Strauss, Lewis L. *Men and Decisions.* New York: Doubleday, 1962.

Stueck, William. *The Korean War: An International History.* Princeton, NJ: Princeton University Press, 1995.

Sulzberger, C. L. *A Long Row of Candles: Memoirs and Diaries, 1934–1954.* New York: Macmillan, 1969.

Summersby, Kay. *Eisenhower Was My Boss.* New York: Prentice-Hall, 1948.

———. *Past Forgetting: My Love Affair with Dwight D. Eisenhower.* New York: Simon & Schuster, 1976.

Taft, Robert A. *A Foreign Policy for Americans.* New York: Doubleday, 1951.

Takeyh, Ray. *The Origins of the Eisenhower Doctrine.* New York: St. Martin's Press, 2000.

———. "What Really Happened in Iran: The CIA, the Ouster of Mosaddeq, and the Restoration of the Shah." *Foreign Affairs,* July–August 2014, 2–12.

Talbot, Strobe, ed. *Khrushchev Remembers.* Boston: Little, Brown, 1970.

Tananbaum, Duane. *The Bricker Amendment Controversy: A Test of Eisenhower's Political Leadership.* Ithaca, NY: Cornell University Press, 1988.

Tanenhaus, Sam. *The Death of Conservatism.* New York: Random House, 2009.

Taubman, William. *Khrushchev: The Man and His Era.* New York: Norton, 2003.

Theoharis, Athan, et al. *The Central Intelligence Agency: Security under Scrutiny.* Westport, CT: Greenwood Press, 2006.

Thomas, Evan. *Ike's Bluff: President Eisenhower's Secret Battle to Save the World.* New York: Little, Brown, 2012.

Thompson, Kenneth, ed. *The Eisenhower Presidency: Eleven Intimate Perspectives of Dwight D. Eisenhower.* Lanham, MD: University Press of America, 1984.

Thompson, Nicholas. *The Hawk and the Dove: Paul Nitze, George Kennan and the History of the Cold War.* New York: Henry Holt, 2009.

Truman, Harry S. *Memoirs of Harry S. Truman, I: Year of Decisions; II: Years of Trial and Hope.* New York: Doubleday, 1956.

Truman, Margaret, ed. *Where the Buck Stops: The Personal and Private Writings of Harry S. Truman.* New York: Warner Books, 1989.

Tudda, Chris. *The Truth Is Our Weapon: The Rhetorical Diplomacy of Dwight D. Eisen-hower and John Foster Dulles.* Baton Rouge: Louisiana State University Press, 2006.

Tyson, Timothy. *The Blood of Emmett Till.* New York: Simon & Schuster, 2017.

Urban, Wayne J. *More Than Science and Sputnik: The National Defense Education Act of 1958.* Tuscaloosa: University of Alabama Press, 2010.

U.S. Department of State. *Foreign Relations of the United States.* Washington, D.C.

U.S. Senate. *Alleged Assassination Plots Involving Foreign Leaders: An Interim Report of the Select Committee to Study Governmental Operations* (Church Committee). Washing-ton, D.C.: GPO, November 1975.

———. *Communist Threat to the U.S. through the Caribbean.* Hearings before the U.S. Sen-ate Committee on the Judiciary, Subcommittee to Investigate the Administration of the Internal Security Act and Other Internal Security Laws. 86th Congress, First Ses-sion. Washington, D.C.: GPO, July 14, 1959.

———. *Executive Sessions of the Senate Foreign Relations Committee.* Vol. 6. Washington, D.C.: GPO, 1976.

———. *Executive Sessions of the Senate Foreign Relations Committee.* Vol. 12. 86th Con-gress, Second Session, 1960. Washington, D.C.: GPO, 1982.

———. *Hearings before the Preparedness Investigating Subcommittee of the Committee on Armed Services.* Part 1. Washington, D.C.: GPO, 1958.

Vigers, T. W. "The German People and Rearmament." *International Affairs* 27, no. 2 (1951): 151–55.

Von Tunzelmann, Alex. *Blood and Sand: Suez, Hungary, and Eisenhower's Campaign for Peace.* New York: HarperCollins, 2016.

Wacker, Grant. *America's Pastor: Billy Graham and the Shaping of a Nation.* Cambridge, MA: Harvard University Press, 2014.

Wall, Wendy L. *Inventing the "American Way": The Politics of Consensus from the New Deal to the Civil Rights Movement.* New York: Oxford University Press, 2008.

Warner, Roger. *Back Fire: The CIA's Secret War in Laos and Its Link to the War in Vietnam.* New York: Simon & Schuster, 1995.

Warren, Earl. *The Memoirs of Earl Warren.* Garden City, NY: Doubleday, 1977.

Webb, Willard J. *The Joint Chiefs of Staff and the Prelude to the War in Vietnam, 1954–1959.* Washington, D.C.: Office of Joint History, Joint Chiefs of Staff, 2007.

Weiner, Tim. *Legacy of Ashes: The History of the CIA.* New York: Anchor Books, 2007.

Wells, Christopher. "Fueling the Boom: Gasoline Taxes, Invisibility, and the Growth of the American Highway Infrastructure, 1919–1956." *Journal of American History* 99, no. 1 (2012): 72–81.

West, J. B. *Upstairs at the White House: My Life with the First Ladies.* New York: Coward, McCann, 1973.

Westad, Odd Arne. *The Global Cold War.* New York: Cambridge University Press, 2005.

White, Theodore. *The Making of the President, 1960.* New York: Atheneum, 1961.

White, William S. *The Taft Story.* New York: Harper and Brothers, 1954.

Whitfield, Stephen J. *The Culture of the Cold War.* Baltimore: Johns Hopkins University Press, 1996.

Whyte, William. *The Organization Man.* New York: Simon & Schuster, 1956.

Wicker, Tom. *Dwight D. Eisenhower.* New York: Times Books, 2002.

Wiesner, Jerome B. *Where Science and Politics Meet.* New York: McGraw-Hill, 1965.

Wilkins, Roy, and Tom Mathews. *Standing Fast: The Autobiography of Roy Wilkins.* New York: Viking, 1982.

Wills, Garry. *Nixon Agonistes: The Crisis of the Self-Made Man.* New York: Mariner Books, 2002.

Winkler, Allan M. *Life under a Cloud: American Anxiety about the Atom.* New York: Oxford University Press, 1993.

Witte, John F. *The Politics and Development of the Federal Income Tax.* Madison: University of Wisconsin Press, 1985.

Woodhouse, C. M. *Something Ventured.* New York: Granada, 1982.

Woods, Randall Bennett. *Quest for Identity: America since 1945.* New York: Cambridge University Press, 2005.

Wukovits, John. *Eisenhower.* New York: Palgrave Macmillan, 2006.

Wyden, Peter. *Bay of Pigs: The Untold Story.* New York: Simon & Schuster, 1979.

Yaqub, Salim. *Containing Arab Nationalism: The Eisenhower Doctrine and the Middle East.* Chapel Hill: University of North Carolina Press, 2004.

York, Herbert. *Race to Oblivion: A Participant's View of the Arms Race.* New York: Simon & Schuster, 1970.

Young, Nancy Beck, ed. *Documentary History of the Dwight D. Eisenhower Presidency.* Vols. 1–12. LexisNexis, 2005–9.

Zelizer, Julian E. *Arsenal of Democracy: The Politics of National Security from World War II to the War on Terrorism.* New York: Basic Books, 2010.

Zhai, Qiang. *China and the Vietnam Wars, 1954–1975.* Chapel Hill: University of North Carolina Press, 2000.

Zhang, Shu Guang. *Deterrence and Strategic Culture: Chinese-American Confrontations, 1949–1958.* Ithaca, NY: Cornell University Press, 1992.

Zhang, Xiaoming. *Deng Xiaoping's Long War: The Military Conflict between China and Vietnam, 1979–1991.* Chapel Hill: University of North Carolina Press, 2015.

INDEX

PHOTO CREDITS

1. Eisenhower Library
2. Eisenhower Library
3. Eisenhower Library
4. U.S. Army, Eisenhower Library
5. U.S. Army, Eisenhower Library
6. UP, Eisenhower Library
7. Harris & Ewing, Inc. Library of Congress
8. Eisenhower Library
9. Morgan Fitz, Library of Congress
10. Library of Congress
11. Library of Congress
12. New York World-Telegram, Library of Congress
13. Keystone-France/Gamma-Keystone via Getty Images
14. Thomas O'Halloran, U.S. News and World Report, Library of Congress
15. Thomas O'Halloran, U.S. News and World Report, Library of Congress
16. Eisenhower Library
17. Library of Congress
18. National Park Service, Eisenhower Library
19. Carl Iwasaki/The LIFE Images Collection/Getty Images
20. Library of Congress
21. Hulton-Deutsch Collection/CORBIS/Corbis via Getty Images
22. Hulton-Deutsch Collection/CORBIS/Corbis via Getty Images
23. National Park Service, Eisenhower Library
24. National Park Service, Eisenhower Library
25. U.S. Army
26. National Park Service, Eisenhower Library
27. UP, Library of Congress

28. Warren K. Leffler, U.S. News and World Report, Library of Congress

29. Marion Trikosko, U.S. News and World Report, Library of Congress

30. Library of Congress

31. Warren K. Leffler, U.S. News and World Report, Library of Congress

32. New York World-Telegram, Library of Congress

33. National Park Service, Eisenhower Library

34. National Park Service, Eisenhower Library

35. Paul Vathis, AP, Eisenhower Library

36. Library of Congress